GOVERNOR GEORGE M. TROUP

THE OFFICIAL HISTORY of
LAURENS COUNTY GEORGIA

1807-1941

BERTHA SHEPPARD HART, M.A.

Author of "Introduction to Georgia Writers"

Southern Historical Press, Inc.
Greenville, South Carolina

This volume was reproduced from
An 1972 edition located in the
Publisher's private library,
Greenville, South Carolina

All rights reserved. No part of this publication may be reproduced,
stored in a retrieval system, transmitted in any form, posted
on to the web in any form or by any means without
the prior written permission of the publisher.

Please direct all correspondence and orders to:

www.southernhistoricalpress.com
or
SOUTHERN HISTORICAL PRESS, Inc.
PO BOX 1267
375 West Broad Street
Greenville, SC   29601
southernhistoricalpress@gmail.com

Originally published: Dublin, GA. 1941
Copyright 1941 by:
John Laurens Chapter D.A.R.
Reprinted by: Southern Historical Press, Inc.
Greenville, SC
ISBN #0-9308-888-9
All rights Reserved.
Printed in the United States of America

FOREWORD

As the John Laurens Chapter of the Daughters of the American Revolution reaches the quarter-century mark of her existence, she sees the fulfillment of her hopes, plans and aspirations of nearly two score years in the publication, in book form, of the official History of Laurens County, Georgia, 1807-1941; and it is the Chapter's happy privilege to present, as her Silver Anniversary offering, to the people of Dublin and Laurens County, and to friends in other cities, counties and states, this volume in which are preserved, for all time to come, Laurens County's valuable records and rare documents.

In 1922, during the regency of Mrs. M. A. Shewmake, a committee was appointed, with Mrs. S. M. Kellam chairman, to bring in subjects for study for the ensuing year. From the four subjects submitted by this committee, the Chapter chose the "History of Laurens County." This study proved so interesting and informative, that, from time to time, there was discussion in the Chapter of having these articles published in book form as a County History. No definite action was taken however until 1925 when Mrs. M. J. Guyton, at that time Regent, appointed a committee, with Mrs. J. A. Carswell chairman, to "collect and compile all papers written on Laurens County in 1922." From that time forward old letters, newspapers and other records were searched for; aged citizens were interviewed for their wealth of memories of days gone by; and with unabating interest and zeal, research was continued and the original material augmented, both by the History committee and by members of the Chapter.

Mrs. Carswell remained chairman of this committee until illness forced her to give up this important work in which she had taken such active interest, and Mrs. T. J. Blackshear was made chairman. She continued as the highly efficient History chairman until failing health preceding her death, compelled her to relinquish the task to which she had given so freely of her time and ability.

Mrs. E. B. Freeman, Regent, 1930-1931, 1931-1932, appointed Mrs. John S. Adams, who had imbibed, since childhood, County lore and traditions, to succeed Mrs. Blackshear as chairman. Great strides were made under her capable leadership; the mass of collected data was revised, increased and put in manuscript form. The Chapter was highly gratified when Judge Ira Stanley Chappell of distinguished County lineage, agreed to take over this manuscript and, from it, compile and write the History of Laurens County. Ere his work was well begun the Chapter's plans for a published County History were disrupted and her members' hearts saddened by the illness and death of their chosen author.

In 1932, Mrs. Freeman still Regent, fresh impetus was given the work in the appointment, by the Grand Jury, upon recommendation of Judge R. Earl Camp, of the John Laurens Chapter as the official Historian of Laurens County. This appointment was part of Georgia's state-wide Bi-Centennial Program, in which each County was asked to appoint an official historian of his or her County.

Following is Judge Camp's recommendation to the Grand Jury of Laurens County in session at its regular February term, 1932: "This great organization, the Daughters of the American Revolution, distinguished throughout America, and its especially notable local Chapter, is singularly worthy and deserving of this local distinction, having gathered at its own expense a wealth of material during past years preparatory to the publication of a History of Laurens County; and the Grand Jury of this term of Laurens Superior Court is cordially solicited to ratify immediately this designation by the Court; and that upon its ratification and election this order and the Grand Jury's action be spread upon the minutes of the Laurens Superior Court, this February 2nd, 1932."

(Signed) R. EARL CAMP, *Judge.*

"This appointment of the John Laurens Chapter of the Daughters of the American Revolution as Historian of Laurens County approved by the Grand Jury, this February 2nd, 1932."

(Signed) T. C. METHVIN, *Clerk.*

"Filed in office of the Clerk of Laurens Superior Court, No. 29, page 28, February 2nd, 1932."

(Signed) E. S. BALDWIN, *Clerk.*

The Laurens County History Committee continued their research into the County's files and have availed themselves of all known sources of information. During the chairmanship of Mrs. Adams, typed copies, in duplicate, were made of all collected data; one copy retained by the Chapter for future publication; the other forwarded to the Department of Archives and History of the State of Georgia.

In 1940, when Mrs. A. J. Toole assumed the regency of the Chapter, desiring to commemorate the Chapter's 25th anniversary, the plan was revived of publishing the official History of Laurens County as the Chapter's Silver Anniversary Project, also as the Chapter's contribution to the Golden Jubilee Projects of the State and National Societies of the Daughters of the American Revolution. Mrs. E. B. Freeman, a member of the History committee since its original formation, was appointed chairman of the publication committee. It is largely due to the interest, enthusiasm and untiring efforts of Mrs. Freeman that the Chapter's long, long dream of a published County History has become a reality.

In October, 1940, the services of a Chapter member, Bertha Sheppard Hart, M.A., an author and historian of recognized ability, were secured to compile the records collected by the Chapter and to prepare this material for publication. Mrs. Hart has verified, enlarged and brought to date these historical collections, and this, the official "History of Laurens County, Georgia, 1807-1941," is the result. The Family History Section, which was made available to all Laurens County families, is of especial personal interest, and the Chapter regrets that other families entitled to representation did not submit their histories for publication.

For publisher, the Chapter chose Mr. W. W. Hayes, of The McGregor Company of Athens, Georgia, and credit for the success of this publication is due Mr. Hayes for his helpful suggestions and superior workmanship. The full and detailed Index is the work of Mr. Frazier Moore, also of Athens. This will greatly enhance the value of the book for reference purposes.

The Chapter extends thanks and appreciation to the Dublin *Courier-Herald* for excellent publicity so generously given.

To Mrs. J. E. Hayes, State Historian and Director of Archives and History of the State of Georgia, who supplied information that otherwise could not have been obtained.

To the City and County officers; to the Superintendents of the City and County Schools; to the County Commissioners and to the Historical Records Survey organization whose local work has been done by Mrs. Helen McCall Bashinski and Mrs. Julia Franklin Rountree.

To certain departments of the Federal Government.

To Miss Leah Kittrell for group pictures of the public buildings.

The Chapter is greatly indebted to Mrs. A. A. Coleman and Mrs. Herman Balsley who typed the complete manuscript for the book.

To Chapter members who have contributed written articles and other aid and information, we are most grateful.

To Mrs. Walter A. Hobbs the Chapter extends especial appreciation for her splendid work as treasurer of the finance committee.

With pride in their glorious past and looking forward to an even greater Dublin and Laurens County in the years to come, I am,

                      Yours faithfully,

                      MAY LAND TOOLE (Mrs. A. J.), *Regent*.

                      John Laurens Chapter

                      Daughters of the American Revolution.

Dublin, Georgia
August 15th, 1941.

ACKNOWLEDGMENTS

The Author, Mrs. J. F. Hart, acknowledges with gratitude valuable information received from the following: T. J. Blackshear, Mrs. Enda Ballard Duggan, Stanley Reese, Joe Chappell, R. C. Coleman, Ernest Clark, J. L. Allen, Vernon Chavous, James L. Keen Sr., L. H. Keen, Cone Thigpen, E. G. Simmons, C. H. Kittrell, C. C. Crockett, M. H. Blackshear, Walter Daniel, F. N. Watkins, Mrs. J. B. Fordham, Lamar Currie, Mrs. E. B. Mackey, and Honorable Tom Linder.

PUBLICATION COMMITTEE

Mrs. E. B. Freeman, *Chairman*

Mrs. J. F. Hart   Mrs. M. J. Guyton

Mrs. A. J. Toole

TABLE OF CONTENTS

Chapter		Page
I.	THE INDIAN PERIOD	1
	1. Mounds and Relics	1
	2. DeSoto in Laurens County and Georgia	3
II.	WHITE MEN IN THIS SECTION	7
	1. Before and During the Revolution	7
	2. The Oconee War	9
III.	FORMATION OF THE COUNTY, LOCATION OF COUNTY SEAT	12
	1. Laurens, Sumpterville, Dublin	12
	2. John Laurens	14
	3. Blackshear's Ferry	15
	4. Revolutionary Soldiers in Laurens County	18
IV.	PIONEER PERIOD	23
	1. Pioneers	23
	2. War of 1812	28
	3. Indian Troubles after War of 1812	30
	4. Land Lottery List	34
V.	A LAURENS COUNTY GOVERNOR WHO DEFIED THE PRESIDENT	39
	1. Governor George Michael Troup	39
	2. Governor Troup Defies the President	41
	3. Children of Governor Troup	42
VI.	THE PERIOD OF 1812 TO 1860	44
	1. Growth	44
	2. Indian Troubles	46
	3. Through the Forties	49
	4. The Fifties	50
VII.	THE PERIOD FROM 1860 TO 1870	56
	1. The Confederate War	56
	2. Laurens in the War	57
	3. Record of Laurens County Companies Found in the Clerk's Office	58
	4. Additional Information Concerning War Between the States	60
	5. Confederate Army—Soldiers from Laurens	61
	6. An Episode of the War	63
	7. Jeff Davis in Laurens County	66
	8. Gentlewomen of the Sixties	69

Chapter		Page
VIII.	COUNTY GOVERNMENT AND COURTS	72
	1. Inferior Court and Court of Ordinary	72
	2. Board of Commissioners of Roads and Revenues	74
	3. Laurens County Court System	75
	4. Court House and Jail	85
IX.	PERIOD OF 1870, 1880, 1890	88
	1. In the Eighteen Seventies	88
	2. The Eighties	92
	3. The Nineties	95
	4. In Retrospect	98
X.	THE TWENTIETH CENTURY	103
	1. The Period of 1900-1920	103
	a. Growth	103
	b. Recreation Resorts	106
	c. Laurens County in the World War	108
	d. General Matters	111
	2. The Period of 1920-1941	112
XI.	LAURENS COUNTY—GEOGRAPHICAL AND AGRICULTURAL	118
	1. Geographical	118
	a. Population and Civic Divisions	118
	b. Militia Districts	120
	c. Tributary Waterways	122
	d. The Oconee River	123
	e. Boats of the Oconee	123
	2. Agricultural	125
	a. Soil and Cotton Production	125
	b. Crop Diversification	129
	c. Flora of Laurens	133
	d. Fauna of Laurens County	134
XII.	STATE AND FEDERAL AGENCIES IN LAURENS	135
	1. Federal Loan Agencies	135
	2. The Triple A	135
	3. Federal Surplus Commodities	136
	4. NYA	136
	5. PWA and WPA	136
	6. Georgia State Employment Service	137
	7. The Laurens County Welfare Department	137
	8. Farm Security Administration	138
	9. Local Selective Service Boards	139
XIII.	INDIAN TRAILS, ROADS, AND HIGHWAYS	141

Chapter		Page
XIV.	LAURENS COUNTY CHURCHES	144
	1. Baptist Churches	144
	2. Primitive Baptist Churches	161
	3. The Methodist Church in Laurens County	163
	4. Other Denominations	170
	6. Recent Churches (white)	175
	7. Colored Churches	175
	8. Defunct Churches	177
	9. Preachers of Laurens County	177
XV.	SCHOOL HISTORY OF LAURENS COUNTY	181
	1. 1807 to 1870	181
	2. The Public School System	184
	3. The Industrial School at Poplar Springs	186
	4. Consolidation	188
	5. The Schools of Dublin	189
XVI.	POST OFFICES, TOWNS AND COMMUNITIES	192
	1. The Dublin Post Office	192
	2. Post Offices in Laurens County	194
	3. Towns and Communities	197
	a. Lovett	197
	b. Brewton	198
	c. Dexter	199
	d. Rockledge	203
	e. Dudley	204
	f. Montrose	206
	g. Rentz	208
	h. Minter	211
	i. Cadwell	212
	j. Laurens Hill	215
	k. Cedar Grove Community	219
	l. Cross Roads Community	220
XVII.	IN PUBLIC SERVICE	221
	1. In the State	221
	2. In Service Beyond Laurens	222
	3. In the County	223
XVIII.	PROFESSIONAL MEN IN LAURENS COUNTY	225
	1. Lawyers	225
	2. Physicians	227
XIX.	GENERAL	232
	1. Laurens County Banks	232
	2. Military Companies	234
	3. Newspapers of Laurens County	235

Chapter		Page
	4. The Carnegie Library	237
	5. Longevity in Laurens	239
XX.	CLUBS AND FRATERNITIES	241
	1. John Laurens Chapter D. A. R.	241
	2. Oconee Chapter, U. D. C.	243
	3. United States Daughters of 1812	245
	4. Woman's Study Club of Dublin	246
	5. Parnassus Club	247
	6. Dublin-Laurens County Council of Parent-Teacher Associations	249
	7. The Dublin Garden Club	252
	8. A Short History of Laurens Lodge No. 75 F. and A. M., Dublin, Ga.	253
	9. Order of Eastern Star in Dublin	254
	10. The American Legion	255
	11. The American Legion Auxiliary	255
	12. The Lions Club	255
	13. Exchange Club of Dublin	256
	14. Rotary Club of Dublin	257
	15. Woodmen of the World	258
	16. Former Fraternities and Clubs	258
	17. Boy Scouts	259
XXI.	NEGROES IN LAURENS COUNTY	261
	APPENDIX	267
	Early Wills	269
	Early Marriages	280
	Family Histories	301
	INDEX	527

ILLUSTRATIONS

Governor George M. Troup	*Frontispiece*
Map of Laurens County	6

Facing Page

Dublin and Laurens County Buildings	72
A Group of Dublin Churches	144
Dublin City Schools	184
Laurens County Consolidated Schools	188
Dublin Public Buildings	232
Judge John Samuel Adams	306
Judge R. Earl Camp	336
Edward Burton Claxton, M.D.	342
Alfred Tennyson Coleman, M.D.	348
Judge John Thomas Duncan	362
Colonel Cincinnatus Saxon Guyton	390
Judge Mercer Haynes	398
Judge James B. Hicks	402
James Richard Hightower	404
Shady Valley—Country Home of Dr. C. H. Kittrell	426
Mrs. J. A. Peacock	242
Colonel Whiteford S. Ramsay	452
Thomas Randolph Ramsay	456
Judge Thomas H. Rowe	468
Judge James Barnes Sanders	472
Captain Hardy Smith	484
Captain Rollin Adolphus Stanley	496
Colonel John M. Stubbs	512
Lucien Quincy Stubbs	514

Chapter I

THE INDIAN PERIOD

1. MOUNDS AND RELICS

It is an established fact that this county was originally occupied by the Indians. We know this, not on the evidence of written records or oral traditions, but from material remains. Among the many various customs practiced by the American Indians, that of mound building was one of the most important because it is from these old mounds which are left standing today that historians have been able to learn much about the Red race.

On the banks of the Oconee River, four miles south from Dublin, two Indian Mounds, evidencing the former occupation of the river banks by the Red men, lie yielded to the guardianship of trees. The larger of the two mounds commands a view of the river and the surrounding plains, and is the type of mound that the Indians built for signal fires and watch-out posts. On one end of the mound, on the side next to the river, there is a gentle slope from the river up to a high ledge on the mound. Here, on the highest point, long ago, was the place where some Indian brave built signal fires, took his blanket to inclose the smoke, only to let it rise in billowy clouds to the sky, so that the hunting expedition up the river might return to defend the encampment from warring tribes. Here was the place, when the tribes were on the warpath, a sentinel kept watch on the river while standing on the edge of the steep descent of the ground toward the river.

Following the ledge of this mound, one comes to the far end from the river, where huge bowlders lie against the steep side. Farther on, where the mound slopes down again, there is a pond, to which the canals that were built from the river were connected. The traces of these canals are still to be seen. It was the custom of the Indians when they built mounds near rivers and streams, to dig narrow canals leading up to the mound. These canals were used as fish reservoirs, and were filled with growing and breeding fish which were caught with nets made by the Indians. The mouths of these canals were closed with gates which they made of reeds and clay. For this reason the white man gave the name "Fish Trap Cut," to the place on the river where the mounds are situated.

The second mound, situated not far from the first one, is oval shape, and was either originally intended for the type of mound built for the camp site of the chief of the tribe and his family, or for the council of the tribes as a peace-treaty mound.

The different types of flint arrows turned up by the plows in the fields beside and around the sides of this mound lead us to believe that it was used as a council ground for many tribes. These arrows are made up of flint foreign to our native county, flint from quarries in various parts of Georgia, so a state geologist who has visited the place has stated. Some of the arrows were of clear flint, some cloudy, all specimens of different quarries. Here many a brave may have smoked the symbolic peace pipe with his red brothers from the far parts of Georgia.

There is another mound near Diamond Landing on the Oconee. The ground is still covered with flint arrowheads and bits of Indian relics which differ so in nature as to suggest that this spot was a common meeting place for Indians from all sections of the state. Pieces of pottery and flint are such that the oldest inhabitant cannot remember any such in our section.

These mounds are about a thousand yards apart, with level fields between them, suggesting the idea that it was perhaps used as a "Council ground." It is in the form of a triangle with a bubbling spring forming the apex.

While this field has been cultivated for many years, every year the plowman turns up numbers of arrowheads and bits of pottery, worked or carved with symbols suggestive of the swastika. The age of these mounds may be only imagined, when one sees full grown trees protruding from their tops.

This section of Georgia was thickly populated by the Creek Indians according to Jones in the first volume of his "History of Georgia." He says: "... when the colony of Georgia was founded, the ceded lands lying between the Savannah and the Altamaha rivers and extending toward the west were occupied by Indians whose principal settlements were established in the vicinity of streams, in rich valleys and upon the sea-islands. The middle and lower portions of this and the adjacent territory were claimed by the Muskhogees, or Creeks, consisting of many tribes and associated together in a strong confederacy." That the banks of the Oconee were thickly settled by these Creek Indians is shown further by Mr. Jones when he says: "The many traces of the early constructive skill, ancient relic beds and old Indian fields along the line of the Altamaha and of the Oconee River give ample token that in former times the aboriginal population dwelling here was by no means inconsiderable."

Indian names given to creeks and other spots in Laurens County are still used today. Mr. Victor Davidson in his "History of Wilkinson County" tells of the naming of one creek near Dublin by the Indians as follows: "There is a tradition that once a tribe of Indians built their village on the creek which flows into the river just above Dublin and that a great drought came, preventing any crops from being grown and the whole tribe almost starved, so that the survivors moved away, but before leaving named the creek, Hunger and Hardship, which name it bears to this day."

Other mounds believed to be of Indian construction may be found near the Oconee River north of Dublin on the Blackshear Ferry Road six miles from town. Four miles from Dublin on the Blackshear Ferry Road there is a burial mound that is situated near what is now believed to be the Indian village Kitchee. This village was on a tall bluff overlooking the river. Here are found ancient trees around whose bases are expanded rings, as if a rope might have been tied around them, yet the rings are not broken. This was a way the Indians had of marking the place of burial of their dead. One of these trees stood at the head of a grave.

2. DeSOTO IN LAURENS COUNTY AND GEORGIA

It is interesting to know, from facts recorded by various writers of early times, that the first white man to march through the forests of this section which we now call Laurens, and the first to look upon the muddy waters of the Oconee was Hernando DeSoto.

DeSoto landed in Florida in the year 1539 with six hundred brave soldiers, two hundred horses, a great number of savage bloodhounds, fleet footed greyhounds, a vast drove of hogs, artillery, weapons, handcuffs, chains, neck-collars, and the necessary implements for refining gold, because that was the purpose of their march. They thought they would find large deposits of gold from which they would reap a much greater harvest than even DeSoto did in the realms of Atahualpa. He came from Tallahassee into Decatur County, on through Irwin and into Laurens.

DeSoto's march northward was comparable to that of Sherman when he devastated Georgia in his march to the sea during the War Between the States; so cruel and inhuman was his treatment of the Indians, and so great was his destruction to their homes and crops as he passed through their settlements.

A Spanish historian tells of him as he reached the Indian town of Toalli, where he was informed that farther northward lived a powerful king, or chief, whose country was called Ocute, which was inhabited by the Oconees, a tribe of Creek Indians.

DeSoto reached this locality in April,-1540, and according to the description of it, there can be little or no doubt that the people of Laurens County are now occupying the section called Ocute, and that Dublin is built on or near this Indian village.

On approaching Ocute, DeSoto was met by two thousand Indians bearing a present from their chief. This present consisted of many conies, patridges, bread made of maize, dogs, and two turkeys. Historians tell us that the dogs were welcomed as much as if they had been fat sheep, because there was such a scarcity of meat in the country.

When DeSoto resumed his march on April 12th, he obtained from this friendly chief four hundred burden bearers, with potatoes, corn and other foodstuffs.

This friendly treatment of DeSoto and his band by the Indians at Ocute is worthy of commendation, because in spite of the fact that DeSoto had treated the Indians so cruelly, they were hospitable to him and the suffering of these Spaniards was greatly relieved by their gifts of food.

Dr. John R. Swanton, of the Smithsonian Institution, says that DeSoto and his followers journeyed over land from a point where Hawkinsville now stands, going east and crossing the Oconee at Carr Shoals six miles above Dublin, and two miles from Blackshear's Ferry.

"When DeSoto landed in Florida and set out on his notable exploration of Florida he had also in mind to find the fabled Fountain of Youth which Ponce de Leon had failed to find. The Indians were smart enough, however, to carry him along the Tallahassee Trail across the Altamaha River instead of letting him turn northward to the wonderful fountain which he was seeking. The Indians in Florida had told DeSoto of the wonderful clear waters of the river that flowed from the Fountain of Youth, and when DeSoto reached the Altamaha River and saw that the waters were muddy he concluded that the Indians were carrying him in the wrong direction. He then turned northward again, passing through Laurens County at a point known as Old Condor, and immediately in front of the present home of Mrs. Nannie J. Linder and across Big Creek; the log of DeSoto showed that after crossing Big Creek he came upon what he described as a 'great sandy desert.' This is known today by all residents of that section of Laurens County as the Sand Ridge. Here he concluded to turn westward again.

"After crossing the Oconee River at Carr Shoals, DeSoto journeyed on along the Indian trail to Nacoochee Valley and there he heard great stories of gold to be found in the hills to the west. In Habersham County, at Clarkesville, Georgia, where the highway turns northward to Clayton, Georgia, there is a stone bearing a marker which shows that DeSoto passed that spot in May, 1540.

"DeSoto journeyed west through the gold country along the Indian trail leading to what is now called Fort Mountain. A great stone fortress is still to be seen, which was built by some prehistoric race, at Fort Mountain. Fort Mountain is only about twelve miles from Dalton, Georgia, and can be clearly seen from Dalton on a clear day. The scenic highway from Chatsworth to Ellijay over the mountains passes within two miles of this old prehistoric rock fortress and there is a side road leading out to the old rock fort.

"From Fort Mountain looking westward, the rugged mountains to the north and a line of mountains to the south enclose a long level valley leading to the Tenenssee River at Chattanooga. This inviting scene caused DeSoto to continue his journey westward; this finally led him to discover the Mississippi River, where he died and was buried in its waters.

"In the hills of North Georgia, especially around Cleveland in White County, and Dahlonega in Lumpkin County, was the industrial section of the Indians where implements of the chase were fashioned. Indian arrowheads were formed out of a special kind of flint, and they were shaped in a most ingenious manner. Long-handled gourds are native to this section of the country and Indian gunsmiths or arrowhead makers took a long-handled gourd and fixed a hole in the end of the handle so that the icy cold spring water would run out of the gourd one drop at a time. The flint to be fashioned was placed in the fire and heated. It was then held under this icy water and each drop was permitted to fall on the high places of the flint. Every time a drop of the cold water would strike this hot flint a small part of the flint would be sheared off. This, of course, was a very tedious process, but it was the best that the Indian had, and it is better than the white man has because the white man has never learned any system by which he can shape a flint into an arrowhead."

—By Hon. Tom Linder, Commissioner of Agriculture.

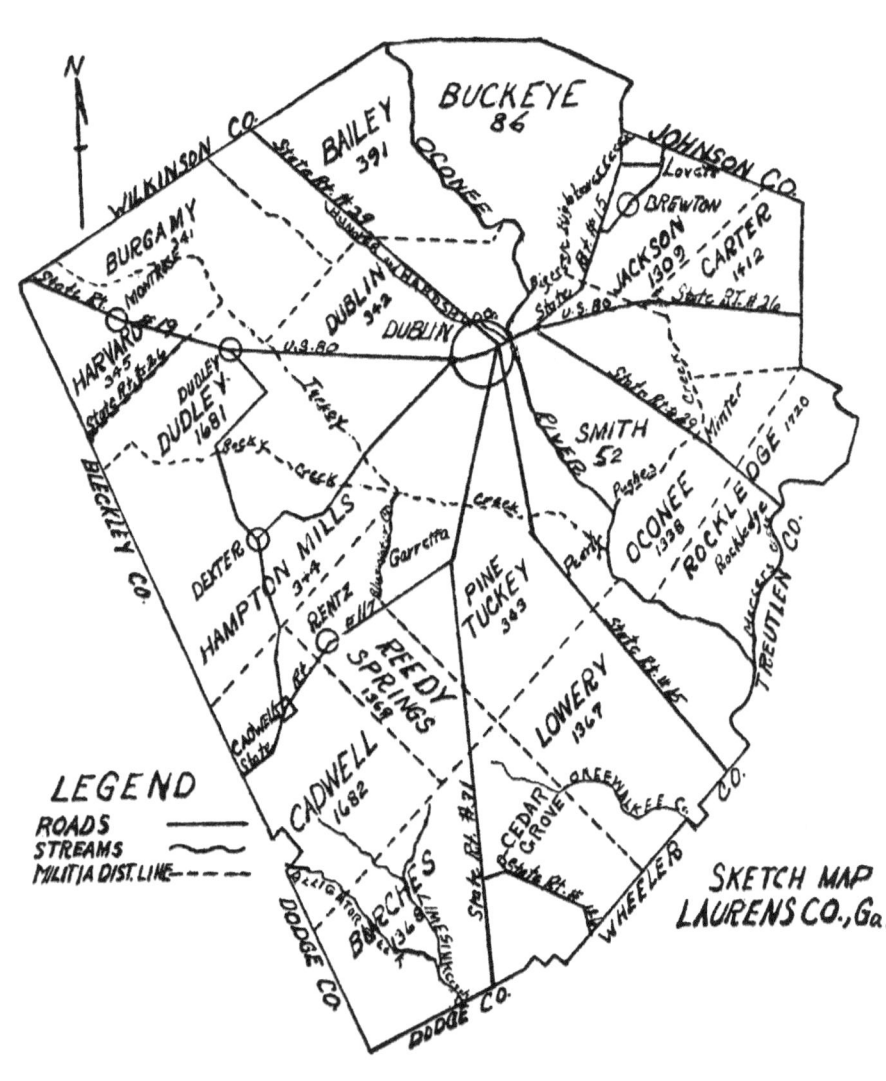

CHAPTER II

WHITE MEN IN THIS SECTION

1. BEFORE AND DURING THE REVOLUTION

In this section lying between the Oconee and the Ocmulgee Rivers there are no authentic records that white men lived here during the Spanish period. It is thought that there was a Spanish mission below the junction of the Oconee and the Ocmulgee; the priests probably visited northward for here and there in the history of this Mission there are references to Oconee Town. For some reason the Indians in this section became the enemies of the Spaniards and that would explain why there were made no Spanish settlements. (Davidson's History of Wilkinson County).

The patent granting a charter to the Trustees of Georgia in 1732 included all lands between the Savannah and the Altamaha Rivers, and their headwaters to the Pacific Ocean. This, of course, included the Oconee lands.

After the immigrants reached Savannah in February, 1733, they made a treaty with the Indians. In the treaty mention is made of the Oconee River; in the sixth article occur these words: "any runaway slave is to be returned by the Indians and a reward is to be given to the Indians for his return, provided he was taken on the farther side of the Oconee River." In this treaty the Indians agreed to allow the settlers the use of certain of their lands lying between the Oconee and Ogeechee Rivers.

The Indian signees of this treaty were the chiefs of the eight tribes of the Lower Creeks. The principal man among them was Oueekachumpa from the tribe of the Oconas, the Oconee River bears the name of this tribe. This old man was a relative of Tomochichi, that old chief who for some reason had suffered banishment at the hands of the Lower Creeks. But he had not lost his influence among them and used it to great advantage in aiding Oglethorpe.

Here and there were scattered villages, the fine hunting grounds and fertile soil made it a land congenial to Indian tastes so there was in this Oconee region a rather heavy Indian population. Here they remained undisturbed after the Spanish menace had passed over until the last quarter of the eighteenth century when white families began to push in. At first the Indians showed no objection till the number began to increase. To protect these families the colonial government built a few rude blockade forts on the Oconee and Ocmulgee. In these forts were a few huts, the owners had small clearings nearby; when they went out to work them guns were carried and careful watch for any Indian signs of approach was made. After the War the Federal Government established small garrisons of United States troops along the Oconee.

During the Revolutionary War the British employed the halfbreed McGillivray to incite the Creeks and keep them making war on the American white settlers; due to this influence there were Indian raids in this section.

One small encounter between the Indians and colonists at the very beginning of the Revolutionary War occurred on the Oconee River in what is now our county at Big Shoals which was situated a short distance from the present site of Blackshear's Ferry. In 1776 Capt. Thomas Dooley having just returned from Virginia where he had been employed in the recruiting service, with about twenty men enlisted for the Continental Brigade in Georgia; anxious to commence his military career with laurels, he advanced against a party of Indians encamped near the Oconee River. Although the enemy outnumbered him four to one he depended on courage and discipline for victory. The Indians had kept their spies on the alert and discovered his approach in time to lay an ambuscade on the route he had taken. About 7 o'clock in the morning of the 22nd of July as he was passing through a cane swamp, near Big Shoals, he was attacked in front and back by a large body of Indians hidden by the cane. Early in the skirmish Dooley received a ball in the leg breaking the bone above the ankle; apparently regardless of his own condition, he encouraged his men to continue the conflict. Discovering the commanding officer had fallen, the Indians rushed from the cane to get him. Lieutenant Cunningham, second in command, did not have his commanding officer carried off the ground but consulted his own safety, being among the first to make a disorderly retreat. When the retreat commenced Dooley called to his men and requested them not to leave him in the hands of the Indians. The last man who saw him said he was endeavoring to defend himself with the butt end of his gun although unable to stand. Dooley and three other men fell into the hands of the Indians and were murdered. Cunningham was afterward arrested and tried for cowardice but was acquitted. *(McCall's History of Georgia)*.

After the Revolutionary War, the Georgians coerced the Creeks into ceding the land between the Oconee and Ogeechee Rivers to the State. This treaty of 1783 fixed the boundary line of the frontier. In the earlier treaty of 1733 the Creeks had given over or lent to the Whites this land of theirs for use. Now they were forced to surrender it. The Creeks were not reconciled to this and went on the war path. For several years the Oconee War raged between the Creeks and the Georgians.

2. THE OCONEE WAR

During the Revolutionary War many Tories fled from the eastern part of the Georgia Colony and settled on the eastern side of the Oconee where the Indians were, because the Creeks had sided with and aided the English during the War. But Tory lands were confiscated when peace permanently came, and treaties were made with the Indians which carried them farther from the Whites. Then there was a rush of settlers and homes were made along the Oconee. But many difficulties assailed them because the State Government was too weak to protect them from Indian attacks. The half-breed McGillivray returned from Florida where he fled during the War and incited the Indians to many massacres, this menace lasted till McGillivray's death. For over ten years there was a reign of terror throughout Washington County. More memorable was the Oconee War to the people of this section than was the Revolutionary.

During this period Benjamin Harrison, a well-to-do settler of Washington County, lived opposite Carr's Bluff (six miles above Dublin). "Time after time his horses were stolen, his cows killed, his neighbors scalped."

"Harrison had no compunctions against going direct to the Indian town and taking redress. We thus find that in 1792 having lost six horses he called together his command and set out to the Indian nation across this section. Arriving at their towns on the Flint, he was promised by Uchee king and the Cussetah king that they would help him get his horses. At another time, having had a horse stolen and a cow killed by the Uchees, he gave chase with his command, overtaking them, and had a skirmish with them taking three of their guns. The Uchees in a rage returned to the nation and began raising a force to return and take vengeance upon Captain Harrison. However, through the influence of Timothy Barnard, who had married a Uchee squaw, they were induced to delay their hostile expedition. Barnard wrote to Harrison explaining the situation and asked him to give back the guns, which he did." (As the incident is recorded in Davidson's History of Wilkinson County).

When the land between the Ogeechee and the Oconee was surrendered by treaty to the State, in 1783, immediately two counties were created from it—Washington and Franklin. A part of that which is now Laurens—in fact all of Laurens east of the Oconee, was included in the county of Washington.

It was about the time of this treaty of 1783 that Laurens County began to be settled. To reward the brave patriots of the Revolution a tract of land was given to each for a new home to be located in these new counties of Washington and Franklin. This was done through Head Right Land Warrants. In 1777 the Georgia Assembly set up the Head-right system; every head of a family could have 200 acres of land, 50 additional acres for each member of his family, also 50 acres for each slave, not exceeding ten. He must settle within six months, this time was later extended to nine months. After the War a Revolutionary soldier was to have 250 acres exempt from taxation for ten years. If he desired more than this a small price was charged for each additional acre.

As a result of this in 1789 a number of settlers from North Carolina and Virginia came to Georgia. Many of these new settlers, some of them being of Scotch-Irish descent, some of Huguenot descent, settled in Washington County—a number taking up land on the east banks of the Oconee River, the frontier line.

Soon after this came the celebrated Yazoo Fraud, concerned with lands which the State of Georgia claimed. This Fraud had its climax in the burning of the papers of the Act in 1796. From Memoirs of General Blackshear, one of the original settlers of Laurens County, we find that it is probable that he was a member of the Legislature at the time and witnessed this famous bonfire.

From the time of the treaty of 1783, which made the Oconee the boundary between the Whites and the Indians, there had been trouble between the two, the settlers on the east side and the Indians on the west side. The Indians would slip across the river and steal, the Whites would retaliate. The Whites would entice the Indians across, make them drunk and rob them. The Indians would in turn retaliate.

Finally, in 1802, the United States extinguished the title of the Creeks to the lands lying west of the Oconee River. Georgia's boundaries as a state were fixed that year also.

This land obtained by treaty with the Indians at Ft. Wilkinson was divided into the counties of Wayne, Wilkinson and Baldwin. The lands were distributed by a land lottery. From part of the land of Wilkinson County, that part of Laurens west of the Oconee was made.

We see that the lands in Laurens County east of the Oconee River were to a great extent settled through Head-right land grants, while those west of the Oconee were distributed in large measure through the land lottery system. A part of Laurens was included in those lands which were concerned in the Pine Barren Frauds about this time. These lands lay in Montgomery County. There were granted 7,000,000 acres of land in excess of the actual acres, that were there. This was known as the Pine Barren Speculation of 1795.

The Head-right system was so susceptible to fraud that the method of distribution was changed by the Government to the Land Lottery system. This Act was passed in 1803. It provided that land acquired by Indian cessions should be divided in lots of 202½ acres, each lot to be given a number and a map of the whole to be made. These numbers with many blank slips were placed in a box and people were allowed to draw them. The Land Lotteries were in 1806, 1819, 1821, 1827, and 1832.

In 1794 Elijah Clarke, feeling that the Federal Government was not taking severe enough steps to destroy the Spanish menace from Florida, collected hundreds of men to lead personally in an invasion against the Spaniards. The French at enmity with Spain encouraged Clarke's expedition and planned to reinforce him at St. Mary's with a fleet that would join his forces in beseiging St. Augustine. Across the Oconee Clarke led his men and on down the western side; one of his camps was at Carr's Bluff (near Blackshear's Ferry), which was maintained till the expedition was ready to march. From a fort about where Milledgeville is now located Clarke's forces marched on passing through Laurens and arrived at St. Mary's. Then the Federal Government ordered him to stop and as the French withdrew aid, Clarke led his men back to the west side of the Oconee.

Having failed in the Florida invasion, General Clarke decided to encourage the men that he had collected, to set up an independent republic along the western side of the Oconee. Had he been successful Laurens County would probably now not be in the State of Georgia, but in the Trans Oconee Republic. But the Federal Government put an end to this, and Clarke's dream of a republic never became a reality.

In October, 1795, Benjamin Harrison almost plunged Georgia into another Creek War when he with others fell upon a number of Indians who were making merry in one of the Indian homes at Carr's Bluff. He massacred seventeen, twelve of them being Uchees. The Indians retaliated by burning the blockade that Harrison had built to protect his farm, but Harrison was not at home. Even the Whites did not blame the Indians for this raid, for they felt there had been great provocation.

Fortunately Benjamin Hawkins was made Indian agent among the Creeks, and by his tact and kindness to the Indians he brought about peaceful conditions between Whites and Indians.

Chapter III

FORMATION OF COUNTY AND LOCATION OF COUNTY SEAT

1. LAURENS, SUMPTERVILLE, AND DUBLIN

At the close of the Revolutionary War all Georgia was divided into eight counties, but a movement was soon on foot in this section, as in other sections, to create a new county in order to centralize business which was increasing each year. In this part of the State farmers were owners of vast estates which could easily be divided and sold for profit to immigrants who were eagerly looking for fertile lands along waterways.

On December 10, 1807, the General Assembly of Georgia passed an Act to lay out and identify new counties out of the counties of Baldwin and Wilkinson. One of these new counties was to be called and known by the name of Laurens in honor of John Laurens of Revolutionary fame. John Laurens, a native of South Carolina, was of Huguenot ancestry, and had the honor of being aide to General Washington. He was held in high esteem by the people of this section. The new county of Laurens was to consist of "all that part of Wilkinson County lying between the Oconee and the Ocmulgee Rivers, beginning at the mouth of Big Sandy Creek on the Oconee River running thence sixty degrees west to the Ocmulgee, thence down the course of the same to the upper corner of the Fourteenth District on said river, then up the same to the point of beginning." The population of the county at the time of its formation was 1795, of this number 485 being slaves. On December 13, 1808, by an Act of the General Assembly of Georgia about one-half of its original territory was taken from Laurens and formed into Pulaski County. This left Laurens County comparatively small and the people were dissatisfied, so in 1811 portions of Washington and Montgomery Counties on the west side of the Oconee River were added to Laurens. In this form it remained until 1858 when an Act was approved giving a strip of the eastern portion of Laurens County to Johnson County. This strip was two miles wide and nine miles long, extending from the present Dublin and Wrightsville public road, in an easternly direction, to the Emanuel County line and parallel with the original eastern boundary of Laurens. A minor change was made in 1906, but only to settle a matter of disputed territory.

Sumpterville, was the first county seat of Laurens County. It was located on the west side of the Oconee River, on Turkey Creek, where at that time the home of Major Peter Thomas was situated.

This site was eight miles west from the present site of the city of Dublin. The General Assembly of 1807 passed an Act contained in these words: "The site for the public buildings in and for the county of Laurens shall be in the town called and known by the name of Sumpterville. Between Rocky and Turkey Creeks the forest growth was largely oak and hickory and early settlers soon discovered that where there was such timbered land the soil was unusually fertile. This section thus became the most populous part of the county.

For the location of the county seat a beautiful spot was chosen near where the clear waters of Turkey Creek flowed between its banks shaded with lofty trees. The first court was held in the home of Major Thomas, the first grand jury was:

Benjamin Adams, Benjamin Brown, William Boykin, Robert Daniel, Joseph Denson, Benjamin Dorsey, Simon Fowler, Henry Fulgham, John Gilbert, Thomas Gilbert, Leonard Green, Edward Hagan, Andrew Hampton, Charles Higdon, Mark May, Gideon Mays, George Martin, William McCall, Charles Stringer, John Speight, James Sartin, Jesse Stephens, Samuel Stanley, Samuel Sparks, George Tarvin, Joseph Vickers, Jesse Wigins, Nathan Weaver, David Watson, Joseph Yarborough, William Yarbrough. (Taken from G. C. Smith's "The Story of Georgia and the Georgia People").

On December 10, 1811, when the above mentioned portions of Washington and Montgomery Counties were added to Laurens, taking in a considerable territory on the east side of the Oconee River, it became necessary to change the county seat from Sumpterville to a location nearer the center of the county. Consequently, the county authorities purchased from Joseph L. Hill the present site for the city of Dublin; it lay west of the river adjacent to what was known as the Sand Bar on the eastern side. The deed to this land was dated March 11, 1811, and recorded September 23, 1812, in Book of Deeds "B" on page 174, in the office of the Clerk of the Superior Court of Laurens County. It was made to John G. Underwood, William H. Mathers, Jethro B. Spivey, Benjamin Adams, and John Thomas, as Commissioners of the County of Laurens. The consideration expressed therein is one hundred dollars cash in hand paid, and the deed conveys "one hundred acres of the southeastwardly side of Lot No. 232 and adjoining Lot 233 in the first land district." An Act of the General Assembly was passed on December 13, 1811, authorizing the public buildings for the new county to be located on this tract of land.

The town of Dublin was incorporated by an Act of the General Assembly of Georgia, approved December 9, 1812 (Lamar's Compilations, page 951). It was perhaps the smallest town ever created by the Legislature of a sovereign state, for the Act provided that "The said incorporation shall extend to and include all the inhabitants living within 250 yards of Broad Street and within 400 yards of the

Court House in the said town of Dublin." Jonathan Sawyer, a pioneer citizen of the county, was granted the privilege of naming the new county seat of Laurens and he called it Dublin in honor of the capital of his native land, Ireland.

The site chosen, was directly on the west bank of the Oconee River, giving it a good location in South Central Georgia, where its commercial interests could be carried on by river transportation until a railroad could be built. Then both would make it an ideal place for business. Time has proved that its location has many advantages for its growth and general development.

Some historians say that Jonathan Sawyer presented the land for the county seat, but there is no record of such a gift. Sawyer married the daughter of David McCormick and beause she had been born in Dublin, Ireland, Sawyer asked that the town might be named Dublin in her honor.* There is a record that Jonathan Sawyer, who was made a County Commissioner in 1812, sold in the name of the county one acre of land to Eli S. Shorter.

2. JOHN LAURENS HERO OF THE REVOLUTION

"Lieutenant Colonel John Laurens, whose name the county bears, was the son of Honorable Henry Laurens. The Laurens family was descended from an old Huguenot family that had come to America in the earlier part of the 18th century. John Laurens was born in Charleston, S. C., in 1755. He received his early education in his native city, but as was the case with most of the more wealthy families of the day, Henry Laurens sent his son to London to be educated, and at the outbreak of the Revolution John Laurens was a law student at the Temple. When it became evident that a rupture between the colonies and the mother country was inevitable, the young student begged his father for permission to return to America that he might cast his lot with his countrymen in their struggle; but the elder Laurens was one of those who held tenaciously to the belief that all differences should be settled without bloodshed, and he refused his son the desired permission. But when a few months more had destroyed all hope of peaceable settlement, and soon after the guns of Lexington had sent their echoes reverberating into the remotest corners of the British empire, John Laurens waited no longer for his father's consent, but taking his fate in his own hands, stole away from England and on neutral vessels worked his way from France to America. He at once enlisted in the patriot army, and was soon after attached to Washington's personal staff.

"He showed the most undaunted courage in various engagements

---

* In a correspondence between H. M. Stanley and a descendant of Jonathan Sawyer, living at Hutchinson, Kansas, the latter stated that David McCormick was the ancestor of the McCormicks who established the McCormick Reaper Company.

of the war, from Brandywine to Yorktown. He was at Germantown, where he was severely wounded; he was at Monmouth; he fought gallantly in the attack on Savannah and was one of the brave defenders of Charleston where he was included in the surrender and subsequent exchange. At Yorktown he was among the first to enter the British lines and was one of the commissioners to receive the surrender of Cornwallis.

"In 1781 he was sent by Congress on a special mission to France to ask for a loan of money, and to procure military stores. For his part in this business he was honored with the thanks of Congress. Upon his return, he immediately rejoined the American army, which was then commencing the seige of Yorktown. The terms of the capitulation were arranged by him, and he received with his own hand the presented sword of Cornwallis. After this he repaired to South Carolina, a portion of which was still in the possession of the enemy; and while leading a detachment against a foraging party of the British army near Combahee in South Carolina, the 27th of August, 1782, he received a wound which terminated his life. His character was thus given by Allan: 'Colonel Laurens uniting the talents of a great officer with the knowledge of the scholar and engaging manners of a gentleman, was the glory of the army and the idol of his country'."

Laurens County is proud of the fact that it bears the name of so noble a patriot who gave his life for his country. "Such a name and such deeds should live and ever be honored."

NOTE—The above article was taken from an account of John Laurens written by G. O. Mudge in Bob Taylor's Magazine and published in the Laurens Centennial Edition of the Dublin *Courier-Dispatch*, December, 1907; and from an account written by George White in 1848.

3. BLACKSHEAR'S FERRY

In the history of Georgia, and possibly of the entire Southland, it is probable that no landmark is more fascinating, more romantic, than that of an old river ferry known as "Blackshear's Ferry." Located four and one-half miles north of the city of Dublin, in Laurens County, this flat boat still plies its way across the muddy waters of the Oconee River, carrying its human, mechanical and animal cargoes as it did a century ago. Many generations and many races have stood on its deck and watched the waters ripple in its wake; red man, white man and black man have depended upon it.

In fact, the history of Blackshear's Ferry will never be known in its entirety, for no man knows who first built it. It may be safely stated, however, that it was serving the red man under a white master before Oglethorpe settled at Savannah. Who that master was, nobody knows, for there are no records, but in history there is recorded the story of the "lost colony" that wandered south from

Virginia, and was never heard from again, and it is firmly believed by those who know something of the legend that the traces of the white tribe even now found near this spot are those of this lost colony, settled here among the friendly Cherokee Indians of the tribe of Chief Kitchee, who, together with the white leaders of the colony, constructed this ferry.

This utility, according to the oldest records available, was first known as "Tramble and Batey" Ferry, operated by these two pioneers of Georgia for many years. So closely were these white masters of the craft allied with their Indian brothers, that when the Colonial Government sent General David Blackshear here for the purpose of driving out the Indians and to survey the lands, that, under orders from his government, the General took over the river boat, and it became "Blackshear's Ferry." This name it has held on down to the present day, although it has long since been purchased by the County in which it is located, and its services made free to the people it serves. The May Term of Court, 1874, ordered purchase from E. J. Blackshear "the ferry including the landings and ferry privileges on both sides of the river and also his ferry house on this side of the river, and the land around the house, to-wit, 100 yards square."

The story of the expulsion of the red man is in itself interesting enough with its drama, its tragedy, and its pathos to fill many an hour with its telling. However, in this brief article, it will suffice to tell of the wonderful people of red skins, who lived upon the tall bluff overlooking the Oconee, just one-half mile from the present site of the ferry. Presided over by Chief Kitchee, himself a scion of many generations of chiefs, these people have left marks of advanced civilization, traces of culture, and unmistakable indications of intelligent development, both in industry and philosophy. In accordance with their custom, the red people gave this village the name of its founder, and was known as "The village of Kitchee;" it was a town of several hundred braves, and its grounds, even yet cleared and bare, cover some ten acres. Bits of pottery, tomahawks, and hundreds of arrowheads even now lie strewn about the place, unfound by relic-seekers, and left alone to tell the tale of a vanquished race.

When the Colonial Government sent its soldiers and guardians of its majesty under General Blackshear to this peaceful land to drive out these red men, the village of Kitchee was doomed. Tepees, flimsy and cold, but still to these simple children of the forest, homes, were reluctantly folded up by their owners under the grim orders of their white brothers, and loaded on the gaunt backs of Indian ponies, to be carried off to strange lands, where their hunting grounds were to be restricted, and where these children of the woods were to be shut in, like caged beasts who have never before known confinement.

And now comes one of the most touching incidents in the racial life of these sentimental and reverent people, for with their expulsion, came the realization that they must leave to the cold mercy of the white invaders, that hallowed spot on the edge of their village, that was the burial grounds of their dead. To the red man, the departed is never dead, but living as guardian angels over the mortal, living a beautiful life in the "Happy Hunting Grounds." Thus, it is said that the final council was held over the graves of their departed; the results of that council convince us that these people were both sentimental and reverent, for soon after, three old Indians came before the white commander, General Blackshear, and requested that of all this great tribe, they be allowed to remain so long as they might live, close by the graves of their fathers, guardians over their peaceful sleep. Not even a General could turn deaf ears to such a plea, and so, while their people were conveyed by the whites over the red waters of the Oconee on the old ferry, these three red men stood silhoueted against the rising sun in the East, majestic, though conquered, sentinels over sacred ground. When the last of these died, loving hands of white brothers laid them away by the side of the graves they guarded. Today, this burial ground offers a mystery yet unsolved by the highly developed minds of the white race.

For his services to his government, General Blackshear was given an area of 17 square miles, reaching out on either side of the river, and he built his beautiful home just half a mile from the site of his ferry. About this home, a village sprang up, known as "Springfield." Its postoffice was served by the old "pony express" system in its first days, but later followed by the stage coach. Today, there is no house nor evidence of this town, except a field in which farm negroes labor, and on the hill, a tiny cemetery, wherein are the graves of the old General himself, and his family, and the graves of the General's aides.

Among the mysteries of the southland, none is more baffling than that of "Indian Spring Rock" located one mile north of the present site of the ferry. The tiny trickle of crystal clear water comes flowing from the rock itself. This rock is about four feet high, and about seven feet long, and on one of its sides, it has been made as smooth as if it were turned out of one of our marble plants. Across the wide face, written, or carved into its hard surface, are characters never put there by nature. These hieroglyphics are carved in a long line across the entire surface; they have the appearance of Egyptian character, yet they have never been deciphered. Who knows but that some race of whom history has never known, sought to leave for us, in this rock, an indestructible story of former life?

To the aged man who now serves as Ferryman. his charge is sacred; it is, to him, something almost animated. He will sit and tell you, for an hour, of its legends; of its proud record of service to mankind throughout these many ages. His name is R. A. Watson, and his people have been ferrying this boat for many years—in fact, his father before him, and his grandfather before that. It is to this man, devoted to his charge, devoted to the beautiful history of this Southland, and devoted to the service of his fellowman, to whom I am indebted for my knowledge of this story. Though his years have brought him almost to his allotted time, his giant body still handles his craft with the skill of experience. His loving hands guard every board in its flat hull, and his mind still cherishes its imperishable legends.

In time of depression, Blackshear's Ferry almost lost its existence, for in an effort to cut governmental expense, the Commissioners of Laurens County considered its abolition. To the rescue of this famous landmark, came two young lawyers of Dublin, backed by the old ferryman, who plead that this utility—the oldest of its kind in America, by my knowledge—be allowed to continue to serve. The ferry was saved, and each day there are from sixty to one hundred crossings, with old Mr. Watson straining at the ropes and pulleys that pull the flat with its cargo across the river.

During the first years of the nineteenth century the ferryman was William Beaty. His home stood near the old blockhouse. It was a scene in 1808 of one of the county's largest social affairs when his daughter married Abner Hicks. Mrs. L. B. Linder, an old resident, today has in her possession an urn that was one of the bridal presents on this occasion.

The most unique character among the former ferrymen was Irwin Calhoun, his strong forte and pastime was singing. It is said that he could sing from sunset to dawn and never repeat a song.

Other ferrymen have been: S. L. Weaver, E. M. Lake, Joseph T. Watson, D. M. Watson, J. C. Jones, J. L. Bostwick, and D. W. Skipper.

The first mention of a ferry that was made on the county records is found on the Minutes of the Inferior Court under date of February 2, 1808:

"Ordered that a ferry be established across the Oconee River at Blackshear's landing at the following rates to-wit, for a loaded wagon fifty cents, empty wagon thirty-seven and half cents, loaded cart twenty-five cents, empty cart $18\frac{3}{4}$ cents, pleasure carriage waiter and horses thirty-seven and half cents, man and horse $6\frac{1}{4}$ cents, led horse and footman, all black cattle, 2 cents per head, sheep, hogs, and goats one cent each."

—*By Julia Thweatt Blackshear (Mrs. T. J.)*

4. REVOLUTIONARY SOLDIERS IN LAURENS COUNTY

Much of the land awarded soldiers for Revolutionary service in early Washington County Bounty Grants lay in what later became the county of Laurens. Thus in the early days of Laurens County many Revolutionary soldiers were numbered among her inhabitants and some of these found their last resting place within her borders. Many of the first immigrants to this county came from North Carolina and settled in a colony (Story of Georgia and Georgia People, G. G. Smith); records of their Revolutionary service are found in the "Roster of Soldiers from North Carolina in the American Revolution," published by the Daughters of the American Revolution of that state.

In the list of 600 Revolutionary soldiers living in Georgia in 1827-1828, compiled by Miss Martha Lou Houston, from original records in the National Capitol, four residents of Laurens County are listed: Jonathan Branch, Thomas McCall, Solomon Williams, and Elizabeth Keen, the widow of a North Carolina Revolutionary soldier, who was entitled to draw land in the Cherokee Land Lottery of 1838. Elizabeth Keen is buried in the old Ballard family burial ground in Laurens County, near Brewton.

With few exceptions, the names listed below, as Revolutionary soldiers from Laurens County, are recorded in Book I, "Early Wills of Laurens County, 1809-1840;" some as makers of their own wills, others as executors or witnesses to wills of relatives or friends. Indication of this is made following each name, together with the date the name appears in the records in the office of the Ordinary of the County. Unless otherwise stated, proof of Revolutionary service for these men is found in "Georgia Roster of the Revolution" by L. L. Knight. This list is incomplete, as, with few exceptions, only the names found in court records of this county are included.

ANDERSON, HENRY—Will, 1815; soldier Georgia Militia.

ANDERSON, JOHN—Early settler, Laurens County, soldier Georgia Militia.

ARLINE, JOHN—Received headright of land in Washington County, Georgia, 1784, for Revolutionary services (Ref.: Story of Georgia and Georgia People, by G. G. Smith); named in will of Thomas Pullen, 1828; buried in that part of Laurens County which later became Johnson.

BACON, JONATHAN—Will, 1832; refugee soldier, Certificate of Col. John Baker, Lieut. Col. of Militia, given at Sunbury, May 10, 1784.

BECK, SIMON—Witness, 1815; Certificate of Col. G. Lee, April 12, 1784, entitled to a Bounty Grant.

BENNETT, JOHN—Witness, 1816; granted 230 acres (on reserve) Washington County.

BLACKSHEAR, DAVID—Voucher 390 North Carolina Militia (later rose to rank of General in Indian Wars); reference: N. C. D. A. R. Roster; buried in Blackshear family burial ground, "Springfield," Laurens County, Georgia.

BRANCH, JAMES—Name on Cherokee Land Lottery List for Rick's District, Laurens County, 1838.

BUSH, WILLIAM—Listed as one of the original settlers of Laurens County; half brother of David Blackshear, and accompanied him when he immigrated from North Carolina to Georgia, reference: "Landmarks, Memorials and Legends," Knight; name listed on Pierce's Register as soldier from North Carolina, reference: N. C. D. A. R. Roster.

CARY, ALEXANDER—Name recorded in Laurens County, Georgia, Land Lottery List for 1819, under Captain Leroy G. Harris' Militia District, with the word "Revolutionary" and the numeral "4" opposite his name, indicating that he was entitled to 4 draws in this Land Lottery for Revolutionary services.

CASON, SAMUEL—Witness, 1822; Georgia soldier of the line.

COATS, JOHN G.—Will, 1837; Georgia soldier of the line; Certificate of Col. E. Clarke, Feb. 2, 1784, entitled to a Bounty of land in Washington County; also 287½ acres in Washington County, April 17, 1785.

COLEMAN, JONATHAN—Witness, 1816; name on Harvey Certified List of Georgia Revolutionary Soldiers.

COLEMAN, THEOPHILUS—Will, 1816; Lieutenant of the North Carolina Militia, November 28, 1776; reference: N. C. D. A. R. Roster.

COOKSEY, JOHN—Name recorded in Laurens County, Georgia, Land Lottery List for 1819, under Captain Hardy Griffin's Militia District, with the word "Revolutionary" and the numeral "4" opposite his name, indicating that he was entitled to 4 draws in this Land Lottery for Revolutionary services; name also appears on the Cherokee Land Lottery of 1827.

CULPEPPER, SAMSON—Will, 1823; executor, 1826; Lieut. Georgia Militia, received Bounty Warrant for Revolutionary service.

DANIEL, BENJAMIN—Will, 1816; Minute Man; on Certificate of Gen. John Twiggs, March 4, 1784, entitled to Bounty of 287½ acres in Washington County.

DARSEY, BENJAMIN—Will, 1820; Bounty of 287½ acres in Washington County, March 4, 1784, and an additional grant of 287½ acres in same county, April 26, 1785; member first Grand Jury, Laurens County, 1809, Reference, Story of Georgia, by G. G. Smith, page 284.

DARSEY, JAMES—Name recorded in Laurens County, Georgia, Land Lottery for 1819, under Captain Hardy Griffin's Militia District, with the word "Revolutionary" and the numeral "4" opposite his name, indicating that he was entitled to 4 draws in this Land Lottery for Revolutionary services; also received Bounty Grant of land in Washington County; certificate of Revolutionary service on file in the office of the Secretary of State.

DAVIS, BENJAMIN—(of Burke County)—Witness, 1798; Bounty Grants in Washington County of 287½ acres, each, March 2, 1784 and July 4, 1784.

DEAN, JOHN—Witness, 1817; Georgia soldier of the line; Bounty Grants in Washington County, of 287½ acres, each, August 12, 1784, June 7, 1784.

DEAN, WILLIAM—Witness, 1817; Sergeant under Col. Marberry; entitled to Bounty of 250 acres in Washington County.

DUNCAN, THOMAS—Will, 1823; Georgia soldier of the line; granted Bounty of 250 acres in Washington County, December 10, 1784.

FARMER, THOMAS—Will, 1817; North Carolina soldier; Reference: N. C. D. A. R. Roster.

FULLWOOD, JOHN—Will, 1828; executor, 1815; witness, 1816; name on Lottery List, 1827, Laurens County.

GLASS, JAMES—Witness, 1830; Private, Col. John Stewart's Regiment; received Bounty Warrant for Revolutionary service.

GOODMAN, HENRY—Will, 1816; Lieutenant in North Carolina Militia; reference, North Carolina D. A. R. Roster.

HAGAN, EDWARD—Georgia Soldier of the line; certificate as refugee soldier, April 7, 1785; Bounty Warrant 287½ acres in Washington County; also 287½ acres June 17, 1784; member first Grand Jury, Laurens County, 1809; reference: History of Georgia by G. G. Smith, page 283.

HAMPTON, BENJAMIN—Witness 1820, 1826, 1828; name on Certified List of Georgia Troops.

HOLLY, JONATHAN—Will, 1809; name on Certified List of Georgia Troops.

HUDSON, JOHN—Witness, 1828; Will, 1838; name on Cherokee Land Lottery List, 1838; buried in old Hudson estate (now owned by the Browning family) in southern part of Laurens County, near Cedar Grove.

HUTCHINS, EDWARD—Name recorded in Laurens County, Georgia, Land Lottery of 1819, under Captain Hardy Griffin's Militia District, with the word "Revolutionary" and the numeral "4" opposite his name, indicating that he was entitled to 4 draws in this Land Lottery for Revolutionary services. Name also appears in the Harvey List of Georgia Revolutionary soldiers.

JOINER, JESSE—Will, 1827; Witness, 1813; certified list of Georgia Revolutionary soldiers; Lottery, 1827, Laurens County.

JONES, JONATHAN—Will, 1827; Captain; Bounty Grant of 287½ acres in Washington County, June 5, 1784.

KINCHEN, WILLIAM—Early settler, Laurens County; soldier, North Carolina Militia.

LIVINGSTON, WILLIAM—Witness, 1813; listed on Harvey List as Lieutenant; Bounty Grant in Washington County, April 26, 1784.

MCCALL, THOMAS—Named as husband in Will of Elizabeth Mary Ann McCall, 1830-1840; Certificate as refugee soldier, May 22, 1784; Bounty Grants in Washington County, June 12, 1784; name on Cherokee Land Lottery List, 1838, for Hobbs' District, Laurens County. Buried in old cemetery at Dublin, Georgia, by side of his wife Elizabeth Mary Ann McCall.

MANNING, BENJAMIN—Witness, 1816; name on Cherokee Land Lottery List, 1827, Bibb County.

MANNING, DRURY—Heir in Will of John Manning, 1813; Bounty Grant of 287½ acres, Washington County, April 26, 1784.,

MANNING, JOHN—Will, 1813; Georgia soldier of the line; Bounty Grant, Washington County, June 16, 1784.

MATTHEWS, WILLIAM H.—Member Board of Commissioners, Laurens County, December 10, 1810; Listed in Knight's Roster under "Georgia Revolutionary Pensioners Living in Other States," as living in Florida.

MCLENDON, DENNIS—Listed as one of the first settlers of Laurens County by G. G. Smith in "Story of Georgia;" received Bounty Grant of 287½ acres for Revolutionary service.

MOORE, THOMAS, DR.—Witness, 1823, 1826, 1829; Georgia soldier of the line; Bounty Grant of 287½ acres, Washington County, Oct. 18, 1784; 287½ acres, same County, Jan. 29, 1785.

O'NEAL, WILLIAM—Will, 1826; private, Ballard's Company, North Carolina Militia, July 20, 1778, served for nine months; reference: N. C. D. A. R. Roster.

PHILLIPS, BURRELL—Executor, 1814; Georgia soldier of the line; Bounty Grant, Washington County, Dec. 10, 1784.

PHILLIPS, MARK—Will, 1814; Georgia soldier of the line; Bounty Grant of 575 acres, Franklin County, Feb. 2, 1784.

POPE, WILEY—Witness, 1824; Colonel, Georgia Troops, received Bounty Warrant for Revolutionary service.

PULLEN, THOMAS—Will, 1828; name on Lottery List, 1827, Laurens County.

ROBERTS, FREDERIC—Early settler, Laurens County; buried in an old cemetery (since discarded) located where W. & T. depot now stands; native of Virginia, soldier of South Carolina Militia; received grant of 300 acres in Burke County, Georgia, in 1784.

Rowland, John—Will, 1829; Witness, 1818; name on Harvey List of Georgia Revolutionary Soldiers.

Ryalls, Wright—Witness, 1813; name on Lottery List, 1827, Telfair County (This county joins Laurens to the south).

Shine, John—Name on Harvey List of Georgia Revolutionary Soldiers, buried in the Blackshear Family Burial Ground, Springfield, Laurens County.

Smith, Hardy—Soldier, North Carolina Militia, Wilmington District; Reference: North Carolina D. A. R. Roster; buried in the Old Smith Burial Ground 10 miles south of Dublin near the old River Road.

Spear, David—Will, 1820; Soldier, Continental Line of North Carolina; Reference: North Carolina D. A. R. Roster.

Swilley, Nicholas—Name recorded in Laurens County, Georgia, Land Lottery for 1819, under Captain Adam Jones' Militia District, with the word "Revolutionary" and the numeral "4" opposite his name, indicating that he was entitled to 4 draws in this Land Lottery for Revolutionary services.

Tarvin, George—Georgia soldier of the line; Bounty Grant of 287½ acres in Washington County, February 23, 1784; member first Grand Jury, Laurens County; Reference: "Story of Georgia" by G. G. Smith, page 284.

Thomas, John—Witness, 1808, 1823; name on Harvey List of Georgia Revolutionary Soldiers; member Board of Commissioners, Laurens County, December 13, 1810.

Thomas, Peter—Witness, 1816; Georgia soldier of the line; received two warrants for 500 acres land in Washington County; first Superior Court of Laurens County was held in his home.

Vickers, Thomas—Witness, 1828; Georgia soldier of the line; Bounty Grants in Washington County, 287½ acres, each, March 11, 1784, and July 9, 1784.

Warren, Eli (Elias)—Witness, 1826, 1838, 1830; Bounty Grant, Liberty County, July 22, 1785, for Revolutionary service.

Warren, Josiah—Name on Harvey List of Georgia Revolutionary Soldiers, rank of Captain; buried at Poplar Springs Cemetery, Laurens County; Reference: "Landmarks, Memorials, and Legends," Knight.

Whitehead, William—Will, 1817; private, Continental Line of North Carolina, June 1, 1779, 18 months; received Bounty Grant of 250 acres, April 30, 1783.

Williams, Solomon—Name on Cherokee Land Lottery List, 1838, Nick's District, Laurens County; member first Grand Jury, Laurens County, 1809; Reference: "Story of Georgia" by G. G. Smith.

Yarbrough, William—Name on Lottery List, 1827, Laurens County; member first Grand Jury, Laurens County, 1809; Reference: "Story of Georgia" by G. G. Smith.

Young, Oben (Ween)—Will, 1826; Georgia soldier of the line.

Young, Phirson—Name recorded in Laurens County, Georgia, Land Lottery List for 1819, under Captain Hardy Griffin's Militia District, with the word "Revolutionary" and the numeral "4" opposite his name, indicating that he was entitled to 4 draws in this Land Lottery for Revolutionary services.

Family data for some of the Revolutionary Soldiers listed above will be found under "Early Wills of Laurens County."

—By Henrietta Sanders Freeman (Mrs. F. B.)

CHAPTER IV

PIONEER PERIOD

1. PIONEERS

The outstanding figure in Laurens County history in the first decades of the 19th century was General David Blackshear, born in North Carolina. He was only twelve years old when the Declaration of Independence was signed but he was present at two battles. His educational advantages were confined to a few months in crude pioneer schools. He learned the art of surveying and this occupation led him to Georgia. In 1790 with some of his relatives he moved from Carolina to the Georgia frontier.

In the oak and hickory woods of what later became Laurens County he made a settlement near the banks of the Oconee and named it Springfield. He became a leader in the Oconee Wars and through the dangers of Indian attack and massacres he maintained a home for himself and relatives. He became a man of honor in Georgia and was held in high esteem by the Governors. He held appointments under Jared Irwin and James Jackson. When there was a prospect of war with France in Washington's administration he was ordered by the Adjutant General of Georgia to raise a body of soldiers.

So busy had his life been in fighting Indians and establishing civilization that he did not marry till he reached his 38th year. In 1802 he married Miss Fannie Hamilton of Hancock County. She possessed six stalwart brothers who became well known as warriors and statesmen.

David Blackshear was active in exposing the Yazoo frauds and stood by the Governor when fire was brought down from heaven to destroy the iniquitous papers in front of the capitol at Louisville. During the War of 1812 he was appointed Brigadier-General by Governor Mitchell. He served as war correspondent during the war.

In 1816 he was elected to the Senate, a position he held until 1825 when he voluntarily gave up public office. Early the next year he resigned his commission as a general of the state militia. On July 4, 1837, he died, a man of wealth, of honor, and of high esteem, and was buried on the land on which so long he had lived.

General Blackshear and Governor Troup were close personal friends, and the official esteem in which he was held by the Governor is shown in Governor Troup's letter to him on the occasion of his resignation as Brigadier-General. (Here follows copy of letter)

"Executive Department,
Milledgeville, Ga.
February 21st, 1826.

"Dear Sir: It would be ungenerous, after you had filled so many offices of trust and honor, civil and military, and all to the satisfaction and advantage of your country, to deny you, in the decline of life the privilege to retire from your military command. I regret, notwithstanding, the infirmities of age or any other causes, should deprive the public of your usefulness in any sphere of action. It is known that if your strength has departed, your patriotism remains unquenched, and that in any peril or danger threatened to the country, we can still confidently appeal to that first of virtues which has never failed you in the worst of times, and which you will carry with you to the grave. Your resignation is accepted with the sincere hope that many days of happiness remain to you.

GEORGE M. TROUP

To Brigadier-General Blackshear:"

In Laurens County today are prominent citizens related to the intrepid David Blackshear, but only the remains of the family burial ground are left as reminders of this famous Georgian.

An admirer of Blackshear, Stephen H. Miller, in his "Bench and Bar of Georgia," (Vol. I) gives a picture of General Blackshear's plantation, Springfield.

"Besides his grapery of several acres, General Blackshear owned large orchards, from which he distilled apple and peach brandies of the purest kind. Nothing was neglected in the manufacture, from the gathering of the fruit to the dropping of the rectified spirits from the tube. He usually gave morning drams to his slaves; and whenever, from exposure to cold or water, they required a tonic, he ordered them to receive it from his cellar. It was often the case that, in heavy work—raising houses, building mill-dams, and adjusting timbers—they were in condition to receive it; but he never permitted them to have it in such quantity as to produce intoxication, and he saw nothing to regret from the custom.

"He also cultivated the cane, making more than enough sugar and syrup for his own use. It was his rule to let his neighbors have whatever he could spare from his farm. He never profited by scarcity and high prices in the market. His rates were just fairly remunerative. He never speculated on the necessities of the people. Being a first rate judge of human nature, he was not often deceived. To the honest and industrious he was ever a friend; to the idle and dissolute he showed no favor. Though obliging in his disposition, he adhered to certain rules which he adopted early in life:

"1. Never spend any money before you get it.
"2. Never pay other people's debts.
"3. Never pay interest.

"Much is comprehended in these words. They reveal the secret of his prosperity. General Blackshear was governed by principle —not by impulse, hence this great influence and success."

That General Blackshear was a great example of southern hospitality is revealed by Major Miller:

"It was customary for the court, including both the judges and the bar, while journeying on the circuit, to stop with General Blackshear at leisure intervals. The dignified Early, the jovial Strong, and other high functionaries, who enjoined silence in court and held the multitude in awe, laid aside official consequence and shot duck and angled with as much glee as the boys who were furnished them as guides and companions. The judges would go to the mill and wade upon the sheeting or creep softly upon the dam, spearing the finny tribe or harpooning a turtle, with perfect relish for the sport. After such achievements, the sideboard was called for its quota of refreshment. It was all right then, but a very decided change has since taken place; and sideboards, wine, brandy, and such old-fashioned luxuries have been dispensed with—certainly an improvement on the virtues of our predecessors."

Among the pioneers are the names of David Blackshear, William Bush, Amos Love, Henry Fuqua, Eli Warren, John Clark, Jethro Weaver, Colonel McCormick, Benjamin Hampton, Hardy Smith, Jethro Spivey, Thomas Moore, Gilliard Anderson, Alexander and Noah Stringer, Benjamin Daniel, Elisha Ballard, Dennis McLendon, John, Charles and Moses Guyton, Samuel and Jeremiah Yopp, James Ira Stanley, and Thomas McCall.

David Blackshear came from North Carolina to this territory before the county was created; with him came William Bush, his half brother, and later his brother, Joseph Blackshear.

Elisha Ballard came from Virginia before the county was created, and developed large plantings east of the Oconee River.

Noah Stringer, a farmer, was active in county affairs, at one time serving as a judge of the Inferior Court.

Hardy Smith came to this section soon after the Revolutionary War. Gilliard Anderson became one of the county's largest slave owners.

Benjamin Daniel came from North Carolina to settle on a bounty tract on Buckeye Creek. These "bounty lands" were granted by the National Government as a reward to Revolutionary soldiers. From the five children of this Daniel are many descendants in the county today.

Henry C. Fuqua owned farm lands on each side of the Oconee.

It is said that it was he who first discovered that cotton seed was a fertilizer, and that this discovery was made by accident. Some of his descendants live in Laurens at the present time.

Robert Coats came from Savannah with many slaves and became a large planter in the Poplar Springs community. The Stringers also lived in this community.

John, Charles, and Moses Guyton came from South Carolina and purchased large holdings on the Buckeye Creek. Their father, Moses Guyton, had won for himself an enviable fame in the Revolutionary War and his descendants have figured prominently in county affairs. Descendants are still living in Laurens County.

Dennis McLendon was a Revolutionary soldier who settled on a bounty tract in Laurens. He and his descendants have been large land owners in the part of the county in the neighborhood of Blue Water Creek.

Samuel and Jeremiah Yopp came to Laurens about 1815 from North Carolina. Samuel settled on Turkey Creek and Jeremiah in Dublin. They became extensive landowners and were among the wealthiest men of the County.

James Ira Stanley came to Laurens County from his native state, North Carolina, and became a large land owner. His descendants have been prominent citizens here for many generations.

John Clark came to Laurens from Burke County about the year 1800 and settled on what is now the Telfair Road in the Cedar Grove community. Some of his descendants are still living in the county.

One of the earliest settlers, in what was afterwards Laurens County, was Amos Love. He was the third in a direct line bearing the same name, all natives, probably of Salisbury District, North Carolina. The North Carolina Historical and Geological Register for April, 1900, page 220, exhibits the abstract of the will of Amos Love I. It was dated August 15, 1770, and probated October 30, 1779. In this will the first Amos mentions his son by the same name, and names him co-executor, with the testator's wife, Mary.

Amos Love II served in the War of the American Revolution as First Lieutenant in a regiment raised in the Salisbury District, according to Wheeler's History of North Carolina, Volume I, page 80. He afterwards moved to Onslow County, North Carolina, where he died in 1798. He was there Judge of the Court of Common Pleas and Quarter Sessions, and the minutes and judgments of the Court bearing his signature are still extant. He was possessed of many acres and many slaves, as indicated by his will; for, besides providing for his wife, Mary, and daughters, he gave a plantation and negroes to each of his three sons, Amos, John, and Charles. (Records of Onslow County Wills published by the North Carolina Historical Commission.)

Amos Love III. and his two brothers removed, shortly after their father's death, to that part of Wilkinson County, which afterwards became Laurens County, in this State. Amos Love acquired large land holdings—thousands of acres—a few miles north of Dublin, on the west side of the Oconee along Hunger and Hardship Creek. He married Margaret James. He was an active Baptist, and gave the land on which Poplar Springs Church was built. He was the first clerk of the Superior Court of Laurens County, serving from its organization.

He was one of those who were appointed commissioners of the Court house and jail of the county upon the passage of the Act to make permanent the site of the public buildings in Dublin, his fellow-commissioners being John G. Underwood, David Blackshear, Neill Monroe, Thomas Moore, Archibald Griffin, George W. Welch, Lunsford C. Pitts, and John Guyton, the last named being appointed in the place of Noah Stringer, who had removed to Mississippi. (Lamar's Digest, p. 22). Benjamin Adams and Jethro B. Spivey had originally been named as two of the commissioners, but they resigned. (Lamar's Digest, p. 1227).

It may be declared therefore that Amos Love was one of the fathers of Dublin—one of the founders— for he was one of those to decide just where the permanent buildings should be fixed definitely—the precise location of the county site—that afterwards became the City of Dublin.

Mr. Love became a leading merchant of Dublin—"A. Love & Co.," being a well known house.

In 1819 he was elected to represent the county in the General Assembly and served for three years.

He is represented as having been a gentleman of wide reading—and the inventory of his estate and the returns of his administrators indicate that he was fond of books and periodicals—and of gentle, engaging manners. Certain it is that he played a large part in the beginnings of the county's history, and enjoyed the confidence and esteem of his neighbors.

Thomas McCall was born, in 1764, in North Carolina. He was a Revolutionary soldier and after the War came to Georgia. In 1818 he moved to Laurens County and became a large planter and winegrower. He lived on a large plantation east of the Oconee which he called "Retreat" and here he reared five lovely daughters whose marriages have furnished well-known names in Dublin and Laurens County—the Moores, the Stanleys, the Yopps, the Rowes, the Burneys, the Guytons, the Chappells, the Hicks, the Kellams, and the Stevens.

Thomas McCall, after coming to Georgia, held the office of State Surveyor-general for nine years. His brother was Major Hugh McCall, who wrote the first history of Georgia.

2. THE WAR OF 1812

The settlers along the Oconee were making headway in building better homes and clearing broad acres when they were again threatened with Indian attacks, and were made anxious by the turn of foreign affairs against our young republic. The Napoleonic War was on in Europe, again England and France were enemies, and America knew that each of these countries would threaten the trade of our young nation, and would contend for supremacy in the New World. The remembrance of Indian attacks and atrocities that had prevailed in the Revolutionary War was fresh in the minds of the frontier settlers. They knew that Britain and possibly France would again send their agents to incite the Indians. The Central Government was weak so the State Government resolved to protect itself, and military companies were organized and forts ordered by the Governor to be built.

David Blackshear of Laurens County, who had distinguished himself in Indian warfare, was put in charge of forces at Fort Hawkins. At this time the remotest settlement of the country between the Oconee and Ocmulgee was Hartford, Pulaski County (now Hawkinsville). The Governor of Georgia knew that forces and supplies would have to be hurried from Milledgeville, Georgia's capital, to Hartford, so he ordered a road to be built. This became the famous Hartford Road which passed through Baldwin, Wilkinson, Twiggs, and Pulaski counties. The road was finished just before the War of 1812 was declared; it was a rush job and every able-bodied man between sixteen and fifty living within three miles of the road was drafted in its building. Laurens County men were too far to be used. General Blackshear made important use of this road during the War, for it became his principal line of communication.

During this war, Tecumseh, chief of the Shawnees, incited by the French went through the Creek lands fomenting anger against the American white settlers. His powers stirred the Creeks in the Ocmulgee area and even the Seminoles in Florida.

In 1813, under the influence of Tecumseh, the great chief of the Tallassees went on the war path and turned his face eastward. Creeks and Cherokees friendly to the whites took up arms against him, but the Federal and Georgia governments sent them no help. Not until an August day when his forces made a surprise attack and massacred the men at Fort Mims did the white government wake up. Then, as the hostile Indians started for Coweta Town (now Columbus) and what they deemed would be a triumphant march of destruction through Georgia to the Savannah, the Governor of Georgia sent General Floyd with the Georgia Militia against them; David Blackshear in command of the Second Brigade of the Fifth Division was sent with Floyd. His division was composed of men from Laurens, Wilkinson, Twiggs, Pulaski, and Telfair counties.

Before the attack on Fort Mims, Blackshear had been ordered by Governor Mitchell to fortify the frontier. In Twiggs County he built three forts along the Ocmulgee, and seven forts in Pulaski and Telfair, and men from Wilkinson and Laurens, under Colonel William Cawley, guarded these garrisons. When Floyd was sent to Alabama General Blackshear was sent with him, and when Floyd was wounded in the attacks on the Indian towns of Autossee and Tallassee, Blackshear was appointed to take his place. When Floyd was again able to take active service, General Blackshear assembled his forces with Hartford as headquarters, and was in complete charge of the Georgia frontier.

By the middle of 1814, Washington, the nation's capital, had been taken by the English and Georgia feared invasion from the British on the southern Atlantic coast or from the Gulf. Soon news came that British ships had landed at Apalachicola and were preparing the Seminoles to attack Georgia. To add to this terror it was learned that the Creek Indians who had been driven off by the forces of General Jackson were hastening to join with the Seminoles. Laurens County men were in the companies sent to reinforce the frontier forts and join General Jackson in defending New Orleans, also in the forces sent by Governor Early to Mobile. General Blackshear's division was sent from Hartford to a position on the Flint River. From here he was ordered by the head of the Federal forces to Mobile, the point where the British were to attack after their attack on New Orleans.

But even while General Blackshear was on the march, a contradictory order came to him from the Governor of Georgia.

Governor Early learned that the British troops had landed on Cumberland and were inciting the Seminole Indians and run-away slaves to make attacks. Immediately he sent word to General Blackshear to change his course and march for the Atlantic Coast. Realizing how grave was the threat General Blackshear turned about, making his way from Fort Hawkins, through Telfair County, and on to Darien. For many years the road over which he passed was known as the Blackshear Road.

Just before he reached Darien he received news of the victory at New Orleans, and he knew the war was virtually over. He occupied Sapelo Island and cut off the British lines; before he made battle on them, news of peace came.

To follow the course and accomplishments of this able Laurens County man is to learn almost the whole story of the War of 1812 in Georgia.

Little has been written concerning the land activities during the War of 1812. George Michael Troup of Laurens County, was re-elected to Congress October 1810, and on the 26th day of May, 1812, Col. Troup was appointed chairman of the committee on Military Affairs. At the time of this appointment there was on the

Republican side of the house men of marked ability. Laurens County was proud of her son who held this appointment during the entire war. In the "Life of Troup," by E. J. Harden, he says, "Col. Troup was at the seat of the national government when the British took possession of the city of Washington, burned the Capitol and other buildings, and committed other acts of outrage unknown to civilized warfare." His proud spirit was fired with indignation at these atrocities. We have it from good authority that among the few persons in Washington at the time who did not forget their propriety in the general panic which pervaded all classes, were: James Monroe, then Secretary of State, and George Michael Troup, Congressman from Laurens County, Georgia.

Troup being chairman of Committee of Military Affairs was the principal director in the War of 1812.

AN INCIDENT OF THE WAR OF 1812

It was in the attack on Autossee that a Laurens County man, Ezekiel Attaway, distinguished himself for bravery. The incident is thus recorded by Frances Mitchell in her "Georgia Land and People":

"In this battle, Captain John Irwin commanded the cavalry, and Captain Jett Thomas the artillery; the latter, marching in front of the right column, elicited great praise from General Floyd for his gallantry in the action. He possessed the art of inspiring his men to brave deeds on the battlefield. In the heat of the combat, one of his cannons had but three men left. At this moment it seemed that the Indians would certainly capture it—for ten men out of the thirteen who had defended it were weltering in their gore, when Ezekiel Attaway, with heroic firmness, wrested the traversing handspike from the carriage of the gun, saying to his two brave comrades: "With this, I will defend the piece as long as I can stand. We must not give up the gun, boys. Seize the first weapon you can lay your hands on and stick to your post until the last!" Is it any wonder that the Indians gave way before such determined courage?"

3. INDIAN TROUBLES AFTER THE WAR OF 1812

In 1818 when the Indians were again giving trouble, General Rabun requested General Jackson, in charge of the Federal Indian suppression, to protect Georgia's exposed area; when he received no answer from Jackson he sent Captain Obed Wright against the Felemna and Hopaunee towns. Wright, with two companies of mounted men under Captain Rogers, and Captain Robinson and infantry forces under Dean and Childs, marched from Hartford (Hawkinsville) to Fort Early (Cordele). There he learned that the chief of the nearby Indian town had joined a hostile force at Chehaw or

Cheraw (near Leesburg). Captain Wright followed him to Chehaw and deeming that this was a Hopaunee town attacked the village and destroyed it with fire. Although these Cheraw Indians tried to raise a flag of truce, Wright ruthlessly pushed the attack. This act of the Georgia troops angered the whole country, for the Chehaws were a friendly people of the Creeks and had aided General Jackson with food and horses when he was fighting the hostile Creeks.*

Laurens County furnished troops and wagons for this expedition; below follows a list of soldiers and property furnished.

MUSTER ROLL OF CAPT. ROGERS' COMPANY OF GEORGIA CAVALRY ORDERED INTO SERVICE BY THE EXECUTIVE

FROM CAPT. HEAD'S COMPANY (Militia District)

No.	Grade	Name	Commencement and Expiration of Service
	Captain	Timothy L. Rogers	April 18, 1818-April 27, 1818
	1st Lieut.	Samuel Calhoun	April 18, 1818-April 27, 1818
	2nd Lieut.	George Powell	April 18, 1818-April 27, 1818
	Cornet	Isaac Welch	April 18, 1818-April 27, 1818
	1st Sergt.	Elisha Debose	April 18, 1818-April 27, 1818
	2nd Sergt.	John Sperlin	April 18, 1818-April 27, 1818
	3rd Sergt.	Charles Davis	April 18, 1818-April 27, 1818
	4th Sergt.	Epharim Sanders	April 18, 1818-April 27, 1818
	1st Corpl.	Charles Broocks	April 18, 1818-April 27, 1818
	2nd Corpl.	Joseph Slaton	April 18, 1818-April 27, 1818
	3rd Corpl.	Goodridge Driver	April 18, 1818-April 27, 1818
	Trumptor	Seborn Durham	April 18, 1818-April 27, 1818
1	Private	Alpherd, Jephthy	April 18, 1818-April 27, 1818
2	Private	Brooks, Samuel	April 18, 1818-April 27, 1818
3	Private	Booth, John T.	April 18, 1818-April 27, 1818
4	Private	Booth, Wiley	April 18, 1818-April 27, 1818
5	Private	Barefield, Sampson	April 18, 1818-April 27, 1818
6	Private	Cox, Waide P.	April 18, 1818-April 27, 1818
7	Private	Caliway, Wm.	April 18, 1818-April 27, 1818
8	Private	Caliway, Benjn.	April 18, 1818-April 27, 1818
9	Private	Caliway, Josiah	April 18, 1818-April 27, 1818
10	Private	Corethers, George	April 18, 1818-April 27, 1818
11	Private	Cormer, James	April 18, 1818-April 27, 1818
12	Private	Champin, William	April 18, 1818-April 27, 1818
13	Private	Corethers, Andy	April 18, 1818-April 27, 1818
14	Private	Caten, Head Williams	April 18, 1818-April 27, 1818
15	Private	Davis, Williams	April 18, 1818-April 27, 1818
16	Private	Durham, Sanders	April 18, 1818-April 27, 1818
17	Private	Davis, Joshua	April 18, 1818-April 27, 1818
18	Private	Driver, Jules	April 18, 1818-April 27, 1818
19	Private	Driver, Giles	April 18, 1818-April 27, 1818
20	Private	Eles, Joshua Y.	April 18, 1818-April 27, 1818
21	Private	Feltes, Cary	April 18, 1818-April 27, 1818
22	Private	Finey, Henry	April 18, 1818-April 27, 1818
23	Private	Gammon, Joel	April 18, 1818-April 27, 1818
24	Private	Gammon, Willis	April 18, 1818-April 27, 1818
25	Private	Gun, Moses	April 18, 1818-April 27, 1818

* White's—"Historical Collections of Georgia."

No.	Grade	Name	Commencement and Expiration of Service
26	Private	Hester, William B.	April 18, 1818-April 27, 1818
27	Private	Harderson, Cullen	April 18, 1818-April 27, 1818
28	Private	Hill, Wm. B.	April 18, 1818-April 27, 1818
29	Private	Hancock, Simeon	April 18, 1818-April 27, 1818
30	Private	Hunt, John R.	April 18, 1818-April 27, 1818
31	Private	Isleants, Stephen	April 18, 1818-April 27, 1818
32	Private	Jones, Wm.	April 18, 1818-April 27, 1818
33	Private	Jones, John B.	April 18, 1818-April 27, 1818
34	Private	Low, Wm.	April 18, 1818-April 27, 1818
35	Private	Ledlow, Lewis	April 18, 1818-April 27, 1818
36	Private	Long, Philip	April 18, 1818-April 27, 1818
37	Private	More, Samuel	April 18, 1818-April 27, 1818
38	Private	McLendon, Lewis	April 18, 1818-April 27, 1818
39	Private	Marchel, Chesley	April 18, 1818-April 27, 1818
40	Private	McLemore, Jesey	April 18, 1818-April 27, 1818
41	Private	McLendon, Hugh	April 18, 1818-April 27, 1818
42	Private	Medlock, George D. F.	April 18, 1818-April 27, 1818
43	Private	McCardel, Charles	April 18, 1818-April 27, 1818
44	Private	McLemore, William	April 18, 1818-April 27, 1818
45	Private	Picket, Martin	April 18, 1818-April 27, 1818
46	Private	Pleaseants, Thomas	April 18, 1818-April 27, 1818
47	Private	Parmer, George	April 18, 1818-April 27, 1818
48	Private	Pedey, Bradford	April 18, 1818-April 27, 1818
49	Private	Roberts, Luke	April 18, 1818-April 27, 1818
50	Private	Roberts, Reuben	April 18, 1818-April 27, 1818
51	Private	Stubbs, John	April 18, 1818-April 27, 1818
52	Private	Striplin, Benjamin	April 18, 1818-April 27, 1818
53	Private	Stephens, Liles	April 18, 1818-April 27, 1818
54	Private	Stewart, John	April 18, 1818-April 27, 1818
55	Private	Stewart, Samuel D.	April 18, 1818-April 27, 1818
56	Private	Tamplin, John	April 18, 1818-April 27, 1818
57	Private	Tripp, Samuel	April 18, 1818-April 27, 1818
58	Private	Turner, James	April 18, 1818-April 27, 1818
59	Private	Word, Wm.	April 18, 1818-April 27, 1818
60	Private	Wimberly, Titus	April 18, 1818-April 27, 1818
61	Private	Wilder, Werd	April 18, 1818-April 27, 1818
62	Private	Wilder, Green	April 18, 1818-April 27, 1818
63	Private	Watley (or Wotley), Willmoth	April 18, 1818-April 27, 1818
64	Private	Wilson, Reding	April 18, 1818-April 27, 1818
65	Private	Woodsworth, Elbert	April 18, 1818-April 27, 1818
66	Private	Williamson, Wm.	April 18, 1818-April 27, 1818
67	Private	Woodsworth, John	April 18, 1818-April 27, 1818
68	Private	Woodsworth, Daniel	

I do hereby certify that this Muster Roll is a true statement, this 16th day of July, 1818.

TIMOTHY L. ROGERS, Captain.

(Military Records, 1799-1839, pp. 271-272, Georgia Department of Archives).

MUSTER ROLL OF THE LAURENS TROOP OF LIGHT DRAGOONS, GEORGIA MILITIA, COMMANDED BY CAPTAIN JACOB ROBINSON AND ORDERED INTO SERVICE BY HIS EXCELLENCY THE GOVERNOR

No.	Rank	Name Present	Time in Service
1	Capt.	Jacob Robinson	30 days
2	1st Lieut.	Charles S. Guyton	30 days
3	2nd Lieut.	John I. Underwood	28 days
4	Cornet	Lewis Joiner	28 days
5	Trumpter	Terrel Higden	28 days
6	1st Sgt.	Wm. A. Underwood	31 days
7	2nd Sgt.	John Anderson	31 days
8	3rd Sgt.	John Fort	31 days
9	4th Sgt.	Frederick Carter	31 days
10	1st Corpl.	Clement Fennel	28 days
11	2nd Corpl	David Speairs	28 days
12	3rd Corpl.	Nicholas Baker	28 days
13	4th Corpl.	Wm. H. Parimore	28 days
14	Private	Speir Knight	28 days
15	Private	John Cory	28 days
16	Private	Robert Knight	28 days
17	Private	John Armstrong	28 days
18	Private	Wm. Fountain	28 days
19	Private	James Knight	28 days
20	Private	John Spicer	28 days
21	Private	Joel Ware	28 days
22	Private	Henry C. Fukeway	28 days
23	Private	John Underwood	28 days
24	Private	Robert Coats	28 days
25	Private	William Carson	28 days
26	Private	James Pickeron	28 days
27	Private	Samuel Hill	28 days
28	Private	James Glass	28 days
29	Private	John N. Martin	28 days
30	Private	William Oliver	28 days
31	Private	Eli Ballard	28 days
32	Private	Robert Thomas	28 days
33	Private	John G. Petre	28 days
34	Private	William Cauthron	28 days
35	Private	William Fulwood	28 days
36	Private	Thomas Riggins	15 days
37	Private	Thomas W. Anderson	8 days
38	Private	Littlejohn G. Hall	15 days
39	Private	Jones Levingston	15 days
40	Private	Joel Culpeper	15 days
41	Private	Lanier Smith	8 days
42	Private		
43	Privtae	Levan Adams	8 days
44	Private	Daniel W. Duffie	6 days
45	Private	William Picket	6 days
46	Private	James Beaty	28 days

I certify on honor that the within Muster Roll exhibits a true and fair statement of the Laurens Troop of Light Dragoons Georgia Militia ordered into Service by his Excellency, the Governor, under my command. April 27, 1818.

JACOB ROBINSON, Captain,
Comdg. L. D. G. Militia.

(Military Records, 1799-1839, p. 273—Department of Archives of Georgia).

OWNERS OF BAGGAGE WAGON—TIME IN SERVICE EACH

Isaac Robinson, 1 Wagon—Seventeen days.
John Barlow 1 Wagon—Ten days.
Mrs. Anderson 1 Wagon—Thirteen days.

Captain's pay 30 days at $56.00 per month, is $56.00; 1st Lieut. pay 30 days at $46.00 per moth, is $46.00; 2nd Lieut. pay 28 days at $41.00 per month, is $38.26; Cornet pay 28 days at $36.00 per month, is $33.60; 4 Sergeants pay 31 days at $26.00 each, $26.86 is $107.44; 4 Corporals and 1 Trumpter pay 28 days $24.00 per month each, $22.40 is $112.00; 24 Privates pay 28 days $21.00—$19.60 is $470.40; 4 Privates pay 15 days, $21.00—$10.50 is $42.00; 3 Privates pay 8 days $21.00—$7.46 is $22.38; 2 Privates pay 6 days $21.00—$4.20 is $8.40.
Total $936.48
Isaac Robinson's Wagon and team, 17 days at $5.00 per day $85.00
John Barlow's Wagon and team, 10 days at $5.00 per day $50.00
Mrs. Anderson's Wagon and team, 13 days at $5.00 per day $65.00
Total $200.00
Total amount of pay..$1,136.48

The payment for rations and forage due and which ought to have been paid when the within account was discharged was this day paid to Captain Jacob Robinson by a warrant No. 219 for $8.61 on the Treasurer and delivered to L. Q. C. Lamar agreeably to Captain Robinson's letter of the 2nd Sept. inst.

EXECUTIVE DEPARTMENT.
22nd Sept. 1819.

4. LAND LOTTERY LIST

GEORGIA—LAURENS COUNTY

LAND LOTTERY, 1819

Copied from the original records in the office of the ORDINARY of LAURENS COUNTY, GEORGIA, by HENRIETTA SANDERS FREEMAN (MRS. E. B.)

GEORGIA, LAURENS COUNTY

PERSONS ELIGIBLE TO DRAWS IN LAND LOTTERY, 1819.
CAPT. LEROY G. HARRIS DISTRICT

Names	Draws	Names	Draws
Armstrong, W. James	1	Cary, Alexander, Revolutionary	4
Algiers, D. William	2	Cook, Elizabeth, orphan of Edmund Cook	1
Adams, Benjamin	2	Coleman, Josey	1
Adams, Lemach	1	Coleman, John	1
Adams, Peter	2	Coleman, James	1
Bowlin, Richard	2	Clements, Cornelius, orphans of	1
Butts, Wilson	1	Champion, Micajah	2
Butts, David	2	Colley, George	2
Butts, James	2	Coleman, Jonathan	2
Blair, George	2	Coleman, W. Wade	1
Bell, Lewis	(torn)	Carrel, Thomas	2
Barefield, William	2	Coleman, R. Wright	2
Barker, Nicholas	2	Cooper, Henry	1
Barker, Murrill	(torn)	Clements, Joseph	1
Brantley, Benjamin	2	Cicaty, D. Augustin	2
Chisolm, B. Edmund	2	Crawford, Archibald, orphans of	1
Cooper, B. John	1	Clark, G. W. Solomon	2
Cooper, Eli, orphan of Cannon Cooper	1	Cannon, D. Robert	1
Cary, John	1	Crews, Jesse	2
Cary, Tyre, orphan	1	Clark, Warren	1

Names	Draws	Names	Draws
Cato, William	2	Nelson, James	2
Clark, Thomas	2	Outlaw, Alexander, orphan of Benjamin Outlaw	1
Crawford, Nancy, widow	1	Price, Sarah, orphan of Zach Price	1
Davis, B. John	2	Pitts, C. Lunsford	2
Daniel, John	1	Price, John	1
Daniel, James	(torn)	Pope, Jacob	1
Duke, Shadrich	2	Perry, Joseph	2
Duke, Isham	1	Perkins, Job, orphans of	1
Duke, Eliza, widow	1	Pitts, Henry	2
Duke, P. Leonidas, orphan of Wm. P. Duke	1	Parrott, William	2
Duncan, Thomas	2	Passmore, James	1
Die, John	2	Roach, John, orphans of	1
Evin, John	(torn)	Roberts, Nancy, widow	1
Fullwood, John	2	Register, John	2
Field, Owen	2	Roberts, Harrel, orphan	1
Fullwood, William	1	Rye, William	2
Folsom, Nathaniel	1	Roach, William	1
Fuqua, C. Henry	2	Roberts, Daniel	2
Finney, John	1	Roach, Charley	1
Guyton, John	2	Robinson, James, orphans of	1
Gibson, William	2	Russell, Lourana, orphan of Jackson Russell	1
Guyton, Charles S.	1	Shannon, J. Edward	2
Gilstrop, Peter	1	Shoary, Joseph	1
Grinstead, Robert	2	Spicer, John	2
Harris, G. Leroy	1	Sikes, Joseph	1
Howard, James	2	Stephenson, Silas	2
Hale, Jonathan	2	Stucky, Mary, widow	(torn)
Hale, William	2	Stucky, John	(torn)
Hargrove, B. Harrison	2	Stucky, Lewis, orphans of	1
Higdon, Sealy, widow	1	Seward, William	2
Higdon, Budd, orphan	1	Smith, John	1
Hamock, John	2	Sikes, Winey, widow	1
Hogan, John	2	Snellgrove, Edward	2
Hampton, Andrew	2	Snellgrove, Jesse	2
Hampton, Wade Benjamin	1	Smith, Matthew, orphans	1
Hampton, Leroy Joseph	1	Sikes, Redon, orphan of Jacob Sikes	1
Hale, Solomon	2	Story, Richard	2
Hale, Lazarus	2	Sanders, Wright	1
Hale, Thomas	2	Solomon, James	2
Hobbs, Bowling	1	Spear, David	2
Hobbs, Lary	1	Smith, Unity, widow	1
Horn, Joel	2	Sweary, Judith, orphan of Geo. Sweary	1
Horn, Josiah	2	Solomon, Mary, widow	1
Hood, C. Robert	1	Thomas, John	2
Horn, Beady, orphan of Joshua Horn	1	Taylor, Susannah, widow	1
Hobbs, Drury, orphan	1	Tippet, Nancy, widow	1
Higdon, Terrell	2	Thompson, Alsace	2
Jones, C. Solomon	2	Woodrow, Simon	2
Johnston, William	1	Woodyard, Young	2
Jenkins, Uriah	2	Woodyard, William, orphans of	1
Ludlow, M. John	1	Woodyard, Nancy, widow	1
Love, Amos	2	Warren, Reuben	2
Lowther, John	1	Waller, Martha, widow	1
Moore, Syntha, widow	1	Waller, Samuel, orphans of	1
Moore, Edward	1	Willis, Benjamin	2
Moat, Nancy, widow	2	Williams, Sarah, widow	1
Maddox, Jane, widow	1	Williams, W. Henry, orphans of	1
Maddox, Alexander, orphan	1	Warren, James	2
McDaniel, John	2	Williamson, William	2
McBain, John	1	Williamson, Margaret, widow	(torn)
McCullers, Britton	4	Weeks, Michael	2
McCullers, D. John	1	Watkins, Thomas, orphans of	1
Mayo, Bray	1	Welch, W. George	2
Moat, Abel	1	Yonn, Jesse	2
Moat, Jethro, orphans of	1		
Nelson, Charles	1		

CAPTAIN SION SMITH'S DISTRICT

Names	Draws	Names	Draws
Alburson, Arthur	2	Burch, John	1
Armstrong, James	1	Burch, Mary, widow	1
Alburson, Joseph	2	Burch, Michael, orphans of	2
Alburson, Sarah, widow	1	Brown, Lovett	2
Attaway, Ezekiel	1	Brown, Jesse	2
Bell, Zachariah	2	Blanchard, Robert	1

Names	Draws	Names	Draws
Brantley, James	2	Loftin, James	1
Burch, Benjamin	2	Morris, Jonathan	2
Bowery, William	2	Miller, John	1
Benefield, Elizabeth, widow	(torn)	Miller, Charles	1
Benefield, Needham, orphan of S. Benefield	(torn)	Miller, F. Levi	1
		McCullers, Malcolm	2
Benefield, James	1	Miller, James	1
Blanchard, Nancy, widow	1	Miller, Lewis	1
Blanchard, Joseph, orphan of B. Blanchard	1	Miller, Amos	1
		Miller, Jonathan, Sr.	2
Creach, Joshua	2	Miller, William	2
Creach, David	2	Miller, Jonathan, Jr.	2
Cobb, Thomas	2	Miller, Elias	2
Carey, Rebecca, widow	1	Northcut, Robert	2
Carey, Mary, orphan of Jesse Carey	1	Odom, Emera	2
Caldwell, Micajah	2	Poythress, Edward	2
Cawthorn, Stephen, orphans of	1	Padgett, William	2
Daniel, William	2	Peters, G. John	2
Dickson, Thomas	2	Roberts, Richard, orphans of	1
Douglass, Wilson, orphan of M. Douglass	1	Roberts, Dempsey	1
		Roberts, Drew	2
Driver, Lemach	2	Regins, Thomas	2
Douglass, Hezekiah	1	Rabb, Hezekiah	2
Duncan, Elbert	2	Robertson, Shadrach, orphans of	1
Fennell, Rutha, widow	1	Robertson, Isaac	1
Fennell, Clement, orphans of	1	Smith, Simon	2
Fennell, Dempsey	2	Shannon, Uzail	2
Faircloth, Allen	2	Smith, Sion	1
Gaines, Bartholomew	2	Swearingen, Bailey	2
Gay, Josiah	2	Swearingen, Frederick	2
Harrison, Reuben	2	Swearingen, Elizabeth, widow	(torn)
Henly, Orten	1	Swearingen, Benjamin, orphan of John Swearingen	(torn)
Hamilton, John	2		
Holton, Nathaniel	1	Swearingen, Martin	2
Hudson, John	2	Swearingen, Thomas	2
Hall, Nathan	2	Turner, Joseph	2
Hamilton, Benjamin	2	Turner, Millard	1
Holton, Samuel	2	Underwood, A. William	1
Ivey, John	1	Underwood, J. John	1
Ivey, Robert	2	Underwood, L. Daniel	1
Johnston, David	2	Vaughn, David	1
Jordan, D. Elizabeth, widow	1	Vaughn, Michael S.	2
Jordan, S. Ann, orphan of Edw. Jordan	1	Vaughn, Michael, Jr.	1
Joiner, Levy	2	Wright, William	2
Johnston, Eady, widow	1	Wright, Kinson	2
Knight, Spier	2	Wright, Abel	1
Knight, Robert	2	Young, Benjamin	2
Kittrell, Jonathan	2		

CAPTAIN HARDY GRIFFIN'S DISTRICT

Names	Draws	Names	Draws
Alligood, Hillery	2	Boyett, Thomas	2
Alligood, Daniel	1	Cawthorn, William	2
Averett, Banjamin	2	Creach, Noah	2
Andrews, Frederich	1	Cawlwell, Samuel	2
Averett, India, widow	1	Cooper, Henry	2
Averett, William, orphans of	1	Cobb, Job	2
Anderson, John	2	Clinch, Edward	2
Anderson, Mary, widow	1	Collier, James	2
Anderson, Henry, orphans of	1	Cooksey, John, Revolutionary	4
Anderson, A. Worthy	1	Creach, Charles	2
Barlow, Richard	2	Covey, John	2
Benton, Isaac	2	Darcey, Benjamin, Jr.	2
Barlow, James	2	Darcey, Willis, orphans of	1
Barlow, Mary, widow	1	Darcey, James, Revolutionary	4
Barlow, Thomas, Jr., orphan of Thos. Barlow, Sr.	1	Darcey, Benjamin, Sr.	2
		Darcey, Joel	1
Brumbly, Baptist	2	Darby, Timothy	1
Brumbly, James	2	Darcey, Joseph	1
Barlow, James	2	Dreding, Samuel	2
Barlow, John	2	Daugharty, John, orphans of	1
Boyett, Isaac	2	Duren, Thomas	1
Boyett, Arthur	2	Daugharty, Latia, widow	1
Baswell, David	2	Evins, Elisha, orphan of John Evins	1
Boyett, Josiah	1	Fountain, Esaeas	2
Bidgood, James	2	Fountain, Noah, orphans of	1

Names	Draws	Names	Draws
Fountain, William	2	Phillips, E. Daniel	2
Faircloth, Robert	1	Phillips, John	1
Faircloth, Benjamin	2	Phillips, Samuel	1
Faircloth, Caleb, Sr.	2	Perkin, S———	(torn)
Faircloth, Davis	(torn)	Pittman, B. Albert	2
Faircloth, Peter	2	Pew, Thomas	2
Faircloth, Caleb, Jr.	1	Ritter, William	2
Faircloth, Joshua	1	Roberts, Mark	2
Faircloth, John	1	Roach, John	(torn)
Faircloth, Richard	2	Sanders, Robert	2
Faircloth, Ethelred	2	Sanders, Benjamin	2
Faircloth, William	1	Sealy, Edward	2
Faircloth, Frederick, Sr.	2	Sanders, John	1
Faircloth, Frederick, Jr.	1	Sanders, Thomas	1
Faircloth, Thomas	2	Sanders, Coleman	1
Fossett, Abraham	2	Swearingen, John, orphans of	1
Farmer, Andrews	1	Sheffield, Wright	2
Godwin, Silas	1	Smith, Abigail, widow	1
Griffin, Archibald	2	Smith, James	1
Ganghy, Milikiah	2	Smith, Mary, widow	1
Griffin, William	1	Smith, Benjamin, orphans of	1
Griffin, Hardy	1	Smith, R. William	2
Hains, Baysard	2	Trammell, Daniel	2
Hutchins, Edward, Revolutionary	4	Trammell, Jared, Jr., orphan of Jared Trammell, Sr.	2
Harrod, Nathan	2	Tucker, James	1
Harrod, John	1	Thompson, Jainy, orphan of	2
Hunt, William	2	Tucker, Matthew	1
Howe, Edward	2	Tucker, Henry, Jr.	1
Hair, Edward	2	Whitehead, William	2
Ingham, David	2	Wood, Hardy	2
Jackson, James	2	Whitehead, Bennett	1
Knight, William	1	Whitehead, Reason	1
Knight, James	2	Wood, Jonathan	1
Linsey, Tempy, orphan of John Linsey	1	Williams, William	2
Miller, John, Jr.	2	Young, Oren	2
McCullers, H. James	1	Young, Phirson, Revolutionary	4
McIvin, G. Angus	1	Young, Margarit, orphan of	4
McDaniel Elijah	2	Young, John	1
Perkins, William	2		

CAPTAIN FRANCIS J. ROSS' DISTRICT

Names	Draws	Names	Draws
Averett, Abner	2	Manning, Reuben	1
Anderson, John	1	McGriff, William	2
Bush, Lewis	1	Phillips, Susannah, widow	1
Battels, John Joseph	2	Phillips, Dicey, widow	1
Bender, Parker	2	Pickering, Namon	2
Bailey, Wineford, widow	1	Powell, John	2
Bush, Zachariah	2	Powell, Rebecca, orphan of Benj. Powell	1
Brown, Daniel	1	Phillips, Gabriel	2
Beaty, Mary, widow	1	Phillips, Mark, orphans of	1
Beaty, William, orphans of	1	Pickering, James	1
Chairy, Mary, widow	1	Phillips, H. Henry	1
Cason, Willis, Jr.	1	Powell, Charity	1
Cameron, James	1	Ramsay, Lewis	1
Cason, Charity, widow	1	Ramsay, Isaac	2
Collier, John, Jr.	2	Spann, H. Benjamin	2
Cason, Samuel	1	Spurlock, Britton	1
Cason, Nancy, orphan of A. and M. Cason	1	Speigh, Thomas	2
		Slaughter, Beth, widow	1
Collier, Thomas	2	Slaughter, George, orphans of	(torn)
Collier, Thomas, Jr.	1	Smith, Isaac	2
Collier, Probate	1	Smith, Mary, widow	1
Cason, Whitehouse	1	Sutton, John	1
Chanaway, Charles	1	Smith, David	1
Dickson, James	2	Smith, William	1
Guyton, Joseph	2	Smith, John	2
Hay, James	1	Thomas, Peter	2
Hay, Davis	2	Thomas, Mary Ann, orphan of Micj. Thomas	1
Hogan, Isham	1	Tison, Moses, Jr.	1
Hart, Warren	1	Tison, Aaron	1
Hart, Robert, orphans of	2	Thomas, Robert	1
Jones, Jonathan	1	Thomas, Patrick	1
Jones, O. Aaron	2	Tyson, Moses, Jr.	2
Lambert, John, Jr.	1	Varnado, John	2
Moat, David	1	Varnado, Henry	1
Matthews, Thomas	1	Varnado, J. Henry	1
Moore, Alfred	1	Vickers, Joseph	2
Mooey, John	1	Willis, George	2
Moore, James	2		
Moore, William	1		

CAPTAIN JONES' DISTRICT

Names	Draws
Allen, Eason	2
Allen, Bryan	2
Allen, John, orphans of	1
Adams, Lewis	2
Ard, George	2
Anderson, Thomas	1
Braezeal, Willis, orphans of	1
Brown, Sarah, orphan of Daniel Brown	1
Boyett, Lock	1
Brookering, Edwin	1
Coats, Robert	2
Coats, G. Thomas	2
Culbertson, S. John	2
Calhoun, Axom	1
Calhoun, Samuel	1
Calhoun, Lidia, widow	1
Calhoun, John, orphans of	1
Crabb, Prudence, widow	1
Calhoun, Joseph	1
Coats, Josiah, orphans of	2
Fountain, Susannah, widow	1
Fountain, Noah, orphans of	1
Fort, John	1
Grantham, Nathan	1
Gibson, Sampson	1
Howard, Nancy, widow	1
Howard, John	2
Howard, Josiah	1
Hollinger, Littleton	1
Hollinger, Berry	1
Hickman, Stephen	2
Harden, Eliza, widow	1
Harden, Hugh, orphans of	1
Ingham, James	2
Jones, Adam	2
Johnston, William	1
Johnston, James, orphans of	1
Lawson, James	2
Law, Stephen	2
Leonard, Henry	1
Morris, Thomas	1
McDaniel, David	2
Mills, Jemimah, widow	1
Mobley, Hiram	1
Manning, Thomas	2
Moore, Jacob	1
Moore, Mary, widow	1
Miller, David	1
Mills, Harrod	(torn)
Morrell, Levi	(torn)
Morrell, Aseanith, widow	1
Nutt, Matthew	2
Newburn, John	2
Newburn, Thomas	1
Nutt, William	1
Payne, George	2
Perkins, Nancy, widow	1
Perkins, Joshua, orphans of	1
Peake, William	2
Ramsay, Penelope, widow	1
Ramsay, Benjamin, orphans of	1
Roe, Enoch	1
Rowland, John, Jr.	2
Rowland, John, Sr.	2
Rowland, Edmund	1
Ramsay, H. James	2
Rowland, Sarah, widow	1
Smith, William	2
Sanford, Samuel, orphans of	1
Smith, Isham	2
Smith, Robert	2
Smith, W. John	1
Spivey, Jethro B.	2
Smith, P. Thomas	1
Shiver, Jacob	2
Swilley, Nicholas, Revolutionary	4
Shiver, Abraham	2
Shiver, Burrell	2
Shiver, Daniel	2
Shiver, James	2
Thomas, Daniel	2
Thomas, John, Sr.	2
Underwood, John	2
Vickers, Stephen	2
Vickers, James	1
Wood, Willis	2
White, James, orphans of	1
Week, Sarah, orphan of David Week	1
Williams, James	2
Yates, John	2
Yates, Jesse	2

"GEORGIA, LAURENS COUNTY

WE

JOHN THOMAS

and

HENRY PITTS

do hereby certify that the foregoing list of names and numbers as they now stand registered are correct of the persons entitled to draw in the contemplated land lottery of this State and the number of draws thereto of the Eighty-first battalion of Georgia Militia.
Given under our hands this 8th March, 1819."

(Signed) JOHN THOMAS

HENRY PITTS

CHAPTER V

A LAURENS COUNTY GOVERNOR WHO DEFIED THE PRESIDENT

1. GOVERNOR GEORGE MICHAEL TROUP

Governor George Michael Troup, one of the State's most illustrious sons, was for years a resident of Laurens County, and was one of Georgia's noblest statesmen. He was born a Georgian, September 7, 1780, at McIntosh Bluff on the Tombigby River, which later became Alabama territory. His father was an English naval officer; his mother, Catherine McIntosh, was a descendant of John McIntosh, an officer in General Oglethorpe's regiment as commander of the Scotch Highlanders. His parents lived in McIntosh County, at their residence called "Belleville," a beautiful site on Sapelo River. They had six sons, no two were born in the same place, except the two youngest.

George M. Troup was sent to school at Princeton and upon graduating, studied law in Savannah. In 1800, before he was twenty-one years of age, he was invited to represent Chatham County in the Legislature. This he declined. In 1806, he was sent to Congress and remained a member until 1815. In 1816 he was elected United States Senator and held office two years, and afterwards became one of the outstanding early executives of Georgia.

During his administration as Governor, he took a bold stand in the Indian affair and successfully supported the rights of Georgia in a controversy with the United States Government. He held the office of Governor for four years, and was then returned to the Senate. Troup was the last Governor of Georgia elected by the Legislature, and in October, 1825, was the first Governor elected by the people. His opponent was his old enemy, John Clark—his supporters were called "Troupers." Bitter hatred sprang up even in families and among friends. This has made stirring and interesting chapters in Georgia's political history.

In 1803, the General Assembly sat at Louisville, Georgia, and there on the 30th of October, Troup was married to Miss Ann St. Clare McCormick. They lived at a place near Hardwick in Bryan County, then known as "Troup's Old Field." His wife lived less than a year. In 1809 he married Miss Carter of Virginia. Six children were born to them. Only three lived to maturity.

An interesting event of this time was the visit to Georgia of the famous LaFayette, who in his old age desired to behold again the scenes of his many triumphs during the war of the Revolution.

Governor Troup welcomed him on his arrival in Savannah, March 19, 1825, as the guest of the State.

After a most brilliant career in the political life of Georgia, it is interesting to recall the latter days of this scholarly statesman, who passed his remaining days on his plantation, "Valdosta," in Laurens County, a few miles southeast of Dublin. Originally, this plantation was "Valde Osta." Today, nothing is left in Laurens County to carry the beautiful name "Valdosta" but a negro church, built by descendants of the Troup slaves. However, the city of Valdosta, Georgia, in Lowndes County, is named for this once famous plantation.

Description of the mansion that was built in this place is given by H. B. Folsom, writing for the Macon *Telegraph*. "The large living-room was twenty-five by forty feet. Italian plasterers had been employed to decorate the frescoed walls. The structure was of heavy timbers. The framing was spiked together with hand-forged nails, the greater number of them being five inches long." Nothing remained for many years of the once hospitable home of Georgia's famous Governor but the old office or den. There were no windows to this room, because here state secrets were discussed. The office was built of heavy timber as a protection from the attack of the Indians.

Another plantation home of the Troups' was "Vallambrosa," named for a noted retreat near Florence, Italy. This home, just ten miles of Dublin, was the scene of many gatherings with lavish entertainment. Of this once beautiful place, nothing remains but the magnificent water oaks, the garden wall that is standing here and there, and the old burial lot.

Several years ago, the John Laurens Chapter Daughters of the American Revolution undertook the task of preserving the few remaining treasures of this place, a special sum of money being set aside each year for this duty. A beautiful spring house of rock, built by Miss Oralie Troup, daughter of Governor Troup, was put in perfect state of preservation and kept so by the members of the local D. A. R. Chapter. The name and date can be clearly seen in the massive rock that surrounds this marvelous piece of work.

Also the burial lot has been restored. Miss Oralie is the only member of the Troup family buried at this place. The John Laurens Chapter, under the regency of Mrs. E. T. Barnes, in 1938 erected a handsome bronze roadside marker at the entrance of this home place on the Federal Highway.

The Montgomery County plantations were the "Rosemont" place, the "Horseshoe Bend" place, now in Wheeler County, also the "Mitchell" place. The Troup slaves ran into the hundreds, and descendants of these may be found on these different plantations today.

From private letters written by Governor Troup, all of them dated, "Valdosta, Laurens," we know that he spent the last twenty-five years of his life in Laurens County.

He was at his home place in Laurens, when he received a message to come to Rosemont in Montgomery County. He was taken sick while there, and died within a few days. He was given a simple burial. The casket was improvised. On the coffin lid lettered in brass tacks, was the inscription, "An Honest Heart." He was buried in the family burial lot at Rosemont, on the twenty-sixth day of April, in the year of our Lord 1856.

A life size portrait of Governor Troup hangs on one side of the President's chair in the Senate Chamber of Georgia. The picture reproduced as the frontispiece of this book is said to be an excellent likeness.

—*By Augusta Stanley Adams (Mrs. J. S.)*

NOTE: Material for this paper has been taken from "Reminiscences of Georgia" by H. B. Folsom, and "The Life of George Michael Troup' by Edward Harden, "the only authoritative biographical account in existence of one of the most commanding figures in the history of Georgia." Written three years after his death.

2. GOVERNOR TROUP DEFIES THE PRESIDENT

Over twenty years had passed since Georgia had sold her vast western acres to the Federal Government with the understanding that the Indians would be at once removed from Georgia soil. But the government at Washington was playing between Georgia and the Indians in an effort to get the Indians to go voluntarily. Troup was determined to bring the matter to a head if it meant a war between the State and the Nation.

President Monroe appointed two Georgia men, Meriwether and Campbell, to treat with the Creeks. At Indian Springs they met in council with the representatives of the Lower Creeks and made a treaty by which the Creeks agreed to give up all their lands in Georgia for an equal amount in the West and in addition $400,000. William McIntosh, a half breed Indian, and the cousin of Governor Troup, influenced the Indians to make the treaty, but it so angered the upper Creeks they refused to stand by the Treaty and killed the brave McIntosh.

When John Quincy Adams became President he declared that the treaty had been secured by bribes and ordered Governor Troup to stop the survey he was having made. Troup was angered and sent a message to the Georgia Legislature saying, "It is not too late, step forth, and having exhausted the argument, stand by your arms."

Adams, fearful of civil war, made a treaty with the Indians by which they gave up all Georgia lands except a strip along the Chattahoochee, but Governor Troup felt that this was a compromise and would agree to nothing but the old treaty; ignoring the new treaty he ordered all lands to be surveyed. The President threatened to stop the survey with the army; in answer Troup wrote thus to the Secretary of War:

"You will distinctly understand, therefore, that I feel it to be my duty to resist to the utmost any military attack which the government of the United States shall think proper to make on the territory, the people, or the sovereignty of Georgia, and all the measures necessary to the performance of this duty, according to our limited means, you will be considered and treated as a public enemy, and with the less repugnance, because you, to whom we might have constitutionally appealed for our own defense against invasion, are yourselves the invaders, and what is more, the unblushing allies of the savages, whose cause you have adopted."

President Adams saw that Troup was in deadly earnest so he influenced the Creeks to agree to give up all lands east of the Chattahoochee; soon the Creeks were removed and, thanks to Governor Troup, Georgia was in possession of all lands occupied by the Creeks.

3. CHILDREN OF GOVERNOR TROUP

The plantation on Turkey Creek which Governor Troup named Vallambrosa became the home of his youngest daughter on his death. This land had been owned and occupied by Joseph Blackshear, brother of General David Blackshear. His bones rest there in the old graveyard. Miss Oralie lived here in a white two-story house, at the end of an oak bordered lane. A winding shady path led down to the spring, over which till this day stands a stone arch carved with the word "Oralie." She was tall and graceful and her fondness for dancing made her a social favorite. Romance for her budded but never flowered, she became engaged, the brocaded satin wedding dress had been made, but before the wedding day, death called the prospective bridegroom. The satin gown was put away and some years passed, but a widower, Dr. John A. Vigal, with two sons moved to Dublin and in time he came a-courting to Vallambrosa. The satin gown did fulfill its mission; though past her days of youth, Miss Oralie married Dr. Vigal.

A brilliant reception at Vallambrosa followed the wedding. It was a social occasion and assembled the elite of Laurens County. Many years after, an old lady who was a guest on this occasion related these memories to her niece:—

"Among the guests were Mary Lowther, Ella Lowther, Minkie Currell, Clara Guyton, Belle, Zoe and Mosley Blackshear (granddaughters of General David Blackshear). The Misses Blackshear wore pink merino dresses trimmed in black velvet. Mary Lowther wore a white lace dress trimmed in blue silk hand-made leaves. Ella Lowther wore a white mull made low neck and short sleeves. The girls wore satin coronets in their hair to match their dresses. Other guests were Jerry Yopp, Henry Duncan, Jim Thomas, Peter Sarchett, Moses and Cincy Guyton and Gus Whitehead.

"An orchestra from Macon furnished the music, a harp, a violin, and a bass viol were the pieces and the Lancers was danced. Refreshments consisted of turkey, ham, salad, pickles, cake and boiled custard. There was pound cake, yellow loaf cake, and sponge cake, fruit and nuts."

Governor Troup's only son, George, died without issue.

The oldest daughter of Governor Troup was named Florida. She married Thomas Bryan, a descendant of Jonathan Bryan, and had two sons and two daughters. While her daughters were young girls, she changed by law the name Bryan to Forman. The two older children, the two sons, kept the name Bryan. Both of these after reaching manhood came to Dublin to live. It seems that neither was ever married. Jack Bryan is buried in the old cemetery in Dublin.

One of the granddaughters, Augusta, married Robert Wayne of Savannah. The Waynes moved up from Savannah and established a large plantation above what is now Dudley and it is known today as the Wayne Place. The other granddaughter, Georgia, married Holmes Conrad and lived in Virginia.

Jack Bryan is remembered still by some of Dublin's old residents as the village entertainer. On the piazza of one of the little Dublin stores he would assume an elocutionary attitude and eloquently render Hamlet's soliloquy or some other classical masterpiece.

Governor Troup nor his family seem to have been church people, there is no name of his family that appears on Laurens County Church rolls. There is a long list of names of slaves of Mrs. Forman (Bryan) on the rolls of the Poplar Springs Baptist Church (white).

In her late years Governor Troup's younger daughter Oralie became mentally unable to look after her large affairs and her niece's husband was put under a heavy bond as her guardian.

Chapter VI

THE PERIOD OF 1812 TO 1860

1. GROWTH

The years of prosperity that came to Georgia after the War of 1812 were shared by Laurens County. After the purchase of Florida by the United States Government, the Spanish menace was no more and the southern part of the State began to prosper. The wave of population swept from the east and southeast to northwest; in 1821 the town of Dublin was larger than Macon.

At the end of the first quarter of the 19th century a prominent visitor to the county seat thus described the town:

"Dublin contains a courthouse, a jail, an academy, thirty-five houses and stores. Considerable cotton was formerly deposited in the warehouses here to be taken down the river, but at present little is received and the warehouses are going to decay." (Adiel Sherwood in "The Georgia Gazetteer").

Trails had become roads. Instead of paying road tax, the men made and worked the roads. A legislative Act passed in December, 1815, provided that road service should be rendered by "all able-bodied, effective white male inhabitants, mulattoes, free negroes, and slaves, from age of sixteen to fifty years."

Corn was the universal crop throughout the country, and much of it was used for making whiskey. The small farmer, unable without slaves to produce cotton, used his extra corn in this way to secure a little money.

An historian says of the period of the first decades of the 19th century— "Nothing was produced in the county for market except horses, cattle, hogs, and whiskey." (G. G. Smith's "History of Methodism in Georgia").

In the second decade there began a comparatively large production of cotton in the northern part of the county. Men owning slaves came into this section because of the fertile land adapted for cotton production. They prospered and built comfortable homes and developed estates. General Blackshear was a surveyor and surveyed roads for the section's development. Some of these followed old Indian paths. Today there is a road passing the home of J. B. Fordham near Poplar Springs Church known as the Blackshear Trail, which was surveyed by General Blackshear and followed an Indian Trail.

In the southern part of the county the settlers, few and far between, made a living with range cattle, sheep, and cows, and hogs in the swamps. Early settlers in this section were the Clarks, the Noles, the Burch families. For a long time these lands were considered almost worthless, sometimes many acres were sold before the courthouse door to pay overdue taxes, for twenty-five cents an acre. Several years passed before the owners of these pine acres realized the value of the timber; then they began to cut it, draw the pines to the river and making a raft piloted it down to Darien, and lumbering became a real industry.

Cotton farmers made long hauls carrying their cotton to Savannah or rafting it down the Oconee. Through these early decades settlements were increasing, lands were being converted into fields, cotton and corn were being cultivated as the farm crops, the Oconee was becoming an artery of trade, but there were no industries. Laurens, together with other counties of Georgia and southern states, was becoming vocal against the tariff acts, which they felt were being passed by the Federal Government for the benefit of the northern states that were busily engaged in manufacture.

The principal subject for thought and discussion was the expulsion of the Indians, for a Laurens County man was heading the movement, so the history of the county through the third and fourth decades was concerned with the acts of George M. Troup. As early as the second decade political divisions began to appear. James Jackson of Savannah, was the father of political parties in Georgia. He was an ardent supporter of the Anti-federalist or Jefferson Party. George M. Troup was his political son who became the party leader as opposed to the Federalist leader in Georgia, who, was John Clarke, the son of the famous Revolutionary soldier, Elijah Clarke. Under these two men political parties became localized and came to be called the Troupers and Clarkites. During the Twenties and Thirties political races and enmities between the followers of these leaders were the order of the day. The principal contests were the races for the governorship between Clarke and Troup. One can imagine the heated agitations that were in Laurens, since this was the home of Troup. Finally, in the latter part of the Thirties, the local parties, obscured by the tariff opposition, were lost in the National parties. The Troupers became the States Rights party and later the Whig; the Clarkites became Democrats. These were the two parties in Georgia until War becam imminent.

In November, 1833, an act of nature provided this date as a boundary line of events, and for many years men said "This thing happened before the stars fell" or "It was after the stars fell." This brilliant meteoric shower was seen all over the State, for several hours the air was full of falling stars. Blacks and superstitious Whites were full of terror for they feared "Judgment Day" had come. Another date long remembered was a Saturday in January, 1835, declared to be the coldest day ever known in Georgia.

2. INDIAN TROUBLES

Between 1830 and 1840 the question of transporting the Cherokees from Georgia was a constant source of trouble. The unrest of the Cherokees spread to the Seminoles in Florida. They took up arms under their famous chief, Osceola, murdered the United States agent among them and planned to invade Georgia. The Upper Creeks of Alabama, hearing of this, resolved to make opportunity of the Seminole uprising and strike a blow in Georgia. The Governor of Georgia, William Schley, ordered volunteer companies to be formed all over the State to crush this Seminole and Upper Creek uprising. The military activities of this period are known as the Seminole War.

The following is a letter to the Governor from General Eli Warren, head of the militia in Laurens; the others were written to the Governor on his request for volunteer companies to be formed in Laurens.

"Dublin, January 31, 1836.

"To His Excellency
William Schley

"Sir. The orders of your Excellency under date of 23rd Inst requiring the raising by voluntary enlistment or draft, thirty five hundred militia &c &c came to me through Majr. Genl. Wimberly on the night of the 29th Inst. Unless some unexpected and unavoidable delay has happened to those by whom I have dispatched orders—the Colonels Commanding the several Regiments composing my Brigade will receive their orders by ten o'clock today—I have ordered, that so soon as the men are detailed from the several Regiments—that each company of men so detailed, meet and elect officers to command them, until a more full and complete organization of the companies takes place. This was done because I through the men so detailed, by having officers immediately on their enlistment or draft—would be under better discipline and organization when called into actual service—It is hoped that this measure will meet the approbation of your Excellency.

"The call that your Excellency has made upon the militia of the state—for the protection of the frontier of Georgia, and our brothers of Florida ought and I hope does meet a hearty and patriotic response on the bosom of every Georgian and should a sufficient number of the militia be called into service to make it necessary for the command of them to devolve upon an officer of my rank, and your Excellency should think proper to confer the command of them upon me, which is most respectfully solicited—its duties will be attended to with undeviating firmness and the best abilities I possess.

"I am very Respectfully
Your Excellency's Mo. Ob. st.
ELI WARREN."

"Letter
Genl. Eli Warren
31 Janry, 1836
"Draft
Vol. Florida Expedition
(On Reverse)

Dublin, Ga.
Feb. 3d
Excellency William Schley
Milledgeville
Georgia

To Genl. Warren

(Original letter on file in office of Georgia Department of Archives).

Head Quarters,
39th Regiment Georgia Militia
Dublin   February 6, 1836

"Dublin Volunteers
To His Excellency
William Schley
Sir

By the order of your Excellency under date of the 23rd of Last month, I ordered the raising to-day from the 39th Regiment G. M. Forty One Militia by enlistment or draft for the protection of the South Western frontier of Georgia and the people of the Territory of Florida against the invasion of the Hostile Indians. I have the honor of reporting to your Excellency the names of fifty-eight militia who voluntarily enlisted for the service contemplated under your Excellency's orders alone referred to. And who are ready to march at a moment's warning. After the company had enlisted the men composing it elected a captain and other officers to command them, who together with their rank are designated in this report to your Excellency:

1. George M. Troup Jr., Captain.
2. Newnan McBain 1st Lt.
3. Thomas N. Guyton, 2nd Lt.
4. Edward J. Blackshear, Ensign
    PRIVATES
5. Hardy Alligood
6. Henry Alligood
7. Joseph Aycock
8. Samuel Baker
9. Washington Baker
10. William Barrick
11. Daniel Bullock
12. Littleton B. Burch
13. George Ballard
14. Caraway Brown
15. Alexander Bussel
16. James Cunningham
17. Irvin Calhoun
18. Jacob Clements
19. Josiah S. Dickson
20. William Y. Dorsey
21. Rufus M. Dorsey
22. William M. Goff
23. James M. Goff
24. John G. B. Goff
25. William Grant
26. William Griffick
27. William Grey
28. Stephen B. Hester Junr.
29. William L. Hampton
30. Phillip Herndon
31. James Hudson
32. Charles S. Holmes
33. Hezekiah Jones
34. Eldridge R. Kellum
35. Isaac Layton

36. Lewis McDaniel
37. Joseph S. Mason
38. Abraham L. Moore
39. James Nobles
40. Henry H. Phillips
41. Elisha Phiney
42. Moses Pullen
43. Elias Pullen
44. Robertson J. Rauls
45. Nathaniel Russel
46. Tilman Rouland
47. Reden Register
48. Silas Simmons
49. Daniel Thompson
50. Allen W. Thomas
51. John B. Thomas
52. Bartlet Thomas
53. Joseph A. Turner
54. David Thompson
55. Gillis Wright
56. Alexander Wright
57. Gilbert Willey
58. Thomas Wates

All of which is most respectfully submitted to your Excellency
Charles P. Cruch, Colonel
39th Regiment G. M."

"P. S. It is the wish of the volunteer company from this regiment to be equipped with Rifles if it be consistent with your Excellency's views." C. P. C. C. G. M.

Comd., 8th Febry. 1836

To His Excellency
William Schley
Milledgeville
Georgia

Lieut. McBain

On Reverse
Laurens
Dublin Volunteers
attchd. to 39th Regt.
George M. Troup Jr., Capt.
Newnan McBain, 1 Lt.
Thomas N. Guyton, 2 Lt.
Edward J. Blackshear, Ens.
Comd. 8th. Febry. 1836

(Original letter on file in office of Georgia Department of Archives).

"His Excellency William Schley, Governor and Commander-in-Chief of the State of Georgia—
Sir:
I am instructed to inform your Excellency that 45 young men of the county of Laurens have embodied & enrolled as a rifle corps of which you will receive an official & detailed account from the Col. of the regiment, have elected Geo. M. Troup Jr their Captain, Newnan McBane 1st Leut, Thomas Guyton 2d Leut, Jefferson Blackshear 3d Leut or ensign. That they do hereby tender their services to the state of Georgia or the United States & at

the same time to make known to your Excellency that they will be ready to march at a moment's warning—
I have the honor to be your Excellency's most obedient Servant
George M. Troup Jr."

"P. S. The company may be designated as the Laurens rifle company & will require arms & accourtrements—"
G. M. T. Jr."

Letter
George M. Troup Jr.
9th Feby 1836
(Vol. Comps
Florida Expedition)
Ansd 12th Febry 1836

On Reverse

Dublin, Ga.
9 Feby   10 Geo M Troup Junr.
To
His Excellency
William Schley
Milledgeville
Georgia

(Original letter on file in office of Georgia Department of Archives.)

3. THROUGH THE FORTIES

In the latter Thirties the state was giving its attention to construction of railroads. A company was organized to build a line connecting Macon and Savannah; the proposed line would have come through Laurens and Dublin, but fearing that a railroad might be an invasion of private rights and would give unpleasant publicity, the citizens of the county refused a right of way and, when surveyors came in 1834, they ran the road through Washington County.

Through the Twenties and Thirties large plantations of cotton had been developed in the northern part of the County by Governor George M. Troup, John, Charles and Moses Guyton, Robert Coats, Jeremiah Yopp, Ira Stanley, Joel Coney, John Thomas, William O'Neal, and David Blackshear.

The county suffered a financial panic in 1839, brought on by rife speculation, and cotton dropped to four and five cents a pound.

When Texas was admitted to the Union in 1845 troops were sent to protect the Texas frontier; this enraged Mexico and she declared war. When the War Department called on Georgia for a regiment of infantry, many volunteers from Laurens were entered.

By 1840 the South looked on slavery as a national institution. In Laurens County a large part of the population was not slave owners, but all were loyal to the principle and resented any opposition to slave owning. But the disrupting work of the Abolitionists was poisoning friendly relations between North and South as early as the third decade. In the latter part of 1840 the Laurens County Baptist churches drew up resolutions and entered on their minutes a scathing rebuke of a Northern periodical, "The Christian Reflector," which expressed "sentiment abhorrent to our views and certain threats against the holders of slaves." The speech of the president of American Baptist Convention, who was one of the Vice-Presidents of the Board of American Baptist Foreign Missions, was so objectionable that southern churches refused to co-operate further in the foreign mission program.

By 1845 the county had a population of 3,258 whites and 2,760 blacks. Although there was such a large black population there were few large slave owners; these were the great cotton plantation operators.

Dublin at this time had "a good courthouse, several stores, 65 houses, and 180 inhabitants." (White's "Statistics of the State of Georgia.")

By the fourth decade lumbering was the principal industry and some half dozen sawmills were operating in the County. (White)

The first record of organized aid for the poor of the County is found on the minutes of the Inferior Court under the date of March 4, 1817: "Ordered that Burton H. Pitts, Joseph Yarbrough, Lewis Linder, Needham Cook, and William Mason be and are hereby appointed overseers of the poor in and for this county, and they, or a majority of them, are authorized to transact the business of their appointment."

Concerning a Poor House, the following is recorded under date of June, 1854: "It is ordered that Francis Thomas, T. N. Guyton, and Andrew Fuqua be appointed commissioners to select some suitable location for the erection of a poorhouse for the accommodation of the paupers of this county, and that they make an estimate of the cost for the purchase of land, construction of building and report upon the same at the next term of court." The houses were built a few miles from Dublin and maintained till about 1934.

4. THE FIFTIES

By 1850 Dublin had become the market of a splendid agricultural section, cotton being the main article of sale. Sheep raising was also an important industry and wool was a staple of commerce. In the upper part of the county Thomas N. Guyton's large sheep herds necessitated the employment of trained shepherds. In 1860 agricultural statistics showed there were 6,379 sheep and 16,553 pounds of wool produced.

Throughout the county there were large planters in the front ranks of the State's agricultural life. Through many years the Guytons, Kellams, O'Neals, Coats, Stanleys, and others, in the northern part of the county, had expanded their plantation area.

In the eastern part Frank and Laurence Ballard, the Smiths, the Hightowers, C. L. Holmes, Dr. Jacob Linder, and the Kinchen family were large landowners.

In the southern part Wright Noles and Alfred Burch had vast ranges of cattle.

In the western part of the county Hayden Hughes (grandfather of Dudley Hughes) owned a plantation of such extensive acreage that it required hundreds of slaves for its cultivation. Other families owning large plantations and many slaves were: the Brazaels; the Hamptons; the Ashley Vickers, near the present site of Montrose; the Harvards and Walkers of Laurens Hill; the Daniel Combs and David Ware, on Rocky Creek.

The largest planter, Ex-Governor Troup, though old, kept active supervision over four plantations. In the first half of the Fifties he was a familiar figure on the road through Dublin, passing from his Valdosta to his Vallambrosa plantations, with a menage of several slaves, horses and wagons carrying even household furnishings, dogs, and other equipment. He rode on horseback in the van, or in later years in his carriage with a driver of long years of service. Had he not been distinguished by his personality, he would have been by his dress—an odd figure wearing a blue coat with metal buttons and buff vest and a fur cap.

Two other large plantations lay between Governor Troup's Valdosta place and Dublin: the Fuqua place, now known as the Fuller place, and the plantation of Thomas M. Yopp, now known as the Hightower place.

In the Fifties Laurens County had nearly a half-slave population, for the preceding census showed 3,468 whites and 2,974 slaves. The slave owner regarded his slaves as his most valuable property. The following tax list returned by a Laurens County farmer shows how greatly the slave property exceeded land, household goods and other possessions.

In the South slaves were regarded as more valuable than land or houses, as this tax list shows.

E. J. Blackshear's Tax List for 1861

For the first year of the War and first of Confederate States.

Slaves

1. Nathan $1,000.00
2. Ringold 1,200.00
3. Riker 1,000.00
4. Big Fed 800.00
5. Bill 900.00
6. Reuben 200.00
7. Isaac 200.00
8. Joe 1,100.00
9. Andrew 1,200.00
10. Old Ben 10.00
11. Jarvis 1,100.00
12. Will 1,200.00
13. Old Anthony 700.00
14. Tom Anthony 1,200.00
15. Cupid 1,200.00
16. Viney 400.00
17. Dinah 400.00
18. Milly 700.00
19. Chany 800.00
20. Jake 300.00
21. Atley 200.00
22. George (born 1861) 100.00
23. Rose 1,000.00
24. Little Anthony 300.00
25. Anna 200.00
26. Hagar 200.00
27. Aimey 700.00
28. Venus 200.00
29. Little Sarah 800.00
30. Phoebe 800.00
31. Old Harriet 1,000.00
32. Mary Ann 100.00
33. Rindy 800.00
34. Martha 700.00
35. Fanny 600.00
36. Dick 700.00
37. Frank 500.00
38. Ellis 400.00

Slaves

39. Brogdon 150.00
40. Drusy 800.00
41. Candace 600.00
42. Charles 600.00
43. Little Harriet 300.00
44. Emmeline (lit) 200.00
45. Lucy 150.00
46. Hector 700.00
47. Lizzy 500.00
48. Jennette 600.00
49. Nancy 500.00
50. Tom 200.00
51. Wally 600.00
52. Little Fed 400.00
53. Henry 300.00
54. Big Sarah 800.00
55. Judy 600.00
56. Rachel 500.00
57. Big Emeline 800.00
58. Ella 500.00
59. Bob, born April 100.00
60. Annis, dead 700.00

Total $35,310.00
Deduct 3,900.00

Taxable $31,410.00

To Be Deducted
(Come from Texas since Christmas)
Cupid $1,200.00
Anthony 1,200.00
Emeline 800.00
George 100.00
Ella 500.00
Bob 100.00

Total $3,900.00

LANDS

	Acres
Kilgore tract, I live on	287
Gray tract, next to Glass	287
Braswell tract, Will Dean	287
Part of Berryhill (Maddux lives on	200
A strip of Marshall and another Gray	650
John Roach, at Brewton's Mill	10

Value $6,000.00

Linder land, mouth of Big Creek	287

Value $1,000.00

John Brewton land	150
Lee land	650
A slice of Ben Brewton	50
Ben Brown or Glass land	200

Value $2,100.00

Old Springfield	1,000

Value $4,000.00

Total Acres	3,460
Total Value	$13,100.00

HORSES

Old Doc	$ 50.00
Bill	165.00
Gardner	165.00
Joe, mule	180.00
Tom, mule	180.00
Brandy	170.00
Paddy	40.00
Jack	150.00
Pete	150.00
Sophia	130.00
Pidgeon	120.00
Puss	130.00
Kate	150.00
Racy	150.00
Diamond Soph	160.00
Snowball	75.00
Charles, stud	100.00
Ball Pigeon	60.00
Tim Racy	60.00
Blazer Pigeon	30.00
Riley Puss	50.00
	$2,435.00

STOCK OF ALL KINDS

Cows, 30 head	$180.00
4 yoke of oxen	160.00
39 sheep	78.00
Hogs, 200	400.00

Solvent note—W. G. W.	$300.00
One pleasure carriage	$300.00
Household and kitchen furniture, big kettle, old still, clock &	$450.00

TOTAL TAXABLE PROPERTY

Slaves	$31,410.00	All Other Property	$17,403.00

ANTE-BELLUM MILLS

The principal large grist mills in Laurens before the "War" were the Stanley Mills, the Hampton Mill, the Yopp Mill, Blackshear's Mill, and the Israel Johnson Mill.

Historic Chappell's Mill had its origin in the early days of the County. Though originally built by a Mr. Gilbert, it soon came into the possession of the Ira Stanley family and for years was known as Stanley's Mill. When the Stanley estate was divided, this old mill became the property of Ira Stanley's son, James Rowell, who later disposed of it to his brother-in-law, Dr. James Thomas Chappell, and thus it gradually came to be called Chappell's Mill. The mill site is on South Sandy Creek, in Bailey's District, near the Wilkinson County line. The mill has been in constant operation since its beginning, and is now (1941) owned and operated by Mayo Dixon.

Blackshear's Mill was built and operated by Daniel Blackshear. It ground both meal and flour, the flour bolted by hand. The power also ran a saw mill. It was located on Big Creek, in Buckeye District.

Yopp's Mill was built by J. W. Yopp. It was located near the Yopp plantation, on Turkey Creek, about five miles from Dublin.

Hampton's Mill was built by A. Y. Hampton, on Buckhorn Creek, in the Hampton Mill District.

Johnson Mill was built and operated by Israel Johnson. It was located on Messer Creek, in the Oconee District.

The Shewmake Mill was at Shewmake Springs, near where New Bethel Baptist Church is located. There is a story that seems authentic to the effect that the miller lived near a large limesink near the mill site, and one morning when the owner went to the mill he found that the miller's house had been swallowed by the limesink. These limesinks belong to an underground river that runs through Georgia and on into Florida.

It was in the last decade before the War that the stately primeval pines were commercially attacked. It is said that the largest commercial lumber mill was located near Blackshear's Ferry, about 1858. Many sold their timber at $2.00 per acre and felt that they were receiving gifts from heaven. A few years after the timber cuttong began, turpentine stills were set up. *(Information from James L. Keen, Sr.)*

Iu 1860 Dublin was incorporated. James F. Robinson, George Currell, W. S. Ramsay, Joel E. Perry, and John B. Wolfe were appointed commissioners, with full power to make all by-laws and regulations necessary for the government. They were to remain in office until the first Monday in January, 1862, when all voters were to meet and elect commissioners by ballot.

The principal merchants of this period were: Freeman H. Rowe,

Martin Dasher, Thomas N. Guyton, John Lowther, and George Currell. Some of these continued business after the War. George Currell was a merchant for forty years.

When the Republican Party, in 1860, elected Abraham Lincoln President, Laurens County men, along with all of the South, felt that those who opposed protection for slave property by the National Government were in power, and that measures would be taken to emancipate all slaves; so, to slave-holding states, secession from the Union was the only means by which they could hold and protect their property.

There was no newspaper published in Laurens County before the War but there were many subscribers to the Milledgeville paper, and during the latter part of the Fifties, men of Laurens congregated at stores on the day the mail brought the weekly edition. They had listened with great interest to the reports on the Lincoln-Douglas debates, and when Lincoln was elected President they felt that he would free the slaves and would compel the slave-holding states to stay in the Union. For had he not said on his nomination:

"A house divided against itself cannot stand, I believe this government cannot endure permanently half-slave and half free. I do not expect the Union to be dissolved. I do not expect the house to fall—but I do expect it will cease to be divided. It will become all one thing or all the other. Either the opponents of slavery will arrest the further spread of it, and place it where the public mind shall rest in the belief that it is in the course of ultimate extinction, or its advocates will push it forward till it shall become alike lawful in all the states, old as well as new—North as well as South."

Chapter VII

THE PERIOD FROM 1860 TO 1870

1. THE CONFEDERATE WAR.

South Carolina seceded in December and Governor Brown, Georgia's war governor, not waiting for the inauguration of Lincoln, seized the Federal Fort Pulaski at the mouth of the Savannah River and called for a convention to meet at Milledgeville to decide on secession.

Every county sent delegates to this convention at Milledgeville in January 16, 1861. Moved by the flaming eloquence of Toombs, Herschel V. Johnson, Benjamin H. Hill, T. R. R. Cobb and others, secession was formally declared. When Laurens' delegate, John W. Yopp, brought back the news that Georgia had left the Union, there was great rejoicing and a celebration was staged in Dublin with torch light processions and bonfires.

All seceding states sent delegates to a convention at Montgomery, Alabama, in February. At this convention the "Confederate States of America" was formed, with Jefferson Davis, President; Alexander Stephens of Georgia, Vice-President; another Georgian, Robert Toombs, Secretary of State.

Richmond, Virginia, became the capital of the Confederacy about the middle of the first year of the War, so Virginia furnished the fields for most of the battles.

All the able-bodied men of Laurens County were active soldiers; all her best horses were carried away for use of the cavalry and for draft animals. The women, children, and old men were not able to raise crops sufficient for home use and the last two years of the War brought great privation. Due to the blockade there was a great dearth of salt. Women dug up the dirt floors of long used smoke houses, boiled it and, evaporating the water, secured small amounts of the precious article. Old spinning wheels and looms were brought out and women began to make cloth; every available moment was spent in knitting for the soldiers; housewives sent their precious stores of linen to be used for dressings for the wounded.

Georgia became a battleground in 1864 when Federal forces were ordered to pass through from the mountains to the sea. When, in a series of battles, the Union General, Sherman, had conquered Georgia resistance and almost destroyed Atlanta, he divided his army into three sections, with orders to plunder all property on their march to the sea. These three divisions came together near Milledgevile and passed through Sandersville, but only foraging parties passed through

Laurens, thus there was not great devastation by burning of property here as occurred in those counties on Sherman's line of march.

In April, 1865, Lee surrendered. Slowly the soldiers drifted back to their homes, many never came back, many came back maimed or wounded, all emaciated and discouraged. With the few poor horses on which they rode home and the few they found upon their return, Laurens County men turned again to the soil.

The next ten years were almost as hard as the four years of actual combat. The Federal Government was determined to make it hard for the seceding states to be restored to the Union with full rights of citizenship. The entire South was put under military control. There was no Freedman's Bureau put up in Laurens, as there were in other counties, and white men would have had little trouble with former slaves had it not been for straggling Yankees who went through the county formenting dissatisfaction and strife among the negroes. So Laurens men organized a Ku Klux Klan and thus kept the negroes in hand.

By 1869 Georgia had ratified the 13th and 14th Amendments to the National Constitution and Georgia men were in control of the Legislature. These white members expelled the negro members from the Assembly. This Act angered the Republicans, who were in control at Washington, and Georgia was put back under military rule. It was not until 1870, after Georgia had ratified the 15th Amendment, that the state was restored to the Union.

2. LAURENS IN THE WAR.

Extracts from a letter written by Major T. D. Smith many years after the War.

"The Blackshear Guards was the first volunteer company to enter the War from Laurens County; they left in July, 1861. This company was organized by Captain Everard Blackshear and named in honor of him; Captain Blackshear being then too old to enter the service, W. S. Ramsay was elected to the captaincy and, under orders from Governor Brown, we were taken to Atlanta, where the 14th Georgia Regiment was made up of ten companies from different counties of the State. Colonel A. V. Brumby was elected Colonel and W. S. Ramsay Lieutenant-Colonel of the Regiment.

"The captaincy of Company H (Blackshear Guards) became vacant on the election of W. S. Ramsay to the lieutenant-colonelcy. Captain T. M. Yopp was elected captain. The brigade was then ordered to Lynchburg, Virginia, where we were mustered into the Confederate service.

"After the campaign in northwest Virginia (where we went after being mustered in) we returned to Davis' Ford on the Occuguan River. From Davis' Ford we went to Fredericksburg, from there to Yorktown. After the evacuation of Yorktown we went back via.

the Chichahominy to Richmond, meeting McClelland at Seven Pines and giving him a licking.

"The Seven Pines engagement (1862) was the beginning of the Seven Days around Richmond, and the first great victory of the Confederacy. After the Seven Days fight the enemy tried to reach Richmond by another route and was met by Lee at every point, and defeated.

"Finally the War was shifted to Petersburg. After being overpowered Lee surrendered at Appomatox on the 9th day of April, 1865.

"Of the one hundred and twenty-four men that went from Laurens County in the Blackshear Guards, these returned to live several years after the War: Col. W. S. Ramsay, Hardy Smith, T. D. Smith, W. E. Duncan, John W. Jones, R. H. C. McLendon, T. P. Register, D. J. Bush, L. C. Jenkins, G. W. Jenkins, Terrell Perry, J. F. Scarboro, John D. Bates, U. G. B. Faulk, E. Y. Woodward, J. A. Coleman, John Register, Elijah Coleman, L. O. Coleman, A. G. Register, J. R. McDaniel, T. M. Yopp, T. H. Rowe, B. C. Atkinson, Benjamin Dominey, Andrew Berryhill, James Williams, P. W. Douglas, T. R. Dixon, Frank Fullford, M. V. B. Smith, W. J. Hall, B. B. Linder, W. T. Haskins, John U. Hutchinson.

"The next company to leave for the War was the Laurens Volunteers, J. T. Chappell, Captain; it was put in the 49th Georgia Regiment in 1862, as Company G, one hundred twenty-five men, rank and file.

"The next was the Barkaloo Rifles, Captain G. W. Bishop, 57th Georgia; it was in the Western army and carried off ninety-nine men, rank and file.

"The next was the Troup Volunteers, J. M. Smith, captain, Company B, 57th Georgia Regiment, ninety-seven men.

"Next Infantry was organized from Laurens County, April 1862; Captain, L. Q. Tucker, ninety-nine men, rank and file.

"Company A, organized from Laurens in May, 1864; Captain R. A. Stanley, one hundred three men, rank and file.

"Aggregate number of men from Laurens County enlisted for the War, 657."

Captain L. C. Perry was severely wounded in an engagement and carried the scars till his death.

3. RECORD OF LAURENS COUNTY COMPANIES FOUND IN THE CLERK'S OFFICE.

Blackshear Guards, Company H of Northern Virginia, 14th Georgia Regiment, Thomas Brigade, Army, W. S. Ramsay, captain; Thomas M. Yopp, first lieutenant-captain, transferred to the Navy. Thomas H. Rowe, second lieutenant; Hardy Smith, third lieutenant, became captain at Mechanicsville; Henry Currell, first sergeant; L. C. Perry, fourth sergeant; R. D. Davis, first corporal; Irwin Calhoun, second corporal; James C. Lee, third corporal; L. C. Jenkins, fourth corporal.

All entered on July 23, 1861.

This company lost more heavily in battle than any of the Laurens County companies.

Laurens County Volunteers were recruited with J. T. Chappell, captain; J. A. Daniel, first lieutenant; R. H. Duncan, second lieutenant; Calphrey Clark, third lieutenant.

This company was formed March 4, 1862, under a call from the Governor, at Savannah. It was formed into the 49th Georgia Regiment at Camp Davis and drew the number G. They left Camp Davis, April, 1862, for Goldsboro, N. C., and thence to Richmond in May 24, 1862.

Barkaloo Rifles, organized from Laurens and Wilkinson, May 2, 1862, was known as Company J, 57th Georgia Regiment. This company was in the Battle of Baker's Creek in 1862, in the Battle of Vicksburg, 1863, and in the battles of the North Georgia Campaign in 1864.

Troup Volunteers were organized, 1862, as Company B, 57th Georgia Regiment, in Mercer's Brigade. This company was in the Battle of Baker's Creek, Battle of Vicksburg, in the Tennessee Army, and in the North Georgia battles in 1864.

A body of Infantry was organized April, 1862, as Company C, 57th Georgia Regiment, Ledbetter's Brigade, Army of Tennessee. This company was principally engaged in battles in the West. Although in action at Vicksburg, very few lost their lives.

Company A was organized in May, 1864, Georgia Regiment 2, First Brigade, Army of Tennessee. In this company there were several volunteers over the age, fifty-five.

In Laurens Volunteers J. W. Jordan was conspicuous for his bravery as bearer of the regimental colors; he enlisted in March, 1862.

OFFICERS OF COMPANY H. 14th GEORGIA REGIMENT

Captain T. M. Yopp, commissioned 1863.
1st Lieutenant P. W. Douglas, commissioned 1863.
2nd Lieutenant H. B. Smith, resigned 1864.
3rd Lieutenant L. C. Perry, promoted captain 1864.
1st Sergeant, J. M. Stanley.
2nd Sergeant, James Davis, killed Dec. 13, 1862.
3rd Sergeant, R. F. Hall.
4th Sergeant, F. D. Smith, promoted May, 1864.
5th Sergeant, John W. Jones, elected 2nd Lieutenant 1864.
1st Corporal, C. B. Linder.
2nd Corporal, Dennis McLendon, elected 1st Lieutenant, 1863.
3rd Corporal, James Lee, killed, 1862.
4th Corporal, L. C. Jenkins.

W. J. Hall, appointed 4th sergeant, 1864.
H. M. Stanley, appointed 5th sergeant, 1864.
Jeff Howard, discharged, 1862.
Irwin Calhoun, 3rd corporal, discharged, 1862.
John B. Wolfe enlisted as a private, became 2nd Lieutenant. He served at Bakers Creek at Vicksburg, and at Jonesboro, Ga.

4. ADDITIONAL INFORMATION CONCERNING WAR BETWEEN THE STATES.

The high officers of the Blackshear Guards in 14th Georgia Regiment:

MAJORS: Felix L. Price, Robert W. Folsom, James M. Fielder, William A. Harris, Richard P. Lester, Washington L. Goldsmith, Charles C. Kelley.

COLONELS: A. V. Brumby, Felix L. Price, Robert W. Folsom, Richard P. Lester.

LIENTENANT-COLONELS: W. S. Ramsay, Felix L. Price, Robert W. Folsom, William A. Harris, James M. Fielder, Richard P. Lester, Washington L. Goldsmith.

On account of his health, Thomas H. Rowe, second lieutenant of the Blackshear Guards, resigned in August, and in December Dr. Frederick Douglas, who prior to this time had been serving in the 3rd Georgia Regiment, but had now succeeded in being transferred to the 14th, was elected first lieutenant when the company was at Huntsville, West Virginia.

During this war Laurens had three "Yankees" who made most devoted Confederate soldiers. Freeman H. Rowe came to Dublin about twenty years before the War from his native Connecticut. His son, Tom, was a captain. Sometime before the War, Captain Louis C. Perry came from Hartford, Connecticut. Dr. Nathan Tucker came from Rhode Island; his son Lucian was a captain.

There was no Red Cross in those days to sponsor making supplies for wounded soldiers, but women took out their linen sheets and table cloths and sent them to the Army hospitals. They cut the wool from the backs of sheep, carded, spun, and knitted it into socks. Women even took their husband's places in the fields. Women of wealth who had worn only imported clothing, got out old looms and, putting them up, sat on the loom bench and wove cloth for their families and for uniforms for soldiers. Hardship and sacrifice became the order of the day. Even nature seemed unfriendly. A drought in 1862 cut down the corn crop. Legislative Acts were passed restricting distillation to keep the corn for food.

In the early years of the War, when there was still wealth in the county, the people at home raised several hundred dollars to provide comfort for the Blackshear Guards and sent the purse to Lynchburg by Judge Freeman Rowe.

A precious heirloom of the War Between the States is today in the possession of the Guyton family. It is a flag of the Confederacy. Colonel C. S. Guyton's company in the 57th Georgia Regiment was known as the "Dixie Boys." The flag which they carried was presented by Miss Seward of Thomasville. When the company surrendered at Vicksburg, Miss., the flag was placed on a stack of arms. The gallant Captain Davis could not bear to have the flag fall in the hands of the enemy. He seized it and sewed it up in the saddle blanket of Lieutenant-Colonel C. S. Guyton without the owner's knowledge. Colonel Guyton discovered the flag when he arrived at Enterprise, Miss., and proudly brought it home.

ROSTER COMMISSIONS OF LAURENS COUNTY

Number I. Roster Commission Company H, 14th Regiment—Georgia Volunteers, Hardy Smith, Wm. Duncan, T. D. Smith.
Number II. Roster Commission Company C, 57th Regiment—Georgia Volunteers, W. B. Smith, A. L. Morgan, W. A. Witherington.
Number III. Roster Commission Company B, 57th Regiment—Georgia Volunteers, J. W. Carter, J. E. Jackson, W. B. F. Daniel.
Number IV. Roster Commission 37th Georgia State Troops, A. J. Hilbun, J. S. Drew, W. R. Hester.
Number V. Roster Commission Company I, 57th Regiment—Georgia Volunteers, J. B. Wolfe, Wm. Gilbert, R. D. Dixon.
Number VI. Roster Commission Company G, 49th Regiment, Dr. J. T. Chappell, J. F. Fuller, John Burch.

5. CONFEDERATE ARMY—SOLDIERS FROM LAURENS

D. F. Attaway, C. A. Alligood, D. B. Attaway, E. C. Allen, B. C. Atkinson, John W. Bedingfield, Hardy Bellflower, J. T. Bender, Andrew Berryhill, William Berryhill, W. B. Bostwick, James Branch, F. D. Beall, Jacob H. Barber, H. H. Blankenship, W. W. Bailey, — Blankenship, G. W. Brooks, G. W. Belcher, J. J. Bowen, John Burch, W. M. Beasley, B. F. Brown, J. C. Bracewell, N. F. Brown, R. M. Benford, W. C. Bishop, J. A. Bracewell, Henry Beacham, D. J. Bush, Green W. Bustell, Cone E. Bryant, N. B. W. Bracewell, M. M. Burch, E. L. Beacham, L. C. Beacham, W. S. A. Bracewell, H. T. Bush, — Bedgood, T. B. Bland, H. C. Black, T. F. Brown, J. A. M. Butler, J. M. Bass, G. F. Bass, J. D. Bates, B. F. Ballard, John T. Balts, Oswell Beall.

L. J. Cullen, E. H. Cullens, N. S. Chafin, I. S. Chappell, E. W. Cullen, J. W. Carter, E. C. Coleman, John Coleman, Joseph Coleman, L. D. Coleman, L. A. Chapman, N. R. Camp, J. C. Chipley, J. F. Colley, Allen Cowart, J. F. Coney, J. G. Carter, E. W. Cummins, R. W. Cullens, N. M. Corder, J. R. Chapman, G. W. Conner, Wm. Conley, Irwin Calhoun, Henry Currell, James P. Chappell.

Lot N. Daniel, Carswell S. Davis, Thomas R. Dickson, Benj. Dominy, John J. Dominy, Peyton W. Douglas, Willie E. Dunkins, J. A. Dixon, W. E. Duncan, B. F. Dixon, John Davidson, L. A. Dreyer, Dr. J. B. Duggan, James W. Daniel, Olin Daniel, W. B. F. Daniell, John I. Dixon, Richard Davis, R.H. Dunkins.

Joe M. Ellington, J. F. Ellington, W. E. Edge, J. T. Elliott, John C. Edwards, J. F. Edmonson, J. M. Everett, J. E. Elliot, James F. Faulk, Elkania Faulk, G. B. Faulk, James T. Faulk, William G. Faulk, C. F. Fullford, Francis E. Fullford, Valentine Fullford, W. H. Foxworth, E. W. Fordham, Jas. M. Fordham, Jeremiah Fordham, J. T. Flanders, W. J. Fordham, E. M. Floyd.

N. C. W. Graham, Duncan Graham, John M. Graham, J. C. Graham, B. R. Graham, Elia Graham, Jas. R. Graham, Wm. Gilbert, W. F. Geffckins, J. L. Gufford, J. W. Grines, Henry Gray, Jas. B. Gay, Josiah Gay, Wm. J. Gay, W. H. Griffin, C. S. Guyton, — Green, I. H. Hall, Joel G. Hall, Jonathan G. Hall, William J. Hall, Thomas W. Haskin, P. W. Hendricks, J. H. Herrington, Robert F. Hill, Ebenezer Hilliard, G. B. Hollingsworth, Jeff Howard, John Hutchinson, W. R. Hester, T. H. Hall, H. P. Hall, F. M. Hightower, G. S. Holland, J. M. Hutchins, J. W. Hawkins, Thomas Hart, J. R. Holcomb, E. M. Holmes, J. R. Holmes, W. T. Haskins, M. D. Heath, A. J. Hilbun, H. M. Hornburry, Thad Herrington.

James V. Ive, Little C. Jenkins, George W. Jenkins, John W. Jones, Thomas A. Jones, William L. Jones, H. I. Jones, H. T. Jones, J. B. Jones, M. L. Jones, W. R. Jackson, B. I. Johnson, N. A. Johnson, William Kea, Wesley Kea, T. D. Keen, Wilen Keen, J. D. Keen, J. L. Keen, W. D. King, J. L. Kinchens, John S. Knight, Z. Kennedy, G. T. Kinchen.

G. E. Lanley, W. J. Lanley, L. B. Linder, W. Z. Lynn, J. Y. Lee, E. L. Lock, W. H. Long, J. E. Lord, E. M. Lans, B. B. Linder, Dr. J. L. Linder, W. A. N. Lowery, Doc Linder, Lumpkin Linder.

D. B. Maddox, Jas. W. Maddox, Warren W. Maddox, William H. Mimms, Amos M. Moore, Andrew H. Moore, Capt. H. M. Moore, Lewis Metts, John McCant, Jas. T. McDaniel, John C. McDaniel, John I. McDaniel, John Y. McDaniel, Washington W. McDaniel, Dennis McLendon, Richard McLendon, W. H. H. McClendon, A. H. McClendon, G. W. McDay, Wiley Martin, L. A. Matthews, Wm. M. Mathias, James Mincey, J. A. Minter, R. E. Miller, Lewis Metts, G. A. Marchman, W. J. Massey, J. R. Miller, J. M. Minor, J. C. Mackey, W. K. Methvin, H. W. Moorman, J. K. Mills.

A. M. Nash, J. F. Nelson, Robt. Nobles, Willie Nobles, Jeff Nobles, J. B. Newman, Jas. C. Nealey, A. J. Odum, Beatty Outler, Rufus A. Outler, Joseph H. Padgett, John T. Perry, Terrell Perry, W. J. Perry, B. F. Parker, J. C. Parker, L. C. Perry, J. M. Parks, S. K. Passmore, Ernest L. Perry, Daniel G. Pope, Thomas H. Pope, Joseph P. Powell, J. I. Pharis, T. W. Pritchett, A. L. Pridgen, V. E. Purvis.

Wm. Register, Wash Register, T. S. Register, Jas. P. Register, Alfred G. Register, Dave Register, Elijah F. Register, Jas. L. Register, John Register, John M. Register, J. C. Register, W. S. Ramsay, L. L. Raffield, J. W. Raffield, J. R. Rawls, Noah Rowe, Thomas H. Rowe, Wallace Rowe, A. L. Rowland, G. W. Rowland, A. L. Rogers, Charles Rowland, Wm. C. Robinson.

J. P. Scarborough, Wm. M. Scarborough, L. F. Scarborough, J. F. L. Scarborough, W. R. Scarborough, Newton Scarborough, John Scarborough, David Scarborough, D. J. Scarborough, Jethro F. Scarborough, J. M. Scarborough, J. W. Spell, Jack Saturday, J. R. Stewart, W. R. Stewart, J. B. Silas, Benj. C. Shepard, E. Shepard, Hardy Smith, W. B. Smith, T. D. Smith, W. W. Smith, J. Z. Smith, Emory Smith, Henry Smith, Martin V. B. Smith, William H. Smith, W. L. Strickland, John M. Stubbs, J. C. Stinson, P. R. Shy, W. J. Stafford, G. M. Sanders, W. F. Snellgrove, J. N. Snellgrove, E. M. Stanley, Jas. W. Stanley, Hardy M. Stanley, R. A. Stanley, James Stephens, Joel Stephens, George Slaughter, William Slaughter.

M. Thigpen, Richard Thigpen, E. H. Thomas, W. J. Thomas, James A. Thomas, W. A. Thomas, Ezekiel H. Thompson, H. M. Thornburg, T. M. Tarpley, R. F. Tidwell, G. B. Towns, Calvin Tyre, J. F. Ussery, J. F. Venson.

K. A. Walker, R. H. Walker, W. E. Warren, Jas. J. Warren, Thomas J. Warren, K. B. Ward, Henry M. Watson, D. M. Watson, D. L. Warnock, W. R. Warnock, W. A. Warrington, G. S. Watkins, W. T. Wilkes, John Wilkes, Alex P. Wilkes, J. F. Willis, R. A. Williams, R. J. Williams, Thomas Windham, W. A. Wilson, W. J. Williford, W. G. Webb, J. A. Williams, G. W. Webster, Drew Williams, W. A. Witherington, J. B. Wolfe, Pleasant Wood, T. A. Wood, T. J. Wood, G. A. Wood, W. J. Wood, J. B. Wood, E. Y. Woodard, J. W. Woodard, S. A. Whitfield, Jack Wilkerson, H. H. Wynn, J. L. Wynn, W. H. Wright, J. N. Wright, John E. Woodward, Thomas M. Yopp.

This list is incomplete—it was not made till years after the War, and then from the memory of living soldiers.

6. AN EPISODE OF THE WAR

The Lone Vidette

An unwritten episode of the Great Civil War, 1864

By William Gove

The period of time covered by the War Between the States presented many opportunities for the display of individual bravery and pluck on both sides. Where the horrible carnage was most frequent, these instances of valor and courage were more numerous, but for cool, deliberate daring, under the greatest risk, the following incident will easily rank among the first. The writer had the account from the lips of the chief actor on the occasion and it has been verified by many responsible people who personally know of it.

Last Fall, sitting by his hospitable hearth, while the crackling logs in the broad, open fireplace made sport of the howling wind outside, the hero of the event told the story of long ago. At the time of the daring adventure, Dr. D——, a young surgeon in the Confederate Army, was home on a furlough on account of wounds. His home was in one of the counties immediately below Macon, Georgia, and he lives today, honored and respected by all who know him, within twenty miles of the scene of that eventful day. Retired from the active practice of his profession, with ample of this world's goods to keep him and his good old wife in comfort, he passes his days in peaceful ease, surrounded by his children and children's children, keeping "open house" to all who come.

Though now an old man, "while on his temples grow the blossoms of the grave," his eyes are undimmed by age, and as memory recalled the events of those stirring days, his face lit up with the fire of youth. So, holding the old musket across my knees while "I watched the purple wreaths of smoke" curl up from my pipe, I heard the following tale:

In the Fall of '64, when Sherman was making his famous "march to the sea," his army passed down the line of what is now the "Central of Georgia Railway," leading from Macon to Savannah, Georgia. According to the usages of war, the invaders not only destroyed the track of the railroad, but also destroyed or appropriated, all munitions of war, and everything which might be used for the benefit of the enemy. All grist mills and cotton gins, with all cotton, were especially objects devoted to destruction.

When the Federal Army reached a small station about forty miles from Macon, the leaders learned from some "run-a-way negroes" that there was a large, well appointed mill which ground both corn and wheat, situated about fifteen miles south of the railroad and that several hundred bales of cotton belonging to the Confederate Government were stored there.

Immediately a large detachment of Cavalry was detailed to go and burn both mill and cotton. They had as guide a mulatto negro named "Jim" who belonged to the family who owned the mill and who had run away and joined the Yankees, as soon as he heard of their nearness. As it was known that the tireless and dashing Confederate General Wheeler, with his seeming ubiquitous body of horsemen was hanging on the flank of the Federal Army, the detachment of raiders kept a sharp lookout for an ambuscade and moved very cautiously. My home, at the time, was situated nine or ten miles from the railroad and on the direct road the raiders must follow. Knowing my uniform would cause my arrest, if discovered, I had mounted my horse, and with my musket across my saddle-bow, I had "taken to the woods" as soon as the Yankees had approached my neighborhood. That morning I had ventured home for a few minutes, but as soon as arrived I learned of the coming of the detachment guided by the negro, so it was without any great delay I was back in the saddle and galloping down the road at the best pace my horse could go.

Within a short distance of my house, and between me and the mill, was a large creek which at point divided into two prongs and was crossed by six or seven bridges, connected by a series of embankments and known locally as "Big Sandy Creek" and "Lightwood-knot Bridges."

As I dashed down the road it occurred to me that if I could destroy the bridge, or at least a portion of it, I could stop the oncoming force as the creek was swollen by recent rains to the size of a very respectable river with a swift and deep current.

Living just at the end of the bridge on the side from which I was coming was an old negro woman. As I reached her house I saw that she was doing the periodical clothes-washing and had a large fire of pinewood around the pot out in the yard. My plan was formed on the instant. It was nearly half a mile from the beginning of the first bridge to the end of the last abutment on the farther side with a raging torrent covering the space between, the creek now being high above its banks and both prongs joined in one rolling tumbling mass of muddy water.

Checking my horse at the cabin of the old woman, I hurriedly explained my plan as follows: I was to dash on across the bridges to the other side and there stop as if I were a soldier on the lookout while she was to seize the flaming pine from around the pot, fire the first bridge in one or more places, then run on, setting fire to the others as she came to them. The mention of the fact that "the

Yankees are coming and are just up the road" was sufficient to put the vigor of youth into her old frame.

The poorer class of the whites in the South at the time and most of the negroes had the greatest horror of the "Yankees," a current belief among them being that the Yankees had horns and that they killed and burned for the pure love of it.

Knowing that when the Federal soldiers discovered the part the old woman had taken, they would burn her little shanty and therewith all her earthly possessions, I told her that I would see to it that she was reimbursed. She quickly agreed to do her part. It took less time to explain the plan and to put it into operation than to tell it, for the hoofs of my horse had scarce ceased to sound on the first bridge, before the old woman had set fire to the end nearest her, and was running with the flaming brands in her hands on to the other side. Reaching the farther bank, I brought my horse round to face the bridges, buttoned up my coat, adjusted my cap, and, altogether made as soldierly appearance as possible. There was an abrupt turn in the road on both sides of the creek, so that one coming from either direction could not see the bridge till they came within a few feet of it. I had scarcely reined my horse into proper position when the head of the raiding force came into view.

They were riding four abreast. Astride a mule, riding with the first four, was the informer and guide, "Yaller Jim," as he was generally known.

Seeing the blazing bridge directly in front of them, the column halted and several of the soldiers sprang from their saddles to try to put out the fire. The smoke at first so obscured their vision that they did not see the old woman fleeing for her life, far ahead, nor the Confederate soldier on picket duty on the other side. But they were speedily advised of both, for the men had hardly torn at the first blazing plank when a shot startled them and a bullet whizzed by with its vicious sound. Looking along the bridge they saw the old woman running for her life and just reaching the farthest bridge, while a Confederate soldier was sitting on his horse just at the bend in the road, wildly waving his hand to some person or persons unseen around the bend. Between the soldiers and them, the bridges were blazing in several places. While yet they looked, another shot came whizzing by, and another, and another, from my gun.

The soldiers who had dismounted fired a shot apiece at the two figures on the other side and then hastily scrambling back into their saddles, the whole detachment wheeled and galloped madly back along the road they had come, never doubting but that they had run into the hated Wheeler and his men.

The idea was accentuated by several shots in rapid succession from the bridge and the wild yell of the Confederate boys, accompanied by hoof beats on the bridge.

The detachment never drew rein till they were safe with the main force which spent an uneasy day and night, expecting each moment an attack from the enemy. "Yaller Jim" was left far in the rear, and fearing capture, if he continued in the road, he abandoned his mule and took to the paths through wood and field which every negro knows by heart and can find day or night.

"Did I feel nervous?" said the Doctor in answer to a query. "Well, I should guess so. I knew there were two or three hundred soldiers over there and I knew that if my ruse did not work that would shortly become a very unhealthy neighborhood for me. Like a flash I thought of every road leading away from that bridge and its possibilities of leading to a hiding place. I knew the country like a book and in my mind's eye I could see several places where a blood hound could hardly trail me. And I tell you, if that bugle of theirs had sounded a 'Charge' instead of a 'Retreat,' as it did, I should have proved the going qualities of my horse that day. I could hardly credit my eyes when I saw them all going, but you may rest assured I felt greatly relieved."

The Doctor pursued the flying column across the bridge and on in sight of his house, which he found has not been burned. On the way he picked up the mule abandoned by the negro which he succeeded in keeping during the rest of the war and which he used on his farm for several years afterward.

Returning to the bridge, he found the shanty of the old woman in flames, one of the soldiers having paused long enough to hurl a blazing brand into it. The house and its poor contents were entirely consumed. He then turned his attention to the bridges.

Owing to the recent rains the planks in the bridges were wet and burned slowly and he was able to put out all the fires before the bridges were seriously injured.

Often on winter nights the old soldiers living around the neighborhood tell to gaping youngsters tales of the war, but none do they repeat so well as the one of how Dr. D— saved old Lightwood Knot Bridges and Stanley's Mill* from the Yankees.

7. JEFF DAVIS IN LAURENS COUNTY.

If the passing of DeSoto through this section, long years before Laurens County was formed, adds interest to Laurens County history, then the passing of Jeff Davis through the same section more than fifty years after it became the county of Laurens, has increased that interest many times.

Davis, the President of our Southern Confederacy as we love to call it, but strickly speaking, The Confederate States of America, the man who had nobly responded to his country's call, and accepted the presidency of the new government, founded in defense of justice

---

*Chappell's Mill in upper part of Laurens.

and honor, the man who had risked all and lost; that man was now fleeing for his life, with the enemy in hot pursuit. Yet the people of Laurens County love to know that in his flight fate brought him this way; and the ground over which he passed is hallowed ground.

It has been handed down from father to son, from mother to daughter; so that all know that Mr. Davis represented that government which came into existence for the protection of States Rights against the Union that had ignored those rights, even as England, our mother country, had done.

Hence, after the War Between the States was over, and the Confederate States of America had lost, Mr. Davis and his cabinet were hunted as if they were rebels or criminals: but to the people of our Southland, these men had only added glory to their names; and the passage of Jeff Davis through Laurens, will linger in the memor of Laurens County citizens as a matter of much significance.

But let us begin at the beginning, which was in the state of Virginia. As soon as it became inevitable that Richmond, the capital of our Southern Confederacy, would be taken by the enemy, Mr. Davis began to make plans for the safety of Mrs. Davis and family, while he endeavored to reach some port on the Gulf, and from thence, sail to England.

A closed carriage was secured for Mrs. Davis, with a trusty servant John Davis as driver. A suitable escort was provided, and the party started southward. Mr. Davis and two or more close friends followed, taking precaution to attract as little attention as possible. They traveled in small groups, and avoided taking a special escort, as there were spies scouting the country, and the enemy might, at any time, become aware of the whereabouts of the Davis party. Yet the many groups of southern soldiers returning from war, helped to make the members of this group feel comparatively safe, while they continued to be cautious. It was even deemed best that Mrs. Davis and escort should take a different road from that taken by Mr. Davis; but all go southward with the understanding where they would meet, if possible, on certain dates.

Now as the small group, in which Mr. Davis rode, moved onward, it so happened, that on Saturday just before nightfall, Mr. Davis, in company with Judge Reagan and a few friends, reached the east bank of the Oconee River, which runs through Laurens County close by Dublin. The road they traveled ran down to Ball's Ferry. There they were to camp for the night.

About the same hour Mrs. Davis' party came out of a densely wooded road near the home of Mr. E. J. Blackshear, ten miles from Dublin. There she was given that genuine welcome for which so many Laurens County planters were famous; and was entertained for the night with true Georgia hospitality.

As Mr. Davis neared the ferry already mentioned, they heard

humors of a plot to rob a wagon train which had attracted much attention on account of the fine looking stock and general appearance of all concerned. It was very probable that there was plenty of money as well as provisions along, so the robbing would prove very profitable. On questioning the ferryman the report was verified.

Mr. Davis, believing that Mrs. Davis and party must be somewhere in the vicinity, became much alarmed for fear she had joined the wagon train; so the idea of camping was abandoned, while he and his friends spent the night on horseback scouting the country to render assistance to Mrs. Davis.

It was a long and lonely ride that night for Mr. Davis and friends. Only ten miles, but having no guide through the dense woods they found it difficult to make their way. A short while before daylight, however, they reached the road they were seeking; and strange as it may seem they, even as Mrs. Davis' party had done the afternoon before, came into the main road not far from the home of Mr. E. J. Blackshear.

One can only imagine the great joy of Mr. Davis when he found that his family were there, and that they had not been harmed during the night. After an early breakfast, and securing all the information they could concerning the roads and the location of the Federal troops, the party left the Blackshear home and continued their journey southward, Mr. Davis riding in the carriage with Mrs. Davis. The carriage was driven by the negro, John Davis.

About 11 o'clock Sunday morning of the same day the party drove into the town of Dublin, where they made a brief stop at the store of Judge F. H. Rowe. The judge, learning that some travelers wanted a supply of provisions, went down to his place of business, and there found that the party was led by Jeff Davis. Judge Rowe not only supplied their wants, but gave them a cordial invitation to dinner, which they deemed prudent to decline; so after getting directions for further procedure, the journey was resumed.

It might be pertinent to mention here that Judge Rowe was a native of Connecticut, yet he was careful to direct the Davis party the safe way southward, while the Federal soldiers who came by a few hours later, and were in pursuit of the Davis party, as Judge Rowe suspected, the judge gave them directions to go west; otherwise the Davis caravan might have been captured in Laurens County instead of Irwinville several days later. Had the party adhered closely to directions given in Dublin, Mr. Davis, in all probability, would have reached his port, and sailed to England; thereby avoiding capture.

There is a little romance connected with the Davis party, which concerns the negro population of Laurens County. While the Davis carriage was waiting in front of the store already mentioned, a number of people gathered near to ask questions concerning the war and soldiers. In the crowd gathered there, there were many negroes.

One of them, a comely young woman, attracted the attention of the driver, John Davis. In the free and easy way of the southern negro, he entered into conversation with her and found that her name was Della Connoway. During the brief time of waiting he began to talk love to her, for she had really made a deep impression upon him, and he had, in like manner, impressed her as young man of more than usual importance, since he was driving for such fine folks, behind such fine horses.

So as John Davis, the young driver, traveled back to Macon, where the party was broken up, he was thinking about the young girl he had seen in Dublin. As soon as he was relieved in Macon, he made his way back to Dublin, found the girl, courted her, married her and settled down on a farm in Laurens County, where he reared a family of ten children. Among them was one named Jeff. The old driver lived to be eighty years old; enjoying a vigorous life, the latter part of which was spent near Eastman in Dodge County, where he moved about twenty years before his death.

It is not our purpose to follow Davis to the time of his capture in Irwinville, but we will mention this coincidence. The Michigan Cavalry that made the capture, the following Tuesday, had camped in Dublin the night after the Davis caravan had passed. When the Cavalry overtook them, the arrest was easily made, as the Confederates made no resistance.

The capture of the Davis party reflected no glory upon the captors. There was no cause for the Federal officers to make a display of heroism; for when the party was overtaken, they surrendered in a most practical way. If there was any manifestation of heroism, it must be accorded the Confederate group who maintained their perfect equilibrium under the trying circumstances.

There was another member of the Confederacy that came to Dublin in the terrible days after the Surrender, Robert Toombs on his way out of Georgia, came to the house of his friend Everard Blackshear and spent a night in the old house that stood near the mill. It is claimed that Robert Toombs stayed in Dublin for three weeks, hidden in the house of Major Hugh Moore. The old house still stands, but it was removed several years ago to Brantley Street.

—*By Julia Thweatt Blackshear (Mrs. T. J.)*

8. GENTLEWOMEN OF THE SIXTIES.

In the beginning of this county's making, pioneer women with undaunted courage, grim determination, and never ceasing tact, ably aided and abetted their sturdy, heroic men as they hewed out and laid the foundation of Laurens County. Together they dreamed, planned, prayed, and worked at the stupendous task of building homes, churches, schools, and in a few years settling the county site, Dublin, on the banks of the Oconee.

Memory oft-times paints a picture of "Old Miss" of the "Big House" in her billowing skirt, tight basque, black silk apron, lace cap, dainty feet carefully shod, and in her hands the inevitable bunch of keys; for she carried the keys in those days to the smoke house, pantry, linen press, and store room. The houses amid the stately trees bore euphonious names such as "Doll Neck," "The Oaks," "The Hermitage," "The Pines," "Rose Cliff," "Frog Level," "Valambrosa," "Bellevue," and many others. They were homes in which our Grandmothers and Great Grandmothers ruled as queens. Note the well ordered house, the gracious welcome and charming hospitality for which they were famous. The social calendar full of dinings, quiltings, house-warmings, balls, and Christmas celebrations, a time of feasting and good cheer. The table filled with delicious viands that only "Molly" in the kitchen and "Miss" in the parlor knew how to prepare.

Their devotion to the children sometimes eight, ten, maybe a dozen, has been handed down in song and story. Mammy in full charge in the day, but as the shadows of night begun to fall, "Mother," would gather the little ones around her knee and in the gentlest of southern voices teach them from God's Holy Word, lessons of truth, honor, integrity, and love. Theirs a simple faith, they loved their homes, a golden axis on which their little world revolved. On the plantations scattered over the county they reared a race of stalwart sons and goodly daughters.

The picture would not be complete were not mention made of the kindly relations that existed between Mistress and slave, her compassion for them was shown in her readiness to minister to their needs in sickness and health, sorrow and old age. The pious instruction of these godly women, their solicitude and interest created in the bosom of the negro an age long devotion and loyalty to their "White folks." Many of them were faithful unto death during the trying days of the 60's.

To more vividly bring to mind the gracious ladies of long ago let fancy weave a miniature picture of: "Old Miss," Mrs. Thomas McCall; "Miss Jerusha," Mrs. William O'Neal; "Miss Margaret," Mrs. Jeremiah Yopp; "Miss Betsey," Mrs. Samuel Yopp; "Miss Elizabeth," Mrs. Thomas Moore; "Miss Emily," Mrs. Byron Whitehead; "Miss Mabel," Mrs. Andy Fuqua; "Miss Jane," Mrs. F. H. Rowe; "Miss Rachel," Mrs. Robert Robinson; "Miss Jane," Mrs. J. L. Linder; "Miss Janet," Mrs. Ira Stanley; "Miss Marianna," Mrs. Elijah Blackshear; "Miss Belle," Mrs. Everard Blackshear; "Miss Elvira," Mrs. Thomas Guyton; "Miss Elmina," Mrs. Charles Guyton; "Miss Pollyana," Mrs. Moses Guyton; "Miss Lizzie," Mrs. David Daniel; "Miss Caroline," Mrs. R. A. Bedingfield; "Miss Anne," Mrs. William Hester; "Miss Mary," Mrs. George Currell; "Miss Liza," Mrs. Lowther; "Miss Lula," Mrs. Geffckens; "Miss Ann," Mrs. Hardy Smith; "Miss Anne," Mrs. Dr. Tucker; "Miss

Elizabeth," Mrs. J. E. Perry; "Miss Nancy," Mrs. J. T. Duncan, Sr.; "Miss Anna Eliza," Mrs. David Clark; "Miss Frances," Mrs. Frank Thomas; "Miss Mary Frances," Mrs. Andrew Hobbs; "Miss Frances," Mrs. James M. Fordham; "Miss Nancy," Mrs. J. T. Register; "Miss Mat," Mrs. R. A. Stanley; "Miss Lizzie," Mrs. B. F. Stanley; "Miss Athalia," Mrs. J. T. Chappell; "Miss Nettie," Mrs. W. S. Ramsay; "Miss Emma," Mrs. Thomas H. Rowe; "Miss Ella," Mrs. Hardy Smith; "Miss Mary," Mrs. J. B. Wolfe; "Miss Maria," Mrs. Dr. McCullough; and many others of blessed memory.

No word so aptly describes these women as found in Holy Writ: "Strength and honor are her clothing, she openeth her mouth with wisdom, and in her tongue is the law of kindness. She looketh well to the ways of her household, and eateth not the bread of idleness. Her children arise and call her blessed, her husband also, and he praiseth her." She believed her mission was to soothe and to solace, to help and to heal, the sick world that leaned on her. When the war of the 60's came, some of the dear women mentioned had gone to their reward, but the majority with their brave and courageous daughters exhibited a heroism and devotion to principle scarcely equalled and never surpassed in the world history. Aching hearts bade the soldiers good-bye, with tear dimmed eyes gave a smile of hope, and words of cheer, that would in the days to come nerve them to deeds of unparalleled daring. Bravely through the four years these women bore privations, perils, and heart breaking bereavement. When the war was over, the men returned to find nearly everything they possessed swept away, it was the wives, mothers, sweethearts, daughters, who as in the days of yore worked together to build anew a bigger and better town and county.

> *"Soft benediction from their hands*
> *Have sparkled like the sea-side sands.*
> *Their lives like some sweet story reads*
> *A fairy wonder book of deeds.*
> *Time e'ers its bare recital bars,*
> *To tell it all would tax the stars."*
>
> —By Josephine Rowe Carswell (Mrs. J. A.)

Chapter VIII

COUNTY GOVERNMENT AND COURTS

1. INFERIOR COURT AND COURT OF ORDINARY.

In the beginning of the colony of Georgia a General Court and Inferior Courts were created, the latter to be in control of the minor affairs of the Colony. As the colony grew into parishes the Inferior Courts became the ruling power of the division.

When Laurens County was created in 1807 justices were elected for the Inferior Court; there were five of these and the term of office was four years; they were elected by the voters. This court exercised a three-fold power that is now vested in an Ordinary, a Board of County Commissioners, and the lower courts.

The Inferior Court of Laurens County had control of all fiscal affairs from the time of the county's creation till it was abolished by legislative act of the State Constitution of 1868. In 1852 the Court lost jurisdiction over probate and estate matters and this power was vested in the Ordinary. In 1866 all court cases were taken over by the County Court.

Here follows a list of the Inferior Court Justices:

Beginning in 1808:
Thomas Gilbert served 2 years.
Peter Thomas served 2 years.
Thomas Davis served 4 years.
William O'Neal served 10 years (2 terms).
Edmund Hogan served 6 months.
Ashley Wood served 1 year.
John Thomas served 4 years.
John B. Spivey served 1 year, and 1 month.
Adam Jones served 9 years.
George Linder served 13 years (at different times).
John Love served 4 years.
Noah Stringer served 4 years.
John Fullwood served 7 years.
Archibald Griffin served 1 year, 1 month.
John G. Underwood served 3 years, 1 month.
George W. Welch served 4 years.
Thomas Moore served 3 years.
John Guyton served 4 years.
Amos Love served 3 years.
Jacob Robinson served 3 years.
Neil Munroe served 6 years.
Edward St. George served 8 years.

Jethro Weaver served 1 year, 1 month.
Matthew M. Kinchin served 3 years.
Russell Kellam served 1 year.
Jordan Baker served 4 years.
George W. Daniel served 1 year, 1 month.
John Ricks served 2 years.
David Maddox served 4 years, 1 month.
Elbert Duncan served 2 years.
J. H. Fondrew served 1 year.
E. J. Blackshear served 11 years
John W. Smith served 1 year.
John T. Wright served 4 years.
Robert Robinson served 13 years.
A. G. Hampton served 2 years.
T. H. Rowe served 5 years.
Hardy Smith served 5 years.
John W. Yopp served 5 years.
William Adams served 6 years.
C. B. Guyton served 6 years.
Daniel Anderson served 4 years.

Between 1865 and 1868 the following were Justices:
W. S. Ramsay, H. M. Burch, B. A. Herndon, J. B. Wolfe, Wiley McLendon, James I. Robinson, C. L. Holmes.

DUBLIN AND LAURENS COUNTY PUBLIC BUILDINGS

Thomas H. Wilkinson served 5 years.
Henry Bohannon served 7 years.
Benjamin Hampton served 10 years,
1 month.
Robert Coats served 1 year.
Jacob Horn served 5 years, 1 month.
Jeremiah H. Yopp served 7 years.
H. C. Fuqua served 3 years.
H. B. Hathaway served 3 years.
Lewis Linder served 8 years.
M. G. O'Neal served 3 years.

Clerks of the Inferior Court were:
1809-1818, Amos Love.
1818-1825, Neil Munroe.
1825-1827, Geo. Mather, who died in office.
1827-1833, Thomas Moore, who died in office.
1834-1860, Francis Thomas, who died in office.
1860-1868, John T. Duncan.

The last session of the Inferior Court was held in July, 1868. The control was then taken over by the Ordinary, who at that time was Washington Baker.

In 1852 the Court of Ordinary was created and was given jurisdiction over probate of wills, testamentary letters, administration, disposition and sales of property of deceased persons, appointment and control of guardians, control of mental incompetents, orphans, fi. fas., subpoenas, marriage licenses, records of bonds, registries, and files; these powers had been previously exercised by the Inferior Court.

The full control of county affairs after 1868 was in the hands of the Ordinary. Early in the 1870's agitation began for the creation of a Board of County Commissioners, whose duty would be the control of the county's financial affairs and the roads.

In 1873 there was an Act passed by the General Assembly creating an Advisory Board for Laurens, which was to consist of three members. This Board was to sit with the Ordinary in the control of county affairs. This body could be said to be the first Board of County Commissioners; it consisted of Thomas H. Rowe, David H. Coombs, and C. S. Guyton.

This Act of 1873 was repealed in 1875 and the same Act created "the County Board of Laurens County to be composed of one member from each Militia District in said county, who shall be elected on the fourth Saturday in April, 1875, by an election held at the precincts of each militia district, under the form and regulations required by law for the election of other county officers."

This Board has power to govern and control all property of the county; to levy both general and special taxes; to establish, alter or abolish all roads, bridges, ferries, or to lease or rent same; to establish, change, or abolish election precincts and militia districts; to elect the County Board of Education; to examine and audit the accounts of all officers having the care, management, keeping, "collecting and disbursing of money belonging to the county, or appropriated to its use and benefit, and bringing said officers to a settlement; to regulate the disposition of all estrays taken up in the County; to make rules for the marking and branding of all livestock; to abolish, alter, or regulate the alms house of said county, and make such rules and regulations for the support of the poor of the county as are authorized by, and not inconsistent to law; to regulate and fix the fees for all license for peddling and retailing of spirituous liquors, taking bond and security of the parties applying for the same. Said Board shall appoint Road Commissioners, and shall require them to make to them their returns; and shall have all other powers as were by law vested in the Inferior Court prior to the adoption of the present State Constitution and shall have no jurisdiction, except such as pertains to county matters.''

The members elected to this Board were: J. M. Lowery, Iverson H. Harvill, A. J. Thompson, W. W. Smith, B. F. Stanley, and Enoch M. Lake. The Clerk of the Superior Court served as clerk of the body and the Sheriff was required to sit in.

In 1877 this Act was repealed and jurisdiction returned to the Ordinary.

2. BOARD OF COMMISSIOERS OF ROADS AND REVENUES.

In 1893 Thomas Rowe introduced an Act which was enacted by the General Assembly providing for a Board of Commissioners of Roads and Revenues which would have the same powers as the Board of 1875 had. The first members of this Board were: J. F. Fuller, Chairman; W. A. Witherington, W. J. Fordham, T. J. Blackshear, and J. C. Powell; Mr. Powell removed from the county and was replaced by J. M. Finn. These members were named in the bill.

The following men have served as members of the Board of Commissioners of Roads and Revenues from 1896:

1896—J. F. Fuller, Chairman; J. M. Finn, T. J. Blackshear, M. S. Jones, J. R. McDaniel.
1898—M. S. Jones, Chairman; W. W. Smith, W. J. Thomas, J. R. McDaniel, J. H. Yopp.
1900—W. W. Smith, W. J. Thomas, J. H. Yopp, W. H. Mullis, Chairman; A. J. Weaver.
1902—A. J. Weaver, Chairman; Wm. Kea, J. E. Stanley, Albert Arnau, J. M. Blackshear.
1904—Wm. Kea, Chairman; J. E. Stanley, Albert Arnau, J. M. Blackshear, Wm. Gilbert (later J. L. King).
1905—E. R. Orr, Chairman; J. L. King, John M. Blackshear, L. O. Beacham, A. W. Davidson. J. Ira Moore, appointed to fill unexpired term of J. M. Blackshear.
1906—E. R. Orr, Chairman; L. O. Beacham, A. W. Davison, J. Ira Moore, W. B. Taylor.
1907—E. R. Orr, Chairman; L. O. Beacham, A. W. Davidson, W. B. Taylor, Wm. Kea.
1908—E. R. Orr, Chairman; L. O. Beacham, W. B. Taylor, Wm. Kea, Jeptha Tingle.
1909—Wm. Kea, Chariman; W. B. Taylor, J. J. Wynn. In September, 1909, there was added to the Board: J. J. Bowen, John S. Drew, H. C. Burch, J. T. Walden, J. W. Guest.
1911—H. C. Burch, Chairman; J. J. Wynn, J. J. Bowen, J. S. Drew, J. T. Walden, A. K. Spivey, Ernest Clark.
1912—H. C. Burch, Chairman; J. J. Wynn, Ernest Clark.

1913 and 1914—J. J. Spivey, Chairman; C. T. Beacham, W. M. Herndon.
1915—D. R. Coleman, Chairman; C. T. Beacham, J. J. Wynn.
1916—D. R. Coleman, Chairman; C. T. Beacham, J. M. Thigpen.
1917-1920—H. C. Burch, Chairman; R. F. Garner, O. W. Parker.
1921-1924—D. R. Coleman, Chairman; A. J. Weaver, G. W. Granger.
1925-1928—J. F. Graham, Chairman; Robert M. Lord, C. L. Thigpen.
1929-1932—J. M. Cannon, Chairman; V. J. Taylor, C. L. Thigpen.
1933-1936—J. M. Cannon, Chairman; V. J. Taylor, C. L. Thigpen.
1937-1940—J. F. Graham, Chairman; Robert M. Lord, L. O. Beacham, Jr.
   J. R. Lord appointed at death of R. M. Lord in 1940.
1941-1944—Lamar Thigpen, Chairman; J. F. Graham, J. L Allen.

Clerks to the Board of Commissioners since 1893 have been: T. J. Blackshear, W. C. Solomon, T. J. Blackshear (again), E. D. White, J. H. Witherington, James L. Keen, Jr., Walter Daniell, James L. Keen, Jr. (again).

Two members of this Board are from the territory west of the Oconee, one from the east. The Board holds monthly sessions. The term of office of each Commissioner is four years, and members are now elected by the people at the same election.

3. LAURENS COUNTY COURT SYSTEM.

To witness the first court ever held in Laurens County, we must turn our thoughts to the year 1808. If we are to appreciate and understand the beginning of our Court system, we must acquire a proper background, otherwise the incidents related in connection with the first sessions of the Court would seem highly amusing. The conditions under which Court was held then were far different from those of the twentieth century. There were no electric lights, no telephone, telegraph, automobiles, or even typewriters to aid and facilitate the procedure of the Court. The petitions of the litigants, instead of being typed and filed with the clerk, were written in long hand on the minutes of the court, either by the parties themselves or the clerk. Since there were no paved roads it was by no means certain that the Judge would arrive on the day set for court or even later, as riding the circuit required months of travel over hundreds of miles where there were but few bridges and the road was often only an Indian path. In 1818 Laurens County became a part of the Ocmulgee Circuit, comprising a territory equal to the combined area of the states of Maryland and Delaware, so we can readily see the difficulties of holding court.

Under such circumstances, the first term of the Laurens County Superior Court convened on April 25, 1808, in an out-house near the home of Major Peter Thomas, with Peter Early, who in 1813 became Governor of the State, presiding as Judge. John Clark, son of Elijah Clarke, was the first solicitor-general to try a case in Laurens County. At this particular time Thomas Jefferson, the father of democracy, was serving the last year of his second term as the third President of the United States. The Sovereign State of Georgia, under the leadership of Governor James Jackson, having ceded her "Yazoo Lands" to the United States Government in 1802, was barely recovering from this horrible nightmare which nearly wrecked the honor of the State. At this term no business was transacted except the finding of six true bills by the grand jury. The first indictment was against Charles Higdon, charged with bigamy, and, strange as it may seem, this defendant was a member of the same grand jury which indicted him. The charge was stated in the following language, "We, the Grand Jury of Laurens County, indict Charles Higdon, for marrying a woman while his first wife is alive."

To the modern legal mind of today, with its love of technicalities, this indictment seems defective in the respect that it fails to allege that he was not divorced, since, if he were, it would be no crime to marry while your first wife was alive. At this time Judge Early fined four grand jurors twenty dollars each and twelve petit jurors ten dollars each for failing to attend court.

The October term began on the 24th day of October, 1808. For the time being, its organization was hindered and frustrated by a very stubborn and unruly character who no doubt was of the opinion that courts did very little good anyway. Finally, quieting the fellow, the judge passed the following judgment: "Cader Mann, having, during the sitting of this court, committed a most outrageous contempt of authority thereof by profanely cursing and swearing in the court yard, and by standing in defiance of the high sheriff endeavoring to arrest him under the immediate order of the court, and having added to the contempt by cursing and swearing in the immediate presence of the court when brought there to be punished; it is further ordered that the said Cader Mann be imprisoned in the common jail in the county of Washington for the space of three calendar months, and that, at the expiration of his imprisonment, he do enter into recognizance with the clerk of this court or the Superior Court of Washington County, himself, in the sum of five hundred dollars and two securities being freeholders in the sum of two hundred and fifty dollars each, conditioned to be of good behavior to all persons for the term of five years " Since nothing is found to the contrary we may presume that the three months in jail taught Mr. Mann to be discreet. He, along with many others, as will be shown later, had little regard for the coming of a court which had the power of interfering with the God-given liberties of man. This little episode created such excitement among the citizenry of the county that the judge adjourned court "until to-morrow morning at Nine O'clock." On Tuesday, October 25th, the first case was tried and the jury returned a verdict of guilty against William Parker for assault. Judge Early sentenced the defendant as follows: "The defendant, William Parker, having been convicted upon the charge of assault, it is hereby ordered that he pay a fine of $15 and that he stand committed to the custody of the sheriff until paid.'" Next the case of State vs. Tarvin was disposed of, with a verdict for the state, and the imposition of a fine of $50 and commitment to the custody of the sheriff until the fine was paid. We note that all the sentences were so worded that the defendant remained indefinitely in the custody of the sheriff if the fine was not paid.

That the grand jury believed in brevity can be seen in the presentments for the October term, 1808, in this language:

"First: We present Amos Forehand for publicly speaking in the presence of Alexander Blackshear, and saying, that if the prisoner then in the fence, were a brother or relation of his, he wished hell might be his Heaven if he would not kill a judge at a flash of a gun as he came out of the court house."

"Second: We present Samuel Riggins for insulting the clerk of the court by kicking him as he was passing from the house of Maj. Thomas to the courthouse, Monday evening, before the court adjourned."

"Third: We present Michael Horne and Samuel Riggins for fighting in the courthouse yard during the sitting of the court, on information of Daniel Scarborough, one of the grand jury."

"Fourth: We return our sincere thanks to his Honor, Judge Early, for his prompt and impartial discharge of the duties assigned him at the present term."

The records indicate that before 1811 there was no jail in Laurens County. The prisoners were either taken to Sandersville or kept in the "Rail fence." It was not at all unusual for the Judge to order that the head of the prisoner be inserted between two of the upper rails of the fence, thus placing the offender in such a predicament that his misfortune was a warning to all the pioneer public who saw him there. It was for commenting upon this that the grand jury preferred a charge against Amos Forehand. It is interesting to note here that Arter Sheffield contracted to build the county's first jail in 1811, using as his material huge pine logs. After completing his arduous task he decided to celebrate, so "tanking up" on an excessive quantity of home-distilled liquor, he took charge of the town until he was finally captured and placed in the jail as its first prisoner. With reference to this, Judge Hawkins states that Sheffield so keenly felt the humiliation to which he had been subjected and the indignities thus visited upon him, that he shook the dust of Laurens County from his feet and left, never to return.

The first new trial ever granted in Laurens County was in the case of State vs. Green. Immediately after the defendant was found guilty of cattle stealing, the judge passed an order reciting that the verdict was without evidence to support it and was against the evidence, and ordered that "it be set aside and a new trial granted." Under present rules motions for a new trial are passed upon at a later date, and the defendant is at an added advantage by reason of the fact that he may secure a record of the case and pick the flaws of the trial after an exhaustive study of the evidence.

At the October term, 1809, His Honor, the judge, failed to appear, and the clerk, Amos Love, entered the following order upon the minutes: "Monday, October 30th, 1809. The Honorable Judge of the Court failed to attend. The court in terms of law in such cases made and provided a postponement until to-morrow morning at nine o'clock, Tuesday, October 31st. The judge having failed to attend, the court is adjourned until court in course." Why the judge failed to appear is not given.

The first murder trial in Laurens County was that of Hansell Roberts, charged with killing Benjamin Harrison on the 14th day of August, 1811. The case resulted in a mistrial. James Miller, who was convicted of assault and battery at the May term, 1808, and sentenced to pay a fine of fifty dollars and costs, was pardoned by Governor David B. Mitchell, on the condition that he pay the court costs. This was the first occasion on which executive clemency was extended in Laurens County.

At the April Term, 1812, Judge Early imposed the following sentence on Ralph Hicks, convicted of cattle stealing:

"You, Ralph Hicks, are to be taken and forthwith tied to a tree in the public square in the town of Dublin and there receive thirty-nine lashes on your bare back with a cat o'nine tails, and you are in the same manner at the same place to receive another thirty-nine lashes at the hour of twelve o'clock on to-morrow, the 16th inst., and you are in the same manner at at the same place to receive thirty-nine more at the hour of twelve o'clock on Friday the 17th inst., and you are then to be branded on the shoulder with the letter 'R' and then be discharged upon the payment of the costs."

Grand jury presentments for the October Term 1812 show that it was still difficult to compel proper respect for the dignity of the court. Their language was as follows:

"We present as a grievance and disorder that William Monroe insulted the jury, by standing in the door of their room cursing and swearing, and would not depart when ordered by the bailiff and also some of the jurors. We also present Christopher Edwards for mocking the bailiff of our body when calling Burke Chisholm, and also for cursing in the presence of the jury. We also present James Drake for hanging about the door of the jury room, and when requested to leave, he refused to do so, and cursed the bailiff and the jury together. We also present Stephen Law for cursing in the presence of the jury and after being ordered off by the bailiff stated that he would say what he damn pleased. We also present Benjamin Faircloth and Drury Roberts for an affray committed in the court yard on the first Monday in September last while the court of Ordinary was sitting, to the great interruption of said court and other good citizens." At this term the grand jury stated that they were happy to say that the records of the county appeared to be in good order and that there remained unappropriated the sum of $120.33.

Other matters disposed of at the October Term, 1812, were the trial of a divorce case and the foreclosure of fifty-five mortgages. The county's first divorce case was that of William Grady vs. Sarah Grady; the first verdict was granted at this term, but it does not appear the second decree was ever given. It appears that the State had loaned money to various individuals taking, as security, mortgages upon their lands. These were foreclosed upon the petition of David B. Mitchell, Governor and Commander-in-Chief of the Army and Navy of the State and the Militia thereof, praying for foreclosure on mortgages given to John Milledge, Governor of the State, and his successors, etc.

That there were those who still refused to pay the court proper respect is again shown in the grand jury presentments of the October Term, 1814. "We approbate in the highest terms the prompt and judicious conduct of His Honor, Judge Harris, in taking notice of and inflicting proper punishment on Ashley Wood of Twiggs County, for an unparalleled and outrageous contempt of the court and for insulting his Honor while in the impartial discharge of his duties in Laurens County." Wood was reprimanded for boisterous talking and took offense, telling the judge he would "see him later after the court was over." His impertinence cost him three months in jail.

As most of our information as to the deliberations of the Court is derived from the grand jury presentments, we turn our attention to other reports. In the March term, 1820, we find the following return: "We present Archibald Dougald Wilkerson for trading with a negro belonging to Wilbur Smith for money to the amount of $2.75, on Sunday, the 13th of February, and also for frequently keeping tipping Shop door open on the Sabbath, Elijah Deen, one of our body informed." David Blackshear, Foreman. Again at the April Term, 1828, with the same foreman as above. "We, the grand jury for the body of the people of the county of Laurens take pleasure in saying that we have nothing of a grievous nature to present. There are no instances of public gaming nor of trading unlicensed with negroes that comes within our knowledge. We recommend that sealed weights and measures such as are acknowledged by the name of this State shall be procured by the proper authority in our county by which to prove and adjust the various weights and measures used in the exchange and sale of grains and liquids. We recommend to the Judges of the Inferior Court to have the court house repaired and made comfortable before the next term of the court and that the common jail be made decent for its objcets."

At the April Term, 1830, this return is found: "We, the grand jury, after examining the clerk's books and accounts, find them correct. We, the grand jury, present George Payne for killing hogs on Sunday, the 13th day of December, 1829, in the County of Laurens and when called on by some of the members of the church where he then belonged, answered he had done so, and would do it again, and was expelled from the religious denomination; but still makes a common practice of having his slaves labour on the most Holy Sabbath in defiance of the laws, good order, peace and dignity of this State, witness Thomas Barbour and others.''

There were many terms when the grand jury had no criminal charges to prefer as is seen from these returns. "October Term, 1830, we the grand jury chosen and selected for the county of Laurens feel much gratified to have it in our power to say that we have no presentments to make—Wingfield Wright, Foreman.'' In 1831, "We are happy to say that we have no presentments which it is our duty by law to make—Benjamin Hampton, Foreman.''

Another interesting feature is the form which the clerk always used to record the opening of the court, the following language being invariably used: "The Honorable the Superior Court for the county of Laurens met agreeable to adjournment, present his honor———— judge of said court.''

Briefly reviewing other incidents of the first court terms we find that a true bill was returned against Alexander Smith in 1814 for retailing liquor without a license, that in 1817 William McCullers was convicted of larceny and sentenced by Judge Harris to receive thirty-nine lashes at the public whipping post, then to be released upon the payment of costs. The first lawyer admitted to the bar in Laurens County was Daniel McNeal of South Carolina, who was admitted at the October Term, 1818. The first white man, and probably the only one to be hanged in the county, was a tobacco dealer by the name of Tarrell who was executed in 1848. The victim with a few friends were gathered around the wagon of the dealer, on the banks of Hunger and Hardship Creek. An argument arose, and Tarrell slew his visitor and escaped. For a while the search for him was futile until some one thought of the faithful dog tied to the wheels of his master's wagon. They released the dog and followed on fast horses until the dog was successful in the search for his master. Tarrell was then tried, convicted, and sentenced to be hanged.

Among other important events incidentally connected with the Laurens County court history was the controversy which arose out of the slaying of Letcher Tyre by Fluker and Tarbutton in 1906. After Tarbutton had been placed in jail, he was able to secure, through the influence of Charlie Rawlings, a brilliant array of lawyers as ever defended a citizen of these parts. The defense counsel included Thomas W. Hardwick, Judge J. K. Hines, later a member of the Supreme Court of Georgia, T. L. Griner and Judge John S. Adams. Laurens County was represented by K. J. Hawkins and its county attorney, M. H. Blackshear. As this killing happened near Lovett, a spot close to the Johnson County line, Hardwick made the point that the venue was in Johnson rather than Laurens County.

Under the prevailing law the Secretary of State was the sole arbiter of boundary disputes between counties, thus the matter was placed before him. Under the evidence which Hardwick was able to produce, Phil Cook, Secretary of State, decided that the killing occurred in Johnson County, and that this county had jurisdiction of the case. His decision had the effect of chopping off and placing in Johnson County a small strip of territory which hitherto had always been recognized as a part of Laurens. For years this plot of land was the object of much superstition, being referred to as "no man's land."

The bulk of the civil cases tried in the early days were suits on account, and they were very few compared with those on the dockets of our court later. In the January Term, 1933, the Superior Court had over two hundred cases for trial, while in the December term the City Court surpassed this record with two hundred and sixty-four cases on the docket. The majority of the early criminal cases were for assault and battery, most of them being fist fights. Evidently they thought it cowardly to use a knife or a gun, for very few were employed. From 1853 to 1868, a period covering fourteen years, there were one hundred and thirty-five criminal cases. Of this number, a few filed pleas of guilty, six were discharged on demand, ten acquitted, twelve transferred to the County Court, and sixty-nine cases in which no action was taken. What a contrast with the January term, 1933, with over eighty-five cases on the criminal docket, and fifty-eight transferred by Judge Kent to the City Court to be added to one hundred and seven criminal cases already pending there.

Prior to the formation of the Dublin Judicial Circuit on August 18, 1911, Laurens County had little, if any, influence in the formation of the circuits, as will be shown by the fact that it was "kicked about" from place to place until it was finally given its own circuit. When first created it was put in Ocmulgee Circuit. It had the pleasure of providing one Superior Court judge, Judge Peter Love, who presided from 1849 to 1859. Only three times had its citizens had the office of Solicitor General, though the Dublin bar was among the best in the state. Peter Love was the fourth Solicitor General of the circuit. Hon. Rollin Stanley served as Solicitor General of the Oconee Circuit for one term during the sixties, and Capt. W. C. Davis filled an unexpired term as Solicitor General of the Ocmulgee Circuit in 1902. In the year 1818, Laurens became a part of the Southern Circuit; on December 12, 1881, it was placed in the Oconee Circuit, only to be transferred to the Ocmulgee Circuit on December 9, 1882. Then on December 23, 1884, it was again switched to the Oconee Circuit. Later, on November 26, 1890, it became a part of the Ocmulgee Circuit, being transferred for the third time to the Oconee Circuit on August 19, 1907. Since 1911, Laurens County has remained in its own circuit, the Dublin Circuit.

The list of the judges of the Superior Court of Laurens County is as follows:

Peter Early, 1808 to 1821.
C B. Stone, 1821 to 1822.
Thomas E. Harris, 1822 to 1827.
Moses Fort, 1827 to 1829.
C. B. Cole, 1836 to 1846.
Jas. J. Scarborough, 1846 to 1849.
Peter Love, 1849 to 1859.
A. H. Handell, 1859 to 1868.
J. R. Alexander, 1868 to 1871.
A. C. Pate, 1871 to 1882.
Thomas G. Lawson, 1882 to 1885.
C. C. Kibbee, 1885 to 1889.
D. M. Roberts, 1889 to 1891.
W. F. Jenkins, 1891 to 1895.
John C. Hart, 1895 to 1902.

Thaddeus Holt, 1829 to 1832.
Lott Warren, 1832 to 1835.
James Polhill, 1835 to 1836.

F. C. Foster, 1902 to 1903.
H. G. Lewis, 1903 to 1908.
J. H. Martin, 1908 to Dec. 1911.
K. J. Hawkins, Jan. 1912 to ——.
W. W. Larsen, appointed to fill Hawkins unexpired term.
J. L. Kent, 1913 to 1925.
R. Earl Camp, 1925 to 1933.*
J. L. Kent, 1933 to 1941.
R. Earl Camp, 1941-

In the early days of our court, the sheriff occupied a place of unusual dignity and was given the title of High Sheriff. It has been said that it was the custom for this officer of the court to wear his hat. The first sheriff of the county was James Hampton. Others in the order of their office are:

Isaac Kirksey
Miles Smith
John Thomas
Uriah Kinchen
Ira Stanley (These served from 1808 to 1829).
Moses Guyton, 1830 to 1831.
Chas. S. Guyton, 1831 to 1834.
John H. Hampton, 1834 to 1837.
J. G. Fondon, 1837 to 1838.
T. N. Guyton, 1838 to 1842.
F. H. Rowe, 1842 to 1846.
John W. Yopp, 1846 to 1848.
L. M. Hudson, 1848 to 1852.
Capt. J. M. Smith, 1852 to 1854.
John T. Duncan, 1854 to 1856.
W. S. McLendon, 1856 to 1858.
John T. Duncan, 1858 to 1860.
John J. Keen, 1860 to 1862.
B. A. Herndon, 1862 to 1866.
L. C. Perry, 1866 to 1868.

Joel E. Perry, 1868 to 1870.
George Currell, 1870 to 1872.
W. B. Keen, 1872 to 1874.
Dennis McLendon, 1874 to 1880.
J. C. Scarborough, 1880 to 1882.
J. E. Perry, 1882 to 1886.
J. C. Scarborough, 1886 to 1890.
G. M. Howard, 1890 to 1894.
W. J. Joiner, 1894 to 1898.
E. E. Hicks, 1898 to 1904.
J. D. Prince, 1904 to 1906.
E. E. Hicks, 1906 to 1908.
J. J. Flanders, 1908 to 1914.
W. N. Watson, Jan. 1915 to Dec. 31, 1920.
Lester F. Watson, Jan. 1921 to Dec. 31, 1928.
W. H. Adams, Jan. 1929 to Dec. 31, 1936.
I. H. Coleman, Jan. 1937 to ——.

It is to be noted the list of the clerks of the court is very small, compared to the number of other court officers. Those serving as clerks of the Superior Court are:

Amos Love, 1808 to 1827.
Thomas Moore, 1827 to 1834.
Francis Thomas, 1834 to 1860.
John T. Duncan, 1860 to 1866.
Hardy Smith, 1866 to 1893.

W. J. Hightower, 1893 to 1909.
H. I. Hilburn, 1909 to Dec. 1910.
E. S. Baldwin, Jan. 1, 1910 to Dec. 31, 1940.
J. E. Bedingfield, 1940 to ——.

---

* In Judge Camp's term, Miss Charlotte Hightower was made official court stenographer, the first woman to hold the position.

It seems nothing short of remarkable that Laurens County has had only nine clerks in one hundred and twenty-five years, especially when we note that one served scarcely longer than a year.

Adam Saffold was the first Solicitor General. He was followed in office by Thaddeus Holt, John Gibson, Peter Love, Thaddeus Sturgis, and W. B. Bennett, who served in the order named, but the record fails to disclose the terms of their service. Other solicitor generals are:

Rollin A. Stanley, 1871 to 1876.
Tom Eason, 1876 to 1878.
C. C. Smith, 1882 to 1883.
Robert Whitfield, 1883 to 1884.
C. C. Smith, 1884 to 1887.
Tom Eason, 1888 to 1890.
H. G. Lewis, 1890 to June 1902.
W. C. Davis, 1902 to 1903.
J. E. Pottle, 1903 to 1908.
E. D. Graham, 1908 to Dec. 31, 1912.
E. L. Stephens, Jan. 1, 1913 to Dec. 31, 1924.
Fred Kea, Jan. 1925 to Dec. 31, 1932.
J. A. Merritt, Jan. 1933 to Dec. 31, 1936.
J. Roy Rowland, Jan. 1937 to Dec. 31, 1940.
J. Eugene Cook, Jan. 1941 to ———.

Prior to the formation of our modern Court of Ordinary, the judges of the Inferior Court attended to all county matters as well as holding the trials of slaves. Who the Justices of the Peace have been, as well as exactly what their duties were, does not appear on the records, but Judge Hawkins states that from tradition, it was their authority to grant divorces, settle land title disputes, and try all slaves accused of any offense, less than capital. If the investigation by the Justice of the Peace showed the slave to be guilty of a capital offense, the penalty for which was death, he notified the judges of the Inferior Court who held a trial. If the slave was convicted by the jury, he must be hanged not sooner than five, nor more than thirty days from the date of the verdict. The following was a capital offense when committed by a slave or free person of color: Poisoning or attempting to poison, assault with intent to murder, assaulting any white person with a weapon likely to produce death, maiming any white person, burglary and arson.

The first person to be hanged in Laurens County was a slave by the name of Sharper who was hanged on Saturday, the 26th day of July, 1819, having been convicted of attempting to murder Joseph Perry. The judges presiding at this trial were George W. Welsch, Adam Jones, and John J. Underwood. In the same year, a slave by the name of Jones was convicted and hanged, the place of his execution being the spot where L. A. Chapman's old brick yard was formerly located. The last judges of the Inferior Court were John W. Yopp, E. J. Blackshear, and Robert Robinson, the court being abolished soon after the creation of the Court of Ordinary.

This court was created in 1852, with F. H. Rowe as its first judge. This court attends to numerous county affairs as well as probating wills, appointing administrators for estates, issuing marriage licenses, etc. The judges of this court are as follows:

F. H. Rowe, 1852 to 1860.
Washington Baker, 1860 to 1870.
J. B. Wolfe, 1870 to 1877.
John T. Duncan, 1877 to 1891.
Rollin A. Stanley, 1891 to 1893.
Capt. Hardy Smith, 1893 to 1897.
Jos. M. Fordham, 1897 to 1901.

W. A. Wood, 1901 to 1917.
E. D. White, 1917 to Aug. 22, 1937.
W. H. Adams, 1937 to 1940. (Elected to fill unexpired term of E. D. White).
W. H. Adams, 1941 to ——.

It was during Judge Duncan's administration that fifteen thousand dollars worth of bonds were issued for the building of a bridge over the Oconeee River.

We pass next to a consideration of the County Court. This Court was created in 1866, having as its first judge, Hon. M. L. Burch, who was succeeded by Mercer Haynes, the latter holding office until 1890, when this court was abolished by an Act of the Legislature. Five years intervened before the formation of the City Court of Laurens, which held its first session with Ira S. Chappell as judge. Under the authority vested in him at that time, Judge Chappell appointed E. J. Blackshear clerk, and F. G. Corker solicitor. Judge John S. Adams, who was appointed by Governor Candler to succeed Judge Chappell, served one year when this court was abolished and the City Court of Dublin was established by an Act of the Legislature in 1900. Judge Adams by appointment, became the first judge of the new court and continued in that capacity until 1904, when he resigned. Others who have been judges of the City Court of Dublin are:

J. E. Burch, 1904 to 1908; G. H. Williams, Solicitor; D. L. Emerson, Clerk.
K. J. Hawkins, 1908 to 1911; W. C. Davis, Solicitor; A. H. Grier, Clerk.
J. B. Hicks, 1911 to 1917; Geo. B. Davis, Solicitor; J. N. Donaldson, Clerk.
R. D. Flynt, 1917 to 1921; T. E. Hightower, Solicitor; Sidney F. Brown, Clerk.
S. W. Sturgis, 1921 to 1925; Wm. Brunson, Solicitor; Sidney F. Brown, Clerk.
G. C. Bidgood, 1925 to 1933; J. A. Merritt, Solicitor; Sidney F. Brown, Clerk.
E. L. Stevens, 1933 to 1940; L. F. Watson, Solicitor; Sidney F. Brown, Clerk.
Palmer Hicks, 1941——; Stanley Reese, Solicitor; Johnny Beddingfield, Clerk.

Sheriffs of the City Court of Dublin:
J. D. Prince, 1900 to 1904.
J. A. Peacock, 1904 to 1910.
B. M. Grier, 1910 to 1916.
J. Ira Maddox, 1917 to ——.

(Note: At this time, the office of the Sheriff of the City Court was consolidated with that of the Superior Court).

Clerks of the City Court:
E. J. Blackshear, 1895 to 1899.
Freeman Moore, 1899 to 1903.
L. Q. Stubbs, 1904 to 1913.
D. L. Emerson, 1913 to 1917.
A. H. Grier, 1917 to 1921.
Jos. N. Donaldson, 1921 to 1925.
Sidney F. Brown, 1925 to 1941.
Johnny Beddingfield, 1941——.

The office of Clerk of City Court was abolished by Legislative Act, the duties to be assumed by the Clerk of the Superior Court.
Solicitors of the City Court:

F. G. Corker, 1895 to 1897.	T. E. Hightower, 1918 to 1921.
J. B. Sanders, 1897 to 1899.	William Brunson, 1921 to 1925.
F. G. Corker, 1899 to 1902.	J. A. Merritt, 1925 to 1933.
G. H. Williams, 1902 to 1908.	L. F. Watson, 1933 to 1935.
W. C. Davis, 1908 to 1910.	Joe Chappell, 1936 (resigned).
Geo. B. Davis, 1910 to 1914.	R. I. Stephens, 1937.
S. P. New, 1914 to 1918.	Stanley Reese, 1937.

It will be well to mention here that W. J. Joiner was the first sheriff of both the County Court and the City Court of Laurens. T. B. Hudson succeeded him as sheriff of the County Court and served until it was abolished in 1900.

As an intermediate court, the City Court has done much to alleviate the heavy burden of business which previously had been borne by the Superior Court. This court has both monthly and quarterly terms. Sidney Brown, former clerk, reported that on one occasion twenty mortgage foreclosures were filed in one day, another on which he issued twenty-two criminal warrants late one afternoon, and all the prisoners were in jail by the next morning.

Laurens County should consider herself quite fortunate in having secured for herself a division of the Federal Court. In May, 1926, Congress passed a bill creating the Dublin Division of the United States Court for the Southern District of Georgia. The first officers of this division of the Federal Court are:

> Judge William H. Barrett, Judge, Augusta, Ga.
> Hon. Walter W. Sheppard, Dist. Atty., Savannah, Ga.
> Hon. Scott A. Edwards, Clerk, Savannah, Ga.
> Hon. G. F. Flanders, Marshal, Swainsboro, Ga.
> Hon. L. Q. Stubbs, Deputy Clerk, Dublin, Ga.
> Hon. John S. Adams, Referee in Bankruptcy, Dublin, Ga.

Judge John S. Adams resigned as Referee to accept a position as attorney for the United States Treasury in the Department of insolvent National Banks. Stanley A. Reese, who was appointed to fill his unexpired term, is said to be the youngest Referee ever appointed to this position in the State. Reese resigned and Hardeman Blackshear was appointed in 1938.

At the death of L. Q. Stubbs, Miss Jessie Baldwin became deputy clerk, the first woman to hold this position.

NOTE: Most of the material of this article is from a paper prepared on Laurens County Court History by the late K. J. Hawkins, former Judge of the Superior Court, published in 1914. For additional information, the author is indebted to the court officials of this county.

4. COURT HOUSE AND JAIL.

The first reference to the building of a court house is found in the minutes of the Superior Court under date of February 8, 1808, when it was "ordered that Amos Love, Alexander Blackshear, Andrew Hampton, John Fullwood, Jethro B. Spivey, Simon Smith, Elisha Farnall, Wm. Yarborough, Leonard Stringer and Stephen Vickers be and they are hereby appointed to assist the Justices of the Inferior Court in pointing out and ascertaining the most convenient and eligible site for court house of said county.

"Ordered that the above named persons together with the Justices of the Inferior Court do meet at the house of Andrew Hampton, Esq., on first Monday in April next at 10:00 o'clock in the forenoon to proceed on business aforesaid."

Whether this committee met and what they decided is not recorded, but if the place was chosen there was but little done about a building; the next record is found in the minutes under date of August, 1811, when it was "ordered that the Clerk do pay John Fullwood, Esq., the sum of $36.00 for the building of a temporary court house in Sumpterville, and making table and seats."

It seems that after the county seat was moved to Dublin this same contractor constructed a court house, for there occurs in the minutes of the Inferior Court the record that it was "ordered that the Clerk pay over to John Fullwood, Esq., the amount received for the general tax for the year 1828 on account of his demand against the County for building the court house."

In 1848 the third courthouse was ordered built; the next year the old courthouse was ordered to be sold and removed in two months after the sale; in June, 1849, this house was accepted after being built under contract with George Stephenson. This was a two-story building with court hall on first floor and county offices on the second. It was removed to Franklin Street, where the Bus Station is now located. It was used at different times as a wagon shop, a boarding house and hospital. This building was of wood but well built and of good material as certified by its long life of usefulness.

Under the first Board of County Commissioners the present brick structure was erected in 1895. It was built on a contract price of $22,480 with a levy of tax of $1.40. Marvelous to tell—there was no bond issue for its erection.

JAILS

During the three years the county seat remained at Sumpterville there was no jail. There is a notation on the minutes of 1811 that a jail of great logs was built by Arter Sheffield. This was ordered built after the trial of Hansel Roberts who in October was ordered to be sent to the Washington County jail, "there being no jail in this county." This must not have been considered safe for we find other notations referring to criminals being sent to Washington County or Wilkinson County jails.

In 1829 the Inferior Court let to Charles Guyton a contract for the building of a jail. In 1832 the Court ordered "a ditch to be dug all around the building five foot sufficiently wide to take in two pieces of timber, 1 foot thick each." But even with this timbered palisade the jail was not long considered a safe place for prisoners for, in 1837, T. N. Guyton, Charles Guyton, Robert Robinson, and A. A. Fuqua were ordered to examine and report on the safety of the jail.

The committee reported the structure unsafe and recommended a new jail be built. The new one was constructed in 1838 by Robert Robinson.

In 1851 in June a tax levy was ordered for the building of a jail. The jail was built by A. A. Fuqua in 1852.

This old jail stood on the site of the present jail. It was burned in 1890. The present jail was built by the Court of Ordinary in 1891.

It would seem that as late as 1842 men in Laurens were imprisoned for debt. There occurs in the minutes of the Inferior Court under date of 1842 the following notation: "Ordered that the prison bounds alowed to persons arrested under and by virtue of Ca Sa for debt for the County of Laurens, commence at Mrs. Mary Cooper's on Gaines Street in Dublin, running said street to Guyton's Gin House, thence running along Jefferson Street till it intersects Jackson Street, thence up Jackson Street to Dr. A. T. Brown's house; including the Jail and all houses on said square back to the beginning."

Chapter IX

PERIOD OF 1870, 1880, 1890

1. IN THE EIGHTEEN SEVENTIES.

Following the War Laurens County suffered as did the rest of the State from the privations of war and the rigors of the Reconstruction period. Sherman's armies had not passed through Laurens, but foraging squads ravaged the country, and another scourge was even more destructive, for a Confederate force sent to protect the country from Yankee destruction was Wheeler's cavalry, who came just before the surrender; these hungry discouraged soldiers rode here and there pillaging the fields, seizing gathered crops, and taking every horse that was able to do heavy work and leaving old broken-down animals in their place. Wheeler, the doughty little general with his broad black plumed hat and red sash, was feared as much almost as Sherman.

The soldiers returned to their homes, the home guards were disbanded, and all men started over again with determined hearts. By the latter part of the seventies restoration was well under way, wagons were again hauling cotton to Savannah and business was growing. This enlightening passage is found in the Grand Jury Presentments of April, 1872:

"Labor has been much improved and seems to be in unison with the wants of the county more than at any time before. Like in the halcyon days of Troup our county stands, as is seen, in balance equal in hospitality, purity, and prosperity with sister counties in the State, and preeminently shares unity of action and concern of her citizens in observing law and fostering good."

The same Grand Jury declares at that time that the county is out of debt. The same presentments recommended, "a conference be held between our representatives in the Legislature and the Central Railroad Company to look into the matter of building a railroad." Jonathan Weaver was the foreman of this forward-looking body.

Relations between former slaves and masters remained friendly. In most cases the negroes were unwilling to leave old masters and go out for themselves. They were ignorant and incapable of directing their own lives, yet in most cases white men did not take advantage of them. Below is a contract drawn between a former owner and some of the negroes he had owned. They could not read what was written but as "ole marse" showed them where the name should be, each grown negro made his mark.

June, 1865.

"This is to certify that an agreement is made between myself (A. C. Duggan) and my negroes once but now freed men and women.

"They have agreed to live with me as they always have until Christmas on their part. And I am to feed and clothe them and treat them as before on my part. I will give the name of head of each family and number of children of each.

"Flue and his wife and four children; Amanda and six children; Celah and five children; Wash, a man of 21 years old; John, a boy nineteen years old; Bow, a boy sixteen years old; Bithe, 13 years old, no relation; Sarah five years & Jesse three years old, no relation here; Jack, a boy 14 years old, no relation.

"Witness T. G. Duggan."

About this time there was a negro riot, Tode Norris, a big vicious mulatto led the uprising. It was ended when some of the negroes were killed and a hundred or so of them were arrested and carried to Sandersville jail for safe keeping. Some of these were freed but some were sent to the penitentiary.

Even through the Eighties there was a latent fear of negro uprisings, and when in 1882 there was a negro riot in Eastman in which a young white man was slain by a crazed mob, all the adjoining counties took steps for safety.

Through the Seventies and Eighties the Oconee River was of great commercial importance.

In May, 1872, the Grand Jury recommended "an appropriation of $500 be made to clean out the Oconee River so that a boat company now forming may run a small steamboat between this place and the Oconee Bridge."

John M. Stubbs was a powerful factor in developing transportation lines on the Oconee between Dublin and Raoul's Station before the railroad came. He spent much of his own money in clearing the channel and keeping it navigable. He organized a river transportation company with R. C. Henry as captain.

From the early years of the county the river has been used for trade. For many years before the War there were timber rafts floated on the river and pole boats for carrying cotton and products to market and bringing back supplies. The first boat was named the George M. Troup, built by Judge Freeman H. Rowe, David Robinson, and others.

In 1876 the Grand Jury recommended that the Ordinary establish a chaingang for "The purpose of punishing criminals found guilty of minor offenses." Today the chaingang force is located at the former County Poor Farm and is under a Warden appointed by the State Prison Board, upon recommendation of the County Commissioners. Their work is to take care of all roads not under State control.

In 1879 the Grand Jury recommended that a ferry be made at

Diamond's Landing, a crossing over the Oconee River in the southern part of the county.

Agriculture was fast recuperating. Some of the farmers that were becoming planters were: Thomas H. Rowe, Seaborn Weaver, Andy Hobbs, J. I. Fordham, C. S. Guyton, J. H. Yopp, the Brazeals, E. A. Vickers, and W. M. Kea. Robert Wayne, who married a granddaughter of Governor Troup, was operating a large plantation near Dudley—it is still called the Old Wayne Place.

In 1873, Dublin applied for and received a certificate of incorporation.

A glimpse of the town in the latter Seventies and Eighties would at this point be informative.

A two-story frame courthouse, with a tiny wooden guard house at the rear, was in the center of a square outlined with China berry trees. The business life centered in a few general merchandise stores and its public buildings—a church where the First Baptist Church now stands and a school house called the Academy where the High School is now located. On the corner now occupied by Pierce and Orr was a store owned and operated by George Currell; on the site occupied now by Black's Drug Store stood the store operated by J. B. Wolfe. The present Hicks Drug Store site, once occupied by the store long owned before the war and operated by Judge Rowe, was the Peacock Drug Store. The only other building from there to Franklin Street was Newman's little Harness Shop. Another general merchandise store stood on the present site of Westbrooks. W. B. Jones operated a thriving business at the Lovett & Tharpe site. On the corner of Jackson and Lawrence, Captain Louis Perry built a store about 1873 and operated it for a number of years. All these stores were wooden buildings with piazzas facing the road. The merchants hauled their goods by wagon from the nearest stations on the Central Railroad, usually from Toombsboro.

The first drug store was opened in 1872 by Dr. Harris Fisher on the present site of the Oatt's Drug Store.

The most popular spot in dry, sandy Dublin town in the Seventies was a barroom operated by one Peter Sarchett, there was no other place where men could congregate so comfortably as under the shade of a great oak near the bar. There was a certain fascination for the little boys, too, for Peter Sarchett had a parrot that could shriek swear words as well as her master's name. This "groggery" occupied the site of the old bank building on Jefferson Street next to Hicks' Drug Store.

About 1876 the first brick building was erected; this was Dr. R. H. Hightower's office. Where now Phillips old stables stand, was then a two-story wooden building, a photographer's studio upstairs and downstairs the post office run by "Uncle Willie" Hicks.

The principal residences of that day were few and far apart.

The finest house in town was the Yopp residence on Gaines Street near the Christian Church. The "white house" occupied by the Weavers was located on the site of Tindol Brothers Store.

In the Seventies the hotel, a story-and-a-half unpainted wooden building, was full of life during court; mine host was the amiable John Keen. It stood where McClelland Stores are today. The next house below the hotel was Lige Benton's, an unpainted wooden building standing on the site just north of the railroad tracks.

Dr. Harris Fisher married the community's beloved teacher, Miss Julia Guyton, and built his home on the site of Mrs Jones' apartment house near the High School of today. Up the hill on the road to Macon was the Dasher home, a wide-spreading structure built around a log house, the site now occupied by the Graves' residence.

Across the street was the white house designed and built in 1872 by architect Sutton for Colonel Stubbs. Within a few years its landscaped grounds made it the show place of Laurens County. Colonel Stubbs was a horticulturist by nature and practice.

The first step toward beautifying Dublin was taken when Captain Rollin A. Stanley set out shade trees on each side of the street from the Baptist Church to his residence near the intersection of Bellevue Avenue and the present Coney Street.

The oldest home now standing is the house on Rowe Street occupied by the late Freeman Rowe; Judge Rowe built and occupied this house before the War Between the States. In its kitchen was cooked the meal for President Jefferson Davis when, after the surrender, he was fleeing from the Federal Government.

In a beautiful grove stood the large double-pen log house of George Currell. This old house was the social center of the town; his music-loving daughters, with their piano, attracted the young people to musicals and singings.

Another old home near Dublin was a large log house built and occupied by Andy Fuqua. It is today occupied by Charles Perry. Its lawn is decorated by a giant oak, perhaps, the oldest tree in the county.

On the east side of the courthouse there were no houses, only the cabin of the negro ferryman, "Uncle Billy" Donaldson; the road from the ferry led between fields bounded by rail fences.

The area between Elm and Oak Streets was a fine oak grove. Although it might be dry, hot and dusty, here it was cool and inviting, and through the woodland paths strolled courting couples, and under the spreading trees were held Sunday School picnics, speakings, and festivals. The only house for some years, in this area, was the D. S. Blackshear home, the site now occupied by the residence of M. H. Blackshear.

Another home of historic interest is the Ramsay residence on Bellevue Avenue, built by Col. W. S. Ramsay a short time after the War Between the States, and still owned and occupied by his descendants. This old place is noted for its formal gardens, which were planted by an English landscape gardener, W. F. Higgons, soon after the house was built.

The only houses along Bellevue Avenue, beyond the Stubbs place, were the Hicks, Beacham, Ramsay, Stanley, and Duncan homes. The city limits, on the west, were at the present intersection of West Drive and Bellevue Avenue. To the west of the present home of E. T. Barnes was a pond, and between the pond and what is now McCall's Point was a negro quarter.

In the year 1879 Dublin was governed by Mercer Haynes, Mayor, and Aldermen Peter Sarchett, T. H. Rowe, R. M. Arnau, W. J. Scarborough, J. F. Moore, I. T. Keen, recorder and treasurer, James W. Wright, marshal.

Dublin's first fire company was organized in 1878, with W. H. Tillery, chief. The Dublin Telegraph Company was incorporated in 1878.

2. THE EIGHTIES.

The negroes in Laurens were realizing, by this time, their independence, and certain of their leaders were inciting them to demand political equality. Warren Miller announced for the Legislature in 1882, backed by the prominent negroes, Wm. Harris, Samuel Mitchell, Crawford McCall, James Yopp, Cupid Blackshear, Jack Coney, Lot Conway, Joseph Troup, and George McLendon. There was no longer the "Carpetbaggers" to aid them, so their candidate was not successful.

In the session of the Georgia Legislature, 1882-1883, there was passed an enactment authorizing the Ordinary of Laurens County (John T. Duncan) to make annual assessment on taxable property sufficient to raise $3,000.00 during a term of five years; this sum to constitute a special fund for the purpose of building a bridge across the Oconee, at Dublin. Joel T. Coney, William B. Jones, Berrien B. Linder, Frank M. Taylor, and J. Frank Fuller were appointed building commissioners. The bridge was built and opened to the public on a summer day in 1891 with a great celebration. Ordinary Duncan led the procession over the bridge.

This was not the first bridge built over the river at Dublin. Dr. R. H. Hightower, a few years before, had built a wooden toll bridge, but the Oconee on a rampage swept it away.

In 1882 a catastrophe came to Laurens. About sun-up, on a spring morning, a hurricane swept through the southern part of the county, following a north-easterly direction; not a tree was left in its path. Fortunately the area was sparsely populated. A belt of the finest primeval long-leaf pines was destroyed. For years after the area was a land of desolation in a waste of great clay-roots.

Another calamity was the fire in Dublin in 1885. The only business house left after the fire stood on Laurens Street till 1940 when it was torn down.

The eighth decade is a memorable one in the history of the county, for then the county and city of Dublin really began to grow.

In 1883 the state granted a charter to the Wrightsville & Tennille Railroad Company. The first president was G. W. Perkins, and the first vice-president, W. B. Thomas. The road was planned to connect Wrightsville with the Central Railroad at Tennille. About the time this line was finished the promoters joined with people of Laurens County in organizing the Dublin and Wrightsville Railroad Company; the line was built from Tennille to the Oconee River at Dublin, being completed to that point in 1886.

The two roads consolidated as one company, but the name of the road remained "The Wrightsville and Tennille" and the traffic department was moved to Dublin.

In 1891 the line was extended over a steel bridge across the Oconee. In the meantime, a railroad had been built from Hawkinsville to Dublin, known as the Oconee and Western. In 1899 the Wrightsville and Tennille purchased this road. The stations along the line were: Hutchins, Harlow, Vincent, Springhaven, Dexter, and Alcorns. Presidents have been: G. W. Perkins, A. F. Daley, H. D. Pollard, Charles Molony; now (1941) H. D. Pollard is President and B. F. Lord is General Manager. For many years M. V. Mahoney served as General Freight and Passenger Agent and was succeeded by A. J. Toole, who retired in 1941, after fifty years spent in railroad service.

In the Eighties Dublin's longest rail line had its conception. The Macon, Dublin and Savannah Railroad is a monument to the resolute endeavor of two of south Georgia's most prominent citizens, Col. John M. Stubbs and Honorable Dudley M. Hughes.

In the latter part of the Eighties, Colonel John M. Stubbs, of Laurens, and Honorable Dudley M. Hughes, of Twiggs County, organized the Macon and Dublin Railroad Company Grading was begun at Dublin, but work was stopped within fourteen miles of Macon. The company was then changed to the Savannah, Dublin and Western Short Line Company, with the idea of building a road from Savannah, through Dublin, to Macon, and one from Dublin to Americus. A large sum of money was spent, but the work was never completed. Competition with the Central forced the company to abandon the Americus division. A new company was organized which completed the road from Macon to Dublin and named it the "Macon, Dublin and Savannah."

In the spring of 1891 the first train came into Dublin from Macon. From far and near visitors came for this momentous occasion.

During the time the Macon, Dublin and Savannah was under construction, a company known as the Macon Construction Company surveyed a road from Macon to the Oconee at Carr Shoals, six miles north of Dublin, and thence to Savannah. The road was never built. However, much grading was done between Savannah and Brewton and several miles of rail were laid. Then the company failed, and the part that was graded from Brewton towards Savannah was bought by the Central Railroad and chartered as the Brewton and Pineora Railroad. At Register, the road was turned to the east and completed to Statesboro. This connected it with the Statesboro and Dover line and with the main line of the Central. The name Brewton and Pineora ceased and the road became known as the Oconee Division of the Central, and trains ran from Dublin to Savannah, connections being made at Dover.

In the late nineties the Macon, Dublin and Savannah was extended to Vidalia.

Another railroad was run into Dublin in 1904. E. P. Rentz built, from his large lumber mill, a railroad to Dublin to reduce the cost of freight on his lumber; in 1905 he continued the road to Eastman and it was called the Dublin and Southwestern Railroad. In 1906 the road was sold to the Wrightsville and Tennille and began operation as the Southwestern Division of the W. & T. Stations established along the line were Tingle (Garretta), Mayberry, Rentz, Mullis, Cadwell, and Batson.

By 1885 farmers all over the country began to realize that co-operation would be necessary if their best interests were to be attained. With this realization, a union, known as the Farmers' Alliance, was begun in 1887. It took the form of a class organization but became a political party. The Laurens County farmers were drawn to it by such attractive planks in its platform as "cooperative marketing," and the regulation of currency in such a way that silver could be coined in unlimited amounts. By 1892 the Farmers Alliance had become the Populist Party. At this time the farmers began opposition to jute bagging, which, because there was no other, they were forced to use. The Farmers Alliance taboed the use of jute and was instrumental in introducing a bagging made of cotton thread. This the members of the organization used till they discovered that it was not as satisfactory as the jute, and equally as expensive.

In many near-by towns there were special stores set up as Farmers' Alliance Stores. In Laurens there was no store of this kind but a few of the merchants over the county agreed to sell at special prices to members of the Alliance. Among these were L. B. Lanier's store in Dublin and J. A. Jackson's in Brewton. Cards were issued by the organization to each member and, with such a card, he traded at these stores.

The organization in Laurens County elected for its president, John W. Green with "Bud" Lingo,, vice-president. The second president was J. A. Clark, with T. J. Blackshear, vice-president. J. H. Yopp was secretary. There was a county unit and, under it, an organization in each militia district.

In February, 1886, there was a memorable spell of weather, and a freeze that lasted almost two weeks. In this section there are few freezes and they last for only a day or two.

Fraudulent voting was reduced, when a registration act was passed in 1887, "making it unlawful for any person to vote or attempt to vote at any election in Laurens County without having registered in the manner provided."

In the latter part of the Eighties Dublin floated the first bond issue, under the mayorship of F. H. Burch; a bond was voted for $5,000.00 for erecting a school for whites and one for negroes.

3. THE NINETIES.

The prosperity that began in the Eighties was slowed down by a financial panic in 1893, caused by a business depression largely resulting from the exportation of the country's gold. Laurens especially suffered, since her money source depended on the cotton production and its price; cotton went as low as three cents a pound. The voters in the South felt more than ever that the Nation's financial welfare depended on the free coinage of silver. The champion of this argument was William Jennings Bryan, so in the year 1896 the voters of Laurens gathered in the stores of Dublin or on the yards of the churches, before service, to discuss the "free coinage" of silver at the ratio of 16 to 1," and the election of Bryan for President.

During this period the principal business establishments in Dublin were James M. Reinhart, John B. Wolfe, J. M. Tillery, L. C. Perry & Co., T. M. Hightower & Co., W. B. and M. I. Jones, B. Nance, and E. J. Tarpley.

In the years just before the War the first Jewish family came to Dublin—the Hermans. The family moved from here to Eastman. Dr. J. D. Hermann, one of the leading physicians of this section, was born here. In the Eighties Adolph Baum began a mercantile business here. Soon his brother N. B. joined him and, through the Nineties, this firm, the Dublin Mercantile Company, was one of Dublin's largest business houses.

The public well of Dublin was on the courthouse square for years; or rather two wells, one for people and one for stock; but after John P. Fort had dug an artesian well in Southwest Georgia, Dublin men saw that sanitary conditions would be helped by boring such wells here. About 1892 the first artesian well was dug, the prime spirit in this enterprise being a public-spirited Jew, N. B. Baum.

In the late Nineties Dublin made long strides in improvements—telephones, an electric light and water plant, and a sewerage system were installed, and parts of some of the streets were paved.

During the middle Nineties a newspaper man, Attys P. Hilton, saw the need of a large and modern hotel for Dublin. Securing the services of his brother, a contractor, he built the Hilton Hotel on the site of the present City Hall. This was leased to G. S. Hooks, a man of considerable experience in the hotel business, and came to be known as the Hooks House. Soon after his father's death the hotel was bought by T. W. Hooks, and has been known since as the New Dublin Hotel. It is still owned by Mr. Hooks, who has been for many years the owner and operator of the Hotel Lanier in Macon.

THE SPANISH-AMERICAN WAR

In February, 1898, the United States Battleship, Maine, was sunk by the Spanish, in the harbor of Havana, Cuba. For years the people of the United States had been enraged over the cruel policy of the Spanish Government in Cuba. Now all over the country went up the cry, "Remember the Maine."

In April, 1898, the United States declared war on Spain, and of the 3,500 men that Georgia sent as soldiers, Laurens County gave her quota.

The following sketch was written by a Laurens County soldier, W. W. Ward, and is typical of the experience of the County's men who enlisted in the Spanish-American War.

"At the outbreak of the Spanish-American War, I enlisted for the duration of the war. There were some twelve or fifteen Laurens County boys in that war; among them were John D. McDaniel, Jule B. Green, William Lingo, "Pet" Pritchett, Neal Jones, and others whose names I do not recall.

"I joined the Macon Hussars and we were mustered into the United States Army and known as the 1st Georgia Regiment. After joining the company in Macon we were moved to Griffin, Georgia, where we were mustered into the United States service and then moved to Chickamauga Park where we were brigaded with the 31st Michigan and the 158th Indiana Regiment. Here we went into intense training preparing for foreign service.

"We did not remain at Chickamauga long before we were ordered to Porto Rico. But the events of the war were moving fast on several fronts, and before we could embark, the Battles of Manila and Santiago were fought and the armistice was signed. We were turned back to Chickamauga and afterwards moved to Knoxville, Tenn., to await the outcome of the settlement.

"Later we were returned to Macon and mustered out of the service November 16, 1898."

Other Laurens County men in the war were J. E. Burch, who joined up in Missouri and was encamped on Long Island; Wesley Kea, and "Windy" Williams.

The Whiskey Traffic in Laurens

During the Seventies and Eighties Laurens County knew her most notorious period, for the sale of whiskey was general and unrestrained. During that time Dublin maintained from three to six barrooms, and at every cross road in the county stood small wooden buildings where a few bolts of cloth, a few heavy groceries, some tobacco, and a stock of wines and whiskeys were sold.

After the War distilling was permitted in the State to aid the veterans in turning corn into money; this encouraged the sale, and in a county where there was no prohibition law, the traffic ran to excess. A few laws were passed by the State but they had but little effect in restricting the trade. There was a law requiring an applicant for a license to sell whiskey in Laurens to obtain the written consent of two-thirds of bona fide free-holders within three miles in all directions from the place where he proposed to sell it. Then, the Ordinary, in his discretion, could refuse a license to anyone although he had complied with all provisions.

In 1889, an Act was passed making it unlawful for any person or persons to vend, sell, or exchange any kind of liquor in any quantity within five miles of any of the rural churches in the county.

In the charter of Dublin, there was put in a provision that no barroom could be licensed for less than a tax of $1,000.00.

These "groggeries" furnished places for lawlessness and even crime; and when the people could no longer stand such conditions, they set to work, in the latter part of the Eighties, to stop whiskey sales. The following paper by Mrs. L. L. Porter describes the period:

"The old citizens paint a troublous season while the better people were trying to carry the town for local option. One gentleman said, 'Dublin was the worst drinking town I know of, and good people didn't care to come here. We had lots of strong, fine citizens, but some of them couldn't see why a barroom in every store should worry anyone. One incident paints it pretty plainly: a young man of the town got drunk, took his pistols, and rode horseback through one of the stores. No one stopped him and nothing was done about it, for he was a nice fellow when he was sober, and was very popular.'

"Marshal Nath Watson's throat was cut, and a Mr. Hood was found dead. In a country store twelve miles from Dublin, one night there was a drunken melee in which three white men were killed and two negroes hurt.

"Inspired by the desire to 'clean up' Dublin and Laurens County, a lodge called the 'Independent Order of Good Templars' was organized. It was a State lodge and the one in Dublin became Harmony Lodge Number 81. It began in 1890 and lasted about ten years. The pledge was:

" 'No member shall make, buy, sell, use, furnish, or cause to be furnished to others as a beverage, any spirituous or malt liquors, wines, or cider; and every member shall discountenance the manufacture, sale, and use thereof.'

"In 1893 Frank Corker entered the race for mayor promising a clean town. The vote was also for local option. Frank Corker began his work by having Sol Hattaway clean up the barrooms. This was the stormiest period in Dublin's history. But this and the coming of the railroads began her growth."

In 1897 the telephone exchange was placed in Dublin by a private company, consisting of Wm. Pritchett and J. M. Finn, with W. W. Bush as manager. Mr. Bush bought the Exchange and a line to Macon, then the Macon and Dublin line began to operate in conjunction with the Bell System. Today it is owned by the Bell System, being taken over in 1910.

About 1896 the city of Dublin floated a bond issue for $25,000.00 for the purpose of erecting a light and water plant. In 1897 there was another issue for $12,000.00 for the purpose of erecting a stand pipe, making improvements on the plant, and laying sewers.

4. IN RETROSPECT.

In those beginning years, when the first settlers were thinking of an appropriate name for their new home, it was the usual custom to select a name from the old world; names that were already famous in song and story. Among the early forefathers was a man from Ireland and to him was given the great privilege of naming the town Dublin. Every succeeding generation learned to love its origin and think of our Dublin as the Irish do, "A little bit of Heaven" overlooking the bend in the river they love, the Oconee, which bears the name of an ancient Creek town.

The pioneers soon learned that here, in this favorite spot, was a fine place to settle and carve out for themselves and for their children a home where they could live in friendship, contentment and understanding.

When we contemplate the growth of this little village and realize how it has stretched from the little fringe of its beginning, we are proud to think that the place has been worthy of the dream of those whose toil and sacrifice was great in the creation of those things which marked the beginning of this self-styled small town.

Scenes of frequent great fires, which destroyed the business center, took away the old land marks, but always leaving the historic Court House where all of the public gatherings were held when court was not in session. Later, this old building was moved away, in order that a more modern structure might be built; but the general plan of the village remained the same.

Looking back on an era that has passed, and with what fragrant memories one recalls those gnarled old mulberry trees that once shaded the middle of Jackson Street, with a fine well of drinking water, conveniently placed about midway.

Many of the first stores were built with broad porches. Here the natives gathered to discuss politics, local and state problems, their river activities as they built their flat boats and steam boats when they were at their peak. These were the people we loved, who made the days and years rich beyond any telling in those beautiful old fashioned days we now recall.

In the old cemetery, situated in the heart of the city, rests in peace the remains of hosts of notables marked by stones of simple dignity, shaded by spreading cedar trees and fine old fashioned shrubs placed here by tender and loving hands. There is a personal affection about this hallowed spot which speaks eloquently of the passing of time, and changes wrought by the years.

The first person to be buried in this memorable spot was a young man from South Carolina, Laurens Vivian, who, while on a visit to his relatives, the McCalls, became ill and died. The distance was too great to take his body back to his old home, and the burial was in Dublin. With painstaking accuracy this old rock grave which seems to stand guard to this place of tender memories, was always pointed out to strangers.

This old cemetery is "thickly sown with the historic dust" of Dublin and Laurens County, for many of our pioneer citizens found their last resting place here. Among those interred in this sacred spot were the Revolutionary soldier, Thomas McCall, and a Real Daughter of the Revolution, Nancy Lancaster Duncan.

In turning the pages of the past, there is a great temptation to wander into the sacred associations of those heroic people of other days; space permits the mention of only a few incidents. Today we find Dublin 130 years old, modern, proud and progressive, taking her place among the small cities of our country. If we have given to Dublin and Laurens County the choicest place in our hearts, it is because history will not let us forget the men and women who pioneered in our behalf. Their names once occupied a high place in the world's thoughts and admiration. I would like to dedicate these pages to your forefathers and mine, who in those joyous days of long ago, placed the whole of their courageous skill and talents upon this fascinating little city we call home.

Through contact with the younger generations of this proud City, who have provided us with such keen inspiration, I have the feeling that they will go forward to greater triumphs in their service to our country.

—By Augusta Stanley Adams (Mrs. J. S.)

> The following article was written by Mrs. E. C. Campbell, one of Dublin's most loved ladies, several years before her death, and was printed in a special edition of the Dublin *Courier-Herald*. It is reproduced below as a part of this history, because it gives us such a clear picture of the happy, tranquil life led by the Dublinites of many years ago.

"The short period it has taken for Dublin to attain her lofty place in the galaxy of Georgia's most progressive towns is really very surprising. There are now very few landmarks of the old Dublin left. All have gone down before the scythe of progress.

"I remember that about seventy-five white families comprised the citizenry during my childhood, living for the most part blocks and blocks apart. There was plenty of room for each family to have cows, pigs, chickens and, be it said, those animals had all the privileges of the streets they desired. They browsed along the streets and obstructed the sidewalks at their own sweet will. The neighbors' swine disturbed our midnight slumbers with gruntings and squealings.

"The vacant blocks and seldom used streets grew up in weeds, and the pedestrians often appeared to one another, on different streets, as folks do when walking through snowdrifts—just hats, heads, and umbrellas visible and bobbing up and down over the tops of the weeds.

"All streets were in total darkness (except when the moon was gracious) with the exception that on the corners of streets 'up town' posts holding kerosene lamps were placed to illuminate the business section. The wide distances, together with the dim and beclouded flickering, made these lamp posts seem like ghosts.

"At the corner where the Union Dry Goods Company now stands, was the only brick building in town. It was a most unpretentious affair—store below, residence above—and belonged to Mr. Lassiter.

"Near Folsom mercantile house, Mr. W. W. Robinson kept a small department store—the nucleus of his present big hardware enterprise. About the spot where Keith & Waddell's attractive business now stands was a tiny 10x16 wooden structure which answered very well as post office. Mail was brought by a mule from the towns around, and the trip required one whole day to go and another to return. It was never a voluminous mail pouch. That slowness was characteristics of the general trend.

"The Hicks Drug Company was at home on its present site in a wooden building, and for the ability to survive through thick and thin, I must say it reminds one of the Brook in that it goes on forever, while others have sunk into oblivion.

"Plum trees flourished where the Episcopal Church stands and many a luscious blackberry I've gathered from the patch covering the site of Charlie Cain's home.

"One church accommodated the entire village. It was a one-room wooden structure just where the Baptist Church now stands. Here we attended the Baptist Sunday School in the morning and the Methodist in the afternoon. There was not even an organ to furnish the music. Judge Wolfe led all the singing. He stood, a sober look on his benign countenance, and ran the gamut of 'do re mi' until he struck the right note and then he led off in a loud triumphant voice, the congregation following as if singing peans of victory. No one ever doubted Judge Wolfe's ability to master the most intricate trills, and we watched eagerly for the pleasant twinkle of his eye, which announced he had struck the right pitch.

"Captain Rollin Stanley was superintendent of the Sunday School. I remember him as wearing a patriarchal beard and having a face radiant with love. So interesting did he make the study that the naughtiest boy and girl became serious.

"After Sunday School, Colonel W. S. Ramsay delivered the sermon replete with wisdom and couched in the most beautiful phraseology, for, be it known, he was master of English.

"And then the school! Just where the High School now is was the old wooden structure—just one big room where all classes sat from the primary to the Trig.

"Boys and girls. played together and not once did I hear a boy say an ugly word, or know one to be rudely ill-mannered.

"The room was large, and the professor's desk was far from the entrance. Between the two front doors was the water bucket and dipper. We never had our serenity disturbed by microbes in those days, and if ever that bucket and dipper were sterilized, the deed never came to my knowledge. Young Dublinites were proof against germs and beyond a doubt the thirstiest set of youngsters that ever lived. A perfect stream went to and from the bucket continuously.

"Cupid was there plying his trade in hearts, too. If Johnnie had an apple or a bag of peanuts, which he wished to give to Mary, he gave her a wink and nodded toward the bucket. Then he proceeded, hid the gift behind the bucket, drank, and went back to his seat demurely. Mary then became instantly thirsty.

"In this sequestered spot, there was nothing to see but the earth beneath, the sky above, and the river rolling by. So on Sunday afternoon late, the road to the river became the boulevard, and everybody promenaded by everybody else and passed a pleasant greeting. The ferry was manipulated by 'Uncle Bill,' whose feet would have put Charlie Chaplin out of business, had the movies been a reality then. How the children loved Uncle Bill. He carried them across the ferry Sundays without pay.

"The social calendar was limited to a picnic now and then, and a party. The calico party was quite an exhilarating amusement. Every young lady made a calico dress, and a tie of the same material for her escort. The tie was placed with her name in an envelope and sold to some young man for ten or twenty-five cents—said sum going for refreshments for the party. The young man would escort the young lady whose name he drew. Of course, the mystery attached caused a fluttering of hearts and an almost unendurable suspense on the part of the girls for they speculated wildly as to who had purchased their ties; and 'twas said the young men sometimes swapped.

"No circus ever came nearer than Macon. Think of children never having their pulse thrilled by the scream of a calliope, or the roar of a real sure-enough lion, or the wild ecstacy of following a parade.

"Once a tramp came through with a machine to take tin-type. His tent became a rendezvous for lovers and fond parents with their off-spring.

"Those were placid days and a beautiful spirit of harmony pervaded the community. Yet there was one degrading feature—open barrooms. There were several of these places of debauchery in the otherwise serene and happy village—places where the Devil plied his trade in ruining hearts, and souls, and happy homes. To combat this permiscious influence, the temperance society was formed.

"I can't refrain a smile at the awesome secrecy of those meetings, its officers of high-sounding titles, its passwords, signs, raps, etc.

"Surely I must tell you of the time when we Dublinites ate only corn meal breads for six weeks. You see the river was too low for the boats to come or go. Flour was merely a pleasant memory. We ate muffins of corn meal, hoe cake pones, crackling bread, Johnnie cake and every conceivable thing that can be concocted of corn meal. At last it rained! O joy! The river rose, the boat came up. What a delightful sensation permeated our being when the sonorous sound of the boat's whistle fell upon our eager ears. That night the citizens smacked their lips over hot biscuits! Editor Hicks wrote a glowing and lengthy editorial on the festive occasion, while the more poetic geniuses tried to immortalize the event in song.

"On the southeast side of the railroad, there were not even a half-dozen houses. There Captain Tom Rowe lived in ante-bellum comfort, surrounded by his sturdy boys and girls who have contributed so largely to the progress and culture of Dublin. Captain Rowe owned a saw mill by the branch on Saxon Street.

"Colonel Stubbs had a grist mill in Stubbs Park.

"Every house had its well of water and no one ever thought of ice excepting when reading of Arctic explorations. What we did not have we didn't bother about. It seems now that everybody followed the line of least resistance. Neither did we hurry in those days. Maybe the rest of the world did, but Dublin, nestling on the banks of the calm Oconee, shut in by forests and great stretches of farm lands, remained imperturbed by the scurrying of the outside world. The days were deliciously long and a dreamy, drowsy contentment seemed to envelope the village. But one day, the screeching of a locomotive pierced the stillness, the clicking of the telegraph aroused the citizens from their dreaming, and then the restless tide of humanity from the world outside began to pour in, bringing multitudes of innovations."

CHAPTER X

THE TWENTIETH CENTURY

1. THE PERIOD OF 1900-1920

a. GROWTH

The turn of the century found a progressive Laurens County and Dublin. Laurens County stood in the head rank of the States agricultural interests. County and city in the first quarter of the Twentieth century reached their highest degree of prosperity.

In 1902 Dublin issued bonds for $25,000.00 for erecting a school building, laying sewers, and other improvements, A. T. Summerlin, Mayor. In 1904 there was an issue of $45,000.00 to erect a grammar school building, a city hall, to improve the light and water plant, extend water mains and sewers, and improve the fire department, E. R. Orr, Mayor.

Under the mayorship of Albert R. Arnau was the first establishment of a sinking fund.

About the turn of the century, the old cemetery at the rear of the Methodist Church had become inadequate and being too near the heart of town for expansion, a tract in the northern part of the town was purchased and Northview Cemetery was begun.

By the time its first centennial, 1907, had arrived, Dublin was a considerable business center. Its first department store was the Four Seasons, which began in 1903, with a capital stock of $50,000; in four years the capital stock was doubled and there were six large departments. It occupied the building now partially used by the McClelland stores. J. E. Smith (Banjo) was president, J. H. Witherington vice-president, and R. M. Arnau general manager.

Running a close rival to the Four Seasons was another department store, the Jackson Stores, organized in 1906 by W. C. Tompkins, C. S. Pope, Dr. J. M. Page, F. H. Keen, and D. R. Jackson. The store bore the founder's name; a few years before this, Allen Jackson had come from Brewton and established a business in Dublin that culminated in this large store.

Other large dry goods establishments were the Sam Weichselbaum Company conducted by N. B. Baum; the W. F. Schaufele Company and the Outler, Arnau & Outler Company. There were over a hundred retail stores and eight wholesale grocery stores. The largest of these was the Brandon & Dreyer, which has continued in business and is operating today (1941) as the Hilbun-Bobbitt Company. The Brigham-Jones Company was both retail and wholesale. Outler,

Arnau & Outler also operated a wholesale business of heavy groceries, hay, and grain, under title of the South Georgia Grocery Company.

W. W. Robinson was the pioneer in hardware, operating through more than three decades; another large business was the Gilbert Hardware Company, operated by D. W. Gilbert and H. G. Stevens, opened in 1897.

Dr. C. H. Kittrell came to Dublin in the later years of the Nineties, being the first optometrist in the County; by 1907 he was also operating one of the largest jewelry businesses in the State.

A large buggy and harness business was operated by C. W. Brantley; another buggy and carriage store was run by M. A. Kendrick. R. F. Deese and Company was a large furniture business operated by R. F. Deese, established in 1896. So substantial has this store been that it is still in operation (1941) by Mr. Deese, who has associated his son, Tom, with him in business.

In 1904, the automobile had not arrived, the horse was at the height of his popularity as a traffic animal. A large livery and sale business was conducted by Brown and Phillips which was begun in 1891; another livery stable was that of the W. S. Burns & Company, under the management of William Bales. A blacksmith and carriage shop was conducted by Rachels and Jordan.

Dublin had become an industrial center. In 1898 a large furniture factory had opened. Within a few years, under the direction of J. M. Simmons, it was one of the largest in the South. The company bought large tracts of timber for furnishing raw material. They erected a boarding house and several cottages for employees.

In 1899 a hame factory had been established. Laurens' largest factory was a cotton mill begun in 1900. The president was Wm. Pritchett; treasurer, J. M. Finn; directors, Wm. Pritchett, J. M. Finn, C. W. Brantley, W. F. Schaufele, R. C. Henry, J. D. Smith, T. J. Pritchett, and F. G. Corker. The mills represented an investment of $250,000.00. They were equipped with 8,120 spindles and 260 looms. Neat comfortable houses were built for the 250 operatives.

In 1900 an oil mill and ice factory began operations and there were also an iron foundry and two machine shops in operation.

Attractive drug stores were—the Emerald City, Tarpleys, the Hicks Drug Store, the Taylor-Coleman Pharmacy and the Oconee Pharmacy. The Hicks Drug Store is still in operation (1941), the oldest drug store in this section, having come into existence more than sixty-five years ago as the J. W. Peacock & Company. Next it became the Hicks, Peacock, and Hicks, and in 1909 was incorporated as the Hicks Drug Company by F. H. Rowe, II.

Near the turn of the century, progressive Dublin men began to realize that the business of the town and county could be vitalized only through cooperative effort and advertising. The first organization for this purpose was The Young Men's Business League, composed of such men as J. S. Simons, Jr., J. M. Finn, H. M. Stanley, L. L. Linder, C. A. Weddington, T. V. Sanders, James B. Hicks—at that time Mayor of Dublin—and A. W. Garrett.

About the same time there was organized a Board of Trade. These two bodies inaugurated several enterprises of civil and agricultural importance.

One of the first movements of the League and Board of Trade was to institute a Chautauqua, erecting for it a commodious building. For several years there were annual meetings, a week in length, for which were employed the best entertainmnt and educational talent in the country.

Under the auspices of these civic bodies, leading agricultural and fraternal organizations held meetings in Dublin. In August, 1900, the Georgia Horticultural Society convened here, and a week later came the State Agricultural Society. In 1901 the Grand Lodge Royal Arcanum met in Dublin.

Evolving from the Board of Trade and the League, about 1912, was a Chamber of Commerce. Hal M. Stanley was one of the prime leaders in this movement. Though called for duty to Atlanta about this time, he had the pleasure of seeing the organization off to a fine start. The first secretary was Bob Martin, the second was Charles B. Caldwell, who was followed by N. G. Bartlett, former principal of the Dublin High School. Mr. Bartlett was a live wire and, under his direction, the Chamber of Commerce was unusually active, instituting many progressive movements, in which the principal objective was the development of marketing and agricultural possibilities.

Mr. Bartlett served till 1922 when he was called to a larger field in North Carolina. Other secretaries have been C. W. Philips, W. H. Proctor and Miss Blanche Metts. Among those serving as presidents were: W. W. Robinson, S. M. Kellam, D. S. Brandon, E. G. Simmons, Fred Roberts, E. D. White, and Milo Smith.

In 1941 the Chamber of Commerce was reorganized. H. M. Simmons became secretary, W. W. Brinson, president, with the following directors: W. W. Brinson, Cecil Carroll, R. H. Hightower, Earle Hilbun, Wilber S. Jones, L. P. Keen, Dr. C. H. Kittrell, B. H. Lord, J. H. Mahoney, J. F. Pierce, W. S. Reese, E. W. Vaughn, C. U. Smith, and L. D. Woods.

By 1917 hard times were well over and prosperity was coming in at a rapid pace. Cotton prices were climbing to heights before unreached. At the close of business, December 31, 1917, the First National Bank had the largest deposit ever made before that time, $201,808.28.

Improvements in Dublin were going rapidly forward. In 1905 there was an issue of $45,000.00 in bonds for city hall, lights, school, and fire improvement. The complete issue has since been retired.

In 1904 there was an issue of $65,000.00 in bonds for fire, water, light, school, and park improvement. This issue has been retired.

In 1910 there was a $30,000.00 issue in bonds for waterworks, light, sewerage and street improvement. This issue has also been retired.

In 1918 there was an issue of $75,000.00 for schools, water, sewerage and paving. Of these, $45,000.00 have been retired.

In 1919 there was an issue for school extension and improvement bonds of $50,000.00. Of these, $24,000.00 have been retired.

By 1917 the farmers were organized and launching progressive movements; the principal organization was the Farmers' Union, under the leadership of Ira N. Eubanks, C. H. Kittrell, and W. D. Dixon. Soon there was erected a grain elevator, and a potato-curing house was made available. The Laurens County Livestock Association was organized, sales of cattle and hogs sponsored, and stock yards built. In all these developments the Chamber of Commerce took a leading part.

Tick eradication became effective in 1915, the County Commissioners cooperating with the state.

In 1918 the County Commissioners turned over certain leading roads of the county to the State Highway Commission, and the era of good roads began. Long before this the old method of working roads had been done away with and regular road forces kept the roads. This consisted of the chain gang controlled by wardens; the force was under the direction of a competent overseer, the county furnishing mules, scrapes, and road machines.

The roads leading to Dublin had been straightened and hardsurfaced, and most of the roads had been clayed. In 1919 the County floated $500,000.00 in bonds for permanent bridges. In this year the County Commissioners slightly changed a disputed boundary line between Laurens and Dodge Counties.

About 1905 the first moving picture show opened in Dublin, owned and operated by the widow of Dr. Hightower, "Miss Genie," as she was popularly known. This show house was called the Theatorium.

Since then there have been the Crystal, the Amuzu, the Dublin, and others. Today there are two theatres, the Ritz and the Rose. These are owned by the Martin Company and directed by Bob Hightower. The Ritz was opened in 1935.

The first opera house, built by Dr. C. H. Kittrell on the corner of Madison and Monroe Streets, was burned. The same fate befell the Bertha, a theatre built by Steve Lord about 1918 and named in honor of his wife.

b. RECREATION RESORTS

By this time Laurens County people were becoming out-door minded, and began the developing of recreation centers.

Dublin's pleasure ground, at the turn of the century, was the Pavilion, in a forest of pine, in the eastern part of the city.

On Turkey Creek, at the Robinson Bridges, a pavilion was built; the beautiful setting, the clear water for swimming and its easy accessibility made it a popular resort. It was called, at different times, Peacock's and Spivey's.

Laurens County possesses natural phenomena in the form of large springs flowing hundreds of gallons of water. These have been used for recreation purposes. The waters are cold and crystal clear and appear like bottomless blue pools. In their sylvan setting of pine and hardwood trees, often festooned with gray moss, they are places of beauty. They are near the right bank of the Oconee, a few miles below Dublin, and are approached by winding country roads leading from the left of the Glenwood Road. Nearest Dublin, is Wells Spring, at one time a popular resort for picnics and camping parties.

In the third decade of the 19th century, William McIntosh, famous half-breed Indian chief of the Lower Creeks, maintained a reservation at Wells Spring. He was a cousin of Governor Troup and a very strong attachment existed between them. While living at Wells Spring, he sent his children to school in Dublin. One of these was his son, Chilli McIntosh, who later escaped from a burning house, in Carroll County, when his father was killed by unfriendly Indians. Chilli became the first superintendent of education in the state of Oklahoma. (Information given by Lucien Lamar Knight.)

Wilkes Spring, a few miles to the south, is even larger and more beautiful than Wells. Rock Springs is smaller but equally as attractive.

On the left side of the Oconee, and often reached by a boat trip down the river, are Dead River Spring and Troup Spring. Both are similar to Wells, Wilkes, and Rock. Many people declare these waters to have medicinal value, but scientific tests have never been made. Dead River Spring is, by water, seven miles from Dublin. Troup Spring is two miles below. It is much smaller than Dead River, but its setting is more picturesque; its water boils up two feet above the surface. The great volume of boiling water makes it impossible to sink in the spring. This spring lake was Governor Troup's favorite fishing ground. It was the scene of his only diversion. Here with Captain Yopp or Thomas McCall, he spent many hours.

All these springs have been popular for camping and picnicking parties. Especially popular in springtime was the Dead River Spring when its banks are white with wild Easter lilies.

Other points of interest in Laurens County that are natural phenomena, are Boiling Springs and Thundering Springs. Thundering Springs are in the upper part of Laurens, near the county line of Johnson. An old authority said that at one time the spring was 18 to 20 feet in diameter, and that rheumatic patients often came to plunge themselves into its boiling heart. It was impossible to sink, although the spring seemed bottomless. The water boils with a sound that may be heard at some distance, hence the name Thundering Spring.

Near the Dublin-Wrightsville Highway, about six miles from the Laurens-Johnson line, are Boiling Springs, so called because of the numerous springs which boil up through white, sandy depths. A little white church stands nearby, and until a few years ago, its pine grove furnished a site for a popular camp-meeting ground.

A popular recreation ground is Sessions Lake. About 1933, Mr. Dee Sessions chose a sylvan setting on Rum Creek, and by sinking nine artesian wells converted the whole into a swimming and boating lake. It continues under the Malone management.

In 1917, artesian wells were dug, and the Dublin Natatorium was built by C. D. Hilbun, S. M. Alsup, H. T. Pullen, M. W. Kassell, A. D. Blackshear, S. V. Conyers, and N. G. Bartlett.

In 1919, the General Assembly passed a law providing that all counties have Boards for equalizing valuations of property. The County Commissioners appointed as the first Board of Equalizers, J. Warren Carter, H. R. Bedingfield, and J. E. White.

In 1914, Laurens County was overtaken by the financial crisis that was general over the South. Cotton prices went to a low level, and the Buy-a-Bale movement was initiated to boost the price. The banks of Dublin were driven to use clearing house certificates.

c. Laurens County in the World War.

From the nation's capital in April, 1917, President Woodrow Wilson sent the ringing announcement: "We are at War, God helping us, we can do no other." Both men and women of Laurens County responded freely to the call.

Every form of activity was undertaken. The quotas for Liberty Bonds were oversubscribed, and the county took an apportionment of $10,000.00 in thrift stamps. Dublin subscribed $3,000.00 for Y. M. C. A. work. George B. Davis was appointed food administrator and J. M. Finn, chairman of the County Council of Defense. In June, 1917, 3,294 men registered from Laurens County.

Mrs. T. H. Smith was appointed Red Cross chairman, with Mrs. Thomas Gibson in charge of the woman's work. The following is a summary of woman's Red Cross work in Dublin, rendered in February of 1918:

"The work was organized in May, 1917, and by February the following work was accomplished:

"Eleven dozen sheets, 12 dozen huck towels, 4 dozen bath towels, 3 dozen wash cloths, 48 pairs of pajamas, 24 hospital sheets, 36 draw sheets, 1 complete hospital outfit for one patient consisting of a cot, mosquito net, pillows, sheets, blankets, shirts, pajamas, slippers, etc.; these were contributed in the spring and summer.

"During the fall these were sent in:

"One hundred seventy-nine hospital bed sheets, 1 entire emergency cot outfit, 4 dozen pairs pajamas, 25 comfort kits, 60 Christmas packages, 27 convalescent robes. At the time the summary was made there were in the making many garments and other supplies, with 60 pairs pajamas and 60 hospital shirts.

"In knit articles 148 sweaters, 14 helmets, 12 pairs socks, 10 mufflers, 10 pairs wristlets sent off, 56 sweaters almost completed." (*Courier-Herald*, February 5, 1918).

Mrs. E. S. Street was chairman of the Civilian Relief Committee of the Red Cross, and Miss Frances Webb, Chairman of Publicity. The Laurens County quota was oversubscribed.

Beginning in January, the merchants and business men of Dublin, for ten weeks, observed Monday as a holiday in order to conserve fuel; before that time most of the merchants had begun closing business two hours earlier than usual. War gardens were planted on vacant lots. Laurens County housewives cheerfully observed food-conservation rules—Monday, wheatless; Tuesday, meatless; Wednesday, wheatless; Saturday, porkless.

Beginning in August, 1918, a prayer service was held each day at 12 o'clock in Dublin. Rallies and campaign meetings were held all over the county to stimulate food and fuel conservation and increased production of food crops. In the spring when the Liberty Loan train and, in the autumn, when the Victory Loan train came to Dublin, they were visited by large and enthusiastic crowds.

On September 16, 1918, the City Council of Dublin passed an ordinance declaring it to be the duty of all persons in the City of Dublin between the ages of 16 and 55, physically able to work, to engage in some useful employment for at least 40 hours each week.

During this war 1,138 men went into service from Laurens County.

THE WORLD WAR DEAD

John W. Adams, Dublin, died December 1, 1918; George L. Attaway, Dublin, died December 1, 1918; Leon F. Brannon, Dublin; Linton T. Bostwick, Dexter; Tom Watson Bryant, Dexter, died October, 1918, in Washington, D. C.; David Burton Camp, Dexter, died December 12, 1918; Ashley Collins, Dudley, died November 9, 1918; Clarence David Fordham, Dublin, died September 29, 1918, of wounds; Oscar Fulwood, Dublin, died November 16, 1918; John W. Green, Lovett; Joseph C. Hall; Archie Hinson, Dudley, died of pneumonia in a hospital Overseas; Syl. P. Hodges, Dublin; Charlie Huffman, Dublin; Ed McLendon, Dublin.

Walter E. Martin, Dublin, died August 7, 1918; James Mason, Co. B 151st M. G. Rainbow Division, Dublin, died July 29, 1918—killed in action in France; Jesse A. Mercer, Dublin; Rayfield Meacham, Dublin; George C. Mitchell, Rentz; Robbie D. New, Dublin; Cecil Preston Perry, Dublin; Flanders Pope, Dublin; John H. Sanders, Montrose; Roger O. Sellers, died in a military hospital, New York City, 1918; Louis M. Thompson, Dexter; George Windham, Dublin; Henry K. Womack, Dublin, died August 7, 1918, at Camp Gordon; McKinley Yopp, Dudley; Fleming du Bignon Vaughn, Dublin.

Only a few of the Laurens County men in War Service are referred to below:

Otis Woodard, Dexter, second lieutenant in quartermasters' corps of National Army.

James Mason of Company B, 151st M. G. Bat. Rainbow Division, killed in action in France, July 29, 1918.

Walter E. Martin, wounded July 18, 1918, in France.

Lieutenant Randolph R. Sanders was wounded in an aviation field in 1918; was in Air Service, Military Aeronautics Branch of the Army from November 7, 1918, until honorably discharged on June 19, 1919, by reason of the demobilization of the emergency forces.

O. K. Jolley of Dexter, was in a German prison camp.

Among others who went over were: Wiley C. Phelps, Frank C. Simmons, Jas. Barnett, Sig Knight, Alex. L. Davis, Arthur S. Underwood, Marshall H. Hogan, Robert E. Ballard, Durell W. Knight, Marvin J. Thigpen, Dennie C. Tracy, L. O. Mosely, Martin Alsup, Peter Twitty, Milo Smith.

Joseph A. Hesse enlisted in the United States Navy in 1913, became an ensign.

Palmer Currell was assistant band master at Camp Hancock.

Lieutenant L. B. Whipple of Dudley, was wounded in France.

A. P. Whipple, Jr., was in the navy.

E. B. Gibson was a corporal in France when Armistice was signed.

Laurence Walker was in the famous 82nd Division.

From the Dublin High School went Burke Corker to the regular Army, Nathan Holleman to the Navy, Chris White to the Navy, Griswold Satterfield to the regular Army, Theron Smith to the National Guard, and Henry Johnson to the Cavalry.

Felton Pierce rendered service overseas in the 122nd Infantry, 31st Division.

Roy Lewis, a Dublin boy, was a member of the gun crew of the steamer Boringuen that sank a German submarine near the British Coast.

Prentice Adams saw service on the U. S. Destroyer Gregory, as gunner's mate; was also stationed in Adriatic waters; service extended from June 20, 1917, to July 16, 1919.

William Brunson also rendered service in the U. S. Navy.

James Weddington, in the hospital corps of the Marines, was in the great France-American offensive in the Soissons-Rhemis sector. He was commended for gallant conduct.

Louis E. Gordy belonged to the famous Rainbow Division.

Parker New resigned as solicitor of the City Court to volunteer in the United States Navy. He was in the Officers' Training School at Newport, R. I. His commission as Dock Ensign was issued just after the Armistice. James C. and Herbert S. Matthews of Lovett, were in the aviation service. One received training at Rockwell Field, San Diego, Calif., the other in the aeronautics school at Austin, Texas.

Dublin doctors who served in the Medical Corps were: Sidney Walker, Major, who served in a British hospital at Leeds, England, for many months; Charles A. Hodges, 1st Lieut., 20 months' service overseas; Landrum Page, 1st Lieut.; Ovid Cheek, 1st Lieut.; J. W. Edmondson, 1st Lieut.; G. R. Lee, 1st Lieut., 13 months' service in the Dental Corps.

d. GENERAL MATTERS

In 1920 Dublin entertained the Reunion of Confederate Veterans. General James A. Thomas led the colorful parade on May 12th; at that time General Thomas, a Dublin man, was State Commander.

In 1927 the John Laurens Chapter D. A. R. unveiled at McCall's Point, a marble seat as a memorial to Laurens County World War soldiers.

In 1921 the Dublin Country Club was organized. Several acres near the northern section of the city were turned into golf links and a club house was erected. The project was incorporated by E. G. Simmons, H. G. Stevens, and F. B. Reins.

In 1914 the General Assembly passed a law called the Ellis Health Act. The Act provides that a Board of Health consist of the Chairman of the Board of County Commissioners, the County Superintendent of Schools, and a physician elected by the Grand Jury. Dr. Ovid Cheek, a veteran of the World War, was appointed physician in charge of the county's health affairs. Dr. Cheek has served since his appointment in August, 1919. Typhoid fever, malaria, and hookworm infection have been reduced; epidemics of small pox, diphtheria, and other contagious diseases have been prevented and infant mortality reduced. This department keeps check on the water and milk supply; has supervision of camps, dairies, cafes, drug stores and all places where foods are sold. A record is kept of all births. Clinics are held and children are vaccinated for small pox, diphtheria and typhoid. Dr. Cheek is assisted by a staff consisting of F. R. Goulding, Jr., sanitary engineer and research worker; Mrs. Edna B. Grove, nurse; and Miss Annie K. Henderson, clerk.

If prosperity could be judged by the number of automobiles in use, the year 1918 could be placed in a high rank—for in that year 9,000 were returned for taxes in Laurens County. A long cry from that day in 1902 when Ernest Rawls frightened all the farmers' mules hitched in the public square with a chugging Locomobile car which he proudly guided with a lever. Though horse-driving people thundered anathemas on this unhallowed form of locomotion, John Duncan and Harry Stephens soon became car possessors and led a rapidly-growing procession of automobile owners.

2. THE PERIOD OF 1920-1941

The "Roaring Twenties" swept in on a wave of prosperity, only to end in the financial fiasco that began in 1929 and lasted till about 1934.

Since 1920, there have been five bond issues made by the City of Dublin. Bonds for $55,000.00, dated January 1, 1921, were issued for bridge and culverts, school, water, and sewerage. Of these, $20,-000.00 have been retired. Four bond issues were made in the 1930's.

On January 1, 1936, water bonds were issued for $57,000.00 and Public School Improvement bonds for $18,000.00. Refunding bonds, dated July 1, 1937, were issued for $38,000.00. There was another issue of Refunding bonds for $39,000.00, dated January 1, 1939.

In 1925, the City of Dublin sold its light plant to the Georgia Power Company. Transmission lines were brought to Dublin from Milledgeville, and Dublin was made a central point for distribution.

In the same year there was great agitation over locating, at Dublin, a pulp mill for the whole Southeastern part of Georgia. A site was presented by the Chamber of Commerce, and work was begun on the half-million dollar plant. The venture failed because it was under-financed, and because it was based on a false theory—a belief that high class paper could be made from pine stumps after the resin had been distilled from them.

Nineteen twenty-six saw the erection in Dublin of a modern brick hotel, with a 60 room capacity. The Chamber of Commerce, headed by a young man of public spirit and tireless energy, initiated and sponsored the building of The Fred Roberts Hotel. Dublin was saddened, before the structure was finished, by the death of the man who had been so largely responsible for the building, and whose name it bears.

The Atlantic Ice and Coal Company erected a large ice factory and meat curing plant in Dublin about 1920. The Crystal Ice Company established a plant in 1927. The first ice factory in Laurens was begun by the Dublin Telephone and Telegraph Company about the beginning of the century. It had a capacity of fifty tons. Before that time ice was sold by grocery and drug stores. Till the latter part of the 19th century there was no sale of ice except in cases of sickness or other emergencies.

The year 1925 is memorable for furnishing the highest and lowest water marks in the history of the river. In February, the Oconee's waters on the west extended far up into Scottsville; on the east, beyond the river bridge. In the summer of that year a lad waded across the river at Dublin.

A tornado, on a summer afternoon in 1929, making its way from Bleckley County, swept through the western part of Laurens County, with destruction in its wake. There was a property damage of over $60,000.00; in the Mount Carmel community the Church and several residences were blown down. The Red Cross immediately began restoration, and in a short time new buildings were erected.

The latter years of the 1920's will be remembered as a blue period. Cotton production and cotton prices were at a low ebb. There were few building improvements in the county; residence were needing paint and out houses falling into decay. Insurance and loan companies were taking over many Laurens farms. The decade of the Twenties was the period of bank failures. Crop failure in 1921, and a heavy slump in the price of cotton, lead to a depreciation of property values, and since bank collateral was based on property, it was made almost worthless.

In an effort to restore prosperity by aiding the farmer, in 1933 a group of business men organized the Dublin Production Credit Association which would provide a permanent system of agricultural credit for Laurens, Johnson, and Treutlen Counties. There was an authorized credit of $75,000.00. M. H. Hogan was made president and M. E. Everett, secretary-treasurer. The directors were: E. T. Barnes of Laurens, Judge Will Stallings of Treutlen, H. L. Fulford and M. T. Rhiner of Johnson. An office is maintained in Dublin with T. A. Arnold, secretary-treasurer, and J. R. Murphey, assistant secretary.

Many Dublin people visiting New York City in the summer of 1934 felt a great pride in seeing a Dublin girl make her debut on the legitimate stage when Eugenia Rawls played in Lillian Hellman's "The Children's Hour." A few years later she made her first appearance in Atlanta in "Little Foxes."

In October, 1931, the State organization of the United Daughters of the Confederacy held its annual convention in Dublin. At this convention, Mrs. Izzie Bashinski, of Dublin, was elected State President. The hostess was Mrs. B. B. Page, President of the (local) Oconee Chapter.

The Knights Templars held the annual State Convention in Dublin on May 10th and 11th, 1933.

The most famous ball team that ever played in Laurens County was the St. Louis Cardinals. The team was brought to Dublin by the Lions Club and played in April, 1933, against Oglethorpe University. In 1935, the Cardinals again played in Dublin, this time against the University of Georgia.

During the Thirties, bus lines became popular through the country. The first bus was operated in 1926 between Macon and Dublin by J. D. Bass and Irwin Montford. The Greyhound Lines, now operating over Federal Highway No. 80, and the Service Coach Lines connect Dublin with neighboring towns, as well as Atlanta. The Bus Station was built in 1939, and from it six buses leave daily for Macon, Atlanta, and points North, as well as making connections in other directions.

In April, 1926, the Twelfth District High School meet was entertained in Dublin.

In March, 1933, the initial act of the Roosevelt administration was to guarantee bank deposits up to $5,000.00, and immediately the condition of banking institutions began to improve. Statements of local banks in 1934 showed total resources of $1,099,063.96; in January, 1935, they were $2,830,805.80.

Laurens County's industrial growth has depended upon products of field and forest.

The only industry that began in the last century, still operating, is the Southern Cotton Oil Company. This institution boasts a history of fifty-seven years. In 1928 the Southern Cotton Oil Company absorbed the Empire Cotton Oil Company, which in 1912 had taken over the Laurens Cotton Oil Company. The company today not only operates a seed-crushing plant but also a fertilizer plant and large ginneries. W. S. Reese, the present manager, believes that this company operates the largest ginneries under one roof, east of the Mississippi.

Other large ginning plants in Dublin are operated and owned by Lovett-Brinson, W. P. Roche and Cecil Carroll.

The Lovett-Brinson plant includes gins, fertilizer mixing plant, and bonded cotton warehouse. Operations began in 1930. Other gins are operated at Garetta, Cedar Grove, and Minter.

The Roche Manufacturing Company was established in 1930 and includes gins, fertilizer-mixing plant and bonded cotton warehouse.

The Dublin Gin Company, organized in 1931, includes, with the gin, a bonded cotton warehouse, established in 1927, and a fertilizer mixing plant. Cecil E. Carroll is owner and operator.

Furnishing markets for the hardwood and pine products are several mills, factories and resin stills.

The Georgia Plywood Corporation took over a large veneer mill that began in the early years of the present century. The factory uses mainly the wood of gums and oaks. In the average working season there are over two hundred laborers on the yard and in the woods. The present company was organized in 1932, with James Allen president.

In 1915, Mark Lester and son took over the Hardwood Manufacturing Company which had been organized in 1913. At first, the factory manufactured only rims, but it now makes more handles than rims. Woods of ash, oak, and hickory are used. The largest output consists of lumber, cut in pieces and tied in bundles to be shipped to foreign markets.

Cutting both hardwood and pine are several large lumber companies in Dublin.

The J. M Gettys Lumber Company took over the Gragg Lumber

Company, which began operation about 1924. The E. B. Mackey Lumber Company's plant has expanded over five acres since it began operation about 1925. The Dublin Sash & Door Company was established in 1920 by J. H. Beacham. The C. T. Alexander & Sons Lumber Company has been operating since 1932.

The Census of 1940 shows that in Dublin there are twenty-two wholesale establishments, and six in the remainder of the county.

The wholesale grocery business was begun in Dublin in the last century by The Pritchett Grocery Company. They brought much of their freight up the river.

Five large wholesale grocery establishments are located in Dublin.

The oldest of these began in the latter part of the 19th century as Brandon and Dryer, then became the D. S. Brandon Company. In 1940 the business was sold to the Hilburn-Bobbitt Company.

About 1910 Alsup & Williams Wholesale Grocery Company began business. In 1914 it continued as a partner business with A. D. and S. M. Alsup. In 1920 it was incorporated as the Alsup Grocery Company.

The W. R. Werden & Company began business about 1908 as the E. S. Street Company. It was taken over by W. R. Werden about 1930.

In 1916 Cochran-Smith and Company opened a wholesale business, which has since been incorporated as the Cochran Bros. Company.

The Cash Wholesale Grocery Company was established in 1926 by Smith and Brandon. It is now operated under the same name by Smith and Register.

A grain and fruit wholesale establishment is the O. L. Chivers Company. It began in 1907 as the Black-Chivers Grain Company.

The 1940 Census shows that there are 169 retail stores in Dublin, and 156 in the remainder of the county.

The oldest department store in the county is Churchwell Brothers, established about 1911, and taken over by Churchwell in 1913. It has been directed for over twenty years by M. W. Jordan and Coke Brown.

The J. C. Penney Company was established in 1926. A. W. Vaughn is the present manager.

The R. L. Stephens Department Store was established in Dublin about 1935 under the management of Mr. and Mrs. R. L. Stephens. The oldest dry goods store now operating in Dublin is that of H. V. Westbrook, which opened in the late years of the 19th century.

Other dry goods and ready-to-wear stores in Dublin are: The United Department Store, the A. Lease Department Store, the I. E. Thigpen Department Store, the Kaplan Stores.

The oldest grocery store in Dublin is the Charlie Keene Grocery which has been in continuous operation since 1898; first, as Keene Brohters; since 1912, owned and operated by Charlie Keene.

Leading grocery stores are: Pierce & Orr, the Jernigan Grocery, Rutland's Grocery Store, the Charley Keen Grocery, the Hudson Grocery and Market, and Tindol Brothers. The great chain grocery companies, Atlantic & Pacific, Rogers, and Sims operate large branch stores in Dublin. The Keen Grocery and Tindol Bros. began operation in the last century.

"Dime Stores" are Woolworth and McLellan. The McLellan was opened in 1916.

Meat markets are: The Guy Scarborough Market, the Shuman Market, and J. A. Stinson Market.

The Blue Ribbon, owned and managed by M. E. Cochran, is the leading bakery of all this section. Previously Dublin has had the Lafferty Bakery and the Oconee Bakery.

Pharmacists of Dublin today are: Dr. E. L. Black, who came to Dublin in 1905. He conducts Black's Pharmacy, and together with Emmett Black and Lucian Malone, operates the Black Seed Store.

The Beddingfield Pharmacy was established in 1920 as Beddingfield & Green. In 1932 it took its present name, with Dr. J. E. Beddingfield, owner and manager.

In 1923 the Dixie Drug Company became the Coleman & Claxton; in 1927 it became the Claxton Drug Company and is operated now by Dr. M. Z. Claxton.

In 1937 the Keith-Waddell Drug Store became the Oatts Drug Company. It is owned and operated by Dr. E. W. Oatts.

In 1926 the Oconee Pharmacy became the Service Drug Store, owned and operated by Dr. Johnnie Jordan.

Since 1912 there has been a large and flourishing Coca-Cola plant in Dublin. The present manager, W. L. Holmes, succeeded J. B. Kendrick in 1938.

Many Dublin companies are dealers in all standard automobiles.

The first large agency for the Ford cars, in Laurens County, was incorporated as the Ford Service Company by Watkins and Street; it next became the E. S. Street Company; then Marshall & Peacock took it over; since 1926 it has been the Morris Motor Company, George T. Morris, owner and director.

In 1926 the Chevrolet agency was bought by the Marshall & Peacock Company; since that time it has become the Peacock Chevrolet Company, owned and operated by R. T. Peacock.

In 1933 the Laurens Motor Company was named dealers for Plymouth and Chrysler cars. In 1939 the firm became Brigham-Stevens Company. In 1940 the Stevens Motor Company became dealers for Plymouth and Dodge cars and trucks. Pontiac cars are sold by the Wynn-Balsey Company.

A Laurens County establishment furnishes flowers for the territory between Macon and Savannah. The Dublin Floral Shop, operated and owned by Mr. and Mrs. Joe Middleton, has expanded since its beginning in 1927 to three large green houses.

Large hardware stores in Dublin are the Laurens Hardware Company, established about 1914 by Hall, Shewmake and Hilbun, now owned and operated by S. T. Hall and Earle Hilbun. The Lovett-Tharpe Hardware began in 1894 as the Gilbert Hardware Company, in 1913 it became the Stevens Hardware Company, and in 1929 it was taken over by W. H. Lovett and Henry Tharpe.

OFFICIALS OF THE CITY OF DUBLIN—1873-1941

The 1940 Census gave Dublin a population of 7,814. It was first incorporated in 1812 and the corporate limits made in 1820. The present form of government was embodied in a charter which was granted in 1873; it was again incorporated in 1882, reincorporated in 1893. A new charter was granted in 1905, another in 1910, which, with amendments, is the charter of today.

The city control consists of a mayor, aldermen, police department, attorney, fire department, water department, health department, and Recorder's court.

The mayors since 1873 have been: Dr. Peyton W. Douglas, Joel E. Perry, M. L. Burch, J. J. Connor, Mercer Haynes, John B. Wolfe, Jas. C. Scarborough, K. H. Walker, J. E. Hicks, Thomas B. Felder, Jr., David Ware, Jr., Lucius Q. Stubbs, F. H. Burch, D. S. Blackshear, Frank G. Corker, Jas. B. Sanders, J. S. Adams, Jas. B. Hicks, A. T. Summerlin, E. R. Orr, Albert R. Arnau, W. S. Phillips, C. A. Weddington, W. W. Robinson, P. S. Twitty, Izzie Bashinski, Jas. B. Jones, H. R. Moffett, T. E. Hightower, T. C. Keen, C. A. Hodges, Dee Sessions

City clerks have been: Hardy Smith, Isaac T. Keen, E. J. Tarpley, W. A. Wood, A. R. Arnau, Mercer Haynes, T. D. Smith, E. D. White, V. L. Stanley, A. P. Hilton, C. A. Weddington, A. H Graham, A. H. Grier, M. A. Rogers.

Those serving as chief of police have been: J. A. Peacock, J. B. Hightower, J. F. Flanders, J. J. Flanders, E. S. Ennis, E. C. Pierce, H. I. Robinson, E. C. Pierce, J. W. Robertson.

The period of the last twenty years has brought more comfort and luxury in the lives of the people than did the preceding hundred years. Paved roads and electric power lines have penetrated almost every section of the county. In 1927 the Georgia Power Company began to supply electricity; in 1939 the REA began to build lines, with offices in Dudley, Sandersville, and Alamo.

The Dublin water department has been headed for a number of years by D. F. Sams. Lynwood Hodges is water plant operator; Otis Sanders is chief of the fire department.

The present board of control is composed of Honorable Dee Sessions, mayor; 1st ward alderman, Martin Willis; 2nd ward, Milo Smith; 3rd ward, P. C. Hutchinson; 4th ward, M. Z. Claxton; from the city at large are E. B. Mackey, W. P. Tindol, Bruce Suggs. City clerk is M. A. Rogers; assistant clerk, Miss Gussie Bell Rawls; recorder, Dawson Kea; city attorney, Carl Nelson.

CHAPTER XI

LAURENS COUNTY—GEOGRAPHICAL AND AGRICULTURAL

1. GEOGRAPHICAL.

a. POPULATION AND CIVIC DIVISIONS.

Some twenty-nine counties had been created in Georgia before 1807; in that year, by legislative Act, Laurens, Telfair, Putnam, Morgan, Randolph, and Jones were formed.

Laurens County is bounded on northwest and north by Wilkinson, on the north by Washington, on the northeast and east by Johnson, on the east by Treutlen, on southeast by Wheeler, south and west by Dodge, and on northwest by Bleckley. In the early years the southeastern and southwestern boundaries were Montgomery, Telfair, and Pulaski. The county lies well toward the center of the State and contains 796 square miles, or 509,440 acres.

The United States Government report gives a forty year average rainfall of fifty-one inches. Temperature is relatively high, the annual mean, as reported at Dudley, is 65.5°. The mean temperature for the winter is 58.6°, for spring, 66.8°, for the summer, 80.1°, and for the fall, 66.4°.

The growth of population has been slow but steady. From a population in 1810 of 1,975 (465 of that number slaves) it had grown in 1910 to 35,500. The most rapid growth was between 1890 and 1900. In 1930 the population decreased to 32,693. In 1940 it increased to 33,606.

In 1940 the population of Laurens in the militia districts was: District 52, Smiths, 1,599; District 86, Buckeye, 1,264; District 341, Burgamy, 1,143; District 242, Dublin, 10,896; District 343, Pinetucky, 1,746; District 344, Hampton Mill, 2,551; District 345, Harvard, 810; District 391, Bailey, 982; District 1309, Jackson, 1,346; District 1338, Oconee, 1,060; District 1367, Lowery, 1,437; District 1368, Burch, 2,184; District 1369, Reedy Springs, 1,561; District 1412, Carters, 831; District 1681, Dudley, 1,340; District 1682, Cadwell, 1,935; District 1720, Rockledge, 921; Total population 33,606.

Laurens, in the list of Georgia counties, is seventh in size and about seventh in population. It is forty-three miles in length and thirty-five miles in width—almost an empire within itself.

The county has been in different congressional districts, and associated at different times with different counties in the same congressional district.

A Legislative Act passed in December, 1825, reads: "The counties of Emanuel, Scriven (sic), Bulloch, Effingham, Chatham, Bryan, Liberty, McIntosh, Tattnall, Montgomery, and Laurence (sic) shall form and compose the first congressional district."

Legislative Act of December 23, 1843, provided: "the counties of Camden, Glynn, Wayne, McIntosh, Liberty, Bryan, Chatham, Effingham, Bulloch, Montgomery, Tattnall, Appling, Ware, Laurens, Emanuel, Lowndes, Telfair, and Thomas shall compose the first congressional district."

Legislative Act of January 22, 1852, provided: "The counties of Chatham, Effingham, Bryan, Liberty, McIntosh, Tattnall, Bulloch, Emanuel, Montgomery, Lowndes, Telfair, Appling, Glynn, Camden, Wayne, Ware, Laurens, Clinch, Thomas, and Irwin shall compose the first congressional district."

In the Code, 1861, Article II, Section 44, we find: "The fourth district shall be composed of the counties of Jasper, Putnam, Jones, Baldwin, Bibb, Crawford, Wilkinson, Twiggs, Houston, Laurens, and Pulaski."

Confederate Records, Vol. IV, show that Laurens, Johnson, Brooks, Colquitt, Thomas, Montgomery, Telfair, Glynn, Camden, Ware, Pierce, and Chatham Counties constituted the First District.

Legislative Act, July 30, 1872, provides: "The Sixth District shall include the counties of Baldwin, Bibb, Butts, Jasper, Jones, Laurens, Newton, Putnam, Rockdale, Twiggs, Walton, and Wilkinson."

Act of August 28, 1883, provides: "The Third Congressional District shall be composed of the following counties: Coffee, Dodge, Dooly, Houston, Irwin, Laurens, Lee, Macon, Montgomery, Pulaski, Schley, Stewart, Sumpter, Telfair, Webster, and Wilcox."

Act of September 26, 1891, provides: "The Eleventh District shall include Glynn, Johnson, Laurens, Montgomery, Dodge, Telfair, Irwin, Coffee, Appling, Wayne, Pierce, Ware, Clinch, Echols, Lowndes, Brooksfi Charlton, and Camden Counties."

Act of August 19, 1911, provides: "Twelfth District: Twiggs, Houston, Pulaski, Wilcox, Dodge, Telfair, Laurens, Johnson, Emanuel, Montgomery, and Toombs."

Act of August 25, 1931: "Sixth District: Balwwin, Bibb, Bleckley, Crawford, Glascock, Hancock, Jasper, Jefferson, Jones, Johnson, Laurens, Monroe, Putnam, Twiggs, Washington, and Wilkinson."

When we consider the fact that Congressional districts depend upon population, the large number of changes will be understood.

Laurens County is now, and has been since 1861, in the 16th (State) Senatorial district (Constitution of 1861). Prior to 1845 Georgia's representation in the Senate was by county; in the Act of December 23, 1843, Laurens was placed in the Tenth (10th) District. It remained in that district until January 19, 1853, when the districts were discontinued and the representation was again made by counties.

b. Militia Districts.

In the early years of the Republic, the Federal Government seemed a long way from the people of Georgia and the Indians were close by; so the State took steps for its own military protection with the organization of militia districts in each county. Laurens laid off its territory into military sections. When a certain area had as many as a hundred fighting men, it was organized into a militia district and a corps of military officers was elected.

The State organization was composed of divisions, brigades, and regiments, with battalions and companies in each county. Men between the ages of 18 and 45 were members. There were battalion musters twice a year and company musters four times a year. The company, at these times, met at a designated spot in the militia district. The battalion musters were held at the county seat.

Militia muster days were red-letter days at the county seat. From their homes, the men came on horseback or on foot, each man carrying a weapon which might be a single-barrel shotgun, a rifle of ancient style, or a strong, long stick, previously cut and hardened. There was a great ado of drilling and reviewing, interspersed with drinks of whiskey or home made beer. When the muster was over the men celebrated with wild revelry stimulated by copious drinks of corn whiskey or peach brandy.

The early half of the nineteenth century was the period of a young and growing republic. Military organizations were the natural requirements.

Each militia district was given a name by the County and a number by the State, but the district was more often known by the name of the Captain of the Company. In an old land lottery list for Laurens County, the militia districts are known as Captain Leroy G. Harris District, Captain Sion Smith District, Captain Hardy Griffin District, Captain Francis J. Ross District, and Captain Adam Jones District.

The old muster ground, at the county seat, was located on the east side of Hunger and Hardship Creek, near the end of Jefferson Street. Laurens Hill and Boiling Springs were also muster sites. It was on the muster grounds at Boiling Springs that a great barbecue was given to the first company that left for Confederate War Service. During the War, Everard Blackshear turned his own front yard in Buckeye into a muster ground and drilled the men himself.

After the Confederate War, there were no more muster days or militia drills, but the militia districts today form the County's divisions. Each militia district has a Justice of the Peace Court and a Notary Public. The Justice of the Peace is elected, the Notary is appointed by the Judge of the Superior Court, on nomination of the Grand Jury. Each militia district has a building where the court is held.

These are the Georgia Militia (G. M.) Districts today in Laurens:

Dist. No. and Name	Date of Commission of First J. P.	Dist. No. and Name	Date of Commission of First J. P.
52—Smith	Aug. 10, 1812	1309—Jackson	Oct. 19, 1879
86—Buckeye	Aug. 10, 1812	1338—Oconee	March 29, 1881
342—Dublin	Feb. 1, 1808	1367—Lowery	Oct. 8, 1883
343—Pinetucky	Feb. 1, 1808	1368—Burch	Oct. 5, 1883
341—Burgamy	Feb. 1, 1808	1369—Reedy Springs	Oct. 5, 1883
344—Hampton Mill	Feb. 1, 1808	1412—Carter	July 11, 1887
345—Harvard	Feb. 1, 1808	1682—Cadwell	created in 1903
391—Bailey	Nov. 20, 1813	1681—Dudley	created in 1909
		1720—Carter	created in 1914

The first five militia districts were established in 1808. They are now called Dublin, Pinetucky, Burgamy, Hampton Mill and Harvard Districts, though they were laid out as District 1, 2, 3, 4, 5. The description of their location is found in the minutes of the Inferior Court under date of February 1, 1808.

"Ordered that the County of Laurens be laid off into five districts in the following manner, to-wit:

"1st Beginning on the Oconee at the mouth of Wamuchs Mill creek, thence to where Folks trail crosses the south prong of Hunger and Hardship, thence to Josiah Stringer's, thence down Stringer's branch to the Mouth, thence up Turkey Creek to the boundary line and up that to the county line, thence along said line to the Oconee River and down said river to the beginning shall form district No. 1.

"2nd Beginning on Turkey creek at the mouth of Stringer's branch, thence down said creek to the upper line of the 17th district, thence including the seventeenth and twelfth districts to the Oconee River and up the same to the mouth of Wamucks Mill Creek and along the lower line of District No. 1 to the beginning shall form District No. 2.

"3rd Beginning on Turkey Creek where the upper line of the 17th district intersects the same, thence leaving out the 17th and 12th districts, to the county line, thence along said line to the little Ocmulgee, thence up the same to the upper county line, thence along same to the old boundary line, thence down the same to Turkey Creek, and down the same to the beginning, shall form District No. 3.

"4th Beginning on the Little Ocmulgee at the Uchee Path, thence along said path to Hogany trail, thence along said trail to the main prong of Jordan's Creek, thence down said creek to the mouth, thence up the Ocmulgee River to the upper county line, along said line to the little Ocmulgee, thence down the same to the beginning shall form District No. 4.

"5th Beginning on the little Ocmulgee at the Uchee path and thence down said creek to the lower county line, thence along said line to the Ocmulgee River, thence up the same to the mouth of Jordan's Creek, thence along the lower line of District No. 4 to the beginning shall form District No. 5.

"Ordered, That James Bracewell and Alexander Blackshear be and they are hereby appointed Magistrates for District No. 1, and that John McBane and John Pollock be appointed Constables for said district.

"Ordered, That John Fulwood and Andrew Hampton be and they are hereby appointed Magistrates for District No. 2 and that Gideon Mayo and John Williams be appointed Constables for said district.

"Ordered, That Elisha Farnall and Joseph Denson Sr., be and they are hereby appointed Magistrates for District No. 3 and that James Moore and Joseph Denson be appointed Constables for said district.

"Ordered, That Needham Stevens and Samuel Jones be and they are hereby appointed Magistrates for District No. 4 and that John Jeon and Henry Duett be Constables for said district.

"Ordered, That William Hall and Robert Duett be and they are hereby appointed Magistrates for District No. 5 and that John Grenstead and Wm. Morris be Constables for said district."

c. TRIBUTARY WATERWAYS

Streams flowing into the Oconee River, beginning at the North, are: Big Sandy Creek; Deep Creek, Dry Creek; Buckeye; Hightower; Kellam's; Upper Rocky and its tributary, Deep Branch; Still Branch; Fort Creek with its tributaries, Big Creek, Little Creek, Big Branch and Brewton Creek; Rum Branch; Hunger and Hardship Creek with its tributaries, Strawberry Branch, Bud Branch and Sandy Ford Branch; Long Branch; Shaddock Creek; Pugh's Creek with its tributaries, Cull's Creek, Indian Branch, Randall Creek and Messer Creek; Turkey Creek with its tributaries, Walnut Creek, Palmetto Creek, Horse Branch, Crooked Branch, Spring Branch, Blue Water Creek and Mosquito Branch; Flat Creek.

Mercer Creek, with its main tributary, Red Hill Creek, forms part of the boundary line between Laurens and Treutlen Counties, and empties into the Oconee River.

Pendleton's Creek drains a portion of the eastern part of the County and forms part of the boundary line between Laurens and Emanuel Counties, but does not empty into the Oconee River.

The Oconee River, changing its course, left two Dead Rivers, one in Buckeye District, the other in Smith's. In the Buckeye District the water of the Oconee, depositing a rich silt in a depression, produced a thick vegetation and a treacherous soil that was given the name Cow Hell.

After the Oconee River leaves Laurens County it receives streams that belong to the County—upper Whitewater Creek and Okewalkee Creek.

Laurens County streams flowing into the Ocmulgee are Alligator Creek, with its tributaries; lower Whitewater Creek; and Limesink

Creek, with its tributaries Big Branch, Land Branch, and Long Branch.

Flowing across the extreme southern corner of Laurens County is Joiner Creek. Into Alligator Creek flows Batson Creek, with its main tributary, Bay Creek.

A large tributary of Turkey Creek is lower Rocky, draining the western part of the county, its tributaries being: Whitley Creek, Stitchihatchee Creek, Boggy Creek, Buckhorn Creek with its tributaries Long Pond and Mar Branch, Bay Branch, Hogan's Branch, and Little Rocky.

d. The Oconee River

The principal stream of Laurens County is the Oconee River. In the "Gazeteer of Georgia," published in 1825, it is thus described: "The Oconee River rises N. E. of the Ocmulgee in the mountainous country which separates the waters flowing into the Atlantic from those that flow into the Gulph of Mexico. Two considerable streams, the head waters of the river, the North and Middle Forks, unite below Athens, and the Appalachee from the S. W. falls in opposite Greensboro 35 miles further south. In removing obstructions from the river in 1820 a large keel boat, 60 feet long, ascended to Barnetts Shoals, near Watkinsville; but no produce has been floated upon it above Milledgeville. To this town they bring 70-ton boats. The general course of the river is S. S. E. till it unites with the Ocmulgee 200 miles below Milledgeville (a gentleman who has sailed on its surface each way, thinks it 280) and here they both lose their names in the Altamaha." (Adiel Sherwood, Author).

Almost from the beginning of the County the Oconee River has been used for transportation; in the early years it carried timber rafts, then, as the Government began to clear its bed, boats began operation. From the point where it passes from Laurens to the point where it enters are these old landings: Baunauclaughbauh (Bonny Clabber), Stave Landing, Shady Fields Landing, Fish Trap Landing, Fuller's Landing, Dublin, Dominy Landing, Hobbs Landing, Guyton Bluff Landing, Deep Creek Landing, U. S. Government Landing, Hall's Landing. The County has maintained three ferries, Diamond Landing Ferry (near Wilkes Spring), the Dublin Ferry and Blackshear's Ferry. Only the last mentioned is still operated.

e. Boats of the Oconee.

The fall of the year had come—one of those years between 1870 and 1880.

Cotton picking was over and the ginning was about finished. A few bales had been hauled to Savannah to be sold, but many planters were waiting to send their cotton to market by boat down the Oconee.

A boat would be coming up the river before many days. There

was no regular schedule, but it was about time for one to show up. So said the wise ones among the groups of men here and there, gossiping about the weather, the crops and boat that was due. Business was dull and times were hard, for Reconstruction days were just over.

A far-off whistle broke the sleepy quiet of the little town of Dublin. It could mean but one thing. Again the sound of the steamer whistle came, clearer this time. Men started down to the boat landing. The small town had waked up, for this was an event.

The coming of the river steamer meant new merchandise, supplies of many kinds, and often fresh oysters. The steamer whistle spoke to the women of the town as well as the men, and more than one small boy thrilled to its sound.

Soon the boat was in sight. It proved to be the *Two Boys*, bringing freight and expecting to return with cotton. The *Two Boys* had made the trip to Dublin many times before.

By the time the steamer had come to a stop, a good share of the masculine population of Dublin was on hand to greet her, with a good sprinkling of the ladies. Such was the importance of the river traffic in an earlier day.

The first record of a steamboat on the Oconee was in 1819. When the *Lady Washington* came steaming up the river, it is said that people were waiting all along the banks to see it pass.

There must have been steamboats to make occasional trips up the river from Darien after that, but the next record is that of the *Governor George M. Troup*. It was built in Dublin a short time before the War Between the States by Freeman H. Rowe and David Robinson. When the war began, it was either given or sold to the Confederate Government.

The boats used before the time of the *Governor George M. Troup* were mainly pole boats; it was a slow laborious job to pole up the river to Dublin. The trip back was much faster, requiring little more than one third of the time.

These boats brought supplies and carried back cotton. The main freight brought was salt. The boat landing was between the former ferry and the present county bridge, near where the plywood mill now stands. At the landing was the salt house where salt brought for merchants and farmers was stored till called for. The old salt house stood there for many years after it ceased to be used.

One of the Oconee's most famous boats was *The Colville*, which was purchased by a company headed by Colonel John M. Stubbs, and brought from Wilmington, North Carolina, by Captain R. C. Henry and a Mr. Skinner. This boat was used for several years between Dublin and Raoul Station and was later sold and transferred to the Ocmulgee River. Colonel Stubbs was also the prime mover in the construction of *The Rover* and *The Gypsy*, which were operated by Captain W. W. Ward. These boats were built by the Forest and Stream Club as pleasure boats, but they were used for freight service, as well.

Other steamers built in Dublin were: *The Louisa, The Laurens, The R. C. Henry, The City of Dublin, The Gypsy, The Rover, The New Dublin,* and the *Wm. M. Wadley.* Most of the steamers built here, and the light draught steamers built for Georgia, Florida, and South Carolina rivers, were constructed by Captain John M. Graham, Dublin's famous boat builder. He could build a boat to meet any requirement. All he needed to know was the amount of water the boat was to draw when loaded.

Captain R. C. Henry was manager of the boats on the Oconee for many years, and made a fortune on the river. He was a public spirited citizen and contributed much to the city's progress.

Other boats which have plied trade on the Oconee were: *The Nan Elizabeth, The Southland, The Clyde, The Cumberland,* and *The Silverside.*

When *The Colville* was brought to Dublin it was not an easy matter to navigate the Oconee. At considerable expense, the Oconee River Steamboat Company made improvements on the river, and later the Government aided. Congressman James H. Blount secured the first appropriation ever given to the Oconee. The Federal Government appropriated $10,000.00 for this purpose. Later Charles F. Crisp, James G. Turner, and Wm. G. Brantley secured appropriations. In 1874 the County appropriated $500.00 "to clean out Oconee River bed."

When the railroads began to haul freight, river commerce became less and less; now, with railroads and highway trucks, one sees few steamers on the river, save a pleasure boat or a river boat bringing in timber for the plywood mill.

One of the last boats was the *Katherine S.*, owned by J. A. Kelly, which made her maiden trip in 1917.

—*By Jane Roberta Smith.*

2. AGRICULTURAL

a. SOIL AND COTTON PRODUCTION

Lying in the Atlantic Coastal Plain, the County has a sandy loam soil; the Norfolk, Orangeburg, Ruston, Grady, Thompson and Tifton are the prevailing types. The soil is especially adapted to agriculture, being easily cultivated and capable of high fertility. The northern part of the county has a red subsoil with pebbly, dark sandy loam with lime content; the southern part of the County was once known as the "pine barrens," but when the pines were cut and the land opened up, the gray pebbly soil with a clay subsoil proved to be susceptible to high fertility. Laurens lies in that part of Georgia known as the Altamaha uplands with an elevation above sea level between 200 and 400 feet.

Laurens is one of the high-ranking agricultural counties. It was thus described by D. G. Bickers, associate editor of the Savannah *Morning News*:

"Climatic conditions, variety of soils, and fertility all combine to make Laurens County one of the best farming counties in all of the State. It is one of the few counties where farmers feed themselves as well as grow cash crops. Two crops may be grown on Laurens County lands each year. All general farm crops thrive here; cotton, tobacco, corn, soy beans, peas, hay, oats, rye, wheat, sorghum cane, sugar cane, peanuts, sweet potatoes, Irish potatoes on a commercial scale, watermelons and peaches on a commercial basis, cantaloupes and permanent pastures for beef and dairy cattle.

"Tobacco, to the extent of 1,000 acres, will be grown in Laurens County this year, and on a safe basis, for there are several veteran demonstrators in the County to assure quality and price." (Savannah *Morning News*, April 25, 1927).

Cotton is now, and has been in the past, the main money crop, for the county lies in the tertiary plain, rich in lime, that aids cotton growth. Geological investigations show that a line of calcareous rock passes through the county.

Long before the War Between the States the production of cotton was the chief occupation and source of wealth. In 1860 the production was 6,934 bales of 400 pound weight. War almost stopped production and Reconstruction retarded it, but by 1880 there were 20,689 acres growing cotton; these rapidly increased till by 1910 there were 100,253 acres producing 41,884 bales.

By 1900 Dublin had become a cotton market and headquarters for several large exporters whose buyers paid as high prices as those in Atlanta, Macon and Savannah. This encouraged cotton production. In the early Nineties, cotton receipts in Dublin amounted to approximately 5,000 bales; by 1907, receipts had increased to 30,000 bales.

Many farmers were progressive and conducted large and profitable farming operations. Joel Coney, in the Poplar Springs community, was, in the Nineties, the largest farmer in the County, operating between fifty and sixty plows. C. W. Brantley was owner of 4,000 acres in active production. J. D. Smith had large farms producing grain and hogs. J. A. Hogan, in the Dudley community, in the second decade of the present century, was the largest planter in the county; in a certain year his plantings were: 2,000 acres in cotton, 2,000 acres in corn, 1,000 acres in peanuts, 500 acres in oats, 600 acres in peas, 150 acres in wheat, 250 acres in rye, 125 acres in potatoes, 15 acres in watermelons.

In 1906, the Laurens County Farmers' Club was organized, with

W. J. Joiner, president, W. F. Higgins, secretary, and H. M. Stanley, treasurer.

Four cotton warehouses were taking care of the farmers' cotton and a cotton exchange aided his safe selling. The Farmers' Supply Company, managed by B. H. Rawls, supplied their implements. Of great encouragement to the production of cotton was the Georgia Warehouse & Compress Company, established in 1895. The compress had a capacity of 71 bales per hour. Able directors were T. J. Pritchett, J. M. Finn, and H. A. Knight.

Another encouragement to the production of cotton was the coming to Dublin of the Southern Cotton Oil Company, which provided a steady and dependable seed market.

The cotton market was built up through cotton export firms headed by James S. Simons, Jr., John W. Byrne, W. B. Rogers, Izzie Bashinski, H. H. Coley, Hack Robinson, Thomas R. Ramsay, J. R. Powell, J. M. Couric, and A. C. Scarboro.

In 1911, Laurens reached its peak production of cotton, 61,000 bales. In 1914, G. L. Cullens hauled in, at one time. to the Dublin market, sixty bales.

With the depredations of the boll weevil, cotton production began to fall. The last large production was in 1918, when 55,858 bales were raised. Not knowing how to combat the weevil, farmers made the lowest production in 1921 of 11,112 bales. Then the County, led by the County Agent and the Chamber of Commerce, began strenuout fighting of the weevil. Now, with favorable weather conditions, production climbed back; in 1940, the County's production was 25,611 bales.

Laurens County ranks among the three highest cotton-producing counties in the state.

Cotton made its record price in Laurens County on August 29, 1918, when two bales sold for $500.00, 35 5/6 cents per pound.

The great improvement in gin machinery was another stimulant to large cotton production. The old horse and hand power gins began to give way when steam power came into use in the 1880's. Captain T. H. Rowe was the first Laurens County man to install a steam gin.

OUR OLD GIN AND SCREW.

The old-fashioned gin and screw, with their wooden machinery, assisted by mules and human strength of brawny negroes, would be objects of amusement to our present generation.

A big two-storied gin house covered all the machinery for ginning cotton. The gin was upstairs, and here a man stood and fed its sharp teeth with handfuls of cotton. The feathery lint flew backward through an opening into the "lint room." The seeds fell to the floor and were swept downstairs into the seed pen.

Downstairs, the wooden machinery consisted of a huge post, in the center of a large rotunda. Three feet from the ground two levers, fifteen feet or more in length, were attached to the center post, extending in opposite directions. Near the top of this central power, wooden cogs fitted into a wheel dropped through the floor from above. This wheel, connected to the gin with a leather band, was all that was needed.

The ginning was simple. A mule was hitched to the end of each lever. A half-grown colored boy seated himself on a lever to guide the mules. "Get up," he cried. The mules began their tramp round and round. The wooden wheel began to turn. The gin began to whir, and the ginning was begun.

The old-fashioned "screw," which packed the cotton into bales, reminded one of a windmill in Holland, with its two giant arms hanging from on high and extending from each side at an angle of perhaps 45 degrees.

On a low platform rested a large strong box, the shape and size of a bale of cotton. This box was neatly lined with cotton bagging with the necessary extra length falling over the sides and ends. The box was filled with cotton brought in baskets from the lint room.

About sixteen feet above the box was suspended a huge iron screw, ten inches in diameter. Attached to the end of the screw was a heavy block of wood the shape and size of the box, though smaller. The long levers held the screw in place directly over the box. Strong hands pushed, or mules puled the levers round and round. The block descended, and by its pressure, the cotton was packed.

The two longest sides of the box were laid flat, and cotton ties were forced under the cotton. The jute bagging was folded and stretched neatly about the packed cotton. The ties were drawn and fastened tightly. The bale of cotton, perfectly made, stood free, weighing the average five hundred pounds.

—*By Elizabeth Duncan Lanier (Mrs. W. R.)*

Early in the second decade the Chamber of Commerce and leading farmers set a movement on foot to secure for Laurens County a farm agent. A committee composed of T. J. Blackshear, W. B. Rice and E. T. Barnes recommended J. B. Tyre for the office. He served the county until 1922 when J. F. Hart, Jr., a graduate and former teacher of the State College of Agriculture, was employed by the County Commissioners. He continued in this work till 1939.

Shortly after the employment of a Farm Agent, the women of Dublin prevailed upon the County Board of Commissioners to put on a home demonstration agent. Miss Martha Philbuck was employed. Since then, the following have served the county in that capacity: 1918, Miss Pearl Gillman; 1918, Miss Bernice Sammons;

1919, Miss Ethel Shelor; 1920, Miss Edith Robertson; 1922, Mrs. E. O. Ward; 1925, Miss Bernice Echols; 1928, Miss Pauline Derrick; 1931, Miss Opal Ward; 1936, Miss Dorothy Kellogg; 1938, Miss Nelle Robinson; 1941, Miss Bobby Hicks.

b. CROP DIVERSIFICATION.

After the coming of the boll weevil farmers began raising, on a large scale, many products that had previously received but little attention. Among these was the sweet potato; in 1917 a potato curing house, with large storage facilities, was erected.

Farmers awoke to the need of legume crops for cattle feed and soil enrichment, and began to plant velvet beans in the corn crops. In 1917, the Oconee Milling Company erected one of the largest velvet bean mills in the world. Livestock production has been greatly aided by the velvet bean. It resists the wear of weather and clinging to the corn stalks, furnishes a protein food for cattle in winter.

Improved pastures are seen throughout the County. In 1923, under the direction of the County Agent, farmers bought and planted 30,000 pounds of lespedeza seed and 15,000 pounds of carpet grass.

In the 1920's watermelons began to be grown for shipping. In 1923 there were over a thousand acres planted. In 1934 there were shipped 418 cars of watermelons. In 1940, a third of the farmers were raising peanuts on a commercial acreage; 23 per cent of the crop area was devoted to cotton, and 61.8 per cent to corn.

The greatest hindrance to the County's agricultural progress is the large amount of tenantry. The records of 1935 show only one farm out of every four to be operated by the owner. The Farmers' Union became the Farmers' Cooperative Association and instituted several progressive movements to aid the farmer. A Farmers Cooperative Store was established in 1916, with J. R. Cherry, manager. In 1918, an elevator was built in Dublin; the Association put in a peanut-shelling plant about the same time, and the Sanitary Canning Club was established.

Stock raising began to be an important agricultural industry about 1917. The Farmers Live Stock Association and a live Chamber of Commerce, with N. G. Bartlett, secretary, built stock yards. A meat curing plant was established and operated by R. E. Braddy. Today there are, in Dublin, four meat-curing plants.

Hog-raising is now one of the leading money crops, and Laurens is the second largest hog-raising county in Georgia. In 1922, under the direction of the county farm agent, J. F. Hart, and the secretary of the Chamber of Commerce, C. W. Phillips, cooperative hog sales were inaugurated. A sale was held each month, from October to April. At one sale there were nine carloads of hogs, 1,017 head.

Dairying, in the Twentieth Century, has come to be a strong industry. Foremost in this was Captain W. B. Rice, who was the leader of crop diversification in the County. Captain Rice assembled a fine herd of pure Jerseys; in 1923, there were fourteen cars of grade Jerseys brought in, and small farmers began securing herds.

Beginning about the same time as the Rice Dairy was the Perry Brothers' Dairy. Perry Brothers have made a specialty of fine pasture lands. Stumps and obstructions were removed and broad acres planted in carpet and other grasses. The farm agents employed by the Central Railroad for several years used these pastures for model demonstration areas. Flowing artesian wells, improved grass lands free of bitter weed, and grain crops give the Perry Dairy herd ideal conditions.

These first dairies used almost entirely the Jersey, now two large dairy farms are using only the Guernsey. Dr. E. B. Claxton supplies a large trade from a herd of Guernseys on his farm to the north of Dublin. The Parker Dairy Farm, with Duren Parker, manager, maintains one of the finest Guernsey herds in the State and supplies a large number of families. Mr. Parker specializes, not only in high class milk, but also in breeding pedigreed cattle. The Parker Guernsey Farm consists of over 100 acres situated two miles north of Dublin. Three artesian wells and a modern freezing plant provide germ-free milk.

Another dairy herd is maintained by J. A. Stinson.

The first creamery in the County wes established in 1923 by J. W. Geeslin, through the aid of the County Agent. The plant had been started in 1920 as an ice cream factory, but when Laurens County farmers began to buy dairy herds, it was changed into a creamery. It is believed to have been the second creamery in Georgia.

The Armour Packing Company established a creamery in Dublin in 1928; this was also a poultry market. In 1941, the large plant was discontinued and a station established by Swift. Today there are two cream stations in Dublin—Swift's and Lifsey's.

In contests sponsored by the *Southern Ruralist-Progressive Farmer* and the State Agricultural College, two Laurens County farmers won the title "Master Farmer of the South-Eastern District:" U. G. B. Hogan of Dexter, in the year 1928, and Hiram Joiner of Montrose, in the year 1930. In other years, J. B. Fordham and Duren Parker were named "Master Farmers" of Laurens, though they did not win the district award.

In the five-acre corn production contest of 1929, E. T. Barnes won second place in the South Georgia Upland Group, with a yield of 115.03 bushels per acre. The Georgia State College of Agriculture put on these contests to encourage increased production.

In 1923, a system of crop rotation was emphasized by farmres.

The county agent outlined the folowing program which was used by many farmers, with excellent results.

FIELD No. 1

First Year—Oats, Wheat, Rye, followed by Spanish Peanuts or pea hay.
Second Year—Cash Crops—Cotton, Peanuts, Melons, Potatoes, Cane, Etc.
Third Year—Corn, Beans, Peanuts.
Fourth Year—Velvet Beans, Cow Peas, Soy Beans, one or all; to be plowed under.

FIELD No. 2

First Year—Velvet Beans, Cow Peas, Soy Beans, one or all; to be plowed under.
Second Year—Oats, Wheat, Rye, followed by Spanish Peanuts or Pea hay.
Third Year—Cash Crops—Cotton, Peanuts, Melons, Potatoes, Cane, Etc.
Fourth Year—Corn, Beans, Peanuts.

PERMANENT PASTURE

FIELD No. 4

First Year—Cash Crops—Cotton, Peanuts, Melons, Potatoes, Cane, Etc.
Second Year—Corn, Beans, Peanuts.
Third Year—Velvet Beans, Cow Peas, Soy Beans, one or all; to be plowed under.
Fourth Year—Oats, Wheat, Rye, followed by Spanish Peanuts or Pea Hay.

FIELD No. 3

First Year—Corn, Beans, Peanuts.
Second Year—Velvet Beans, Cow Peas, Soy Beans, one or all; to be plowed under.
Third Year—Oats, Wheat, Rye, followed by Spanish Peanuts or pea hay.
Fourth Year—Cotton, Peanuts, Melons, Potatoes, Cane, Etc.

Laurens County was a pioneer in the peach growing industry. Col. John M. Stubbs set out many acres in peaches on his estate in the Montrose community.

A fruit growing industry of vast proportions, which attracted the attention of the State, was a fruit farm, planted in the first years of the Twentieth Century at Kewanee on Rocky Creek, twelve miles southwest of Dublin.

Several thousand acres of land were purchased here by a midwestern group of men, organized as the Georgia Fruitland Company, whose aim was to create a large colony of fruit producers. Their plan provided a home and competency for those who had no capital save a small monthly salary. For each member who joined the colony there was to be an orchard planted by the company and cared for till bearing age, then delivered to the owner for its income. The land was surveyed into lots of twenty acres, each of which was sold on monthly payments of $10.00. Taking over his orchard, the buyer received the income of the fruit, and on that finished paying for his lot. Hundreds of acres were planted in peach trees, but the San Jose scale soon began its deadly work and the orchardists, not being able to cope with it, lost the trees, and the lands were, in time, sold for taxes.

During the first quarter of the century many pecan trees were planted. Growing pecans has greatly increased the farmers' income. The largest pecan market in the County is the P. M. Watson Company of Dublin. In the 1940 season, this firm bought over 800,000 pounds of nuts and Mr. Watson estimates that 60 or 70 thousand pounds were produced in the county. At 1940 prices, the income, to Laurens growers, was approximately $100,000.00.

A stimulant to stock raising in Laurens is the weekly auction sale. Large barns and sale yards were built in 1940 by M. E. Cochran, in Dublin, and here each Thursday afternoon throughout the year the Dublin Live Stock and Commission Company (owned and operated by Mr. Cochran) holds an auction, with Clayton Nicholson, auctioneer. Stock yards are maintained in Dublin by M. H. Hogan and G. A. Jepeway.

There are no longer heavy losses to farmers in curing meats, as the curing house is independent of weather. In Dublin are the Braddy Curing Plant, the Geeslin Curing Plant, the Crystal Ice Company, and the Atlantic Ice and Coal Company. In recent months a curing plant has been established in Cadwell.

The 3,573 farms of the County are aided by the County Farm Agent who acts as adviser, demonstrator, and organizer. Harry Edge, employed by the County Commissioners, maintains an office in the Federal Court Building, aided by a full-time secretary, Miss Thelma Hester.

Miss Bobbie Hicks, the home demonstration agent, maintains an office in the old Post Office Building and is employed by the Board of Education. Miss Hicks is adviser for fifteen 4-H Clubs for girls and eight community clubs for farm women.

Mr. Edge is a graduate of the State College of Agriculture; he came to Laurens in 1939 after serving as county agent of Cook County. In the year 1940, the county agent succeeded in organizing a one-variety cotton community with 65 members; emphasis was given to terracing, building of trench silos, and planting of winter cover crops. Two hundred seventy-one boys belong to four 4-H Clubs.

In 1940, farm wives received direct aid through a mattress-making project; 1,620 matteresses were made.

One of the greatest aids to farm women was the installation of a farm market in Dublin, in 1940, under the direction of Miss Nelle Robinson (Mrs. Stanley Reese). The men's clubs of Dublin assist in paying the expense of renting the building.

Much of the wealth of Laurens County has come from the pine. The long leaf, or yellow, pine finds in the southern half of the coutty an ideal habitat. Lumbering and turpentining were the first industries in the county.

c. Flora of Laurens.

Three varieties of gum trees—sweet, black, and tupelo—ash, cypress, magnolia, poplar, maple, elm, hickory, catalpa, redbud, persimmon, locust, tuliptree, sycamore, cherry laurel, dogwood, and wild tea olive flourish in Laurens County. There are several varieties of the oak—red, white, water, post, and black jack. The coast live oak grows in profusion around certain old settlements; it is said that Thomas McCall, a great lover of trees, brought young trees from the coast and distributed them among his planter friends.

Among the woody plants or shrubs are: the sassafras, so well adapted to the soil it sometimes grows into a tree, the mimosa, gall berry, old man's beard, buckeye, sweet shrub, bush honeysuckle or wild azalea, sweet bay, sumac, alder, willow, French mulberry, catalpa which grows into a tree, the holly which becomes a tree, poison oak, crabapple which grows into a tree, huckleberry, bush blueberry, blackberry, chokeberry, and elderberry.

From early spring through early autumn wild flowers bloom. Some found here are: wild Easter lilies, the magnolia tree which furnishes a large handsome blossom, and the sweet bay, a similar but smaller and more fragrant flower. There are also violets, pink azalea, fragrant sweet shrub, purple gerardia, wild asters, wild verbena, golden rod, wild carrot, butterfly weed, mock pennyroyal, bouncing bet, hog peanut, sensitive pea, sundrops, fly catcher, burdock, Indian pipe, ground or moss pink (wild thrift), rattle box pea, and dandelion, and false sunflower. Among the woodland vines are: honeysuckle, yellow jasmine bamboo, smilax, poison ivy, sarsaparilla, muscadine grape, and cowitch.

Burning the woods is a custom that has come down from the County's early history. There grows in the County the famous wiregrass; when young it is tender and makes good grazing for cattle. As this was the principal sustenance for the range cattle, each year the woods were burned off that the cows might have good grazing. This custom still persists, although the county requires that cattle be kept within fence. When the boll-weevil came, the farmer, to destroy his winter home, burned the woods. For these two reasons, millions of pines have been destroyed and are still being destroyed.

Long leaf pine areas are sadly depleted. A second growth of pine still supplies the turpentine industry. In the County today are four large stills.

The slash, the loblolly, and short leaf pine are now being heavily cut for pulp wood. Despite the ravages of lumbermen and pulpwood cutters, there still may be a future for the pine. Many farsighted people of the County are replacing the loss of long leaf pines with fast-growing slash. With the encouragement given to reforestation by the State and the Agricultural Division of the Federal Government, large areas in the county have been planted in young pines.

Approximately 5,000 acres have also been set out in slash pines. The County Agent purchased, in 1940, for 77 farmers, 259,500 pine seedlings. The largest reforestation area, by one individual, is that of T. R. Gilder.

In the 1930's, the Phoenix Mutual Life Insurance Company began, under the direction of C. W. Philips, reforestation of over 1,200 acres of Laurens land, believing this to be the crop most suitable to the type of soil.

The pine lands of Laurens County still furnish one of the County's main industries, the turpentine farms. Two large stills are located near Dublin; on the west of the town is the E. T. Barnes plant; near the river, on the east, is the still of Carter and Burns. The largest turpentine plant in the County is the Buie Still; other plants are the Weatherly Company near Cadwell, the Gilder Still in the southern part of the County on the Glenwood road, the Laurens Turpentine Company near Rockledge, and the Lamar Currie Still at Cedar Grove.

—By Helen McCall Bashinski (Mrs. I.)

d. Fauna of Laurens County.

There are no deer in Laurens County, but wild turkey abound in the thick swamps. Quail is abundant. Gray and fox squirrels, raccoon, o'possum, red and gray fox, cotton-tail rabbit, and a few wild cat may be found in this district. Otter, muskrat in abundance, a few mink, and summer or wood duck are here in season, also the mallard.

Snipe and woodcock immigrate here, and a few woodcock nest here. The meadow lark, brown thrasher, mourning dove, mocking bird, shrike or butcher bird, Wilson thrush, blue jay, humming bird, cardinal, and any number of song birds, may be found In the heavily-wooded swamps may be found a few very rare ivory bill woodpeckers.

Among the poisonous snakes are the highland rattler and water moccasin. Only a few coral snakes and black widow spiders are found.

In the streams of Laurens County are many varieties of fish—namely, perch, bream, trout, several varieties of cat fish, black fish, and jack.

There are no game preserves or fish hatcheries in the county.

—By Helen McCall Bashinski (Mrs. I.)

CHAPTER XII

STATE AND FEDERAL AGENCIES IN LAURENS

1. FEDERAL LOAN AGENCIES

Federal loan agencies have aided, and are now aiding farmers. In 1916, the Federal Land Bank began assisting farmers to secure long loans and low interest advantages. At first, through lawyers designated for the purpose, a farmer could secure a Federal loan; about 1925, an office was established in Dublin with J. R. Cherry, secretary. In 1937, the office was enlarged and is now the National Farm Loan Association, with Fred L. Brown, secretary-chairman.

In 1928, the Seed Loan was begun, loans applied for, and affairs managed through the Laurens farm agent. Fred L. Brown was put in charge. It has since been consolidated with the offices in Bleckley, Dodge, Laurens, and Telfair counties, Eastman being used as headquarters.

The First Federal Savings and Loan Association of Dublin was chartered under the Federal Government in January, 1935. Deposits are insured by the Federal Savings and Loan Insurance Corporation. The president is Cecil Carroll and F. N. Watkins is secretary-treasurer.

2. THE TRIPLE A.

The agricultural crisis of 1932-33, brought about by a burdensome surplus and depressed farm prices, led to the passing by the Federal Government of the Agricultural Adjustment Act of 1933. Under This Act, the United States Department of Agriculture began, in each State, programs to control production and to encourage beneficial use of farm land not in cultivation.

Since the cotton control program could not be begun in time to control planting, farmers were asked to plough up a certain acreage then growing cotton; so, 1933 is remembered as "the Plough-up campaign year."

The administration of the AAA program was placed in the hands of the county agent, J. F. Hart. The agent's office was enlarged and several assistants were employed. In 1934, farmers began to shift their acreage from soil-depleting crops to other crops that were soil-improving or erosion-preventing. In December, 1934, Laurens County farmers, in a referendum, voted for government control of the cotton production. The droughts of 1934 and 1936 aided in reducing cotton production.

In 1933, Fisher Strickland was employed as assistant to the county agent, to aid in administering the Government program. In 1939, he was sent to Coffee County as farm agent. In the summer of that year, the Federal Government sent Travis Taylor to help with the AAA program; he was followed by Z. S. Norville. In 1940, the work was separated from the County Agent's territory and offices were established in the old Post Office Building. Z. S. Norville is Administrative Assistant; he has for assistants: Mrs. Grace Branch, Mrs. Louise Scarborough Parker, Mrs. Saralyn White, Mrs. Martha Fincher, Miss Mary Moorman, Miss Martha Rountree, Miss Lucia Stevens, M. A. Stewmake, and Donald Lamb.

That the Government has dealt generously with Laurens County farmers is shown in the total amounts the County has received, annually, as of February 20, 1941:

1933, $328,200; 1934, $207,400; 1935, $341,300; 1936, $229,861; 1937, $169,546; 1938, $481,070; 1939, $536,236; 1940, $204,001*; Total, $2,497,614.

3. FEDERAL SURPLUS COMMODITIES.

The Welfare Department of Georgia and the Federal Surplus Commodities Corporation have distributed food to hundreds of Laurens County's needy and unemployed. H. G. Stevens, county commodity foreman, is now furnishing supplies to eighty Laurens County schools for school lunches, to four hundred families, and five hundred Farm Security farmers. Each month about three thousand people receive aid.

4. FEDERAL NATIONAL YOUTH ASSOCIATION.

In 1939, headquarters for eight counties was located in Dublin by the Federal National Youth Association. Under the direction of Miss Alexa Daley, area director, with Mrs. Edith Mae Allgood, area secretary, many projects have been initiated and completed, including a vocational building at Cedar Grove, a gymnasium at Brewton, a vocational building at the colored school, St. John, and a shop at Cadwell.

Unemployed students have been placed in business offices to gain experience in clerical work. For some time a NYA resident-project was maintainedd for thirty-six girls, whereby they received domestic and commercial training. The home was located in Dublin, with Miss Virginia Graves in charge.

5. PWA AND WPA

During the latter half of the 1930's, Dublin has been greatly improved by Federal and State aid. In 1935, the City, with the State Highway Department, paved road and sidewalks of Jefferson Street.

With Federal aid, through PWA, the city expanded and improved

---

* Does not include 1940 agricultural conservation program payments.

the water system. With WPA work, four and eight-tenths miles of paving were laid in 1936. In 1939 and 1940 there were three additional miles laid. The Parks were improved with recreational facilities.

For several years WPA operated sewing rooms in Dublin. Here unemployed women made garments and household articles for distribution to needy families.

Library workers were furnished the Carnegie Library to catalogue and mend books, and aid in circulation. A traveling library for the county is financed by the Federal Government, aided by the County.

6. GEORGIA STATE EMPLOYMENT SERVICE.

The passage of the Wagner-Peyser Act on June 6, 1933, inaugurated a Federal-State system of public employment offices. These offices are not to be confused with relief agencies. They have as their work the selection and recommendation of unemployed people who are qualified for available positions.

The National Reemployment Service established a local office in Dublin on December 1, 1933, to serve Laurens County for four months, with Aubrin U. Hogan, Dexter, appointed manager. At the end of that time Wheeler, Treutlen, Bleckley, Dodge, Washington, Johnson, and Wilkinson counties were added. After a year's time, Montgomery, Telfair, and Emanuel counties were also added. The Dublin office served these eleven counties until August, 1938.

At this time, the State of Georgia was able to meet the requirements imposed by the Federal Government, and the National Reemployment Service became the Georgia State Employment Service, affiliated with the United States Employment Service. With the establishment of additional local employment offices, Toombs, Washington, Wilkinson, and Emanuel counties were transferred to more convenient offices.

Since January 1, 1939, when benefits became payable by the Georgia Unemployment Compensation Act, the Georgia State Employment Offices have, together with their work of "matching men and jobs," handled these unemployment compensation claims for persons out of work.

Personnel of the Dublin office are: A. U. Hogan, manager, Miss Winnelle Wilkinson, W. S. Calloway, Miss Margaret Thompson, and Paul Ward.

7. THE LAURENS COUNTY WELFARE DEPARTMENT.

The Laurens County Welfare Department was created in July, 1937. The five Welfare Board members, appointed by the County Commissioners, were: Dr. J. E. New, Dexter; H. M. Currie, Route 1, Alamo; J. W. Geeslin, Dublin; N. P. Metts, Route 4, Dublin, and

John D. Smith, Rockledge. This Board has remained intact, with the exception of the resignation of John D. Smith and the appointment of Ellis Wilkes, Rockledge, as his successor.

In July, 1937, the Welfare Board appointed Miss Essie Mae Cobb as Director of the County Department, which position she still holds. As the case load increased additional personnel was employed and the Director is now assisted by three investigators, Mrs. Sara Jo Powell, Miss Frances Lanier, Miss Virginia Graves, and two secretaries, consisting of Mrs. Mattilu Burch Brown and Mrs. Christine S. Tingle.

The primary function of the Department is taking and investigating applications for old age assistance, blind assistance, and aid to dependent children. In addition, applications for other types of assistance, such as WPA, CCC, Surplus Commodities, Crippled Children's treatment and free cancer treatment, are taken.

One of the first steps of the Department was the abolition of the County Almshouse and the placement of its inmates in the homes of relatives. This afforded a substantial saving to the county and at the same time gave a more desirable home life to the inmates.

Since the inauguration of the Welfare Program there have been 7,000 families in Laurens County who have applied for assistance.

—*By Essie Mae Cobb.*

8. FARM SECURITY ADMINISTRATION.

In 1934, under the Emergency Relief Administration, the Georgia Rural Rehabilitation Corporation set up a program to help farmers help themselves by lending them money to buy livestock and farming equipment, fertilizer and other necessities for carrying on a farming program. A Farm Plan was worked out with the borrower by the supervisor in each case. This program has been known since 1937 as the Farm Security Administration.

Since it was about July, 1934, when the Georgia Rural Rehabilitation Corporation was set up, the balance of the year was spent in selecting suitable farms and the type of families needed, or families who needed assistance most. This work was done by the Relief Administration, under the supervision of a County Administrator.

In 1935, Laurens County assisted 56 families on this program. Ed Rivers, whose home is Louisville, Georgia, was engaged as Farm Supervisor. Miss Opal Jordan was in his office as clerk. Mrs. Reba B. Page was Supervising Aide at that time. In November, 1935, Ed Rivers resigned and H. L. Cordell was transferred from Jessup, Wayne County, Georgia, to Laurens County, as Rural Rehabilitation Supervisor.

In January, 1936, Miss Audrey Morgan was sent here as Home Supervisor. On February 1, 1936, Richard McDonald was sent as Assistant Supervisor. At that time the FSA office in Dublin worked

Treutlen, Johnson, and Laurens counties. During 1936 Laurens County made about 70 loans to people who were unable to secure credit from any other source.

In 1937, about 90 loans were made in Laurens County. In the fall of 1938, demand for this type of loan was so great that the State Office increased the personnel. Given below is the personnel who worked from this office in 1939: Thomas N. Balkcom, Grady B. Crowe, Wesley W. Moore and William J. Roberts worked as Assistant Rural Rehabilitation Supervisors; Miss Lucia B. Monroe and Miss Velma L. Dunaway were employed as Home Management Supervisors; Misses Evelyn C. James, Mary C. Smith, and Lucia F. Stephens were clerks.

With this increase in personnel, the FSA program was extended in 1939 to take care of 419 borrowers. Under the Bankhead-Jones Act, Laurens County made nine tenant purchase loans, which give the farmers selected by the County Advisory Committee 40 years to make equal payment on their farms after the Government has purchased them. These payments are about the same as a normal rental.

The personnel working from this office in 1941 is as follows: Thomas N. Balkcom, Rural Rehabilitation Supervisor; William J. Roberts, Rural Rehabilitation Supervisor; Howard L. Cordell, Unit Supervisor in Charge; Ray Bell, Bruce H. Moore and Lucius T. Bacote, Assistant Supervisors. Mrs. Frances S. King, Miss Velma L. Dunaway, Mrs. Elvie M. Johnson, and Dannie M. Denson are Home Management Supervisors. Misses Mary C. Smith, Sara F. Brookins and Emma C. Chavous worked as clerks. Dannie M. Denson and Lucius T. Bacote are negro supervisors, working with negro clients in the Buckeye community.

During the time the Farm Security program has been in effect in Laurens County, 40 farms have been bought through the Tenant Security Program and the Bankhead-Jones Act. Both of these programs are administered through the Farm Security office.

For the past two years, Farm Security Administration has extended help to the very lowest income families of the county to the amount of approximately $250,000.00 each year.

—*By Howard L. Cordell.*

9. LOCAL SELECTIVE SERVICE BOARDS.

During the year 1940, the second World War was raging in Europe and country after country was forced into the conflict in an effort to protect their freedom and democracy. It became apparent to the people of this country that the United States should increase her armed forces and, in other ways, provide for National Defense. This came to be considered as an emergency, both as to training additional men for the armed forces as well as increased production of all materials and supplies that would be needed in the event of war.

Therefore, the 76th Congress passed the Selective Service and Training Act of 1940, which was approved on September 16, 1940, and, as a result, President Roosevelt declared October 16, 1940, Registration Day, on which day every male between the ages of 21 and 35 was required to register for selective service training for one year.

To administer the selection of registrants for one year's training under this law local boards, advisory boards, medical examiners and appeal agents were appointed by the Governor for each county.

Two local boards were appointed for Laurens County, each board having jurisdiction over approximately 2,050 registrants. The offices of both boards are now (1941) located in the Federal Building, Dublin, Georgia.

a. Local Board No. 1.

The following members were appointed to serve this board: Carl K. Nelson, Chairman; Will Avery and George Foster.

Examining Physicians appointed for this board were: Doctors A. T. Coleman, H. G. McMahon, and R. G. Ferrell.

Harry L. Taylor, attorney, was appointed Appeal Agent.

Clerks serving this board are I. F. Maddox and Miss Mae Allen Jordan.

b. Local Board No. 2.

The following members were appointed to serve this board: Lewis K. Smith, Chairman; Joel A. Coleman, and H. D. Joiner.

Examining Physicians appointed for this board were: Doctors E. B. Claxton, O. H. Cheek, C. G. Moye, G. R. Lee, and Wm. C. Thompson.

C. C. Crockett, attorney, was appointed Appeal Agent.

Clerks serving this board are: Walter Daniell and Mrs. A. A. Coleman.

The first call for trainees was issued December 4, 1940, and through April 8, 1941, 55 white and 25 colored boys have been sent to induction stations for military training from this county, approximately 90 per cent of this number being volunteers.

c. Advisory Board.

The following men were appointed as advisors to assist registrants in filling out their selective service questionnaires: G. B. Parrott, E. F. Moxley, L. D. Woods, C. D. Devereaux, O. B. Overstreet, and M. S. Mullis.

Although the duties of board members, examining physicians, appeal agents and advisory board members require a great deal of their time and efforts, these patriotic citizens are serving their government in this capacity without compensation.

—*By Walter Daniell.*

CHAPTER XIII

INDIAN TRAILS, ROADS AND HIGHWAYS

Because of its location, the part of Georgia now known as Laurens County seems to have been a popular habitation of the Indians, for many Indian trails passed through the County.

"At the time DeSoto landed in Florida, there was an Indian trail from what is now St. Augustine, Florida, to a point in Georgia near the present site of the city of Hazlehurst in Jeff Davis County. There it intersected another Indian trail called the 'Tallahassee Trail,' which came from a point on the Gulf of Mexico, crossed the Altamaha River a short distance below the junction of the Oconee and Ocmulgee, and extended to a capital of the Indian Nation called Yamacraw, on the banks of the Savannah River where the city of Savannah now stands.

"On the north side of the Altamaha River this (the Tallahassee) trail intersected another trail running parallel to the Altamaha River and Oconee River. This trail extended from the mouth of the Altamaha River where Darien now stands, to a point of land which now belongs to J. B. Hicks of Dublin. From there this trail extended up through Morgan County, through Athens and into Nacoochee Valley, which is famous for Indian legends, mounds, etc., as well as for its natural beauty and fertile soil.

"Another trail extended from Yamacraw along what later became known as the old Savannah Road, extending from Yamacraw in a northwesternly direction and crossing the river at what is now Dublin, Georgia, and extending to Indian Springs, a health resort of the Indian tribes. From Indian Springs this trail extended to the capital of the Cherokee Nation at a point about twenty miles northeast of Rome, Georgia." (From a sketch written by Hon. Tom Linder).

INDIAN TRAILS, OLD ROADS, HIGHWAYS.

The Lower Uchee Trail lead from the Ogeechee River to the Oconee; crossing the river at Carr's Bluff, it passed on, crossed Turkey Creek, passed through what is now Cochran, on to Hawkinsville (then an Indian trading post) and crossed the Ocmulgee at that point. It was named for Uchee Tustenaggie who was the chief of the Uchee Indians in the last years of the eighteenth century and first quarter of the nineteenth. (Davidson's History of Wilkinson County).

The Jameson Trail led from Carr's Bluff westward. Lower on

the Oconee, Indians crossed at what is now Dublin, which was known as Jenc's Ferry. (Davidson).

An ald Uchee Trail led from Uchee Town (situated southwest of what is now Columbus) to the southeastern coast and crossed the southeastern part of what is now Laurens County. It was used as a part of the boundary line between Laurens and Montgomery counties. (Mrs. J. L. Walker, Waycross).

The Sunbury Trail passed through what is now Dublin and connected old Sunbury, in the southeastern part of Liberty County, with Louisville, when Louisville was the State Capital.

The first stagecoach line to run through Laurens County united Savannah with Louisville and passed through Sumpterville, the first county seat, which was used as a relay station. These old stage coaches could carry ten or twelve persons and were drawn by four horses. An old hitching post, claimed to have been used at this time, still stands at the site of Sumpterville.

In the second decade of the nineteenth century, the building of turnpike roads was begun, and stage coaches were put in operation to carry mail and passengers.

An Act was passed by the General Assembly of Georgia in 1818, providing that "John Coats and his heirs, for the term of ten years, have the sole and exclusive right of running a line of stage carriages between the towns of Darien and Milledgeville by way of Dublin." It also provided that "any person who presumes to run any stage or carriage in any manner for fare or hire between these two towns, other than John Coats, and without his consent, shall pay to John Coats the sum of $20.00 for every passenger carried."

John Coats was a Laurens County man and quite able to buy horses, coaches, and hire drivers.

An old Indian trail was followed by David Blackshear in making a road from Blackshear's Ferry on the Oconee, near his old home, Springfield, to old Hartford, now Hawkinsville. This is still used and is known as the Blackshear Trail. It passes through the settlement known as Elmwood.

The Darien and Milledgevile Road entered Laurens from the southeast, crossed Mercer's Creek, followed a northerly course past the Tweed community and Valdosta, the old home of Governor Troup, across Shaddock's Creek, over the W. & T. Railroad near old Condor, crossing Big Creek, Kellam's Mill Creek and Buckeye Creek into Johnson County, partially following the old Sunbury Trail. Over this road stage coaches operated from Milledgeville to Darien and Savannah. It followed, for the most part, the old Indian Trail from St. Augustine, Florida, upward through North Georgia.

The Old Savannah Road entered Laurens from Emanuel County at Pine Stump corner, running a northwesterly direction across Pugh's Creek, on across branches of Shaddock's Creek, running into the Old Darien and Louisville Road, crossing the W. & T. Railroad and joining the old Snell's Bridge Road. Through heavy sand beds, it led down to the Oconee River, and crossed the Dublin Ferry.

The old Louisville Road entered from Johnson County, passed Blackshear's Mill, crossed the Oconee at Blackshear's Ferry, and ran southwesterly to Dublin. This road partially followed the old Indian Trail running from South Carolina to Alabama.

The Sandersville Road entered the northeastern part of the county, intersected the Buckeye Road at Tucker's Crossroads, passed Marvin Church and entered the Darien Road.

The Dublin and Wrightsville Road entered Laurens County near Boiling Springs, crossed Hightower Creek, a branch of Big Creek, not far from the county line, and on into Dublin by the Old Savannah Road.

Snell's Bridge road entered from the east, passed through the Lem Keen lands, and ran into the Wrightsville road that leads through Lovett.

All these old roads, except the Blackshear Trail, were on the east side of the Oconee.

The most famous road on the west is the Old Chicken Road. It entered from Pulaski County, now Bleckley, passed through the Buckhorn community, crossing Big and Little Rocky creeks, entering what is now the Macon and Savannah Highway at Turkey Creek bridge. There are various theories as to why it is called the Chicken Road; the most far fetched is that it was, in years past, a trail of the Chickasaw Indians; the most probable is that it was a market road leading to old Hartford, over which peddlers carried their wares and exchanged them for poultry.

Many towns no larger than Dublin had paved roads in the 1920's, and by the latter part of that decade the Highway Board began paving the road from Macon to Dublin; a few years later the paving was carried on to Savannah. This is now Federal Route 80, also State Highway 26.

The next paving was between Dublin and Wrightsville and is a part of State Highway 15. This has been marked by the D. A. R. Society as part of the Nancy Hart Highway. This is also a part of the Jeff Davis Highway.

State Route 29 is paved from Dublin to Milledgeville, by way of Irwinton. It is a part of the Wilson Memorial Highway.

State Highway No. 31 is now paved, and connects Dublin and McRae.

Paving has also been finished on State Highway 29, connecting Dublin with Vidalia, by way of Soperton.

A farm-to-market road between Dublin and Dexter has been paved.

Paving is now (1941) under way on State Highway 15, connecting Dublin and Glenwood.

A farm-to-market highway is under construction, supplying a paved road between Dexter and Dudley.

Paving on State Highway 117 is completed between Dublin and Rentz; this is the Dublin-Eastman Road.

CHAPTER XIV

LAURENS COUNTY CHURCHES

The first denominations to establish churches in this section were the Baptist and Methodist, and till this day these denominations lead in numbers. There were a few members of these churches in this territory before the County was created.

The father of the Baptist Church in Georgia was Daniel Marshall; the founders of the Methodist Church were Thomas Humphries and John Major. These pioneer preachers came to this locality in the last quarter of the Eighteenth Century. Suffering hardships of every kind, their zeal was unabated. The first preachers who came to this territory made their way on foot from one pioneer cabin to another, holding services in the homes. The first pastors went on foot or horseback; for the most part they were unmarried men, for the life they were forced to lead was too strenuous to be shared by a wife. The following is typical of the experience of early preachers in our section:

"My circuit abounded with rivers and creeks which in winter overflowed their banks but never prevented the punctual fulfillment of my appointments. Sometimes they were swum on the back of my faithful 'Darby,' at other times crossed in a dug-out. Women and children would walk for miles with shoes and stockings in hand in very wet weather, putting them on before arriving at the church. Having lived mostly in the cities, the habits of my parish in the wire-grass region were rather novel to me. The whole family was often quartered in one room, but a more kind and courteous people I never saw. Some of my congregations were made up of the most wealthy and cultivated people in the State. My work included twenty-eight appointments, so that I had but little time or opportunity for pastoral visiting and rest. My health, not very robust in early life, by horseback exercise, eating sugar cane, and sleeping in well-ventilated houses, lighted and warmed by pine knots, astonishingly improved under my arduous labors." (Experience of a Methodist Preacher, J. Knowles, in "History of Methodism" by G. C. Smith.)

1. BAPTIST CHURCHES.

POPLAR SPRINGS BAPTIST CHURCH

Poplar Springs Church is the oldest Baptist Church in Laurens County. In the early records we find no reference to correspondence with Laurens County churches, but we do find record of correspondence with churches in Bibb, Washington, Burke, Pulaski, and Wilkin-

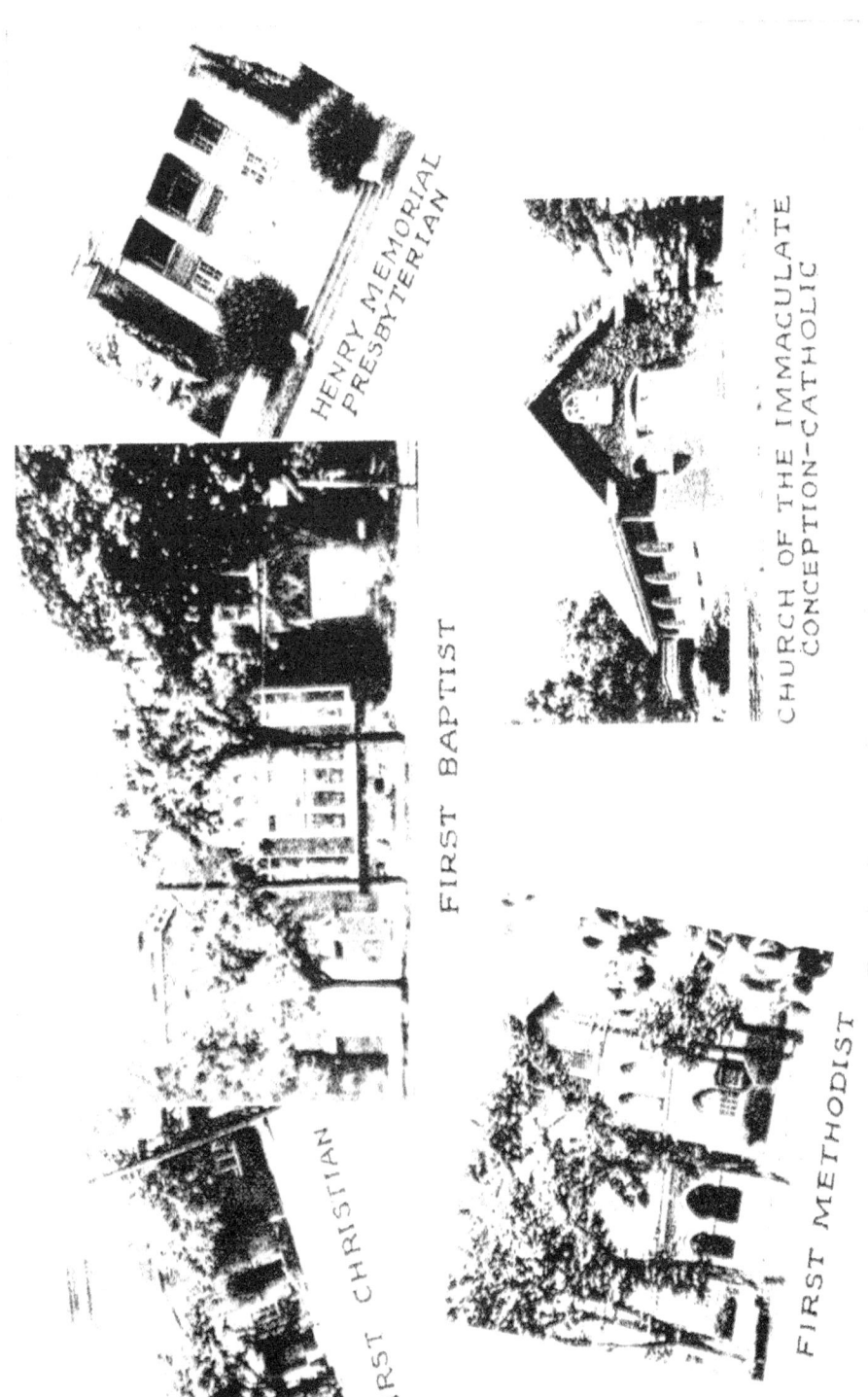

A GROUP OF DUBLIN CHURCHES

son counties. This church has an unbroken records since its constitution, August 1, 1807. The old minutes were well kept and are perfectly legible. They are indeed a treasure-house of information as to local conditions, as well as Baptist usage of that period.

At the time the church was constituted Laurens County had not been formed, and the church was in Wilkinson County. The presbytery consisted of Charles Culpepper, Isaiah Shirley, and Charnic Tharpe. The first conference was held August 22, 1807, with John Albriton as Moderator. The Clerk is not named but the first minutes were doubtless recorded by Amos Love, who never added his name to minutes, for the records show that he was Clerk until 1833. At that time Hardy B. Stanley became Clerk.

In almost every instance before the church went into the call of a pastor, the whole church would observe a day of fasting and prayer "for guidance in this important step." One set of minutes records a resolution saying: "We do hereby set apart Friday before our next conference as a day of fasting and prayer, that the Lord will direct our minds to a pastor."

In the early days, members were being received into the church at almost every conference by letter from Buckhead Church in Burke County, or from Deer Creek Church in Pulaski County, or from a church of similar faith in Washington County.

Church discipline was rigidly but kindly enforced in the early days of the church. From its beginning, slaves were admitted into the membership of the church and were baptized by the same minister in the same pool as the whites. Occasionally a slave-owner would be disciplined by the church for cruelty to slaves. The colored people continued their membership in the church for quite a while after freedom. In the year 1873, they withdrew and constituted churches of their own with the aid of the whites. Two colored churches were constituted largely by members from Poplar Springs, namely, Spring Hill and Sandy Ford. Before freedom there were as many colored members as whites—probably more. They had to be disciplined regularly, but the church seems to have been kind in its dealing. A good portion of the old minutes is taken up with discipline—much of it with slaves.

So far as can be gathered from the records, there have been only three houses of worship. The first, tradition says, was a log house which was used until 1830, when the second was built. This building was never heated, yet they had long-drawn-out preaching services, winter and summer, and seem to have good crowds. The second building was a frame structure, unceiled but well built. There was no meeting or conference in November, 1864, "on account of excitement occasioned by the passing through the county of Sherman's army."

The present house of worship was begun in 1886. The work was done largely by the membership of the church, several of whom were experienced carpenters. The floor was laid and sash and doors put in in 1889. They began holding service at once in the new house. The first service was held in July, 1889. The house was ceiled in January-February, 1891. The pews were built in January, 1894. The present baptistry at the spring was built in 1895. The old pews were given to the colored church at Spring Hill and are still in use.

The new house was never publicly dedicated until it was remodeled and painted. The dedication service and home-coming were held on August 1, 1923—the 116th anniversary of the church. The centennial anniversary of the church was celebrated on August 1, 1907. Invitations were sent to all former members and former pastors. They came from far and near. The crowd was conservatively estimated at 2,500 people. It was an all-day meeting with "dinner on the ground." Rev. A. B. Campbell, one of the noted Baptist ministers of Georgia, preached the centennial sermon. Rev. S. F. Sims was pastor at that time and made an address in the afternoon. It was truly a great day in the church's history.

Though 126 years old, Poplar Springs church is still active and is a light-house on the sea of life to those in its territory.

Poplar Springs church is the mother-church among Baptist churches in Laurens County. Dublin, Oconee, Bethsaida, Marie, and Centerville churches were largely constituted by members carrying letters from Poplar Springs. We cannot close this sketch without mentioning Rev. W. S. Ramsay, who was identified with the church as its pastor longer than any other minister. He served the church faithfully as pastor for twenty-six years, and was still pastor at the time of his death in 1900.

This church has licensed many preachers who have served churches in Laurens and neighboring counties; at times her own sons returned to her as pastors. This was true of William Baker.

The slaves constituted a large percentage of members; at the beginning of the War Between the States, there was a colored enrollment of about two hundred. Sometimes there were slave members whose owners were not members. Dr. Nathan Tucker's slaves were members, and the largest number of slaves belonging to one estate were the slaves of Governor Troup's married daughter, Florida Bryant. Other large slave owners who were members of the church were: Robert Coats, John G. Coats, James Blackshear, the Coneys, Ira Stanley, the O'Neals, Yopps, Ashleys, Ellingtons, W. A. Knight, John Thomas, and James Lock.

—By *Emma Hobbs Fordham (Mrs. J. B.)*

BETHLEHEM BAPTIST CHURCH

Bethlehem Baptist Church is the second oldest church in the County now active. The following sketch of its history was written by Mrs. L. B. Linder and read by her at the dedication of the present building in 1920. Mrs. Linder is still the most active member of the church, a leader of the Missionary Society, and a teacher of the Sunday School. She has been a member at Bethlehem since Reconstruction Days.

"Bethlehem Church was constructed at the Fork Road Meeting House, four miles from Dublin, on the river road leading from Milledgeville to Darien. There were thirteen members, eleven whites and two colored, all dismissed from Buckeye Baptist Church for the purpose of constituting a Baptist Church at the Fork Road Meeting Place, to be called 'Bethlehem.'

On the fourteenth day of July, 1821, those thirteen members were organized to constitute a regular Baptist Church, Brethren John Whittle, Benjamin Manning, and Levi Bush acting as presbytery.

In the year 1882, Solomon Williams made the church a deed to three acres of land at Holmes Cross Roads, and the church was moved to its present site.

The settlement went to work to build a house; the contract was let to Young Keen, a deacon of the church. A small log house was built at a cost of sixty-nine dollars; some still remember the high pulpit which scarcely showed the preacher's head when he was seated.

The first pastor was the Reverend John Whittle. The first clerk was George Daniel, who served for eighteen years. The first deacon was James Kinchen.

The church held monthly meetings, and as time went by this little church in the wildwood gained in membership, but who knows the obstacles that beset this band of faithful followers of the Lord when the spirit of anti-missionary was strong, education at a low plain, and intemperance rife in the land!

The country was sparsely settled, many had to ride for miles, braving cold and storm; but they came on horseback, in carts, and in other rude vehicles, even buggies were scarcely known. Some walked perhaps for miles.

A number of deacons were ordained, among them was Richard Graham, father of our present clerk, G. F. Graham; Lawrence Keen was made a deacon and was afterwards ordained to preach, which he did for long years.

Pastor after pastor served this church. The fourth pastor was the Reverend David Daniel, a man of deep piety and broad views of the Bible. It was he who gathered the children into the first Sunday School of the church. This was the first organized Sunday School of the county. Through his loyalty to Baptist principles and elevated aims, he lived to see his name placed among the eminent preachers of Georgia.

In 1872, the Reverend L. J. Harrison was called for the second time; he served for three years. Following him was the Reverend J. M. Donaldson, who served for six years.

Next came J. T. Smith who was licensed to preach and served the church for three years.

In 1885, the Reverend W. S. Ramsay was called to the pastorate and served till his death in 1900, serving the church for fifteen years.

Reverend Ramsay was a scholarly man, of high intellect and dignified mein, possessing a lovable personality. He resigned the charge of the First Baptist Church of Dublin in order to accept the call to this church, being urged by a number of members who felt that he would be a great help to Bethlehem. Words are inadequate to express the love and high esteem of the church for him.

During his pastorate the log house of worship was found inadequate to accommodate the large crowds, and it was decided to build a new church. In 1887, a large frame building was erected, costing $1,800. At this time a large and flourishing Sunday School was held each Sunday afternoon. An auxiliary to the church was organized—a Woman's Missionary and Aid Society. Its first meeting was held November 27, 1897, with seven members: Mrs. H. H. Martin, Mrs. Jane Keen, Mrs. Annie Brett, Mrs. Nannie Bell Linder, Miss Latha Graham. Mrs. L. B. Linder was elected president, and Mrs. L. H. Linder, secretary and treasurer.

The deacons, at this time, were Frank Fuller, for a long time Superintendent of the Sunday School, J. M. Guest, W. I. Taylor, Horace Jones, and Isaac Keen. These deacons were loyal to their trust and strong to defend the principles of the church.

In 1901, the Reverend O. O. Williams was called to the pastorate and served for five years. J. R. Kelly followed and served two years.

The church has ordained to the ministry these men: H. S. Scarboro, Charles Ricks, J. T. Smith, J. D. Smith, Charlton Smith, and Turner Smith.

Reverend W. E. Harville was the seventeenth pastor. His pastorate began March 5, 1915, after resigning from Shady Grove, where he had served for twenty years. From 1866 only two clerks have served: James Bush, who served for eleven years, and G. F. Graham, forty-two years.

In 1918, the church building was pronounced unsafe, and a new building was erected. The building has since been enlarged and six Sunday School rooms added. It maintains a Sunday School, Woman's Missionary Union, and a Baptist Training Union. The Rev. C. E. Vines is now (1941) pastor.

BLUE WATER BAPTIST CHURCH

On the old Telfair Road, near the banks of Turkey Creek, stands Blue Water, one of the oldest churches in the county. In 1938 her members observed their centennial anniversary, and the following sketch was read by Mrs. R. L. Dawkkins.

Twelve men and women met on Monday, April 9, 1828, and organized the Blue Water Baptist Church; four men—Davis Joiner, Marbar Hudson, John Woodard and Daniel McDaniel—and eight women—Elizabeth Joiner, Jane Sanders, Elizabeth Miles, Mary Hudson, Laura Ann Hudson, Dilion Grinstead, Polly Ann Warren, and Mary Woodard. They set as their first meeting day Saturday before the third Sunday, which was April 14, 1838.

Reverend L. B. Lee was called as the first pastor, and they elected two deacons: Davis Joiner and John Woodard.

The first church building was a small log structure located near Blue Water Creek.

In this same year correspondence was opened with Rocky Creek and the Dublin Church. The records show that they continued to receive and appoint correspondents with sister churches until recent years.

Reverend Lee served as pastor for two years; at the close of his ministry, forty-seven members had been added to the church, making a total of fifty-nine.

Records show that members were received by experience at almost every meeting. In February, 1840, Lucindy, a colored woman, was received by experience; she was the first negro member.

The Reverend Larry Hobbs was called in 1840 and served seven years. In 1845 Davis Joiner was ordained by this church; he was called to be the pastor and served six months. An arm of the church was extended to the young church of Rock Springs in 1848; in 1885, an arm of the church was extended to Bay Creek.

In 1865, the church ordained B. A. Bacon who was called to be pastor at New Hope.

The Reverend W. J. Baker was the pastor during the dark war days; he served the church for fifteen years.

In 1867, the colored membership had increased to forty-one members; the church then gave them the privilege of electing their own officers. Three years later they were granted letters that they might organize their own church.

The records show that in 1874 W. M. Williamson was licensed to preach, and in that year appears the first record of the organization of a Sabbath School; but there must have been one before that time, for in an associational letter there is a reference to "two Sabbath Schools in healthy condition."

In 1875, the church called one of its sons for pastor, the Reverend W. M. Williamson, who served for a year, then became missionary for the Ebenezer Association. Other pastors of this church were J. L. Pharis and N. E. Joiner.

The records fail to show how long the first building was used, but the second church was located near the present site. It also was a log building. The funds were raised during the ministry of Reverend Green, and the building was completed in October, 1881. Reverend Green passed away in 1937, at the age of ninety-two.

In 1884, Reverend J. T. Smith came to the church and served for five years.

In 1888, the church decided to have services twice a month; Reverend Smith was called for the third Sunday, and Reverend M. A. Currie for the first Sunday. In this year, the church donated the old seats to the colored church, Robinson's Chapel. In 1891, a committee was sent to Big Sandy Church in Wilkinson County to organize a Sunday School convention. In 1892, there occurs the first mention of a public offering being taken at the service. In 1901, T. M. Tamlinson was licensed to preach.

Nineteen hundred two was a memorable year—the first organ was bought; in July a revival was held that resulted in the reception of forty-three members; correspondence was opened with Marie Church; the church went to half-time with a salary of $152.00.

In 1907, the church was painted and an annex built. In 1915, the Spring Hill Sunday School was made an arm of the church.

In 1918, the initial movement for a new building was made by the pastor, Reverend T. E. Toole; and it is largely due to his interest and generosity that the present handsome church became a reality. The building was completed and the first service held in the new church, March 19, 1922. The next year Reverend Toole resigned and was followed by C. W. Pope.

The church, on March 7, 1926, licensed Cecil Daniel to preach; since that time he has studied at Mercer University and at the Southern Baptist Seminary; he has served several churches in this County and is now serving a church in Atlanta.

In its first century, the church has been served by thirty-two pastors. Reverend Vergil Vickers, the present pastor, came in September, 1937. The church has ordained seven men to the ministry. At the present time there are three hundred members, a good Sunday School, a B. Y. P. U., a Woman's Missionary Union, and a board of six deacons, consisting of E. A. Joiner, J. J. Joiner, R. E. Brown, E. D. Barron, J. L. Brown, and A. L. Currie.

FIRST BAPTIST CHURCH OF DUBLIN

The minutes of the Poplar Springs Church, under date of the February meeting of 1831, record the fact that brethren from Dublin asked the help of this church in the organization of a church at Dublin. The official deed book records the sale of one acre of land by Jeremiah Yopp to Bolin Hobbs and John Woodard, deacons of the Dublin Baptist Church. The consideration was ten cents, the date, February 9, 1831.

On this acre of land was erected the first Baptist Church in Dublin. The first pastor was the Reverend Buchanan; Jordan Baker was the second. James Williamson came next, his broad Scotch brogue attracting the interest of the most unconcerned listener. The third was a young preacher destined to write his name among Georgia's famous preachers, David G. Daniell. Other pastors of the early period were: Larry Hobbs, Bolin Hobbs, L. B. Lee, W. J. Baker —son of Jordan Baker—and W. D. Horn. The earliest clerks were Bolin Hobbs and Elijah Benton. At that day a church had but two deacons, and they served for life. The first deacons were Bolin Hobbs and John Woodard, followed by F. C. Hightower and Nunan Scarborough.

During the ante-bellum period the church was very small, the largest portion of the membership were women. At no time were there more than twenty voters, and from 1850 to 1860 not more than fifteen.

The first building was a small unpainted house, the interior as plain as the rude exterior; unceiled walls and overhead; wooden benches, often of puncheon, sawed out by hand; the pulpit, a high-up, close, boxed thing; a little window just over the preacher's head, which could hardly be seen when he was sitting. This was used until a much larger building was constructed in 1867.

With the new building new life came into the church. The Sunday School soon became self-sustaining and ran the year round; the Saturday meeting and monthly conference remained a custom for many years.

Prominent members during the War period were J. J. Rivers, R. A. Stanley, Wright Stanley. Capt. R. A. Stanley was the beloved Superintendent of the Sunday School for many years. Wright Stanley was clerk and contractor of the new church building. The Reverend E. B. Barrett was pastor from 1865 till 1869. He was a young man full of vigor, a recent graduate of Mercer University. He was an earnest and deeply spiritual man. His eloquence drew large congregations and he was held in love and high esteem by all who came his way. The Reverend Barrett was followed by the Reverend W. L. Geiger, who held the pastorate for several years. Under his preaching W. S. Ramsay was converted, being ordained to the ministry in 1870, in the Dublin Baptist Church. He became its pastor and served till 1891.

The second building served the church as a house of worship for forty years, an annex being added during this time to accommodate the growing congregation. It was during the pastorate of the Reverend Millard A. Jenkins that the present building was begun, and during the incumbency of the Reverend Allen Fort that it was completed. This imposing edifice follows the Gothic type are architecture. It was modeled after Melrose Abbey, of Scotland.

The church has been served by these pastors: Dr. Buchanan, James

Williamson, David G. Daniel, Larry Hobbs, Bolin Hobbs, L. B. Lee, W. G. Baker, W. D. Horn, E. B. Barrett, W. L. Geiger, W. S. Ramsey (the longest pastorate), W. N. Hurst, J. Ware Brown, E. W. Marshall, J. C. Solomon, R. E. Neighbor, Millard A. Jenkins, Allen Fort, W. A. Talliaferro, T. W. Callaway, R. L. Baker, C. D. Graves, and Grover Tyner.

Noteworthy for length of scholarly service are two pastors of the First Baptist Church—Colonel Whiteford S. Ramsay and Dr. Clarence D. Graves—both, powerful factors in the spiritual, intellectual and physical well-being of this community. Colonel Ramsay, a graduate of old Oglethorpe University, with post-graduate work at Princeton, served the church for twenty-two years during the last decades of the Nineteenth Century. Clarence D. Graves, D.D., graduate of Wake Forest College and of the Southern Baptist Seminary, held the pastorate for twenty years, from January, 1921, to January, 1941.

A large group of deacons and associate deacons is now (1941) headed by the senior deacon, B. F. Cochran.

This First Baptist Church became the mother of other churches in Dublin. In 1902, the West Dublin Baptist Church was built. This was a mission church for the Dublin Cotton Mills District. In 1919, a second Baptist Church was organized in Dublin by members of the First Church; this is the Jefferson Street Baptist Church.

The Woman's Missionary Society of this church was organized in August, 1887, with these charter members: Mrs. Thomas Rowe, Mrs. Mercer Haynes, Mrs. A. A. Cowart, Mrs. M. E. Martin, Mrs. J. B. Wolfe, Mrs. G. W. Belcher, Mrs. W. W. Robinson, Miss Mattie Ramsay. The organization was first called the Woman's Aid Society. In 1908, the Society was divided into five circles, which have grown to eight.

Presidents who have served since organization have been: Mrs. Thomas Rowe, Mrs. Mercer Haynes, Mrs. J. W. Walker, Mrs. W. W. Robinson, Mrs. J. R. Hightower, Mrs. J. A. Carswell, Mrs. W. E. Harville, Mrs. W. C. Floyd, Mrs. J. C. Pittman, Mrs. G. H. Williams, Mrs. Freeman Rowe, Mrs. Vernon Charous, Mrs. I. S. Chappell, Mrs. B. F. Cochran, Mrs. R. C. Coleman, Mrs. J. F. Hart, Mrs. Carl Nelson, Mrs. A. J. Hargrove, Mrs. Guy V. Cochran, Mrs. R. C. Garrard, Mrs. Milo Smith.

BETHESDA BAPTIST CHURCH

In Pinetucky District, on the Scotland Road, stands Bethesda Church, a large white-painted frame building; this is the fourth house that has been erected.

The church was organized in 1838 and a log house was built on the McDaniel place in the Browning settlement; the next house was a frame building on the Dixon place near the spring, built about

1880. This was burned, but rebuilt in 1888. In 1892, the chucrh was moved and the building on the present site erected.

The first pastor was Reverend Tolbert Kinchin; another beloved pastor was Reverend W. E. Harville.

The present pastor is the Reverend H. L. Maddox; there are about 140 members, and an active Sunday School of about sixty members.

New Hope Baptist Church

One of the oldest churches in Laurens County is New Hope, in the Burch District. Records have been lost, but it is known to have been in existence as far back as the 1830's. There is a record on the minutes of the Ebenezer Association of Wilkinson County that this body was entertained by the New Hope Church in 1839.

In the years when the practice of foreign missions was growing in Georgia this church suffered a division; those opposed to missions withdrew and established a church elsewhere, taking the name Primitive Baptist; those favoring missions remained at New Hope as Missionary Baptists.

One of the old and prominent members of this church was Alfred Burch, who was rich in sons and daughters and ranging herds of cows and sheep; he and his sons were the sustaining members of the church for many years. Two long-term and beloved pastors were the Reverend Frank Gay and John T. Rogers. (Information from Clayton Burch).

Centerville Baptist Church

In 1846 there is a reference on the minutes of old Poplar Springs Church that "an arm of aid was extended to Centerville school house" but there is no record of the constitution of a church till 1903. The church building stands in a grove of trees, on the Centerville Road, in the Bailey's District.

Rock Springs Baptist Church

The Rock Springs Baptist Church was organized in 1848 with ten members. Assisting in the presbytery were D. Joiner from Blue Water Church, and Reverend Lee. The first two houses were built of logs, but the present church is a large frame building.

The first pastor was the Reverend L. B. Lee and the first clerk was Hiram Kinchin.

Pastors during the ante-bellum, war and Reconstruction periods were: L. B. Lee, D. Joiner, Bolin Hobbs, William Baker, Killiam Windham, J. T. Kinchin, Larry Hobbs, D. J. Thompson, W. M. Williamson.

A custom of the church is to have an annual Homecoming Day. This day has been celebrated on a Sunday in August since 1915.

Mount Carmel Baptist Church

In March, 1857, the Mount Carmel Baptist Church was constituted. The covenant was signed by fifteen members, one of whom was a colored woman. They are as follows:

Hardy Allagood, James M. Shepard, James Hill, Berry Hobbs, James R. Witherington, R. T. Grimsley, Sealey, a woman of color; Nancy Witherington, Easter M. Grimsley, Sarah Allagood, Mary Ann Shepard, Susan C. Hill, Harriet Hobbs, Amanda Fountain, Sarah Grimsley.

At the next meeting, a month later, Hardy Allagood was chosen deacon, and James Shepard, clerk. In the May meeting, churches chosen for correspondence were: Rocky Creek, Blue Water, Laurens Hill and Poplar Springs. In the minutes of August, 1857, among the names of those added to the membership was "Gilbert, a black brother, the property of Francis Clark, by experience."

In August, 1857, the church agreed to attach itself to the Ebenezer Association, Wilkinson County, and at the same meeting "two brethren were appointed to lay plans for the accommodation of the Blacks."

Larry Hobbs served as the first pastor; so beloved was he that in September, 1858, he was called for life, or "so long as Church and Minister shall remain satisfied."

This church in conference, May, 1858, passed this resolution: "Resolved, That we take up the duty of feet-washing and that we commence that duty at our next communion season."

On the second Sunday in March the church established a "Sabbath School with a Bible Class attached to the same." In May, 1861, the church voted to establish a prayer meeting.

In November, 1861, the minutes reveal that the menace of war was in the land; Thursday, November 28, was appointed as a day for assembling at the church to observe a day of fasting and prayer. Excuses for absence from church attendance were entered on the minutes for—John Hobbs, William A. Witherington, and M. L. Allagood, "in the Confederate Army, until they return." The church met on March 7, 1862, in response to a national proclamation that "all Christian Churches join in a day of humiliation, fasting, and prayer." Before the volunteers from this district left for the War, the pastor preached to them. Letters were written by the church to the men in the army.

The Mount Carmel Church has been located on two sites. The first was near Dexter, where the old graveyard is located. Then a house, built at the present site, was blown down by a tornado. The present house was built in 1931; later a parsonage was built on the church grounds.

Shady Grove Baptist Church

Shady Grove Church was constituted in 1858, the Reverend Harrison being the first pastor. Two acres on Bruton Creek were obtained by the trustees for church and school purposes. In 1860, the first church, a log building, was completed. The church became a member of the Mount Vernon Association in October, 1859.

The first trustees for the church were Z. B. Keen, James S. Chipley, and Young B. Keen.

A Prayer Service was observed on November 15, 1861, to petition "the Lord to prosper our cause in the present struggle, bless our arms, and restore peace."

Reverend Harrison served six years. Then came one of the best beloved of all the pastors, the Reverend J. M. Donaldson.

The frame building, completed in 1900, was burned in 1910. The present building was then erected. In 1892, the church established a mission station at Ellington School house.

Among the pastors of the church are: the Reverend Louis Harrison, J. M. Donaldson, Joseph M. Smith, G. W. Smith, Joseph M. Wood, J. T. Smith, W. A. Harrison, H. T. Smith, W. R. Cox, E. W. Marshall, J. H. Oliver, T. E. Toole, and R. T. Baker. Reverend W. E. Harville was called to the church in 1896 and was the pastor for a score of years. The present pastor, Reverend R. W. Eubanks, has served twenty years.

OCONEE BAPTIST CHURCH

In Bailey's District, on the Toomsboro Road, stands an old Baptist Church. In the minutes of the Poplar Springs Church, 1869, is found a notation to the effect that J. I. C. Stanley, Jesse Metts and others were dismissed to establish a church at Mount Pleasant. The first preaching was done by John Dupree, a missionary. This church was known for several years as Oconee Church.

PLEASANT SPRINGS BAPTIST CHURCH

Pleasant Springs, a small church, on the old Savannah Road, was constituted in 1870, in the Johnson community, Oconee District.

The first building was located on the John A. Johnson place, near the Spring which gave it its name; the second house stands a half-mile from the original site on land given by Jim Johnson. Near by is the old graveyard where the head of the Johnson family, Israel Johnson, lies buried.

The first deacons were: Ben Graham and H. H. Wynn, Sr. Early clerks were: Sherman Johnson and E. Z. Young. Among the early pastors were: The Reverend Donaldson, Tom Windham, Dick Windham, Billy Harrison, and J. R. Harvey.

Baptism was administered in the old Johnson Mill Pond, an historic spot.

Among the pastors have been: the Reverend J. M. Donaldson, L. J. Harrison, J. W. Johnson, I. T. Chipley, J. A. Webb, M. Davis, G. W.

Smith, J. Z. Bush, G. R. Watson, J. R. Harvey, S. D. Walker, H. T. Smith, G. W. Smith, T. A. Smith, and W. W. Pierce.

This church entertained the Mount Vernon Association in 1879.

SNOW HILL BAPTIST CHURCH

Snow Hill Church was established in 1871. The first services were held in the log school house near the spot where the church now stands; then a log church was built; the third and present house was a frame building constructed by Bob Faircloth and John Baggett; some years later an annex was added. The leading spirit in the establishment of the church, and the first pastor, was Reverend Tolbert Kinchin, who taught school in the little log house. The first deacons were R. A. Bedingfield and John Grinstead. The ordinance of baptism was administered in the Kinchin Limesink. Bob Register served for many years as superintendent of the Sunday School. Among the long-term pastors were Reverend Tolbert Kinchin, Frank Gay, Jordan Hobbs, John Green, and David Green.

This church has, from time to time, divided its members and sent them out to Baker, Mount Zion, Rentz, Cadwell, and Pleasant Hill to organize churches.

BLUE SPRINGS BAPTIST CHURCH

Blue Springs Baptist Church, established in Reconstruction Days, 1875, is located in the Rockledge District. The building in use today was dedicated in 1897. The land on which the church stands was given by John Smith; the first pastor was L. J. Harrison. The church was organized through its leading spirit, the Reverend Jim White, with eleven members. Among the pastors were: the Reverend J. B. Windham, O. O. Williams, J. T. Jones, W. S. Brantley, W. A. Harrison, Joseph Tyson, J. Z. Bush, G. R. Watson, and J. R. Harvey.

MOUNT ZION BAPTIST CHURCH

Mount Zion Church was organized in 1876. The first congregation worshipped in the Willis School Building, near Turkey Creek. The present site was then obtained and a log house built farther from the road than the present building. The first pastor was the Reverend John T. Rogers. In 1934, an annex was built. Early pastors were: the Reverend C. B. Smith, J. W. Green, and Jordan Hobbs. Among the prominent early members were D. W. Thomas, J. W. Barron, and D. J. Thompson.

WHITE SPRINGS BAPTIST CHURCH

White Springs Church, located in the Lowery District off the Glenwood road, was organized in 1882. The church was organized under a brush arbor. The first church, a log building, was used for about fifteen years, then the present frame building was constructed.

The first pastor was C. R. Windham, and J. E. Walden was the first clerk.

Poplar Springs (South) Baptist Church

Poplar Springs South, so called to distinguish it from another Baptist Church of the same name, is located in Oconee District, on the Savannah road. It was established in 1886.

It was first built near the spring on the W. E. T. J. Harden place, but was torn down and removed to its present location in 1891. The first pastor was the Reverend J. F. Wynne.

Bethsaida Baptist Church

Bethsaida Baptist Church was organized July 7, 1888.

Presbytery: Rev. Charlton B. Smith, Rev. James T. Smith, Rev. John Dupree.

Charter members were:

A. J. Hilbun, Jerry Y. Lee, John W. Horn, John N. Brown, Samuel Charters, Henry M. Burch, John L. Pharis, John C. Register, Brancy B. Horn, Mary Etta Brown, Eliza R. Burch, Frances C. Pharis, Carrie A. Charters, Eliza Scarborough.

The first church was built in 1889 and remodeled in 1930. Pastors were:

1888—John A. Clark (First Pastor)	1914-17—T. J. Barnett
1894—J. Z. Bush	1917-18—J. C. Solomon
1894-98—D. E. Green	1918-20—Frank Cochran
1898—J. B. Brookshear	1920-23—C. W. Pope
1899-1903—Geo. W. Tharpe	1923-24—E. M. Palmer
1903-07—T. J. Holmes	1924-25—A. V. Pickron
1907-09—W. E. Harville	1925-26—J. G. Paige
1909-10—J. R. Lunsford	1926-31—E. A. Kilgore
1910—W. A. Taliaferro	1931-33—S. J. Baker
1910-12—R. O. Martin	Present Pastor—Kendall Everett
1912-14—F. B. Asbell	

New Bethel Church

New Bethel Church, located on the Dublin-Dexter Road, was established in 1895. The church now occupies its second house of worship, the first having been burned. Among the early members were the Lees and Edwards.

Among those who have served as pastors are Reverend W. R. Lanier and Reverend J. W. Parker.

Marie Baptist Church

During the summer of 1899 Reverend R. E. Neighbor came to Marie community and preached in a dilapidated, unceiled, unpainted school house to a group of needy, unorganized people. He would preach at the morning hour to his own flock, the Dublin First Church, being the pastor of that church. In the afternoon he would preach to the Marie group. If the little school house overflowed, he stood in the door and preached to those inside and out. During that same summer he took a tent, lights, and song books, from the First Baptist Church and conducted a revival for two or three weeks, preaching three times daily.

Reverend Neighbor was furnished a horse and buggy by his church to use in his rural work. At the close of the afternoon service he drove home to visit his sick members.

Converts were received into Dublin Church, during the tent meeting. At the close of that meeting, September 21, 1899, Marie Church was constituted with 27 charter members, some coming from Poplar Springs Church, and some from Dublin.

The first conference was held in the new building on October 14, 1899. No preacher was present. It was ready for services in less than a month after the organization. The first converts were baptized in Hunger and Hardship Creek, four miles away. Later a pool was built at M. S. Jones' home. A. J. Hobbs was the first church clerk, and J. T. Smith was the first pastor.

Before the church was organized, Sunday School, of a very crude type, was held in the school house.

On July 8, 1900, the first revival began and lasted fifteen days. Fifty people presented themselves for baptism. The Reverend R. E. Neighbor and W. L. Walker preached three times daily. The house was dedicated on October 21, 1901. During the first few years weekly prayer meetings were held. Later the service was omitted, still later it was revived. In the early history of the church delinquent members were disciplined.

Nine pastors have served this church: J. T. Smith, J. E. Duren, H. T. Smith, T. Bright, T. E. Toole, O. O. Williams, J. E. Townsend and Charles Maples.

The Sunday School was continued in the one-room building, doing poor work, failing to enlist many, until the Sunday School Board sent Reverend Tom Harville, Reverend E. A. Kilgore, and Reverend J. J. Brock to teach improved methods. Meanwhile, on September 28, 1924, Marie celebrated her 25th anniversary. Reverend Claude Coalson, of Wadley, preached the sermon. A congratulatory letter from Reverend Neighbor, the founder of the church, was read at that service.

On October 2, 1927, a committee was appointed to remodel the church. As a result, eight Sunday School rooms were provided. The interior was very much improved in appearance. Mr. J. J. Brock and Mr. George Andrews spoke on the occasion of the dedication of the rooms, May 13, 1928. Mr. Otto Daniel drew the plans for remodeling the building.

—By Emma Perry.

Olivet Baptist Church

Olivet Baptist Church, on the Glenwood-Dublin road, in the Dublin District, had its origin in a tent meeting, conducted by the Reverend Millard A. Jenkins. The house of worship was completed in 1903, a spacious annex being added later.

The first pastor was the Reverend B. G. Smith. The present pastor (1941) is the Reverend C. E. Vines, who has served for several years. The church maintains a Sunday School, a Woman's Missionary Union, and a Baptist Training School. Service is held twice a month.

Baker Church

The Baker Baptist Church was constituted in 1905; a church was built between the Rentz and Telfair roads in the Reedy Springs section.

Union Springs Baptist Church was constituted in 1905 in the Lowery District.

Pleasant Hill Baptist Church

Pleasant Hill Baptist Church, located five miles southeast of Cadwell, was constituted in the year 1912. Placed in a community where there was much need of a Baptist Church, it has made great progress.

Though small, originally, in building and membership, it has, through the courageous efforts of the faithful few, obtained a modern building, with an enrollment of 246 members. Pleasant Hill building is a wooden structure capable of seating 500 people, with Sunday School rooms to accommodate eight classes. It is provided with comfortable pews, a piano and an organ.

Pleasant Hill Church has a Sunday School averaging from 75 to 100 in attendance from an enrollment of 125. It is a graded Sunday School and uses the program laid out by the Southern Baptist Convention.

Commendable work has been done by the different B. Y. P. U. and mid-week Prayer Meetings. The Women's Missionary Union has served as important place in the church.

Pleasant Hill Church has been served by some of the most able ministers of this section of Georgia, namely, the Reverend T. J. Hobbs, George Coney, Eli W. Evans, W. W. Grant, Dr. J. C. Solomon, N. H. Burch, J. F. Jones, H. L. Avery, and C. H. Renfroe of Kite, Ga.

Oakdale Baptist Church was established in 1914.

Antioch Baptist Church

The Antioch Church is in the Hampton Mills District, in a quiet spot between the Rentz and Dexter roads. It was organized in 1916.

Services were held in the Wilkins School House until the present house was built. This house has been occupied since 1928. The Reverend C. D. Lowery has been a long-term pastor.

JEFFERSON STREET BAPTIST CHURCH (DUBLIN)

The Jefferson Street Baptist Church was organized October 12, 1919, with fifty charter members. The organization sermon was preached by Dr. R. L. Baker, pastor of the First Baptist Church. The first and only pastor is Reverend R. W. Eubanks, who has served for 22 years. The first deacons were: W. T. Dupree, R. M. Duggan, and J. R. Cherry.

Those serving as clerks have been: J. D. Hobbs, L. H. Holland, James Joiner, Dr. J. L. Smalley, J. H. Hobbs, W. B. Bryans. Serving as treasurer have been: J. R. Cherry, H. V. Joiner, E. J. Hudson, W. H. Hobbs; C. M. Chastain was first Sunday School superintendent.

The church still occupies the building in which it was organized, although several additions have been made. This building was purchased from the Presbyterians by the First Baptist Church of Dublin, which aided in organization and also presented the building.

Soon after the church was established, a Missionary Society was organized. This has grown into a Missionary Union with four circles and junior auxiliaries. The presidents of the society have been: Mrs. D. C. Shea, Mrs. Herschel Jenkins, Mrs. James Hobbs, Mrs. W. B. Smith, Mrs. L. R. Bright, Mrs. R. W. Eubankks and Mrs. R. L. Tindol.

BAPTIST ASSOCIATIONS

The first Baptist Church of Laurens County was organized in 1807. If it became a member of an Association for the first five years, it was probably the Ocmulgee Association in Wilkinson County.

The Ebenezer Association held its first meeting with the Cool Springs Church in the year 1813. The Laurens County churches that were members of this Association were: Poplar Springs, Blue Water, Rocky Creek, Laurens Hill, Oconee, Dublin, New Hope, Bethsaida, Dudley, Marie, and Centerville.

The Laurens County Association held its first meeting on November 30, 1911, convening with the Blue Water Church. W. E. Harville was elected Moderator and Judge W. A. Wood, of Dublin, the clerk. The introductory sermon was preached by the Reverend W. A. Taliaferro, pastor of the Dublin Church. Reverend W. E. Harville, who served for nineteen years as Moderator, preached the missionary sermon. J. H. Witherington was clerk for seventeen years. Since the death of Mr. Witherington, B. C. Keen has been clerk.

The Association is composed of five districts:

District 1: Bethlehem, Blue Springs, Brewton, Minter, Pleasant Springs, Shady Grove.

District 2: Bethsaida, Centerville, Dublin First, Jefferson Street, Marie, New Bethel, Poplar Springs North.

District 3: Antioch, Dexter, Dudley, Laurens Hill, Montrose, Mt. Carmel.

District 4: Baker, Cadwell, Mount Zion, New Hope, Oak Dale, Pleasant Hill, Rentz, Snow Hill.

District 5: Blue Water, Bethesda, Olivet, Poplar Springs South, Rock Springs, Union Springs, White Springs.

Annual meetings of the Association are held for two days in the month of October.

The Woman's Missionary Union of the Laurens County Association was organized in Dexter in 1911. Annual meetings of one day have been held each January at different churches of the Association. The organization has had the following superintendents: Mrs. W. C. Floyd, Mrs. J. C. Pittman, Mrs. L. B. Linder, Mrs. R. W. Eubanks, Mrs. Henry Wood, Mrs. U. G. B. Hogan, Mrs. O. L. Anderson, and Mrs. Talmadge Williams. Mrs. J. Tom White has served for several years as secretary.

The Baptist churches east of the Oconee belonged to the Mount Vernon Association, which was constituted in 1859; one of the churches that took the initiative in the new organization was Shady Grove Church, in Laurens County. The fifth annual meeting of the Association was held in October, 1862, with the Shady Grove Church. Other meetings were held here in 1867, in 1883, and in 1894.

Pleasant Springs Baptist Church of Laurens County, which had been organized by the Reverend J. R. Wood, joined the Mount Vernon Association in 1865. The Association met here in 1880.

The Bethlehem Baptist Church joined the Mount Vernon Association and entertained the body in 1870 and again in 1891.

At the session of the Association in 1891 the church at Brewton was admitted as a member.

The church of Bethlehem was first a member of the Hepzibah Association, then a member of the Union, till she withdrew to join the Mount Vernon.

2. PRIMITIVE BAPTIST CHURCHES

In the second decade of the nineteenth century the heart of the Baptist denomination was set on fire as to the responsibility of foreign missions by the stirring call of Luther Rice, a returned foreign missionary. From the Atlantic sea board to the Mississippi the movement swept. It reached the churches of Laurens County and became a dividing force that led to Missionary Baptists and Primitive Baptists. Those who opposed foreign missions, Sunday Schools, and the use of musical instruments in the church service withdrew and organized separate churches, adding the word Primitive to the Baptist name. Because they were opposed to movements that other denominations regarded as progressive, these Baptists were ridiculed as "hard shells," and were most often called Hardshell Baptists. Several of these old Primitive churches in Laurens County have disappeared, and there is no record of them.

Following are a few Primitive Baptist Churches in Laurens County today:

Silver Leaf Primitive Baptist Church in the Rockledge Community was organized about 1879 on land near Pugh's Creek, sold to the church by A. G. Odom. The Reverend J. M. Thomas is the pastor, H. E. Stewart is clerk.

Norris Chapel Primitive Baptist Church is in the Rockledge community. The first church stood among the pines, a little distance from the town of Rockledge. It was moved to the town in 1906 and occupied the Masonic Hall. This building was blown down and the church erected the present building on the same site. The church was named for its first pastor, Jordan Norris, who served it for twenty years. C. L. Thigpen is the present clerk.

Another Primitive Church in the Rockledge community is Union Church, established about thirty years ago. The present pastor is Elder N. F. Mims, the clerk is Jerry Browning.

These churches were formerly in the Gum Log Association but later became members of the Upper Canoochee. This Association was constituted in Washington County in 1829 at Limestone meeting house. The Association became so large that it was divided into Upper and Lower Associations in 1847.

Old Primitive families in the Rockledge community were: the Thigpens, Odoms, Bushes, Foskeys, and Spiveys. Among the well-known former Primitive preachers were: Elders Jordan Norris, John Steptoe, T. A. Smith, Joe McDaniel, J. B. Thomas, and W. H. Stephens. The Primitive churches of this county aid in support of the Orphans' Home at Vidalia. (Information from C. L. Thigpen).

Members of the Primitive Baptist Church in the upper part of Laurens hold membership in Mount Olive Church near the Laurens-Wilkinson line. It is over a hundred years old, having been established in 1836. Some of the early members were Wesley Daniel, Zenas Fordham, the Allens, and Towsons.

Bay Springs Primitive Baptist Church was constituted May 14, 1898, by members from Cool Springs Church. Names of members in the constitution were: Lafayette Allen, Anna Allen, John Arnold, Mollie Arnold, Matilda Allen, S. M. Fowler, C. F. Powell, Susan Powell, and M. C. Scott.

Names of ministers who served as supplies were: Elders James P. Barrs, G. F. Powell, G. W. Floyd, and J. N. Nobles. Elder James P. Barrs served as pastor from October 15, 1898, until December 15, 1900. Elder J. A. Taylor served as pastor from May 18, 1901, until April 14, 1928, when Elder J. F. Dykes was called to assist him. They served together until Elder Taylor's death July 6, 1928. Elder Dykes served until August 19, 1939. Elder J. B. Glisson served from October 14, 1939, until the present time, March 7, 1941.

Names of those who have served as Deacons of Bay Springs Church: C. F. Powell from September 17, 1898, until his death, May 18, 1923; John E. Lord from January 17, 1903, until his death, June 13, 1914; J. D. Faircloth from March 14, 1925, to present time, March 7, 1941; J. B. Lord, Sr., from September 20, 1930, to the present time.

Names of clerks who have served Bay Springs Church: S. M. Fowler, from May 14, 1898, to April 15, 1905; John E. Lord, from May 20, 1905, until his death, June 13, 1914; W. G. Fowler, from June 20, 1914, to January 16, 1915; T. J. Lord, from November 18, 1916, until the present time, March 7, 1941. (Information furnished by John E. Lord.)

The Reedy Springs Primitive Baptist Church is located three miles from Rentz.

3. THE METHODIST CHURCH IN LAURENS COUNTY.

Methodism came to Laurens County in the first quarter of the 19th century. This area was included in the Ohoopee Circuit, and Angus McDonald was sent through the country as a missionary. As there were no schools and no churches, he traveled with difficulty over blazed trails to the far-apart log cabins of the settlers. (G. G. Smith's "History of Methodism in Georgia").

Through the section west of the Oconee, in 1883, passed Lorenzo Dow, one of the most powerful evangelists of the Methodist Society. He declared that he had been ordered by John Wesley, in a vision, to preach to Georgia frontiersmen. He was a New Englander, who made two trips to Georgia, having been converted by Hope Hull, a pioneer preacher who visited New England. On his second trip to Georgia the Governor gave him a pass through the Indian country. He preached in the cabins of white pioneers along the Oconee and Ocmulgee Rivers.

At first, the Methodist denomination was called the Methodist Society.

For the most part, Methodist converts were made at camp meetings. When small houses had been built by Baptists, the Methodist worshipped in them also.

Growth and inspiration came to Methodism in Laurens County, and the entire Dublin District, through the labors of the Reverend J. D. Anthony, lovingly known as "Uncle Jimmy" and "the Bishop of the Wiregrass." Between the years 1879-1882 he was presiding elder of the Dublin District, which, at that time, "embraced the territory now in the McRae and Dublin Districts, also Darien, Jesup, Hinesville, Taylor's Creek, and Jonesville, which are now in the Brunswick District, and Crisp and Douglas of the Valdosta District." (Life and Times of Rev. J. D. Anthony.)

Many people living in Laurens today were christened or baptized by this famous preacher, who was connected with the South Georgia Conference for more than fifty years, and during most of that time labored in the Wiregrass Region. In the year 1846, he joined the South Georgia Conference and served as presiding elder in several of the districts.

The first preachers were unmarried. They received little more than $50.00 per year and traveled on horseback. The circuits had two preachers. Each preacher had about a dozen churches and preached twice each month at each appointment, preaching every day in the week except Monday.

Till 1830, all Georgia Methodist churches belonged to the South Carolina Congress. About the middle of the fourth decade two Georgia conferences were made, the North Georgia and the South Georgia.

Buckhorn Methodist Church

Believed to be the oldest Methodist Church in Laurens County is the old Dorsey Church, now called Buckhorn Church, probably because Buckhorn School was built near it, and also because it is on Buckhorn Creek. According to tradition, the first house of worship was built by Seth Dorsey on what was known as the John Lord estate, and called Bethsaida.

"The earliest written records were destroyed while in custody of Mrs. J. R. Faircloth, when her home was burned at Dexter, Georgia; the only written record dates back to 1856, when all the South was in the shadow of impending civil war.

Buckhorn Church prospered under the care and guidance of such class-leaders as Robert A. Dorsey, John McCrackin, T. J. Bryant, J. J. Bryant, S. A. Clark, Claud Pope, J. W. Dorsey, W. V. Bryant, and Wm. Stripling.

"In 1885, the church was on the Buckhorn charge, in the Brunswick District; in 1886, it was in the Frazier Mission in the Brunswick District; in 1887 to 1889, on the Buckhorn charge; from 1890 to 1893, on the Dempsey charge in the Eastman District; from 1893 to 1895, on the Empire charge in the Eastman District; from 1895 to 1907, on the Dexter charge in the McRae District; 1907 to 1940, on the Dexter charge in the Dublin District.

"Below are the pastors since 1869:

"1869, J. J. Morgan; 1870-1871, H. C. Fentriss; 1872, L. A. Dorsey; 1873, W. D. Bussey; 1874, Daniel C. Pope; 1875, J. E. Rorie; 1876, W. F. Bearden; 1877, G. B. Walter; 1878, Joseph Langston;

1879, Charlie A. Moore; 1880, H. A. Hodges; 1881, F. W. Flanders; 1882-1884, D. G. Pope; 1885, Geo. M. Prescott; 1886, D. G. Pope; 1887, J. G. Cooge; 1888, Gordon F. Roberts; 1889, L. R. Allison; 1890-1891, E. L. Phillips; 1892, E. L. Phillips and D. G. Pope; 1893-1894, C. C. Hines; 1895, E. M. Wright; 1896, Guyton Fisher; 1897-1898, H. C. Fentriss; 1899-1900, E. L. Tucker; 1901, M. L. Watkins; 1902, W. O. Davis; 1903-1904, L. A. Snow; 1905, L. A. Snow and H. C. Ewing; 1906, J. P. Dickinson; 1907, J. P. Bross; 1908-1909, C. C. Lowe; 1910, J. W. Bridges; 1911, S. S. Bridges; 1912-1913, C. S. Bridges; 1914, Silas Johnson; 1915, L. E. Brady; 1916, Geo. R. Stephens; 1917, O. S. Smith; 1918-1919, Thos. H. Tinsley; 1920-1921, J. C. Griner; 1922-1923, H. E. Wells; 1924, M. P. Webb; 1925-1926, E. A. Sanders; 1927, Ralph Crosby; 1928, J. M. Thompson; 1929, J. S. Willis; 1930, Frank Gilmore; 1931, S. James Brown; 1932-1933, R. L. Harris; 1934-1935, C. J. Mallette; 1936-1938, O. H. Rhodes; 1939-1940, C. C. Long.

Gethsemane Methodist Church

Gethsemane is the second oldest Methodist Church in the County, still active. It was organized in 1850. Among the early members were: Benjamin Pope, Edmond Holmes, Kindred Jones, and William Brantley. A little log house was the first church. It was also used as a school house. Two of the early pastors were the Reverend Fred Flanders and Charley A. Moore.

In 1878, a frame building was constructed on the original site. Near by was the graveyard in which many well-known Laurens County people rest. In the early years of the twentieth century a new frame house was built. The church was later moved to the present site on the Soperton Road, a short distance east of Dublin.

Boiling Springs Methodist Church

Boiling Springs Church was established about 1851. The land was donated by Everard Blackshear, who sawed the lumber for the church at his own sawmill from great pines cut on the Parson's place and rafted down the river. John Scarborough, a carpenter of the day, was in charge of the building. The studding was hewn from near-by pines.

The presbytery establishing the church was headed by the Reverend W. M. B. Moorman. Among the early members were Louis Linder, James L. Clark, John P. Maddux, James R. Maddux, and William Barwick.

First Methodist Church of Dublin

There is no record available of the beginning of the First Methodist Church of Dublin, but in the year 1852 or 1853 Reverend John McGehee, passing through Dublin, stopped with a classmate, Hon.

John B. Wolfe, and preached here. In 1867 there were seven charter members of the church. Their names are as follows:

Mrs. Wm. G. Wright, Mrs. Ella Smith, Mrs. K. H. Walker, Mrs. Eliza Smith, Mrs. Tom Rowe, Mrs. Anna Jeffkin, Mrs. Phoebe Douglas.

Reverend Daniel G. Pope was pastor of the newly organized church and preached three times a year, ill health preventing him from preaching oftener. The services were held in the Baptist Church, which was located in the same spot where the present First Church now stands. At first services were held once a month; later they were held twice a month, until 1891. The next place of meeting was the old Academy, which stood where the High School now stands. The Academy was used until 1894, when the present brick building was erected.

Captain Hardy Smith donated the lot for the new church building, giving a part of the plot on which his own home stood. His daughter, Mrs. Claudia Smith Bishop, still lives in the old Smith home next to the parsonage. Reverend Geo. C. Thompson was the architect for the new church building, and Col. John M. Stubbs was a very liberal contributor. Reverend M. A. Morgan and Reverend W. F. Smith, who was pastor in 1890, 1891, and 1892, were instrumental in the building and completion of the edifice.

The building of the church occupied many years, for the town was small and the members few.

The Sunday School was organized in 1874 with seventeen members. Dr. Wall Johnson, Prof. W. E. Thompson, J. M. Minar, A. R. Arnau, C. Whitehurst, A. W. Garrett, M. H. Blackshear, and Dawson Kea have been superintendents.

Since the early days of this church music has been an outstanding feature of worship.

The church has had four organist, Mrs. Hardy Smith was the first. Miss Daisy Graham, now Mrs. L. V. Stone, of Augusta, succeeded Mrs. Smith. For over thirty-five years Mrs. J. A. Peacock was the organist, and it was through her tireless effort that a pipe organ was obtained. Through her instrumentality, Andrew Carnegie gave $750.00, with the understanding that the local church give the same amount, which they did.

Mrs. Annelie Peacock Brown, daughter of Mrs. J. A. Peacock, is carrying on a beautiful service in song with her very lovely voice.

Mrs. James F. Flanders, the present organist, succeeded Mrs. Peacock and is ably assisted by Mrs. J. L. Laney.

The church was greatly revived in 1884-1885, during the pastorate of Reverend T. D. Strong. Mrs. Strong, the wife of Reverend Strong, was a woman of unusual character and ability. Her fine intellect, gracious manner, and spirit-filled personality, endeared her to the town. It was during this time that Reverend John B Culpepper conducted a sweeping revival, but there was no steady growth until the year 1901-1902, under the pastorate of Reverend W. F. Smith, when the membership reached one hundred seventy-five. The membership at prsent is 1,137.

The church was remodeled in 1909-1910, and the educational building added, during the pastorate of Reverend John M. Outler. All indebtedness was paid in full during the pastorate of Reverend W. H. Budd, in 1918.

The arrangement of the church property in Dublin is ideal. The church stands in the center; on the right is the District parsonage, on the left is the church parsonage. The church property is free of debt.

The list of pastors since 1867, in order of service, follows:

1867—Daniel G. Pope	1899—P. S. Twitty
1868—Charles A. Moore	1900-1901—W. N. Ainsworth
1869-1870-1871—John J. Morgan	1902-1903—Geo. W. Mathews
1872—H. J. Ellis	1904-1905-1906—E. H. McGehee
1873—G. W. Callaway	1907-1908—W. F. Smith
1874—J. C. Jordan	1909-1910—Jno. W. Outler
1875-1876—A. M. Williams	1911-1912—A. M. Williams
1877—E. M. Whiting	1913-1914-1915—Whitley Langston
1878-1879—Chas. A. Moore	1916-1917-1918—W. H. Budd
1880—H. A. Hodges	1919-1920—L. A. Hill
1881—F. W. Flanders	1921-1922—J. M. Glenn
1882-1883—Daniel G. Pope	1922—Leland Moore
1884-1885—T. D. Strong	1923—E. M. Overby
1886—Charles H. Branch	1924-1925-1926-1927—J. C. G. Brooks
1887-1888—Geo. C. Thompson	1928-1929—O. B. Chester
1889—Joe C. Parker	1930—L. A. Harrell
1890-1891-1892—W. F. Smith	1931-1932-1933-1934-1935—Lawrence Gray
1893-1894—M. A. Morgan	
1895-1896-1897—O. B. Chester	1936-1937—C. B. Harbour
1898—J. W. Domingoes	1938-1939-1940—J. N. Peacock
	1941—Anthony Hearn

Three times Dublin has had the honor of entertaining the South Georgia Annual Conference. The first Conference in Dublin was held in 1899, with Bishop Wilson presiding. The second Conference was in 1919, with Bishop Warren A. Candler presiding. The third Conference to which this church was hostess was November 3rd to 7th, 1937, Bishop William N. Ainsworth, assisted by Bishop Arthur J. Moore, presiding. Two occurrences made this Conference a memorable and historic session, and the church an historic building—first, the voting on unification by the Conference, and second, the retirement of Bishop Ainsworth because of declining health.

It was also at this session of the Conference that a group of ministers, among whom were Dr. J. A. Thomas, Rev. O. B. Chester, and Rev. H. W. Joiner, who, from the standpoint of service, were its oldest members, agreed on the following fact: That the most powerful sermon to which they had ever had the privilege of listening was delivered in the First Methodist Church in Dublin, by Bishop Alpheus W. Wilson, during the Conference of 1899.

In 1887, the Woman's Work was first organized as the "Parsonage Aid Society;" there were twelve members, with Mrs. K. H. Walker, president, and Mrs. R. H. Hightower, treasurer. Under the pastorate of the Reverend M. A. Morgan, the Foreign Missionary Society was organized in 1893, with Mrs. M. A. Morgan, president, and Mrs. L. B. Lanier, treasurer. In 1901, the Home Missionary Society was organized. In 1912, the two united as the Woman's Missionary Society, with Mrs. D. A. Smith, president. Other presidents have been: Mrs. H. C. Thompson, Mrs. T. J. Pritchett, Mrs. C. H. Kittrell, Mrs. Z. Whitehurst, Mrs. T. B. Brantley, and Mrs. Viola Neal.

—*By Kellie Ballard.*

MT. ZION METHODIST CHURCH

In 1866 there was constituted a small church called Sandy Mount and a log house was built on the McLendon place. Later the location was changed. John Wilkes gave three acres of land and the present house was built. The name was changed to Mount Zion. The first pastor in the little log church was the Reverend Charles Moore. The church is in the Rockledge community.

No Methodist preacher has ever been loved more than "Uncle Charlie Moore." He was pastor of almost every Methodist Church in the county. He joined the Conference before it was divided and, on its division, became a member of the South Georgia Conference. He came to the Dublin circuit about eighty-one years ago. The Dublin circuit, at that time, was composed of the Dublin Church, Boiling Springs, Marvin, Mount Zion, Darsey Church in Laurens County, and Wrightsville and Mason's Bridge in Johnson County.

MARVIN METHODIST CHURCH

Marvin Methodist Church is a frame building in Buckeye District, whose uncared for appearance tells of its abandonment. Occasionally there is a service, but its members have nearly all left the community. Its history dates back to about 1868, when it was built through the efforts of D. S. Blackshear and A. L. Morgan. Among its members were: the Kellams, the C. S. Guyton family, W. B. (Coot) Smith's family, the George M. Prescott family, and the Ellington family.

PLEASANT HILL METHODIST CHURCH

Pleasant Hill Methodist Church was built about 1875. Among the early members were Joseph H. Page, Elbert H. Flanders, George Morris, Riley Stewart, and John Hutchinson.

CARTER'S CHAPEL

On Route 80, in Carter's District, stands a small white church known as Carter's Chapel, organized over sixty years ago. Among the early members were the Carter, Thomas, Holmes, Hilbun and Stewart families. Among the former pastors were: the Reverend C. A. Moore, J. C. Wardlaw, W. N. Ainsworth, R. M. Booth, and S. A. Hearne. The present building is the second house of worship.

NEW EVERGREEN METHODIST CHURCH

The New Evergreen Methodist Church was organized August 30, 1891, with W. F. Smith, pastor of the Dublin Methodist Church, as its first pastor; Reverend J. C. Keemer was Bishop, and J. W. Hinton was presiding elder. This church was organized at the precinct or court house in Bailey's District, G. M. (391) of Laurens County, and services were held here until the church now standing was built.

The charter members were:

E. M. Whitehead, by certificate, now dead; Edward Whitehead, by certificate; Mrs. O. A. Bower, by certificate, now dead; Omer Bower, by certificate; Dr. James L. Linder, by certificate; James N. Linder, by certificate; Lewis Metts, by profession of faith; Mrs. Zena Metts (Whipple), by profession of faith; Mrs. L. A. Stanley, by profession of faith, now dead; George Bower, by profession of faith, now dead; James Castle; Coney Watson.

Under the pastorate of the Reverend W. F. Smith, eighteen members were added. In 1893, the Reverend M. A. Morgan was made pastor at Dublin, which included New Evergreen Society. Reverend Morgan was a consecrated man and, under his guidance, the church building was erected and the church grew and prospered.

On July 7, 1892, Joel W. Hilliard, having joined the Society, donated two acres of land for the church building: the deed was made, E. M. Whitehead, Lewis Metts, F. E. Griffin, D. James, L. Linder, and J. H. Stanley, acting as trustees.

The Reverend O. B. Chester served three years as the next pastor, but in 1897, the Dublin Church went to full-time and the New Evergreen Church has been shifted from one circuit to another.

T. D. Bailey is the present secretary. He has held this office for twenty years, has been a trustee for forty-two years, and a steward for forty years.

—*By T. D. Bailey.*

THOMAS CHAPEL

Thomas Chapel, a small Methodist Church, in the Adrian community, is sometimes known by the name of Pine Grove. It was organized in 1905. The church was dedicated in 1907, and improved in 1939. It was named for Billy Thomas, who preached the first sermon in the church.

Pine Hill Methodist Church

On the Telfair Road, about five miles from Dublin, a small Methodist Church has stood since 1895. From its location, it was given the name Pine Hill. Among the early members were the Moyes, V. O. Hall, S. L. Veal, J. B. Veal, D. J. Spivey. Among the early pastors were: Reverend C. A. Moore, Reverend Bickley, Reverend Scruggs. V. O. Veal has served as church clerk for many years. The church was formerly in the Dublin charge but is now in the Dexter.

Harmony Methodist Church

The Harmony Methodist Church was built about 1898. Among the early members were John A. Salter, W. H. Wynn, E. A. Wynn, and M. A. Maddox.

The Centenary Methodist Church

The Centenary Methodist Church was organized by Reverend N. H. Williams, presiding elder of the Dublin District, and Reverend L. A. Hill, pastor of the First Church, on Sunday night, November 9, 1919, with thirty-one members. The church is a white wooden building with Sunday School rooms, located on the corner of Telfair and Saxon Streets in Dublin. The land was bought by the Dublin First Methodist Church. The first pastor was the Reverend E. L. Wainbright. The Woman's Work was organized in 1920 as the Missionary Society, ten members constituting the group. The first president was Mrs. S. W. Adams; other members holding this office have been: Mrs. Bartow Jones, Mrs. G. W. Bedingfield, Mrs. G. C. Bidgood, Mrs. A. W. Thomas, Mrs. I. C. Huffman, Mrs. Sieberman, and Mrs. Charles Tripp.

4. OTHER DENOMINATIONS

Christ Episcopal Church

(This sketch was written by James A. Thomas in 1907).

In the early Nineties the first Episcopal rector was sent to Dublin to cover the field as a mission. In 1905, Arch Deacon Walton commended a movement to erect a house of worship.

Big hearted Dr. R. H. Hightower donated the site, and the good people of Dublin, without regard to their religious views, made common cause with the few Episcopalians, and the present structure on the corner of Church and Academy Streets was the result.

Mr. Little, E. J. Blackshear, Dr. A. T. Summerlin, and J. S. Simons, Jr., as wardens and vestrymen, were active and indomitable workers in the movement. Through Mr. Little, whose genial disposition and pleasing address made him dear to Dublin people, all classes became interested. The artisan gave his labor, the mill man his lumber, the professional man and general public their money to the cause.

But, no church was ever built without the aid of woman, and to Mrs. E. J. Blackshear, Mrs. P. L. Wade, Mrs. Paul Hough, Mrs. J. S. Simons, Jr., Misses Maud and Bertha Brantley too much credit cannot be given.

In 1898 the building was completed and all debts paid. On the 5th day of February, 1899, the building was dedicated by Right Reverend Bishop Nelson, assisted by Arch Deacon Walton, Rectors F. E. Reese, Knight and others. The members were to know their house of worship for all time as "Christ Church of Dublin."

THE DUBLIN CATHOLIC CHURCH
Contributed

The Mass, which is the universal service of the Catholic Church, has been said and sung in Dublin by mission priests for over thirty years. However, it was not until 1911 that a church was built. Prior to this time hardy priests traveled by train, horseback or carriage to reach Dublin where services were held in private homes. There are still sideboards and buffets which served as altars. Candlesticks bedecking dinner tables and holding Yuletide tapers now, held Mass candles and Benediction lights years ago. White, snowy altar cloths were laundered immaculately by Dublin's pioneer Catholic women. Thus began Catholicism in Dublin and Laurens County.

In 1911, due to the zeal of one woman, Mrs. Victoire Lowe Stubbs, the cornerstone was laid for the local Catholic Church. A location overlooking Stubbs Park had been selected and Mrs. Stubbs, a daughter of one of Maryland's ante-bellum governors, had approached influential friends in the east for help in building a church. George Duval, a monsignor of the church, responded generously to Mrs. Stubbs' plea, requesting only that the church be named The Church of the Immaculate Conception in honor of the Mother of God. In June, 1911, simple and impressive ceremonies of dedication were held, the church being dedicated by Right Reverend Benjamin J. Kelly, Bishop of Savannah, with Catholic laymen and clergy from all over the state in attendance.

A moving spirit in the building of the church was the late M. V. Mahoney, who, together with Mrs. Stubbs, zealously pushed plans for the new church until a dream became a reality with the dedication in 1911.

The first pastor was Father Richard Harmilton.

HENRY MEMORIAL PRESBYTERIAN CHURCH

From time to time, Presbyterian families coming to Dublin and finding no church of their own faith in which to worship, affiliated themselves with the Baptist and Methodist denominations, until, in the early part of the year 1897, Reverend J. B. Mack, at that time Evangelist for the Synod of Georgia, came to Dublin for the purpose of establishing a Presbyterian Church, provided a sufficient number of persons could be found who desired such an organization.

Dr. Mack found only thirteen Presbyterians in the City but they represented some of the most influential families in the community. Among this number were: Captain and Mrs. R. C. Henry, Mr. and Mrs. Alex Moffett, Mr. and Mrs. L. G. Moffett, Dr. and Mrs. Chas. Hicks and Col. and Mrs. Alex Akerman. The desire to organize a church and establish regular worship was found to be unanimous. Both Methodist and Baptist churches welcomed the idea of this denomination founding a church in their midst and cordially opened their doors in an effort to assist them in perfecting necessary plans for their organization.

Captain Henry made arrangements for a meeting, at which the organization was effected in the latter part of the year 1897 by authority of Macon Presbytery, which body appointed Dr. C. H. Hide of Macon, Georgia, to assist Reverend Mack in perfecting a constituted church, and at this meeting the following officers were elected, ordained and installed: Alex Moffett and Alex Akerman, Elders; Captain R. C. Henry and J. D. Robertson, Deacons.

For about two years services were held in the old Masonic Hall. Then, through the great interest and liberality of Captain Henry, a house of worship, at the corner of Jefferson and Columbia Streets, was erected and dedicated in the year 1899. Soon after this building was completed, Captain Henry died, and, as a token of affection and gratitude, the congregation voted unanimously to change the name of the church to Henry Memorial Presbyterian Church.

Mrs. Henry, widow of Captain Henry, continued for a number of years the generosity begun by her late husband, and it was through her liberality that it was possible for the church to retain a full-time pastor.

The most consistent and active forces in the history of this church, for its maintenance and development, have been the Sabbath School and the Woman's Work. The Sabbath School, from the beginning, has been officered with men of courage, faith and hope.

The Woman's Work was first organized under the name, Ladies Aid Society. They continued their work under this name for a number of years, then became known as The Woman's Missionary and Aide Society, the Missionary functioning under one head and the Aide under another, but composed of the same membership and meeting on alternate Mondays. It was during this period that the Aide Society bought and paid for a manse located on the corner of Johnson and Franklin Streets. This property was later sold and the proceeds applied on the construction cost of the new church building. These societies labored under separate heads until the

General Assembly ordered that the work of the women of the Presbyterian Church, under their jurisdiction, be co-ordinated under one name, "Woman's Auxiliary," which name they bear at the present time (1941).

The guiding heads of this branch of the church's activities since formation have been: Mrs. Alex Akerman, Mrs. R. W. Alexander, Mrs. B. H. Russell, Mrs. A. J. Toole, Mrs. B. A. Hooks, Mrs. E. Ross Jordan, Mrs. L. G. Moffett, Mrs Harry Eagan, Miss Susie Carrere, Mrs L. C. Pope, Mrs. Morton Mason, Mrs. Thos. Gibson, Mrs. Elbert Brunson, Mrs. J. H. Balsley, Mrs. Paschal Phillips, Miss Vera Pierce, Mrs. J. M. Couric and the present efficient incumbent, Mrs. C. C. Crockett. (1941).

During the forty-four years of the life of this church it has been served by the following pastors:

Revs. W. F. Strickland, W. C. Stevens, R. W. Alexander, J. W. Stokes, C. M. Chumbley, Dr. J. G. Patten, Rev. W. M. Pease (supply), Dr. D. McIntyre, Rev. W. M. Crofton, Dr. J. D. McPhail, Rev. W. James Hazelwood, Dr. Ralph Gilliam (stated supply), and Rev. R. P. Walker, lately called to the pastorate of this church and who will be installed at a date to be set by Presbytery.

In the year 1919, during the pastorate of Dr. J. G. Patten, who was beloved by every denomination and every citizen of the city, the first church building was sold to the Baptist denomination, and a year later the beautiful, new Henry Memorial Presbyterian Church was erected on its present site on Bellevue Avenue. During the erection of the new church the Episcopalians extended a cordial invitation to the Presbyterians to worship with them. The invitation was accepted and for a year the Episcopalians had services one Sabbath and the Presbyterians the next, using the same building and choir for each denomination. This proved to be a delightful arrangement and created a bond of lasting friendship and appreciation between the two denominations.

It was in 1935, when the church found it necessary to make drastic cuts in expenses, that Rev. W. James Hazelwood, pastor of the Presbyterian Church of Eastman, accepted the task of serving both churches, giving one Sabbah to the Eastman Church and the next to the Dublin Church, and, succeeded during his little more than two years of service, in almost clearing the church debt, installing an adequate heating system, and leaving the church building in good repair.

Rev. Hazelwood accepted a call to the pastorate of the Presbyterian Church in Hapeville, Georgia, during the fall of 1937 and the Henry Memorial Church was without a pastor for more than a year; but the Sabbath School, under the leadership of Col. C. C. Crockett, superintendent, and Mr. J. F. Hart, teacher of the Adult Bible Class, together with the departmental teachers, succeeded in sustaining interest and keeping the spiritual fires burning.

Undaunted by the hardships of a "flock without a shepherd," it was during this period that the membership, in concerted effort, lifted the remaining indebtedness on the church building; and in January, 1939, dedication services were conducted by Dr. Rutherford E. Douglass, of Henderson, Kentucky.

The church rejoices that one of her sons, Alfred G. Moffett, early felt the call to enter the ministry, and is now (1941) pastor of one of the leading Presbyterian Churches in the State of North Carolina.

Through shadow as well as sunshine, the congregation has maintained a good hopeful spirit, and has done with efficiency, the part of the work in the city which seemed allotted to her.

The First Christian Church

The First Christian Church of Dublin was organized in August, 1898, by the Reverend E. L. Shellnut, in a tent on the grounds of the present high school building. The charter members were: Mrs. M. A. Smith, T. B. Hicks, Jas. B. Hicks, Mr. and Mrs. H. T. Jordan, Mr. and Mrs. E. J. Holland, Mrs. A. M. Prince, Mrs. A. T. Summerlin, Mrs. E. F. Bailey, Mrs. J. T. Smith, Lyda Prince and Sherman Prince.

The first elder was E. J. Holland; the first deacons were N. B. Rawls and H. T. Jordan; Jas. B. Hicks was the first church clerk, and Mrs. T. B. Hicks the first treasurer. The first pastor was the Reverend S. P. Speigel.

The church held services in the Masonic Hall, located then at the corner of Jefferson and Madison Streets.

Pastors who have served the church are: S. P. Speigel, T. L. Harris, P. M. Mears, B. H. Morris, G. W. Mullins, W. A. Cassaboom, C. S. Jackson, W. F. Mott, John W. Tyndall, E. W. Sears, James O. Moore, Dr. E. L. Tiffany, James Lawson, E. L. Sharpe, Robert Bennett.

In 1908, the church building on the corner of Jefferson and Gaines Streets, a handsome structure of hydraulic stone, was completed.

In 1901, the Christian Woman's Board of Missions was organized, with Mrs. T. B. Hicks, the first president. The charter members were: Mrs. Mary Smith, Mrs. T. B. Hicks, Mrs. McPherson, Mrs. Summerlin, Mrs. Carter, Mrs. John Williams, Mrs. Dent, Mrs. Jordan, Mrs. Rawls, Mrs. J. A. Rachels, Miss Winnie McPherson, Mrs. E. F. Bailey, Mrs. Tom Smith, Mrs. Harpe. In 1921 the organization became the United Christian Missionary Society. In 1927 the Society celebrated the Golden Jubilee of women's activities in the church. Among those who have served as presidents are: Mrs. Tom Hicks, Mrs. McPherson, Mrs. H. T. Jordan, Mrs. T. K. Tharpe, Mrs. Gratt Holt, Mrs. M. A. Shewmake, Mrs. C. H. Jones, Mrs. J. M. Page, Mrs. J. J. Jordan, Mrs. I. G. Prim, Mrs. L. L. Porter, Mrs. Doyle Knight, Mrs. B. W. Johnson, Mrs. H. W. Jordan, Mrs. B. L. Tingle.

6. RECENT CHURCHES (White)

Church of the Nazarine, located on Telfair Street, Dublin.
Church of God, located in the Pinetucky District, Glenwood Road.
Church of God, located on Telfair Street, Dublin.
Gospel Center, located on Madison Street, Dublin.
Glad Tidings Tabernacle, located at Dexter.
Church of the Full Gospel, located on the Cadwell-Chester-Mt. Carmel Road.

7. COLORED CHURCHES

COLORED BAPTIST CHURCHES

Holly Springs, Dublin District, Toomsboro Road
Pinelevel, Oconee District, Route 2
Hat Off, Lowery District, Glenwood Road
Liberty Hill, Oconee District, old Savannah Road
Rose Hill, Dudley District, Dudley
Brown Chapel, Jackson District, Lovett
Mount Green, Jackson District, Manning
Brown Grove, Buckeye District, Buckeye Road
Evergreen, Carter's District, Dublin-Scott Road
Valdosta, Oconee District, River Road
Barbara Chapel, Rockledge District, Rockledge
Bird Hill, Dudley District, Joiner Road
Williams Chapel, Dublin District, Soperton-Vidalia Road
Turkey Creek, Pinetucky District, Garretta
New Evergreen, Bailey's District, old Stevensville Road
Middle Ground, Hampton Mills District, Dexter
Sun Hill, Cadwell District, Cadwell
New Friendship, Montrose
Rice Hill, Dublin District, Dexter Road
Mount Calvary, Reedy Springs District, Rentz-Cadwell Road
Driskell Tabernacle, Belfry Street, Dublin
Buckeye, Buckeye District
Mount Moriah, Academy Street, Dublin
New Providence, Burch District
Green Grove, off Telfair Street, Dublin
Barnes Springs, Rockledge District, inactive
Brown's Grove, Buckeye District, inactive
Bryant's Gift, Dudley District, inactive
Burch's Gift, Reedy Springs District, inactive
Cave Springs, Jackson's District, inactive
Eason Hill, Harvard District, near Allentown, inactive
Hick's Grove, Pinetucky District, Glenwood Road, inactive
Jones' Gift, Dudley District, Dublin-Cochran Road, inactive
Olive Springs, Buckeye District, inactive
Reese Chapel, Jackson's District, inactive
Shepard Chapel, Dudley District, inactive
Springhill, Dudley District

The Springhill Baptist Church is the oldest negro church in Laurens County. It was constituted in Reconstruction days by the Poplar Springs Baptist Church (white), under a brush arbor. Joel Coney, a wealthy planter, gave the land. The first church building was burned in 1893; a new church was built the next year;

Council Oliver preached the first sermon in the new church. The first pastor was Joe Cooper, whose term of service was from 1865 to 1867. This old church had a large membership from its beginning. Many of the slave members of the Poplar Springs Church (white) became its members. The Poplar Springs Church had over two hundred negro members at the beginning of the War Between the States.

The second oldest negro church in Laurens County is Turkey Creek Church, organized in 1867 by the Blue Water Baptist (white) Church in a brush arbor on land near the white church. The first pastor was a white man, the Reverend Tolbert Kinchin. The present house was dedicated in 1911. The first building was of logs, the second, a frame building, was erected in 1886. It was given the name Turkey Creek to distinguish it from the Blue Water white church.

Colored Baptist Churches, Continued

Shady Road, Dublin District, Dudley-Shewmake Road
Mount Zion, Jackson District, Dublin-Wrightsville Road
Williams' Grove, Mary Street, Dublin
Saint Luke's, Dexter
Ebenezer, Jackson District, Brewton
Good Will, Gaines Street, Dublin
Beulah Hill, Hampton Mill District, Dexter
Spring Hill, Bailey's District, Irwinton Road
Millville, Burgamy District, Irwinton Road
Macedonia, Harvard District, Montrose
Hogan's Grove, Dudley District, Dudley-Dexter Road
Holly Grove, Bailey's District, off Toomsboro Road
Montford Grove, Dublin District, Elmwood Road
Sandy Ford, Dublin District, Macon-Dublin Road
Pleasant Grove, Harvard District, out from Montrose
Laurens Hill, Dudley District, Dudley-Rebie Road
Rock Creek, Dudley District, Dublin-Dexter Road
Fountain, Pinetucky District, off Glenwood Road
Batson, Jackson District, out from Adrian
Reedy Springs, Reedy Springs District, Telfair Road
Pearly Chapel, Pinetucky District, Glenwood Road
Robinson Chapel, Pinetucky District, 3 miles off Dublin-Glenwood Road
Woodard Grove, Dublin District, off Glenwood Road
Second A. B., Decatur Street, Dublin

Colored Methodist Churches

Strawberry, Dublin District, Blackshear Road
Bethel, Buckeye District
Mount Pullen, Jackson District, Wrightsville Road
Zion Hill, Jackson District, Dublin-Wrightsville Road
Saint James, Brewton District
Condor, Smith District, Condor
Fleming Chapel, Pinetucky District, Dublin-McRae Road
M. E. Washington, Washington Street, Dublin
C. M. E., Gaines Street, Dublin
Saint Paul, Rowe Street, Dublin

OTHER COLORED CHURCHES

Church of God in Christ, Alabama Street, Dublin
Church of God, Wabash Street, Dublin
Church of God in Christ, Montrose, Macon Road

8. DEFUNCT CHURCHES

In the minutes of the Poplar Springs Church, under date of July 11, 1812, there accurs this notation:

"On motion of Brother Alexander Stringer the following members were dismissed in order to assist in the constitution of a church at Big Rocky Creek, Laurens County, viz., Alexander Stringer, Thomas Barton and wife, Richard Barlow, Simon Stringer and wife, John Bowen (sic), and Jeff a colored brother." Rocky Creek Baptist Church was established in 1812 and for a century was active. The old church stood at Kewanee and was burned a few years ago. Prominent in this early church were: J. Barlow, J. Sheppard, B. Whitehead, J. W. Yopp, R. Faircloth, Wm. Scarborough, D. H. Combs, and Barnett.

One of the most prominent pastors of this church was the Reverend George Robert McCall.

Before the War (1861-1865) there was a Baptist Church six miles west of Dublin, known as the Limestone Church. It was burned in 1878 and was never restored.

Another old Baptist Church west of the River, in the days before the War, was old Calvary Church.

An old Baptist Church was incorporated at Holly Springs in 1831.

In the 1820's there was a small Baptist Church on the Oconee River above Blackshear's Ferry. In the 1850's there was an old church in the northern part of the county known as Buckeye Baptist Church. One of its pastors was James Sharp Chipley.

What is believed to be the oldest Methodist Church ever established in Laurens County has been out of existence so long that no one remembers it. The only trace is an old deed dated August 21, 1830, made by Turner Mason to John Webb, M. Fisher, Joseph E. Plumer, William L. Mason, and James Glass as trustees. It was four or five miles east of Dublin. Turner Mason was the maternal great grandfather of Turner, J. T., Hardy, and Dan Smith. Dr. William L. Mason was their grandfather; their mother was Martha Mason, a member of the Methodist Church.

9. PREACHERS OF LAURENS COUNTY

Outstanding in length of service and loyalty to the Master's service in Laurens County have been several men whose names will be long remembered.

Among Georgia's most prominent preachers during the middle of the 19th century was David G. Daniell, whose parents moved to Laurens County from North Carolina in his infancy. He was ordained to the ministry at Bethany Church, in Washington County, and, soon after, settled in Dublin. He served as pastor of the Dublin Church and of other Laurens County churches; was pastor of Bethlehem Church for several years. After leaving Dublin, he resided, first, in Hancock County and, later, moved to Atlanta, where he organized the First Baptist Church.

Reverend E. B. Barrett was a brilliant young preacher who served as pastor of the Dublin Baptist Church and as teacher of the Academy. He served through the Confederate War as Chaplain. Another pastor of the Dublin Church was Washington L. Geiger. After leaving Dublin he opened a school in Bulloch County and became the editor of a paper called "The Excelsior News," the first paper ever published in that county.

A well-beloved Baptist preacher was J. M. Donaldson whose name and work were known in Laurens for half a century. He was born in Screven County in 1816, and about 1845, moved to Laurens. He organized Shady Grove Church and was Moderator of the Mount Vernon Association for many years.

Serving the Methodist Church for many years was William B. Moorman. He was a charter member of Boiling Springs Church and prominent as a Mason.

Long-term pastors of Laurens County churches who served in pioneer days were: L. B. Lee, Jordan Baker, Larry Hobbs, Bolin Hobbs, Wm. J. Baker, William Windham, Tolbert Kinchin, Davis Joiner.

Beloved Laurens County men preaching in Laurens and adjoining counties in the last quarter of the century were: Col. W. S. Ramsay, T. Turner Smith and his brother, James T. Smith, J. Z. Bush, John W. Green, John T. Rogers, W. A. Harrison, J. H. Oliver, and N. F. Gay.

Col. W. S. Ramsay holds a distinctive place among the preachers of Dublin and Laurens County. Of high intellectual attainments, he gave a life of consecrated and scholarly service from young manhood until his death in 1900, as pastor of the First Baptist Church of Dublin for more than two score years, also serving other churches in this section of the State.

Deserving more than passing mention is a family that lived four miles east of Dublin during the period of War and Reconstruction.

The widowed wife of a Confederate soldier whose oldest son was but twelve years of age at his father's death, reared five sons to useful manhood. Two of them became outstanding preachers—James Thompson Smith and H. Turner Smith. Their educational advantages were meager for the mother needed the help of the sons on the farm. But against all odds, Jim and Turner Smith, after reaching manhood graduated at Mercer University, the first Laurens County men to receive diplomas from this institution. Two younger brothers, Hardy and Dan, became financiers and contributed greatly to the growth of Dublin.

Beginning his ministerial service in the Nineties, W. E. Harville continued to serve Laurens County Baptist Churches till his death. He served as Moderator of the Laurens County Association from its organization through 1929. He married a daughter of Captain Thomas Rowe and made his home in Dublin.

H. S. Scarboro lived near Dublin and served churches in the Mount Vernon Association.

Beloved ministers, now living, who have served churches in Dublin and Laurens County are Dr. C. D. Graves, R. W. Eubanks, J. E. Townsend, C. L. Lowery, H. L. Maddox, W. R. Lanier, G. G. Harrison, C. E. Vines, and J. L. Allen.

Prominent in the ministry today are the following Laurens sons, born and reared in the county:

Guy M. Hicks, son of Mr. and Mrs. E. E. (Pomp) Hicks (now deceased), of Dublin, is a prominent Methodist preacher in Louisiana.

Robert H. Blackshear, son of Mr. and Mrs. D. S. Blackshear (deceased), of Dublin, is a Presbyterian preacher who has been serving churches in New York State for years.

Dr. Leland Moore, son of J. Ira Moore (deceased), was born and reared in Laurens County. He has served leading Methodist churches of Georgia, both as pastor and as presiding elder.

William M. Haywood, son of Mrs. J. H. Haywood, reared in Laurens County, has been pastor of prominent churches and has held the office of presiding elder in the South Georgia Conference.

Nathan Burch was born and reared on a Laurens County farm, a son of Mr. and Mrs. Galden Burch. He lived at Cadwell and served several churches in the Laurens County Association.

Alfred M. Moffett, son of Louis G. Moffett and wife (deceased), has served leading Presbyterian churches in North Carolina and Tennessee.

Tom Harville, son of Reverend and Mrs. W. E. Harville (both deceased), was pastor for several years of the First Baptist Church at Millen, and is now pastor of Prince Avenue Church in Athens.

Cecil Daniel, son of Mrs. Henry Daniel, lived near Garretta; he has been pastor of Laurens County Baptist churches, and of churches in Waycross and Atlanta.

Walter Knight was a Dublin boy brought up by a widowed mother. He was a member of the First Baptist Church of Dublin; is now pastor of a church in Atlanta.

Frank Cochran, D.D., son of B. F. Cochran and Rebecca Vason

Cochran (deceased), has served as pastor of Georgia Baptist churches. He is now Chaplain in the U. S. Army.

Blewster Knight, son of Mr. and Mrs. R. W. Knight, was reared near Dublin, and was ordained to preach by the Bethsaida Church. He was serving as pastor at Eatonton, Georgia, at the time of his death.

James A. Sconyers, son of John S. and Ella Sconyers (deceased), lived near Brewton. He died at the age of fifty years while serving as district evangelist of the South Georgia Methodist Conference.

Merlin Bishop, son of Mr. and Mrs. W. A. Bishop, is a missionary, now teaching in a mission school in China.

Reginald Russell, son of Mr. and Mrs. L. R. Russell, is a Baptist minister, well known in Georgia and Florida. He has served as pastor of the Tabernacle in Macon, and is now pastor at Waycross.

Davis Knight was reared in Dublin by a widowed mother, Mrs. Mamie Kelley Knight, and was ordained to the ministry by the Jefferson Street Baptist Church. He is pastor of a church near Macon.

Kendall Everett, son of Mrs. Alma Everett Cullens, attended Moody Bible Institute and is today serving as pastor of Bethsaida Baptist Church in this county.

Howard C. Scarborough, son of Mr. and Mrs. W. P. Scarborough, was ordained to the ministry at Bethsaida Church. Though under twenty-one, he is serving Oconee Baptist Church.

In the 1870's, two Laurens County men were ordained to the ministry by the Mount Vernon Association: J. T. Chipley and J. L. White.

Local preachers who resided in Dublin were W. C. Floyd, Baptist minister, and Bob Arnau, Methodist.

CHAPTER XV

SCHOOL HISTORY OF LAURENS COUNTY

1. 1807 TO 1870

Struggling with the hardships of frontier life and the vicissitudes of the ten-year Oconee Indian Wars, the people along the Oconee River had no time for establishing schools, but by the time Laurens County was created parents were becoming anxious for educational advantages for their children. Little groups of settlers began to build small log huts and employ teachers.

In 1817, the State made provision for schools for poor children. The small amounts contributed by the State were controlled by the Inferior Court. Laurens County had a few of these Poor Schools, and in these there were not only the children of the indigent, but abler citizens were content to place their children in them, and let the State bear all expense. In the homes of the well-to-do families there was employed a tutor or a governess, and when the sons and daughters required more advanced education, they were sent elsewhere to school.

The Inferior Court appointed a man in each militia district to take the names of the poor children and report their eligibility for help. On June 15, 1823, they named this list of districts:

        Captain Guyton's District—Uriah Kinchen
        Captain Calhoun's District—Eason Allen
        Captain Stephen's District—Henry Bohannon
        Captain McLendon's District—G. W. Daniel
        Captain St. George's District—Edward St. George
        Captain Tyson's District—William Moore
        Captain Dean's District—Vinson Calhoun
        Captain Hogan's District—Davis Smith
        Captain Swearingin's District—Curtis Joiner

In 1817, the following were appointed by the Inferior Court as trustees of the Poor School Fund: Burton H. Pitts, Joseph Yarbrough, Lewis Linder, Needham Cook, and William L. Mason.

In 1819, the following were appointed as trustees: Joseph Horn, Lewis Linder, Amos Love, Charles Moorman, and John Spivey.

On May 10, 1824, the Inferior Court ordered these men appointed as trustees for the Poor School Fund: Lott Warren, Daniel McNeel, and Henry Pitts.

Later the Academy and Poor School Funds were consolidated and the Inferior Court, in 1839, appointed the following as school commissioners:

John F. Spiers, Benjamin W. Hampton, Daniel Roberts, Nathaniel Tucker, and John G. Anderson.

In October, 1839, two hundred and twenty-two (222) children were reported as approved for participation in the Poor School Fund.

Freeman H. Rowe (Sr.) was appointed to receive the fund and was put under a thousand dollar bond.

On March 12, 1849, the first mention of a county levy appears on the minutes of the Inferior Court: "It is ordered that the tax collector levy a tax of one hundred per cent on the State Tax for county purposes and 25 per cent for education."

In the second decade of the nineteenth century the State provided for the support of academies in each county.

"An Act to incorporate Trustees of the Laurens County Academy.

"Section 1. Be it enacted by the Senate and House of Representatives of State of Georgia in General Assembly met, and it is hereby enacted by authority of same, that John Fullwood, John G. Underwood, Jacob Robinson, John Guyton, Amos Love, Lunsford C. Pitts and George W. Welch and their successors in office shall be and they are hereby declared to be a body corporate by the name and style of the Trustees of Laurens County Academy; and the said trustees and their successors in office are hereby declared to be able and capable in law of suing and being sued, pleading and being impleaded, and to have and to hold, and enjoy real and personal property for the use, purpose, and benefit of said Academy.

DAVID ADAMS,
Speaker

MATTHEW TALBOT,
President."

Assented to December 14th, 1819
JOHN CLARK, Governor.

Sometime during the Thirties the Dublin Academy was incorporated. Since tuition was required, only children of well-to-do parents attended the Academy. The Director made a small charge for the teaching of reading, writing, and arithmetic; a higher charge was made for grammar, geography, and algebra.

The first Academy in Dublin was built on the site of the house now occupied by Mr. and Mrs. W. S. Reese, on Academy Street. It was a long two-room log house with a chimney at each end. (Information from R. M. Stanley).

The second building was a frame structure on the site of the present High School campus.

During the Eighties a Mr. Allen was in charge of the Dublin Academy and was one of its best remembered teachers. He held an unusual philosophy for that day, for he believed that a child should be led, not driven; his creed was "Trust a child's honor and he will not betray it."

During the Sixties, Seventies, and Eighties, there were private schools. A noted teacher of one of these private schools was Richard Niles, who came from the North and married Miss Clifford Yopp, daughter of one of the wealthiest and most prominent of the Laurens County families. Beloved by the whole community was another private school teacher, Miss Elizabeth Stokes, who married John T. Duncan.

In 1819, there was a legislative Act passed to this effect:

"That it shall be duty of commissioners John G. Underwood, D. Blackshear, Neil Monroe, Amos Love, Thomas Moore, and Archibald Griffin to lay off a lot of 4 acres in some suitable situation on public lands and convey same to trustees of Laurens County Academy on which to erect an academy and other such buildings as may be necessary."

Other legislative Acts concerning academies in Laurens County were passed. In 1836, there was an enactment to corporate trustees of Troup Academy and Dublin Academy:

"Also be it enacted by Senate and House of Representatives of State of Georgia in General Assembly met that Barlow Bennett Whitehead, Benjamin Dorsey, Kindred Partain, Sugar Forest, A. Y. Hampton and J. M. Hampton and their successors in office be declared a body corporate by the style of the Trustees of Troup Academy in the County of Laurens."

"Also that Charles B. Guyton, Francis Thomas, John Lowther, John G. Forderin, and Jeremiah H. Yopp be, and they are hereby appointed five additional trustees to the Dublin Academy in Laurens County together with Eli Warren and Robert Robertson (sic), heretofore appointed."

         JOSEPH DAY,
          Speaker of House

         ROBERT M. ECHOLS,
          President of Senate.

Assented to December 27, 1836.
WILLIAM SCHLEY, Governor.

"Be it enacted, etc., that Winfield Wright, Alexander Merriwether, Echols Hightower, William Bridges and Russell Kellum (sic), be, and they are hereby appointed and their successors a body corporate by the name and under the title of the Trustees of the Buckeye Academy in the County of Laurens."

         THOS. GLASCOCK,
          Speaker of House

         JACOB WOOD,
          President of Senate.

WILSON LUMPKIN, Governor.
December 21st, 1833.

"Be it enacted, etc., that Thos. H. Wilkinson, Kindred Partain, Lenoir E. Smith, David Harvard, and John T. Spicer—trustees of the Laurens Hill Academy in County of Laurens."

         JOSEPH DAY,
          Speaker of House

         CHARLES DOUGHERTY,
          President of Senate.

GEORGE R. GILMER, Governor.
December 31st, 1838.

Before the War Between the States, there were a few common schools over the county. The men of a community would build a rude house—generally a log house with a stick-and-dirt chimney—and employ a teacher to be paid a small salary and to be boarded in their homes. In 1859, the Inferior Court appointed John W. Yopp to examine teachers for common schools. The more able families engaged tutors or governesses; sometimes a few families would combine and employ a teacher. This was the general plan of education in Laurens County till the 1870's. In Dublin, there was the Academy, also private schools.

The Southern School Journal was established in Columbus in 1853 for the purpose of exciting interest in public education. About the same time a State Teachers' Association was organized, and while these two progressive movements lasted for only a few years, their influence led indirectly to legislative action. In 1858, the Legislature set aside a large part of the rent of the State Railroad for financing a public school system, but further progress was arrected by the turbulence of secession, war, and reconstruction.

In 1867, the Georgia Educational Association was organized. This body formulated a public school system which was incorporated in an Act passed by the Legislature in 1870 providing for the establishment of free common schools; a law was passed in 1872 providing that one-half of the rental of the Western and Atlantic Railroad be given to the public school fund.

2. PUBLIC SCHOOL SYSTEM

In the Grand Jury Presentment in the Laurens Superior Court in April, 1867, there appears this action:

"We recommend the Inferior Court to levy a tax of 100% upon the poll tax to educate indigent children of the county and advise our people in every district to establish schools for the children of the Freedmen."

The Justices of the Inferior Courts and the Ordinary constituted the Board of Education for the county. The Ordinary was virtually county school commissioner. He kept all records of children entitled to benefits of the school fund and made reports on the school fund, teachers, pupils, necessities and probable revenues of the school year.

A Board of Education, whose members were to be elected by the people, was provided for by legislative Act in 1870; a commissioner of schools was provided for in the same Act. The Act was so changed in 1872 that the Board would consist of five members to be appointed by the Grand Jury. At the April term of court, in accordance with this Act, the Grand Jury thus went on record: "We have elected five freeholders as our county board of education, namely, W. W. O'Neal, J. I. C. Stanley, R. A. Odum, B. F. Stanley, and M. L. Burch." This is the first record of a Board of Education for the county. The first record of the appointment of a county school commissioner was in the same year. The Board of School Commissioners appointed Col. W. S. Ramsay. In 1876, appointed for a

CALHOUN STREET SCHOOL
GRAMMAR SCHOOL AND JUNIOR HIGH

SAXON HEIGHTS GRAMMAR SCHOOL

JOHNSON STREET
GRAMMAR SCHOOL

DUBLIN HIGH SCHOOL

DUBLIN CITY SCHOOLS

Board of Education were: B. H. Blackshear, Edw. Perry, Andrew Thompson, John T. Rogers, and Q. L. Harvard.

When we consider the efficiency of present day schools in Laurens County, it is interesting to note this first record of a school report, returned to the Grand Jury in April, 1877:

"For year ending December 31.
Number of children attending schools—
White 1,403
Colored 1,201

Total... 2,004

"Board of Commissioners authorized
White Schools 28
Colored 9

Total... 37

"Schools were in operation during July, August, and September.
"Teachers licensed by Board........................ 76
Certificates renewed 120
Licenses revoked 2

"One license was revoked because of incompetency, the other for immoral conduct.

"Funds received for educational purposes from all sources.
From State by draft of Tax Collector .... $ 985.77
From Poll Tax of 1876................................. 168.35
Unexpended balance of 1875 .... 116.08

Total... $2,270.20

"Teachers were paid $2.40 for each pupil for the 3-month term.
"The county school commissioner was paid $180.00 yearly salary.
"The increase of pupils has been more than doubly enlarged in the past ten years."

In 1878 the Board of Education reported 2,719 children and 39 schools in operation. In 1883 the Board of Education reported $3,243.97 received for school purposes.

The first county school commissioner, Col. W. S. Ramsay, served continuously during the last quarter of the 19th century.

The Board of Education required the applicant for school commissioner to take an examination on the same subjects as teachers. That Col. Ramsay was exceedingly thorough in those subjects is shown by the grades he made on an examination: School Law 99 1/3, Orthography 100, Arithmetic 100, Grammar 100, History 100, Science and Practice Teaching 100, Geography 100.

Before the century ended the following white schools were in operation in the county:

White	Browning's Flat	Condor
Herndon Spring	Willis Academy	North Condor
Cedar Grove	Union Academy	Dexter
McRay's Mill	Pine Hil	Silver Leaf
Pearly	Chaney	Valambrosa
Moffatt's Spring	Gethsemane	Bay Springs
Dodo	Boiling Springs	Unity
Poplar Springs	Evergreen Academy	Metts

Temperance	Union	Kinchen
Garbutt's	Lovett	Snow Hill
Oak Grove	Summer Retreat	Marie
Gum Spring	Piney Mount	Centreville
Cave Spring	Salem	Roache's
Pleasant Hill	Moore's	Shady Grove
Westbrook	Coleman's	Brewton
Mount Carmel	Ballard's	New Hope
Haskin's	New Alligator	Beulah
Elsie	Buckeye	Harmony
Laurens Hill	Marvin	Pleasant Springs
Montrose	O'Neals	Dublin Academy
Mount Zion	Warnock's	Jones
Eula	Nameless	Eureka
Bethsaida	Suburban	Tittle Institute
	Lee Academy	

Beginning in the Seventies with a three-month school, by 1898 the schools were running six months in the year.

Teachers' Institutes, a week in length, under the direction of an expert educator, were held annually in Dublin. Teachers, at first, were fined for failure to attend.

In the Nineties Hawkinsville held annually a Chautauqua Week which Laurens County teachers attended. A Chautauqua Week was also held in Wrightsville, and Laurens County teachers attended this. In the first decade of the twentieth century, Dublin began to hold annual Chautauquas which continued until the World War. Teachers now attend summer schools at State Universities.

One of the first schools in the State to include manual training and home economics in the curriculum was the school at Poplar Springs in Laurens County.

In the opening years of the twentieth century the Ebenezer High School was established by the Ebenezer Baptist Association at Dudley. It was largely supported by tuition fees with some assistance from the County Board. In 1907 it was burned.

3. THE INDUSTRIAL SCHOOL AT POPLAR SPRINGS

(Contributed)

In 1906, when Poplar Springs patrons asked Miss Emma Perry take charge of their school, there was a new two-room school building on the grounds hard by the grand old church which had been in existence 99 years.

Miss Perry agreed to accept on condition: That a trained teacher be employed on same salary as her own; that an industrial cottage be built and equipped; that teachers be allowed to teach whatever they saw fit to teach. These conditions were accepted, but three weeks later a meeting of Principal and patrons was held. It was then proposed to omit the cottage and all industrial work for fear of ruining the school. Miss Claude Martin had been employed as assistant. In her absence, Miss Perry pledged $50.00 for Miss Martin and $50.00 for herself toward the construction of the cottage. She also offered to go outside the community for donations of equipment. Patrons agreed to the plans with misgivings. All were afraid industrial work would crowd out literary work and drive many from the school.

Before the opening of school the Principal gathered 40 people to clear the grounds of stumps and have a general cleaning. Teachers visited every home. A school improvement club was organized and affiliated with the State Club. A $25.00 prize was won for the greatest improvement of any school in Georgia.

Dublin people took a lively interest in the school. They gave unstintedly their moral and financial support. Dublin merchants donated many pieces of valuable equipment.

In renewing her contract, from year to year, the principal exacted promises of needed and possible improvement. By degrees, a third class-room was built; a music department added; a piano bought; with the third room came the third trained teacher. Another grade was added, making the school a Junior High School.

Dr. C. H. Kittrell gave a large clock, the Singer Sewing Machine Company gave a new Singer. The Keen Cutter Tool Company gave a chest of shop tools valued at $50.00. Local hardware people gave tools. Individuals in Dublin gave money.

An hydraulic ram to pipe spring water up the hill into an elevated tank, was the gift of Atlanta club women.

Greatest of all was the gift from the Dublin Chamber of Commerce of $500.00 to pay off the notes on the teachers' home, which had been built during the fifth year. It was designed by Fred Orr of Athens, and planned to accommodate 20 teachers and pupils.

Dr. A. P. Bourland of the Peabody Board, and Dr. E. C. Branson, late head of the Department of Sociology and Social Economics of the University of North Carolina, were guests of the school during the fifth year. The Hon. Thomas E. Watson was a visitor at the school on one of his speaking tours. He wrote an account of the work in his paper and established a scholarship here.

Only one class graduated during the six years Miss Perry served as Principal: Misses Hattie Lee Miller, Euri Belle Bolton, and Dan Metts. Many others entered higher grades, but for various reasons dropped out. (The larges enrollment was 70).

Miss Miller became an efficient teacher and studied at the University of Georgia. She later married and fills a useful place in her home and community.

Miss Bolton graduated at Georgia State College for Women, Milledgeville; taught in her home county Terrell, and did such an excellent work that her Alma Mater called her back to do extension work for the college; later she became a member of the faculty, which position she still holds. She received her Doctor's degree at Peabody College.

Mr. Metts graduated from Gordon Institute; was a student at Emory when the World War began. He volunteered, trained at Harvard for service on a submarine chaser, went over seas and returning to College, took his Master's degree. Taught at Massey College, Tennessee, and at Tifton Agricultural School. For several years he has been Dean of Sullins College, Bristol, Virginia. (He was the first teacher to transport pupils to schools in Laurens County, which he did by wagon).

Anyone of the three has been worth more to society than all the money that has been invested in Poplar Springs School. Scores of other students have been to college. Many have held places of distinction. More have gone from that school to College than from any school in the rural districts.

4. CONSOLIDATION

An impetus was given to the movement of industrializing the common school of the County when a philanthropist, N. O. Nelson of New Orleans, at his own expense, in 1912, sent Miss Josephine Jordan to introduce industrial work in the Laurens County schools.

Early in the twentieth century the Extension Department of the State Agricultural College began to encourage agricultural and home training work in the schools. In 1911 there were 30 Boys' Corn Clubs, and 64 girls were engaged in the Girls' Canning Club Work. Real improvement began when local taxes were levied. In 1914 there was made a special school tax levy in these districts: Rentz, 5 mills; New Salem, 5; Brewton, 5; Shady Grove, 5; Rose Hill, 5; Hurrican, 5; Lowery, 5; Grinstead, 5; Poplar Springs, 5; Rockledge, 5; Marie, 5; Dudley, 5; Lovett, 5; Cadwell, 5; White Springs, 2½; New Bethel, 3; Excelsior, 3½; Olive Grove, 3; Union, 3½.

Agricultural and home economic work was begun in the Twenties, in the schools of Rentz and Cadwell.

Consolidation of schools began in earnest during the administration of Z. Whitehurst, as County School Commissioner. This movement has grown till the one hundred schools which existed in the early years of the century have been consolidated into twenty, under Elbert Mullis, superintendent, and the present Board of Education. Today in the county system there are 20 white schools, and 61 colored. The two largest colored schools are Millville near Dudley, with five teachers, and St. John near Cadwell, with four. These schools have agricultural and home economic departments.

Schools in the Laurens County System today (1941) are: Baker, Bethsaida, Brewton, Cadwell, Cedar Grove, Cross Roads, Dexter, Dudley, Harmony, Lovett, Lowery, Main, Montrose, New Bethel, Olivet, Pine Forest, Pine Grove, Rentz, Condor, and Wilkes.

LAURENS COUNTY CONSOLIDATED SCHOOLS

Rentz, Cadwell, Dexter, Dudley and Cedar Grove schools have agricultural and home economics departments.

The following men have served as members of the Laurens County Board of Education since 1892: G. W. Bishop, J. F. Fuller, J. H. Yopp, Dr. John Carter, W. L. Geiger, P. L. Wade, J. F. Moore, D. J. Clark, A. B. Clark, Dr. J. T. Chappell, T. J. Blackshear, John Burch, J. W. Warren, Dr. W. A. Thomas, R. J. Chappell, W. A. Witherington, James L. Keen, E. C. O'Neal, R. H. Duggan, M. S. Jones, M. M. Hobbs, J. P. Howell, B. F. Cochran, W. R. McDaniel, A. J. Weaver, E. A. Avery, W. A. Bedingfield, D. M. Kersey, T. A. Clark, J. A. Youngblood, H. I. Joiner, D. S. Blackshear, W. M. Harndon, J. P. Mathis, L. O. Beacham, Jr., J. W. Alligood, T. D. Bailey, T. M. Hicks, H. M. Blankenship, W. O. Prescott, J. B. Fordham, W. D. Parkerson and Leo Kight.

The present County Board of Education is composed of F. A. Josey, H. M. Blankenship, W. M. Herndon, C. J. Bedingfield, and Dr. C. G. Moye.

County School Commissioners, known now as School Superintendents, have been: Col. W. S. Ramsay, J. T. Smith, Z. Whitehurst, R. L. Sumner, T. M. Hicks, and Elbert Mullis. Whitehurst was the first commissioner to be elected by the people.

Mr. Mullis is serving his second term. He is assisted by Mrs. W. T. Roach, secretary, and Mrs. W. W. Wells, director of Negro Education. He maintains offices and a book supply department in the old post office building.

5. THE SCHOOLS OF DUBLIN

The rude double-pen log house which served as the first Academy of Dublin was replaced about 1855 by a better building, the number of pupils long since having outgrown the first quarters.

This was a two-story frame building that stood a little east of the location of the present High School. The lower floor was used for school purposes, the upper for a Masonic Hall. This building was outgrown, moved to the lot where the Carnegie Library now stands, and converted into a City Hall. Later it was sold and moved to Gaines Street to be used as a private dwelling. During the Seventies and Eighties there were several private schools. One of the best attended was that taught by Dick Hicks, in a little two-room house on Bellevue Avenue.

The next Academy was a much larger structure, built on the southeast corner of Academy and Palmer Streets, the first principal being W. V. Lanier. This was burned on a January morning in 1901. Until a new building could be erected, the school occupied two buildings—a large two-story residence on Bellevue Avenue, owned by Mrs. Maud Stubbs Pritchett, and the old City Hall, on the present site of the Carnegie Library. The first graduating class in the history of Laurens County was in 1894, in the Dublin Academy, when it was located on the corner of Academy and Palmer Streets. The members were: Minnie Stokes (Mrs. Frank Bright), Eva Wolfe (Mrs. Thomas Hooks), Jennie Pate Robinson (Mrs. Freeman Rowe), Maude Walker, Julius Walker, and Pearl McCray.

A $25,000 bond issue was floated, and the present high schoo building was begun and ready for occupancy in 1902. This was considered at the time a very spacious structure with its thirteen class rooms and auditorium. The Board of Trustees at that time was composed of J. T. Smith, J. H. Witherington, A. P. Hilton, W. P. Clements, H. M. Stanley, Dr. Charles Hicks, F. G. Corker, B. H. Rawls, F. W. Powell, T. J. Pritchett, with J. C. Wardlaw, principal.

But the builders had not reckoned on so rapid a growth in population. In three years more room was needed, and a new building was erected on Johnson Street, at a cost of $10,000, to serve the purpose of a grammar school. The present Public School System was begun in 1895, when a local tax law was passed. The funds from this taxation, increased by the amount paid by the State, enabled Dublin to have an independent school system.

In 1907, to the high school curriculum was added an eleventh grade, and a progressive movement took the form of domestic science and manual training departments. A little later, a chemical laboratory and a department of public speaking were added.

As the population continued to grow two other grammar schools were built; Saxon Heights, a large two-story frame building, in 1907, and a modern stucco building on Calhoun Street, in 1920.

The progress of the high school is told in the following sketch from "The Public Schools of Dublin," by Katherine Orr.

"In 1913 the Dublin High School was placed on the accredited list of the Association of Colleges and Secondary Schools of the Southern States; it is still on the accredited list and is now a member of the Association.

"Under the New Deal the schools of Dublin have had about $10,000 in improvements from the CWA and WPA and approximately $35,000 through the PWA. The Home Economics and Commercial Departments have been provided with modern equipment of the highest quality, and all other departments have been furnished with whatever was needed.

"Besides high attainment along academic lines, many extra curricular opportunities are offered in the high school. In addition to athletics, a field in which the maximum of interest and development is reached, the extra-curricular program includes the following clubs: Practical Arts, Dramatics, Fine Arts, Senior Hi-Y, Junior Hi-Y, Music, Senior Girl Reserves, Junior Girl Reserves, Writers, Band, and Orchestra. Under the sponsorship of the Economics Class, a high school bank is operated. The plan of the high school is one that lends itself to the complete training of the student, so that in those cases in which college is not the subsequent step, he has the benefit of a well-rounded course of study."

The Dublin School System was organized nearly fifty years ago and since that time it has had the following superintendents: J. C. Wardlaw, Kyle Alfriend, W. R. Lanier, W. E. Thompson, A. B. Clark, W. C. Wright, R. E. Brooks, Paul King, Prof. Garrett, W. P. Martin, H. B. Carreker, Knox Walker, and A. J. Hargrove. Mr. Hargrove held this position from 1930 to August, 1941, at which time Selwyn Howard Sherman, M.A., was elected to succeed him.

Chapter XVI

POST OFFICES, TOWNS AND COMMUNITIES

1. THE DUBLIN POST OFFICE

Sometime between April 25th and May 6, 1811, the Dublin Post Office was established. The first account was submitted July 1, 1811. For the first fifty years the receipts were so small only a scant living was furnished the postmaster.

The records indicate that a contract was made with Levin Moore to transport the mails between Milledgeville and Darien once every two weeks from April through December 31, 1814; with mail coming in only every two weeks, the postmaster had an easy job.

There is a report made for the period from June 1, 1815, to December 31, 1816, that reads: "From Milledgeville by Montgomery Court House, Irwinton, Dublin, Tatnall Court House, to Darien, Ga., William Ball, contractor."

For years mail was carried to Toomsboro by private conveyance three times a week; later, it was carried daily. At Stephensville, an intermediate point, the postmaster opened the pouch from Dublin, inspected the contents and dispatched it on to Toomsboro; it is said that often he did not find a single letter. Tremendous strides have been made since then; in 1940 the total receipts of the Dublin office were $34,151.47. This growth has been attained largely in the present century; in 1897 receipts were only $3,423.02.

In 1893 the office still belonged to the fourth class; in 1894 it was raised to third class; in 1905 it climbed to second class. At the present rate of growth it will soon be first class, since it now lacks only about $6,000.00.

In 1905 a free city delivery was inaugurated. Two deliveries daily have since that time been made in the residential section. There were originally three routes; since 1912 there have been four.

Laurens County has had free rural deliveries since 1900, almost from the date the bill was passed creating them. The Congressman at that time was William G. Brantley and he was highly instrumental in obtaining these routes.

Dublin postmasters since the creation of the office have been:

Jonathan Sawyer	July 1, 1811	Francis Thomas	July 10, 1840
William W. Talbot	April 24, 1817	Joel E. Perry	Jan. 30, 1860
Wright H. Coleman	April 8, 1818	John J. Keen	Oct. 8, 1866
Thomas Moore	July 19, 1822	Henry Herman	July 6, 1869
Henry B. Hathaway	Jan. 31, 1829	Miss Maggie Hester	Oct. 17, 1870
Marcus Gilbert	Jan. 31, 1836	Isaac T. Keen	Feb. 27, 1872
Charles B. Guyton	Dec. 13, 1836	Josiah S. Horn	Feb. 19, 1875

Isaac T. Keen	Dec. 31, 1877	Erwin E. Stone	July 12, 1898
Mercer Haynes	May 26, 1880	Clark Grier	June 2, 1892
Bryant A. Herndon	Jan. 3, 1881	Mrs. George B. Grier	Sept. 8, 1908
Thos. M. Hightower	Aug. 31, 1881	Vivian L. Stanley	Aug. 15, 1913
Wm. P. Hicks	Jan. 25, 1887	Edwin R. Orr	May 23, 1922
Clark Grier	June 2, 1892	Moses Josiah Guyton	June 9, 1934
Vivian L. Stanley	Dec. 20, 1893		

The first woman to serve the post office was Maggie Hester. She was appointed when Reconstruction laws were rigidly enforced upon Georgia. At that time there were no men eligible for the office, since every man had taken part in the "War of the Rebellion." A woman was made postmistress, and she chose a minor, Isaac Keen, as Assistant.

The first Air Mail Service was August 16, 1937, during National Air Mail Week. The dispatch was made at 8:00 A. M. to Macon terminal and consisted of 1,388 pieces of first class mail.

The second Air Mail Service out of Dublin was made May 19, 1938. The dispatch was made over the same route as the first and consisted of 12 pounds of first class mail.

Employees in Dublin postoffice are: M. J. Guyton, postmaster; James W. Long, assistant postmaster; John A. Peacock, Jr., clerk; Andrew J. Cooper, clerk; W. E. Thagard, clerk; W. B. Seymour, clerk; Edmond F. Brown, clerk; Albert L. Thomas, substitute clerk; Julian W. Jones, substitute clerk; George R. Carr, special delivery messenger.

City carriers are: Route 1, J. Alton Dominy; 2, George Outlaw; 3, Chappell Garner; 4, Jesse W. Gibson.

Rural carriers are: No. 1, R. O. McDaniel; No. 2, John W. Thompkins; No. 3, Vernon Chavous; No. 4, Excell E. Prescott; No. 5, David A. Moorman; No. 6, Francis N. Hancock; No. 7, Early E. Warren.

Montrose, Dudley, Dexter, Cadwell, Rentz, Rockledge, each, has one rural delivery.

Rural routes from Dublin have increased from four to eleven. These were later consolidated into the seven routes that are covered today. Early rural carriers were A. M. Black, A. T. Black, H. D. Jordan and Richard Blackshear.

The Dublin post office for one hundred and one years occupied numerous buildings. Its last location in rented quarters was an old building which stood on the site of the present Citizens & Southern Bank Building. In 1911, through the efforts of the late Honorable William G. Brantley, then Congressman of the 11th Congressional District, an appropriation of $65,000 was secured for the building of a Dublin post office. Late in 1912 the office moved into the new quarters.

Early in 1935, Congressman Carl Vinson was instrumental in securing an appropriation of $165,000 for the erection of a new Post

Office and Federal Court Building. This was completed January 18, 1937, with a total investment estimated at $175,000.

The site was acquired from the County by exchange of the old Post Office property for the east portion of the Court Square. The new Federal Building with its massive Corinthian columns is one of the largest and most complete of all the federal buildings erected in this era in cities of the United States, with classification as second class post offices.

2. POST OFFICES IN LAURENS COUNTY
(In order of establishment)

DUBLIN. Jonathan Sawyer, the first postmaster appointed to serve at this office, rendered his first account as of July 1, 1811.

BUCK EYE. The Buck Eye office was established January 15, 1833, with Alexander Merriwether as postmaster. This post office was discontinued on June 12, 1867.

LAURENS HILL. This office was established August 20, 1835, with David Harvard as postmaster. The Laurens Hill post office was discontinued August 25, 1868, and reestablished January 3, 1870. This office was finally discontinued on September 14, 1903. Mail was ordered sent to Montrose.

BAY CREEK. The Bay Creek post office was established November 17, 1851, with Michael Livingston as postmaster. On February 18, 1854, this post office was discontinued.

LIME SINK. This office was established May 14, 1857, with Henry M. Burch as postmaster. The Lime Sink office was discontinued March 29, 1860, and reestablished June 28, 1893. On January 12, 1894, this post office was finally discontinued. Mail for former patrons of the office was ordered sent to Reedy Springs.

REEDY SPRINGS. The Reedy Springs office was established October 27, 1873, with John T. Rogers as postmaster. This office was discontinued December 31, 1901. Mail was ordered sent to Dexter.

BLACKSHEAR'S MILL. This post office was established July 5, 1878, with Josiah D. Horn as postmaster. The Blackshear's Mill office was discontinued December 17, 1879.

CONDOR. The Condor post office was established September 17, 1878, with Dennis Kea as postmaster. On June 15, 1917, the Condor office was discontinued. Mail for former patrons of the office was ordered sent to Dublin.

WYLLY. On February 5, 1879, this office was established with John A. Weaver as postmaster. The Wylly post office was discontinued September 29, 1900. Mail was ordered sent to Dublin.

BUCK HORN. This office was established May 1, 1879, with Andrew J. Thompson as postmaster. The Buck Horn post office was discontinued September 14, 1903. Mail was ordered sent to Dexter.

PICCIOLA. This office was established June 30, 1879, with Jeremiah H. Yopp as postmaster. On June 15, 1889, the name of the Picciola post office was changed to Valambrosa. The Valambrosa office was discontinued August 15, 1899. Mail was ordered sent to Dublin.

TWEED. This office was established April 13, 1880, with Rufus T. Beacham as postmaster. The Tweed office was discontinued July 30, 1904. Mail for former patrons of the office was ordered sent to Rockledge.

ARTHUR. The Arthur post office was establishhed June 29, 1880, with Daniel W. Burch as postmaster. On April 30, 1908, this office was discontinued. Mail was ordered sent to Depue, Dodge County.

BRANCHVILLE. On February 15, 1882, this office was established with Lofton M. Smith as postmaster. This post office was discontinued July 26, 1889. Mail was ordered sent to Condor.

LOVET. This office was established July 1, 1884, with John M. Hutchinson as postmaster. The name of this office was changed to Lovett May 11, 1885.

INEZ. The Inez post office was established May 7, 1883, with James R. Shepard as postmaster. This office was discontinued April 21, 1884. Mail was ordered sent to Reedy Springs.

HATOFF. On June 6, 1883, the Hatoff post office was established with Eujenue E. Thomburg as postmaster. This office was discontinued July 30, 1904. Mail for former patrons of the office was ordered sent to Dublin.

BEULAH. The Beulah office was established January 24, 1884, with John F. Currie as postmaster. On October 31, 1904, this office was discontinued. Mail was ordered sent to Mount Vernon, Montgomery County.

TURKEY. This post office was established January 24, 1884, with Dennis McLendon as postmaster. The Turkey office was discontinued June 6, 1889. Mail for former patrons of the office was ordered sent to Dublin.

DODO. On July 1, 1884, Henry T. Jones was appointed postmaster and this post office was established. The name of the Dodo office was changed to Brewton on June 25, 1894.

NAMELESS. This office was established February 12, 1886, with James R. Shepard as postmaster. The Nameless post office was discontinued December 31, 1901. Mail was ordered sent to Dexter.

DONALDSON. The Donaldson post office was established February 7, 1887, with John L. Keen as postmaster. This office was discontinued January 15, 1895. Mail was ordered sent to Lovett.

PEARLY. This office was established May 20, 1887, with William L. Green as postmaster. The Pearly office was discontinued July 30, 1904. Mail was ordered sent to Dublin.

WALKEE. This post office was established July 21, 1887, with Samuel L. Miller as postmaster. On July 30, 1904, this office was discontinued. Mail for former patrons of the Walkee post office was ordered sent to Dublin.

BRUTUS. The Brutus post office was established February 18, 1889, with James A. Beaty as postmaster. This post office was discontinued September 30, 1890. Mail was ordered sent to Regnant, Johnson County.

DEXTER. The Dexter post office was established January 31, 1890, with James H. Witherington as postmaster.

WESTBROOK. On April 4, 1890, the Westbrook post office was established with Elijah A. Butler as postmaster. This office was discontinued February 15, 1902. Mail was ordered sent to Dexter.

SPRINGHAVEN. The Springhaven office was established June 3, 1890, with Japheth Rawls as postmaster. On June 29, 1907, the Springhaven post office was discontinued. Mail for former patrons of the office was ordered sent to Dexter.

GRIMSLEY. This office was established August 4, 1891, with Edwin O. Powell as postmaster. The Grimsley post office was discontinued December 14, 1901. Mail was ordered sent to Dublin.

DUDLEY. The Dubley post office was established October 9, 1891, with Mrs. Elsie L. Walker as postmaster. The name of this office was changed from Dudly to Dudley on February 12, 1907.

MONTROSE. On October 28, 1891, the Montrose post office was established with James M. Scarborough as postmaster.

BENDER. The Bender post office was established November 18, 1891, with William Gilbert as postmaster. This office was discontinued August 31, 1905. Mail was ordered sent to Dudley.

GARBUTT. The Garbutt office was established September 28, 1892, with Thomas W. Garbutt as postmaster. This post office was discontinued September 29, 1900, and reestablished February 15, 1901. On October 15, 1902, the Garbutt office was finally discontinued. Mail was ordered sent to Meeks, Johnson County.

LOLLIE. The Lollie office was established October 15, 1892, with Henry E. Pritchett as postmaster.

ELMWOOD. On September 7, 1893, this post office was established with Robert D. Dixon as postmaster. The Elmwood office was discontinued July 15, 1899, and reestablished February 15, 1900. On September 29, 1900, this office was finally discontinued. Mail for former patrons of the post office was ordered sent to Dublin.

MUSGROVE. This office was established September 13, 1893, with Madison Alcorn as postmaster. The Musgrove office was discontinued December 15, 1905. Mail was ordered sent to Dexter.

MAGGIE. On September 29, 1893, this post office was established with W. Henry Warren as postmaster. The Maggie office was discontinued February 15, 1895. Mail was ordered sent to Westbrook.

HARLOW. This office was established March 1895, with Columbia Lee as postmaster. This office was discontinued February 28, 1902. Mail was ordered sent to Dublin.

MARTHA. The Martha post office was established June 6, 1895, with John W. Cox as postmaster. On January 27, 1898, the Martha office was discontinued. Mail was ordered sent to Tweed.

ITVILLE. The Itville office was established July 14, 1897, with William L. Pridgen as postmaster. This office was discontinued December 31, 1897. Mail was ordered sent to Lovett.

KEWANEE. On June 21, 1898, the Kewanee post office was established with Carrie B. Rude as postmaster. This post office was discontinued May 31, 1904. Mail was ordered sent to Dudley.

ORIANNA. This office was established May 16, 1899, with Lucien Thigpen as postmaster. The Orianna office was discontinued December 15, 1904. Mail was ordered sent to Adrian, Emanuel County.

ROCKLEDGE. On September 6, 1899, the Rockledge post office was established with William Smith as postmaster.

PINEHILL. Leah L. Hughes was appointed postmaster at Pinehill when this office was established on October 14, 1899. The Pinehill post office was discontinued September 29, 1900. Mail was ordered sent to Dublin.

THAIRDELLE. The Thairdelle post office was established March 5, 1900, with William R. Harrell as postmaster. This office was discontinued April 15, 1902. Mail for former patrons of the Thairdelle post office was ordered sent to Rockledge.

UNIT. This office was established April 12, 1900, with Thomas J. Blackshear as postmaster. The Unit office was discontinued April 15, 1902. Mail was ordered sent to Omecron, Wilkinson County.

SHEWMAKE. This post office was established April 27, 1900, with George A McKay as postmaster. The Shewmake office was discontinued January 15, 1903, and mail was ordered sent to Dublin.

CATLIN. On May 23, 1902, this office was established with Julius A. Dunn as postmaster. The Catlin post office was discontinued May 30, 1907. Mail was ordered sent to Dublin.

KEMPER. The Kemper post office was established October 6, 1902, with James T. Coleman as postmaster. On April 30, 1903, the Kemper post office was discontinued. Mail for former patrons of the office was ordered sent to Rockledge.

ELLISTON. This office was established November 15, 1902, with Ellis W. Bullock as postmaster. This office was discontinued on July 30, 1904. Mail was ordered sent to Dexter.

RENTZ. The Rentz office was established March 11, 1905, with John S. Edmundson as postmaster.

MULLIS. The Mullis post office was established June 17, 1905, with Hiram Mullis as postmaster. The name of this office was changed to Cadwell on August 17, 1908.

BATSON. The Batson office was established September 27, 1905, with Benjamin F. Duggan as postmaster. This office was discontinued October 30, 1909. Mail was ordered sent to Dexter.

3. TOWNS AND COMMUNITIES

a. LOVETT

In 1884 the W. & T. Railroad had been constructed to a point a little below the Johnson-Laurens line, but the first station in Laurens County had not as yet been decided upon, although construction work had advanced eight miles into the county.

One morning the construction train had arrived and the crew was working near a little log store operated by J. M. ("Sug") Hutchinson. On that particular morning a prominent Sandersville man, Warren P. Lovett, came down on the construction train to inspect progress. While in the little store in conversation with Mr. Hutchinson and several other community citizens, he remarked that this was the logical place for a station, and suggested that its name be Hutchinson. The store-keeper, to be equally courteous, replied that Lovett would be a good name. The men were impressed with this suggestion and began to bring pressure to this end on the directors. The station was granted and named Lovett, not so much for Warren P. Lovett as for a long time resident, Irwin Lovett, whose home was a log house nearby. (Information from Mr. Leo Kight.)

The town was incorporated in 1889. Mr. Hutchinson (Sug) was the first railroad agent. His store served for both ticket office and post office since he was also the first postmaster.

The first Mayor was Wm. Bales; the Aldermen were: P. M. Johnson, E. A. Lovett, Z. M. Sterling, M. R. Rachels, and E. J. Hutchinson.

The first stores were operated by Jordan Lyons, Wm. Bales, James Kessler, E. J. Hutchinson, E. P. Rentz, B. B. Wynn, Wm. F. Schaufele, E. A. Lovett, and B. T. Kight.

In 1885, Lovett was a town of considerable size. In 1889, a barroom was opened. Lovett has had three fires, the first about 1886, others in 1895, and 1896.

Prominent early families were the Lovetts, Parkers, Moormans, Hardeways, Stewarts, and Kights.

Prominent early physicians were Dr. P. M. Johnson and Dr. L. P. Fordham, the latter being both physician and druggist.

About 1908 a bank was established which continued till sometime in the Twenties. One of the principal enterprises was the Farmers and Merchants Bonded Warehouse.

In the early years a house was built in which all denominations worshipped and which was also used as a school. Later, a Methodist Church was built and Baptists also worshipped here.

b. Brewton

In 1884 the Wrightsville and Tennille Railroad created a station eight miles from Dublin and named it Bruton, because of its proximity to Bruton Creek. The name was later changed to Brewton.

The most prominent early resident was David Williamson, who operated a large turpentine still in the edge of the village. Other pioneers were the McGowans, Keeens, Kesslers, Griffins, and Curls.

At the turn of the century there were several mercantile houses in Brewton. Among the merchants were: F. H. Brantley, Irwin Jackson, James L. Keen & Son, J. M. Lovett, I. E. Thigpen, and M. G. Thigpen.

One of the first merchants was Allen Jackson, who began with a business valued at about $250.00. The store grew so rapidly that in the early years of the Twentieth Century Mr. Jackson moved to Dublin and opened one of the largest stores in the history of the county.

About 1889 a small frame church was built in Brewton and was used by both Baptists and Methodists. In 1891 Brewton Baptist Church was admitted to the Mount Vernon Association.

In 1895 the Methodists organized and built their own church; this was blown down, but another was built in 1921; this, proving inadequate, was torn down and the present structure was completed in 1936.

The Baptist people of Brewton constituted a church in 1890, and in 1897, built the house now used. Among the pastors who have served this church are: The Reverend Duran, J. H. Oliver, J. A. Blount, James G. Page, G. S. Allen, J. I. Chipley, G. G. Ward, J. R. Kelley, G. G. Harrison, Joe M. Branch, W. C. Culpepper, W. F. Chambliss, E. A. Kilgore, J. E. Townsend, D. W. Edwards, C. E. Vines. J. W. Holland served for several years as clerk.

In 1921 Brewton floated a bond issue of $30,000 for a school building. A commodious brick structure was erected in 1922. Brewton had the first large consolidated school of the County; united with it were the Shady Grove and Leach Schools. This building burned because of a faulty hot air system; in a short time the building was restored; this in turn was burned in November, 1938. Another building was soon constructed similar to the first brick building, and is now in use.

The W. & T. Railroad established a station in the Condor community, called New Condor. A few stores were opened, but the village did not become permanent.

c. DEXTER

The town of Dexter is situated in the western part of Laurens County, twelve miles west of Dublin. The first settlement was made in 1889 by the Reverend John W. Green, who built the first dwelling, a two-room structure. This building still stands just outside the town limits. In 1880 a post office, hotel and several stores were opened to serve the rapidly growing community. The town of Dexter was incorporated August 22, 1891, with T. A. Wood as Mayor, and J. H. Witherington, W. W. Wynne, W. L. Herndon, J. H. Smith, and T. H. Shepard as Aldermen.

About 1890 the W. & T. Railroad extended their line as far west as Dexter, and beyond this to Empire. The road at that time was known as the Oconee and Western, and was built chiefly for the transportation of logs and lumber. For a time lumbering was the main industry and Dexter was a flourishing town, having a population of about six hundred.

Among the oldest families in this community are the McDaniel, Bryan, Blankenship, Davis, Mullis, Joiner, Clark, Darsey, Warren, Lord, Alligood, Hobbs, Green, Kemp, Shepard, and Witherington. Among the older citizens are: Dr. W. B. Taylor who came from Washington County in 1892; Dr. J. E. New, also from Washington County, who came here as a boy in 1895; F. M. Daniel, who located here about 1897; R. C. Hogan and U. G. B. Hogan, brothers, who came about 1900; and John A. McClelland, about 1897. All of these are now living in Dexter.

Among the early settlers, now deceased, are: Ben C. Green, J. Warren Joiner, J. G. (Bud) Thomas, H. F. Maund, T. C. Methvin, J. Tom White, H. S. Chadwick, Joe B. Daniel, George B. Malone, W. L. (Dash) Digby, and Jerry Ussery. There are no minutes prior to 1911, but it is known that Dr. J. E. New served several terms as mayor before this time; H. F. Maund and T. C. Methvin also served as mayor before 1911. The town minutes of 1911 show that J. J. Phillips, who still lives in Dexter, at the age of eighty, was marshal; C. A. Shepard was mayor; E. J. Woodard, who is now operating a mercantile business in the neighboring town of Rentz, was town clerk. Town officers have always been elected annually and, in the earlier days, exciting elections took place. Dr. New was, after a hard race, elected mayor at the age of twenty-one. Mayors since 1911 in the order in which they served are: J. B. Daniel, Jerome Kennedy, W. B. F. Daniel, C. A. Shepard, Jerome Kennedy, R. C. Hogan, L. Taylor, J. G. Thomas, R. C. Hogan, H. I. King, H. W. Daniel, T. C. Methvin, W. H. Faircloth and the present mayor, C. R. Shepard, who is a son of T. H. Shepard, one of the first aldermen. Mr. D. W. Knight, present postmaster, served as town clerk, from 1921 to 1935.

The Dexter Banking Company was the first chartered bank in the county, outside of Dublin, having been organized in 1904 by Dr. Taylor and others. Dr. J. E. New was the first president, and H. F. Maund, the first cashier. Another bank, the Farmers State Bank, was organized in 1910, but was absorbed by the Dexter Banking Company in 1914. D. W. Knight came to Dexter in 1919 as cashier and the bank was voluntarily liquidated in 1933. Depositors were paid in full and stockholders received over par for their stock. However, the bank was continued as a private institution and is now operating as the Taylor-Knight Banking Company, composed of W. B. Taylor, L. Taylor, and D. W. Knight. It is the pride of this community that no money has ever been lost to depositors in their banks.

Among the first business firms in Dexter were: J. H. Witherington, Henry McDaniel, J. W. Joiner & Son, T. W. Turt, R. C. Hogan & Bro., H. S. Chadwick, T. J. Hunnicutt, Shepard & Mullis, Taylor, Currell & Rowe, F. M. Daniel & Son, and Malone, Woodard & Company. The oldest drug store in the county is located at Dexter, having been opened by Dr. W. B. Taylor in 1894, and now operated by Dr. Taylor and his son, L. Taylor.

A small water system was installed by the town in 1910 without issuing bonds. Over a period of fifty years no bonds have been issued against the town.

The Georgia Power Company extended its lines to Dexter in 1929, and in 1936, the WPA paved the road from Dexter to Dublin. A paved post road is now in process of construction from Dudley through Dexter to Cadwell.

Dexter is located in a rich agricultural section and the community is composed largely of small land owners. Cotton has always been the principal crop and the territory is well served by two modern gins and two cotton warehouses, one of these being Federal licensed. In recent years more hogs, cattle and peanuts have been raised, giving increased farm incomes.

Present business firms in Dexter are: Dexter Service Station, Candler Shepard, E. E. Gilbert, Thomas Methvin, Bridger's Barber Shop, W. B. Taylor & Company, Dexter Bonded Warehouse, George Witherington, Mrs. R. M. Green, David Collins, E. P. McDaniel, T. R. Johnson, C. R. Shepard, and J. Kennedy's Warehouse.

Dexter at one time had four rural mail routes, served by J. T. Register, W. P. English, G. F. Shepard, and B. H. Green, but is now served by one carrier, B. H. Green, who is now eligible for retirement after more than thirty years' service. W. P. English and G. F. Shepard retired in recent years after thirty years' service. H. I. King served as postmaster for nearly thirty years, until 1935, when he moved to Washington, D. C.

Members of the present town council are. C. R. Shepard, mayor; W. P. English, W. G. Smith, J. J. Phillips, R. L. Collins, and L. Taylor, aldermen; T. L. Graham, marshal; Donald Underwood, night watchman; Miss Doris Shepard, clerk. Miss Doris Shepard is the only woman ever to have held the office of clerk.

Dexter operated an independent school system until 1938 when it was voted to enter the county system. O. K. Jolley, present principal of the new consolidated school, came to Dexter in 1916 as principal of the town school and served until its consolidation, with the exception of four years teaching in the schools at Rentz and two years during the World War, 1917-19, during which he served with the A. E. F. in France, was taken prisoner and held for nearly a year in Germany. The first P.-T. A. was organized in 1925, with Mrs. Loomis Taylor as president, Mrs. U. G. B. Hogan as vice-president, Mrs. E. A. Sanders as secretary, and Mrs. C. S. Thomas as treasurer. There were thirty-five members, and many helpful things were accomplished. The following have served as president of the P.-T. A. while the town school was in operation: Mrs. C. S. Thomas, Mrs. H. W. Dozier, and Mrs. George Witherington.

The new high school is a consolidation of Mount Carmel, Buckhorn, New Salem, and the old Dexter High School. The new brick school building was erected in 1939-40, at a cost of $30,000, with the school district bearing all costs. The local Board of Trustees were: T. J. Lord, Chairman; F. R. Witherington, W. T. Mackey, R. L. Kitchens, and D. W. Knight, Secretary-Treasurer. The new school opened September 6, 1940, for regular school work with approximately five hundred students and nineteen teachers.

The present P.-T. A. was organized in September, 1940, with Mrs. C. S. Thomas as president, Miss Eleanor Woodard, vice-president, Mrs. H. S. Peek, secretary, and Miss Flaura Mae Coody, treasurer.

The Dexter Baptist Church was organized the fourth Sunday in July, 1893, with twenty-one members. Revered P. A. Jessup was the first pastor, followed in order by the following: J. T. Rogers, J. A. Clark, J. T. Smith, S. F. Simms, E. F. Dye, F. B. Asbel, George W. Tharpe, Q. J. Pinson, T. J. Barnett, J. L. Ivey, E. H. Dunn, R. B. Harrison, J. W. Wambee, O. A. Grant, J. Cecil Daniel, W. J. Williams, and E. A. Price. Present church membership is one hundred sixty-eight.

The Dexter Baptist Sunday School is a graded school, with one hundred twenty-three members enrolled. E. P. McDaniel is superintendent.

The Baptist Woman's Missionary Union was organized in 1908 with Miss Mary Francis Green as first president. Others having served as president are: Mrs. Thompson, Mrs. U. G. B. Hogan, Mrs. J. J. Phillips, Mrs. T. W. Hatch, and Mrs. C. S. Thomas.

The Dexter Methodist Church was organized in 1893 with five members. Mr. and Mrs. Jake Rawls were the first leaders. Mr. J. W. Warren gave the land for the church and Mr. Rawls gave the lumber. In the winter of 1904, the old church building was partially destroyed by a windstorm, and the following winter another storm completed its destruction. The present church was built in 1906, during the pastorate of Reverend J. L. Dickenson. Soon after the first church building was erected, Mr. Jake Rawls, with the help of others, bought the present church parsonage for a preacher's home, and the Woman's Society has had the care of it. In 1909, the Woman's Missionary Society became a Church Aid Society, under the name of Willing Workers, with Mrs. H. I. King, as president, and Mrs. J. E. New, as treasurer. The following have served as leaders in this workk since 1921: Mrs. R L. Harris, Mrs. O. L. Rhodes, Mrs. H. W. Dozier, and the present pastor's wife, Mrs. C. C. Long.

Among the leaders of today in the Methodist Conferences of Georgia is Reverend Silas Johnson, who served as pastor in Dexter as a young man. The present pastor is Reverend C. C. Long, who is serving his third year in the Dexter circuit, at the request of the entire community.

The Dexter Methodist Sunday School was organized in August, 1893, with fifty members enrolled. Elizabeth Rawls, E. P. Warren and B. F. Harvey served as class leaders.

Among the oldest members of the Methodist Church was Mrs. J. W. Warren, now Mrs. J. R. Faircloth, of Dexter.

The Glad Tidings Assembly of God was begun in Dexter in 1932 with an open air revival led by Reverend C. D. Bigbee of Hawkinsville. A Union Prayer Band was organized and meetings were held in the City Hall. Later, gospel meetings were held in the school building and also in a gospel tent, led by Reverend O. L. Kelly and his co-workers of Atlanta, Ga. At the close of this meeting, in October, 1936, a Pentecostal Church was organized, with eighteen charter members. Reverend O. L. Kelly, of Atlanta, was elected pastor, and Miss Ruth Taylor, assistant. Mr. J. L. Hilson donated a lot. Other friends gave material, money and labor, and in April, 1937, a church building was completed, free of debt, and dedicated. The church has a membership of fifty-four at the present time. Reverend H. D. Brown, of Experiment, Ga., is the present pastor.

The first Order of the Eastern Star was organized in Dexter in the summer of 1911; among the charter members were: Mrs. F. M. Daniel, Mrs. H. I. King, Mrs. U. G. B. Hogan, Mrs. R. C. Hogan, Mrs. Jerome Kennedy, Mrs. J. A. Warren, and Mrs. Ernest

Clark. The Chapter was disbanded, but in 1937 it was re-organized as Dexter O. E. S., No. 280, with nineteen women and seven men as members.

The Dexter Lodge, Free and Accepted Masons, No. 340, was chartered in 1891. W. A. Witherington was the first Worshipful Master; J. E. Grinstead was first Senior Warden, and W. F. Woodard was the first Junior Warden. The records prior to 1910 are incomplete, but it is understood that they are enclosed in the cornerstone of the new two-story brick building, erected in 1910, jointly by the Masonic Lodge, the Independent Order of Odd Fellows, and Dr. W. B. Taylor . Some years later the I. O. O. F. was dissolved and the Masonic Lodge assumed the outstanding obligations against the Lodge Building, which were later paid off.

Worshipful Masters of the Masonic Lodge, since 1908, are as follows: J. A. Warren, 1908-09-10-11; E. L. Faircloth, 1912-13; W. A. Witherington, 1914; Ernest Clark, 1915-16-17-18-19-20; D. F. Thomas, 1921-22; H. W. Daniel, 1923; U. G. B. Hogan, 1924-25; H. W. Daniel, 1926; G. W. Edwards, 1927-28-29; U. G. B. Hogan, 1930-31-32; R. C. Hogan, Jr., 1933; I. J. Stripling, 1934; Calhoun Hogan, 1935; C. S. Thomas, 1936; U. G. B. Hogan, 1937-38; W. H. Faircloth, 1939; Herbert Faircloth, 1940, and the present Worshipfl Master is J. A. Stripling. The Lodge has a membership of seventy-five.

Calhoun Hogan, of the Dexter Lodge, is present Worshipful Master of the Twelfth District Masonic Convention.

—*By Mrs. Loomis Taylor.*

d. ROCKLEDGE

Rockledge is located thirteen miles from Dublin on the Macon, Dublin and Savannah Railway. It derives its name from a ledge of rock which crops out along the Dublin and Mount Vernon highway, and runs across the State.

The post office was established in 1899 with William Smith as postmaster, assisted by William Penn Currie.

Before the railroad to Savannah went through Rockledge, it was a terminus of the Wadley & Mount Vernon Railroad.

The churches are a Primitive Baptist and a Methodist. Rockledge is a member of the new consolidated Wilkes High School. The old families are the Thigpens, Wilkes, McLendons, and Salters. The first merchants were R. M. Keen, Ben Newton, R. V. Odom, and W. H. McLendon.

The Rockledge Methodist Church was organized in 1886. For several years a brush arbor was used for services. A church was built in the town about 1908. This building was converted into the present house about 1938.

In the Rockledge community stands old Mount Zion Church, one of the County's oldest Methodist Churches. It was organized soon after the Confederate War; one of its first pastors was C. A. Moore, known as "Uncle Charley." The old Mount Zion congregation, and the congreagtion of another old Methodist Church, known as Salters, have consolidated into the Rockledge Church.

e. Dudley

It was on the day of April 16th, 1888, and in the town of Winchester, Virginia, that Holmes Conrad and his wife Georgia Bryan Conrad signed the deeds that made the Honorable Joshua Walker owner of all that tract of land which now comprises the town of Dudley and its outskirts. At the time Mr. Walker was owner of an estate known, then and now, as "Laurens Hill," and made his home there. One of the signers of this deed, Georgia Bryan Conrad, was the granddaughter of Governor Troup and had come in possession of the property through her mother, Mrs. Florida Troup Bryan, daughter of the governor.

Both traditions and records bear out the fact that there has always been a road where the Macon-Dublin Highway is today. It is possible that this was originally an Indian Trail.

During Governor Troup's lifetime, a plantation road had been made to "fork off" from this main road near where Miller's Filling Station stands today. This plantation road ran in a southwesternly direction by the spot where Dr. Woodard resides and led to the negro quarters of the plantation. During recent years remains of stick-and-dirt chimneys and other relics of these negro cabins have been ploughed up.

About 1885 Honorable Dudley M. Hughes, of Twiggs County, and Colonel John M. Stubbs and Joshua Walker, of Laurens County, began to meet and plan the building of the Macon-Dublin Railroad. Sometimes these gentlemen would meet at the home of Mr. Hughes, sometimes at the home of Col. Stubbs, but, since it was more centrally located, most often at Mr. Walker's store at Laurens Hill.

During the construction of the road, an effort was made by some leading families to place the station at Whipple's Crossing rather than at the present site of Dudley. Mr. Walker was disappointed over the fact that they were not able to build the road by Laurens Hill, and was desirous to have the station adjacent to this particular property, so he made the railroad company the following proposition: That, if they would place the station on its present site, he would lay out a certain number of lots (all to be the same size) and deed every other lot to the company. The proposition was accepted and when the railroad was opened in 1891,the station was placed as stated, and named Elsie for Mrs. Walker. After a time, it was found that there was another station and post office in the State by this name and, since the other town was older, the one in Laurens County had to give way and bear another name. And so, Dudley, the name of Mr. Hughes, who had given untold labor, time and devotion to the building of the road, was the name chosen, and today the town and station bear that name.

One of the first families to live in the new town was that of Ben Fuqua. His home stood to the rear of the present Duggan's Warehouse, and the holly tree by the side of the warehouse was in the Fuqua yard. It was the grandfather of Ben Fuqua who, here in Laurens County, was the first person to discover the value of cotton seed. Before this, farmers, in order to dispose of the seed, had them burned.

Another early family was that of Ben Walker, brother of Joshua Walker. His house stood on the south side of the railroad and is now occupied by the family of Ira Davis.

Other early settlers were the R. J. Chappells, I. J. Duggans, C. J. Johnsons, W. B. Haskins, William Gilberts, Jack Gilberts, A. P. Whipples, Felix Bobbitts, J. W. Guests, H. T. Hooks, and A. J. Cook. Families who came later were those of E. C. O'Neal, Joe Fordham, Joe Johnson, J. A. Hogan, William Methvin, A. J. Weaver, J. G. Donaldson, Dr. J. B. Duggan, W. R. Cook, H. S. Cook, and C. C. Piece.

Not only is Dudley on the Macon-Dublin & Savannah Railroad, but is also on Federal Highway No. 80, about ten miles northwest of Dublin. The population of the town is about 500, and its main business streets and sidewalks are paved. Headquarters for the Oconee Electric Membership Corporation are located here and are housed in a modern brick building.

Other enterprises are: Farmer's Livestock Sales Company, Potato Curing Plant, and cotton warehouses of J. W. Duggan, R. L. Hogan and W. T. Chappell. A modern cotton gin serves the farmers of the surrounding territory.

On December 17th, 1902, the Legislature passed the Act which made Dudley an incorporated town. The charter named T. H. Hooks as the first mayor and the following men to compose the first council: Felix Bobbit, I. J. Duggan, W. J. Gilbert, R. J. Chappell, and W. R. Cook. This mayor and council were to serve until the first regular election, which was the first Wednesday in July, 1903. I. J. Duggan was chosen as first town clerk and Ben Walker was first postmaster.

The first school building stood in a grove adjacent to the lot where the R. J. Chappell residence stands today. It was a one-teacher school, and some of the earliest teachers were: Mrs. Paul Duggan, Jack Gilbert, Allen Whipple, Miss Pauline Thaxton, Miss Jessie Brundage, Mrs. Henry Carroll, Miss Cora Gilbert (now Mrs. Will Keen), and Miss Leila Smith (now Mrs. J. A. Hogan). The land for the first school building was given by Joshua Walker and the M. D. & S. Railroad. Later, I. J. Duggan donated the land on which the present school buildings stand. On this site was erected a two-story wooden building and the school was known as the Ebenezer High School. O. A. Thaxton, now a member of the faculty at Georgia State College for Women, was the first principal. In 1907, this building burned and another of brick was erected on the same site. In the spring of 1936 this building was also destroyed by fire. In the fall of 1937, the school went into the present buildings, and today Dudley enjoys the advantages of one of the largest and best equipped schools in this section of the State. Its faculty consists of 20 members, and the school's enrollment is approximately 500. The buildings which house its commercial and vocational departments, as well as its academic department, are large, comfortable and well equipped. Members of the school board who had charge of building this plant were: R. L. Hogan, T. C. Bobbitt, and J. W. Duggan.

The Bank of Dudley is the oldest bank in the county under its original name. It was organized in 1905. Its first president was J. A. Hogan, its first cashier, T. A. Suttles. There have been only two other presidents: H. D. Joiner and U. G. B. Hogan. Those who have served the bank as cashier, other than Mr. Suttles, are: M. G. Knight, H. T. O'Neal, J. C. Williamson, D. W. Knight, R. L. Sumner, and Rubert L. Hogan.

Churches and church buildings in Dudley are the Methodist and Baptist. The Baptist Church was organized in 1893. The present building is the second house of worship, the first having been destroyed by fire in 1907. The present building was erected in 1913. The land was donated by Joshua Walker and the M. D. & S. Railroad.

The Methodist Church of Dudley was originally located on the Cochran-Dudley Highway near the residence of H. D. Joiner. This building was torn down and the material used in the erection of the first Methodist Church in Dudley. This was on land donated to the church by I. J. Duggan. About 1912 the old building was replaced by the present one.

The town of Dudley is surrounded by territory unusually fertile and therefore well suited to agriculture. Diversified farming is practiced by the progressive farmers in this section, and the result of this is seen in the prosperity which prevails here.

—*By Enda Ballard Duggan (Mrs. J. W.)*

f. MONTROSE

Contributed

The ambitious little town of Montrose, 38 miles south of Macon and 16 miles west of Dublin, on the Macon, Dublin & Savannah Railroad, has nestled itself for more than a quarter of a century beneath the spread of giant oaks and graceful elms.

This village was named in honor of Hon. Dudley Montrose Hughes, a late resident of Twiggs County who, at that time, was an extensive land-holder in both Laurens and Twiggs counties. In its early history Col. John M. Stubbs of Dublin, acquired a great deal of property in Harvard District and devoted much of his talent and wealth to the planting of peach orchards and otherwise landscaping his property with avenues of perpetual beauty, which still stand as monuments to his artistic temperament.

The first mercantile business operated here was under the management of John T. Hughes of Irwinton, who later disposed of it to W. J. Cook during the same year of its establishment.

Many pioneer citizens of Montrose came from Wilkinson County; among them were D. J. Pierce, B. K. Holder, and W. J. Cook. Dr. C. B. Wall, of Jeffersonvile, was the first professional man to locate here, and remained until his death in 1913. T. J. and E. L. Wade, of Washington County, also pioneer citizens, became influential factors in the development of the town. Both had substantial farming interests, and the latter was also engaged in mercantile business. The family of W. G. Thompson of Pulaski (now Bleckley) County, came soon after. Mr. Thompson was both a farmer and a merchant.

The first residence stood near the present site of the Methodist Church, facing the railroad. It was owned by W. M. Scarborough, who lived there during the erection of his home, now known as the Gordon Wade place.

In 1891, the M. D. & S. Railroad was built through the town, and J. M. Scarborough served as agent.

The first school was located at the site of the old school building, now used as Masonic Lodge. Miss Mamie Bell of Brewton, was the first teacher.

The town of Montrose was incorporated in 1919, with M. V. Pickron as mayor, and the following aldermen: Messrs. W. G. Thompson, R. B. Simmons, E. L. Wade, and Dr. Wm. M. Puckett. Dr. Shellnut served as recorder.

There are three churches in Montrose. The Methodist Church was built during the pastorate of Reverend Murray in 1925. The Baptist Church was remodeled in 1925, during the pastorate of Reverend Tharpe of Macon. The Primitive Baptist Church came a few years later, when Reverend Taylor was serving his pastorate. Two active Sunday Schools, three B. Y. P. U., Epworth League, and two Missionary Societies compose the religious organizations.

The outstanding event of 1936 was the sale of bonds for the erection of a consolidated school building, costing $20,000. Prof. E. L. Cates was superintendent. Trustees were: A. J. Weaver, chairman; J. W. Payne, W. R. Cook, W. G. Thompson, and W. S. Williams. This structure was of hollow-tile, with six class rooms, library, two rooms equipped for domestic science, a superintendent's office, and an auditorium which served as a community center. This school building was burned in November, 1938. Almost at once a new building, on the same lines as the first, was constructed and ready for use in December, 1939.

Five teachers, headed by Miss Marguerite McKinney are employed. Two school buses transport pupils. The present school board consists of Jesse Cannon, R. L. Hodges, E. L. Wade, W. G. Thompson, and Wade Dominy.

As an agricultural center Montrose community stands out prominently. Her farm lands and crops attest the highest state of cultivation and progressive methods. Diversified farming is practiced in a conservative manner; several men are turning their attention to the possibilities of dairying and the growing of live stock. Mr. Thompson has proven most successfully that this new venture in the South may herald a better day for Laurens County farmers. He has at various times shipped carloads of cattle. Peanut raising on a large scale has been followed since the early years of the century.

The cutting of hardwood has been of great financial aid; sycamore, poplar, oak, and sweet gum are brought in from the swamps and shipped to Macon. Much pulp wood has been sold in recent years.

Two rural mail routes from Montrose have been consolidated into one.

The Montrose Banking Company was established about 1911 as a chain bank, with C. R. Williams as president, and J. R. Cherry cashier. It is no longer in operation.

Montrose is today (1941) governed by Mayor R. B. Simmons and Councilmen Wade Dominy, C. G. Wade, J. J. O'Neal, D. L. Green, and W. G. Thompson.

g. Rentz

In 1899 Harper and Simpson established a saw mill about thirteen miles south of Dublin. In 1904 E. P. Rentz bought an interest in the mill, which was later changed to the Rentz Lumber Company. The same year the company built a railroad from Rentz to Dublin, and in 1905 the line was extended to Eastman. On February 28, 1941, service was discontinued on the entire line, by the W. & T. Railroad, which had subsequently acquired the line.

The town of Rentz was incorporated August 21, 1905. The first mayor was J. P. Pughsley; councilmen were: J. L. Proctor, A. W. Davidson, J. E. Guy, Dr. C. E. Rentz, and Dr. W. E. Bedingfield.

A. W. Davidson built and operated the first store in Rentz in 1904. He also built the first home in the town.

Doctors W. E. Bedingfield and T. J. Taylor established the first drug store and began the practice of medicine in Rentz in 1905.

The same year the post office was changed from Reedy Springs to Rentz; J. S. Edmondson was the first postmaster.

The first bank was established in 1910 and was known as the Bank of Rentz. Dr. T. J. Taylor was president. This bank was closed in the spring of 1914, and on May 5, 1914, the present Rentz Banking Company was organized, with Dr. J. M. Page as president, H. D. Barron vice-president, H. K. Murckison, cashier. At the present time O. D. Barron is president, Barron Smith vice-president, and Theron Woodard cashier.

In 1905 J. P. Pughsley established a large general store in the young town; in the spring of 1906 fire destroyed this store together with the store of A. W. Davidson and the drug store of Doctors Bedingfield and Taylor. Dr. Taylor then erected the first brick building which is now occupied by Barron's Pharmacy and the post office.

John Rigby built a cotton gin, which was soon bought by a stock company; it burned about 1908. In 1909, Dr. Taylor located a ginnery at Rentz. Later, the present gin, known as the Planters Gin Company, was built by M. E. Burts; and in 1923 O. D. Barron built a modern ginning plant. In 1910, the Farmers Union Warehouse was organized, and began business. Fire destroyed the original building in 1940, with more than 800 bales of cotton. The building was replaced.

In 1923, H. Y. Grant established a cotton warehouse. Additional buildings were soon necessary to store the large cotton crops ginned at Rentz.

At the present time the business established in Rentz are as follows:

Rentz Banking Company, chartered May 2, 1914; Grant Warehouse Company; Farmers Union Warehouse Company; Barron's Pharmacy; J. R. Chambless, hardware and electrical contractor; Rentz Market, groceries and meats, operated by J. R. Chambless and J. A. Daniel; E. J. Woodard, general merchandise; J. A. Davidson, dry goods and notions; James L. Davidson, groceries; Allen D. Davidson, hardware; J. G. Register, groceries; Z. C. Register, groceries; Eugene Couthern, groceries; P. R. Coleman, groceries; R. A. Register, groceries, gas and oil; Mack Strozier, lunch room; Rentz Service Station, O. D. Barron, owner; F. R. Phelps Service Station; Z. C. Register, barber shop; Rentz Wagon Works, blacksmith and general woodwork, owned by J. E. Chambless; Theron Woodard, insurance agent; O. D. Barron Gin Company; Planters Gin Company, R. A. Register operator; Horse and mule sales stables, O. B. Barron. A Livestock Sale Barn was erected by a group of citizens in 1939 as a non-profit enterprise to create a local market for farm live stock. The United States post office, J. E. Chambless postmaster, is a fourth class office, with one rural route. George P. Bugg, the present carrier, succeeded the late J. F. Silas who retired in 1934 on account of ill health, after almost thirty years of service.

J. S. Edmondson was the first postmaster, and J. E. Chambless, the second. Others were: G. M. Knight, L. N. Mullis, O. D. Barron, and C. T. Grainstead.

The present mayor and councilmen are: O. H. Grant, mayor; councilmen, Foster Taylor, A. O. Hadden, H. H. Bedingfield, Barron Smith, and Allen Davidson. W. H. Coleman is town marshal.

The town at one time operated a Delco lighting system, but the Georgia Power Company began supplying electricity to the town April 1, 1927.

The town established a cemetery in 1900.

The population of Rentz is about 400 with 67 residences.

Citizens of Rentz have always been interested in education. About 1914 a two-story brick building was erected and by legislative action, the school became an independent system. Reverend N. H. Burch and O. K. Jolly served as superintendents for a number of years. Others who served during this period were: Miss Carswell of Atlanta; Dan Metts of Winston-Salem, N. C.; Miss Ida O'Neal, Mr. Miller, Mr. Lawson, and Mr. Murchison.

In 1924, courses in home economics and agriculture were added. Miss Sadye Wilkerson, of Utica, Miss., was the first teacher of home economics, and C. A. McMillan was first to serve as teacher of vocational agriculture.

In 1927 the town realized the necessity of broadening its field of usefulness and consolidated with the Laurens County system of schools. This brought in a number of schools in the adjoining territory. L. H. Cook was made superintendent. Later superintendents have been E. A. Rusk and W. M. Ouzts.

In 1939, a vocational building was added. This department is under the direction of Miss Martha Sue McElveen and L. H. Cook.

In 1940, commercial training was added, directed by Miss Gladys Fields of Macon.

The Rentz Methodist Church was organized in 1905 or 1906. Among the early members were: Mr. and Mrs. C. E. Rentz, Mr. and Mrs. J. D. Warthen, Mr. and Mrs. J. S. Pughsley, Mr. and Mrs. Joe Keen. The first pastor was the Reverend Ira Chambers. The first stewards were: David Warthen and Joe Keen. This church, with others, constitutes the Rentz Charge.

Mr. and Mrs. B. O. Rogers were deeply interested in securing a Baptist Church for the town of Rentz so, on the night of Wednesday, June 28, 1905, a small group met in the home of L. G. Knight and organized the Rentz Baptist Church. There were thirteen charter members: Mr. and Mrs. B. O. Rogers (now Mrs. J. E. Chambliss), Mr. and Mrs. W. F. Cooper, Mrs. George Coleman, Mrs John T Rogers, Mr. and Mrs. L. G. Knight, Mr. and Mrs. G. M. Knight, Mrs. John T. Rogers, John S. Knight, D. J. Knight, and G. W. Knight.

The first pastor of the new church was Reverend J. T. Smith, of Dublin. Not owning a building, the church worshipped in the Methodist Church for about a year, until they erected a building of their own in 1906.

The first Sunday School was organized in 1906.

Pastors of the church, since Reverend J. T. Smith, the first pastor, are named below in the order in which they served: T. J. Hobbs, J. Z. Bush, T. Bright, O. O. Williams, T. E. Toole, J. R. Kelly, L. M. Jesup, T. J. Barnette, W. E. Harville, Frank Snyder, C. H. Hornsby, J. C. Daniel, Otis Garland, J. B. Pickern, E. A. Urice, W. O. Brown, and J. W. Harper. C. E. Vines is the present pastor.

During the pastorate of Reverend C. H. Hornsby a movement was started to build a new church. The old wooden structure, becoming dangerous, was torn down and the church again held services in the Methodist Church until, under the leadership of Reverend J. C. Daniel as pastor, the present brick building was completed at a cost of approximately $4,500. The building has a large auditorium which will seat 400 people. There are seven Sunday School rooms and a baptistry built in the rear of the pulpit. The Southern Baptist Convention advanced $1,500 to help finish the building. This has been fully repaid and there is no indebtedness on the property. The notes were destroyed at an impressive dedication ceremony on Sunday, November 29, 1936.

The present board of deacons are: J. E. Chambless, chairman; L. H. Cook, H. Y. Grant, L. A. Gibson, E. J. Woodard.

The present membership of the church is 165. An active Sunday School of eight classes has an enrollment of 120. L. H. Cook is superintendent.

—By L. H. Cook.

h. MINTER

Minter, a small town, in the eastern part of Laurens County, was incorporated in 1906. Among the early settlers were: M. D. Vickers, C. S. New, Dennis Small, W. W. Smith, W. D. Mimbs, J. B. Thomas, L. C. Stewart, John A. Johnson, Sr., John Beasley, W. R. Allen, and the Clements family.

The Minter post office was established in 1892, under the name of Lollie, and Henry E. Pritchett was first postmaster.

The principal church is the Baptist. The present home of this church was built in 1923. Previous to its building the members worshipped in a small frame building called Ann Grove, where the church was organized in 1915. Among the first members of this church were: J. F. Harville and wife, N. Y. Harville and wife, Johnnie Harville, J. J. Young, Dennis Young and wife, J. B. Young and wife, J. C. Clements and wife, R. M. Clements and wife, D. N. Graham and wife, J. F. Graham and wife, J. C. Graham and wife, C. M. Graham and wife, H. J. Sterling and Mrs. Elmina Holmes.

i. CADWELL

Cadwell is located on State Highways Nos. 117 and 126, seventeen miles southeast of Dublin, and is also on the Wrightsville & Tennille Railroad.

The town was incorporated under an Act of the Georgia Legislature in 1907 (p. 500), Amended 1909 (p. 579). This charter and amendment were repealed under Acts of 1912 (p. 681), and on the same date a new charter was granted. (See Acts 1912, pp. 682-691). In 1914 the charter was again changed. Acts of 1925 (p. 916) abolished the Cadwell School System.

The 1907 Act appointed the following governing body: J. W. Warren, mayor; James Burch, Joe Ethridge, C. C. Cadwell, Ed (Sic) Walden, councilmen.

The sale of liquor in the town was prohibited by Act of Incorporation. The 1912 Act appointed the following governing body: H. C. Burch, mayor; A. T. Coleman, A. McCook, H. R. Bedingfield, J. A. Burch, councilmen.

The 1914 Act appointed the following governing body: H. C. Burch, mayor; A. M. Johnson, L. T. Harrell, H. R. Bedingfield, E. E. Hicks, councilmen.

The present government (1940) consists of the following officials: C. J. Bedingfield, mayor; L. K. Smith, Elmer F. Rivers, J. P. Carter, Sr., Allix Colter, councilmen.

When incorporated (1907) the town was to include all the Land Lots 11 and 20 in the 17th land district of Laurens County. Since amendment of 1909, 1,000 square yards comprises the territory of the town, which is described as follows:

> "Commencing at a point in the center of Burch Street where Dexter Street crosses Burch Street, and running southeast down Burch Street five hundred yards; thence up Burch Street northwest five hundred yards; thence up Dexter Street northeast five hundred yards; thence down Dexter Street southwest."

The town was laid off by Galdon Burch and the oak trees along the streets which add much to the beauty of the town were planted at the suggestion of John Burch.

Land for the town was donated by Mrs. Rebecca Lowery Cadwell Burch, and was named for her first husband, Matthew Cadwell, who was the father of Burch Cadwell, C. C. Cadwell, and Victoria Cadwell Lowery. (Being on Burch property, the name Burch was considered until it was learned that there was another post office in the State by the same name.)

The first settlers in Cadwell consisted of the men named in the governing bodies appointed under the Acts of 1907 and 1912 (listed above), also: A. B. Daniel, Luther Clarence, John Burch, R. H. Duggan, J. D. Daniell, E. E. Hicks, T. J. Fann, Bob Ridley, John

Ridley, Walter Mullis, Warren Butler, Burch Cadwell, Mrs. Victoria Lowery, Clarence Sikes, B. B. Jackson, H. C. Coleman, John Weaver, Mack Johnson, T. G. Wade, Warren Joiner, Francis Joiner, Mr. Manning, S. E. Vandiver, and Lem Harrell.

Professional men of Cadwell (early and present) are as follows: Doctors S. D. Bland, J. A. Fort, Butler, G. R. Lee, R. C. Coleman, A. T. Coleman, I. J. Parkerson, R. A. Bedingfield, C. J. Bednigfield. (The last two mentioned are still living and practicing in Cadwell.)

The first buildings in Cadwell were erected by Burch Cadwell and H. R. Bedingfield. The first business was Bedingfield Mercantile Company, owned by H. R. Bedingfield and Luther Clarence.

Being an agricultural section there is located here: two cotton gins, saw mill, peanut sheller, grist mill, cotton seed breeding farms, meat curing plant, two turpentine concerns, two cotton warehouses, and telephone exchange.

Following are some of the leading business men and farmers of Cadwell: H. C. Burch, J. B. Bedingfield, C. J. Bedingfield, W. D. Parkerson, Jr., L. K. Smith, Walter Daniell, W. J. Daniell, G. N. Weatherly, J. P. Carter, Sr., M. H. Sikes, B. J. Bedingfield, Elmer F. Rivers, Allix Colter, H. F. Wynn, C. B. Hudson, A. L. Cameron, R. B. Bedingfield.

BAPTIST CHURCH: This church was organized in 1909; first pastor was Eli Evans; first deacons: John Burch, A. S. Jones; clerk, H. C. Burch. Others who have served as pastors are: J. M. Henderson, A. V. Pickron, T. J. Barnett, J. W. Parker, O. A. Grant, N. H. Burch, O. W. Garland, J. B. Pickron, Charlie Jones, Gus Peacock, and R. L. O'Brien, the present pastor. The present deacons are: Walter Daniell, chairman; L. K. Smith, W. D. Parkerson, Jr., G. C. Williams and S. G. Burch. The church has grown from seven male charter members to a present membership of one hundred seventy-five. The present brick church building was erected in 1919-20, with A. V. Pickron pastor, at a cost of $12,000.

METHODIST CHURCH: This church was organized in 1913. The first pastor was Silas Johnson; first stewards, W. J. Ballard, Mack Johnson, and Mrs. R. E. Burch. The present pastor is C. C. Long, and the present stewards are Mrs. J. B. Bedingfield, Mrs. Belah Burch, and L. J. Flanders. This church has a membership of thirty-five.

It has been reported to the writer that the Cadwell school was begun in 1911, and reference to the Act of 1912, granting a new charter, will show that power to devise a system of public schools in the town and the right to issue bonds was given. Trustees for one-year terms were to be elected by the Mayor and Council.

The Act of 1925 (p. 916) abolished the school system of Cadwell and permitted the town authorities to sell or otherwise dispose of the property. It was then, the year 1925, that other schools in the district were consolidated with the Cadwell School, creating the Cadwell Consolidated School. Under the consolidation the first trustees were: H. C. Burch, chairman; J. B. Bedingfield, secretary-treasurer; J. T. Jones, D. W. Alligood, J. F. Rivers.

The school has grown from its original enrollment of fifty to its present enrollment of approximately 350, with thirteen teachers of whom J. Wilkins Smith is superintendent. Present trustees are: J. B. Bedingfield, chairman; C. J. Bedingfield, secretary-treasurer; Walter Daniell, L. K. Smith, N. J. Stuckey.

(Note: H. B. Graham and Freeman Mullis have been elected to begin term 1941, due to the resignations of first two trustees listed).

Cadwell Consolidated High School has operated since 1939 as a four-year accredited high school; the first diploma issued as an accredited high school was to WalterDaniel, one of its trustees.

With the assistance of WPA four class rooms were added in 1939. This completed a modern brick building with a separate class room for each grade, and an auditorium. Additional departments are: agricultural, home economics, work shop, gymnasium, and a canning plant in which approximately 7,000 cans of fruit, vegetables, etc., were put up for the community in 1940.

The agricultural and home economics departments were added in 1928, and its first teachers were Mr. and Mrs. J. B. Pullen. Present teachers of these departments are Mr. and Mrs. Clyde Greenway.

A course in public music and a band have also been added to the school.

Cadwell Banking Company was organized in 1910 with Mr. Holt of Sandersville, as its first president. Among its officers and directors were: H. C. Burch, D. W. Alligood, H. R. Bedingfield, B. J. Bedingfield, R. J. Register, W. B. Coleman. Those serving as cashier were J. A. Burch, H. H. Burch, and Walter Daniell.

The Citizens Bank was organized about 1912 by a Mr. Williams with A. McCook as president, and W. J. Ballard cashier. A few years later this bank merged with the Cadwell Banking Company.

The Cadwell Banking Company operated until 1928 when it closed after a run was made on it by depositors, caused by the closing of the First National Bank of Dublin, one of its depositories.

In 1929, J. F. Graham, M. H. Sikes, J. B. Bedingfield, W. D. Parkerson, and L. K. Smith organized a private bank, known as the Farmers Clearing Bank, which is operated with L. K. Smith, cashier; W. D. Parkerson, Jr., and J. B. Bedingfield, owners.

In 1913, the town installed a water and light plant which was operated until 1927 when Georgia Power Company lights were secured for the streets and homes.

With the assistance of WPA, a modern water system was secured in 1939, and a modern sewer system for the town is being installed.

All streets are surfaced with sand clay gravel and a highway project for paving, installing curb and gutter and paving sidewalks through the town, on State Route 117, have been approved for immediate construction.

State Route 126 is being graded for paving into Cadwell from the South by State convict forces.

—By Walter Daniell.

j. LAURENS HILL

One of the outstanding landmarks which time has spared to Laurens County is an old estate known as Laurens Hill. This old Colonial home faces the highway, which was originally the Blackshear Trail, about half-way between Cochran and Dublin. The stately old house, with its white columns, stands embowered in a grove of magnolias, cedars, and live oaks. It was built between 1833 and 1843 by David Harvard. He directed the work himself and saw that the house was not only handsomely but substantially built, for nothing was allowed in its erection, except the very best of materials. It was modeled upon the plan of a typical southern home. This old house is still in a perfect state of preservation and, with the exception of slight changes, is just as it was in the Forties.

The grounds surrounding the house are beautified, not only with magnolias, cedar and oaks, but also with choice shrubbery. Here, also, are walks bordered with boxwood more than seventy-five years old. It was Mrs. David Harvard, wife of the builder of Laurens Hill, who planted the circle of cedars on the grounds directly in front of the house.

Mr. Harvard died in October, 1865, and sometime thereafter the house and lands were acquired by Joshua Walker, of Wilkinson County, who with his family resided here and dispensed to all visitors that hospitality characteristic of a gentleman of the old South. His death occurred in 1897. The property then passed into the hands of Mr. Walker's children and most of it is still owned by his descendants. J. W. Whitaker, the present owner, is a grandson of Mr. Walker and makes his home here.

With the exception of Dublin, it is doubtful if any other community in the county can boast of being the place where as many interesting and historical events transpired as Laurens Hill. The store located not far distant was the largest between Dublin and Cochran, and enjoyed a large patronage. It was here that people from miles around gathered to discuss questions of the day and to transact business. It was in this store that Hon. Dudley M. Hughes, Col. John M. Stubbs, and Joshua Walker often met when planning the building of the Macon, Dublin & Savannah Railroad.

Here too, was established a United States post office which was named Laurens Hill.

Across the Highway cut by General David Blackshear, and almost directly in front of the store, the Confederate government erected a building during the war, in which to store supplies. This building still stands, and is known as the Confederate Commissary.

This old house has been the scene of many and varied gatherings. Many times has the congregation of Laurens Hill Church gathered here for its regular service, and for several years the Cool Springs Masonic Lodge held its meetings here.

Almost directly in front of the store at Laurens Hill was the entrance to the old cemetery. Today the store has disappeared and in its place stands a barn. On the south side of the highway (Blackshear Trail), and adjacent to the old Confederate Commissary, lies an old cemetery which holds the dust of persons prominently identified with the history of the County and State. An interesting tombstone in this old cemetery is that of David Harvard, born May 7, 1809; died October 29, 1865; a member and Deacon of Laurens Hill Church.

One of Laurens County's most noted educators, Mrs. Harriet Bates Summers, is buried in this cemetery. Not only was she a teacher of note, but she was also a member of the first Board of Visitors of the Georgia Normal and Industrial College (now Georgia State College for Women), at Milledgeville, Georgia.

The oldest grave in the cemetery is that of a child, Hannah Harvard, who was buried there August, 1837. Other families who rest here are: Summers, Floyds, Wades, Harvards, and Barkwells.

—*By Enda Ballard Duggan (Mrs. J. W.)*

LAURENS HILL BAPTIST CHURCH

Hard by the old Laurens Hill plantation, and on the original Blackshear Trail, stands old Laurens Hill Baptist Church, the fourth oldest church in the county. It was organized in 1843 with the following charter members: David Harvard, Mary Ann Harvard, Mary C. Williamson, Charles Powel, Mary Powel, Robert Higdon, Jr., Emily Higdon, John Higdon, and Matilda Higdon.

It was on December 9th, 1843, that the membership met for the first time and, from the inference made in the minutes, the meeting was held in the plantation home of David Harvard. At this meeting the following were received by letter: Daniel Powel and his wife Frances Powel, Wethy Leonard, Rebecca Jones, Benjamin Powell and Tabithy Bullock. Also "received by experience was Disey, colored woman-servant of Brother D. Harvard." The writer quotes from the minutes of the old journal of the church: "December 9th, 1843, Conference opened by Brother Joseph Ross. The church then proceeded to the choice of a pastor and resulted in the choice of Brother Joseph Ross and Brother John M. Hampton in connection with Brother Ross."

Quoting further, January 20th, 1844: "The church then proceeded to elect a deacon and clerk and resulted in the choice of Brother John Higdon for deacon, and Brother Robert Higdon Junior for clerk. The church then proceeded to appoint a committee to make arrangements for the building of a meeting house and appointed Brother David Harvard, Robert Higdon, Charles Powell, Benjamin Powell and John Higdon the Committee . . . ."

The minutes of October 18th, 1845, show that "letters of correspondence from the sister churches at Rocky Creek, Poplar Springs and Mount Calvary were read," and that "the committee appointed to select a place to build the meeting house reported that their selection was a place near Mrs. Mary Hampton Mills." For some unknown reason the building committee was unable to secure the deed to the land selected, for the minutes of December 20th, 1845, tell us that "on motion of Brother David Harvard, one of the committee, it was agreed to build the house near the bridge on Rocky Creek on the road leading from Blackshear's Ferry to Hawkinsville." This was the logical place for the building because in those early days most of the church buildings of the Baptist denomination were built on or near the banks of some stream. This was true because the water of the stream was used for baptismal purposes. The old journal of this church records frequently the fact that an applicant for church membership, by experience, agreed to meet the pastor and deacons at a certain time at the "stream by the bridge."

Thus the first church building for old Laurens Hill congregation was erected. This was in 1846. The writer has been unable to ascertain the kind of church building this was, except that it was a wooden building, for the journal records a bill of lumber and materials that went into its erection. Evidently it contained a gallery for the negro slaves.

One thing certain about this first church building is that it accommodated the congregation only twenty-seven years, for we read in the journal "the church becoming old and thought to be dangerous it was decided to remove and repair the house." This was February 22nd, 1873, and on October 18th, 1873, the congregation met in the new church for the first time. This second building was a very imposing one for its time. Across the front was a porch of Greek style architecture. Its facade was triangular and the roof was supported by white columns. Like all churches of that day, it had a side door. Since the Emancipation Proclamation was ten years old by this time and the slaves all free, this building contained no gallery for them.

However, the congregation of the church grew until the building would not accommodate it. So, about 1897 or 1898 the porch was removed in order that an addition might be made to the front, and today old Laurens Hill Church stands without the original porch or the side door.

Many and interesting were the events that occurred here, as recorded in the journal. In one place we find: "Saturday, April 15th, 1848—A colored servant of Gov. Troup's, by the name of Dick, received by experience." In another place is recorded, "Received by experience Matilda, a colored sister, servant of Bro. Robert Higdon, Senior, and Green, a colored Bro., servant of Bro. W. G. Philips." Often letters and messengers were received from the following churches: Rocky Creek, Poplar Springs, and Mt. Calvary. Laurens Hill Church elected delegates to union meetings held at the above churches, later to the church at Hawkkinsville, and still later to the church at Dublin. At the meeting of the church conference held August 19th, 1848, there were present 37 white members and 15 colored members, a total of 52 present.

The minutes of the church make no reference to the Emancipation Proclamation, but they show that, "colored members" began asking for letters of dismissal in 1867. This continued until Bro. A. E. Vickers, on October 5th, 1872, made a motion that letters of dismissal be granted to all colored members who requested them. However, the records show that during this same year (1872), and even later, negroes applied for membership and were received. Bro. Jas. R. Williamson served as pastor of the church before and throughout the War (1854 to 1868), but meetings were seldom and irregular.

Those who served the church as pastors were: Joseph Ross, 1843 to 1844; L. B. Lee, 1844-1848; Wm. R. Steeley, 1848-1850; L. B. Lee, 1850-1854; James R. Williamson, 1854-1868; Richard Smith, 1868-1869; Moses N. McCall, 1869-1874; E. B. Barrett, 1874-1875; W. D. Horne, 1875-1877; Thomas W. Dupree, 1877-1878; J. L. D. Miller, 1878-1879. The church became disorganized about 1879 and had no pastor. In 1882 a reorganization occurred and J. Z. Bush was chosen pastor.

The clerks, up to the year 1884, were as follows· Robert Higdon, 1843-1844; C. C. Harvey, 1847; David Harvard, 1848-1856; John R. Coombs, 1856-1867; Quin L. Harvard, 1867-1868; W. C. Harvard, 1868-1871; Quin L. Harvard, 1871-1877; John W. Barkwell, 1877-1883; W. F. Harvard, 1884-

Among the members of the church who were prominent and often mentioned in the minutes are: Robert Higdon, Jr., John Love, John Love, Jr., David Harvard, A. E. Vickers, Kindred Partain, C. Powell, Joshua Walker, and W. M. O'Neal. Of these, David Harvard, Joshua Walker, and W. M. O'Neal often served as Moderator when the Pastor was absent.

The journal of this church, including the minutes of its meetings from May, 1883, to August, 1884, was lost and the clerk,

W. F. Harvard, began recording the minutes in a new book. This book has not been available to the writer. So the recent history of this old church is somewhat obscure except as to its oldest members and attendants. For many years during this period (1883-1941) Isaac J. Duggan and J. A. Hogan were its clerks, and Rev. Geo. W. Tharpe and Rev. J. E. Townsend served as pastors. Reverend C. E. Vines is the present pastor.

Today Laurens Hill Church stands as a silent testimony to those pioneer members, who so nobly and bravely labored, that a Christian civilization of the highest type might be planted on the soil of Laurens County.

k. CEDAR GROVE COMMUNITY

Midway between the Scotland and Telfair roads in Burch's District, is the little community of Cedar Grove, consisting of a few homes, two stores, and three school buildings grouped around a lietle white church.

One looks for a cedar bordered avenue but not a cedar is to be seen. 'Twas thus the name originated: Some half century ago a wealthy church-loving man, Cornelius Clark, wanted a church built in his community. He chose a spot where cedar trees were growing in a graveyard and decided that the church should be built here and named Cedar Grove. But his choice met with opposition from neighbors who wanted it nearer the center of the community. B. L. and Lamar Lowery offered to build the church if placed on the present site. Mr. Clark consented to their choice of location, but insisted that the church carry the name he had chosen, Cedar Grove. This building was burned; a log church was built, and it was burned. Later, Osford's Mill sawed the lumber and David and Warren Pope built the house now in use.

Earliest settlers of this community were the Clarks and the Alfred Burch family, later were the Lowerys, Parishes, John Gay, Sam Harrison, Lamar and S. L. Miller.

Purvis' Store was the first business established; other stores have been operated by Sam Mackey, Russell Howell and Cordie Joiner.

A school was begun while the log church was in use; in 1924, the schools of Oakdale, Union Springs and Whitewater were consolidated at Cedar Grove. In 1926, a bond issue was floated, the first large unit of the building program was constructed and a teachers' home built. In 1939 the community voted a bond issue of $6,000, secured federal aid for $4,909, and two new buildings were erected. The school has fourteen teachers, directed by Principal G. E. Currie.

The Whiteford Masonic Lodge was organized about 1885 in the home of the Reverend Wash Geiger; it was chartered about 1888; the first hall was built near Pine Hill Academy. This building was burned. The Lodge was soon reorganized at Lowery Church; a house was built, the lower floor used as a school, the upper as a lodge hall, but this also was burned. The Lodge then moved to Cedar Grove and erected a new hall. The Odd Fellows have an organization at Cedar Grove and share the Masonic Hall. This organization has been in existence about twenty-five years. Whiteford Lodge is the parent chapter of the Glenville, Alamo, and Rentz Lodges.

Among the outstanding farmers of today are: R. T. Gilder, a large land-owner and naval operator; Clayton Clark, W. M. Clark, W. A. Hill, L. L. Howell, J. C. Davidson, Miller Sears, Morris and Lanier White, and Mrs. A. P. Perdue.

Harlow Currie is a large land-owner, progressive farmer, cattle raiser, and operates the H. M. Currie naval stores plant.

Two old churches, once prominent in the Cedar Grove community, are now defunct. The old Clark Baptist Church, built by descendants of John Clark, ceased to function nearly sixty years ago. Here George Clark was ordained; after he became a minister he moved to Colquitt County and became one of the best loved preachers of that section.

Old Lowery's Church stood for many years in this community. This was a pioneer Methodist Church. Old preachers who served in this section were: the Reverend Galloway, Wash Greiger, and W. E. Kinchen.

1. CROSS ROADS COMMUNITY

Cross Roads community lies in the center of Pinetucky District and has assembled there because of the fertile lands. It lies thirteen miles south of Dublin on the Alamo Road, eight miles from Rentz, and fourteen miles from Cadwell.

In the near area are one Methodist and two Baptist churches. The heart of the community is the Cross Roads Consolidated School; three school buses furnish transportation for the pupils.

A local tax is levied in addition to County and State support for the school's maintenance. Leading citizens of the community are the Lowery, Dixon, Fordham, and Herndon families.

Chapter XVII
IN PUBLIC SERVICE

1. IN THE STATE

In the House of Representatives

1808-1809, Peter Thomas; 1810, Charles Strange; 1811, Elisha Farnell; 1812, Wm. O'Neal; 1813, Wm. O'Neal; 1814, Wm. O'Neal; 1815, Green Wood; 1816, Green Wood; 1817, Lunsford C. Pitts; 1819, Amos Love, Leroy G. Harris; 1820, Josiah Horn, John Thomas; 1821, Josiah Horn, John Thomas; 1822, John Thomas, Josiah Horn; 1823, John Thomas, Josiah Horn; 1824-25, Josiah Horn, Lott Warren (resigned), Neil Munroe; 1825, Neil Munroe, Josiah Horn; 1826, Russell Kellam, Neil Munroe; 1827, Eli Warren, Edward St. George.

1828, Eli Warren, Russell Kellam; 1829, Eli Warren, Russell Kellam; 1830, Russell Kellam, Benj. W. Hampton; 1831, Eli Warren, Benj. W. Hampton; 1832, Eli Warren, James H. Blackshear; 1833, Eli Warren, Jas. H. Blackshear; 1834, Ira Stanley, Jeremiah H. Yopp; 1836, Bryan Allen, Andrew Y. Hampton; 1837, Bryan Allen, Andrew Y. Hampton; 1838, Hardy B. Stanley; 1839, Robert Robinson, Allen Ashley; 1840, Robert Robinson, Allen Ashley; 1841, Robert Robinson, Chas. B. Guyton; 1842, Robert Robinson, Allen Ashley; 1843-1844, Charles B. Guyton, Robert Robinson.

1845-46, Robert Robinson, Charles B. Guyton; 1847-48, Robert Robinson, Charles B. Guyton; 1849-50, Robert Robinson, John W. Yopp; 1851-52, Robert Robinson, John W. Yopp; 1853-54, John W. Yopp; 1855-56, Charles B. Guyton; 1857-58, C. L. Holmes; 1859-60, C. L. Holmes; 1861,62, Robert Robinson; 1863-64, J. M. Smith; 1865-66, Robert Robinson; 1868-69, George Linder (colored), E. D. Barfrett; 1871-1872, C. S. Guyton; 1873-74, J. T. Duncan; 1875-76, J. T. Chappell; 1877, C. S. Guyton.

1880-81, Henry M. Burch; 1882-83, J. B. Wolfe; 1884-85, J. E. Hightower; 1886-87, Joel T. Coney; 1888-89, A. B. Clark; 1890-91, James T. Chappell; 1892-93, T. H. Rowe; 1894-95, John R. Baggett; 1896-97, John R. Baggett; 1898-99, L. Q. Stubbs; 1900-01, L. Q. Stubbs; 1902-03, J. B. Hicks, H. P. Howard; 1905-06, G. W. Williams, D. J. Clark; 1907-08, G. W. Williams, L. A. Matthews (died), D. J. Clark.

1909-10, J. E. Burch, M. S. Jones; 1911-12, W. B. Taylor, E. D. White; 1913-14, W. B. Taylor, W. B. Coleman; 1915-16, W. B. Coleman, G. B. Davis; 1917-18, Geo. B. Davis, L. Q. Stubbs; 1919-20, W. B. Rogers, L. Q. Stubbs; 1921-22, C. H. Kittrell, Hal B. Wimberly, Jerome Kennedy; 1923, (Extra '24), Ernest Clark, Stephen Parker New, Henry (Hal B.) Wimberly; 1925-26, (Extra '26 2nd Extra) Ernest Clark, S. P. New, J. Marion Peacock.

1927, John B. Bedingfield, Reese C. Coleman, S. P. New; 1929-31, (Extra) J. B. Bedingfield, R. C. Coleman, S. P. New; 1931, William Brunson, J. Franklin Graham, Carlton K. Nelson; 1933, Joseph J. Chappell, William Brunson; 1935, Rubert L. Hogan, Rufus I. Stephens; 1937, ('37-'38 Extra) William Arthur Dampier, William Washington Larsen, Jr.; 1939, Ed L. Evans, William Herschel Lovett; 1941, Dawson Kea, William Herschel Lovett.

In the Senate

1808, Edmond Hogan; 1809, Jethro B. Spivey; 1810, Henry Sheppard; 1811, Henry Sheppard; 1812, John Fulwood; 1813, John Fulwood; 1814,

John Fulwood; 1815, Jacob Robinson; 1816, David Blackshear; 1817, David Blackshear; 1818, David Blackshear; 1819, Jacob Blackshear; 1820, David Blackshear; 1821, David Blackshear; 1822, David Blackshear; 1823, David Blackshear; 1824, David Blackshear; 1825, David Blackshear.

1826, Josiah Horn; 1827, Neil Munroe; 1828, Neil Munroe; 1829, Neil Munroe; 1830, Neil Munroe; 1831, Edward St. George; 1832, Russell Kellam; 1833, Russell Kellam; 1834, Eli Warren; 1835, Russell Kellam; 1836, Wingfield Wright; 1837, Wingfield Wright; 1838, Wingfield Wright; 1839, Wingfield Wright; 1840, Wingfield Wright; 1841, Wingfield Wright; 1842, Wingfield Wright; 1843, Nathan Tucker.

1844, Nathan Tucker; 1845, Wesley King; 1846, Wesley King; 1847, Augustus B. Raiford; 1849-50, E. J. Blackshear; 1851-52, James Ross; 1853-54, Charles B. Guyton; 1855-56, Robert Robinson; 1857-58, Robert Robinson; 1859-60, H. M. Moore; 1861-62, John B. Wright; 1863-64, John B. Wright; 1865-66, Lott Barwick; 1868-69, H. Hicks; 1870, H. Hicks; 1871, H. Hicks; 1872, H. Hicks; 1873, J. F. Robinson; 1874, J. F. Robinson; 1875, J. F. Robinson; 1876, J. F. Robinson; 1877, Neill McLeod; 1878-79, Neill McLeod; 1880-81, James H. Hicks; 1882-83, C. S. Guyton; 1884-85, George S. Rountree; 1886-87, John A. Douglas; 1888-89, Charles L. Holms; 1890-91, E. W. Lane; 1892-93, A. F. Daley; 1894-95, James L. Keen; 1896-97, W. R. Kemp.

1898-99, R. J. Moye; 1900-01, George Carter; 1902-03, C. S. Rountree; 1903-04, Robert J. Williams; 1905-06, B. G. Fortner; 1907-08, C. W. Brantley; 1909-10, W. R. Kemp; 1911-12, W. N. Kight; 1913-14, Fred Kea; 1915-16, N. L. Gillis; 1917-18, M. T. Rhiner; 1919-20, Fred Kea; 1923 (Extra '24), James L. Gillis (Montgomery); 1925-26 (Extra '26, 2nd Extra), Manning Alonzo Rountree (Emanuel); 1927, Joseph M. Page (Laurens); 1929-31 (Extra), Felix Carlton Williams (Emanuel); 1931, Sewel Murdock Courson (Treutlen); 1933, William Herschel Lovett (Laurens); 1935, William Washington Larsen, Jr. (Laurens); 1937 (Extra); 1937-38, John B. Spivey (Emanuel); 1939, John B. Spivey (Emanuel); 1941, J. H. Rowland (Johnson).

2. IN SERVICE BEYOND LAURENS

Many Laurens Countians have held positions of honor and distinction in the State and Nation, among these are:

Peyton L. Wade, a leading lawyer, resided in Dublin until made a judge in the Court of Appeals in 1914. He came to Dublin in 1886 from Athens. He was one of the members who organized the Weekly Press Association in 1887.

In 1912 Harris McCall (Hal) Stanley, a Dublin newspaper man, born and reared in the County, became Commissioner of Commerce and Labor; he held this post and the chairmanship of the State Industrial Board continuously until he retired in May, 1940.

Vivian L. Stanley, brother to H. M. Stanley, became Prison Commissioner in 1928, and moved from Dublin to make his home in Atlanta.

Peter S. Twitty was State Game and Fish Commissioner from September, 1923, till January, 1934.

W. W. Larsen served as Representative from the Twelfth District in the United States Congress for nine terms—1916 to 1933. He came to Dublin in 1911 and began the practice of law. In 1914 he was appointed judge of the Laurens Superior Court. His death came while he was Director of Unemployment Compensation. Judge Larsen was the agent who secured the location of a Federal Court at Dublin.

John S. Adams received an appointment in the U. S. Treasury Department, in Washington, D. C., and resided there until his resignation and his return to Dublin to resume his practice of law.

Parker S. New, in July, 1936, was appointed an attorney for the Interstate Commerce Commission, and moved from Dublin to Washington, D. C. Before that time he represented Laurens County four terms in the Georgia Legislature.

Joe Chappell, a former Dublin lawyer, has served as secretary to Senator Richard B. Russell for several years.

Laurens County has been the home of people well known beyond Georgia. Hon. W. G. Brantley, a famous United States Congressman, at one time lived in Dublin; Hon. Thomas W. Hardwick, former Governor of Georgia and United States Senator, lived here in the 1920's; Hon. John T. Boufeuillet, journalist and railroad commissioner, was also a former resident; Ernest Camp, prominent newspaper editor and poet, formerly made Dublin his home; John M. Simmons, nationally prominent manufacturer, lived in Dublin and owned and operated his first factory here. Judge Alex Akerman, United States Judge, Florida, (retired) was also a former resident of Dublin.

Tom Linder, born of one of the old families of Laurens County, has been honored twice by the State. He was elected Commissioner of Agriculture; after serving one term, he retired to private life; but in 1940 was again elected to this responsible office.

3. IN THE COUNTY.

Tax Collectors of Laurens County

The following officers are found in the county records (possibly incomplete).

Edmund Hogan, Elisha Farnall, Robert Coleman, Joel Williams, Charles P. Creech, A. A. Fuqua, William Adams, James A. Thomas, Edmund Perry, Seaborn A. Bracewell, M. L. Burch, B. B. Linder, R. T. Dominy, P. B. Linder, A. J. Hilbun, J. B. Jones, O. W. Linder, O. W. Keen, John Wilkes, Jr., F. M. Daniel, C. H. Adams, E. Darius Keen, M. C. Dominy, Charles E. Baggett, filled unexpired term of M. C. Dominy; Morris Baggett who died in office, his wife filling unexpired term; Trammell C. Keen.

Tax Receivers of Laurens County

James Yarbrough, Ashley Wood, Hugh Thomas, Joel Williams, Andrew A. Fuqua, John Raffield, Washington Baker, Elijah Benton, Edward Perry, Daniel G. Pope, H. Currell, J. B. Jones, A. J. Hilburn, F. D. Beall, Elijah B. Jones, D. H. Barkwell, J. N. Adams, T .G. B. Law, S. F. Brown, James Warren Rowe, John G. Thomas, J. B. Keen, A. E. Haddon.

Four year terms began for these offices about 1920.

CORONERS

John B. Bennett, W. Wright, William Bohannon, Eason Green, Coleman Sanders, Hiram Kinchen, Edward Shepherd, W. E. Jeffeken, William R. Hester, James Wyatt, William Gilbert, James Barfield, Seaborn Jones, Eli M. Keen, David J. Darsey, J. L. Linder, J. C. Donaldson, D. C. Shea, R. J. Rault, S. T. Cordell, L. J. Thomas, Judson L. Jackson, William C. Perry, died in office; Ben C. Edwards appointed to fill unexpired term of Wm. C. Perry; J. K. Rowland appointed to fill Edwards' place, who died in office; O. D. Knight.

COUNTY TREASURERS

Thomas Moore, Robert Roberson, Thomas N. Guyton, Francis Thomas, Freeman H. Rowe, John J. Keen, James W. Stanley, W. J. Scarborough, Joel E. Perry, M. L. Jones, Hardy Smith, William J. Hightower, Tilden Hall, L. C. Pope.

In 1916 this office was abolished and the clerks of the county commissioners acted as Treasurer and gave bond.

The law abolishing the office of County Treasurer was later repealed and the office restored. Since 1924 these have served as Treasurers: William Allen Burch, John R. Daniel, W. S. Thomas, Mrs. Henrietta Bidgood.

Among those who have served as County Surveyors are: David Blackshear, Thomas McCall, Jacob T. Linder, Wm. B. Snell, Frederick W. Flanders, James W. Daniel, K. H. Walker, B. B. Linder, B. H. Blackshear, Elijah Benton, J. W. Barkswell, Ira E. Hilbun, B. W. Burch, John H. Clark, J. D. McLendon, H. H. McLendon, M. C. Carter, J. T. Flanders, Z. Whitehurst, E. H. Green, C. H. Colquhoun, W. H. H. McLendon, D. R. Jackson, Andrew Duffie.*

---

* Sheriffs are listed in the Court section.

Chapter XVIII

PROFESSIONAL MEN IN LAURENS COUNTY

1. LAWYERS

Laurens County has been unusually rich in the number and excellence of its professional men. On Georgia's legal and political stage Laurens County lawyers have played prominent parts.

As early as the third decade of the 19th century Dublin possessed a lawyer known over the State for his knowledge of the law, and law aspirants from adjoining counties came to study criminal and civil law under him; this man was Daniel McNeel.

The most illustrious pupil of Dan McNeel was Lott Warren. Born in Burke County, in 1797, he came as an orphan, at the age of twelve, to the territory that soon became Laurens County. He was working as a clerk in a small store when he was drafted for the Seminole War, and was soon made second lieutenant. After returning to Dublin, he worked on a flat boat on the Oconee River. In 1820, after studying law under McNeel, he was admitted to the Bar. In later life he served as solicitor-general on the Southern Circuit, also as Judge of the same circuit. After he left Laurens County he represented Georgia in the National Assembly.

Eli Warren, a brother of Lott Warren, practiced law in the Dublin Bar before and after the War Between the States.

Peter Early Love, the son of Amos Love, became one of Georgia's leading lawyers and a successful politician. He served in the State Legislature, and became Judge of the Superior Court, Southern Circuit, after a successful career as solicitor-general. He was representing Georgia in the National Congress at the time of secession, and was one of the six members from Georgia who withdrew.

Other men practicing at the Dublin Bar in the Fifties were: E. T. Sheftall and his brother, John R. Cochran, Y. J. Anderson, James C. Borner, E. C. and W. H. Croker.

In 1849, John T. Duncan came to Laurens County. He was elected Sheriff at the age of twenty-one, and, from then until his death, was in active service for the County. He was a judge of the Inferior Court in its latter days. He represented Laurens County in the Legislature and served as Ordinary for twenty-two years. During his administration, the bridge over the Oconee River was constructed and the jail built.

The parents of John B. Wolfe were pioneers in the village of Dublin; he was born in 1838 and educated at the University of Georgia and the University of South Carolina. He was a leading lawyer, farmer and merchant. He represented his County in the Georgia Legislature in 1882.

In April, 1867, Henry Currell was granted a license to practice law. In 1868, James A. Thomas, having studied under the leading lawyers of this section—Eli Warren, Iona Reeves, J. G. Ackington and Eli Cumming—was admitted to the Bar. James A. Thomas was a war veteran and a descendant of Peter Thomas. He made his home in Dublin till his death. His wife was a daughter of one of the County's old families, the Corbetts. He was Commander-in-Chief of the Confederate Veterans for several years.

A prominent Laurens County lawyer who began practice before the War was Mercer Haynes. He came as a young man to the County, became judge of the County Court and served Dublin as Mayor. Other lawyers of this period were Jonathan Rivers, William H. Wylly and R. A. Stanley; the latter was captain of a company in the Confederate War and for many years a leader in the Dublin Baptist Church. He was solicitor-general for this circuit for many years.

Among the leading lawyers of the latter years of the nineteenth century and the beginning of the twentieth were: Colonel John M. Stubbs, Thomas B. Felder, James B. Sanders, and Peyton L. Wade.

Col. John M. Stubbs came to Dublin in 1870 and became recognized as one of Georgia's leading attorneys. He was exceedingly public spirited. He was active in promoting transportation on the Oconee River. Colonel Stubbs was the father of the peach industry in the County; with J. P. Berckmans he organized Georgia's first horticultural society.

Thomas B. Felder, a native of Waynesboro, Georgia, was a prominent figure in the legal profession; after leaving Dublin he became a widely known corporation lawyer, with offices in Atlanta, Memphis, Washington, D. C., and New York City.

James B. Sanders came to Dublin from Penfield, Greene County, Georgia, following his graduation from the University of Georgia, and became director of the Dublin Academy. In 1886, he was admitted to the Bar and began the practice of law in the well known firm of Felder and Sanders. He also served as mayor of the city of Dublin and judge of the City Court.

Peyton L. Wade came to Dublin from Athens, Georgia, and had a large and successful practice. He continued his residence here until his appointment as Judge of the Court of Appeals necessitated his residence in Atlanta.

Other prominent lawyers of this period were: Frank G. Corker, J. E. Hightower, Phil Howard, and David Ware.

In the first quarter of the Twentieth Century, among Laurens County citizens practicing at the Dublin Bar, were: John S. Adams, R. Earl Camp, M. J. Carswell, Ira S. Chappell, George B. Davis,

W. C. Davis, N. B. Eubanks, T. L. Griner, K. J. Hawkins, J. E. Hicks, T. E. Hightower, T. V. Sanders, C. A. Weddington, and Hal Wimberly.

John S. Adams was one of the leading lawyers of the State, and a loving cup was presented him as the outstanding citizen of Dublin. Upon receiving the appointment as Assistant to the Comptroller General, in the department of liquidation of National Banks, he was located for two years in Washington, D. C.

R. Earl Camp is known throughout the State as a lawyer and jurist of exceptional ability. For many years he has served as Judge of the Superior Court, and is holding this important post at the present time (1941).

Lawyers of Dublin of the present time (1941) are: Charles Baggett, E. S. Baldwin, Jr., M. H. Blackshear, Sr. and Jr., J. D. Braswell, Sidney Brown, William Brunson, R. Earl Camp, C. C. Crockett, R. M. Daley, W. A. Dampier, A. L. Hatcher, J. B. Hicks, Palmer Hicks, Dawson Kea, W. W. Larsen, J. A. Merritt, Carl Nelson, James Nelson, James Ogburn, Stanley Reese, E. L. Stephens, Sr. and Jr., R. I. Stephens, Harry Taylor, Lester F. Watson, Herschel W. White, and G. H. Williams. Other lawyers of the Twentieth Century who formerly practiced here, now deceased or residing elsewhere, are: Grover Bidgood, Lawton Bracewell, Joseph J. Chappell, Roger D. Flint, Rowe G. Hicks, George L. King, Charles Molony, S. P. New, Rollin A. Stanley, II., and Berner Williams.

Dublin has the distinction of having a successful woman lawyer —Miss Aretha Miller.

2. PHYSICIANS OF LAURENS COUNTY.

Pioneer doctors and those who have followed have made valuable contributions to the County's welfare.

Dr. Thomas Moore came to Laurens County when the County was in its infancy. Little is known of his early life, but tradition tells us that he rode on horseback from Maryland to Laurens County. The horse deserves mention for he was a beautiful spirited animal and did a great part in carrying his master and his master's saddle bags for ministration to the sick. Dr. Moore was a gentleman of refined manner, in bearing, courtly.

On one occasion, his friend, General David Blackshear, was being sued. Dr. Moore was summoned as a witness against his friend, but refused to testify; whereupon the Judge sentenced him to a day's imprisonment for contempt of court. That night his friends gathered at the jail with hampers of food, and a banquet was held in his honor.

Not only was Doctor Moore an outstanding physician but he served the County as Clerk of Superior Court from 1827-1837. (Information from L. Q. Stubbs).

Dr. Charles Guyton was an eminent physician belonging to one of the county's most prominent and wealthy families. He was located in the town of Dublin.

No physician was more beloved than Dr. Nathan Tucker. He was born in New England but came to Georgia as a young doctor and began practice east of the Oconee River. He was a contemporary of Governor Troup, being his close friend and family doctor. His remains lie in the family burial ground at Tucker's Cross Roads in the eastern part of the County. Dr. Tucker owned broad acres in the Buckeye neighborhood and acquired many slaves. He made little claim to being a churchman but sent his slaves each Sabbath to the church of their choice. Some of these were members of the Baptist Church at Poplar Springs and some went to the little Methodist Church called Marvin, standing in the Buckeye District. Dr. Tucker, believing that girls should have equal educational advantages with their brothers, sent his daughters to Wesleyan, where they distinguished themselves in scholarship. His only son, Lucien Tucker, also became an eminent physician.

Dr. Luke Mizell came to Laurens County as a young doctor, and married one of the famous McCall sisters, by whom he had a son who became a prominent physician in Atlanta. His second wife was Mrs. Elmina Horn Guyton.

Dr. Jacob Thomas Linder was a general practitioner in the County for more than sixty years and an extensive land owner and planter. A son of Dr. Jacob Thomas Linder was Dr. James L. Linder, a prominent physician in the County in the last three decades of the 19th century.

An ante-bellum physician was Dr. McCullough. Dr. W. L. Mills was a general practitioner in the Fifties and Sixties. Dr. J. B. Duggan lived near the Wilkinson-Laurens line and practiced in both counties during the last quarter of the 19th century.

Twelve miles west of Dublin, near Dudley, Dr. James C. Carroll practiced in the Sixties and Seventies. His son, C. C. Carroll, was practicing in the same territory in the Eighties.

Dr. Hudson began pratice soon after the War and was one of the leading doctors in the Seventies. He lived a short distance west of Dublin. He died accidentally of a bullet wound.

Dr. Peyton Douglas was a prominent physician during the last quarter of the 19th century. He lived in Dublin and was a man of wealth and influence.

Dr. Harris Fisher was a successful practitioner in Dublin in the years after the War. His son, Guyton, who became a prominent Methodist preacher, was born here. Dr. Fisher went from Dublin to Eastman.

Dr. James Moore, son of Dr. Thomas Moore, was a physician of note. Another Laurens County doctor was Curtis Williamson.

Dr. Benjamin Stanley was a prominent physician with a large practice in both Laurens and Wilkinson Counties, also a large landowner.

I. H. Harrison began medical practice in Dublin during the latter part of the Seventies. Contemporaries with him were two of Laurens County's best known general practitioners: Dr. R. H. ("Scrap") Hightower and Dr. Charles Hicks.

Dr. R. H. Hightower came to Dublin after his graduation from Washington and Lee University. It was his proud boast that he attended this institution when Robert E. Lee was president. Dr. Hightower was one of the most beloved doctors in the County's history; for more than thirty years he served the sick in Laurens and adjoining counties.

Dr. Charles Hicks was prominent in the medical profession of the entire State of Georgia. He was instrumental in founding the State Board of Health and was president of this organization until his death. Associated with Dr. Hicks was Doctor Baker.

Dr. George F. Green moved to Dublin when a young man and gave to the County a long term of usefulness. He served as County Physician.

Dr. T. H. Hall had a large practice in the latter part of the 19th century and continued for many years as a leading physician of this community; he was County Physician in the Nineties.

In the first quarter of the twentieth century practicing in Dublin and Laurens County were these doctors: Dr. G. W. Jenkins, Dr. R. H. Stanley, Dr. Frank Bright, Dr. J. H. Walton—at one time county physician—Dr. J. M. Page, Dr. Ezra New, Dr. L. J. Thomas, Dr. W. R. Brigham, Dr. J. L. Weddington, Dr. J. J. Barton, Dr. Sidney Walker, Dr. Herbert Rushin, Dr. H. L. Montford, Dr. H. T. Hodges, and Dr. J. W. Edmonson. Dr. Thomas Blackshear enlisted with the Royal Medical Corps in 1916 and served overseas till 1918. He returned to Dublin and became a general practitioner. He later became a specialist in ear, eye, throat, and nose diseases, practicing in Dublin during the 1920's.

Dr. H. A. Mathis was an optometrist in Dublin in the 1930's.

In the early years of the twentieth century, Dr. G. L. Chapman and Dr. A. Y. Drake were County Physicians.

In this, the second quarter of the twentieth century, Dublin has a group of physicians and surgeons whose reputations win patronage from the entire state. They are: Dr. E. B. Claxton, Dr. A. T. Coleman, Dr. Charles Hicks (a relative of the first Dr. Charles Hicks), Dr. W. C. Thompson, Dr. J. J. Barton, Dr. R. G. Ferrell, Jr., and Dr. John Bell.

In other towns of Laurens County there have been, and are, successful doctors.

At Lovett were Dr. P. M. Johnson and Dr. L. P. Fordham; at

Brewton were: Dr. S. D. Bland, Dr. W. C. Sessoms, and Dr. G. C. Moye of the present time; at Laurens Hill was Dr. J. M. Wall; at Rentz, Dr. T. J. Taylor and Dr. W. E. Bedingfield; at Dexter, Dr. W. B. Taylor, Dr. J. E. New, Dr. T. A. Wood; at Dudley, Dr. R. J. Chappell, Dr. J. B. Walker; in Carter's District was Dr. J. G. Carter; at Condor, Dr. Barwick; at Mullis, Dr. J. A. Fort; at Hatoff, Dr. Orr; in Oconee District, Dr. M. D. Vickers.

During the twentieth century, Dublin has had several doctors of osteopathy. The first was a woman, Dr. Ida Ulmer; then, Dr. Seay, Dr. Chaplin; and Dr. J. W. Bixler at the present time.

Dr. Sumner was the first exponent of chiropractic work in Dublin. Dr. A. C. Johnson began chiropractic work here about 1937. In the late Twenties Dr. V. H. Lake was chiropractor for this community.

Veterinarian doctors who have served Laurens County are Doctors Balsey, Laurence, and at the present time, Dr. Smalley.

Hospital History

The first hospital in the County was established about 1912 by Dr. H. T. Hodges at his residence on Franklin Street.

In 1913, Dr. W. C. Thompson opened a hospital in the Court Building on Franklin Street. A few years later this hospital was organized as a union hospital, and was incorporated in 1916 as the Dublin Sanatorium, by Doctors E. B. Claxton, W. R. Brigham, J. L. Wedington, W. C. Thompson, and T. J. Blackshear, Jr. The hospital remained here for a few years, moving from this location to the Burch Building.

Dr. J. W. Edmonson opened a hospital at the old Hodges residence on Franklin Street during the period that the Dublin Sanatorium in operation.

In 1923, the Dublin Clinic was incorporated by Doctors J. W. Edmonson, A. T. Coleman, W. C. Thompson and C. A. Hodges and was operated until 1928 in the Burch Building.

Dr. E. B. Claxton and Dr. W. R. Brigham organized the Brigham-Claxton Hospital in the Corker residence on Bellevue Avenue. After some years this became the Claxton-Montford Hospital and was located in the Street Building on Court Square. In 1937, a modern hospital building was constructed on Bellevue Avenue and became the home of the Claxton Sanitorium with Dr. E. B. Claxton, owner and director. This is a sixty bed hospital.

When the Clinic was discontinued at the Burch Building, Dr. Edmonson and Dr. Thompson established a hospital on Bellevue Road. This is now the Hicks Hospital with Dr. Charles Hicks owner and director.

In 1936, the Coleman Hospital was organized. This is a fifty bed hospital and is housed in a new up-to-date building located on Franklin Street. Dr. A. T. Coleman is owner and manager. In 1939, in order to accommodate a rapidly growing patronage, a large annex was built on Jackson Street.

Dr. W. C. Thompson, one of the owners of the Clinic, moved from there and in 1937 established the Thompson Sanitarium in the old Court House Building, later he removed to the corner of Rowe and Madison Streets. This is only an eighteen bed hospital but it has met the standards of registration in the American Hospital Association.

The first dentists in Laurens County were J. P. and N. R. Holmes. Much of the dental work was done by itinerant dentists, among these were Dr. Key and Dr. Will Smith. The first dentist to become permanent in Dublin was Dr. A. T. Summerlin. Other dentists were Doctors J. B. Donaldson, H. M. Moore, C. C. Jordan, O. G. Mingledorf, W. A. Summerlin; dentists in Dublin at the present time are Dr. G. R. Lee, Dr. Frank Zetterower, Dr. Tom Zetterower, and Dr. R. I. Butler.

Dr. C. A. Hodges, after the World War, began practice in Dublin as ear, eye, throat, and nose specialist.

Another specialist in diseases of eye, ear, throat, and nose was Dr. J. H. Moore, who was located in Dublin during the 1920's.

Dr. Charles H. Kittrell, a prominent optometrist of this section of the State, has conducted an office in Dublin continuously since 1897. Dr. William Wright Smith also did optometry practice in Dublin in the 1930's, later moving to Atlanta. Dr. John Duff, optometrist, is now located in Dublin.

Practicing physicians in Laurens today are: Rentz, Dr. T. J. Taylor; Cadwell, R. A. Bedingfield; Cedar Grove, R. G. Benson; Minter, M. D. Vickers; Carter's District, J. G. Carter; Brewton, C. G. Moye; Dudley, D. B. Woodard; Dexter, J. E. New and W. B. Taylor.

Chapter XIX

GENERAL

1. LAURENS COUNTY BANKS

In 1818, an Act was passed by the General Assembly to incorporate the Bank of Dublin, under the direction and supervision of Thomas Moore, Amos Love, John Guyton, and Neil Munroe.

The next record of a bank is found in the Forties and Fifties, when Judge Freeman H. Rowe did a banking business in his store. This was a branch of a Savannah bank.

Throughout the last decade of the century (19th) there was no bank in Dublin; all money was carried to Macon banks for deposit.

In 1892, a private bank was organized in the drug store of Tarpley & Kellam, with J. H. Williams, president; R. C. Henry, vice-president, and James M. Finn, cashier. In 1899 it was incorporated as the Dublin Banking Company, with a capital stock of $50,000. Captain Henry then became president. He was followed by T. J. Pritchett, and W. W. Robinson, vice-president. The directors were: T. J. Pritchett, W. W. Robinson, J. H. Williams, W. N. Leitch, James S. Simons, Jr., J. M. Finn, C. W. Brantley, E. A. Lovett, and A. W. Baum. The store now occupied by Pierce & Orr Grocery Company was built and occupied by the Dublin Banking Company. Company.

The Laurens Banking Company was chartered in 1898, with a capital stock of $25,000. H. H. Smith, a leading financier, was the first president; Frank H. Roberson, the first cashier; succeeding Mr. Roberson was A. W. Garrett, who was outstanding in banking circles for many years. Directors were: H. H. Smith, F. H. Rowe, H. A. Knight, C. W. Brantley, F. J. Garbutt, Joel A. Smith, and S. J. Lord.

The Dublin Banking Company and the Laurens Banking Company were merged into the Dublin-Laurens Bank.

The First National Bank was incorporated in 1902 with a capital stock of $50,000. F. G. Corker was president; W. B. Rice and W. S. Phillips, vice-presidents; A. W. Garrett, cashier; directors: W. B. Rice, D. W. Gilbert, W. R. Birgham, F. M. Daniel, S. M. Kellam, C. W. Brantley, W. S. Phillips, B. H. Rawls, M. V. Mahoney, C. S. Pope, W. W. Bush, and F. G. Corker.

This organization erected and occupied the building now occupied by the Farmers and Merchants Bank. In 1912 and 1913 this bank erected Dublin's most imposing structure, with six stories and a basement, containing besides the bank quarters, some 64 offices.

FRED ROBERTS HOTEL

NEW DUBLIN HOTEL

CONFEDERATE MONUMENT

CITIZENS & SOUTHERN BANK OF DUBLIN

WOMAN'S COMMUNITY CLUB HOUSE

DUBLIN PUBLIC BUILDINGS

The City National Bank, chartered in 1906, with a capital of $100,000, had as its officers: J. E. Smith, Jr., president; M. E. Burts and A. T. Summerlin, vice-presidents; A. R. Arnau, cashier; D. S. Blackshear, assistant cashier. The directors were: J. E. Smith, Jr., M. E. Burts, A. T. Summerlin, T. B. Hicks, D. L. Emerson, T. H. Smith, E. R. Orr, E. Smith, R J. Chappell, E. P. Rentz, W. B. Rogers, Wm. Pritchett, and A. R. Arnau. This bank occupied the building now used by the Federal Savings and Loan Association.

The Citizens Bank began business in Dublin in February, 1904, with E. P. Rentz, president; Wm. Pritchett, vice-president; D. S. Blackshear, cashier; G. J. Flanders, assistant cashier. The directors were E. P. Rentz, J. H. Beacham, J. M. Williams, Wm. Pritchett, W. B. Rogers, A. T. Summerlin, T. L. Griner, and John E. Lord.

The City National and the Citizens Banks were merged.

The Commercial Bank of Dublin was chartered May 27, 1911, with a capital stock of $25,000. The directors were: J. M. Page, E. D. White, R. A. Johnson, C. O. Sikes, J. O. Barnes, A. P. Hilton, E. G. Simmons, J. S. Brown, J. S. Adams, A. L. Keen, Z. T. Thomas, M. A. Shewmake, and E. D. White; president, J. M. Page; cashier, A. P. Hilton.

In 1918, the Commercial Bank and the Southern Exchange Bank consolidated.

The Southern Exchange Bank of Dublin was chartered November 11, 1914, with C. R. Williams, president; B. M. Lewis, cashier. The capital stock was $50,000. The incorporators were: C. R. Williams, Laurens County; B. M. Lewis, Laurens County; N. L. Gillis, Emanuel County; W. R. Proctor, Emanuel County; D. F. Warnock, Montgomery County; M. R. Davis, Montgomery County; D. D. Davis, Montgomery County; H. L. D. Hughes, Twiggs County; Mrs. D. J. Clark, Mrs. Martha Lowery, E. W. Fordham, J. H. Witherington, James B. Jones, E. Smith, Mose Kassell, W. T. Daniel, J. L. Woodard, J. R. Daniel, B. K. Smith, J. A. Peacock, J. F. Nobles, S. L. Veal, M. M. Hobbs, B. F. Harden, N. M. Herndon, George F. Radford, E. G. McLendon, J. S. Padgett, D. J. Spivey, E. E. Montford, and James M. Fordham.

In March, 1921, the capital stock of the Southern Exchange was increased to $100,000, with F. B. Reins, president and James B. Jones, cashier.

The Bank of Dublin was chartered April 24, 1917, incorporated by J. S. Almand, H. V. Westbrook, F. C. Tindol, B. M. Lewis, and C. E. Westbrook of Columbus, Ga. J. S. Almand was president; B. M. Lewis, cashier. The bank was located on Jackson Street, south of the court house.

A branch of the Georgia State Bank opened in Dublin December 4, 1922, and closed July 14, 1926. C. Whitehurst was in charge; D. W. Burch and Arthur Brannen were directors.

In September, 1928, officials of the Citizens & Southern Bank of Savannah came to Dublin and overnight set up a private bank; in November, this bank was chartered as the Dublin Bank & Trust Company, with a paid-in capital of $100,000. At the time this private bank was established there was no bank in Dublin, and the great need was shown when the bank, on its first day of operation, financed more than $50,000 worth of cotton sold on that day.

On December 30, 1929, the charter was amended and the bank became the Citizens & Southern Bank of Dublin. In the first ten years of operation the Bank made total loans of more than fifteen million dollars.

Directors are Mills B. Lane, Victor B. Jenkins; local directors: B. F. Cochran, M. A. Chapman, W. P. Roche, Dr. J. E. New, W. H. Lovett, George T. Morris. Officers are: Charles U. Smith, president; W. S. Simmons, Jr., assistant cashier; W. A. Hobbs, assistant cashier; T. A. Jernigan, teller; C. Marcus Attaway, teller; Henry L. Cox, transit clerk; Lamar Hogan, bookkeeper; Holmes Brantley, bookkeeper; Montelle Cherry, stenographer.

The Farmers & Merchants Bank was chartered at Brewton, May 10, 1910, and began business in July of that year with a capital stock of $15,000. President was James L. Keen; I. E. Thigpen, vice-president; J. H. Curl, vice-president; directors: James L. Keen, Sr., J. H. Curl, H. T. Buch, J. M. Lovett, I. E. Thigpen; Lehman Keen, cashier.

In 1937 the bank was moved to Dublin and the capital stock increased to $25,000. Officers and directors at the present time are: J. L. Keen, chairman of the board of directors, which consists of J. L. Keen, L. P. Keen, O. F. Keen, E. T. Barnes, C. G. Moye, J. H. Curl, and Carl K. Nelson, attorney. B. F. Herndon is cashier, and J. H. Maddox, assistant cashier.

The Bank has been in continuous business through years of financial crisis. Of the original board of directors J. L. Keen and J. L. Curl remain. In thirty-one years (twelve meetings a year) Mr. Curl has never missed a session.

2. MILITARY COMPANIES.

After the Confederate War there were no military companies in Laurens County until the latter years of that century.

The 4th Regiment, Georgia Volunteers, was organized by the Georgia Legislature in 1890; a division of this was organized here as the Dublin Light Infantry. Men of this company attended annual drill week in Griffin, at Camp Northen.

There are now in Laurens County two Companies of the National Guard. Headquarters Company, commanding officers are Ralph L. Webb and William Brooks Bryans. This Company was called out for riot duty during the railroad strike at Waycross, and the cotton mill strikes at Porterdale and Griffin.

Company K, 121st Infantry, Third Battalion, of Dublin, has as its commanding officers, Clifford H. Prince and Christopher G. White, Palmer Currell is Master Supply Sergeant.

Both companies went to National encampment for a year's defense training, in the fall of 1940.

Company K is the oldest federally recognized unit in the State. It began in 1916 as the Home Guards. Then it was federally designated as Company A; in 1922 it was redesignated as Company K. The first captain of the company was L. C. Pope.

This company has been called out for riot duty in a railroad strike at Waycross, also for riot duty at Porterdale, Manchester and LaGrange.

L. Cleveland Pope has attained the highest military rank of any man in Laurens County since the Confederate War. He enlisted in Company A when sixteen years old. From Captain of the Dublin Guards, he has climbed to the rank of Colonel of the 121st Infantry, Georgia National Guard. In 1922, on the death of General J. Van Holt Nash, he was appointed Adjutant General of Georgia.

Charles Flannery Pope is Major of the 121st Infantry.

3. NEWSPAPERS OF LAURENS COUNTY.

Newspaper history in Laurens County began in 1876 with the publication of *The Gazette*. This paper, a weekly, was begun by one of Dublin's most progressive leaders, Colonel John M. Stubbs, without hope of remuneration, but because Laurens County needed a newspaper. The first editor was Arthur Allen of Savannah. Other editors were: J. M. G. Medlock, his son Charles, and R. L. Hicks. David Ware then took it over and conducted it for many years. Several editors followed: L. Q. Stubbs, Dr. H. V. Johnson, and Julius A. Burney. These were succeeded by the firm of Z. H. Burch and G. F. Burney; while they were serving the paper, the building was burned.

While *The Gazette* was being published, *The Dublin Post* was established; the first edition came out on June 20, 1878. It was published by J. W. Peacock & Company; R. L. Hicks was editor, followed by J. A. Peacock.

In 1887, *The Dublin Courier*, absorbing *The Post* and a little sheet called *The People*, began publication under the ownership of D. J. Thaxton from Jackson. A little later Thaxton entered into partnership with E. W. Morcock. The paper was next operated by Morcock and Pierce. In 1898, H. M. and V. L. Stanley assumed control.

In 1894, *The Dublin Dispatch* was established by a stock company, with J. A. Peacock editor. A. P. Hilton next took over the paper and, in time, Ira S Chappell became associate editor.

The Dispatch and *The Courier* were consolidated in 1899 as *The Courier-Dispatch*, under the management of A. P. Hilton, E. W. Morcock, H. M. and V. L. Stanley. In 1900 Morcock withdrew, and until September, 1907, the paper was published by Stanley and Hilton; Hilton later retired and the firm became Stanley and Williams.

In April, 1903, K. J. Hawkins and C. A. Weddington established a semi-weekly known as *The Dublin Times*. Soon George W. Williams purchased the paper and Ernest Camp became editor. He continued as editor when the paper passed into the ownership of W. L. Mason and W. B. Patillo until 1906 when the publication came under the control of Mason, Patillo, and R. Y. Beckham. About 1907 the paper was taken over by A. P. Hilton.

It is interesting to note that Ernest Camp enlarged his newspaper experience begun in Swainsboro and Dublin into a career. Leaving Dublin he became associate editor with Hon. Sam Small at Brunswick; in 1906 he became editor of *The Walton Tribune* at Monroe, which he later purchased. In addition to making this one of the leading newspapers in the State, he has written two volumes of verse—"Sojourns in Song" and "Autumn Odes." Many of his poems have been used in verse anthologies. He has been honored with the presidency of the Georgia Press Association, and is at present poet-laureate of the Association.

The Courier-Dispatch, in 1903, installed a Mergenthaler linotype machine, a modern Babcock press and an Eclipse folding machine. The owners thought that this was the first country newspaper in the South to install a linotype machine.

In the latter part of the 19th century, a weekly paper, *The Transcript*, was published for a short time.

The Laurens County Herald, a weekly, was established in March, 1910, and after a short time was merged with *The Courier-Dispatch*. In 1913, *The Courier-Herald-Dispatch* became a daily paper.

In the second decade of the 20th century there were in Dublin *The Dublin Messenger* and *The Laurens County News*. These were merged into *The Dublin Press*, a weekly, published in 1929. *The Press* was merged with *The Dublin Courier-Herald-Dispatch* and the name became *Courier-Herald-Dispatch and Press*.

The Courier-Herald, as it is today generally called, is the largest daily in Georgia published in a town of less than ten thousand population. It is owned by a stock company, composed of W. H. Lovett, W. M. Harrison, and Mrs. W. M. Harrison—all of Dublin. W. M. Harrison is editor and manager; D. T. Cowart, advertising manager; with a staff composed of Mrs. W. M. Harrison, Mrs. Clarence Green, Mrs. B. B. Page, and Miss Rosa Pearl Harrison.

The Laurens Citizen, a weekly, was established in August, 1930, and continues today. Editor and owner is O. B. Overstreet.

4. THE CARNEGIE LIBRARY.

The year 1904 marked a long stride in Dublin's cultural advancement, for in that year the Carnegie Library was established.

This is the story of its history as written by Hal M. Stanley in 1935.

"One day about thirty-two or three years ago the telephone in my office rang and from the other end of the line came the voice of Dr. J. H. Duggan, who lived at Elmwood near Poplar Springs Church. He asked if there was a public library in Dublin. When I answered that there was not, he then asked if I would not undertake the establishment of one, and that he would be glad to contribute $100.00 as a nucleus.

"Some months prior, Superintendent J. C. Wardlaw of the Dublin Public Schools, now Dean of the University of Georgia Evening School of Commerce of Atlanta, wrote a letter to Andrew Carnegie asking for a donation for the purpose of erecting a library building in Dublin. For some reason nothing came of this letter. After thinking over Dr. Duggan's suggestion, I wrote to Mr. Carnegie myself. Within a few days I received a blank which I filled out and returned, giving the name of the city, the amount of money desired for the library, and other pertinent information concerning Dublin, its growth, population, tax values, etc. Within an incredibly short time after this blank had been returned I received a letter from Mr. Carnegie's office stating that he would contribute $10,000 for the erection of a library building, which must be erected upon property owned by the city and to be supported by an annual appropriation of not less than $1,000. I brought the matter to the attention of the city authorities and was assured by them, that the money would be accepted, the triangle bounded by Church Street, Academy and Bellview Avenues would be set aside as a lot upon which the library could be built and that an annual appropriation of $1,000 would be made.

"Several months elapsed and nothing was done officially by the City Council. Each time members would report that the matter had been overlooked. In order that the proposition might be brought to a head, one day I wrote an ordinance accepting the offer by Mr. Carnegie, setting aside the triangle referred to, making the appropriation for the support of the library of $1,000, and providing for a Library Board of nine members to be named by Council—three for four years, three for two years, and three for one year. I took this ordinance to a meeting of the Council and turned it over to a councilman, W. F. Schaufele, who introduced the ordinance. It was unanimously passed. The following day I secured a certified copy of the ordinance and forwarded it to Mr. Carnegie. Within a week I received a letter from the Home Trust Company of Hoboken, New Jersey, stating that $10,000 was on deposit with that institution for the erection of the library building in Dublin and advising that the amount would be withdrawn in sums of $3,000 upon draft signed by the Treasurer of the Board and countersigned by the supervising architect. As I remember it, three drafts were drawn, two for $3,000 and one for $4,000.

"Several months elapsed before the contract could be let. Morgan & Dillon of Atlanta were selected as the architects. The plans were drawn and accepted and bids advertised for. A number of bids were received, ranging from $10,000 to $21,000. The contract was given to John Kelly of Dublin for $10,000. Mr. Kelly voluntarily contributed $100.00 of this sum to be used in purchasing books. He did a most excellent job, as any one visiting the library can testify. That he did not lose money on this contract was remarkable as considerable water was encountered in making the excavation for the west wall and it required barrel after barrel of cement to close up this spring. John R. Dillon, of the firm of Morgan and Dillon, supervised the construction of this building, visiting Dublin a number of times while the building was in course of construction. As an evidence of the care given by John Kelly, the contractor, Mr. Dillon, informed the Board that Dublin was securing a building worth considerably more than the contract price.

"From its very inception the library proved to be very popular. Books were donated by many people. The late Judge Peyton L. Wade, who possessed one of the best libraries in Dublin, contributed several hundred books. With the $200.00 contributed by Dr. Duggan and Mr. Kelly, a nucleus was formed, and from time to time the latest current fiction was placed upon the library shelves. So popular was this library that shortly after its establishment a prominent citizen of the city ran for the Aldermanic Board on a platform antagonistic to the library. He was badly defeated. This was prior to the passage of the equal suffrage law, or the majority against him would have been very much greater. Dublin had then no community center, and the library was used for meetings of civic societies and women's clubs.

"It is a source of pride and gratification that I had a part in securing the money and in the establishment of the Dublin Carnegie Library."

The library began with about 400 volumes. Miss Anna Stevens, (sister of Harry Stevens of Dublin) who was with the Atlanta Carnegie Library at this time, came here and instructed the librarian in classifying, arranging, cataloguing, and keeping records.

Librarians who have served since 1904 are: Miss Emma Manning, 1904; Miss Lil Hightower, 1904-1921; Mrs. Josie Carswell, 1922-1929; Mrs. A. J. Toole, 1929-1934; Miss Roberta Smith, 1934 to the present time. Night librarians have been: Miss Minnie Buice, Mrs. A. J. Toole, Miss Gladys Wilson, and Mrs. E. B. Freeman; assistant librarians have been: Miss Katherine Orr, Miss Virginia Graves, Miss

Elizabeth Lanier, and Mrs. J. F. Hart. The library board is appointed by the City Council and at present consists of Mrs. L. L. Porter, chairman; Mrs. Clyde Hilbun, treasurer; Mrs. H. W. Waldron, secretary; Mrs. M. A. Shewmake, Mrs. W. M Harrison, and Mrs. J. R. Laney.

On the one hundredth anniversary of the birth of Andrew Carnegie, the Dublin Library observed its 31st year. On November 25, 1935, *The Dublin Courier-Herald* honored these occasions with a special edition.

The first chairman of the Library Board was Mrs. Mary Hicks Thompson; Mrs. C. H. Kittrell also served in this capacity for a number of years. Mrs. O. L. Chivers served the library for sixteen years, first as treasurer, then as chairman. E. R. Orr was Dublin's mayor at the time the library was built. Mrs. J. A. Peacock and Hal M. Stanley were untiring in their efforts to secure funds and build the library.

The library has now on its shelves between 9,000 and 10,000 volumes.

A county-wide service was begun in 1938 with the WPA furnishing a traveling librarian and other workers, which make possible a more general service. The circulation in 1941 was 80,381.

5. LONGEVITY IN LAURENS.

The County has a good record for longevity. Worthy to be mentioned are a few of those who have approached, or passed, the century mark.

In 1936, Mrs. Caroline Barwick Kea died at the advanced age of one hundred and three years. She was born in Buckeye section in the northern part of the County, October, 1833, on the lands of General David Blackshear. Her father, William Barwick, was a soldier in the War of 1812, who began life in Georgia as a farm overseer for General Blackshear. Mrs. Blackshear became godmother to William Barwick's baby daughter and named her Caroline Blackshear Barwick. Caroline Barwick married Bennett Kea and spent practically all of her life in Laurens County.

Zenas Fordham died at the age of one hundred years, six months and twenty days. He lived in the northern part of the County, on the Laurens-Wilkinson line. An outstanding, public spirited man, and father of a large family.

Mrs. Mary Clark Linder, of Buckeye District, reached the age of ninety-two.

William Kinchen was living on Laurens County soil when the County was created. He came from North Carolina about 1791 and became a pioneer in the Indian lands that became Wilkinson County, his home being in the part later apportioned to the new County of Laurens. He was born in 1737 and died in 1835, having reached his 98th birthday. He was the father of Uriah Kinchen, militia officer and county sheriff.

Another pioneer, born before the County was formed, was Green Bury Knight. His life spanned the nineteenth century, for he was born in 1799 and died in 1902. His granddaughter, Seebie Knight, married a Coleman, and became the mother of twelve sons and one daughter. Mr. Knight possessed a sense of humor as well as length of years. He was very proud of his granddaughter's many children and liked to tell that his daughter had twelve sons and every one of them had a sister. It was his pride that he fought with Andrew Jackson.

Mrs. Maggie Jackson, born on April 5, 1842, reached the grand old age of ninety-five. She died in Dublin at the home of her daughter, Mrs. J. W. Cheek, in 1937. She was a daughter of Young Bright Keen, was born in the northeastern part of the County and lived in Laurens County all her life. In 1862 she was married to James Erwin Jackson and reared seven daughters and two sons.

John W. Green of Dexter, had passed 92 at the time of his death. He served in the Confederate Army; for over fifty years he was a Baptist preacher.

G. V. Jenkins was the county's last Confederate veteran; he was born January 27, 1848, in Laurens County, and died near where he was born in 1938. He entered the Army at the age of sixteen.

D. S. Blackshear died April 20, 1940; had he lived till June he would have been 93. He was a grandson of General David Blackshear, was born near Blackshear's Mill and was an outstanding resident of Dublin for the greater part of his life.

In 1911, James Barlow celebrated his 100th birthday in the home of his daughter, Mrs. J. L. Ussery of Dexter.

Captain Thomas McCall Yopp, son of Jeremiah Yopp, was born in Laurens County in 1828. He died at the Soldiers Home in Atlanta in 1920, nearly ninety-two years of age.

Living today in the home to which she was brought as a bride in 1784 is Mrs. Nannie J. Linder. On May 16, 1940, she celebrated her 90th birthday. She has for many years been a leader in the missionary activities of her church. Under her leadership the church organized in 1895 what was probably the first Missionary Society in Laurens County.

Mrs. Annie Perry Rutland celebrated her 90th anniversary on February 20, 1941. Mrs. Rutland comes from an old Laurens County family. Her father, Edward Perry (Uncle Ned), at the age of eighty, was baptized on a wintry day in the outside pool of Poplar Springs Baptist Church.

Father of Edward Perry and grandfather of Mrs. Rutland was John (Jack) Perry, who reached the age of ninety-four.

CHAPTER XX

CLUBS AND FRATERNITIES

Histories of the following Clubs were prepared prior to May 15, 1941.

1. JOHN LAURENS CHAPTER, DAUGHTERS OF THE AMERICAN REVOLUTION

In 1915 the late Mrs. John Asa Peacock was officially appointed Organizing Regent of a proposed D. A. R. Chapter to be formed in Dublin. Prospective members were called together by Mrs. Peacock, and in February, 1916, the required number of application papers were approved at National Headquarters in Washington, D. C., and the privilege of organizing a Chapter was granted. The first meeting was held in October, 1916, at the home of Mrs. J. S. Adams, with Mrs. M. A. Shewmake and Miss Mary Guyton Ramsay as joint hostesses. The following officers were elected for the first year:

Regent, Mrs. J. A. Peacock; Vice-Regent, Mrs. L. Q. Stubbs; Recording Scretary, Mrs. E. B. Freeman; Corresponding Secretary, Mrs. M. J. Guyton; Treasurer, Mrs. B. A. Hooks; Historian, Mrs. E. J. Blackshear; Registrar, Miss Martha Ramsay; Auditor, Mrs. W. W. Ward; Reporter, Miss Eva Blackshear; Genealogist, Mrs. Frank Lawson.

Charter members: Adams, Augusta Stanley (Mrs. J. S.); Blackshear, Eva Bertha (Miss); *Blackshear, Julia D. Thweatt (Mrs. T. J.); *Blackshear, Margaret Milton (Mrs. E. J.); Burch, Annie Laurie (Miss); Butler, Ethel Shannon (Mrs. R. I.); Eagan, Julia Elizabeth Goods (Mrs. H. E.); Freeman, Henrietta Sanders (Mrs. E. B.); Garrett, Della Harris (Mrs. W. T.); Guyton, Leila Vinson (Mrs. M. J.); *Hicks, Margaret Rowe (Mrs. T. B.); Hilton, Luella Gilbert (Mrs. A. P.); Hooks, Lillie Ash (Mrs. B. A.); *Lawson, May Robison (Mrs. Frank); Lanier, Elizabeth Duncan (Mrs. W. R.); McArthur, Lucy Stanley (Mrs.); *Peacock, Anne Boifeuillet (Mrs. J. A.); Pritchett, Maude Stubbs (Mrs.); Ramsay, Martha Bass (Miss); Ramsay, Mary Guyton (Miss); Roberson, Kathleen Peacock (Mrs. George); Shewmake, Emma Cranston (Mrs. M. A.); Simmons, Mary Graham (Mrs. W. T.); Simons, Mary Pickens (Mrs. J. S.); Stevens, Augusta Burney (Mrs. H. G.); *Stubbs, Lula Ramsay (Mrs. L. Q.); Walker, Maggie May (Mrs. W. F.); Ward, Annie Graham (Mrs. W. W.).

The Chapter was named John Laurens, in honor of Col. John

---
* Deceased.

Laurens, the Bayard of the Revolution, for whom this County was named at its formation in 1807.

The State Regent of Georgia, Mrs. Susie Derry Parker, was the guest of honor at the first meeting, installed the Chapter officers and instructed them as to their duties. Since this time, the first Wednesday in October has been celebrated as the Chapter's birthday.

The John Laurens Chapter has sponsored many worthy causes; has given freely to both loan and gift scholarships; has given annually an award of $5.00 to the pupil making the highest average in American History; has given Good Citizenship medals; has located several Revolutionary soldiers graves, and has observed all Patriotic Days. In 1926 the Chapter erected a handsome marble bench at McCall Point in memory of Laurens County boys who gave their lives during the World War. Since 1922 the Chapter has made extensive research in Laurens County history, and has many documents, records, reports and sketches sufficient for a history of the county. On February 2, 1932, the Chapter was appointed by the Grand Jury as County Historian. In 1926 the Chapter entertained the State Regent, Mrs. Herbert Franklin. In Novber, 1928, the State Executive Board was entertained by the Chapter. In February, 1930, the Chapter unveiled a marker for the Nancy Hart Highway, the State Regent and other distinguished guests being present.

There have been only two years that the Chapter has not qualified for the Honor Roll. At the 1933 Conference the Chapter received the State Editor's Award of $10.00 for the splendid work of Miss Katherine Chappell, reporter. In 1933 a D. A. R. Book Unit was established in the Carnegie Library with about one hundred volumes of historical and genealogical nature; the Unit is enlarged each year and a copy of the D. A. R. magazine is kept on the library tables.

In 1938 the Chapter attained one of the objectives it has had since organization. Under the Regency of Mrs. E. T. Barnes, a bronze marker was unveiled with appropriate exercises on the Valombrosa plantation of Governor George M. Troup. The marker stands on the main highway, Federal Route 80, near Turkey Creek bridge.

An important step was taken, in 1939, in the organization of the eighteen young women of the Chapter into a Junior Group, which is affiliated with both the State and National Junior Assemblies of the National Society of the Daughters of the American Revolution.

In observance of the Chapter's twenty-fifth birthday (1941) a valuable contribution to the historical and genealogical records of the City, County, and State was made in the publication, in book form, of this official History of Laurens County, 1807-1941. This history represents the culmination of nineteen years of research into early County records and the collection of all available data pertaining to Laurens County and her people. It is a source of gratification and pride to the Chapter members that their plans for nearly a score of

ANNE BOISFEUILLET PEACOCK
(Mrs. John Asa Peacock)

Organizing Regent John Laurens Chapter
Daughters of the American Revolution

years have materialized, and that these authentic County records are now accessible to all who seek them for all time to come.

Both the Georgia Society and the National Society of the Daughters of the American Revolution have bestowed honors on members of the John Laurens Chapter. Mrs. J. A. Peacock served as State Historian and State Chaplain. Mrs. John S. Adams was State Recording Secretary, State Librarian, State Chairman of International Relations and LaFayette Day, State Chairman of National Defense through Patriotic Education, and received the highest honor of the State organization—State Regent. Mrs. Adams served as National Teller when Mrs. Herbert Fay Gaffney of Georgia was elected Vice-President General, and has served as Chairman of the Georgia Banquet in Washington, D. C.

Mrs. E. B. Freeman has served as State Chairman of Georgia D. A. R. Book Plate, Chairman of the May Erwin Talmadge Loan Fund, State Corresponding Secretary, State Recording Secretary and State Librarian. At the Continental Congress in Washington, D. C., she served as teller when Mrs. May Erwin Talmadge was elected Recording Secretary-General and has had charge of the Georgia Box at National D. A. R. headquarters.

Miss Mamie Ramsey has served as State Chairman of Independence Day and Programs. Mrs. M. J. Guyton has served as State Chairman of Conservation and Thrift, LaFayette Day, Georgia Bell at Valley Forge, Radio, Merchant Marine Library, and Filing and Lending Bureau. Mrs. I. Bashinski has been State Chairman of Wakefield.

Regents of the Chapter have been: Mrs. J. A. Peacock, 1916-1918, 1918-1919; Miss Mary G. Ramsay, 1919-1920, 1920-1921; Mrs. M. A. Shewmake, 1921-1922, 1922-1923; Mrs. Frank Lawson, 1923-1924, 1924-1925; Mrs. M. J. Guyton, 1925-1926, 1926-1927; Mrs. J. S. Adams, 1927-1928, 1928-1929; Mrs. B. A. Hooks, 1929-1930; Mrs. E. B. Freeman, 1930-1931, 1931-1932; Mrs. A. T. Coleman, 1932-1933, 1933-1934; Miss Katharine Chappell, 1934-1935, 1935-1936; Mrs. E. T. Barnes, 1936-1937, 1937-1938; Mrs. J. M. Couric, 1938-1939, 1939-1940; Mrs. A. J. Toole, 1940-1941, 1941-1942.

Honorary Regents are Mrs. J. S. Adams and Mrs. E. B. Freeman.

A member of the Chapter, Lila Moore Keen (Mrs. James L., Jr.), has twice put on exhibits of heraldic paintings at the D. A. R. National Congress in Washington. Mrs. Keen has been recognized as a leading Georgia artist.

—*By Leila Vinson Guyton (Mrs. M. J.)*

2. OCONEE CHAPTER, UNITED DAUGHTERS OF THE CONFEDERACY.

The United Daughters of the Confederacy is primarily a patriotic society, with an outstanding purpose in the hearts of its members for helping our veterans and their widows and for perpetuating the truths of Confederate history, while keeping forever sacred the memory of the dead.

The Oconee Chapter of United Daughters of the Confederacy was organized in Dublin on Saturday afternoon, August 12, 1891, by Col. W. S. Ramsay, one of the most beloved ministers Dublin has ever known. The name of Oconee Chapter was chosen and a charter obtained, but the Chapter did not function in an active manner.

Major T. D. Smith, a Confederate veteran, was so interested in the welfare of his comrades that the ladies who formed the original Chapter applied to the State Division of U. D. C. for a new Charter under the name of the T. D. Smith Chapter. The State President communicated with the applicants, stating that a charter had been granted under the name of Oconee Chapter, officially numbered 58; therefore another charter would not be granted.

The Oconee Chapter was then reorganized. The charter hangs on a wall of the club room in the Carnegie Library of this city and carries the following names as charter members:

Miss Mamie Felder, Mrs. Anna Perry, Miss Mamie Smith, Mrs. R. H. Hightower, Miss Vera Hightower, Miss Martha Ramsay, Mrs. L. B. Lanier, Mrs. Arcada Fell, Miss Carrie Hightower, Mrs. E. K. Bryans, and Mrs. Georgia Wright.

The total number of Chapter members, as listed in the Year Book of 1940-41, is sixty-nine with twenty associate members.

In this brief history, it would be impossible to mention the many worthwhile accomplishments of the Chapter, but it suffices to say that Confederate veterans and widows have been well cared for and the Chapter has cooperated with civic, social and patriotic organizations of Dublin in beautifying our city. At the intersection of Bellevue Avenue, Academy Street, and Jackson Street there is a small plot of ground which is always kept attractive with grass, shrubs and blooming plants. In this triangle the splendid marble shaft to our Confederate dead was erected by the Oconee Chapter.

Another of this Chapter's accomplishments was the placing of the handsome granite boulder bearing a bronze tablet erected to the sacred memory of Laurens County boys who fell in the first World War. This boulder stands on a corner of the Court House lawn. Every Confederate veteran of this County has been awarded his Cross of Honor. The Chapter has had the pleasure of bestowing many crosses of military service on World War veterans, thereby linking the Confederate past with the present.

All Confederate graves in this county have been properly marked by the Oconee Chapter.

The Georgia Division of United Daughters of the Confederacy has been entertained twice by Oconee Chapter. Registration has been completed on 100 per cent basis and many new members are added to the roster each year.

Following is a complete list of the presiding officers from date of organization to the present year:

Mrs. J. A. Thomas, 1903-1904; Mrs. Z. Whitehurst, 1905-1906; Mrs. J. A. Thomas, 1906-1909; Mrs. E. J. Blackshear, 1910-1913; Mrs. C. E. LaFrage, 1914-1918; Mrs. T. J. Pritchett, 1919-1922; Mrs. H. C. O'Neal, 1923-1925; Mrs. Izzie Bashinski, 1926-1929; Mrs. O. L. Chivers, 1929-1930; Mrs. T. A. Curry, 1930-1931; Mrs. Bluford Page, 1931-1932; Mrs. J. M. Couric, 1933-1935; Mrs. Harry Taylor, 1935-1937; Mrs. H. S. Whitehurst, 1937-1939; Mrs. Viola Neal, 1939-1941.

Oconee Chapter has been greatly benefited by the executive ability, loyalty to the cause, and enthusiasm of these noble women. In recognition of their ability, the Georgia Division of U. D. C. has bestowed honors upon members of this Chapter by naming them officers and State Chairmen. Mrs. Izzie Bashinski served two terms as State President and Mrs. O. L. Chivers was State Corresponding Secretary and 3rd Vice-President.

The Oconee Chapter sponsors a large Chapter of Children of the Confederacy, named for Miss Adeline Baum, a beloved member who for a number of years served as State Organizer of C. of C. Chapters. The Adeline Baum Chapter is divided into the Junior and Senior Groups. Miss Maria Waldron is president of the Senior Group.

—By *Clyde Black Chivers (Mrs. O. L.)*

3. UNITED STATES DAUGHTERS OF 1812

The Thomas McCall Chapter, United States Daughters of 1812, was organized on September 2, 1932, in the home of Mrs. J. S. Adams. Charter members are: Mrs. J. S. Adams, Miss Katharine Chappell, Mrs. M. J. Guyton, Mrs. S. M. Kellam, Mrs. S. P. Rice (deceased), Mrs. E. B. Freeman, and Mrs. J. M. Simmons of Bainbridge. This Chapter was the second to be organized in the State.

On December 13, 1932, the following officers were installed by Mrs. Lucius McConnell, president of the General John Floyd Chapter of Atlanta:

President, Mrs. J. S. Adams; Vice-President, Mrs. E. B. Freeman; Recording Secretary, Mrs. M. J. Guyton; Treasurer, Mrs. Izzie Bashinski; Registrar, Miss Katharine Chappell; Reporter, Mrs. S. M. Kellam; Curator, Mrs. J. M. Simmons.

The Chapter has had for its aims—the advancement of educational work and the marking of graves of soldiers of the War of 1812. The colors are blue and grey, emblematic of the united hearts of the North and the South. The Chapter holds quarterly meetings in the homes of its members.

These have served as presidents: Mrs. John S. Adams, Mrs. E. B. Freeman, Miss Katharine Chappell, and Mrs. I. Bashinski.

The Chapter has furnished the following State Officers: Mrs. John S. Adams, State President for three years; Miss Katharine Chappell, State Recording Secretary; Mis Izzie Bashinski, State Historian; Mrs. E. B. Freeman, State Auditor.

4. WOMAN'S STUDY CLUB OF DUBLIN

The Woman's Study Club was organized in 1912 by Dr. Grace Landrum, for study in literary, art, and musical fields. The Club joined the State Federation of Clubs in 1915, but has since withdrawn.

The following were Charter members:

Mrs. H. C. Thompson, Mrs. C. H. Kittrell, Mrs. Frank Watkins, Miss Grace Landrum, Mrs. M. V. Mahoney, Mrs. L. W. Tutt, Mrs. T. J. Pritchett, Mrs. J. S. Adams, Mrs. Tom Hicks, Mrs. D. S. Brandon, Mrs. M. J. Guyton, Mrs. A. J. Toole, Mrs. M. A. Shewmake, Mrs. Frank Lawson, Miss Ruby Hightower, Mrs. I. Bashinski, Mrs. Z. Whitehurst.

The first officers of the Club were:

Mrs. H. C. Thompson, president; Miss Ruby Hightower, vice-president; Mrs. A. J. Toole, secretary; Mrs. L. W. Tutt, treasurer.

Those who have served as presidents are:

Mrs. H. C. Thompson, Mrs. F. N. Watkins, Mrs. C. H. Kittrell, Mrs. T. J. Pritchett, Mrs. J. S. Adams, Mrs. M. V. Mahoney, Mrs. W. C. Thompson, Mrs. B. A. Hooks, Mrs. J. F. Hart, Mrs. M. A. Shewmake, Mrs. J. M. Couric, Miss Leah Kittrell, Mrs. F. H. Rowe, and Mrs. W. R. Lanier.

The first art exhibit was held in the home of Mrs. F. N. Watkins and consisted of masterpieces of Dublin artists. The next year an evening with Wagner was given in the home of Mrs. M. V. Mahoney under the direction of Mrs. Mahoney and Mrs. W. C. Thompson. A Shakespearian ter-centenary celebration was heldd in 1916 in Stubbs Park, with choruses, dances, and impersonations.

The Club emphasized hospital aid during the years of the World War; a surgical dressing class under direction of Miss Blanche Pew met every Thursday afternoon in the Red Cross rooms.

In 1923, under the direction of Mrs. W. C. Thompson, Handel's Messiah was given at the First Methodist Church as a Christmas celebration. At the Christmas season, the following year, the Messiah was again sung as a memorial to Mrs. Thompson, who had herself now joined the Choir Invisible.

Other outstanding programs presented by the Club in open meetings have been: "The Piper" by Josephine Preston Peabody; "The King's Henchman," "The Vagabond King," "The Blue Moon," "Old Soak," and "Sun-up."

During its connection with the Federated Clubs, the Study Club furnished the president for the Twelfth District, Mrs. C. H. Kittrell. It is with pride that the club has included among its members:

Dr. Grace Landrum, Dr. Ruby Hightower, and Nella Braddy Henney. Dr. Landrum has for some years been head of the English

Department of William and Mary College (Virginia). Dr. Ruby Hightower is believed to have been the second woman in Georgia to obtain the Ph.D. degree. She is head of the Department of Mathematics at Shorter College. Miss Nella Braddy (Mrs. Henney) has been one of the editors for the Doubleday-Doran Company, Garden City, Long Island. She collaborated with Helen Keller in her book, "Mid-stream," and is the author of the biography of Ann Sullivan Macey.

In 1941 the Club published as a memorial to Madge Landrum Watkins, one of the organizers, a volume of her selected verse.

5. PARNASSUS CLUB.

In August, 1927, a group of fifty young Dublin women was organized under the name of Junior Study Club, by members of the Senior Woman's Study Club, the purpose of the organization being "the intellectual growth and mental development of its members."

But almost from the beginning, welfare work was inaugurated and some of the most beneficial and worthwhile projects were sponsored by the Club. In addition to the study of art, music, prose poetry, and current events, the club began to study ways to benefit Dublin.

The first officers were Mrs. Bluford Page, president; Mrs. G. C. Ingram, first vice-president; Mrs. Fred L. Brown, second vice-president; Mrs. M. C. Mason, treasurer; Miss Mary Alma Cobb, secretary, and Mrs. Marion Peacock, reporter.

These officers, with three changes, served for a period of two years of splendid activity, the outstanding achievement of their administration being the affiliation with the Federation of Women's Clubs of Georgia in April, 1928. Changes in the staff of officers occurred when Mrs. W. S. Dennis became first vice-president; Mrs. M. P. Daley, reporter, and Mrs. Marion Peacock, corresponding secretary.

One of the first projects undertaken was the sponsorship of a kindergarten in the public school system in 1928. In the fall of that year a kindergarten department was added with the approval of the City Board of Education.

In 1929, the club sponsored "Clean-up and Paint-up" Week, anti-billboard campaign, the fight on malaria, the paving of Route 80, the Lions Club empty stocking fund, aid to tornado victims of this section, and to the Carnegie Library. In addition, contributions were made to the Tallulah Falls Foundation and the State Sanitarium in Milledgeville.

The list of projects grew with the years. During Mrs. Fred L.

Brown's administration, in 1929-30 and 1930-31, organization of a troop of Girl Scouts in Dublin was sponsored. Attention was also given to better homes, shrub planting, the preservation of food, the sale of T. B. Seals, to aid tuberculosis victims, a diphtheria clinic, and a pre-school clinic. Mrs. Brown served capably and was succeeded by Mrs. Murphey Smith.

Mrs. Smith served in 1931-32 and during her tenure in office the club developed in many ways. She was a well informed and capable leader, and under her guidance the club continued along the same lines as those followed in previous administrations.

In 1932, Mrs. Carl Nelson became president. During that year and in 1933-34 she proved to be an earnest worker. She kept the club up-to-date in federated work, fully meeting all federation requirements. She continued the club's policy of meeting human needs of the community; sponsored a project to give equipment to the home economics department of the Washington Street colored school; promoted affairs of a patriotic nature in cooperating with the city in planning a President's Ball for infantile paralysis victims, and in participating in an NRA parade in Macon. The cultural side of the club was by no means neglected, splendid programs being given at each meeting. It was during this period that the club changed its name to Dublin Parnassus Club. Mrs. Marion Peacock was president in 1934-35, and in 1935-36. In 1935, the club tied with the Woman's Club of Macon for the silver loving cup awarded annually for general efficiency, and kept the cup for half a year. The next year, with Mrs. Peacock still president, the club was awarded the same loving cup for excellency for work done during 1935-36. This signal honor came at the convention of the Federated Clubs of the Sixth District held in Wrens, at which time Mrs. Fred L. Brown was elected president of the Sixth District Federation.

The year 1936-37 saw Mrs. T. W. Hill at the head of the club. She was a gracious hostess at open social meetings, and a splendid leader. Her term saw the usual beneficial projects sponsored, and much work was done in connection with NYA boys and girls. Donations were made to lunch rooms which helped feed hundreds of youngsters at lunch time daily. Requirements were also presented in connection with the awarding of the Parnassus Club music award.

Mrs. A. J. Hargrove was elected president for the year 1937-38 and her first thought was to carry on the club's record of service. Work in behalf of a county library, which was begun the year before, was continued and completed. Later this library became a part of the Dublin Carnegie Library. A health drive was endorsed by the club. As a result many servants unfit to take care of the city's babies or handle food were given treatment. A cancer control campaign was also sponsored, and the WPA nursery school received the careful attention of the club.

Miss Virginia Graves succeeded Mrs. Hargrove to serve as president in 1938-39. Miss Graves was keenly interested in all phases of welfare work of the club, and she resigned in September, 1939, to give her services as head of the NYA girls' home here. She also had a splendid record for her work in the county library before it was merged with the city library. Mrs. Brigham White was elected to succeed Miss Graves.

Splendid programs and social meetings, as well as continued welfare work, marked the first year of Mrs. White's presidency, and she was unanimously chosen to serve again in 1940-41. The program for that year was designed to promote friendly relations between North and South America.

Mrs. White attended several state federation meetings and sponsored projects such as rat proofing the business buildings of Dublin, an exhibition of the work of Dublin artists, and ended her second year with one of the best welfare committee reports in the history of the club.

Mrs. Fred L. Brown was first vice-president of the Twelfth District Federation in 1929-30, and in 1936 she was elected president of the Sixth District Federation.

Other club members who have been officers in the federation include Mrs. Marion Peacock, who was district vice-president in 1932-34, and Mrs. Carl K. Nelson who became president of the Sixth District Federation in 1938, and served through 1940, when she became second vice-president of the Georgia Federation of Women's Clubs.

Charter members of the club who are still active members include: Mrs. George Barbre, Mrs. Fred L. Brown, Miss Virginia Graves, Mrs. T. W. Hill, Mrs. G. C. Ingram, Mrs. Hyrell Kendrick, Miss Elizabeth Lanier, Mrs. J. A. Middleton, Mrs. Bluford Page, Mrs. Marion Peacock, Mrs. Clifford Prince, Mrs. Milo Smith, Mrs. Herschel Whitehurst, and Mrs. L. A. Whitlock.

On February 26, 1941, a new slate of officers was elected to serve during 1942 as follows:

Mrs. Alfred Eubanks, president; Mrs. W. M. Harrison, first vice-president; Miss Elizabeth Lanier, second vice-president; Mrs. Jimmy Nelson, recording secretary; Mrs. Roy Orr, corresponding secretary; Mrs. Clifford Prince, treasurer, and Mrs. M. E. Cochran, assistant treasurer.

—By *Lillian Rountree Harrison (Mrs. W. M.)*

6. DUBLIN-LAURENS COUNTY COUNCIL OF PARENT-TEACHER ASSOCIATIONS

The Parent-Teacher Association is an educational organization which seeks to unite the forces of home, school, and community in behalf of children and youth. It promotes interest and stimulates activity in the fields of parent-teacher interest such as family life, health, public welfare and education.

Calhoun Street, Dublin, was the first association organized in Laurens County. After studying publications sent by Mrs. Bruce Carr Jones of Macon, who was state president of the Georgia Congress of Parents and Teachers, a group of twenty-seven mothers and all of the teachers in the school met in Room 10 on the second floor of the Calhoun Street school building and organized a Parent-Teacher Association. The first dues were sent to the state treasurer September 21, 1923.

The first officers were:

Mrs. Otis L. Chivers, president; Mrs. Russell Brinson, vice-president; Mrs. Alice Cox Reins, secretary; Mrs. Dena Dryer, treasurer.

The present officers are:

Mrs. Carl K. Nelson, president; Mrs. R. C. Garrard, first vice-president; Mrs. Vivian Register, second vice-president; Mrs. N. C. King, recording secretary; Mrs. Roy Orr, corresponding secretary; Mrs. W. F. Willingham, treasurer; Mrs. Blewster Knight, historian; Mrs. D. F. Sams, parliamentarian.

The officers of the other associations are given in the order in which they were organized.

Saxon Heights, Dublin, March 13, 1924. The first president was Mrs. L. J. Thomas. The present officers are:

Mrs. U. S. Wynne, president; Mrs. W. D. Pinkston, vice-president; Mrs. D. T. Sutton, secretary; Mrs. Herbert Walters, treasurer; Mrs. Blanche Walden, historian.

Montrose, April 11, 1924. The first officers were:

E. L. Cates, president (principal of Montroses school); Miss Helen Riley, secretary; Mrs. W. G. Thompson, treasurer.

The present officers are:

Mrs. T. R. Napier, president; Mrs. R. T. Hodges, vice-president; Miss Edith Fordham, secretary; Mrs. D. L. Green, treasurer.

Brewton, March 14, 1925. The first officers were:

Mrs. C. G. Moye, president; Mrs. Hartwell Beall, secretary.

The present officers are:

Mrs. B. C. Keen, president; Mrs. J. H. Maddox, vice-president; Mrs. C. G. Moye, secretary; Mrs. B. F. Herndon, treasurer.

Johnson Street, Dublin, November 11, 1925. First officers were:

Mrs. Albert Duncan, president; Mrs. Morris Baggett, secretary; Mrs. W. A. Hobbs, treasurer.

The present officers are:

Mrs. James Hobbs, president; Mrs. R. W. Eubanks, first vice-president; Mrs. W. W. Ward, second vice-president; Mrs. Paul Hutchinson, secretary; Mrs. Ike Coleman, treasurer.

Dexter, February, 1926. The first officers were:

Mrs. Loomis Taylor, president; Mrs. U. G. B. Hogan, vice-president; Mrs. E. A. Sanders, secretary-treasurer.

This Association was inactive for several years, but was reorganized September, 1940. The present officers are:

Mrs. C. S. Thomas, president; Miss Eleanor Woodard, vice-president; Mrs. H. S. Peek, secretary; Miss Flaura Mae Coody, treasurer.

Junior-Senior High, Dublin, April 27, 1927. This was organized as Dublin High School Association but changed to Junior-Senior High in 1934. The first president was Mrs. M. A. Shewmake. The present officers are:

Mrs. Otis L. Chivers, president; Mrs. B. J. Daley, first vice-president; Mrs. F. M. Hancock, second vice-president; Miss Maude New Sheppard, secretary; Mrs. Clarence Burch, treasurer.

Cadwell, April 27, 1927. The first officers were:

Mrs. E. L. Cates, president; Mrs. B. F. Ridley, secretary-treasurer.

The present officers are:

Mrs. W. D. Parkerson, Jr., president; Mrs. R. A. Bedingfield, vice-president; Miss Fannie Jo Bedingfield, secretary; Mrs. Robert Bedingfield, treasurer.

Dudley, October, 1928. First officers were:

Mrs. W. T. Chappell, president; Mrs. Pope Stanley, vice-president; Mrs. R. L. Hogan, secretary-treasurer.

The present officers are:

Mrs. W. T. Chappell, president; Mrs. Doyle Bedingfield, vice-president; Miss Ellen Perry, secretary; Mrs. Gladson Janson, treasurer.

Condor, 1934. Condor first organized a Parent-Teacher Association in 1934, but later became inactive and was reorganized in 1938. The first president (1934) was Mrs. J. E. Beckham. The first officers of the reorganized association were:

Mrs. A. M. Kirkpatrick, president; Mrs. Fred Driver, secretary-treasurer.

The present officers are:

Mrs. H. S. Whitehurst, president; Mrs. John D. Graham, vice-president; Mrs. J. E. Beckham, secretary; J. L. Roberts, treasurer.

Bethsaida, 1938. The first officers were:

Mrs. Margaret Wright, president; Miss Ethel Collins, vice-president; Miss Essie Brown, secretary; Mrs. J. M. Wolfe, treasurer.

The present officers are:

Miss Essie Brown, president; Mrs. J. B. Atkinson, vice-president; Miss Maryene Scarborough, secretary; Mrs. Bryant Garner, treasurer.

Rentz, February, 1940. The first officers were:

Mrs. Theron Woodard, president; Mrs. E. J. Woodard, vice-president; Mrs. Emmett Knight, secretary-treasurer.

The present officers are:

Mrs. Sidney Smith, president; Mrs. Walter Fordham, first vice-president; Mrs. Walter B. Daniel, second vice-president; Mrs. Emmett Knight, secretary-treasurer.

PRE-SCHOOL ASSOCIATIONS

In 1938 two Pre-School Associations were organized in Dublin. The Nursery Pre-School was organized by the Junior-Senior Association; Mrs. E. L. Black, president. The first president of Nursery Pre-School was Mrs. R. L. Bennett. The present president is Mrs. Horace Ethridge.

Dublin Pre-School was organized by the presidents of the three Elementary School Associations. These presidents were:

Calhoun, Mrs. Milo Smith; Johnson Street, Mrs. Horace Ethridge; Saxon Heights, Mrs. B. F. Moxley.

The first officers of Dublin Pre-School were:

Mrs. Wilbur Jones, president; Mrs. Carl Nelson, vice-president; Mrs. Robert Buchan, secretary; Mrs. U. G. Sheppard, treasurer.

The present officers are:

Mrs. H. L. Cordell, president; Mrs. Andy Kingham, vice-president; Mrs. Harry Edge, secretary; Mrs. Fred Driver, treasurer.

Parent-teacher work began in Dublin in 1922, but the Dublin-Laurens County Council was not organized until November, 1937. Mrs. R. L. Tindol, Dublin, was the first president.

The present officers are:

Mrs. T. R. Napier, Montrose, president; Mrs. Milo Smith, Dublin, vice-president; Mrs. B. F. Ridley, Cadwell, secretary-treasurer.

The Council includes twelve Parent-Teacher Associations and two Pre-School Associations.

Parent-Teacher members in Laurens County who are active in district and state work are:

Mrs. A. J. Hargrove, Dublin, director Sixth District, and State vice-president.
Mrs. O. L. Chivers, Dublin, district publicity chairman and state chairman of home education.
Mrs. Myron A. Pickens, Dublin, editor *Georgia Parent-Teacher*.
Mrs. Martin Willis, Dublin, district secretary-treasurer.
Mrs. Milo Smith, Dublin, district chairman by-laws.
Mrs. R. L. Tindol, Dublin, district chairman of publications.
Mrs. W. T. Chappell, Dudley, district chairman of extension.
Mrs. T. R. Napier, Montrose, member district executive committee.

—By Elizabeth Smith Hargrove (Mrs. A. J.)

7. THE DUBLIN GARDEN CLUB.

Under the supervision of Grady Wright, the Dublin Garden Club was organized on February 17, 1939, in the club room of Claxton Drug Company. Those attending the organization were: Mesdames C. U. Smith, Carl Nelson, Earl Hansford, J. K. Griffin, W. H. Shuman, George Walker, Robert West, Bryant Carroll, R. G. Lee, W. H. Adams, D. Z. Lindsey, R. C. Garrard, T. H. Green, Moffett Kendrick, M. G. Combs, A. C. Scarboro, J. A. Middleton, J. R. Broadhurst, C. A. Hodges and Manley Smith.

Officers elected at this meeting were: President, Mrs. Carl K. Nelson; vice-president, Mrs. M. G. Combs; recording secretary, Mrs. Moffett Kendrick; treasurer, Mrs. D. Z. Lindsey; corresponding secretary, Mrs. R. C. Garrard. With a membership of seventy-seven, the Dublin Garden Club became a member of the Garden Clubs of Georgia in March, 1940.

The first Garden Club Floor Show was held on November 9, 1939, in the Woman's Club House. Mrs. Reynolds Flournoy of Columbus, State Garden Club president, was the guest of the club and speaker at the evening meeting. A Spring Flower Show was held on May 3, 1940, in Hargrove Gymnasium.

Interest in horticulture, flower arrangement, and general attractiveness of home surroundings has grown through the influence of the Garden Club, which has also been active along civic lines. Shrubs have been donated for the court house lawn and efforts made to protect trees in the city. A Christmas lighting contest was sponsored by the club in 1939 and again in 1940. Plans are being made to beautify various plots in the city. Members feel that the organization can render a real service by encouraging a greater appreciation of beauty.

8. A SHORT HISTORY OF LAURENS LODGE NO. 75, F. & A. M., DUBLIN, GA.

Prepared by George Currell, Past Master

On August 17, 1848, a group of prominent men banded themselves together and held under disposition the first communication of Laurens Lodge, Free and Accepted Masons, the following serving as officers:

Phillipp Ketterer, Worshipful Master; W. R. Steeley, Senior Warden; Jacob Cohen, Junior Warden; B. H. Horn, Secretary.

An application was made to the Most Worshipful Grand Lodge of Georgia for a charter, which was granted by that august body on November 9, 1848, to Phillipp Ketterer, Worshipful Master; W. R. Steeley, Senior Warden, and Jacob Cohen, Junior Warden, and to their successors in office, same to be known and styled as Laurens Lodge No. 75 Free and Accepted Masons.

Under authority of this charter, Laurens Lodge No. 75 Free and Accepted Masons held its first communication on November 16, 1848, following officers being present: Phillipp Ketterer, Worshipful Master; Charles B. Guyton, Senior Warden; Pro Tem, Jacob Cohen, Junior Warden; T. N. Guyton, Secretary. The first election of officers was held on December 21, 1848, as follows:

Phillipp Ketterer, Worshipful Master; Charles B. Guyton, Senior Warden; Jacob Cohen, Junior Warden; Thomas N. Guyton, Secretary; F. Thomas, Treasurer; F. H. Rowe, Senior Deacon; J. M. Yopp, Junior Deacon; J. M. Dasher, Tyler.

Laurens Lodge No. 75 Free and Accepted Masons has had to date forty-five Worshipful Masters, they being and serving at the following times:

Phillip Ketterer, 1848, 1849; Chas. B. Guyton, 1850, 1851, 1852, 1857; F. H. Rowe, 1853, 1854, 1858, 1859, 1869; Wm. B. Moorman, 1856; J. T. Linder, 1861, 1862, 1863, 1864, 1865, 1866; J. B. Wolfe, 1867, 1868, 1869, 1881; B. B. Linder, 1870, 1872, 1873, 1874, 1875, 1877; J. T. Chappell, 1871; W. E. Duncan, 1876, 1880, 1882, 1883, 1897; J. T. Rogers, 1878, 1879; J. B. Jones, 1884; J. E. Hicks, 1885; I. L. Harville, 1886; W. S. Ramsay, 1887 to 1895, inclusive; W. A. Wood, 1896, 1898; W. W. Bush, 1899; J. H. Witherington, 1900, 1901; E. J. Fuller, 1902, 1903, 1904; W. C. Davis, 1905; Ira S. Chappell, 1906; W. B. Rogers, 1907, 1908, 1909, 1916, 1917, 1921; J. Y. Keen, 1910; J. J. Flanders, 1911, 1912; W. W. Ward, 1913, 1918.

W. B. Atkins, 1914, 1915; J. G. Patton, 1919; C. D. Hilbun, 1920; A. H. Grier, 1922, 1923; C. C. Crockett, 1924, 1925; M. A. Chapman, 1926, 1927; T. Coke Brown, 1928, 1929; Farrell Chapman, 1930; A. T. Duncan, 1931; C. I. Hilburn, 1932; W. H. Southerland, 1933; Chas. E. Baggett, 1934; W. B. Bryan, 1935; George Currell, 1936; Brigham M. White, 1937 (To June 1, 1937); Wallace W. Walke, 1937 (From June 1, 1937); Ralph L. Webb, 1938, 1939;; D. Z. Lindsey, 1940; J. W. Long, 1941.

The following are the officers for the year 1941:

J. W. Long, Worshipful Master; E. A. Dominy, Jr., Senior Warden; Dewey L. Miller, Junior Warden; C. I. Hilbun, treasurer; Z. D. Lindsey, secretary; R. A. West, Senior Deacon; Wilson W. Bush, Junior Deacon; E. E. Hansen, Senior Stewart; J. L. Bracewell, Junior Stewart; T. C. Brown, Tyler; C. C. Crockett, Chaplain.

Lodge No. 75 Free and Accepted Masons now has a membership of one hundred and eighty-six.

The foregoing statements are hereby certified to be correct by Laurens Lodge No. 75 Free and Accepted Masons in regular session this the 18th day of February, 1941.

Signed: J. W. LONG, Worshipful Master.
Signed: D. Z. LINDSEY, Secretary.
(Seal of Lodge appearing).

9. ORDER OF EASTERN STAR IN DUBLIN.

The Dublin Chapter, Order of the Eastern Star, was organized in 1910. Although an independent body it is closely associated with the Masonic Lodge. Masons, wives, widows, sisters and children of Masons compose the membership whose objectives are relief of suffering humanity and living a creed of Christianity and brotherly love.

Past Worthy Matrons are:

Miss Mildred Bishop, Miss Alma Carrere, Miss Gertrude Pierce, Mrs. Linnie Bright, Mrs. Alice Brinson, Mrs. Dena Dryer, Mrs. Agnes Duncan, Mrs. Mamie Jordan, Mrs. Viola Neal, Mrs. Lota Orr, Mrs. Susie Sams, Mrs. Annie Shea, Mrs. Annie G. Ward, Mrs. Mary Rogers, Mrs. Josephine Williams, Mrs. Effie Fort, Mrs. Nancy West, Mrs. Georgia Claxton, and Mrs. Ollie Mackey.

Past Worthy Patrons are:

M. Z. Claxton, C. C. Crockett, George Currell, T. M. Hicks, T. C. Keen, C. C. Jordan, W. W. Ward, W. H. Adams, J. J. Flanders, R. A. West, T. Coke Brown, and Brooks Bryans.

The chapter has been signally honored in having one of its members, Mrs. Annie G. Ward, made Worthy Grand Matron of the State, also a member of the General Grand Chapter. In 1938, the chapter won the State silver loving cup for second place in increase of membership. In 1939 fourteen members received cards for proficiency tests.

The officers for the year 1941 are:

Mrs. Ruth Bryans, Worthy Matron; Mr. Ralph Webb, Worthy Patron; Mrs. Gladys Rawls, Associate Matron; Mr. Farrell Chapman, Associate Patron; Mrs. Effie Fort, secretary; Mrs. Viola Neal, treasurer; Mrs. Thelma Tanner, conductress; Mrs. Fannie Long, associate conductress; Mrs. Ollie Mackey, chaplain; Miss Gertrude Pierce, marshal; Mrs. Agnes Duncan, organist; Mrs. Cora Burch, Ada; Mrs. Dell Chapman, Ruth; Miss Claudia McDaniel, Esther; Mrs. Sara Adair, Martha; Mrs. D. Z. Lindsey, Electa; Miss Juanita Beasley, warder; Mrs. R. A. West, sentinel.

10. THE AMERICAN LEGION, LAURENS COUNTY, POST NO. 17.

The Legion of Laurens County was organized in September, 1919. The first Commander was Roy Flint.

The Post has been active in securing veterans compensation, the privilege of Government insurance, free hospitalization, local charities, and looking after widows and orphan children of ex-service men.

Commanders have been:

Roy Flint, A. A. Burch, Dr. M. Z. Claxton, T. J. Trammell, J. W. Barton, M. C. Holcomb, G. W. Barbre, M. G. Combs, M. A. Chapman, Dr. C. A. Hodges, Peter S. Twitty.

The present corps of officers are:

E. F. Moxley, Commander; T. C. Bobbitt, Vice-Commander; O. C. Roberts, Vice-Commander; W. H. Hobbs, Adjutant; K. S. Moffett, Historian; Marion Peacock, service officer; David Morgan, sergeant-at-arms; M. G. Combs, chaplain; G. B. Parrot, finance officer; C. C. Crockett, judge advocate.

11. THE AMERICAN LEGION AUXILIARY.

The American Legion Auxiliary was organized March 17, 1925, with sixteen charter members; Mrs. A. W. Chaplin, president; Mrs. T. A. Keen, secretary; Miss Picciola Prescott, treasurer.

Later presidents have been:

Mrs. George Ingram, Mrs. Pascall Phillips, Mrs. George Barbre, Mrs. M. H. Hogan, Mrs. Milo Smith, Mrs. Maynard Combs.

Reorganized August, 1940, with thirty-six charter members:

Mrs. E. F. Moxley, president; Mrs. O. B. Overstreet, vice-president; Mrs. Roy Orr, Secretary; Mrs. C. C. Crockett, treasurer.

12. THE LIONS CLUB.

Organization of the Lions Club was perfected in Dublin in September, 1923, and received a charter in May, 1924, with sixteen charter members. Officers were:

C. D. Hilbun, president; Roy A. Flynt, first vice-president; P. M. Watson, second vice-president; E. H. Langston, secretary-treasurer; C. N. Raney, chaplain.

Directors were: M. A. Chapman, H. P. Phelps, T. A. Curry, and S. V. Conyers.

Other charter members were: Guy V. Cochran, J. O. Collier, Fred L. Brown, J. E. Bedingfield, G. R. Powell, C. D. Bailey, and P. W. Alexander.

In February, 1928, the Dublin Club presented the name of Lion T. A. Curry as candidate for District Governor of the Lions of Georgia, and he was elected at the State convention, which was held at Valdosta during June, 1929. He served as District Governor during 1929-1930. Mr. Curry attended the International Convention for four years.

In 1931 the International President was honor guest, and addressed the Dublin Club at a luncheon in the New Dublin Hotel.

The Club has been active in civic affairs; sponsored charity funds, promoted highway development and aided Boy Scout troops. Since 1924 the club has sent out from 75 to 125 baskets to the poor at Christmas time, and aid for the blind has been a main objective.

In 1928 the club initiated a Better Lawn and Garden contest. Members have visited neighboring towns and organized clubs. In March, 1933, the club sponsored "Homecoming Day" and brought the St. Louis Cardinals to play here against Oglethorpe University; the principal speaker of the day was Governor Eugene Talmadge.

Officers for 1941 are:

Dr. C. H. Kittrell, president; R. L. Bennett, first vice-president; Blakely Parrott, second vice-president; B. H. Lord, secretary; C. U. Smith, treasurer; Nelson Carswell, tail twister; R. H. Hightower, lion tamer.

Directors are Dr. C. A. Hodges, T. A. Curry, R. H. Hightower, Carl Nelson.

13. EXCHANGE CLUB OF DUBLIN.

The Exchange Club of Dublin was organized on October 1, 1936, and the following were charter members:

Allen C. Akeridge, Cecil E. Carroll, Joseph J. Chappell, Robert G. Ferrell, Jr., Harry M. Hill, M. J. Guyton, Wilbur S. Jones, James L. Keen, Jr., Hyrell S. Kendrick, John H. Mahoney, George C. Moore, Roderick T. Peacock, W. H. Proctor, E. G. Simmons, Winfield S. Simmons, Jr., Howard C. Waldron, Wallace W. Walke, L. Doughty Woods.

M. J. Guyton was the first president under the original charter; after reorganization the first officers of the club were:

Wallace W. Walke, president; Cecil E. Carroll, first vice-president; Stanley A Reese, second vice-president; Wilbur S. Jones, secretary; James L. Keen, Jr., treasurer.

Among the projects sponsored by the club are: the permanent marking of the principal streets of Dublin; the sponsoring of the Woman's Curb Market, the rat-proofing of the business district for the prevention of typhus fever; financial assistance to the local PWA Nursery School for under-privileged children; securing for Dublin a local unit of the Highway Patrol and later the building of a permanent home for the local patrol unit; the annual participation in the Empty Stocking Fund program; also several individual charity items have been handled by the club.

Those acting as presidents of the club since its organization up to the present time are:

M. J. Guyton, Wallace W. Walke, Cecil E. Carroll, Stanley A. Reese, John H. Mahoney, Brigham M. White, Wilbur S. Jones.

The officers for the year 1941 are as follows:

Wilburn S. Jones, president; Paul Ward, first vice-president; Hyrell S. Kendrick, second vice-president; Howard C. Waldron, secretary-treasurer.

The club membership at the beginning of 1941 consisted of the following:

C. Frank Andrews, Jr., William J. Bixler, Cecil E. Carroll, Spright Dowell, Jr., Harry Edge, Robert G. Ferrell, Jr., Aubrin U. Hogan, Bonnell C. Jarrard, Wilbur S. Jones, Hyrell S. Kendrick, John H. Mahoney, Roderick T. Peacock, Stanley A. Reese, Winfield S. Simmons, J. Brawner Smoot, Wallace W. Walke, Howard C. Waldron, Paul Ward, Brigham M. White, James H. Winn, L. Doughty Woods.

14. ROTARY CLUB OF DUBLIN.

Organized January 19, 1939.

Charter members and first officers were:

Edgar G. Simmons, president; Walter A. Hobbs, secretary-treasurer; L. A. Whitlock, sergeant-at-arms.

The directors were:

James E. Allen, John B. Bedingfield, A. T. Coleman, Elbert Mullis, Harry L. Taylor.

The first members were:

James E. Allen, John B. Bedingfield, W. W. Brinson, A. T. Coleman, Walter A. Hobbs, Rupert L. Hogan, W. H. Lovett, Elbert Mullis, W. D. Parkerson, Jr., J. Felton Pierce, W. H. Shuman, E. G. Simmons, L. K. Smith, Harry L. Taylor, E. Ward Vaughn, L. A. Whitlock.

Present officers:

John M. Couric, president; Marmaduke H. Blackshear, vice-president; Andrew T. Stevens, Jr., secretary; Walter A. Hobbs, treasurer; William D. Parkerson, Jr., sergeant-at-arms.

The directors are:

Marmaduke H. Blackshear, Wesley W. Brinson, John M. Couric, Walter A. Hobbs, Willie L. Holmes, Earnest W. Oatts, Joe A. Middleton, Duren I. Parker.

The present membership roll is:

Lloyd D. Alexander, Johnnie B. Bedingfield, Marmaduke H. Blackshear, Wesley W. Brinson, Ferrell Chapman, John M. Couric, Russell M. Daley, William J. Grantham, Anthony E. Hearn, Earl Hilburn, Walter A. Hobbs, Willie L. Holmes, Harry W. Johnson, Walter A. Kelley, Joe A. Middleton, Bluford B. Page, Duren I. Parker, William D. Parkerson, Jr., J. Felton Pierce, Otis B. Rawls, Edgar G. Simmons, Vincent F. Simmons, Louis K. Smith, Andrew T. Stevens, Jr., Harry L. Taylor, Dr. William C. Thompson.

15. WOODMEN OF THE WORLD.

Dublin Camp No. 189, was organized November 25, 1905, with forty-two charter members. Members now of this original roll are Alfred T. Coleman, Dublin; R. C. Coleman, Atlanta, and S. W. Sturgis, Dublin.

The chief aim of the organization is insurance with fraternal protection for members and their families.

The officers of the local Camp are:

Chas. E. Baggett, counsel commander; D. A. Moorman, adviser lieutenant; J. E. Townsend, banker; M. B. Carroll, past counsel commander; Jas. L. Lord, financial secretary; David Dunn, escort; Johnie Raffield, watchman; J. S. Kittrell, sentry; J. R. Cherry, auditor and field representative; Emory Baldwin, Jr., auditor; S. F. Beasley, auditor.

Dublin Camp has a membership of 375. Meetings are held the second and fourth Monday nights in headquarters located in the Lovett Building, Dublin.

16. FORMER FRATERNITIES AND CLUBS.

Insurance fraternities in the latter years of the nineteenth century and early years of the twentieth were the Royal Arcanum and the National Union. John A. Peacock, of Dublin, was Past Grand Regent; J. B. Daniel, also of Dublin, was Grand Orator of the Grand Council of Georgia.

The Gem Lodge, Number 81, Knights of Pythias was organized in 1895 in Dublin by visiting members from Hawkinsville Lodge. In a few years it dissolved, but was reorganized as the Dublin Lodge, and flourished in the early years of the twentieth century. The charter members were:

Mercer Haynes, J. E. Smith, Jr., L. B. Linder, Ira S. Chappell, S. M. Kellam, J. D. Prince, P. L. Wade, A. R. Arnau, J. H. Lord, J. H. Smith, F. G. Corker, J. M. Outler, W. W. Bush, and J. D. Smith.

The Dublin Lodge, Independent Order of Odd Fellows was instituted in 1896. The charter members were:

C. W. Brantley, W. J. Carter, J. H. Beacham, W. W. Bush, J. J. Carter, Ira S. Chappell, J. H. Lord, W. E. Duncan, M. A. Kendrick, Mercer Haynes, L. Q. Stubbs, F. F. Scarborough, J. H. McDaniel, G. L. Sims, T. V. Sanders, L. G. Moffett, L. B. Lanier.

November 28, 1905, members from the Hawkinsville Tribe came to Dublin and organized the Walkee Tribe, Improved Order of Red Men. It was reorganized in 1906. Early members were:

E. R. Jordan, Frank Bright, John T. Duncan, D. L. Emmerson, H. M. Stanley, J. A. Peacock, A. R. Arnau, O. T. Rogers, Harvey Mathis, O. A. Irwin, J. L. Tyre, M. J. Guyton, E. B. Nelson, T. H. Prince, W. F. Walker, J. E. Inman, Freeman Walker, W. C. Matthews, A. T. Black, J. C. Pittman, A. H. Graham, P. S. Twitty, J. M. Outler, C. C. Gunnin.

In the Nineties there was a Lodge of the Benevolent and Protective Order of Elks, with John W. Byrne, president. A Dublin Lodge of the Loyal Order of the Moose was organized in 1914.

The Fourteen Club was a men's study club that held its sessions in the club room at the Library. Among the charter members were C. C. Crockett, J. E. Burch, R. D. Flynt, William Brunson, Rev. G. L. Patton.

A Kiwanis Club was organized in the early Twenties. Among the charter members were:

Peter Twitty, E. G. Simmons, A. W. Garrett, C. F. Ludwig, Izzie Bashinski, F. B. Reins, Dr. C. H. Kittrell, J. M. Finn, Alex Knight, O. L. Chivers, H. G. Stevens, Dr. W. C. Thompson.

A memorable occasion in the sessions of this club was the bringing to Dublin of W. J. Smith, the president of the old National Bank of Battle Creek, Michigan.

Former social and cultural clubs among the ladies have been:

The Matrons' Club, the Young Ladies Club, the Current Topic Club, the T. B. C. Club, and the Schubert Club.

During the 1920's there was a Woman's Christian Temperance Union in Dublin.

In 1920 the Dublin Business Woman's League was organized.

The Laurens School Improvement Club was organized in 1914. The first officers were: Mrs. T. B. Hicks, president; Mrs. Z. Whitehurst, first vice-president; Mrs. C. H. Kittrell, second vice-president; Mrs. B. A. Hooks, secretary; Mrs. J. S. Adams, treasurer.

The Johnson Street Improvement Club was organized by Mrs. T. B. Hicks. The first president was Mrs. M. W. Jordan.

Mrs. Z. Whitehurst was first president of the Saxon Heights Improvement Club. Mrs. J. W. Gilbert was first president of the Dudley School Improvement Club. These clubs made worthwhile contributions to the schools, but when it was realized that Parent-Teacher Associations would meet the needs more fully, the clubs were merged in the Parent-Teacher Association.

17. BOY SCOUTS.

There have been Boy Scout organizations in Dublin from time to time. The first organization was in January, 1912, with a troop of thirty-two members, with George B. Fort as Scoutmaster. In 1919, another organization was perfected from national headquarters, under the direction of S. V. Conyers, with Radcliffe Ashe as Scoutmaster; this grew into two troops. Among the most active members were Noble Marshall, Richard Blackshear, Baum Dreyer, Horace Bashinski, Edward Jordan; the last named climbed to the honor of an Eagle Scout.

Later, an organization was sponsored by the Kiwanis Club. In February, 1930, Troop 65, was organized. Dr. Frank Zetterower was director; scoutmasters and assistants were Clarence Devereaux, Joe Martin, and Richard Brandon. Among the charter members were Frank Zetterower, Emory Beckham, Billy Hightower, John Wagnon, Jimmie Sanders, Robert Adams, Isadore Bashinski, Jule Green, Ivan Primm, Banks Moorman, McGrath Keen, Bob Hightower. Frank Zetterower and Bill Duncan became Eagle Scouts.

In 1941 there are two troops—Troop 63, with Scoutmaster Emmett Black and sixteen members, and Troop 65, with L. R. Cook, Scoutmaster, and Spright Dowell, Jr., Assistant Scoutmaster; twenty-nine boys are enrolled in the latter troop. The Scouts have regular quarters. Recently Moody Brown, Frarie Smaller, and Brawner Smoot have become Eagle Scouts.

Chapter XXI

NEGROES IN LAURENS COUNTY

There is, and has been from the County's orgaization, a large percentage of negroes in its population.

Slaves constituted the greater part of the wealth of Laurens County in ante-bellum days. During the War they were loyal to the owners, and, even through the Reconstruction period, gave little trouble. Many of the negroes in the County still bear the names of Laurens County slave owners.

There are several negro schools and churches in the county. The largest part of the church population is Baptist, because the greatest number of white churches in the county before the War was Baptist. On the old church rolls of Poplar Springs, Blue Water, Bethlehem, Laurens Hill, Pleasant Grove, Dublin First Baptist and Mount Carmel are the names of many colored members.

There are 61 colored schools in the county today. Millville, near Dudley, has five teachers; St. John, near Cadwell, has four. Both of these schools have agriculture and home economics departments.

Excellent relations exist between white and colored. Negroes are loyal to their white friends and loyal to their country. In the World War many Laurens County negroes enlisted in the Army.

No man has ever exhibited a finer loyalty nor a greater capacity for friendship than Bill Yopp, a negro man born and raised in Laurens County, belonging to Thomas McCall Yopp. When his master left to join the Army in Virginia, in the early months of the Confederate War, Bill went with him. He went through the War at his master's side. When freedom came, poverty overtook Captain Thomas Yopp, and Bill went out into the world on his own responsibility. A varied career led him here and there over the United States. He worked as a bell hop in the old Brown House in Macon; he worked as a waiter on dining cars; served ten years as porter on the private car of the President of the Delaware and Hudson Railway; working on a Navy collier, the Brutus, he went to far places of the earth; as an old man he secured work at Camp Wheeler.

In time Captain Yopp, an old man, went to live at the Soldiers Home in Atlanta; here Bill found him and devoted the remainder of his life to his former master. Because Bill conceived the plan of securing dimes with which to buy Christmas gifts for the old soldiers in the home, he came to be known as "Ten-Cent Bill." Bill had a remarkable memory and when an old man he could name most of the soldiers who went to the War from Laurens County and could trace the battles and incidents that his master engaged in.

"Uncle George" Linder was the only negro ever elected to serve in the State Legislature. He held the esteem of whites and colored and was known over all this section as a preacher. He worked hard and by excellent management acquired a comfortable home. His son, J. W. E. Linder, was educated for the medical profession and set up a practice in Atlanta.

Another negro who became a doctor was B. D. Perry, a son of Ringgold Perry. Dr. Perry practiced among his people in Laurens for many years.

The best known negro in Laurens County history was Norman McCall, a black giant whose physical prowess was the theme of more than three counties; Norman was for the best part of his life a riverboat hand; he could carry a four hundred pound weight on his back. It was no unusual feat for him to carry two sacks of guano—one under each arm. Norman was a tower of strength, not only in the physical but also in the moral realm. He kept order among his own people, and maintained a discipline that was rigid enough to administer physical punishment with his own hands to those who broke his code of manners and uprightness. He reared sons who have been substantial and law-abiding citizens. His mother was due honor for Norman's high ideals; Patsy McCall was thoroughly a trustworthy slavery negress who served in the best families as mid-wife.

An outstanding citizen is Daniel Cummins, a farmer in the Burgamy District. For nearly ninety years he has lived in Laurens. For fifty years he has owned and operated a farm and reared sons who are now good citizens. He built and owned a store building in Dublin at Five Points, in which are the office of the colored farm and home agents.

Lucius Robinson, though deprived of both legs above the knees, has never begged, but takes his place in the ranks of WPA workers.

Adam McLeod in Lowery's District at one time operated a twelve-horse farm near Diamond Landing. He was the first negro to own and drive his own automobile. Adam has reached a goodly age, having been born in slavery.

The First Baptist Church (colored) in Dublin had as its first pastor Fred Robinson, for twenty years he served the church. After his death, Warren Miller was pastor for several years. Other well known preachers are J. D. Daniell, D. B. Cummins, C. H. Harris.

Among the very old negroes of Laurens County are Dave McGirt, who is thought to have reached ninety; Laura Reynolds is confined to her home, but she has been called by the members of the First Baptist the "Mother of the Church." An ancient negro, Mark White, is still living in the Dudley District; Mark was one of the Troup slaves, his mother having been the maid of Miss Oralie Troup. Another old negress in Dudley District is Nancy Fleetwood, who is past ninety.

Dave Linder, a slave of the Linder family, died about 1937, after having passed the century mark.

Well known in Dublin was "Stumpy Bill" Ramsay, who reached the century mark, protected and cared for by his "white folks." Another faithful retainer of the Ramsay family was an old negro man, known as "Uncle Bill." He was about seventy years old when he was killed one Sunday night by a M. D. & S. train as he was on his way to church.

Perhaps the oldest resident Laurens County has ever had was a slavery negroes, Harriet Chappell, whose authentic age was 106. She lived in Burgamy District.

"Laughing Ben" was a slave in the Ellington family; his name came from his ability to burst into a continuous, spontaneous laughter that could continue indefinitely. He became quite famous and was carried as an exhibit to the St. Louis Fair. Ben was trusted by all who knew him.

A unique character is a fortune-teller, known as Penny Wee. So lucrative is her profession she is no longer in home service, but lives in her own home and spends her time keeping her garden. She is believed in, and her fame is known abroad.

Outstanding teachers in the latter part of the 19th century were: L. C. Pinkston, Henry Plummer, and S. H. Darby.

Clarence Williams, head waiter at the Fred Roberts Hotel, is nearly three score, and has served in Dublin hotels since he was thirteen years old. He is very proud of a granddaughter who is in her second year as a nurse in the Henry Grady Hospital in Atlanta.

The first colored farm agent was employed in Laurens about 1917; his name was Robinson; he left the county on account of poor health. A second agent was Carlton of Tuskegee who served only a short period.

In 1930, Essex Lampkin was put on as agent. In 1935, the present agent, Emory Thomas, began work in the county. Thomas is a graduate of Tuskegee, where he spent ten years. He has organized, in the county, fifteen community Farm Clubs, among the men and boys at Mary Grove, Flemon Chapel, St. Stephens, Buckeye, Springhill, Brown Grove, Brewton, Valdosta, Millville, Hat-off, Dexter, Montrose, Laurens Hill, Dudley, and St. Johns. There are 312 4-H boys who are members.

Effie Lampkin, the first home agent, was put on in 1920. Previous to this she had served as supervisor of schools, employed by the Annie T. Jeans Fund in Laurens County. She was educated in Scotia College, Concord, N. C., with training courses at Hampton and Tuskegee.

There are 39 Girls' 4-H Clubs, composed of 870 members, and 23 adult clubs, with 586 members of colored women, functioning today.

This agent was the first in the State to hold a training course for women of the rural sections.

Negroes have been enthusiastic in preparing for and holding fairs and exhibits.

There are many colored farmers in Laurens County who are making good.

J. D. Daniels, in Carter's District, owns and operates a three-horse farm. Henry Josey is making a success of a three-horse farm which he owns in Reedy Springs District.

In Lowery's District are: Tommy Rozier, who owns five hundred acres of land and runs seven plows; Elijah Pearson owns three hundred acres and operates four plows. Henry Pearson owns his land and runs five plows.

An unusually large number of land owners live in Burgamy District. M. C. Beard owns one hundred twenty-five acres in a three-horse farm. Enoch Whipple, owning one hundred twenty acres, operates two plows. A young woman, Emma Ashley, on the death of her father, took over her father's three-horse farm and is making it a success.

In Pinetucky District, Jim Foster owns his own farm of three hundred acres, and is running seven plows. Jim is president of the Laurens County colored Cooperative Marketing Association.

Jim Knight rents and runs successfully a three-horse farm.

Mike Jones, of the Montrose community, owns and operates a four-horse farm. John Irwin, in the Burch District, is a successful farmer on his own land. In the St. John's community lives one of the oldest negroes in the County, Payne, who owns a large farm. Other successful faremrs in this community are the Williams, the Adams, the Shinholsters, the Kellams and the Stanleys. H. L. Long, now deceased, owned 400 acres in the Valdosta community. Other land owners in this community are William O'Neal and Lollie Smith.

In the Zion Hill community, Jim Jones lives in a home that he has built and furnished with modern conveniences, and operates his farm in a progressive manner.

There are 720 colored farmers in the county.

Many stories of the loyalty of negro slaves to their masters during and after the War have been told for many years. There was Wright Adam, a slave of Everard Blackshear, who saved three hundred bales of cotton when a band of Yankee marauders came to the plantation. The cotton was scattered over a field; when Adam learned that the Yankees were coming that way, he tore down a bridge on the creek beyond the field, thereby turning the course of the soldiers.

Known far and wide was the old black ferryman over the Oconee. Bill Yopp, who pulled the old flat for about three decades, assisted by the sturdy July Donaldson. In the same class with Bill was

Adam Blackshear who helped on the Blackshear Ferry for a quarter of a century.

In 1917, the colored Fair Association was incorporated by E. D. Newsome, W. F. Hughes, H. T. Jones, J. J. Jenkins, T. C. Kinchens, John Thomas, Freeman Hill, C. B. Adams, H. M. Clarke, S. D. Kemp, H. M. O'Neal, Joe Hall. It has continued since that time as the Oconee Fair. At the last fair, there were over a hundred exhibitors; seventy-five dollars in prizes was awarded. The fair was attended by three or four thousand people.

Tom Hughes and Tom Golder were among Dublin's first city mail carriers and served faithfully till retired.

Negroes are loyal to their own and provide for days of death and hardship. Laurens County negroes have organized the Woman's Home Mission Society, and for about forty years this organization has cared for the sick and buried the dead. It is inter-denominational.

The Laurens County Burial Association, with Elder Clark, president, takes care of the dead. The American Woodmen is an insurance organization that carries an endowment and death policies.

The adult Home Demonstration Council meets quarterly, under the direction of the home agent.

Colored doctors today in Laurens are H. T. Jones, U. S. Johnson, and B. D. Perry.

The outstanding negro citizen of Dublin is H. M. Dudley, a leader of his people in church and community affairs. He conducts the only negro undertaker's business in the County.

NOTE: Aid in preparing this Chapter was given by Emory Thomas, colored farm agent, and Effie Lampkin, colored home agent.

NEGRO SCHOOLS OF DUBLIN

(By A. J. Hargrove, Superintendent of Schools of Dublin)

The negro schools in Dublin were taught in the different churches beginning in the early '80s. Among the first teachers were R. W. Everett, Jacob Moorman, J. D. Usher, Joseph Daxon and Frank Smith, each serving from one to three terms, varying in length from three to six months.

Later the city local system was organized and the first city school for negroes was built on Telfair Street near the intersection of Smith Street and called by all "The Academy." Among the first principals to serve in this school were: S. H. Daley of Nashville, Tenn.; L. P. Pinckney, Isaiah Hayes, D. M. Smith, Savannah; E. L. Wheaton, Macon; Roscoe Appling, Macon; H. B. Rice, Augusta. All colored children of the city attended this school.

Under H. B. Rice the attendance was very large. The Northeast section was rapidly building for negroes and a petition was presented the Board of Education for a school. The petition was granted and Scottsville School was built on Decatur Street in 1908.

E. L. Hall was the first principal. The school was known as the Scottsville Elementary School. The Telfair Street Hgih School was moved from Telfair Street to Pritchard Street, and for the term 1914-'15, T. J. Turner, of Eatonton, was elected principal.

During the term of 1917-18 Scottsville Elementary School was burned. They taught in churches in the southern part of the city.

For the terms 1918-19, 1919-20, J. C. Brookins served as principal of the Telfair Street High School. During this term the Scottsville pupils were housed in a new building known as Washington Street School with E. L. Hall as principal. The resignation of J. C. Brookins just at this time changed the Washington Street Elementary to Washington Street High School. The Telfair Street High School became Telfair Street Elementary School with Susie W. Dasher as principal, April, 1920.

L. L. Ison succeeded E. L. Hall at Washington Street High School. After three years he was succeeded by the late J. C. Richardson. J. C. Fisher followed and the present principal, M. A. Ingram, is serving his sixth term. The schools have tried to keep pace with the present day requirements. Washington Street High School has been on the list of accredited State High Schools for several years.

Telfair Street Elementary is a member of Group I Standard Elementary Schools of Georgia.

PARENT-TEACHER ASSOCIATION.

In October, 1923, an invitation was extended the patrons of Telfair Street School by the principal, Susie W. Dasher, to attend a meeting at the school to discuss the coöperation of parents and teachers in the training of the child. The main object was to organize a Parents-Teachers Association if the response warranted. The response was all that could be desired and the organization was perfected.

The following officers were elected: Leila Gamble, president; Mattie Beall, vice-president; J. F. Thomas, secretary; Mary E. Perry, assistant secretary; Susie W. Dashier, treasurer.

The following April a representative was sent to the State P.-T. A. and each year since the Telfair Street P.-T. A. has been represented at the State meeting.

Among some of the projects to help the school the P.-T. A. bought window shades, a set of books for the library, play ground equipment and helped pay for a piano for the school.

The spirit and cooperation continues good.

Officers elected for the year 1940-'41 are as follows:

Ruth T. May, president; Mabel Linder, vice-president; Alma Morgan, secretary; J. F. Thomas, assistant secretary; Catharine Griffin, treasurer.

EARLY WILLS AND MARRIAGES

Abstracts Made from Original Records in the
Office of the Ordinary of Laurens County,
Georgia

By
Henrietta Sanders Freeman (Mrs. E. B.)

EARLY WILLS
BOOK I, 1809-1840

Abbreviations used: w. is for wife; s. is for son; d. daughter; ch. child or children; b. brother; sis. sister; f. father; m. mother; h. husband; hr. heir; g. c. grandchildren; g. s. grandson; g. d. granddaughter; nep. nephew; s. l. son-in-law; ne. niece; d. l. daughter-in-law; b. l. brother-in-law; m. l. mother-in-law; fr. friend; exrs. executors; wit. witnesses. First date, signed; second date, recorded. Original spelling has been preserved.

ALBRITTON, AVERILLA, Apr. 7, 1817-March 10, 1823. s. William. Wit.: Wm. E. Dean, John Dean.

ALLEN, BRYAN, Sept. 3, 1818-May 8, 1830. w. Elizabeth; b. Eason; Exr., Eason Allen. Wit.: John Rowland, Stephen Wolfe, Thomas Speigt, J. P.

ALLEN, ELIZABETH, Mch. 11, 1837-July 3, 1837. h. Bryant Allen, decd.; s. Bryant; d. Queen Elizabeth Bacon; six other ch. including Queen Elizabeth Bacon. Exr.: Bryant Allen. Wit.: Eli Warren, A. T. Bowne, W. W. Barlow.

ALLEN, RACHEL, June 20, 1821-March 10, 1823. s. l. James A. Newman; s. l. Ezekiel McLendon. Exrs.: James A. Newman, Ezekiel McLendon. Wit.: L. G. Harris, Uriah Kinchin, Robert Bracewell.

ANDERSON, HENRY, Jan. 20, 1815-May 31, 1815. w. Mary; g. d. Joycey Coursey; s. Wade Hampton; s. l. William Coursey; d. Ginney Barlow; d. Betsy; d. Polly Wood; s. Abraham; s. John; d. Nancy Perkins; s. West; d. Sina; d. Purlina; d. Matilda; s. Jefferson; s. Madison; s. Washington. Exrs.: Mary Anderson, John Fullwood, Amos Love. Wit.: Simon Beck, Wm. McDaniel, Stanmore McDaniel.

ASKEW, FREDERICK, June 23, 1840-Dec. 11, 1840. w. Nancy; d. Elizabeth; s. James; d. Penny Pullen; d. Ann Watts; d. Mary Webb; d. Sarah Law; d. Martha G. W. Linder; s. Frederick W.; d. Eldahess Simmons. Exrs.: J. F. Linder, Nathan Tucker.

BACON, JONATHAN B., Sept. 13, 1822-Mch. 8, 1823. w. Eliza; d. Sarah; s. Edmund. Wit.: J. E. Morris, L. Davis, Isham H. Saffold.

BARLOW, MARY, Aug. 16, 1820-March 10, 1823. s. Thomas; Exr.: Archibald Griffin. Wit.: Eliza D. Griffin, Catherine Green.

BEATY, MARY, Apr. 4, 1822-Nov. 3, 1824. g. s. James M. Vickers; g. d. Mary Beaty Vickers; hr. Avlina Beaty. Exrs.: George Linder, Wm. Cowley. Wit.: I. L. Hall, Charity Dean, George Linder.

BEDDINGFIELD, SOLOMON, Sept. 23, 1817-Feb. 12, 1818. w. Elizabeth; s. James; d. Sally; s. William; s. Needom. Exrs.: James H. McCullers, Elizabeth Beddingfield. Wit.: Charles D. McCullers, Eli Clark, Josiah H. Gray.

BLACKSHEAR, ELIJAH, March 8, 1823. b. Joseph; d. Harriet Brown; sis. Penelope Bryan; nep. Blackshear Bryan. Exrs.: Amos Love, Wm. Hamilton, Joseph Blackshear, Neil Munroe. Wit.: Joel Williams, Lewis Sanders, Mo. Thomas.

BLACKSHEAR, JOSEPH, May 20, 1829-Aug. 20, 1830. w. Elizabeth Hayne; ch. of b. Edward; ch. o b. David; sis. Penelope Bryan; Joseph Bryan and Betsy Bryan ch. of sis. Susannah Bryan; fr. George M. Troup; fr. Thomas Moore. Exrs.: Thomas Moore, Robert Coats, Edward H. George. Wit.: Chas. S. Guyton, John Lowther, Moses Guyton.

CAREY, JESSE, Oct. 21, 1816-Mch. 11, 1817. s. Vincen; g. d. Mary, d. of s. Jesse dec'd.; d. Ruth, w. of Clemment Fennel; d. Nancy; s. John; d. Jane; d. Elizabeth; b. Alexander. Exrs.: John Carey, Samuel Montgomery, Solomon Hall. Wit.: Jane Montgomery, John Guyton, Wm. Roberts.

COATS, JOHN G., Sept. 2, 1837-July 7, 1840. w. Piety; s. Robert. Exrs.: Andrew Y. Hampton, Francis Thomas. Wit.: John F. Spicer, George Hass, John J. Coats.

COLEMAN, THEOPHILUS, Jan. 2, 1816-July 2, 1816. "w. and all my ch." Wit.: Jeremiah Coney, Jonathan Coleman, Josey Coleman.

COLLIER, JOHN, Feb. 16, 1822-May 22, 1824. w. Nancy; d. Elizabeth Matthews; d. Catherine Guyton; d. Maria; d. Wineford Pattee; d. Nancy; s. Joseph J.; d. Diademia. Exr.: Thomas Speight. Wit.: John Tully, Samuel Cason.

COLLIER, THOMAS, May 12, 1829-Jan. 24, 1830. w. Sarah; s. Robert; s. Thomas; s. Needham; s. Bryan W.; s. George W.; s. Andrew Jackson. Exrs.: John Spicer, Sr., Thos. H. Wilkinson, Thomas Collier, Needham Collier.

COOK, THOMAS, June 8, 1813-Jan. 12, 1814. w. Patsy; s. Henry; s. Arthur B.; s. William; d. Deideamia; d. Ginney Warren Cook. Exrs.: Joshua Hightower; Wm. Livingston. Wit.: Thomas Watters, Elizabeth Smith.

CULPEPPER, SAMPSON, March 8, 1823. w. Martha; s. Thomas K.; m. Mary Smith; s. John; s. Joel; g. s. Sampson Blount Culpepper. Exrs. John C. Culpepper, Joel Culpepper. Wit.: John Thomas, David Culpepper, Winfield Wright.

DANIEL, BENJAMIN, Jan. 3, 1816-Feb. 11, 1818. w. Lucy; d. Patsey Brantley, w. of Benj. Brantley; s. John; s. William; s. James; g. d. Lucretia McDaniel; g. d. Lucinda McDaniel; g. s. Andrew Jackson McDaniel; above named g. c. are ch. of d. Polly McDaniel, w. of John McDaniel. Exr.: James Daniel. Wit.: John B. Bennett, Benj. Brantley.

DANIEL, LUCRETIA, Oct. 1, 1828-Jan. 22, 1830. s. John; s. William; d. Betsy Brantley. Exrs.: John Daniel, Wm. Daniel. Wit.: Neill Munroe, Benj. Nalbotton, John B. Hudson.

DARSEY, BENJAMIN, SR., Aug. 1820-Feb. 2, 1828. w. Leodicey; d. Polly Hampton; g. d. Rachel May Hampton; g. s. Benj. Wade Hampton; Exrs.. Benj. Hampton, Amos Love.

DUNCAN, ELLIS, May 3, 1830-Aug. 21, 1830. m. Mary Archer; sis. Easter Johnson; b. Elbert; b. Thomas; sis. Rebecca Miller. Exr.: Elbert Duncan. Wit.: Hall Hudson, Chas. Walden.

DUNCAN, THOMAS, Sept. 23, 1823-July 12, 1823. w. Mary; d. Rebecka; s. Thomas; s. Ellis; d. Elizabeth; d. Easter; s. Elbert. Exr.: Mary Duncan. Wit.: Thos. H. Wilkinson, Robert Turner.

FARMER, THOMAS, Mar. 11, 1817-May 22, 1817. w. Elizabeth; b. Joseph; b. Jesse; b. Joshua; sis. Elizabeth Farmer Barfoot; sis. Naomi; sis. I'olly. Exrs.: Elizabeth Farmer, Jonathan Pope. Wit.: Bray Mayo, John B. Cooper, Wm. Passimore.

FULLWOOD, JOHN, Nov. 22, 1828-Jan. 22, 1830. w. Mary. Exrs. Mary Fullwood, John Spicer, Zachariah F. Barfield, Jeremiah Yopp, Samuel Yopp, Benjamin B. Buchanan. Wit.: B. W. Hampton, A. Y. Hampton, John F. Spicer, Kindred Portain, Hamilton Nobles.

GIBBONS, ANN, July 31, 1826-June 21, 1827. g. d. Sarah Ann Goden; g. s. Joseph Labon; g. c. Sebna Williams; g. s. Wm. Gibbons Saltenstall;

s. Joseph William; s. Charles; d. Mary Saltenstall; g. d. Margaret Elizabeth Gibbons; s. Henry. Exrs.: Mary Saltenstall, Henry Gibbons.

GOODMAN, HENRY, Feb. 6, 1816-Jan. 15, 1817. w. Elizabeth; s. Joel M. Exrs.: Henry Culpepper, James Hogan. Wit.: Davis Smith, John Fullwood, Jeremiah Outlaw.

HAMPTON, ANDREW, Aug. 29, 1839-Mch. 3, 1840. s. Benjamin W.; s. John M.; s. Andrew Y.; s. James D.; d. Rachel; d. Mary; ch. of my four s. and d. Property to be divided into nine equal shares, one of said shares to go to each family of my g. c. Exrs.: four sons above named. Wit.: Warren W. Whitehead, Charles Roach, Daniel Roberts, Rufus M. Darsey, Richard Thomas, James A. Thomas.

HESTER, REBECCA, Aug. 2, 1832-Nov. 10, 1834. Rachel Anderson, Manley Spivey, Rebecca Keen, William Hester, Stephen B. Hester, s. and d. of sis. Nancy Hester; John Redding, David Redding and Rachel Redding, s. and d. of b. Th— Redding. Exrs.: Stephen B. Hester, Huldah Hester. Wit.: Jefferson Allen, Wm. Allen.

HOLLINGSWORTH, GEORGE, Jan. 23, 1835-Sept. 20, 1835. w. Mary; d. Ellender; s. John; s. Kindred; d. Pollie; s. James; d. Abbey; d. Edney. Exr.: Richard Barlow. Wit.: James Barlow, Sr., Caleb Hollingsworth, Everet Dean.

HOLLY, JONATHAN, Mch. 14, 1808-May 1, 1809. s. James; d. Elizabeth Mayo; s. William; d. Nancy; d. Mary Barrow. Exrs: Lewis Holland, Wm. Neel. Wit.: Jonathan Holly, John Thomas, Thomas Mills.

HUDSON, JOHN, July 9, 1838-July 7, 1840. w. Elizabeth; s. James; d. Sarah; d. Mary; d. Ursular; d. Huldah; d. Corinne; s. Leander; s. Green; s. Newton. Exrs.: John Lowther, Jeremiah Yopp. Wit.: Eli Warren, John Woodard, N. McBane, D. P. Robinson.

JOINER, BURWELL, of Nash Co., N. C., Feb. 16, 1813-Nov. 7, 1816. w. Oner; d. Rhoda Pittman; s. Wilie; d. Elizabeth; s. Shadrack; d. Ferabra; d. Mary; d. Charity. Exrs.: Curtis Joiner, Wilie Joiner. Wit. Jesse Joiner, John L. Bottoms.

JOINER, JESSE, Aug. 27, 1827-Jan., 1837. w. Rebecca; s. Bennett; s. Davis; d. Zillah Wells. Exrs.: Bennett Joiner, Davis Joiner. Wit.: Burrel B. McLendon, Stephen Wolfe, Mahala Joiner.

JONES, ADAM, Nov. 25, 1828-Feb. 3, 1830. w. Leresey; s. Seaborn E.; s. John; d. Ellenor Ann; d. Holly Ann; d. Delia Ann; d. Susan; d. Margaret; d. Queen Ann; d. Laura Ann; d. Jane Passmore; d. Liddy Crawford. Exrs.: Benj. Adams, Peter Adams. Wit.: J. Blackshear, Samuel Yopp, M. G. O'Neal.

JONES, JONATHAN, Jan. 31, 1827-June 13, 1836. w. Rebecca; s. Aaron O.; d. Susannah; s. Jonathan; s. Isaiah; s. Jesse; d. Arnia McNair. Exrs.: Rebecca Jones, Richard Barlow. Wit.: Wm. Moore, Noah Powel, Benj. Powel.

KIRKLAND, SAMUEL, Sept. 16, 1809-Mch. 30, 1821. w. Anne; s. David; s. McCullers; b. McCullers; s. l. Charles Collwell; s. Julius; d. Elizabeth Bollenger. Exrs.: Joseph Soultoustall, McCullers Kirkland. Wit.: Wm. Moorman, Dorothy Clements, Charles Moorman.

LIVINGSTON, JOHN, May 13, 1816-Aug. 9, 1816. w. Nancy; d. Kitty; s. Joseph; s. John. Exrs.: Joseph Livingston, Samuel Robinson, Jesse Joyce. Wit.: Matt. H. Rowan, Moses Wilson, Jared Irwin.

LIVINGSTON, JOSEPH, Jan. 4, 1825-July 12, 1825. w. Feriby; d. Hepsey; d. Mary; s. William; d. Eliza; d. Nancy; d. Sarah Elizabeth. Exrs.: Reuben Underwood, Winfield Wright. Wit.: Isaac G. Miller, John Livingston, Mary Livingston.

LONG, NICHOLAS, Wilkes Co., Ga., Apr. 14, 1819. d. Margaret Telfair; s. Richard H.; d. Eugenia; s. John Junius; d. Eliza; d. Sarah; g. s. Nicholas Long; g. s. Benj. Long. Exrs.: Richard H. Long, Jones Winfield, John Broughton, Henry Gibson. Wit.: B. Porter, Johnson Wellborn, Thos. Wooten.

MADDUX, ALEXANDER, Feb. 13, 1815-July 10, 1815. w. Jane; s. James; s. Lewis; "other ch."; b. Lewis. Exrs.: Lewis Maddux, Jane Maddux. Wit.: Thomas Clarke, Mary Cauley, James Beaty J. P.

MANNING, JOHN, Mch. 17, 1813-May 4, 1813. w. Mary; hrs. Mr. Drury Manning, Henry Bohannon, Elisha Gore, Rachel Rogers. Wit.: Wright Ryall, Ann Ryal, David Ryall, Leonard Locke.

MANNING, WILLABY, April 18, 1816-Aug. 9, 1816. w. Frances; b. Sanders; d. Martha; hr. Isaac Hall. Exr.: Col. Archibald Griffin. Wit.: Peter Thomas, Reuben Tucker, Benj. Manning.

MCBANE, JOHN, Dec. 1, 1819-Mch. 30, 1821. w. Mary; ch. referred to but not named. Exr. Mary McBane. Wit.: Amos Love, Alfred Thompson, John Guyton.

MCCALL, ELIZABETH MARY ANN, Dec. 29, 1830-July 21, 1840. "Marriage settlement with my beloved h. Thomas McCall, dated July 6, 1798;" d. Sarah Georgianna Spivey; d. Elizabeth Smith Moore; d. Harriet Moore Mizel; d. Janet Harris Stanley; d. Margaret Sanders Yopp. Exrs.: Neil Munroe, Eli Warren. Wit.: John Lowther, Charles B. Guyton, Duncan D. Munroe.

MCCARMICK, ELIZABETH, Sept. 5, 1798-Nov. 7, 1825. s. Isham; s. Thos.; d. Sally; d. Polly; d. Silvia; s. John. Exr.: John McCormick. Wit.: Martha Smith, Benj. Davis.

MONFORD, THOMAS, March 8, 1821-March 8, 1823. w. Sarah; s. l. Samuel Whitfield; s. Edmund; d. Elizabeth Whitfield. Exr.: Simeon Ellington. Wit.: Wm. B. Hill, W. L. Mason, Wm. Moorman.

MOORE, SINTHY, Nov. 7, 1827-Mch. 4, 1828. g. d. Lucinda Moore, d. of Edward Moore; g. d. Mary Ann Sicity; s. Edward; s. Drewry Eliot; d. Mary Sicity; d. Birdy Finey. Exr.: Neill Munroe. Wit.: Lemuel Johnson, J. H. Yopp.

OLIVER, WILLIAM, Dec. 2, 1812-Sept. 8, 1813. w. Abigail; w's. ch. by former marriage, William Spell, John Cuddy Spell; nep. William, s. of b. McDaniel Oliver; nep. George, s. of b. Reuben Oliver; nep. John, s. of b. John Oliver; nep. William, s. of b. James Oliver. Exrs.: James Oliver, McDaniel Oliver, Abigail Oliver. Wit.: Wm. Livingstone, C. A. Hill. A later will was recorded June 9, 1828, naming same heirs as above.

O'NEAL, WILLIAM, Mch. 29, 1826-May 15, 1826. w. Nelly; s. l. Benj. W. Hampton; s. Martin; s. Cullen; s. William; s. Eliot Love; s. Edmund L.; Exrs.: Benj. Hampton, Eli Warren, Sampson Culpepper. Wit.: John G. Coats, J. B. Spivey, Robert Coats.

PAYNE, GEORGE, Nov. 8, 1830-May 20, 1831. w. Milly; d. Jenney; d. Harriet; d. Maria; d. Catherine; g. s. Zebulon Ard, s. of d. Elizabeth; d. Martha Smith; d. Theny Shiver. Exrs.: Robt. Rozier, Eason Allen. Wit.: Violet Brown, Robert Rozier, Eason Allen.

PHILIPS, GABRIEL, Sept. 29, 1822-May 24, 1824. w. Olive; s. Wiley; other s. and d. referred to here not named. Exrs.: John Collier, Olive Philips, Henry H. Philips. Wit.: Jonathan Walker, John Abrams, Isham Philips.

PHILIPS, MARK, Dec. 7, 1814-Jan. 4, 1815. w. Diza; s. Harrington; s. David Dewleck; d. Claracy; s. Joel Sharrod; b. Gabriel; b. Burrel. Exrs.: Gabriel Philips, Buriel Philips. Wit.: Sharrod Philips, Joseph Philips.

POPE, FLEET, Sept. 17, 1824-Nov. 3, 1824. "w. and ch."; Exrs.: George W. Daniel, Thomas Moore. Wit.: Wm. Bush, George Mimms, Wiley Pope.

PULLEN, THOMAS, Recorded Mch. 21, 1828. s. Henry; s. Moses; heirs of John Arline; d. Margaret Mason; d. Mary; d. Phereby Williams; s. Thos.; step-sons Lewis Linder and George Linder. Exrs.: Henry Pullen, George Linder. Wit.: Lewis Linder, Thomas Vickers, Daniel Mason, David R. Maddux.

RAMSAY, BENJAMIN, Dec. 30, 1815-Jan. 21, 1817. w. Penelope; s. Benjamin; d. Mary; d. Nancy; s. Isaac. Exrs.: Penelope Ramsay, Isaac Ramsay; hr. Abner Averitt; wit.: Joseph Denson, Abner Averitt.

ROBERTS, FREDERICK, May 10, 1823. w. Laney; s. l. Shadrock Duke; s. l. Wright Sheffield; g. d. Mary Ann Harrison; g. s. Thomas R. Harrison; g. d. Sealey L. Harrison; g. s. Hansel Harrison; s. l. Cain Williams; s. l. Alfred Thompson; s. Daniel; d. Mary Thompson, w. of Alfred Thompson. Exrs.: Thomas Moore, Neill Munroe. Wit.: L. G. Harris, P. L. Holy, A. Hunt.

ROWLAND, JOHN, Feb. 28, 1829-May 15, 1829. w. Mary; s. Dogal; s. James; s. Charles; s. l. Wiley Pope; d. Ann Smith, w. of Wm. Smith; g. s. John Pope. Exr.: Mary Stewart. Wit.: B. B. Flanders, Gibson Gray, Dogal Stewart.

RYALS, SOPHIA, Sept. 22, 1830-Oct. 21, 1830. s. l. Samuel Montgomery; s. Abel; s. Travis; s. Gillis; s. James E.; d. Lucy. Exr.: Gillis Ryals. Wit.: Nathan Tucker, Leonard Musselwhite, James Glass.

SEALY, EDWARD, Apr. 1, 1830-Aug. 20, 1830. w. Margaret Sealy. Exr.: Margaret Sealy. Wit.: Thos. H. Wilkinson, Ann Mott, Francis Thomas.

SMITH, BENNET, Dec. 1, 1814-Jan. 4, 1815. Sis. Mourning Smith; b. Archibald Griffin. Exrs.: Archibald Griffin. Wit.: Simon Smith, Samuel Hammock, Sion Smith.

SMITH, ISHAM, SR., Apr. 20, 1834-July 25, 1835. w. Gracey; s. l. Allen Ashley; s. John W.; s. Robert; s. Thomas P.; s. Isham. Exrs.: Allen Ashley, Robert Rozar. Wit.: James Stanley, Jr., George Brack, Jacob Smith.

SOLOMON, WILLIS, May 2, 1809-Sept. 5, 1810. w. Nancy; ch. referred to but not named. Exrs.: Evans Andrews, Nancy Solomon. Wit.: Reddin Stringer, Ashley Cawthorn, W. Cawthorn.

SPARKS, SAMUEL, Recorded July 10, 1818. s. Charles; s. Samuel; s. Thomas Peter; w. and ds. referred to but not named. Exrs.: Amos Love, Neal Munroe, David Hill. Wit.: Nancy Hill, M. G. Sheppard, Thos. Woodard.

SPEAR, DAVID, Oct. 5, 1820-Mch. 30, 1821. s. James; d. Polly M. Palmore; g. s. David Palmore; d. Elizabeth Duncan; d. Lucinda Carey; s. David. Exr.: James Spear. Wit.: Jonas Johnson, Elizabeth Johnson.

SPIVEY, GIDEON A., Jan. 16, 1837-June 12, 1837. sis. Mary; b. J— Benton. Exr.: Edward Swiney. Wit.: Ashley Vickers, Thadeus Barfield.

SPIVEY, JETHRO BENTON, Feb. 13, 1834-Jan. 1, 1836. w. Catherine; s. Eli B. W.; s. Alford Benton; d. Demaries. Exrs.: Hardy B. Standley, John G. Coats. Wit.: Benj. B. Buchannon, James Standley, Ira Standley.

STEWART, JOHN, June 26, 1829-Sept. 1, 1829. w. Mary; s. Dogal; s. James; s. Charles; s. l. Wiley Pope; d. Ann Smith, w. of Wm. Smith; g. s. John Pope. Exr.: Mary Stewart. Wit.: B. B. Flanders, Gibson Gray, Dogal Stewart.

TODD, JOHN, Dec. 5, 1819-Mch. 30, 1821. fr. Wm. D. Algurs; nep. Jas. Todd, ne. Elizabeth Bryan. Exrs.: Wm. D. Algurs, Dr. Thomas Moore, Eliz. Algurs. Wit.: Jonathan Coleman, Rowling Williams.

URSERY, ELIZABETH, Sept. 13, 1820-Mch. 30, 1824. hr. Mary Hutto; b. William Ursery; b. John Ursery; Hansel Lester's ch. Wit.: Milly Hutto, Lany Smith, Jane Ursery.

WEAVER, JETHRO. Wilkinson Co., Ga. May 10, 1806-Dec. 9, 1812. w. Lucy; d. Martha; s. John; d. Lucy Hagle; d. Phebe Baker; s. Nathan; s. Jethro. Exrs.: Nathan Weaver, Jethro Weaver. Wit.: James Pinkham, Amos Love.

WHITEHEAD, BEASON, Feb. 26, 1827-June 18, 1827. b. l. Joseph J. Battle; m. Elizabeth Whitehead; sis. Rhoda Battle; b. Bennett; b. Warren. Exrs.: Josiah Horn, Edward H. George, David Ingram, Daniel Roberts.

WHITEHEAD, WILLIAM, Oct. 20, 1817-Mch. 30, 1821. w. Elizabeth; hr. Joseph J. Battle; s. Bennett; s. Reason; s. Warren. Exrs.: Bennett Whitehead, Joseph J. Battle. Wit.: Coleman Sanders, Right Sanders, Jas. Warren.

WOODARD, YOUNG, May 4, 1834-May, 1834. w. Mary; s. Green; s. John; s. l. Reuben Warren; s. l. Starkey Swinson; d. l. Nancy; s. Thomas; g. s. Young Woodard. Exrs.: Jethro Weaver, Eli Warren. Wit.: Wm. Godfrey, Joseph Holmes, Chesley S. Warren.

YOUNG, OREN (WREN), July 22, 1826-June 18, 1827. Heirs: "w. and ch." Exrs.: Edward H. George, Benj. W. Hampton. Wit.: Thomas Sanders, Z. F. Barfield, Thomas Moore.

EARLY WILLS

BOOK II, 1840-1869

ALLEN, NANCY, June 22, 1854-Dec. 5, 1855. g. d. Mary B., w. of Vergil Childers; s. Green H. Brazeal; s. Willis S. Brazeal; d. Elizabeth; s. of Wm. J. Kurtz; d. Amanda Barlow. Exrs.: Green H. Brazeal, Willis S. Brazeal. Wit.: Wm. W. O'Neal, C. B. Strickland, John T. Brown.

ANDERSON, JOHN G., Apr. 22, 1849-Mch. 11, 1850. w. Rachel; d. Ann Smith w. of Hardy Smith; s. Daniel; s. Young J.; g. s. John Bryant Wolf, only hr. of d. Rebecca, dec'd, w. of Counsel B. Wolf; ne. Rebecca Ann Keen. Exrs.: Rachel Anderson, Hardy Smith. Wit.: George Currell, Wm. Knight, F. H. Rowe.

ASHLEY, ALLEN, Jan. 14, 1851-Apr. 5, 1852. w. Martha "to whom I have been married for 25 years"; s. Pleasant Allen; s. Oliver H. P.; s. John W.; d. Ann Jane Haseltine; s. Robert J.; d. Josephine C.; d. Sarah Ann Frances Rozar; s. William H. H.; d. Eglentine V. L.; d. Teresy P. Exrs.: Pleasant Allen Ashley, Oliver H. P. Ashley. Wit.: Isaac H. Watkins, James Stanley, Jordan Waters.

ATKINSON, JOHN, Sept. 10, 1856-Oct. 1, 1856. Second w. Mary Ann; ch. of 1st and 2nd w. Exrs.: James M. Jenkins, Mary A. Atkinson. Wit.: Washington Baker, Hardy Watson, James M. Jenkins.

BAKER, JORDAN, Jan. 2, 1843-Mch. 16, 1843. w. Cealey; s. Jefferson; s. William J.; d. Elay Nobles; s. Washington's ch.; Eliza Hobbs. Exrs.: John Hobbs (s. l.), Jefferson Baker. Wit.: James Lock, Isaac Layton, Anthony Yonn.

BARLOW, JAMES, Jan. 23, 1854-Nov. 5, 1855. Two d. by my 2nd wife Winifred, viz. Mary J. and Sarah Winifred; s. William W.; s. John H.; s. Wade J.; s. James J.; d. Amelia, w. of Alfred Lester; s. Judson; 4 ch. of d. Louisa, dec'd, w. of Arthur Preston, viz. Susan, Wade Jr., James A. and Richard J. Preston; g. d. Sarah Rebecca Sumners, ch. of d. Susan, dec'd, w. of Joseph Sumners. (all ch. except first two are ch. by first w., name not given). Exrs. William H. Barlow, Wade J. Barlow, David Harvard. Wit.: Bennett Whitehead, Elijah Benton, John R. Cochran.

BLACKSHEAR, EDWARD J., Jan. 27, 1865-Oct. 5, 1868. s. Benjamin H., born 1850; d. Mary P.; s. Edward J.; b. Everard H. Blackshear. Exr.: Evarard H. Blackshear. Wit.: J. J. F. Blackshear, J. N. Blount, D. B. Maddox.

BRANTLEY, JEREMIAH, Oct. 24, 1848-Jan., 1849. w. Harriet; s. James Madison; s. Josiah Green; other ch. Exrs.: Harriet Brantley, Josiah Green Brantley. Wit.: C. B. Guyton, Wm. W. Brantley, C. L. Homes.

BRASWELL, ALFRED P., July 9, 1859-Oct. 5, 1859. w. Mary Ann Jutson; "all my ch." Exrs: Mary Ann Braswell, Wm. H. Darsey. Wit.: Benj. W. Darsey, Robt. A. Darsey, David J. Darsey.

BRYAN, THOMAS, May 3, 1844-July 4, 1844. w. Margaret, g. d. Sarah Ann Higdon; d. Mary Ann; d. Elizabeth; d. Nancy; d. Sarah; d. Martha; s. Thomas; s. John; s. William. Exrs.: Elizabeth Bryan, Nancy Bryan, Martha Bryan.

BURCH, BENJAMIN, Feb. 14, 1862-Oct. 6, 1862. w. Sarah; d. Cynthia, w. of Calfrey Clark; d. Mary Henrietta, w. of William Hamilton; d. Trecia, w. of James M. Goff; d. Charlotte, w. of Eli Sikes; d. Martha, w. of Jesse M. Joiner; d. Eliza, widow of Stringer Calhoun; s. Benjamin; s. John H.; s. William H. Exrs.: William H. Burch, James A. Thomas. Wit.: John R. Cochran, W. C. Knight, Francis Thomas.

CARTER, MARTHA, Mch. 18, 1843-Mch. 13, 1844. b. James Hicks of Emanuel Co. Exr.: James Hicks. Wit.: Jethro Arline, Francis A. Cimmons, Joel Andrews, Alexander Summers.

CARTER, REBECCA, widow of Robert Carter, Dec. 23, 1844-April 30, 1849. b. Benjamin Evans' sons, Solomon and Henry; ch. of b. Hesekiah Evans; ch. of b. Nathan Evans; sis. Margaret Anderson; sis. Elizabeth Outlaw; ch. of b. David Evans; ch. of Joseph Carter; ch. of Giles Carter; sis. Judy Lupers; sis. Mary Mason. Exr.: Alexander Sumner. Wit.: J. W. P. Stevens, Alexander Sumner, Francis E. Flanders, J. P.

CLARK, FRANCIS M., March 3, 1863-Feb. 6, 1865. w. Eleanor; "all my ch." Exrs.: John G. N. F. Clark, Henry S. Clark. Wit.: G. W. Thomas, G. B. Knight, S. M. Knight.

COATS, JOHN G., June 4, 1840-Sept. 7, 1840. w. Piety; s. Robert; s. Edward J.; s. John O. C. Exrs.: Thos. W. Anderson, Joseph R. Ware, Andrew Y. Hampton, Bryan Allen. Wit.: Lindsey Durham, Milledge S. Durham.

COATS, MARTHA ELIZABETH, June 23, 1841-May 6, 1850. s. John J.; d. l. Priscilla H. Coats, w. of John J. Coats; b. John W. Gray. Exrs.: Andrew G. Hampton, John J. Coats. Wit.: J. D. W. Young, John B. Thomas, A. E. Noles, C. Orange McConnell.

COATS, ROBERT T., Sept. 11, 1852-June 29, 1853. "Grandfather Thomas estate;" Aunt Jane Hampton; "little brothers." Wit.: Alexander A. Giltimon, B. A. D. Hampton, Ann J. Hampton.

DANIEL, GEORGE W., Aug. 19, 1845-Sept. 1, 1845. w. Sarah; s. Amos L.; s. Samuel H.; "all my ch." Exrs.: Sarah Daniel, Amos L. Daniel, Samuel L. Daniel. Wit.: Joseph J. F. Blackshear, John Graham, Eli Warmock, Wm. G. Rowland.

DANIEL, NANCY, Oct. 10, 1857-Oct. 4, 1858. nep. James Warren; ch. of dec'd b. and s. Exrs.: Francis Thomas, Andrew Beddingfield. Wit.: Wm. J. Baker, Thomas Scarborough, Thomas Lock, Wm. Fountain.

DANIEL, WILLIAM, May 12, 1852-Nov., 1853. w. Nancy; g. d. Piety Ann Williams; g. d. Sarah Ann Williams; g. d. Charlotte Ann Williams; g. s. John Williams; b. John; nep. Wm. B. F. Daniel; d. Charlotte Williams; s. l. Calvin H. Exrs.: Francis Thomas, John Daniel. Wit.: Edward T. Sheftall, William D. Coney, Washington Baker.

DIXON, GEORGE, Oct. 20, 1865-Jan. 8, 1866. w. Jane. Exrs.: George W. Thomas, Jane Dixon. Wit.: John H. Wynn, Geo. W. Thomas, Levy H. Harrison.

DUPREE, SYNTHA, June 2, 1852-Dec. 6, 1852. d. Nancy Louise, w. of Wm. Bowen; s. l. Wm. D. Coney; hr. John K. Whaley; hr. John Dupree; hr. John Coleman. Exr.: Wm. D. Coney. Wit.: Uriah G. B. Hogan, Jonathan J. Weaver, James H. Loftin.

ENGLISH, ELI, Dec. 6. 1865-May 7, 1866. w. Treacy to whom married for 49 years; d. Eliza Ann; s. Thomas; s. Silas; other ch. Exrs.: Thomas English, Silas English. Wit.: W. J. Bender, W. T. Haskins, William Haskins.

FUQUA, HENRY C., June 13, 1859-May 7, 1860. w. Winneford; s. Henry Currell; s. James C.; d. Sarah C. Joyce and her ch.; d. Rachel S. Robinson and her ch.; d. Mary J. Currell and her ch.; s. Andrew A.; s. Thomas B. Exrs.: Robert Robinson, Freeman H. Rowe. Wit.: R. E. Hudson, Jos. A. Daniel, John T. Duncan.

GOFF, WILLIAM, Nov. 20, 1856-Feb. 2, 1857. w. Delila to whom married for 50 years; hr. Rutha w. of E. S. Odom; hr. Joseph Watson. Exr.: John G. Smith. Wit.: Childers Harvey, V. Hilbun, John G. Smith, Thomas Johnson.

GRIMES, HIRAM, Montgomery Co., Ga., July 7, 1862-June 2, 1863. w. Amelia; f. l. Alfred Burch. Wit.: Jackson Grimes, Jeremiah McDaniel.

GUYTON, ANN ELIZA, Aug. 9, 1856-Oct. 5, 1856. m. E. G. Mizell; sis. Louisa C. Guyton; b. Cincinnatus S.; b. M. S.; hr. Luke W. S. Mizell; Aunt Polly Webber of S. C.; hr. Adeline Cooper. Exrs.: Luke T. Mizell, C. S. Guyton. Wit.: Jonathan Linley, A. Reynolds, A. M. Bradford.

GUYTON, CHARLES B., Jan. 19, 1856-June 14, 1857. w. Lupina; b. Thos N. Guyton. Exrs.: Thomas N. Guyton, Charles L. Holmes. Wit.: John R. Cochran, James A. Thomas, D. M. Sheftall.

GUYTON, CHARLES S., Oct. 28, 1848-Dec. 28, 1848. w. Elmina; d. Ann Eliza; d. Louisa Caroline; b. Moses; nep. Thomas N.; s. Cincinatus; s. Moses Josiah. Exrs.: Moses Guyton, Thomas N. Guyton, Benj. H. Horn. Wit.: C. B. Guyton, A. B. Spivey, F. H. Rowe, J. P.

HALL, ISAAC L., Apr. 7, 1855-May 9, 1855. d. Mary Ann; d. Sarah Ann; d. Elizabeth Ann; s. Joel G.; d. Temperance Ann; d. Fanny Ann; s. John C. Exrs.: Dr. Nathan Tucker, Elijah F. Blackshear. Wit.: Ephraim Turner, George E. Colley, E. J. Backshear.

HIGDON, ROBERT, Oct. 21, 1850-Nov. 9, 1853. m. Mary; d. Sarah Ann. Exrs.: Gen. Eli Warren, Daniel Roberts. Wit.: Wm. O'Neal, John Love, Kindred Partin.

HIGHTOWER, FREDERICK C., Dec. 2, 1857-Apr. 5, 1858. "w. and all my ch.," referred to but not named; youngest s. Robert. Exrs.: Thomas C. Fuqua, George Currell. Wit.; Weaver J. Nicholas, James C. Lee.

HIGHTOWER, JOSHUA, April 19, 1847-Jan., 1849. s. Raleigh; d. Rebecca, w. of James Underwood; s. Gregory; s. Winfield; d. Mary Hicks; s. Josiah Warren; d. l. Mary Martin second w. of s. Josiah Warren; s. Frederick E.; ch. of d. Sarah McDaniel, dec'd.; s. Joshua E. Exrs.: Frederick E. Hightower, Joshua E. Hightower. Wit.: Lewis G. Linder, Wm. Livingston, Hardy McLendon, Green T. Kellam.

HOBBS, LARRY, Oct. 3, 1855-Feb., 1869. w. Mary (Polly); s. John; s. Berry; s. Larry, Jr.; d. Elizabeth; d. Eliza; d. Mary; d. Martha; d. Sarah; d. Nancy. Exr.: s. John Hobbs. Wit.: James M. Sheppard, Hardy Alligood, John Hobbs, s.

HOLLIMAN, JOHN, Feb. 1, 1854-Dec. 3, 1855. w. Mary Ellen; s. T. J.; s. l. John Stanley; s. l. Henry Powell; sis. Sarah Holliman; s. "Boy Child" b. Sept. 1, 1850; g. s. John Jasper Stanley; g. d. Samantha Jane Holliman. Exrs.: David L. Hitchcock. Wit.: Leroy Jordan, Isaac H. Watkins, Louisiana Watkins.

HOLMES, CHARLES L., Aug. 24, 1863-June 1, 1868. w. Mary T.; "all my ch." Exrs.: Freeman H. Rowe, John T. Duncan. Wit.: John J. Keen, Lewis Bashinski, W. S. Ramsy, T. P. Sarchet.

JENKINS, JAMES J., Sept. 26, 1852-Nov. 24, 1852. w. Lucinda; s. James M.; "all my ch." Exrs.: Lucinda Jenkins, Francis Thomas, James M. Perkins, Wm. J. Baker. Wit.: Drury F. Scarborough, Penn Scarborough, Washington Baker.

JOINER, BENNETT, Mch. 20, 1851-Dec. 7, 1853. w. Matilda B.; d. Martha H.; d. Louise H. Woodard; s. Bennett C.; s. Seaborn B. W.; d. Sarah E., w. of E. S. Coleman; g. c. Reason A.; William B.; John W. and Emily N. Beddingfield, ch. of d. Matilda. Exrs.: Seaborn B. W. Joiner, Bennett C. Joiner, George Currell. Wit.: J. M. Hall, Charles Knight, F. H. Rowe.

JONES, JOHN, Aug. 29, 1846-Jan. 12, 1847. w. Ann; d. Nancy G., w. of Wm. G. Rowland; s. John; s. Thomas A.; ch. of s. Hezekiah; d. Malinda, w. of Edwin Homes. Exrs.: John Jones. Wit.: Reuben Rowland, Richard Graham, E. J. Blackshear.

JONES, MARY, July 11, 1855-Apr. 7, 1856. First h. John Fullwood; second h. Henry P. Jones; g. s. John Thomas Fullwood of Bibb Co.; Patsy, Martha, and Ellen Munroe, ch. of Drew and Katharine Munroe. (Katharine Munroe was ne. of 1st h., John Fullwood). Exrs.: Kindred Partain, Frances Thomas, Daniel H. Coombs. Wit.: W. H. Combs, David Ware, John H. Cochran.

KNIGHT, WILLIAM S., Aug. 24, 1867-Oct. 7, 1867. w. Margaret R.; s. Horace A.; d. Florence O. Exr. Margaret R. Knight. Wit.: R. D. Dixon, W. J. Hogan, J. J. Weaver.

LINDER, LEWIS, Dec. 24, 1855-Apr. 1, 1857. w. Elizabeth; s. Enoch H.; s. William F.; s. Charles W.; s. Francis A.; s. Ashley T.; hr. Elizabeth Linder; s. Lewis G.; d. Elizabeth Maddox; d. Mary Clark; s. Jacob T.; d. Susan Rawls; hr. Charles C. Linder. Exrs.: Lewis G. Linder, Wm. F. Linder. Wit.: Wm. A. Smith, Wm. S. Ballard, Francis E. Flanders, J. P.

MADDUX, LEWIS, Mch. 21, 1845-July 8, 1845. s. David R.; d. Rachel B. Ellington; d. Penelope N. Tramel and her ch.; s. John P.; d. Nancy J., w of Wm. Adams. Exrs.: David R. Maddux, Edward J. Blackshear. Wit.: Elijah F. Blackshear, Abraham B. Lamb, Robert Dodd.

MASON, JAMES, Dec. 31, 1853-Nov. 3, 1861. sis. Rebecca, w. of Levi Davis. Exr.: Everard H. Blackshear. Wit.: L. G. Maddox, David J. Moorman, J. L. Maddox, Jacob J. Linder.

MASON, TURNER, May 27, 1835-July 5, 1843. s. Wm. L.; s. James; d. Susan; d. Rebecca Davis; d. Mary Ann. Exrs.: Wm. L. Mason, James Mason. Wit.: James H. Blackshear, Wm. T. Blackshear, E. J. Blackshear.

McLENDON, WILLIAM R., Dec. 19, 1857-Apr. 7, 1862. b. Wiley. Exr.: Francis Thomas. Wit.: John R. Cochran, James A. Daniel, Blackshear Smith.

MONTFORD, HENRY, Oct., 1841-Jan. 3, 1842. w. Agnes; d. Martha Jane; s. Henry Stokes; s. James L.; d. Elizabeth Spell; d. Sarah Ann Adams. Exrs.: Dr. Nathan Tucker, Winfield Wright. Wit.: Moses Guyton, Russell Kellum, Lewis G. Linder.

MOORMAN, WILLIAM B., Mch. 20, 1861-Apr. 3, 1865. s. Simeon J.; d. Harriet Eliza Hartley and her ch.; s. William J. P.; d. Martha Jane Hartley and her ch.; d. Emily Marline; s. Henry E.; s. David J. Exrs.: David J. Moorman. Wit.: E. J. Blackshear, E. H. Blackshear, J. J. Blackshear, Virgil C. Manning.

NOBLES, SARAH, Feb. 8, 1857-Nov. 2, 1857. g. s. Robert Nobles; g. s. Wm. H. Nobles; g. d. Sarah Nobles; g. d. Celia Nobles; g. d. Malitia Nobles; g. s. Jefferson Nobles; g. d. Ellen Nobles; g. s. Joseph Nobles; s. Hamilton Nobles and W. Elvy. Exr.: Washington Baker. Wit.: Wm. J. Baker, Thomas J. Baker, Thomas Lock.

PARKER, JONATHAN, July 3, 1851-Dec. 4, 1854. w. Mary to whom married for 40 years; d. Mary Eunis; d. Jane; d. Sarah Walker; s. Porter; s. Jacob; d. Ann. Exr.: Jacob T. Linder. Wit.: John T. Davis, M. L. W. Linder, Wm. A. J. Britt.

PICKERING, NAMON, Nov. 13, 1857-Mch. 1, 1858. w. Smitty; s. Union; s. Bennett; d. Sarah; d. Hannah w. of Jackson Hudnull; d. Sely w. of John Wade; s. William; s. Bryant; s. Josiah; s. Ira; d. Amanda E. Exrs.: Smithy Pickran, Bennett Pickran. Wit.: Robt. C. Smith, Silas English, Harriet English.

RAWLS, ARTHUR, Dec. 27, 1846-Sept., 1847. w. Milly; d. Elizabeth Smith; s. Daniel; s. Reddick; s. Elisha; s. David; d. Anna; d. Lucy; d. Mary. Exr.: Jethro Arline. Wit.: Levi Davis, Ephraim Hightower, James Hicks.

REGISTER, ROBERT, Jan. 25, 1851-May 5, 1851. w. Catherine; s. Robert; s. William; s. Washington; s. David; d. Tabitha; "older ch." Exrs.: James Register, John Hobbs. Wit.: Starkey Swinson, George J. Turner, William H. Register.

RICKS, RICHARD, Feb. 1, 1844-Mch. 12, 1844. s. Hampton; s. Rutherford; s. Caswell; d. Arcissa. Exrs.: Jeremiah Yopp, Edward J. Blackshear. Wit.: Wm. Bush, Sr., James C. McCullers, E. J. Blackshear.

RYAN, EMILY, Mch. 18, 1844-Sept. 9, 1844. s. Flonnoy Clark; s. Francis M. Clark; s. Henry; d. Elizabeth Gay; s. Calshey; "other ch." Exrs.: Calshey Clark, Flonnoy Clark. Wit.: Vivian Ryan, Samuel Clark, John Clark.

SCARBOROUGH, DRURY F., Jan. 6, 1852-Feb. 6, 1854. w. Mary Frances; d. Valeria Victory; s. Jethro F.; d. Susie Comfort. Exrs.: Jonathan J. Weaver, Mary F. Scarborough. Wit.: Patrick Scarborough, Penny Scarborough, James I. Stanley.

SCOTT, ISAAC, July 12, 1867-Nov. 4, 1867. w. Martha S.; ch. referred to but not named. Exrs.: Martha A. Scott, C. L. Holmes. Wit.: J. T. Linder, W. D. Martin, Wm. Bush.

SMITH, JOHN W., June 15, 1856-Sept. 27, 1858. w. Susan; d. Gracey Ann E., 2nd w. of Greene Adams; ch. of d. Mentney, 1st w. of Green Adams, viz., Mary and John N. Adams; s. Simon H.; d. Amanda Gray; s. Freeman W. Exrs.: Young J. Anderson, Robt. L. Cummings. Wit.: Benj. F. Stanley, Ira C. Stanley, Jacob Belflower.

SMITH, MOURNING, Sept. 30, 1846-Nov. 5, 1849. nep. Bennett Whitehead; Rhody Antoinette, d. of Bennett Whitehead; ch. of sis. Mary W. Brazeal, w. of Green H. Brazeal; nep. Thomas P. Smith; hr. Winiford Hutchins; hr. James R. Smith of Randolph Co., Ga. Exrs.: Bennett Whitehead, Thos. P. Smith. Wit.: James Barlow, Absalom Johnson, Isaac Thomas.

SMITH, WILLIAM L., June 5, 1864-Oct. 2, 1865. w. Eliza; d. Margaret E.; d. Charity Z. Exr.: John T. Duncan. Wit.: John J. Keen, J. M. Hall.

STANLEY, IRA, Mch. 9, 1858-Apr. 5, 1858. w. Janet H.; s. l. John F. Burney; s. l. James T. Chappell; s. Rollin A.; g. s. Green Franklin s. of John F. Burney; s. Benjamin F.; s. Ira E.; d. Georgia J. Exrs. John F. Burney, James T. Chappell, Rollin A. Stanley, Benj. F. Stanley. Wit.: James R. Stanley, R. L. Cumming, F. H. Rowe.

STANLEY, JAMES, Mch. 2, 1841-Jan. 3, 1842. w. Leah; s. Hardy B.; s. Ira; s. James R. Exrs. Ira Stanley, James R. Stanley, James H. Loftin. Wit.: Jordan Baker, S. B. Walder, James H. Loflin.

STANLEY, JOHN, Oct. 6, 1854-Nov. 13, 1854. w. Sarah to whom married for 22 years; s. James H.; d. Mary E. Stokes; d. Sarah C. Smith; s. John J.; s. Nathan Thomas; s. Richard R.; d. Penelope Ann Prudence; s. Benjamin E.; s. Pearcy L.; s. Rowell R. Exrs.: James Stanley, Thomas Holleman. Wit.: Isaac Martin, P. A. Ashley, James W. Stanley.

STANLEY, SUSAN M., Oct. 23, 1865-Dec. 4, 1865. g. s. Benjamin Franklin Smith; g. s. Cincinatus Guyton Smith; s. William Allen Brack. Exr.: William Allen Brack. Wit.: George W. Slaughter, Ira E. Stanley, Rollin A. Stanley.

THOMAS, WILLIAM, Oct. 12, 1842-July 4, 1844. b. John; b. l. Harrison Bailey; b. Daniel R.; sis. Regina; sis. A— Jane; f. William L.; b. Chamer H. Wit.: Henry Misser.

TROUP, GEORGE M., Sept. 20, 1851-June 2, 1856. d. Florida, married 1st —— Bryan, 2nd —— Forman; ch. of d. Florida; d. Oralie, w. of John Vigal; s. George M. Exrs.: G. B. Cumming, James P. Scriven, Thomas M. Forman, G. M. Troup. Wit.: William Winham, Alex A. Giltiman, Thompson Smith.

VICKERS, JAMES, Sept. 24, 1853-Nov. 5, 1853. w. Elizabeth; d. Eugenia Missouri; s. Ashley E. Exrs.: Ashley E. Vickers, John M. Allen. Wit.: Wm. Rouse, Wm. Beall, Willis Allen.

WATTS, MRS. ANN (widow), Aug. 26, 1846-Jan. 15, 1847. Two youngest s., James G and Frederick F. Exrs. and Wit.: Alexander Adair Giltman, Mary Linder, Martha J. W. Linder.

WILKINSON, THOMAS H., Sept. 27, 1842-Dec. 8, 1842. w. Mary; twin d. Ann Thomas and Mary Jane; "other ch." Exrs.: Mary Wilkinson, Thos. C. Spicer. Wit.: Arthur W. Preston, Wiley G. Philips, David Harvard.

WILLIAMS, LOTT, Sept. 22, 1855-Dec. 6, 1858. w. Polly; d. Nancy w. of Thomas Swinson; d. Mary w. of John B. Fountain; s. Brantley; s. Benjamin; s. James. Exrs.: John W. Yopp, Brantley Williams. Wit.: Jesse Woodard, Thomas Lock, Josiah Gay, Andrew Beddingfield.

WOODARD, JOHN, SR., Oct. 4, 1854-Feb. 5, 1862. w. Levicey; s. Jesse; s. John, Jr.; d. Dicey Joiner; d. Mary Joiner; d. Queen Anne Elizabeth. Exrs.: Levicey Woodard, John Woodard, George Currell. Wit.: W. C. Knight, John T. Duncan, James F. Robinson.

EARLY MARRIAGES

(Original spelling has been preserved.)

MARRIAGE RECORDS, 1809-1817

BOOK A

Man	Wife	Date of Marriage
Adkins, Joseph	Polly Grimes	May 22, 1817
Batson, Dennis	Martha J. Corker	1814
Battle, Joseph J.	Rhody Whitehead	Jan. 18, 1810
Beatty, William	Polly Drew	Oct. 18, 1810
Boyet, Lock	Nancy Fort	Feb. 14, 1811
Brooks, David	Mary Peal	Nov. 10, 1816
Bryan, John	Gracey Tuttle	Dec. 24, 1816
Careker, Jacob	Lucy Griffin	Apr. 14, 1814
Carson, Andrew M.	Mrs. Charity Horn	Aug. 11, 1814
Cawthorn, Wm., Jr.	Sarah Smith	Dec. 24, 1813
Center, Jesse	Polly Faircloth	Aug. 5, 1816
Connelly, Michael	Edney Green	Mar. 3, 1816
Connelly, Philemon	Hannah Winston	Sept. 8, 1815
Cook, Asa L.	Betsy Kent	Jan. 19, 1814
Creach, Noah	Sally Tramel	Feb. 15, 1817
Dale, John	Sarah Wright	1813
Daniel, Elijah M.	Polly Batson	Apr. 4, 1815
Davis, John	Sophia Lomax	Dec. 24, 1809
Dean, John	Jane Albritton	Dec. 22, 1814
Dean, Wm. Ennels	Susannah Albritton	July 4, 1816
Dudley, Edwin	Cathrine Kellam	Apr. 22, 1817
Duke, William P.	Eliza Fenn	Oct. 29, 1815
Fields, Owen	Anna Griffin	Feb. 3, 1814
Flowers, Joseph	Charity Spurlock	Apr. 16, 1817
Folson, Ebenezer	Nancy Montford	Mch. 3, 1814
Grantham, Nathan	Susannah Strickland	Apr. 6, 1817
Hare, Raiford	Polly Darby	1817
Hendricks, William	Susannah Webster	Mch. 11, 1817
Hicks, Abner	Mary Beatty	Sept., 1809
Higdon, Robert, Jr.	Elizabeth Green	Nov. 13, 1814
Hogan, John	Luisa Russell	Sept. 25, 1816
Hollinger, William	Rachel Hester	May 19, 1814
Holton, Robert	Margaret Holton	Dec. 15, 1814
Hutto, Elas	Milley Ursery	Oct. 6, 1814
Hutto, Henry	Catherine Bullock	July 21, 1816
Hutto, John	Polly Ursery	Sept. 1, 1816
Jernagan, Joseph	Zany Lindsay	Feb. 16, 1817
Johnson, Lewis	Betsy Carter	Nov. 8, 1810
Johnson, James	Sarah Norton	Sept. 27, 1809
Lambert, Noll	Polly Willis	1817
Love, John	Betsy Hall	May 16, 1814
McLendon, Burrel	Feriby Joiner	July 23, 1816
McNair, Daniel	Celia Yarborough	Feb. 10, 1811
Manning, Thomas	Patsy Hart	Dec. 27, 1810
Miller, William, Jr.	Sally Miller	Mar. 2, 1814
Montford, Henry	Agey Stokes	1813
Moore, Edward	Elvy Newby	Dec. 5, 1816
Morris, Jonathan	Nancy Loftin	Feb. 23, 1817
Perkins, Samuel	Betsy Alexander	1813
Perkins, William	Pernina Anderson	Nov. 28, 1816

Man	Wife	Date of Marriage
Philips, Burrel	Sally Philips	Dec. 24, 1809
Pickering, Namon	Smitty Smith	Feb. 23, 1817
Pittman, Elbert	Nancy Counsel	June 10, 1811
Pope, Fleet	Sally Mims	Nov. 14, 1816
Register, John	Vancey Cane	May 27, 1817
Roberts, Mark	Mitty Smith	Oct. 20, 1313
Roberts, William	Nancy Tucker	July 4, 1814
Roberts, William	Tabitha Faulk	Jan. 11, 1816
Salter, James	Polly Shearly	Apr. 10, 1817
Scott, David	Ann Hutto	Feb. 23, 1817
Sheffield, Nathan	Permelia Philips	Dec. 10, 1811
Shine, James W.	Elizabeth Taylor	July 22, 1810
Smith, David	Hanna Tuttle	July 23, 1816
Smith, Isaac	Milberry Smith	Feb. 13, 1817
Smith, Matthew	Unity Register	Feb. 19, 1809
Smith, Thomas	Abigail Faircloth	Nov. 18, 1814
Stringer, Emory (Burke Co.)	Polly Horn	Dec. 21, 1813
Stringer, Irwin	Nelly Green	June 4, 1809
Swinson, Thomas	Mrs. Sarah Robinson	April 3, 1816
Thompson, Alfred	Mary Roberts	Feb. 7, 1811
Thompson, James	Mary Joiner	Feb. 1, 1814
Trammel, Daniel	Elizabeth Knight	May 18, 1817
Tucker, John	Easter Nobles	Oct. 29, 1816
Ursery, Meridy	Jane Watson	Mar. 8, 1817
Varnedo, John	Jennet Carson	Aug. 25, 1814
Verenedo, John	Honor Hogan	Mar. 7, 1809
Vickers, Elias	Elizabeth Gibbs	Mar. 27, 1811
Vickers, Thomas	Piety Beaty	Feb. 16, 1817
Wallace, Green	Lovina Rowland	June 23, 1811
Ward, William	Nancy Hutchins	Dec. 15, 1811
Warren, Josiah	Margaret Ann Martin	Jan. 11, 1814
Way, Samuel	Rachel Hampton	Oct. 10, 1816
Wood, Wilkes	Mary Anderson	Sept. 25, 1814
Wynne, John	Peggy Clements	Oct. 29, 1816
Yates, James	Agnes Roling	April 25, 1817
Yeats, John	Patsy Hinson	Aug. 21, 1814
Young, Owen Watson	Patsy Howell	May 1, 1814

MARRIAGE RECORDS, 1811-1817
BOOK B

Man	Wife	Date of Marriage
Allen, Eason	Mrs. Nancy Brazeal	Mar. 28, 1813
Bailey, Burrel	Polly Land	Sept. 20, 1812
Bell, John	Nancy Summerlin	July 1, 1813
Burch, Andrew	Milbrey Pittman	Dec. 12, 1811
Bustle, John	Betsy Varnedore	May 28, 1812
Carey, Jesse	Rebecca Driver	Dec. 25, 1814
Chairs, Joseph	Mrs. Mary Fenn	Dec. 25, 1811
Coney, Jeremiah	Sally Higdon	Feb. 23, 1812
Coney, William	Fanny Bell	Aug. 18, 1813
Cooper, Henry	Betsy Tucker	Dec. 10, 1823
Culverson, John	Betsy Mills	Mar. 21, 1813
Gilbert, Thomas	Alsey Fordham	Apr. 23, 1815
Glass, Thomas	Nancy Cane	Apr. 9, 1813

Man	Wife	Date of Marriage
Griffin, Abner	Patsy Branch	Apr. 18, 1823
Hammock, John	Nancy Williams	June 12, 1817
Hardeson, Harvey	Feby Dykes	Dec. 31, 1815
Hargrove, Howell	Mrs. Susannah Harp	Dec. 1, 1811
Howard, James	Mrs. Silvey Bethea	Oct. 23, 1812
Hightower, Charnall	Mary Ware	Dec. 24, 1815
Hubbart, Stephen	Mary Boyle	Dec. 24, 1811
Ivy, Robert	Elizabeth Miller	Feb. 28, 1810
Kent, Abel	Susannah Ammons	Dec. 29, 1811
Lassiter, Jesse	Cathrine Cochran	Mar. 20, 1823
McDaniel, Josiah	Martha Holinger	June 29, 1817
McLendon, Ezekiel	Eliza Caragen	Mar. 28, 1813
Miller, John	Nancy Swearingame	Dec. 31, 1816
Nelson, James	Christian Spivey	July 2, 1815
Omans, John	Mrs. Louisa Harrington	Sept. 24, 1815
Pennington, John	Fanny Smith	Aug. 10, 1812
Pullen, Moses	Ginny Land	Dec. 12, 1813
Rains, John	Milly Watson	June 17, 1812
Sanford, Brittain	Sally Hammock	Aug. 5, 1812
Sears, Harrison	Harriet Tully	Mar. 2, 1815
Shores, John	Edy Daniel	Mar. 31, 1823
Smith, Jacob	Elizabeth Barlow	Sept. 17, 1811
Swinson, Thomas	Elender Warren	Nov. 12, 1812
Taylor, James	Betsy Yates	July 29, 1812
Ursery, John	Cathrine Ursery	Dec. 24, 1812
Watson, Orandatus	Lydia Smith	Apr. 29, 1813
Watson, Reason	Nancy Higdon	May 26, 1816
Watson, Silas	Keziah Ursery	Sept. 13, 1812
Wright, James	Sarah Maddux	Feb. 2, 1815
Young, William	Nancy McLendon	Mar. 25, 1813

MARRIAGE RECORDS, 1813-1830
BOOK C

Man	Wife	Date of Marriage
Albritton, William	Maria Blackshear	June 1, 1820
Alford, Royal	Mrs. Louisa Hogan	Apr. 19, 1820
Allen, Nazra	Thompsey Lindsey	Sept. 28, 1820
Armstrong, John	Sarah Hathorn	Mar. 1, 1818
Baggett, Josiah	Amey Powell	Apr. 18, 1822
Baker, William	Catharine Weeks	Sept. 10, 1818
Banks, Charles	Lucena Morrell	May 30, 1820
Barlow, Archibald	Priscilla Crass	Nov. 6, 1823
Barlow, Thomas	Eliza Caldwell	Dec. 24, 1822
Belcher, Allen	Elizabeth Peacock	Nov. 13, 1813
Bell, Zachariah	Littice Daugherty	Oct. 3, 1821
Blackshear, Robert	Rebecca Davis	Oct. 1, 1821
Bohannon, John	Harriet Riggins	Nov. 14, 1822
Bracewell, Wiley	Aggie Doorman	Nov. 9, 1820
Branch, David	Charity Hogan	May 7, 1818
Branch, Peter W.	Caroline Matilda Miller	Sept. 30, 1819
Brown, Elias	Rebecca Underwood	Jan. 23, 1823
Brown, Hezekiah	Nancy Stanley	Nov. 14, 1822
Brown, Jesse	Polly Harralson	Nov. 23, 1817
Brown, John	Susan Dean	Nov. 25, 1820
Bush, Gideon	Mary Winham	May 27, 1819

Man	Wife	Date of Marriage
Bush, Moses	Julis Calhoun	Apr. 9, 1815
Bush, Zachariah	Polly Dennis	Sept. 23, 1818
Cadwell, George	Polly Turner	Dec. 6, 1821
Calhoun, John	Jinny Clarke	Oct. 27, 1816
Calhoun, Winton	Elizabeth Minton	Feb. 9, 1823
Campbell, David	Elizabeth Cook	Nov. 22, 1818
Cannon, James P.	Charlotte Stoftoe	Jan. 19, 1820
Carson, William	Caty Sheffield	Dec. 22, 1821
Cary, John	Lucinda Speir	June 11, 1820
Cason, Willis	Betsey Boyett	Jan. 29, 1823
Caswell, Sylvanus	Lucy Vaughn	May 21, 1818
Cawley, George	Betsey Keen	July 22, 1819
Cicaty, Augustin D.	Polly Moore	Dec. 30, 1817
Clark, Thomas	Betsey Spikes	May 24, 1821
Clark, Thomas	Polly Register	Apr. 7, 1816
Clark, Warren	Polly Spikes	May 17, 1819
Clements, Joseph	Elizabeth Register	Jan. 29, 1818
Coats, Robert	Margaret R. Cowan	Mar. 29, 1818
Cobb, Thomas	Mary Cason	Dec. 27, 1818
Coleman, James	Dicey Edwards	Jan. 2, 1823
Coleman, Jose	Beady Horn	Mar. 18, 1821
Colley, George	Sarah Winham	May 2, 1822
Coney, John B.	Betsey Gay	Jan. 27, 1820
Cooper, Henry	Jane Maddox	May 18, 1820
Cooper, James	Elizabeth Rowland	Feb. 6, 1821
Cooper, John B.	Ann Williams	July 1, 1819
Crawford, John H.	Liddy Jones	Apr. 1, 1820
Cross, Irwinton D.	Viny Tyler	Dec. 8, 1822
Cross, William	Dicey Tiler	Oct. 24, 1822
Crouse, Joel	Jane Shores	June 18, 1823
Culpepper, John Cowan	Nancy Caroline Lawson	Jan. 9, 1823
Daniel, James	Polly Armstrong	June 21, 1818
Daniel, William	Tabitha Rickett	Apr. 24, 1823
Darby, Timothy	Nancy Stucky	Apr. 29, 1821
Darsey, Joel	Mary Hall	Jan. 6, 1820
Davis, William	Eliza McBain	Dec. 20, 1821
Dean, Elijah	Martha Page	Sept. 27, 1814
Deen, Williamson	Eliza Smith	June 26, 1818
De Grafenreed, John	Anna Collier	July 1, 1822
Dent, John G.	Fanny Watts	Sept. 6, 1821
Dominey, Henry	Louisa Blackshear	Apr. 1, 1821
Drew, Willis	Sally Mills	Dec. 23, 1817
Duce, Robert	Elizabeth Anderson	Mar. 4, 1820
Duke, Isham	Clarissa Williams	June 22, 1820
Duncan, Elbert	Elizabeth Speir	Aug. 19, 1818
Eason, Elijah	Catharine Joiner	Aug. 20, 1820
Ellington, Josiah B.	Rachel B. Maddox	Oct. 3, 1822
Ellison, Wiley	Ellender Blair	May 10, 1820
Ezel, John	Sarah Pope	Dec. 22, 1822
Faircloth, Ethelred	Nancy Holton	Oct. 4, 1820
Faircloth, Frederick	Nancy Hall	Nov. 30, 1823
Faircloth, Joshua	Elizabeth Faircloth	Oct. 18, 1820
Faircloth, Peter	Jinny Faircloth	Jan. 29, 1818
Farmer, Andrew	Temperence Braswell	Jan. 15, 1818
Folsom, Nathaniel	Patsey Brantley	Mar. 19, 1820
Forester, John	Susannah Cooper	July 9, 1818
Freeman, James	Hannah Oliver	Feb. 20, 1819
Fullford, Valentine	Catharine Wilkes	May 17, 1818

Man	Wife	Date of Marriage
Gaines, George G.	Louisa F. McCall	Feb. 4, 1818
Gay, Josiah	Sally Beddingfield	Nov. 13, 1817
Gay, Reuben	Elizabeth Polk	July 20, 1815
Gibbons, Henry	Sarah Parker	Dec. 9, 1819
Glass, Thomas	Kitty Fullford	July 13, 1821
Green, William	Polly Higdon	Feb. 8, 1821
Griffin, Archibald, Col.	Mrs. Lovicy Kirsey	Dec. 4, 1823
Grimes, John	Patsy Ezell	Aug. 16, 1822
Guyton, Joseph	Catharine Collier	Aug. 21, 1817
Hair, Edmund	Mary Forest	Feb. 14, 1818
Hair, Joel	Aley Forest	May 21, 1818
Hall, Solomon	Nancy Sanders	July 4, 1820
Hargrove, Harmon B.	Mary Fenn	Jan. 27, 1819
Harris, Leroy Garland	Ann Shearman Thomas	Jan. 11, 1820
Hart, Warren	Olive Barlow	Jan. 15, 1818
Hendricks, Hezekiah	Mary Burch	Sept. 11, 1820
Hickman, Stephen	Patsey Gordon	Sept. 28, 1818
Higdon, Charles	Nancy Tippett	Mar. 18, 1819
Hightower, James	Sally Culpepper	Aug. 9, 1821
Hobbs, Boling	Sally Clements	July 27, 1820
Hobbs, Larry	Polly Keen (Mary)	Sept. 7, 1820
Howard, James	Lena Snellgrove	Oct. 7, 1822
Hunt, Anderson	Eliza D. Griffin	June 18, 1821
Hutchinson, Asa	Betsey Sparks	June 23, 1822
Hutto, Peter	Betsey Warren	Nov. 1, 1821
Johnson, Daniel	Alsey Snellgrove	June 1, 1823
Johnson, Emanuel	Nelly Varnadore	Jan. 30, 1819
Johnson, James	Elizabeth Farmer	Dec. 13, 1818
Johnson, John A.	Sarah Watson	Aug. 1, 1816
Johnson, William	Esther Duncan	Dec. 9, 1819
Joiner, Joseph	Elizabeth Montford	Apr. 21, 1818
Joiner, Lewis	Elizabeth Roberts	June 27, 1818
Jones, Livingstone	Henrietta Wylie	May 28, 1818
Jones, Samuel	Delilah Matthewson	July 15, 1821
Jones, Solomon	Sarah Davis	Nov. 29, 1821
Jordan, Henry D.	Elizabeth Montford	June 21, 1821
Karaker, Jacob	Mrs. Nancy Thomas	Nov. 8, 1821
Kittrael, Jonathan	Serena Miller	Feb. 8, 1816
Knight, Speers	Nancy Cary	Oct. 30, 1817
Lafever, John	Peggy Newsome	July 16, 1822
Lafrade, William	Elizabeth Loftin	Dec. 17, 1815
Lambert, Lovinsky	Martha Payne	Jan. 15, 1822
Lambert, Noah	Elizabeth Payne	Mar. 29, 1820
Lassiter, Luke	Nancy Cane	Apr. 29, 1821
Lindsey, John	Mary McCraney	June 18, 1817
Loftin, Elkanah	Mrs. Sarah Swinson	Sept., 1823
Mackey, Charles W.	Susan Slaughter	Apr. 27, 1823
Martin, Robert	Charlotte Harrison	Oct. 8, 1818
Matthews, Howell	Malinda Ussery	Jan. 11, 1821
McGinnis, James	Patsey Grimes	June 7, 1816
McLane, Duncan	Catharine Barfield	Oct. 15, 1818
McLaughlin, James	Nancy Spell	Mar. 12, 1821
McNair, John	Amy Jones	Oct. 6, 1815
Miller, David	Vise Twitty	Apr. 15, 1819
Miller, Elias	Mary Miller	Mar. 25, 1816
Mills, Thomas B.	Betsey Hair	Aug. 1, 1822
Moats, David	Elizabeth Duncan	Feb. 12, 1820
Moore, Alfred	Frances Hart	Dec. 24, 1819

Man	Wife	Date of Marriage
Moore, Thomas	Elizabeth McCall	Oct. 19, 1819
Moore, William	Sarah Ann Riggins	Feb. 25, 1821
Moorman, Charles	Elizabeth Nichols	Apr. 1, 1819
Morgan, Charles W.	Charlotte Gibbons	Mar. 1, 1821
Moreland, Jacob W.	Tabitha Bryan	Jan. 9, 1823
Mosell, Thomas	Nancy Stephens	Nov. 10, 1822
Murphy, James	Nancy Blackshear	Dec. 10, 1820
Nelms, Curtis	Mary Faircloth	June 23, 1831
Nelson, Noah	Penelope Todd	Nov. 19, 1823
Nobles, Jesse	Nancy Fountain	Apr. 24, 1823
Oliver, John M.	Milberry Williams	Nov. 6, 1816
Oliver, William	Dorcas Harrison	Dec. 16, 1819
Omans, John	Elizabeth Underwood	Nov. 2, 1819
Page, Jacob	Elizabeth Roberts	Feb. 7, 1820
Palmor, Balaam	Sarah Weeks	Jan. 27, 1823
Parmer, James	Mary Nobles	June 25, 1823
Parrott, William	Sarah Morrison	June 15, 1821
Passmore, Rowland	Celia Sparks	May 6, 1821
Passmore, Stephen	Elizabeth Riggins	Dec. 26, 1820
Passmore, William H.	Jane Jones	Dec. 16, 1818
Pate, Daniel	Mary McDuffee	July 5, 1818
Peacock, Cullen	Polly Allen	June 13, 1820
Phillips, Samuel	Lucy Everitt	Jan. 14, 1818
Phillips, William	Eliza Hains	Apr. 23, 1823
Phillips, William	Fidelity Bush	Feb. 29, 1816
Pittman, John	Eliza Phillips	Apr. 23, 1815
Pitts, Lunsford C.	Ruth Page	Feb. 20, 1818
Pope, John	Dicey Pope	July 10, 1817
Powell, John	Rachael Vernadore	Dec. 25, 1817
Powell, John	Darcas Hughs	Feb. 5, 1818
Powell, John S.	Winnifred Cornilous	Aug. 12, 1819
Purvis, Richard	Sarah Burch	Aug. 29, 1822
P———, Samuel	Betsey Higdon	Jan. 12, 1819
Raiford, Maurice (of Jefferson Co.)	Patience Mote	Jan. 22, 1819
Rawls, Laban	Harriet Underwood	Nov. 19, 1820
Reed, Alfred B.	Mary W. Shearman	Oct. 31, 1821
Ricks, Richard	Nancy Evans	Apr. 8, 1819
Roach, James M.	Sarah Holland	Jan. 22, 1818
Roach, Jonathan	Polly Taylor	Sept. 13, 1821
Roach, Valentine	Polly Thomas	Apr. 8, 1821
Roberts, William	Sarah Grady	Dec. 9, 1818
Roe, Enoch	Nancy Perkins	Apr. 14, 1819
Rowland, Needham	Louisa Carter	Dec. 13, 1820
Royal, Able	Sarah Nelms	Oct. 7, 1821
Ryals, William	Nancy Lock	Apr. 5, 1821
Sanderlin, Jesse	Nancy Faircloth	Mar. 21, 1822
Sanders, Thomas	Jane Cary	Jan. 17, 1822
Savage, Robert	Polly Tucker	Mar. 15, 1821
Scarborough, James	Polly Lambert	Feb. 12, 1816
Scott, Baptist Norman	Elizabeth Page	Feb. 9, 1822
Sealy, Edward	Margaret Moat	July 21, 1818
Shanks, James D.	Mrs. Elender Beaty	Mar. 4, 1822
Sheppard, Edward	Patsey Waller	Mar. 30, 1820
Shores, Joseph B.	Mary Ann Harrison	Feb. 9, 1820
Simpson, Enoch	Rilla Thomas	Nov. 5, 1818
Slaughter, Noah	Rosie Musslewhite	Oct. 2, 1822
Smith, Davis	Elizabeth D. Jourdan	Jan. 6, 1820

Man	Wife	Date of Marriage
Smith, Elisha	Selina Carson	Apr. 3, 1822
Smith, George	Mrs. Selah Moore	Dec. 29, 1816
Smith, Hugh	Catharine Livingstone	Dec. 31, 1820
Smith, Isham	Martha Payne	Apr. 13, 1820
Smith, Miles	Sally Spell	Oct. 21, 1816
Smith, Thomas P.	Margaret Hill	Apr. 1, 1819
Snellgrove, Jesse	Elizabeth Howard	June 30, 1815
Spell, Reason	Elizabeth Braswell	Dec. 16, 1816
Spiers, James	Maria Martin	Mar. 23, 1820
Spivey, Jonas	Matsey Hester	Mar. 7, 1819
Stephens, Bryan	Rachel Watson	Apr. 2, 1820
Stephens, Ebenezer	Susannah Griffin	June 5, 1819
Stephens, Jesse	Polly Dykes	July 29, 1821
Stewart, Charles	Betsey McCullers	Dec. 23, 1819
Swearingen, Benjamin H.	Mildy Padget	May 12, 1820
Swearingen, Thomas	Nancy Miller	Apr. 8, 1815
Swinson, Stark	Julia Woodward	Sept. 21, 1820
Taylor, Richard	Susan Montford	Oct. 3, 1819
Tharp, Elias	Sally Beaty	Mar. 23, 1820
Thomas, Lewis A.	Oliff Beaty	Jan. 1, 1817
Thomas, Richard	Elizabeth Smith	Nov. 22, 1821
Thompson, Benjamin	Sarah Hair	Aug. 30, 1821
Thompson, Henry	Clary Mathis	Apr. 1, 1820
Thompson, James	Elizabeth Strickland	Jan. 29, 1818
Thompson, Stephen	Margaret Bracewell	Mar. 15, 1821
Tomberlin, Aaron	Mrs. Mary W. Smith	July 23, 1830
Tucker, Davis	Polly Mimms	Nov. 6, 1817
Turner, Alexander	Ruth Fennell	Jan. 8, 1821
Turner, David	Susan Dickson	Apr. 26, 1821
Turner, Joseph	Milberry Johnson	Mar. 19, 1815
Turner, Stephen	Elizabeth Swearingen	Feb. 12, 1818
Tyson, Moses	Nancy Sutton	Sept. 19, 1821
Underwood, James	Rebecca Hightower	Oct. 14, 1819
Underwood, John J.	Sarah R. Cawthorn	Jan. 25, 1821
Ursery, Thomas	Nelly Burch	Sept. 19, 1820
Ursery, Thomas	Milly Smith	July 21, 1821
Walker, Rowland	Peggy Underwood	July 13, 1819
Wallace, George	Rebecca Spell	Sept. 13, 1821
Warren, Reuben	Polly Woodward	Oct. 5, 1814
Watson, Asa	Rhoda Watson	Mar. 23, 1819
Watts, William	Anna Askew	Nov. 25, 1819
Way, Edward	Mary Lord	Dec. 31, 1820
Weaver, Jethro	Polly Elison	Jan. 22, 1818
Webb, Jesse	Nancy Sandford	Aug. 17, 1815
Wells, Elijah	Zilla Joiner	July 25, 1819
Whaley, John	Rebecca Dupree	Sept. 28, 1820
Whiddon, John	Elizabeth Ferguson	Oct. 11, 1820
Whitfield, William	Elizabeth Wallace	Sept. 17, 1817
Wilcox, James	Zilphey Bush	Mar. 5, 1818
Wilkes, Silas	Sarah Slater	Apr. 25, 1817
Wilkinson, Thomas	Mary Spicer	Apr. 5, 1821
Williams, Joel	Fereby Arline	Feb. 11, 1816
Williams, Thompson	Eliza Duke	June 24, 1819
Wood, Jonathan	Malinda Montgomery	Dec. 25, 1823
Woodward, Thomas	Nancy Willis	Aug. 25, 1819
Woodward, William	Nancy Warren	July 5, 1814
Wright, Abel	Rebecca Cadwell	Jan. 13, 1820
Wright, William	Matilda Whitley	Oct. 22, 1818

Man	Wife	Date of Marriage
Wynne, James	Winny Lassiter	June 3, 1821
Wynne, Williamson	Louisa Carter	June 29, 1820
Yates, Jesse	Clarissy Mills	Jan. 20, 1815
Yonn, Benjamin	Martha Snellgrove	Sept. 7, 1819
Young, William	Martha Newby	Sept. 5, 1822
———, Eason	Nancy George	Dec. 8, 1823

MARRIAGE RECORDS, 1811-1836
BOOK D

Man	Wife	Date of Marriage
Adams, William B.	Margaret Sealy	Apr. 20, 1834
Adams, William	Nancy J. Maddox	Oct. 13, 1835
Alaway, Roach	Sally Yates	Mar. 13, 1815
Albritton, Richard	Elizabeth Perkins	Dec. 13, 1825
Allen, Gillum	Penelope Smith	Dec. 31, 1827
Allen, Jordan	Jane Higdon	May 15, 1834
Allen, Nazreth	Nancy Peal	Jan. 17, 1833
Alligood, Hillary	Matilda Fry	Jan. 7, 1829
Andrews, William	Elizabeth Flanders	Jan. 30, 1829
Archer, James	Mary Duncan	Dec. 14, 1326
Arline, Jesse	Jack Eliza Kichens	June 10, 1826
Arline, Jethro	Elizabeth Mason	July 26, 1827
Ashley, Allen	Martha Smith	Mar. 4, 1824
Bacon, Thomas	Queen E. Allen	Sept. 1, 1824
Barlow, Anderson	Mahala Adams	Mar. 20, 1827
Beach, William	Mary Dean	July 28, 1825
Bell, William H.	Nelly Spell	Mar. 29, 1827
Blackshear, James	Elizabeth Brewer	Apr. 6, 1826
Blanchard, Joseph	Winneford Ballentine	Aug. 3, 1826
Bohannon, Philemen	Agnes Culpepper	Aug. 22, 1833
Brack, James	Susan Dean	Mar. 6, 1825
Brantley, Lewis	Isabel Luke	Aug. 7, 1835
Braswell, Reddick	Ose Kitchen	Aug. 24, 1824
Bryan, Edward	Eliza B. Ellington	Nov. 11, 1823
Burch, John	Lydia Hendricks	Mar. 2, 1825
Burch, Littleton	Susan Brack	Feb. 29, 1827
Burch, Reuben	Charlotte Cadwell	Dec. 7, 1826
Bush, William	Mary Smith	Nov. 30, 1834
Caldwell, Samuel	Mrs. Margaret Love	June 1, 1826
Caldwell, Spencer	Catharine Young	Aug. 26, 1828
Canady, Allen	Florida Cane	July 15, 1824
Clements, James	Nancy Wilkes	Mar. 28, 1824
Coleman, Rhesa	Eady Green	Nov. 7, 1828
Collier, James	Mrs. Arthour Roach	April, 1811
Cooper, William	Rhoda Gilbert	Feb. 8, 1829
Coward, Allen	Elsey McDaniel	May 29, 1825
Culpepper, David W.	Eliza Smith	Nov. 28, 1833
Culpepper, David	Catharine Livingstone	Jan. 8, 1835
Daniel, John	Elizabeth Hudson	Jan. 22, 1828
Darsey, Joseph	Nancy Johnston	Nov. 6, 1829
Darsey, Thomas	Charlotte Peacock	Feb. 8, 1823
Davis, Levi	Rebecca Mason	Jan. 17, 1828
Dean, Kindred	Elizabeth Brookins	Dec. 16, 1824
Denson, John	Katharine Caldwell	Feb. 25, 1836

Man	Wife	Date of Marriage
Dillard, Sampson	Dradencia Collier	Nov. 24, 1825
Drury, James	Nancy Brooking	Jan. 7, 1826
Dukes, Benjamin	Delilah Ann Jones	Apr. 16, 1829
Duncan, Thomas	Polly Alligood	July 1, 1824
Eason, Isaac	Elizabeth Bellflower	July 22, 1827
Ellington, John E.	Mary Hightower	Aug. 11, 1825
Faircloth, Benjamin	Mrs. Susan Young	Jan. 24, 1826
Faircloth, Robert S.	Matilda Alligood	Mar. 4, 1825
Fennell, Ephriam	Peggy Spisser	Feb. 17, 1828
Fennell, Patrick	Elinor Johnson	Mar. 15, 1826
Flanders, Mark	Mary Wall	Nov. 9, 1828
Floyd, Eli	Mrs. Unity Smith	June 23, 1825
Fullford, Bryan	Eliza Fullford	Jan. 19, 1824
Fullford, Jordan	Peggy Young	Mar. 29, 1827
Fuqua, Henry C.	Elizabeth Webb	Apr. 17, 1824
Futch, James	Eliza Simms	Jan. 18, 1835
Garnto, Nathan	Jemima Mimms	May 6, 1825
Gibson, William	Mildred Finney	May 16, 1828
Glass, James	Sarah Arline	Jan. 14, 1821
Glass, Levi	Sally Martin	Jan. 10, 1820
Glover, Foster	Priscilla Graham	Dec. 24, 1825
Goff, John G.	Eliza Higdon	Feb. 25, 1836
Grantham, Noel	Martha Miller	Jan. 25, 1824
Green, Eason	Eliza Weaver	Nov. 17, 1825
Green, Jesse	Elizabeth Champion	Mar. 1, 1825
Griffin, Bennett S.	Mary W. Brazeal	Nov. 23, 1824
Griffin, Hardy	Rachel Way	Nov. 16, 1825
Griffin, Lunsford	Elinda Fausett	Feb. 17, 1827
Grinstead, Robert	Elizabeth Martin	Dec. 21, 1826
Guyton, Dr. Charles B.	Lupina Horn	Jan. 27, 1836
Hall, I. C.	Temperance Manning	Jan. 4, 1829
Hampton, Benjamin W.	Clementine O'Neal	Aug. 11, 1824
Hampton, Andrew Y.	Eliza B. Coats	Dec. 18, 1828
Hampton, John M.	Miss A. J. Thomas	Feb. 13, 1827
Hicks, James	Mary Pullen	Nov. 21, 1828
Hicks, William	Altis Drinkwater	Dec. 18, 1834
Higdon, Charles	Alley Powell	Jan. 17, 1828
Hightower, Wingfield	Elizabeth Smith	Mar. 9, 1828
Hilliard, Dennis	Margaret Daniel	Jan. 17, 1827
Hines, Thomas	Anna Wright	Jan. 27, 1825
Hodges, Elbert	Silence Culpepper	Dec. 24, 1828
Holliday, Abner	Elizabeth Goodman	Dec. 16, 1824
Hollingsworth, Caleb	Citilly Brookins	July 12, 1825
Holly, Henry	Mary Oliver	Mar. 26, 1826
Holms, Edwin	Matilda Jones	May 8, 1821
Howard, Charles W.	Laura M. Hampton	Apr. 7, 1836
Hudson, Andrew H.	Sarah M. Ingram	Feb. 19, 1835
Hutchinson, Aaron	Elizabeth Niel	Mar. 20, 1836
Ingram, James	Sarah Ingram	Feb. 19, 1828
Johnson, James	Penelope Tucker	Jan. 24, 1825
Johnson, Jesse	Jane Faircloth	Jan. 20, 1824
Johnston, Lewis	Christian Sullivant	Mar. 12, 1829
Joice, William	Sarah Ann Fuqua	Sept. 29, 1824
Joiner, Bennett	Sarah Smith	Dec. 10, 1824
Joiner, Davis	Rhoda Mote	July 22, 1823
Joiner, Gilford	Letitia Ann Riggins	Nov. 6, 1825
Keen, Young	Rebecca Hester	Apr. 15, 1827
Keen, Young	Mary Ann Jones	Apr. 20, 1834

Man	Wife	Date of Marriage
Kellam, Seth F.	Mary Culpepper	Mar. 16, 1828
Lewis, Jesse	Elizabeth Bullock	Feb. 22, 1835
Lewiston, William T.	Mathaly Culpepper	Jan. 24, 1833
Linder, Lewis	Elizabeth L. Hall	Aug. 6, 1829
Livingstone, William M.	Sarah Culpepper	Dec. 17, 1835
Lock, James	Atha Adams	Dec. 23, 1828
Lucas, Jonas	Tabitha Wright	Oct. 30, 1836
Maddux, David R.	Elizabeth Linder	Jan. 1, 1823
Maddux, Lewis	Mary Sparks	Aug. 14, 1828
McDaniel, James D.	Laney Fields	Jan. 24, 1836
McGee, Mial	Susannah Johnson	Dec. 25, 1823
Manning, Reuben	Alsa Curry	Jan. 30, 1827
Marshall, Henry	Maria Ingram	Mar. 18, 1827
Martin, Lemuel	Mertie Oliver	Jan. 10, 1833
Mason, William L.	Tamer Padgett	May 14, 1829
Matthews, William S.	Luthena Tuckston	May 13, 1829
Mazingo, Henry	Mercy Allcock	Dec. 23, 1830
Meek, Noah	Nancy Ramsay	Jan. 22, 1829
Miller, Aaron	Appy Grantham	Feb. 19, 1824
Miller, James	Rebecca Duncan	Jan. 20, 1825
Miller, James R.	Nancy Livingston	Dec. 26, 1830
Miller, Samuel	Mary Clark	Aug. 9, 1827
Mills, Thomas	Matilda Carson	Mar. 20, 1823
Mills, William	Louisa Howard	Jan. 5, 1825
Mimms, George	Ann Eliza Daniel	June 11, 1825
Minton, Jonathan S.	Mary Hall	Jan. 29, 1828
Mizel, Luke T.	Harriott McCall	Mar. 29, 1827
Montgomery, Samuel	Mrs. Elizabeth Howell	May 11, 1826
Moore, Edward	Jane Goodman	Sept. 22, 1824
Moore, Henry D.	Penelope Stephens	Jan. 9, 1824
Moore, Dr. James S.	Theresa C. Delk	June, 1836
Moss, James C.	Ann Marcia Calhoun	Apr. 4, 1825
Musslewhite, Leonard	Nancy Dominy	Sept. 23, 1823
Nobles, Levi	Lucinda Spiers	May 11, 1828
Odum, Elijah S.	Rutha Goff	Oct. 29, 1835
Oliver, James W.	Susan Green	May 1, 1836
Oliver, Joseph	Sarah Hutchinson Martin	Feb. 26, 1824
Oliver, Tyson	Martha Allen Martin	Apr. 22, 1824
O'Neal, Martin G.	Mary Ann Hampton	May 25, 1828
O'Neal, Theophilus	Patsey Culpepper	Jan. 25, 1821
Outlaw, Alexander	Olive Musslewhite	Feb. 8, 1826
Outlaw, Alexander	Elizabeth Fullford	Feb. 25, 1828
Palmer, Jared J.	Hepsibeth Livingston	Aug. 10, 1826
Parker, Jacob	Sarah Bush	Feb. 13, 1834
Parker, Porter	Mary Pope	May 16, 1833
Parkhurst, Jeremiah	Elizabeth L. Ingram	July 15, 1827
Parrott, Ansley	Synthia Finney	Jan. 11, 1829
Payne, George	Milly Shiver	Feb. 9, 1823
Payne, John	Angeline Shiver	May 12, 1836
Payne, Phillip	Nancy Thomas	Mar. 3, 1833
Perry, Charnal	Eleanor Hilliard	Jan. 29, 1836
Perry, Edward	Elizabeth J. Lee	Feb. 4, 1836
Pierce, John	Susan Todd	June 15, 1835
Pope, Frederic	Eliza Watts	Feb. 9, 1834
Pope, Wiley	Mary Stewart	Sept. 11, 1823
Powell, Benjamin	Sarah Mimms	Feb. 24, 1828
Powell, Benjamin	Matilda Forest	Dec. 25, 1835
Powell, Isiah	Frances Spurlock	Jan. 21, 1827

Man	Wife	Date of Marriage
Powell, Lewis	Mrs. Sarah Wilkes	Aug. 8, 1822
Rawls, Joseph	Mary Barlow	Dec. 1, 1827
Register, James	Jane Calhoun	Oct. 6, 1825
Register, Robert	Elizabeth Calhoun	Mar. 11, 1827
Ricks, Daniel	Mary Mason	Apr. 24, 1828
Roberts, Daniel	Elizabeth Carey	Oct. 2, 1826
Rowan, Matthew H.	Temperance Watson	Nov. 7, 1824
Rowe, Freeman H.	Margaret J. Moore	May 16, 1837
Rowland, John	Mrs. Mary Chaires	Sept. 9, 1822
Ryals, Travis	Sarah Jackson	Sept. 9, 1827
Sandford, Keen	Caroline Steptoe	Oct. 6, 1826
Scarborough, Perrin	Penelope Fordham	Dec. 12, 1835
Sheppard, John	Mary Kirksey	Sept. 3, 1829
Ship, David	Susina Anderson	Feb. 22, 1825
Shiver, James	Polly Shiver	June 5, 1823
Shiver, Warren	Mary Delk	Apr. 5, 1835
Simmons, John W.	Penelope Miller	Feb. 24, 1827
Skelton, Robert	Martha Ritter	Aug. 9, 1827
Smith, Charles	Mary Wallace	Nov. 18, 1824
Smith, Hardy, Jr.	Mary Ann Beacham	Oct. 21, 1826
Smith, Willis J.	Charlotte English	Mar. 22, 1835
Smith, Zachariah	Elizabeth Rawls	Dec. 14, 1834
Snellgrove, Solomon	Nancy Hair	Dec. 15, 1828
Spell, William	Edicy Alligood	May 6, 1826
Thomas, Ethelred	Lina Nelms	June 14, 1825
Thompson, Guy	Matilda Anderson	May 11, 1826
Tilby, James W.	Mrs. Elizabeth Russell	Sept. 17, 1826
Tison, Eason	Carissa Phillips	Dec. 26, 1826
Touchstone, Christopher D.	Lucinda Smith	Aug. 20, 1833
Trammell, James I.	Penelope N. Maddux	Jan. 6, 1825
Turner, Joseph A.	Sarah Tucker	Mar. 8, 1835
Vann, Elzy	Rosana Stewart	Apr. 2, 1835
Varnadore, Westley	Winy Wilcox	Mar. 8, 1835
Walker, Noah	Charlotte Calhoun	Jan. 7, 1826
Wallace, William	Mrs. Mary Larkins	Sept. 23, 1826
Warren, Eli	Eliza Jane Love	Apr. 14, 1825
Weaver, Jethro	Mary Bracewell	Oct. 20, 1824
Weekly, John	Lucinda Carey	Dec. 29, 1826
Weeks, Bartemus	Levina Crass	Jan. 28, 1836
Weeks, Bartimus M.	Anna Sauls	Dec. 13, 1827
Weeks, Wm.	Susan Brookins	Jan. 20, 1836
Welch, George D.	Mary T. Griffin	Oct. 28, 1817
Whitfield, Samuel	Margaret Outlaw	Oct. 13, 1825
Williams, John C. F.	Mary Curie	Aug. 9, 1827
Winham, Allen	Bethena Bush	Nov. 21, 1824
Wood, Allen	Elizabeth Mashburn	May 17, 1829
Woodward, John	Vicey Nobles	Jan. 8, 1824
Wright, James	Gilby Burch	Apr. 4, 1826
Yopp, Jeremiah H.	Margaret S. McCall	Mar. 9, 1824
Young, Emanuel J.	Mary Montgomery	Feb. 11, 1836

MARRIAGE RECORDS, 1833-1848
BOOK E

Man	Wife	Date of Marriage
Abbott, Abner A.	Mary Gibson	Mar. 7, 1841
Adams, Cuthbert	Elizabeth B. Culpepper	Jan. 4, 1838
Adams, John I.	Martha Jane Montford	Dec. 14, 1841
Adams, Sumner	Sarah G. Montford	Jan. 25, 1838
Adkinson, John P.	Parthena Yonn	Nov. 13, 1835
Allen, Bryan	Nancy Standley	June 20, 1833
Alligood, Hardy	Sarah Green	Feb. 22, 1838
Alligood, Henry	Sarah Creech	Dec. 29, 1836
Ard, Dr. Andrew W.	Jane V. Payne	Oct. 13, 1836
Askew, Frederick	Mrs. Nancy Maulfress	Apr. 16, 1833
Bailey, Aurelius H.	Sarah Ann Rains	Mar. 7, 1843
Bailey, Cullen D.	Elizabeth Herrin	Oct. 6, 1837
Bailey, Oliver H.	Mary Dynn	May 21, 1839
Bailey, Wynnsford H.	Ann Winn	Aug. 1, 1839
Barlow, William W.	Amanda M. Allen	June 27, 1837
Barwick, Lott	Elizabeth Rountree	Jan. 29, 1835
Barwick, William	Martha Outlaw	Dec. 7, 1837
Bellflower, Jesse	Mahala Horn	May 3, 1837
Bellflower, Samuel	Demarsy Thomas	July 11, 1841
Bender, Wiley J.	Sarah J. Adams	July 5, 1841
Bracewell, Matthew	Riney Keel	July 24, 1842
Bracewell, Redick	Elizabeth McDaniel	Dec. 31, 1836
Bracewell, Seaborn A.	Roxa Ann Woolf	Jan. 10, 1841
Brown, Dr. Alfred Theodore	Emeline S. Davis	Apr. 18, 1838
Brown, James N.	Louisa Cox	Jan. 10, 1841
Bryan, Thos., Jr.	Unity Darsey	May 18, 1837
Bryan, William	Martha Hare	Feb. 22, 1838
Bryant, John	Darsey Allen	Oct. 26, 1837
Burch, Benjamin H.	Mary Jane Daniel	Apr. 20, 1843
Burch, Michael	Susan Smith	Jan. 3, 1839
Bush, James	Celia M. Smith	Feb. 1, 1838
Carter, Elijah	Mary Flanders	Feb. 20, 1840
Cawley, Michael John	Mary Scarborough	June 16, 1842
Clark, James L.	Elizabeth Hightower	Dec. 15, 1839
Clark, Matthew	Ursula A. S. Hudson (Weaver)	July 14, 1842
Clark, William	Sarah Howell	Jan. 23, 1834
Clements, Jacob	Miraza Burgan Turner	June 16, 1839
Clements, Jacob	Sarah Busley	June 1, 1843
Clements, Elias	Elizabeth Turner	June 9, 1839
Coleman, Josey	Sarah Ann Coleman	Oct. 18, 1838
Coleman, William	Nancy S——more	Nov. 16, 1841
Coley, Atlalia	Julia Ann Wilkinson	May 26, 1842
Cooper, William	Mary D. Moore	Mar. 29, 1840
Cross, Cullen	Lucinda Scarborough	June 21, 1839
Culpepper, Eason A.	Queen Ann Jones	Feb. 20, 1838
Cunningham, James	Brancey Bender	Dec. 28, 1837
Cunningham, James	Caroline Swiney	Nov. 12, 1839
Currell, George	Mary J. Fuqua	Oct. 13, 1842
Dadd, Robert	Elizabeth Maddox	July 27, 1836
Daniel, Hiram K.	Katharine McBane	Jan. 24, 1835
Darsey, William Y.	Frances C. Chisholm	Sept. 20, 1833
Davis, Daniel	Elizabeth Miller	May 27, 1837
Doll, Abram	Martha Shiver	Aug. 29, 1841
Faircloth, Robert	Evalina Grady	Nov. 24, 1836

Man	Wife	Date of Marriage
Falk, Thomas	Mrs. Penelope Skelton	Oct. 31, 1841
Fennel, Ephraim	Mattie Moye	Oct. 26, 1843
Forest, James	Elizabeth Bullock	May 9, 1835
Forest, James E.	Tishy Brookins	Jan. 1, 1837
Fordham, Benjamin	Caroline Howard	Mar. 2, 1843
Fuqua, Thomas	Mary M. J. Hightower	Oct. 12, 1843
Garnto, Nathan	Susan Parrott	Sept. 14, 1836
Goff, Madison	Pressia Burch	Jan. 20, 1838
Goff, Washington D.	Marinda E. Thompson	Jan. 19, 1840
Goff, William N.	Joanah Robbins	Oct. 6, 1836
Graham, Alexander	Elizabeth Pope	July 16, 1843
Grant, William	Lucy Jones	July 28, 1848
Gray, William	Amanda Smith	July 16, 1837
Green, Wallace	Deborah Cross	May 1, 1842
Grinstead, William	Delman Warren	May 17, 1836
Guyton, Starling	Mary Williamson	Aug. 31, 1834
Guyton, Thomas N.	Elvira L. Dasher	Oct. 17, 1839
Hall, John H.	Rebecca Snellgrove	Oct. 28, 1838
Hampton, William L.	Louisa Horn	Feb. 8, 1838
Hamuck, R. P.	Sarah Williamson	Mar. 26, 1840
Hand, Henry	Louisa Floyd	July 19, 1840
Haskins, William	Nancy Bender	Sept. 7, 1837
Hicks, James	Mary Ellington	Sept. 5, 1837
Higdon, Robert	Mary Ann Bryan	Oct. 16, 1841
Hogsett, William Wilson	Martha Ann Adams	Dec. 21, 1837
Holland, John	Sarah Ann Higdon	Dec. 29, 1836
Holmes, Charles L.	Mary P. Touchston	Sept. 5, 1839
Hudnal, Jackson	Elizabeth Gaynes	Jan. 23, 1840
Hudnal, Thomas J.	Mahala J. Guyery	Aug. 24, 1837
Hudson, James	Harriet Brantley	Oct. 26, 1836
Joiner, James S.	Elizabeth McDaniel	July 25, 1839
Johns, Elias	Mary Parrott	Feb. 19, 1837
Jones, Henry P.	Mary J. Wells	Nov. 8, 1838
Jones, Hezekiah	Sarah Kinchen	Mar. 19, 1840
Jones, William F.	Mary Jane Bush	Aug. 10, 1837
Kee, Henry	Sarah Carter	Oct. 4, 1836
Kinchen, Thomas H.	Eliza J. Daniel	June 2, 1842
Kinchen, William	Milly Grayham	Dec. 21, 1837
Kiree, Samuel	Penelope Vick	Mar. 9, 1837
Lashly, Hardy	Mary Christian	July 4, 1837
Layton, Isaac	Mabel Strickland	Oct. 30, 1837
Lee, William C. H.	Hester Ann Yopp	July 9, 1835
Leonard, James W.	Nancy White	Dec. 31, 1837
Lewis, Andrew	Comfort Layton	June 9, 1839
Linder, Jacob T.	Martha J. W. Askew	Sept. 28, 1837
Lock, Thomas	Eliza Perry	Jan. 24, 1839
Luke, William	Sarah Rhodes	Feb. 14, 1839
McBane, N.	Nancy Barlow	July 5, 1838
McDaniel, Andrew J.	Mary G. Warren	Mar. 13, 1842
McDaniel, William	Ann Gilbert	Oct. 11, 1835
Mason, Thomas J.	Malinda Freeman	May 13, 1841
Miller, Thomas	Nancy Vick	Sept. 4, 1837
Mimms, Jesse	Rebecca Rye	Apr. 15, 1838
Mindon, John	Sarah Ann Bell	June 22, 1842
Montford, J. L.	Elizabeth Adams	Dec. 19, 1839
Moorman, Thomas J.	Susan M. Linder	Dec. 20, 1838
Morris, Ivey	Susan Goff	Dec. 21, 1837
O'Neal, Cullen	Ethelinda Adams	Dec. 18, 1837

Man	Wife	Date of Marriage
Parrott, John	Mariah Flanders	Mar. 9, 1837
Parrott, John	Rebecca McVay	Nov. 2, 1839
Parrott, William	Mary McVay	June 13, 1839
Passmore, Alexander	Elizabeth Ellington	Dec. 12, 1838
Payne, A. J.	Jane Shiver	Apr. 8, 1834
Perry, Joseph	Harriet Roach	Feb. 1, 1837
Pharis, William S.	Sarah Rhodes	Feb. 14, 1839
Pickron, Bryan	Ann A. Smith	Jan. 25, 1838
Pope, Benjamin	Mariah Hall	Jan. 5, 1837
Powell, Henry D.	Elizabeth N. Holloman	June 12, 1842
Preston, Arthur W.	Louisa Barlow	May 13, 1840
Ramsay, Lewis J.	Mary M. Spears	Oct. 20, 1836
Rawls, Daniel	Margaret Mason	Oct. 31, 1841
Redin, John	Mahala Williams	Jan. 17, 1836
Rentz, John A.	Josephine B. Moore	Apr. 12, 1842
Robin, Tillman	Ann Davis	July 7, 1842
Robinson, James W.	Eliza Ricks	July 2, 1837
Rodes, Joseph	Sally Rye	Oct. 17, 1839
Rooks, John A.	Ellifair Howard	Feb. 23, 1843
Ross, Joseph	Margaret Ingram	June 6, 1843
Rowland, Alexander	Mary Stanley	Aug. 4, 1836
Rowland, William Griffin	Nancy Jones	Apr. 16, 1838
Sandford, Keen	Sarah Finey	Nov. 5, 1840
Sandford, Keen	Sarah Berryhill	Mar. 25, 1838
Scarborough, Daniel N.	Sarah Lee	Feb. 25, 1835
Scarborough, Drury F.	Mary Frances Weaver	May 13, 1841
Scarborough, Henry	Huldah Hudson	Sept. 8, 1836
Scarborough, James	Hannah Fordham	Feb. 17, 1839
Scarborough, Patrick	Eliza Ann Smith	Jan. 9, 1836
Shaw, David D.	Epsey Key	Nov. 21, 1838
Sheppard, Edward	Winneford Sandford	Apr. 3, 1837
Shirley, William	Charlotte Gorman	Aug. 18, 1836
Shiver, Phabian	Angeline Brown	July 11, 1838
Shores, John	Margaret Williamson	Oct. 17, 1839
Singletary, Arthur	John Ann Lock	Oct. 14, 1833
Smith, Aaron	Nancy Allen	Feb. 9, 1837

MARRIAGE RECORDS, 1841-1851
BOOK F

Man	Wife	Date of Marriage
Allen, Gillam	Caroline Mullis	Oct. 4, 1842
Allen, John	Harriet White	Feb. 18, 1849
Allen, William G.	Rachel Hester	Aug. 30, 1851
Alligood, William O.	Eliza Hobbs	Dec. 30, 1846
Atkinson, John	Mary Ann Ursery	June 8, 1845
Barnes, William	Amanda Nelson	Apr. 9, 1846
Barnett, John	Matilda Hair	Mar. 26, 1846
Beasley, John	Jane Vick	Sept. 1, 1844
Beasley, Reuben	Mary Smith	May 10, 1846
Beasley, Wright M.	Jane Johnson	Apr. 19, 1846
Beddingfield, Andrew	Deborah Grinstead	Apr. 23, 1846
Bellflower, Robert R.	Luraney E. Smith	Feb. 18, 1849
Bennett, Samuel	Emeline Brown	Jan. 13, 1849
Bracewell, Alford P.	Mary Ann Judson	Apr. 19, 1845
Brantley, Green J.	Mrs. Elizabeth Ricks	Aug. 30, 1849
Brantley, Joseph M.	Harriet J. Brantley	Jan. 9, 1848

Man	Wife	Date of Marriage
Brantley, William W.	Sarah Ann Warnock	Aug. 14, 1849
Brown, Elijah	Nancy P. Clark	Mar. 4, 1849
Brown, Urban A.	Lucy L. Weaver	Nov. 23, 1843
Smith, George	Jemima Rutha Sumner	Jan. 24, 1839
Smith, Jacob	Elizabeth Morgan	Aug. 8, 1841
Smith, James M.	Lydia Ursury	Dec. 23, 1841
Smith, John W.	Susan McRay	Sept. 10, 1843
Smith, Lewis D.	Sarah Katharine Stanley	Aug. 13, 1843
Smith, William	Harriet White	Jan. 11, 1838
Spell, John E.	Elizabeth E. Montford	Dec. 28, 1833
Spell, George Washington	Eliza Watson	Jan. 5, 1840
Spivey, James B.	Mary A. Smith	Sept. 21, 1837
Taylor, John, Jr.	Naomy Morgan	Jan. 8, 1839
Thomas, Alfred	Elvily Lewis	Oct. 13, 1836
Thomas, Alfred	Malinda Scarborough	Sept. 19, 1838
Thomas, John	Holland A. Jones	Dec. 24, 1835
Thomas, John	Mrs. Lucy Adams	Oct. 3, 1839
Thomas, Richard	Lydia Montgomery	Jan. 5, 1842
Varnadore, Eli	Rebecca Barlow	Aug. 16, 1836
Volotton, Benjamin	Mary Brantley	Dec. 24, 1840
Wadkins, Joseph	Mary Hudnal	Aug. 14, 1840
Warren, James H. M.	Elizabeth Outlaw	Dec. 31, 1841
Warren, Woodard	Mary Cicaty	Sept. 7, 1843
Waters, Jordan	Adeline Smith	Aug. 27, 1840
Weaver, Jesse J.	Mary Ann Perry	May 12, 1841
White, James T.	Clarissa Coleman	Mar. 12, 1837
Wight, Green	Mrs. Susan M. Hudson	Feb. 14, 1837
Wilkes, Malcom	Frances Kirsey	July 28, 1835
Williams, John B.	Beady Gray	Apr. 18, 1837
Windham, William	Nancy Aycock	Jan. 25, 1835
Woodard, Green	Mary Sealey	June 25, 1835
Woolf, Council B.	Rebecca Anderson	June 11, 1837
Wyatt, James	Lucretia Hobbs	July 14, 1842
Yopp, John D.	Mary F. Hampton	Sept. 30, 1841
Burney, John F.	Margaret E. Stanley	Jan. 17, 1849
Bussell, Green	Elizabeth Hollingsworth	Apr. 26, 1846
Carswell, George S.	Elvina Delegall	Dec. 31, 1846
Chancy, William W.	Sarah Hudson	Apr. 14, 1844
Clark, Francis M.	Eleanor Ingram	June 24, 1847
Clark, Henry	Keziah Hudson	Oct. 30, 1845
Coleman, John A.	Nancy Southerland	Dec. 21, 1848
Coleman, William T.	Emily L. Joiner	Jan. 14, 1847
Coleman, Wright R.	Hetta McLendon	Nov. 7, 1844
Cross, James B.	Martha A. Bracewell	June 30, 1848
Cross, John	Mary McDaniel	Jan. 9, 1849
Cross, Samuel William	Milly Luke	Nov. 28, 1841
Daniel, Samuel H.	Elizabeth H. Swinson	Jan. 16, 1843
Daniel, William	Nancy Woodard	Apr. 5, 1847
Darsey, James R.	Louisa Elizabeth Mills	Dec. 26, 1844
Darsey, Joseph	Alicia Peacock	July 29, 1841
Darsey, William H.	Malinda Adams	May 26, 1842
Deferill, John	Agnes Powell	Dec. 18, 1845
Deforal, James	Marjorie Powell	Jan. 16, 1845
Dickson, James	Nancy McBain	Dec. 31, 1843
Drew, Oliver	Claudia Willard	Apr. 7, 1844
Driver, Daniel	Sarah Gibbons	Feb. 11, 1845
Duncan, Joseph R.	Nancy J. Alligood	Sept. 9, 1849
English, Silas	Harriett Powell	Jan. 11, 1844

Man	Wife	Date of Marriage
English, William	Elizabeth C. Livingstone	Oct. 5, 1843
Flanders, Jordan	Mary Ann Parcus	Feb. 29, 1847
Floyd, Eli	Queen Ann Register	June 9, 1848
Floyd, Edward M.	Atsley Hudson	Jan. 13, 1848
Floyd, Jesse	Polly Mimms	May 30, 1847
Forest, Berry	Nancy Bryan	Oct. 16, 1836
Forest, Thomas	Margaret Joiner	Nov. 9, 1843
Foster, James R.	Martha A. L. Cunningham	Apr. 28, 1846
Fountain, John B.	Mary Williams	Aug. 26, 1851
Gay, Jacob	Elizabeth Faulk	Aug. 6, 1846
Goff, Andrew J.	Martha A. Griffin	Dec. 23, 1845
Graham, Richard	Margaret L. Daniel	Oct. 19, 1847
Gray, Willard	Georgian Bush	Sept. 21, 1349
Hall, John	Lucy Ann Moorman	Jan. 10, 1845
Hall, Justant J.	Sarah Pope	Jan. 6, 1845
Hamilton, William G.	Mary Ann Burch	July 14, 1848
Hanchard, Edwin B.	Fanny Benton	Jan. 12, 1845
Hardee, Thomas R.	Mary B. Brown	July 30, 1848
Harvey, Curtis C.	Sarah Jane Forest	June 23, 1845
Herndon, P. W.	Katharine Moore	June 11, 1844
Hester, Jasper	Narcissa Ricks	Feb. 20, 1846
Hightower, Joshua E.	Sarah A. Watts	Mar. 4, 1846
Hilliard, Braxton	Mary Weaver	Jan. 20, 1848
Hilliard, Littleton G.	Mary Roach	Mar. 1, 1848
Hobbs, Drewry	Annie Roach	May 20, 1847
Hobbs, John	Mary M. Faircloth	Jan. 4, 1841
Holley, Rufus	Amanda Moorman	Jan. 26, 1848
Horne, Benjamin H.	Winneford E. A. Yopp	June 6, 1848
Horne, Crosby J.	Mary Roberts	Apr. 3, 1845
Horne, Jonas	Eliza M. Cross	Dec. 31, 1843
Howard, John	Katharine J. Powell	Sept. 11, 1845
Howard, John J.	S. Jane Hampton	Jan. 21, 1845
Hudson, Littleton	Juliann Swinson	Oct. 31, 1848
Hudson, Littleton	Mary Swinson	Dec. 30, 1849
Johns, Elias	Mary Smith	Nov. 13, 1845
Joiner, Anthony	Sarah Smith	Feb. 20, 1845
Joiner, Seaborn B. W.	Dicey Woodard	Nov. 7, 1844
Joiner, William	Angeline Sanders	Dec. 19, 1844
Joiner, William	Mary Woodard	Dec. 11, 1844
Jones, Henry P.	Mary Hampton	July 2, 1846
Jones, Kindred M.	Elizabeth Mimms	Nov. 27, 1845
Keen, Young B.	Melvina Todd	Mar. 25, 1841
Kellam, Armisted R.	Zoe Love Buffington	Nov. 24, 1846
Kellam, James G.	Mary S. Howard	Apr. 5, 1849
King, John C.	Ann Powell	Aug. 29, 1844
Kinchen, Jeremiah F.	Mary Ann Maddox	May 11, 1845
Lamb, Abraham B.	Martha Wyatt	June 16, 1844
Law, Lunsford	Susan Mason	Apr. 6, 1845
Lewis, Milton H.	Rosetta Narworthy	Nov. 7, 1844
Livingston, John M.	Nancy Brown	Mar. 29, 1849
Lock, Leonard	Susan Rebecca Smith	July 16, 1846
Love, Charles	Charity Miller	Jan. 3, 1844
Lowery, Andrew L.	Matilda McLendon	Nov. 3, 1846
Mason, John	Nicey Wilson	Mar. 9, 1845
Mason, Morris R.	Mary Moye	Sept. 8, 1844
McCullers, James C.	Mariah M. Mills	July 19, 1842
McGinnis, David	Rhoda Garnto	Nov. 27, 1845
Moore, Hugh M.	Sarah Jane Rentz	Jan. 7, 1844

Man	Wife	Date of Marriage
Moorman, Simeon J.	Louisa E. Snell	Jan. 31, 1850
Pace, Davis	Sarah E. Wilkinson	Dec. 24, 1844
Parish, John H.	Mary Clark	Mar. 9, 1849
Partain, Enoch	Mary Salter	Mar. 9, 1848
Peacock, John	Caroline Williams	Nov. 5, 1842
Perry, Eason	Mary Metts	Jan. 18, 1849
Pope, John S.	Harriett Brantley	Jan. 23, 1850
Powell, William	Lucinda English	Sept. 14, 1843
Purvis, William H.	Elizabeth Cochran	Apr. 26, 1847
Ricks, Hampton	Lindy Ann Bush	Dec. 13, 1843
Rix, Rutherford	Elizabeth Kinchen	Feb. 27, 1845
Roach, Samuel	Rozella Garnto	Dec. 19, 1843
Robinson, James M.	Mary Ricks	May 21, 1846
Ross, Joseph J.	Mary C. Carey	Dec. 28, 1843
Sanders, Coleman	Mrs. Emily Darsey	Mar. 21, 1844
Sanders, John David Hampton	America Hudson	June 5, 1845
Seers, Harrison	Emilia Miller	Jan. 10, 1850
Shiver, John	Moriah Payne	Jan. 1, 1845
Slaughter, Iverson	Catherine Payne	Oct. 27, 1844
Smith, Thomas M.	Martha Mason	Dec. 24, 1848
Spell, Green	Sarah Tucker	Dec. 31, 1846
Steeley, William R.	Piety Coats	Dec. 21, 1843
Stephens, John	Elizabeth Dorhority	Feb. 9, 1845
Stewart, William J.	Sarah Graham	June 30, 1844
Striplin, Mailon B.	Susannah Abbott	May 16, 1847
Sumner, Joseph	Eady Bridges	Jan. 11, 1846
Thomas, Francis	Catharine S. Lightfoot	May 14, 1846
Thomas, Isaac	Sophia Shirley	Jan. 22, 1846
Thompson, Allen	Mary Darsey	Mar. 16, 1848
Tindol, Alexander	Benita Alligood	Jan. 7, 1846
Truett, William A.	Elizabeth Williams	May 11, 1846
Turner, Ephraim	Mary Jane Colley	Feb. 13, 1845
Underwood, John	Martha Wyatt	Oct. 13, 1844
Walton, Joseph J.	Nancy Wright	Apr. 1, 1844
Warnock, David	Jeannette C. Brantley	Jan. 11, 1849
Warnock, James	Margaret Kinchen	Jan. 7, 1850
Warren, Reuben	Elizabeth Williamson	July 16, 1844
Warren, Reuben	Mary C. Duncan	Feb. 19, 1845
Warren, William J.	Margaret Sandford	Mar. 2, 1848
Watkins, Emmaziah R.	Lucinda Weeks	Oct. 6, 1844
Watson, David	Cynthia Taylor	Dec. 23, 1847
Watson, Lewis	Martha Bird	Feb. 25, 1849
Weaver, Jonathan J.	Amanda E. Hogan	Dec. 29, 1843
Weaver, Seaborn L.	Susan Perry	Jan. 23, 1845
White, Thomas J.	Huldah T. Hester	April 26, 1849
White, William	Margaret Hester	Nov. 22, 1849
Willard, William H.	J. Ellafore Perry	Dec. 24, 1844
Wiliamson, Henry	Nancy Finney	Nov. 12, 1846
Woodard, Jesse	Sarah P. E. Joiner	Feb. 1, 1844
Wright, F. K.	Lucinda Coleman	Sept. 2, 1847
Wright, William G.	Rebecca J. Moorman	Dec. 6, 1849
Wyatt, John	Nancy J. Noles	Mar. 11, 1844
Young, Edward M.	Dorcas S. Alligood	Jan. 8, 1845

MARRIAGE RECORDS, 1840-1855
BOOK G

Man	Wife	Date of Marriage
Adams, Manasseh	Rebecca Ann Keen	Apr. 21, 1850
Adams, William G.	Mentney Smith	Mar. 11, 1847
Adams, William G.	Graceyan E. Smith	Aug. 21, 1853
Adams, Wyatt C.	Martha Ann Wall	Oct. 29, 1846
Alligood, Thomas	Elizabeth Hobbs	Mar. 2, 1848
Anderson, Daniel	Allie Smith	July 25, 1852
Bacon, John	Rebecca Weakly	Feb. 24, 1850
Baker, Thomas J.	Mary Noles	Apr. 14, 1850
Baker, Washington	Katharine Rayfield	Apr. 4, 1852
Baker, William	Elizabeth Jenkins	May 21, 1846
Beasley, Redding	Mary Hart	April, 1853
Beddingfield, Andrew	Delman Grinstead	Apr. 23, 1846
Beddingfield, Reason A.	Caroline Register	Jan. 3, 1855
Berryhill, William H.	Susan English	Oct. 17, 1850
Bracewell, N. B. W.	Frances Harden	July 10, 1850
Bradford, Isaiah	Elizabeth Wood	Jan. 4, 1825
Branch, Isham	Elizabeth Gaines	Oct. 9, 1851
Brown, Dawson	Eliza Butler	Mar. 10, 1853
Brown, Robert	Delilah Cunningham	July 30, 1844
Bush, Charles B.	Caroline E. Kinchen	Jan. 11, 1854
Bush, Henry P.	Frances B. Daniel	Dec. 30, 1846
Bush, Henry M.	Amarantha A. L. Gay	Apr. 24, 1854
Caldwell, George	Mary A. E. Bird	Oct. 19, 1854
Caldwell, Samuel D.	Mary E. Whitehead	Dec. 11, 1851
Clark, William H.	Lucinda J. Stripling	July 27, 1855
Cochran, John A.	Mary E. Palmer	Oct. 12, 1854
Coleman, Andrew B.	Susan C. Southerland	Jan. 1, 1852
Coleman, Leonard	Lucretia Bracewell	May 22, 1850
Coleman, William J.	Emily C. Wright	Oct. 14, 1852
Coney, Joel	Jemiria Howard	Jan. 1, 1852
Conner, John	Susan Williamson	Feb, 1851
Cooper, Eli J.	Florida Ann Hester	Sept. 22, 1853
Cooper, Jarrel T.	Margaret McDaniel	Feb. 13, 1851
Cooper, William	Roxan Rowland	July 26, 1848
Cumming, Dr. Robt. L.	Leah N. Stanley	Jan. 23, 1855
Daley, John T.	Eliza J. Cooper	Aug. 29, 1848
Daniel, Lott M.	Wilantha J. Darsey	Jan. 9, 1851
Darsey, Robert A.	Mary A. Nicks	June 14, 1849
Dasher, John M.	Mary E. McElvain	Mar. 28, 1848
Duncan, John T.	Sarah Amelia Fuqua	Aug. 15, 1854
Duncan, Thomas Strange	Sarah Dominy	Jan. 4, 1855
Dupree, Daniel J.	Susan T. Hogan	Aug. 9, 1853
Evans, John J. G.	Betha B. A. Howell	Feb. 9, 1854
Faircloth, Thomas F.	Mary F. Hobbs	Feb. 15, 1849
Faircloth, William T.	Syntha E. Striplin	Sept. 5, 1850
Fordham, Ira	Rebecca Stephens	Oct. 31, 1850
Fordham, William	Cynthia Hilliard	Dec. 4, 1853
Fountain, David	Amanda W. Faircloth	Feb. 20, 1850
Gay, Josiah	Isabelle Jenkins	Aug. 27, 1854
Glover, James	Catharine Graham	Aug. 22, 1852
Goodman, William	Jane E. Taylor	Nov. 17, 1846
Graham, Alexander, Jr.	Mary Pope	June 3, 1852
Graham, Alexander	Elizabeth Hester	Sept. 13, 1851
Graham, Duncan	Mary A. Stewart	July 29, 1852

Man	Wife	Date of Marriage
Graham, Eli	Nancy Keen	Jan. 13, 1853
Graham, Kellam	Zilla Graham	Jan. 20, 1853
Graves, Thomas	Charity Hair	Feb. 20, 1851
Gufford, Miles	Elizabeth White	Mar. 28, 1840
Hall, Jonathan	Susan Johnson	April 14, 1833
Harden, Leander	Elizabeth Cooper	June 15, 1851
Hester, Henry	Mary Smith	Jan. 25, 1847
Hester, Stephen B., Sr.	Mrs. Hulda S. Drew	Mar. 2, 1851
Hester, Stephen, Jr.	Charlotte Stewart	Jan. 12, 1854
Hilburn, Andrew J.	Mary C. Carter	Mar. 24, 1853
Hilliard, Francis	Susan L. Metts	April 19, 1853
Hobbs, Berry	Harriett S. Witherington	Oct. 18, 1846
Hobbs, David	Matilda A. Bracewell	May 26, 1853
Hobbs, Drury	Sarah Kennedy	Oct. 5, 1854
Hobbs, Larry	Elizabeth Nobles	June 6, 1850
Howard, James F.	Harriet Howard	Dec. 26, 1849
Howard, Jefferson	Ann S. Hilliard	Nov. 11, 1852
Hudson, James F.	Sarah P. Winham	May 22, 1853
Hudson, Littleton	Leah Ann Swinson	May 5, 1852
Ingram, David B.	Mary Ann Frances Hudson	Aug. 28, 1845
Johnson, Robert	Nancy Ann T. Johnson	June 2, 1853
Johnson, Thomas H.	Subray Brown	Dec. 15, 1853
Joiner, Jesse M.	Martha Burch	Oct. 15, 1846
Joiner, Jonathan	Maria Mason	Jan. 27, 1848
Keen, Eli M.	Narcissa Hart	Mar. 18, 1855
Keen, William P.	Zilpha Hart	May 28, 1854
Kinchen, John	Martha Culpepper	May 6, 1852
Kinchen, Thomas	Frances Clark	Dec. 6, 1849
Kitterer, Philip	Sarah A. Wright	Jan. 11, 1845
Leavitt, James	Clara Bates	Aug. 15, 1851
Leonard, Elijah	Nancy Wyatt	Aug. 21, 1850
Linder, Enoch H.	Martha A. Hicks	Oct. 15, 1854
Livingston, Richard S.	Elizabeth Brown	April 2, 1852
Luke, John	Tabitha Jane Graves	Aug. 11, 1850
Maddox, John P.	Elizabeth F. Arline	Sept. 12, 1851
McDaniel, David	Eliza Bracewell	May 16, 1847
McDaniel, Jeremiah	Martha Berryhill	July 20, 1851
McDaniel, Louis	Martha Fountain	Oct. 17, 1850
McCray, Duncan	Queen Ann Evans	Oct. 23, 1851
McLendon, Charlie	Elizabeth Thigpen	Mar. 22, 1849
McLendon, Wesley W.	Rebecca Miller	Aug. 7, 1853
McVay, John A. J.	Elvy Watson	Oct. 31, 1854
Miller, John N.	Mary Miller	Jan. 15, 1854
Mills, Matthew	Martha Howard	July 30, 1848
Mizell, Luke T.	Mrs. Elmina Guyton	Oct. 16, 1851
Montgomery, John L.	Mary Jane Love	April 4, 1848
Mullis, Berry	Martha M. Weekly	Sept. 16, 1854
Mullis, John	Serena Darsey	May 23, 1850
Niles, Alison B.	Caroline C. Yopp	May 21, 1851
Oliver, Dr. James H.	Mary Jane Kellam	Dec. 2, 1850
O'Neal, Cullen	Mrs. Jenesha Coney	Jan. 26, 1854
Palmer, John	Mary A. Mason	Nov. 23, 1848
Perkins, William H.	Sarah Pope	Oct. 16, 1854
Perry, John	Elizabeth Hobbs	Jan. 13, 1848
Perry, John, Sr.	Ann Rawls	Oct. 25, 1854
Pope, Jackson	Harriet Ann Hester	Oct. 5, 1850
Pope, John	Mary A. Bridges	Sept. 4, 1853
Powell, Eustas	Nancy Hollingsworth	Mar. 22, 1853

Man	Wife	Date of Marriage
Powell, Leroy	Ellafair Powell	Oct. 12, 1848
Ray, James C.	Mahala Faircloth	Sept. 17, 1850
Rayfield, John	Sarah Jane Watson	Feb. 19, 1851
Register, Elijah F.	Nancy Y. Coleman	Dec. 27, 1853
Register, Jesse P.	Mary Ann Rowland	Feb. 11, 1851
Register, Robinson	Sarah Graham	Oct. 18, 1852
Register, William H.	Penerily Baraquella Ann Williamson	May 31, 1853
Robinson, Robert A.	Martha J. Daniel	Dec. 14, 1854
Sandford, Henry H.	Martha J. V——	June 22, 1853
Scarborough, James	Mary Fordham	Feb. 15, 1855
Scarborough, Miller	Nancy Spell	Nov. 9, 1847
Scarborough, William H.	Permelia M. Bracewell	Dec. 19, 1850
Scott, Thomas	Narcissa Hudson	Mar. 9, 1849
Smith, Aaron	Lizzie Evans	Dec. 3, 1846
Smith, Carleton B.	Honor McLendon	July 29, 1849
Smith, Henry M.	Sarah M. Scarborough	Nov. 24, 1853
Smith, Robert C.	Sarah Ann Phillips	Dec. 23, 1851
Smith, William T.	Nancy Kea	Oct. 22, 1846
Spivey, Alfred B.	Mary A. E. Moreland	July 27, 1852
Spivey, Daniel	Allie Bush	April 30, 1854
Stanley, James I. C.	Letitia J. Ellington	Feb. 16, 1855
Stripling, Robert F.	Ann J. Witherington	July 13, 1853
Stone, William	Louisa Bellflower	Aug. 4, 1846
Summers, Joseph M.	Mary Ann Flanders	Sept. 13, 1853
Summers, Joseph	Harriet E. Bates	Dec. 4, 1853
Swinson, Thomas	Nancy Williams	Dec. 1, 1850
Swinson, William F.	Elizabeth Scarborough	Jan. 25, 1855
Taylor, Henry	Margaret Register	Oct. 18, 1854
Thomas, Charnol H.	Elizabeth Mills	Sept. 14, 1848
Thompson, Andrew	Frances Partin	Feb. 15, 1855
Thompson, Elisha	Elizabeth Berryhill	Mar. 18, 1855
Thompson, William	Rutha Watson	Nov. 3, 1850
Tousen, Henry	Mrs. Molly Spivey	July 18, 1848
Vann, Elias	Lorena Ursery	Jan. 16, 1851
Wade, John	Celia Pickering	April 30, 1854
Warren, Joshua	Margaret Alligood	Feb. 6, 1851
Watson, Daniel	Milenor F. Bellflower	Nov. 23, 1854
Watson, James F.	Mary Ann Cross	May 1, 1850
Watson, Joel N.	Caroline M. Tucker	Jan. 23, 1851
Watson, Uriah M.	Elizabeth B. Culpepper	June 23, 1852
Weaver, William F.	Martha Watson	Dec. 30, 1847
Whitehead, William B.	Antoinette Whitehead	April 29, 1855
Williams, Joseph P.	Elizabeth Stokes	Jan. 28, 1851
Williams, Lott	Polly Williams	Aug. 6, 1850
Williams, McKinley	Serena Barnett	Sept. 5, 1848
Wood, David	Margaret Glover	Oct. 10, 1851
Worthy, James C.	Lucinda Watson	Jan. 7, 1847
Wright, Felix K.	Sarah Proctor	Oct. 3, 1847
Wright, James A.	Rachel Smith	April 22, 1855

FAMILY HISTORIES

Space in this Section was open to all Laurens County families; on the following pages will be found the genealogies of those families who availed themselves of the privilege of permanently preserving their family records in the official History of their County.

COMMITTEE
Mrs. E. B. Freeman, *Chairman*

Mrs. W. H. Adams	Mrs. M. J. Guyton
Mrs. Helen M. Bashinski	Mrs. Blue Holleman
Mrs. A. T. Coleman	Mrs. Walter A. Hobbs
Mrs. Albert Geeslin	Mrs. Jack Smith

"Non sibi sed aliis"—Oglethorpe's Motto

GENEALOGICAL

ADAMS

Prominent among the early settlers of Laurens County was the Adams family, members of which came to this county in the early 1800's and have lived here continuously for approximately 130 years. In addition to their agricultural pursuits, this family has furnished citizens who have held positions of importance in the business, professional, and political world.

Peter Adams, the progenitor of the Adams family in Laurens County, was born in North Carolina, and in that state he and his wife Lidia Ann were married. When their oldest son William (born in 1809) was a small child, Peter and Lidia Ann came to this part of Georgia and built their home about two miles from historic old Blackshear's Ferry. This old home is still standing and is an historic landmark, dating back to the earliest days of the county.

Peter Adams was an outstanding citizen of the county. His name is recorded in the Laurens County Land Lottery of 1819 as a member of Captain Leroy G. Harris' Militia District.

Children of Peter and Lidia Ann Adams were William, born in North Carolina, and four other children who were born in this county: Wyriott Cason Adams, Manassah Adams, Sarah Jane Adams, and Ethelinda Adams.

Wyriott Cason Adams, son of Peter and Lidia Ann Adams, was born in Laurens County October 2, 1823; married October 29, 1846, to Martha Ann Hall (born January 27, 1828; died October 11, 1903) the daughter of Isaac and Susanna Ross Hall. Their children were: Abilene Horry Adams, Isaac Wyriott Adams, Cuyler Hall Adams, Dorah Adams, Oscar Cason Adams, Edgar Adams, and Josie Homer Adams.

Wyriott Cason Adams was successful planter and was highly regarded by his fellowmen. In the War Between the States he served in Company D, 8th Georgia Regiment as 1st Lieutenant; represented Wilkinson County in the State Legislature in 1873-1874. One of the first bills he introduced was that creating a board of county commissioners.

Abilene Horry Adams, eldest son of Wyriott Cason and Martha Ann Adams, was born September 11, 1848; married in February, 1871, to Elsie Jane Fordham, daughter of Wliey Fordham and Lucretia Cannon Fordham. He moved to Laurens County in 1889 from Wilkinson County, and lived at the Adams home place near Dublin continuously until his death. He was a successful farmer and one of the oldest and most greatly beloved citizens of this section. He lived his religion in the daily walk of life, and found unmeasurable happiness in doing a kindness for his friends and bringing joy to those less fortunate.

Abilene Horry Adams died September 10, 1930, and was buried on his 82nd birthday in Northview Cemetery, Dublin, Georgia. Elsie Jane (Fordham) Adams was born September 16, 1853; died April 5, 1936.

To Abilene Horry Adams and Elsie Jane Adams nine children were born:

I. Cuyler Homer Adams, born December 18, 1873; died August 2, 1938; married Minnie Jane Sheffield (daughter of James Arthur Sheffield and Winifred Cannon Sheffield) on October 26, 1902. To them were born: (1) Cordy Homer Adams, who married Lois Vaughn (daughter of Jack Shine Vaughn and Susie Elizabeth Johnson) November 27, 1929. They have one child, Jerry Cordy Adams, born November 1, 1930. (2) Arthur Abilene Adams, who married Robiclair New (daughter of Dr. J. E. New and Maude Brantley) September 5, 1936. (3) Ernestine Adams. (4) Ruby Jeanette Adams. (5) Atys Weldon Adams. (6) Brigham Sheffield Adams (died October 18, 1923).

Cuyler Homer Adams was a large landowner and planter. At the age of 28, he was elected tax collector of Laurens County and served four terms. He was the youngest tax collector in the State at this time. He was a member of the Board of Stewards of the First Methodist Church of Dublin, Georgia. In 1926 he established the Adams Funeral Home, which he owned and operated jointly with his three sons who have continued to operate this business since his death.

II. Rachel Viola Adams, born June 28, 1876, married Francis Marion Daniels (son of John Wesley Daniels and Mary Watkins Daniels), December 26, 1897. To them were born: (1) Horry Wesley Daniels, who married Marguerite Rawlins. Their children are Horrie Wesley Daniels, Jr., and Beverly Daniels. (2) Bertha Mae Daniels, who married Walter Patillo. They have one daughter, Patricia Daniels Patillo. (3) John Parks Daniels, who married Nellie Rivers. They have two sons: John Parks Daniels, Jr., and Robert Marion Daniels. (4) Elsie Helen Daniels. (5) Dr. Francis Marion Daniels, Jr., who married Frances Schaefer. They have one daughter, Ryan Adams Daniels. (6) Dorothy Daniels, who married Vance Elkins.

III. Eva Bertha Adams, born February, 1878; died May 24, 1904; married in July, 1902, Ira Hall (died 1910). They had one daughter, Edna Hall, who married Elvis Smith of Macon, Georgia. They have one son, Elvis Smith, Jr.

IV. Mattie May Adams, born March 8, 1882; died June 18, 1903; married Charles L. Webb, jeweler, in July, 1902. They had one daughter, Charlie Mae Webb, who married Thomas Haynes White (son of John Thomas White and Anna Haynes White), February 8,

1936. They have two sons: John Thomas White II and Charles Haynes White.

V. Wiley Horry Adams, born June 19, 1885; married Martha Frances Atwater (daughter of Charles M. and Isabelle Matthews Atwater), December 20, 1911. Wiley Horry Adams served two four-year terms as sheriff of Laurens County, and was severely injured in the performance of the duties of his office on October 28, 1935. On September 9, 1937, he was elected to fill an unexpired term of Ordinary of Laurens County, which office he still holds.

Children of Wiley Horry Adams and Martha Atwater Adams are: (1) Charles W. Adams, graduated from Dublin High School in 1931, and from Marion Military Insitute, Marion, Alabama, in 1935; married Ruth Lorena Schoeneman (daughter of George J. Schoeneman and Ruth Rouse Schoeneman), September 3, 1938. Their children are James Gary Adams and Thomas Robert Adams. (2) Charles W. Adams holds a position with the Treasury Department, Washington, D. C. (3) Phil A. Adams, graduated from Dublin High School in 1932, and Presbyterian College, Clinton, South Carolina, in 1936. He is a sergeant with the State Department of Public Safety, and is located at Thomasville, Georgia. (4) Wiley Horry Adams, Jr., graduated from Dublin High School in 1937. He is now connected with Robert & Company, Engineers, Atlanta, Georgia. (5) Robert Thurston Adams, graduated from Dublin High School in 1938, and attended North Georgia College, Dahlonega, Georgia. He is connected with Federal Reconstruction Finance Corporation, Atlanta, Georgia. (5) Martha Frances Adams, graduated from Dublin High School in 1940; married J. Edison Brinson (son of Dr. R. E. Brinson and Sarah Lovett Brinson), July 21, 1940. (6) Callie Helen Adams, born May 17, 1925. (7) Ann Elizabeth Adams, born April 12, 1928.

VI. Ufa Erma Adams, born January 3, 1888; married Erman C. O'Neal in 1916. Their children are: Virginia Erma O'Neal and Jane Adams O'Neal.

VII. Emmett Albert Adams, born October 13, 1891; died March 7, 1937.

VIII. Birdie Jane Adams, born January 3, 1893; married S. Lester Sharpe, pharmacist, in 1912. Their children are: James Lester Sharpe, who married Thelva Horton; William Horry Sharpe; Ann Sharpe.

IX. Algerine Summerlin Adams, born September 10, 1895; married Orion Brown, February 18, 1923.

Oscar Cason Adams, son of Wyriott Cason and Martha Ann Adams, was born October 10, 1861; died January 7, 1939; married January 1, 1898, to Rosia Ellafair Adams (daughter of William Adams and Charity Sheppard), born February 15, 1866; died August 29, 1938. They had three children:

I. Wyriott Cason Adams II, born February 11, 1895; married Kathleen King. To them were born three sons and two daughters: Wyriott Cason Adams III, John Oscar Adams, Mayleen Adams, Sarah Rosilyn Adams, and Allen Wyatt Adams.

II. Todd L. Adams, born August 10, 1905; married Clynton Hamilyn.

III. Augusta Alma Adams, born September 2, 1907; married Thomas Rentz Napier (born April 7, 1900, son of Robert Freeman Napier and Nina Rentz Napier), September 20, 1925. To them were born: Augustus Rentz Napier, born July 16, 1926; Martha Louise Napier, born November 23, 1927; Betty Carleen Napier, born July 15, 1930.

—*By Martha Atwater Adams (Mrs. W. H.)*

Judge John Samuel Adams

Judge John Samuel Adams, son of William Adams and Charity Barbara Ann Sheppard, was born in Wilkinson County, Georgia, on January 22, 1870, and when a young man came to make his home in Dublin. He was educated in the county schools, studied law and was admitted to the Dublin Bar in 1893. Devoting himself principally to civil and banking law he soon became one of the outstanding lawyers of this section of the state. With a fine record of personal service he was elected Mayor of Dublin and was later appointed Judge of the City Court of Dublin by Governor Allen D. Candler, where he served with distinction for five years before resigning to resume private practice.

In 1933 he became connected with the Treasury Department in Washington, D. C., in a legal capacity. This appointment was in recognition of his knowledge of banking law. He remained in Washington until August, 1935, before resigning to return to his old home in Dublin and to private practice.

The position of Judge of Dublin Judicial Circuit was tendered Judge Adams by Governor John M. Slaton, but this appointment was not accepted. He was always interested in young people and many Dublin lawyers owe their start in the legal profession to training received in his office. In 1929 Judge Adams was voted the first citizen of Dublin and was presented with a loving cup at a dinner given in his honor. At the time of his death, March 29, 1938, he was Referee in Bankruptcy for the Dublin Division of the United States Court, a position which he held for several years.

Judge John Samuel Adams will long be remembered for his wit, intellect, the important place he held in the community and in the hearts of his many friends throughout the state. The inscription on the marble door of the mausoleum in Dublin, where he is interred,

JUDGE JOHN SAMUEL ADAMS

bears this inscription: "He loved the Law and through a rich full life gave it of his best."

On January 20, 1895, John Samuel Adams was united in marriage to a member of early county families of prominence and distinction, Lucia Augusta Stanley, daughter of Rollin Adolphus Stanley and Martha Rebecca Lowther (see Stanley history). "Pren-ces," the beautiful Adams residence on Bellevue Road, named for their two children, Prentice and Frances, was the center of social life in Dublin and here many prominent guests from this and other states were entertained.

Three children were born to John Samuel and Augusta Stanley Adams. Prentice, the only son, was born in Dublin, November 7, 1895. He attended the University of Georgia after his earlier education in this city. Deciding upon a diplomatic career, he was sent to Washington and later to New York for training. When war was declared in 1917, he volunteered for service and was sent to Harvard University to train for the radio branch of the Navy. He saw active service on the U. S. Destroyer "Gregory" as gunners mate. He was also stationed in Adriatic waters near Fieume and Trieste, being in service from June 20, 1917, to July 16, 1919. His marriage to Emma Wallace Fickle occurred on March 8, 1931. He was general salesman for the Standard Oil Company, in Marianna, Florida, at the time of his death, March 12, 1934.

Jamie Vivian, the eldest daughter, was born in Dublin, July 23, 1897; died August 7, 1899.

Frances, the youngest child, was born in Dublin, December 28, 1902. After attending Washington Seminary, in Atlanta, and Southern College, in Petersburg, Virginia, she continued her education at Brenau College, Gainesville, Georgia. On November 28, 1923, she was married to Gray Holmes of Rome, Georgia. Two daughters were born to this union: Nell Gray Holmes, born December 2, 1929, and Augusta Stanley Holmes, born July 22, 1932. Gray Holmes is in the hotel business, owning and operating the Hacienda Hotel, at New Port Richey, Florida, also operating the Mountain Ranch Hotel, at Helen, Georgia, and the Walasiyi Inn, at Vogel State Park, Cleveland, Georgia.

—By Maude Stanley Peteet (Mrs. J. C.)

ALSUP

Angus Dillon Alsup was born in Murfreesboro, Tennessee, October 15, 1882. In 1905 he came to Dublin, Georgia, to accept a position with the First National Bank, later with Smith Wholesale Grocery Company. In 1909 he and W. L. Williams became partners in a wholesale grocery known as Alsup-Williams Grocery Company. In 1913, Mr. Alsup acquired the interest of his partner and it became then and is still known as the Alsup Grocery Company. Later his two brothers, William Byrn and Samuel Martin Alsup, came to join him in business and to make their home in Dublin. June 16, 1909, Angus Dillon Alsup married Jessie Halcyon Rice and to this union were born two children: (1) Martha Halcyon, born September 8, 1916, who, in 1935 married Robert Crittenden Bell of Shelman, Georgia, and to them was born a daughter on October 15, 1937, Halcyon Alsup Bell. Martha Halcyon Alsup Bell attended Wesleyan College and is a direct descendant of Benjamin F. Rice and Rebecca Sauls Rice. (See Rice Family). (2) Infant son who died at birth. Angus Dillan Alsup was a consistent member of the Baptist Church and was known for his loyalty, liberality, and generosity. Although a young man he was always on the alert to sustain and help the unfortunate ones. He was active in fraternal orders being a loyal Mason and Shriner. In 1920 he becamea victim of the influenza epidemic and died February 27, 1920; he is buried in Northview Cemetery.

William Byrn Alsup, born in Murfreesboro, Tennessee, December 10, 1884; married Margaret Elizabeth Seward, of Franklin, Tennessee, March 19, 1913, daughter of John C. Seward and Rosa Rivers Seward. They had five children: two daughters died in infancy; William Byrn Junior, born in Murfreesboro, Tennessee, September 16, 1916, graduate of University of Georgia and University of Georgia School of Medicine; Martha Rivers Alsup, born in Dublin, Georgia, September 30, 1918, attended Georgia University; Jack Seward Alsup, born in Dublin, Georgia, November 1, 1932.

Samuel Martin Alsup, born March 15, 1890, married Louise Knight of Dublin, Georgia. They have three daughters. (See Knight Family).

Angus Dillon, William Byrn and Samuel Martin Alsup are the sons of Henry Clay Alsup, born in Statesville, Tennessee, February 19, 1841, and died at Nashville, Tennessee, December 24, 1912. He married Martha Jane Dillon, born at Lascasas, Tennessee, August 21, 1844, and died at Nashville, Tennessee, August 28, 1911. Grandsons of William T. Alsup, born February 5, 1815; died November 11, 1899; married Fannie Byrn of March 18, 1840, she was born August 1, 1819, and died November 23, 1904. Great-grandsons of Samuel Alsup, born March 12, 1782, and Elizabeth Jennings Alsup who married September 6, 1810. All were prominent citizens of the State of Tennessee.

Five children were born to Henry Clay Alsup and Martha Jane Dillon Alsup, the three sons already mentioned and two daughters. Zilla Alsup married James W. Ferrell, of Murfreesboro, Tennessee, they have several children. Gertrude Alsup married J. C. Chabble, they have one son Alonzo Chabble, born 1917, reside in Winter Haven, Florida.

—*By Jessie Rice Alsup Williams (Mrs. G. H.)*

ARNAU

The Arnau family is of Spanish descent. The first of whom we have record is Francis Arnau, who married Clara Petros who, according to family tradition, was a Spanish princess. To this union was born a son Francis Arnau II who married Martina Villalonga, and had three children: (1) Miquel Marie Depalar; (2) Clara, who married a Godolfus; (3) Alberto, who never married.

Miquel Marie Depalar Arnau was born in St. Augustine, Florida, November 10, 1808; died November 15, 1884; married on May 16, 1830, Mary Ann Colbard, born October 28, 1806, was the daughter of Captain William Colboard, a French Huguenot, and Mary Ann Rice, (born July 21, 1786). Mary Ann Rice was the daughter of John Rice and Mary Ann Monk, who were married January 14, 1783. John Rice served in the Revolutionary War as Sergeant in Captain Butler's Company, 3rd Pennsylvania Regiment.

Miquel Marie Depalar Arnau and his wife, Mary Ann Colboard, had nine children, all of whom were born in Charleston, South Carolina. (1) Miquel Villalonga; (2) Isabella, married Robert Addison; (3) Clara, married Edward Quinby; (4) Robert Monk, married Emma Adelaide Jernigan; (5) Alberto; (6) William Pettigue; (7) Francis, married Mary Jernigan; (8) James; (9) Mary.

Robert Monk Arnau was born October 25, 1840. In June, 1861, at the age of 16, he enlisted in the Confederate Army, Company A, Artillery, Battalion, Hampton Legion, South Carolina; discharged in 1865. He married Emma Adelaide Jernigan of Sandersville, Georgia, in 1870, and the same year they came to Dublin to make their home. She was the daughter of Brigadier General Lewis Augustus Jernigan, who was born in Powellton, Georgia, in 1798, and his wife, Martha Milledge Blocksome, who was born in Augusta, Georgia, in 1806; married in Warrenton, Georgia, in 1824, and moved to Sandersville, Georgia, in 1825. Brigadier General Lewis Augustus Jernigan was Ordinary of Washington County, Georgia, for twenty-eight years.

Robert Monk Arnau and his wife, Emma Jernigan, were the parents of four children: (1) Albert Rowe Arnau; (2) Alice Jacques Arnau; (3) Robert Michael Arnau; (4) Emma Belle Arnau.

Albert Rowe Arnau was born May 16, 1871; died April 10, 1938. He was Assistant Cashier of The Dublin Banking Company, the first bank organized in Dublin; was Cashier of the Citizens Bank when it was organized, and later Vice-President; served as City Clerk, Mayor, and as a member of the City Board of Education. Later, held the post of Secretary of the Commerce and Labor Department in State Capitol; was the Executive Secretary of the State of Georgia under Governor Clifford Walker. He married in 1893, Emma Dora Folsom, a native of Goldsboro, North Carolina, and had four children:

I. Mirabeau Lamar Arnau, born May 24, 1894; married Clove Brantley in 1916; they have three children: (1) Patricia Clove, born in 1918, married Raymond Forker of Hempstead, Long Island, in 1940; (2) Maudine; (3) Albert Thomas, born 1931.

II. Augusta Marian Arnau, morried Blakely Parrott, and has two sons, Blakely Arnau Parrott and Albert Reid Parrott.

III. Mildred Elizabeth Arnau, married Lehman Pratt Keen, (see Keen Geneology) and has one son, Lehman McGrath Keen, born November 18, 1922.

IV. Albert Robert Arnau, born November 16, 1906; married May 30, 1940, to Euline Perkins.

Robert Michael Arnau, third child of Robert Monk and Emma Jernigan, was born in 1876; died February 17, 1940. He was a merchant and later in the real estate business; founded the Arnau Tire and Accessory Company. His son, Earl Arnau, is his successor in this business. He was a religious leader and philanthropist; served as lay leader in the Methodist South Georgia Conference, and did evangelistic work. He married Cora Turlington, in 1898, and had five children:

I. Robert Earl Arnau, born May 23, 1899; married Ethel Merritt in 1931, and has one daughter, Beverly Webster Arnau, born in 1935.

II. Martha Elizabeth Arnau, married, in 1922, Sibley L. White, and has a foster son, Thomas Sibley White, born in 1928.

III. Frances Arnau, married in 1924 Ted Wilhite, and has one daughter, Joy Wilhite, born in 1927.

IV. Doris Arnau, married in 1925 Carl Cochran (see Cochran genealogy) and has one daughter, Betty Rose Cochran, born in 1934.

V. Rose Arnau, married Winfield Simmons in 1934; died February 29, 1940.

Emma Belle Arnau, youngest daughter of Robert Monk Arnau and Emma Jernigan, was born in 1883, married Stanley Jernigan and has two sons:

I. Theron Arnau Jernigan, born in 1910; married Mary Weaver in 1938, and has one child, Mary Joan Jernigan, born in 1939.

II. Robert Lewis Jernigan, born in 1915; married Nelle Moorman, January 29, 1939.

—*By Dora Folsom Arnau (Mrs. A. R.)*

BAGGETT

The Baggett family has been outstanding in the upbuilding of Laurens County in a political, business and religious way for generations.

John Redding Baggett, the first to settle in the Rentz vicinity of Laurens County, son of Joseph Baggett and B. Adline Holly, of Warren County, Georgia, was a large land owner and farmer of note. He was co-owner of Thomas and Baggett Mercantile Company, also served as Representative of Laurens County. He was married three times and is buried by the side of his first two wives in Mt. Zion Cemetery, (1) Mattie D. Gay, (2) Mattie E. Blankenship, (3) Mollie Lancaster Buchan.

John Redding Baggett was the father of seven sons, three by the first wife: E. Oscar, Baggett, Clifford A. Baggett, and Homer Baggett. By the second marriage there were four sons: Charles E., Willie F., Harvey and Morris A. Baggett. Charles E. Baggett, prominent Dublin attorney, Consul Commander of W. O. W., and its Head Banker, with jurisdiction over Georgia, Past Master of Laurens Lodge No. 75, is the father of four daughters: Evelyn, Joyce, Ruth and Ann Baggett.

Morris A. Baggett, born November 8, 1894, died April 22, 1935, member of the Baptist Church, W.O.W., and Odd Fellows, was outstanding in the political life of Laurens County, serving as Tax Collector for about eight years. He married Eva Clyde Bass, (born July 28, 1900, died April 8, 1936) at McRae, Georgia, July, 1917. They are buried in Northview Cemetery, Dublin. To this union were born two sons: one who died in infancy and Jack Baggett, born November 30, 1918. Jack Baggett was educated in Dublin Public Schools, Georgia Military College, Daughn's School of Commerce, Atlanta, and Mercer University, Macon.

Eva Clyde Bass Baggett was the daughter of John D. Bass, deceased, who is buried in Mt. Carmel Cemetery, Dexter, Georgia, and Elizabeth Coleman Bass, now residing in Lakeland, Florida. Both were prominent Laurens County citizens. Eva Clyde Bass had five sisters: Ethel, Ruby, Louise, Claudine and Dorothy; one brother J. D. Bass, deceased, who is buried in Mt. Carmel Cemetery.

—*By Jack Baggett.*

BALLARD

Rose Hill was the name of the plantation of the first Ballard that settled in what is now Laurens County (then Washington County). This Ballard's name was Eli or Elisha and he was a native of old Bruton Parish in Virginia where his ancestors and kinsmen were vestrymen in old Bruton Parish Church. So it is no mystery that the stream which flower through his broad acres was named Bruton creek and the railroad station which was located on the stream was called Bruton (the spelling of the name was changed to "Brewton" in 1894). The large tract of land which comprised this plantation included the banks of this creek almost in their entirety, and the bridge across the stream on the highway at this point was known as Ballard's bridge.

Rose Hill derived its name from the red hill upon which the old two-story house stood in the midst of a grove of cedars, water oaks and crepe myrtles. It was located on the south side of the road leading from the Oconee River to Sandersville. (Dublin was formed later). The house stood about the distance of a city block from this road and a "lane" from the road led to the house. Under the grove of trees which surrounded the house were beds of iris, lilacs and other old-fashioned fragrant flowers.

The founder of this old place came into its possession in 1787, but the deeds are dated "eleven years after the Declaration of Independence." They bear no other date of the year.

The children of Eli Ballard were born here and spent practically all their lives either at or near Rose Hill. About 1890 fire destroyed the house and today even the trees and flowers have disappeared. No trace of Rose Hill is to be seen.

The Isle of Wight County (Virginia) records show that under date of June 5, 1777, Elisha Laurence Ballard was "appointed a Lieutenant to the company whereof Mills Lawrence was Captain of the Militia." He thus rendered active service in the American Revolution. This Elisha Ballard of Laurens County was a member of Captain Jacob Robinson's company of Light Dragons which participated in the battle of Cheraw on April 23, 1812. He thus gave active service in the War of 1812.

His ancestor, first to come to America, was William. He came aboard the ship "James" in 1635 and settled at Yorktown. Thomas 1st, son of William, and Thomas 2nd, son of Thomas 1st, were both vestrymen of old Bruton Parish Church and both were buried from there. For over thirty years, the first Thomas served York County and the state of Virginia in some capacity, from Clerk of York County to Speaker of the House of Burgesses. The second Thomas helped in laying out the town of Williamsburg and was one of the directors of the public buildings for this new town (1699). It was from him that 330 acres of land were obtained upon which to build William and Mary College.

Eli (Elisha), the first Ballard of Laurens County. married Zilla Hobbs of Washington County. Elisha L. Ballard died at Rose Hill February 15, 1827. Zilla Hobbs Ballard died December 2, 1869. They had six children: 1. George Clinton (died at age of 23), 2. Lucy Jeffris, 3. William Laurence, 4. Martha Lin, 5. Benjamin Franklin, 6. Elisha Troup (died at 8).

Both William Laurence and Benjamin Franklin Ballard served in the War Between the States. William Laurence fought under Joseph E. Johnston in "the West" and participated in the Battle of Vicksburg. Benjamin Franklin fought in "the East" with the 14th Georgia Regiment, Company H (Blackshear Guards) and participated in the Battle of Gettysburg.

Of all the children of Eli and Zilla Ballard, only Benjamin Franklin had issue.

Benjamin Franklin Ballard was born at Rose Hill September 16, 1824, and died at his home in Dublin August 17 1898. He was thrice married, 1st to Eliza Maddox; 2nd Kate McBain; 3rd to Rebecca Linder (see Linder genealogy). Children by his first marriage were: 1. Elisha Franklin; 2. Edward David; 3. George Robinson; 4. Sarah Josephine, who married 1st Jacob Thomas Linder (see Linder genealogy) and 2nd William Lingo—no children.

Sarah Josephine Ballard Lingo was born September 22, 1859, and died May 5, 1919; buried in Northview Cemetery in Dublin.

I. Elisha Franklin Ballard, son of Benjamin Franklin and Eliza Maddox Ballard, married Julia Prescott and has two children: (1) Theresa and (2) Zack Prescott Ballard, who married Mae Wells.

Eli Franklin Ballard was born July 1, 1861, died March 14, 1939, buried in Northview Cemetery in Dublin.

II. Edward David Ballard, son of Benjamin Franklin and Eliza Maddox Ballard, married Frances (Fannie) Clark (see Clark genealogy) and had eight children as follows:

1. Martha Nell Ballard married Morris Payne Webb and has four children viz., (a) Morris Payne Jr., (b) Mary Clark, (c) and (d) (twins) David and William.

2. Seth Franklin Ballard married Marviree Culver (Holmes) and has one son, David Clark Ballard.

3. Ellen Ingram Ballard married Luciene Emerson Roberts and has one son, Luciene Edward Roberts.

4. Edward David Ballard married Evelyn Gay.

5. Frances Ballard married William Powell and has one son, Ballard Powell.

6. Mary Ballard married Charles Pierce Gordon.

7. Ruth Ballard.

8. Evelyn Ballard married Robert Jackson Webb.

Edward David Ballard, son of Benjamin Franklin Ballard and Eliza Ballard, was born July 4, 1864; died October 9, 1922, is buried in Northview Cemetery in Dublin.

George Robinson Ballard, son of Benjamin Franklin Ballard and Eliza Maddox Ballard, married Emma Fort and their children are as follows: 1. Maud; 2. Claud; 3. Eliza; 4. Robert E.; 5. James Fort; 6. Hoyt; 7. Louise.

George Robinson Ballard was born March 3, 1866; died December 10, 1940; is buried in churchyard of old Bethlehem Church.

Eliza Maddox Ballard, first wife of Benjamin Franklin Ballard, was born September 9, 1836, in Laurens County, Georgia, and died September 2, 1867.

Kate McBain Ballard, the second wife, died May 24, 1874.

There were no children by Benjamin Franklin Ballard's second marriage, but by his marriage to Rebecca Linder (see Linder genealogy) he had one son, who died in infancy, and four daughters who are prominently identified with their various professions and are active and influential members of the First Methodist Church in Dublin. They are:

I. Frankie Folsom Ballard married John Louis Veal (deceased) of Atlanta, where she has resided since her marriage, and has three sons, viz., Floyd Thomas, John Louis and James Magruder Veal. John Louis Veal is in United States service, Staff Sergeant, Medical Department, U. S. Army.

II. Enda Ballard, identified herself with educational circles; was instructor in History Department of the Dublin High School; later principal of the McRae High School; married Jerry Walker Duggan (see Duggan genealogy).

III. Kellie Hinton Ballard, successful business woman of Laurens and surrounding counties; an active member of the Dublin Garden Club and has been awarded many blue ribbons at flower shows for specimen flowers from the Ballard garden; her favorite vocation is catering and by this profession is most widely known.

IV. Cummie Lin Ballard, prominent business woman who has been at the head of the bookkeeping department of Lovett and Tharpe Hardware Company for several years; superintendent of the Junior Department of the First Methodist Church school in Dublin.

V. Benjamin Franklin Ballard died in infancy.

John Louis Veal, husband of Frankie Ballard Veal, was City Forestry for Atlanta for more than a quarter of a century. He was born in 1881 at Stone Mountain, Georgia, and died in Atlanta on December 13, 1938; is buried in Westview Cemetery in Atlanta.

Rebecca Linder Ballard (see Linder genealogy), wife of Benjamin Franklin Ballard, was born August 31, 1854, and died November 7, 1931. She is buried in Northview Cemetery in Dublin.

Children of Elisha (Eli) and Zilla Hobbs Ballard of Rose Hill, Laurens County, Georgia:

1. George Clinton Ballard, born September 20, 1816; died September 24, 1839.

2. Lucy Jeffris Ballard, born July 21, 1818; died October 13, 1875.

3. William Laurence Ballard, born September 24, 1820.

4. Martha Lin Ballard, born September 9, 1822.

5. Eli Troup Ballard, born May 1, 1827; died April 29, 1836.

6. Benjamin Franklin Ballard, born September 16, 1824; died August 17, 1898.

—By Enda Ballard Duggan (Mrs. J. W.)

BAUM

The first of the Baum family to come to Laurens County was Adolph Washington Baum, who was born in Wilkinson County at Irwinton on January 8, 1854, the son of Alexander and Amelia Fried Baum.

Alexander Baum was born in Sohern, Germany, in 1822, and at the age of 25 came to the United States. In 1850, he married Amelia Fried, who was born in Monzinger, Germany, in 1824. They settled in Wilkinson County at Irwinton where Alexander was engaged in the mercantile business. He was of a noble, generous and kindly nature. Even though he was of foreign birth, he championed the cause of the Confederacy. He enlisted in the militia and fought bravely throughout the War Between the States. He was in Company H, 47th Georgia Division. Being appointed keeper of the commissary, he personally looked after the wants and comforts of his comrades as far as it was humanly possible in those trying times. Alexander Baum's family suffered severely at the hands of Sherman's Army. While the court house was burned by the Yankees, they put the Baum family out in the rain and ransacked their home, taking all of their valuables. From this episode, Amelia, the wife of Alexander, was made totally deaf. Alexander Baum died in September, 1885, and is buried in Laurel Grove Cemetery in Savannah.

Amelia Baum was known all over middle Georgia for her kindness and for her charitable deeds. So far as her financial means allowed, she was a philanthropist. Everybody for counties around knew "Mamma Baum" and loved her. She died at Irwinton, Georgia, in October, 1910, and is buried in Laurel Grove Cemetery in Savannah.

Alexander and Amelia Baum had eleven children, ten of whom lived to reach maturity, viz.: 1. Napoleon Bonaparte, 2. Adolph Washington, 3. Matilda, 4. Rebecca, 5. Georgia, 6. Annie, 7. Emmett, 8. Barto, 9. Amelia (died in infancy), 10. Caroline (Carrie), and 11. Warren.

I. Napoleon Bonaparte, the son of Alexander and Amelia Baum, possessed those characteristics outstanding in both parents—charitableness and nobleness. He was born in Irwinton on November 22, 1852, and died in Dublin, on June 19, 1924. As a young man, Napoleon Bonaparte Baum entered the mercantile business in Toomsboro, Georgia. While there, he served the town as mayor in 1873; he also built and donated to the town its city hall. This building still serves the town in the capacity for which it was built. In 1877, Napoleon Bonaparte Baum married Louise Kohn of New York City, whose father was an artist of great renown. The painting and carving on the stair-rail between the President's Chamber and the House of Representatives and that on the exterior doors of the House of Representatives was executed by Philip Kohn, the father of Louise Kohn. In 1892, Napoleon Bonaparte Baum sold his mercantile business in Toomsboro and moved to Dublin where he again entered the same business. Napoleon Bonaparte remained in this business until his retirement, and for a while operated the largest department store in this section of Georgia. Napoleon Bonaparte Baum served the city of Dublin as member of Council, as member of Board of Education, and as chairman of Water and Light Board. He was untiring in his efforts for the city of Dublin. Both Napoleon Bonaparte and Louise Baum were very charitable and kind to all who needed help.

Napoleon Bonaparte and Louise Kohn Baum had six children as follows: 1. Dena, 2. Adeline, 3. Leo Philip, 4. Blanche, 5. Jeannette, 6. Helen.

I. Dena, daughter of Napoleon B. and Louise Baum, taught in the Dublin public schools for many years. She married Emanuel Dreyer, son of Louis A. and Carrie Dreyer. They have two sons: (1) B. Baum Dreyer, and (2) Dean E. Dreyer.

(1) B. Baum Dreyer, son of Emanuel and Dena Dreyer, was graduated from Dublin High School, attended University of Georgia, also Georgia Tech, after which he held a position with the State Highway Department. He now resides in St. Louis, Missouri, where he holds the position of assistant manager of the Men's Department of Boyd's, one of St. Louis' largest stores.

(2) Dean Dreyer, son of Emanuel and Dena Baum Dreyer,, was graduated from Washington University and the University of Georgia Evening School and holds a Master's degree in Fine Arts from Columbia University. He originated and created the first "Everyday Living" class in this country. This was created in Atlanta, Georgia, and has attracted national attention and brought favorable comments from Dale Carnegie and "We the People," who have tried to add him to their programs.

Emanuel Dreyer, husband of Dena Baum Dreyer, was born June 27, 1871, at Thomasville, Georgia. He gave his time and employment to the wholesale grocery business. He died at his home in Dublin, May 29, 1923.

2. Adeline, daughter of Napoleon and Louise Baum, spent her life in untiring efforts to benefit others. Besides being field secretary for Hebrew Orphan's Home in the Southern States, she has worked hard for the cause of the Confederacy. She organized the Chapter of Children of Confederacy in Dublin, which Chapter bears her name.

3. Leo Philip Baum, son of Napoleon B. and Louise Baum, married Lydia McGrath and lives in Wilmington, North Carolina.

4. Blanche, daughter of Napoleon B. and Louise Baum, married Fred J. Schiff and lives in Orlando, Florida.

5. Jeanette, daughter of Napoleon B. and Louise Baum, has fol-

lowed more or less the vocation of a cateress and thus shows the traditional traits of her paternal grandmother.

6. Helen, youngest child of Napoleon B. and Louise Baum, has served as secretary of the Dublin Chamber of Commerce and as registrar of the Oconee Chapter of the United Daughters of the Confederacy.

Louise Kohn Baum witnessed the assassination of Abraham Lincoln in Ford Theater in Washington City, in April, 1865.

II. Adolph Washington, second son of Alexander and Amelia Baum, was engaged in the mercantile business in Dublin. Never has the county of Laurens had the privilege of claiming citizens more charitable, more noble, and more civic-minded than Adolph and Henora DeWald Baum. Their names were known by every person in distress, rich or poor, high or low, especially if they were in need of kindness. No couple who ever lived in Laurens County was ever loved more than they. Adolph Washington Baum died in St. Louis, October 29, 1932, and is buried in Mt. Sinai Cemetery.

Adolph Washington Baum married Henora DeWald, daughter of Solomon A. DeWald and Caroline Wolfe DeWald. They had one daughter, Alva Baum, who married Hiram Baum (deceased), of St. Louis, Missouri, and they had two sons, Adolph Washington and Carl Hiram Baum.

1. A. W. Baum, son of Hiram and Alva Baum, married Marian Katz, daughter of Jay and Ruth Katz, and their children are as follows: (a) Donald Baum, and (b) Edwin Jay Baum.

2. Carl Hiram Baum, son of Hiram and Alva Baum, is now connected with the Mendel Company of St. Louis, Missouri.

—*By Dena Baum Dreyer (Mrs. E.)*

BEDINGFIELD

For over a century and a quarter the Bedingfield family has been prominently identified with the progress of Laurens County, religiously, culturally and politically, members of each generation occupying outstanding positions of leadership.

The Bedingfield family is of ancient Norman origin, deriving its name from a town in Suffolk, England, and tracing its lineage from the era of the Norman Conquest through an uninterrupted line of distinguished ancestors. Sir Peter de Bedingfield, ancestor of the Baronets of Oxburgh, was the founder of the family in England, and the family seat is Bedingfield House, near Eye, in Suffolk. The progenitors of the various branches in America were Sir John, Sir Walter, and Sir Henry Bedingfield, who were among the early colonists of Virginia. A member of the family in Canada established the Bedingfield estate which is now a ranch owned by the Duke of Windsor.

Edna Elizabeth Bedingfield married Josey Coleman and came to Laurens County from North Carolina, about 1818, settling near Rentz, Georgia. Her parents, John and Elizabeth Bedingfield, residents of North Carolina, died, leaving two younger brothers of Edna Elizabeth, John and Andrew Bedingfield, who came to Laurens County when young to live with their sister. John married Elizabeth Jones and settled in Jefferson County while Andrew remained in Laurens. (A daughter of John, Nancy (Mrs. H. K. Brantley) is 92 and living, the youngest of nine children. Dr. Philip Bedingfield, of Wrightsville, is grandson of John.) Andrew Bedingfield, J. P., musician, church leader, farmer, married 1st, Matilda Joiner, daughter of Bennett and Matilda Joiner, Laurens County. Children: ReasonAndrew, William B., John W., and Emily Nancy. Emily married, first, James Warren, second, David L. Coleman. Andrew Bedingfield's second wife, Miss Coleman. Children: Burl, who married Pencie Knight; Lina married Bob Knight; Jane married Joseph Coleman; and Elizabeth married John Knight; but this history deals with descendants of first marriage. Andrew Bedingfield's 3rd wife, was Viney Bass Horn; no children. William B. Bedingfield, unmarried. Lieutenant John W. Bedingfield, Company H, Blackshear Guards, 14th Georgia Regiment, killed in action, Spottsylvania Court House, Virginia, May 26, 1864.

Reason Andrew Bedingfield (b. April 2, 1833-d. Jan. 29, 1919), Confederate soldier, Company A, 2nd Georgia Brigade, First Army Tennessee, in charge of transport train; J. P., farmer, deacon, married January 13, 1853, Caroline E. Register, twin daughter of Robert and Katy Register (b. April 18, 1837-d. Sept. 20, 1907). Children: William Andrew, (b. Oct. 20, 1855-d. Sept. 17, 1929); John Wells, (b. Feb. 8, 1858-d. Sept. 16, 1895); Fannie Elizabeth, (b. May 30, 1860-d. 1916); Bennett Jackson, (b. Sept. 17, 1863-d. Jan. 19, 1941); Mary Caroline, (b. June 20, 1866-d. Feb. 18, 1898); Henry Robert, (b. May 8, 1869-d. March 6, 1928); Edna Cornelia, (b. April 9, 1872-d. Aug. 4, 1924); Sarah Jane, (b. March 10, 1875-d. 1917). Reason Andrew Bedingfield's 2nd wife was Mrs. Hiram Lord; no children.

William Andrew Bedingfield, teacher, deacon, farmer, mayor of Rentz, member Education Boards, merchant, married November 10, 1878, Sarah Elizabeth Rountree, daughter of George William and Eliza (Dadd) Rountree, (b. November 25, 1864-d. August 8, 1937). Children: Walter Eli (dead); George Washington; Reason Andrew, Jr.; William Henry; Hettie (died in infancy); Ettie Eveline; Gertrude (died in infancy); Hattie Elizabeth; John Ethridge; Alma Aulena; Dewey Arnau; Fitzhugh Lee; Olin Jay; Bernard Diaz (dead); Delmas Jerome; infant daughter (dead). Walter Eli Bedingfield, M. D., banker, farmer, merchant, married Julia Taylor. Children: William Osler, M. D., surgeon; Henry Herbert, druggist, farmer; Lillian, teacher; Lucile, teacher; Walter Hilbert, M. D.;

Eloise, teacher; Irma Grace, teacher. William Osler Bedingfield married Caroline Marvin. Children: Linda, Walter. Eloise Bedingfield married Herbert Ira Conner; daughter, Vivien. George Washington Bedingfield, farmer, merchant, married Sally Lucretia Keen. Children: Mae Audley, Delphin (dead), Doyle Eldred, Elta Oleta. Mae Audley Bedingfield married James Alton Dominy. Children: Betty Anne, Virginia Nell, James Alton Jr. Doyle Bedingfield, vocational teacher, married Betty Crocker. Elta Bedingfield married Clarence Roberson. Children: Sally Jo, Elta Sue. George W. Bedingfield's second wife, Annie Susie Warthen, a son, Warthen (dead). Reason Andrew Bedingfield, Jr., M.D., farmer, married Florrie Proctor. Children: Ralph Proctor; Fannie Joe, teacher; James, medical student; Edna. Ralph Bedingfield married Beatrice Barrs, a son, Lindsey. William Henry Bedingfield, deacon, farmer, merchant, married Ellie Warren. Children: Joseph Albert, William Adger, Ruth, Grace (dead), Warren, Walter. Joseph Albert Bedingfield, druggist, married Ruth Bryson; daughter, Joye. William Adger Bedingfield, vocational teacher, married Mary Al Nelson. Ruth Bedingfield married Alton Daniel. Hattie Elizabeth Bedingfield married Obie L. Rowe. Children: Othnie Lee, Oleta Sue, Roscoe, Margarita. Othnie Lee Rowe, machinist, married Evelyn Burch. Oleta Rowe married Elmer Franklin Rivers, a daughter (dead). John Ethridge Bedingfield, druggist, former alderman, Dublin, farmer, World War veteran, married Mamie Rowe. Alma Aulena Bedingfield married Milo Smith, World War veteran. Children: Milo Smith, Jr., William Robert. Dewey Arnau Bedingfield, farmer, civil engineer, married Mary Sally McGlohorn; son, Dewey Arnau, Jr. Fitzhugh Lee Bedingfield, druggist, farmer; Olin Jay Bedingfield, merchant, farmer; Delmas Jerome Bedingfield, alderman of Rentz, Ga., farmer, merchant, member Education Board, married Mildred Buie.

John Wells Bedingfield, farmer, married 1st, on July 3, 1887, Mary J. Bass; 2nd, Nancy Warren; no children. Fannie Elizabeth Bedingfield married James B. Gay, son of Josiah and Isabel (Jenkins) Gay. Children: Joseph C., and Mary, twins (Mary dead), Carrie Selina (dead), James Matthew, Andrew Holland dead), Ordella and Estella, twins, (died in infancy), Idonie. Joseph C. Gay, farmer, married Elena Jones. Children: Arvilla, Ozero, Rozie L. (dead), J. C., Mildred, Eloise. Arvilla married Collie Burch, one child: Floyd. Mary Gay married Willie Wilkie; children: Ethel, Bobbie. Ethel married John White; Bobbie (dead). Carrie Selina Gay married J. Tom Dominy, one child: Thomasine, who married Paul Jones, one child. James Matthew Gay, merchant, farmer, married Pearly Clifford Sapp; children: Curtis Oslar, James Ralph, Florence Lorene. Curtis Osler married Bertie Winfred Jones, one child, C. S. Glenn; James Ralph, teacher, married Bonnie Graham; Florence Lorene married J. Dykes Burch. Andrew Holland Gay, merchant, farmer, married Gussie Johns. Idonie Gay married John Henry Turner, children: Fred, Elouise, Holland Deen.

Bennett Jackson Bedingfield, farmer, merchant, member Education Boards, mayor of Cadwell, married Laura Winifred Fann, January 12, 1888, daughter of Thomas Jefferson and Frances (Shephard) Fann. Children: Mattie Mae, Mamie (dead), Elton (dead), Bertha Etolia, Eva Jane, C. Jackson. Mattie Mae married William Colter, children: Alex, Bernice, Floree, Bennett. Alex Colter, lumberman, farmer, married Mary Lou Thompson, a child: William J.; Bernice Colter married Elbert Mullis, a child: Elbert, Jr.; Floree Colter married J. P. Carter, Jr., a child: Martha; Bennett Colter, farmer, lumberman, married Opielee Jones. Bertha Etolia Bedingfield, teacher, married Charles Bennett Hudson, children: Charles and Winifred. Eva Jane Bedingfield married Alton Cameron, children: Joann, Jack and Judy. C. Jackson Bedingfield, druggist, farmer, mayor of Cadwell, Chairman of County Board of Education, married Ruth Burch, child: Betty Jim.

Mary Caroline Bedingfield married, 1st, Joel Warren, December 24, 1882; married 2nd, Samuel Franklin Woodard, January, 1895, son of William David and Lou Pinie (Sandford) Woodard, son: Odua A. Woodard, insurance salesman, who married Lizzie Thomas, children: Jas. Edwards, Marie, who married Hal Walton.

Henry Robert Bedingfield, banker, farmer, merchant, married Margaret Elizabeth Warren, December 13, 1894, daughter of David Thomas and Mary Jane (Burch) Warren. Children: John Bennett, Essie Cornelia, Mary Effie, Purlie Elizabeth (dead), Murlie Mae, Hal Thomas, Ella Rheta, Robert Bisland, Henry Riley, Margaret Fleta. John Bennett Bedingfield, Legislative member, former Mayor of Cadwell, farmer, banker, Superior Court Clerk, married Gussie Pauline Moye. Children: Warren Parker, NYA director, Roy Edison, Barbara Fay. Essie Cornelia Bedingfield, teacher, married Loomis Taylor, World War veteran, children: Nell, Claudia. Mary Effie Bedingfield, teacher, married Warthen Chappell, World War veteran, sons: Roy James, John Joseph. Purline Elizabeth Bedingfield married Lonnie Daniel, children: Marion Dorothy, married Talmadge Rawlins; Lonnie Pearl. Murlie Mae Bedingfield married Walter Morrison, children: Mary Jane (dead), Murlie Elizabeth, Anne Cornelia. Hal Thomas Bedingfield, engineer, married Anne Marie Windham, two daughters: Anne Elizabeth, Mary Patricia. Ella Rheta Bedingfield married Revered Bennett Pickron, children: David Reviere, Henry Ashley, Rachel Leah, Nancy Rheta. Robert Bisland Bedingfield, farmer, married Fannie Grace Burch, son: Robert Clayton.

Edna Cornelia Bedingfield married Andrew B. Daniel, December 15, 1890, son of Green Berry and Elsie Jane (Dominy) Daniel, children: Cornelia (dead), Joel B. (dead), Durvis, twin girls (dead), Furman, Ethel (dead), Marion Shaw, Vesta, Clydie. Cornelia

Daniel married C. Cadwell, children: Jerry C., Lawrence Burch, Ola Mae, Edna. Joel B. Daniel married Julia Bell Chambers, children: Woodrow, Roscoe (dead).

Wesley Daniel married Hattie Chambers, children: Orita, Janette, Shirley Ann, Randall. Orita married Malcolm Sanders. Durvis Daniel married Irma Lee Barrs, children: Dorothy, Ophelia, Margie, Ruby, Joy. Furman Daniel married Mattie Clyde Goodrum. Ethel Daniel married Matthew Burch. Vesta Daniel married Otha Evans, child: Daniel Otha. Clyde Lee Daniel married Otha Gause, child: Jerry.

Sarah Jane Bedingfield married David Robert Coleman March 14, 1895, son of Henry Clay and Sebie (Knight) Coleman. Children: Celeste (dead), Mamie, teacher; Walter (dead), Gladys, teacher; Henry Alfred, Lettie and Mettie, twins; Lettie married Walter Walker; Metty married Jethro Grinstead, children: Barbara Jane; son (dead), Ruby Coleman, teacher.

Compiled and lovingly dedicated to my sons, Milo Smith, Jr., and William Robert Smith, *by Alma Aulena Bedingfield Smith (Mrs. Milo).*

BLACK

"The Scotch, Irish, and Welsh ancestor of the Black family of Upson County, Georgia, came to America from England in 1620. Tradition says that he came on the Mayflower and settled in Virginia, where he was later joined by six brothers." (See page 880 of the Upson County History).

Thomas Howard, eldest son of James Richardson and Mary Ann Black, was born in 1851. He was married in 1871 to Louisa Marshall Collier, daughter of Amanda Green and Robert Marshall Collier, one of the largest land owners in Upson County.

Thomas Howard and Louisa Collier Black had the following children: Mary Fletcher (the late Mrs. S. E. Wilson of Dublin, Georgia), Earnest Thomas, Edward Howard, Collier Marshall, Emmett Lee, and Clyde (Mrs. O. L. Chivers). These children married and have descendants.

Thomas Howard Black died in May, 1925, and his wife, Louisa Marshall Collier Black, died in 1894.

Emmett Lee Black, youngest son of Thomas Howard and Louisa Collier Black, was born at The Rock, Upson County, Georgia. He finished high school there and graduated from Mercer University, Macon, Georgia, and became a licensed pharmacist in May, 1906. He moved to Dublin in June of the same year, where he became associated in drug business with his father, Thomas Howard Black, the title of the firm being Black's Pharmacy, which he still owns and operates in the City of Dublin. He is a member of Retail Druggists of Georgia and the Woodmen of the World.

In June, 1909, Emmett Lee Black was married to Harriett Elizabeth Wheeless of Thomaston, Georgia, Upson County. Elizabeth Wheeless was the daughter of the late George Thomas and Sara Scott Wheeless, originally from Meriwether County. She was educated at LaGrange College where she finished in art. She is active in civic and religious circles of Dublin.

The children born to Elizabeth and Emmett Lee Black are:

Elma Lee, graduated from Dublin High School and continued her education at Wesleyan College and is now secretary and treasurer of Black's Pharmacy.

Sara Evelyn, graduated from Dublin High School and specialized in music at Lander College, Greenwood, South Carolina. She was married to Augustus Lucian Malone of Monticello, Georgia, February 21, 1937. Her husband is a member of the firm operating as Black's Seed Store. Their children are Carol Anne and Bette Jean.

Emmett Wheeless Black graduated from Dublin High School, attended Teachers College at Statesboro, Georgia, and continued his education at the University of Georgia. He was married to Yvo Richardson of Oglethorpe, Georgia. He is a member of the firm known as Black's Seed Store.

Dorothy Anne graduated from Dublin High School and attended Bessie Tift College at Forsyth, Georgia.

William Howard Black, the youngest child, is now a senior of Dublin High School. He is a member of the Dublin Band and football squad.

All members of this family belong to the First Baptist Church of Dublin.

—By Elma Black.

BLACKSHEAR

General David Blackshear, one of the most illustrious men ever to call and make Laurens County his home, was the first generation of Blackshears in the county and the second in America.

James Blackshear, the father of General David, was the first to come. He was a German immigrant, who came about 1732 and settled near Trenton, North Carolina. About 1758, he married Catherine Francks Bush, the daughter of John Martin and Civil Francks and the widow of a Mr. Bush. To this union there were born eight children as follows: 1. James, 2. Edward, 3. David, 4. Elizabeth, 5. Susannah, 6. Elijah, 7. Penelope, 8. Joseph.

Elijah Blackshear never married, was born July 17, 1771; died in Laurens County in 1821; is buried in the yard of old Valambrosa, the home of George M. Troup.

Joseph Blackshear was born September 7, 1775; married Winifred, the sister of Colonel William A. Tennille, late Secretary of State. He died in Laurens County in 1830 and he, too, is buried in the yard of old Valambrosa, once the home of Governor Troup. It is said that Governor Troup acquired Valambrosa from Joseph Blackshear.

Of David Blackshear's other two brothers, James, the oldest, was killed by the Tories during the Revolutionary War, and Edward moved to Thomas County, Georgia, and died there in 1829. Concerning his sisters, all three of them also came to Georgia and lived in Twiggs County. So, most of his relatives lived within a convenient distance to him.

David Blackshear was the third child and was born January 31, 1764, on the Chinquapin Creek near Trenton, North Carolina.

Stephen F. Miller, in his "Bench and Bar of Georgia," says that General Blackshear and Dr. Benjamin Franklin each bore a strong resemblance of each other; that the full-length portrait of Dr. Franklin that hangs on the wall of the National House of Representatives gives one the correct idea of how General Blackshear looked. These two men, he says, had much in common and were alike in many respects.

On December 2, 1802, David Blackshear was married to Fanny Hamilton, the daughter of John Hamilton of Hancock County. She was born January 22, 1781, and died February 28, 1824. The Hamilton family was one of great influence and position, all six brothers of Mrs. Blackshear being outstanding statesmen and army officers.

General David and Fanny Hamilton Blackshear had three daughters and eight sons as follows: 1. Mary Hamilton (died in infancy), 2. James Hamilton, 3. William Thweatt, 4. Edward Jefferson, 5. Ann Eliza (died in infancy), 6. Eliza Ann (died in infancy), 7. David, 8. Everard Hamilton, 9. Joseph John Floyd, 10. Elijah Francks, 11. John Duke (died in infancy).

It can be seen that all three daughters and one son of David and Fanny Hamilton Blackshear died in infancy, leaving only seven sons, who reached maturity.

Everard Hamilton Blackshear, the fifth son of General David and Fanny Hamilton Blackshear, was born June 19, 1818, and died February 28, 1871. On October 10, 1844, he married Isabella Maria Hamilton, the daughter of Colonel Everard Hamilton who was a brother-in-law of General David Blackshear. Colonel Hamilton had served as Secretary of State for both Governor Forsyth and for Governor Troup. Everard Hamilton Blackshear and Isabella Hamilton Blackshear had eleven children, four of whom died in infancy. The seven who lived to maturity are as follows: 1. Everard Hamilton, 2. David Stout, 3. Isabella Maria, 4. John Marmaduke, 5. Richard William, 6. Georgia Lafayette, 7. Thomas Joseph.

I. Everard Hamilton, son of Everard Hamilton and Isabella Maria Blackshear, was born in 1844, in Laurens County, and died in 1926, in Pulaski County. In 1873 he married Charlotte Reeves of Pulaski County.

II. David Stout Blackshear, son of Everard Hamilton and Isabella Maria Blackshear, was born June 30, 1848, and died April 20, 1940. He is buried in Northview Cemetery, in Dublin, Georgia. On December 18, 1873, he married Pauline Harrison Howard, the daughter of Colonel Thomas C. Howard of Kirkwood, Georgia. To this union were born four sons and two daughters, as follows: 1. Everard Howard, 2. Carrie Bell, 3. Marmaduke Hamilton, 4. Alex Daley, 5. Robert Henry, 6. Henora Pauline.

1. Everard Howard Blackshear, son of David Stout and Pauline Howard Blackshear, never married. He lives on the farm which was his father's.

2. Carrie Bell Blackshear, daughter of David Stout and Pauline Howard Blackshear, married Joseph Eldridge Smith and they had one daughter, Clyde, and one son, William Eldridge. Clyde received A.B. degree, Wesleyan College; degree in library science, Emory University; holds a position as librarian in Raleigh, North Carolina. William Eldridge, alumnus of Emory University, married Elizabeth Camp and lives in Virginia.

3. Marmaduke Hamilton, son of David Stout and Pauline Howard Blackshear, received A.B. degree, Emory College; B. L. degree, Lumpkin Law School of University of Georgia; practiced his profession in Dublin, Georgia; interested in all worthwhile things; identifies himself with church and civic organizations; has served as superintendent of Church School of First Methodist Church, Dublin; is loved and respected by all who know him. He was born September 16, 1878; married Annie Hardeman of Macon, and they have two children, viz., (a) Marmaduke Hardeman and (b) Carolyn. a. Marmaduke Hardeman, A.B. degree from Emory University; practices law in Dublin; active in church work; married August 5, 1937, Elizabeth Blanchard, daughter of Mell and Pamelia Blanchard, of Crawford, Georgia; they have one daughter, Pamelia Ann. b. Carolyn, daughter of Marmaduke Hamilton and Annie Hardeman Blackshear, married John F. Wilson, son of John F. and Mrs. Wilson. They live in Jacksonville, Florida, and have two children, viz., John F., Jr., and Carol Adrienne.

4. Alex Daley Blackshear, a wholesale merchant in Douglas, Georgia, has never married. Rendered active service on foreign soil during World War I.

5. Robert Henry Blackshear, son of David Stout and Pauline Howard Blackshear; a Presbyterian minister at Peekskill, New York;

married Rebecca Branham, of Oxford, Georgia. They have three sons, viz., 1. Hamilton, 2. Robert, 3. David.

6. Henora Pauline Blackshear, daughter of David Stout and Pauline Howard Blackshear, married Carlos Denton Greenway. They now reside at Alma, Georgia, and have two sons, viz.: Carlos Denton Greenway, Jr., and Alex Blackshear Greenway.

Pauline Howard Blackshear, wife of David Stout Blackshear, was born January 23, 1852, and died November 2, 1936; she is buried in Northview Cemetery, Dublin, Georgia.

III. Isabella Marie Blackshear, daughter of Everard Hamilton and Isabella Maria Blackshear, married Louis A. Matthews of Tennille, Georgia, who served in the Confederate Army. They had two sons and one daughter, viz.: William Collins Matthews, Louis A. Matthews, Jr., both of Atlanta, Georgia, and Annie Belle Matthews Galey of Pensacola, Florida. L. A. Matthews, Sr., died in 1902 and his wife, Isabella Maria Blackshear Matthews, died in 1907. Both are buried in Tennille, Georgia.

IV. John Marmaduke Blackshear, the fourth son of Isabella Maria Hamilton and Everard Hamilton Blackshear, was born February 22, 1853, in Laurens County. In early manhood he went to Pulaski County, where he was married to Mary Reeves, the daughter of Thomas Reeves and Mary Taylor. She lived only a few months; the following year he was married to her sister, Carrie Estelle. There were born to this union seven children: Mary Isabella, Mrs. J. P. Wimberly (deceased); Carrie Leolene, formerly Mrs. C. S. Guyton now Mrs. W. B. Jessup; Rosa LaFayette, Mrs. W. R. Cook (deceased); Alma Gertrude, Mrs. T. S. Crawford (deceased); Cora Estelle, Mrs. J. Forrest Beam (deceased); Nina Lurline, Mrs. Otto Diekow (deceased).

Mrs. J. M. Blackshear, nee Carrie Reeves, died in Cochran in 1905. The family then moved back to Laurens, where in 1900 he was married to Ola Baker, daughter of Reverend W. S. Baker of Irwinton. Three children were born to them: an infant who died at birth; John Marmaduke Blackshear, Jr., born September 29, 1903; Ola Baker Blackshear, born June 1, 1905.

Four children survive of the three groups. John M. Blackshear, Sr., died in November, 1913, and is buried in Dublin, Georgia. Children of Mary Isabella Blackshear and James Philip Wimberly are as follows: Philip Wimberly (deceased); Carrie Estelle Wimberly, Mrs. L. O. Jones, Cochran, Ga.; Alma Wimberly, Mrs. J. D. Shelton; Cora Estelle Wimberly, Mrs. Wilbur Thompson; Julia Deese Wimberly, Mrs. N. G. Jordan; James Phillips Wimberly; Kathryn Lucille Wimberly.

Guyton children: John Marmaduke Guyton (deceased); Carolyn Boifeuillet, Mrs. Wilt. Jolly; Mary Kate, Mrs. Henry Wilkinson; Frances Evelyn, Mrs. W. Comer Cherry; Rose Blackshear, Mrs. J. R. Edmondson.

Cook children: William Frederick, Miriam Virginia, Albert Jackson.

Cranford children: Helen Beam and Marion Adele.

Beam children: J. Forest Beam, Jr., deceased.

Guyton grandchildren: Rose Mary Jolly, William Guyton Wilkinson, William Comer Cherry, Jr.

V. Richard William Blackshear, son of Everard Hamilton and Isabella Maria Blackshear, was born January 8, 1855; married Evie R. Ware, daughter of David Ware of Laurens County, Georgia, in 1855. Their children are as follows: (1) Richard William, (2) Annie Blanch Norris, (3) Louise Deal, (4) Pauline Coleman, (5) Margaret, (6) Ware.

VI. Georgia Lafayette Blackshear, daughter of Everard Hamilton and Isabella Hamilton Blackshear, was born in 1861. Never married; died in Pensacola, Florida; is buried in Northview Cemetery in Dublin.

VII. Thomas Joseph Blackshear, son of Everard Hamilton and Isabella Hamilton Blackshear, was born August 13, 1856; married Eva Bertha Stanley (see Stanley genealogy), daughter of Dr. Ben and Elizabeth Bass Stanley, on June 19, 1889. They had the following children: 1. Raphael Semes, 2. Thomas Joseph, 3. Wilhelmina Elizabeth, 4. Paul David, 5. Eva Bertha, 6. Renaldo Franklin.

1. Raphael Semes Blackshear died April 26, 1906, buried in Stanley Cemetery.

2. Thomas Joseph Blackshear, Jr., received degree in Medicine from Atlanta Medical College; served in Medical Department of U. S. Army in England during World War; practiced medicine in Dublin, Georgia, and Wilson, North Carolina; married Rosalie Robinson of Jacksonville, Florida; has one son, Emmett Everard.

3. Wilhelmina Elizabeth Blackshear, daughter of Thomas Joseph and Eva Stanley Blackshear, married Seth Monte Kellam (deceased) (see Kellam genealogy), and they had the following children: 1. Seth Monte, Jr. (died in infancy), 2. Thomas Blackshear, 3. Seth Hamilton, 4. Wilhelmina Blackshear, 5. Paul David, 6. Bettie Eve. Seth Monte Kellam, husband of Wilhelmina Elizabeth Blackshear, died June 28, 1936, and is buried in Northview Cemetery, Dublin.

4. Paul David Blackshear, son of Thomas Joseph and Eva Stanley Blackshear, served in World War until its close; received degree in law from Washington Law School; practices law at Pineville, West Virginia. He has never married.

5. Eva Bertha Blackshear, daughter of Thomas Joseph and Eva Stanley Blackshear, was twice married, first, to Jack A. Street (deceased) of Dublin, Georgia. Jack A. Street died in McRae, Georgia, in 1919, and is buried in Northview Cemetery in Dublin. There were no children by this marriage, but by her second marriage to Major J. E. Graham there is one child, Eva Bertha.

6. Renaldo Franklin Blackshear, son of Thomas Joseph Blackshear and Eva Stanley Blackshear, died in infancy.

Thomas Joseph Blackshear, Sr., was twice married, first, to Eva Bertha Stanley who bore him six children. She died on August 9, 1899, and is buried in the Stanley cemetery, sometimes called "The Ditch" (see Rowell Stanley genealogy) in Laurens County.

On July 9, 1902, Thomas Joseph Blackshear, Sr., married his second wife, Julia D. Thweatt, who bore him no children. She died on October 24, 1932, and is also buried in the Standley cemetery.

Besides the graves of General David Blackshear and his wife, Fanny Hamilton Blackshear, at Springfield, you will also find the graves of two sons, viz.: James Hamilton and William Thweatt, who died in the meridian of life. Another grave is that of Mary Jane, the wife of another son, Edward Jefferson Blackshear. "A half-dozen little graves tell of angelic slumbers here. Dear old spot, hallowed by tender memories!"

The military and political life of General David Blackshear is recorded in the early history of the County.

—*By Marmaduke Hamilton Blackshear.*

BLOODWORTH

John Bloodworth (1730-1808) emigrated from England early in life and settled in New Hanover County, Wilmington District, North Carolina. His name is found on Roster of Captain George Merrick's Company, North Carolina Militia during Colonial Wars. He served as private and lieutenant during Revolutionary War, and Major in North Carolina Militia against the Indians. A marker has been placed on his grave in Morgan County, Georgia. John Bloodworth was a State Senator from Wilmington District, North Carolina, 1804. About 1806 he came to Georgia and joined his sons, Samuel, Thomas and Henry, who had settled in Wilkinson County. He was a Baptist minister and was on a visit to his son, Thomas, who had removed to Morgan County when he died. He married first Tamsie Axon, in 1748, and their children were Samuel (Revolutionary soldier), Thomas (Revolutionary soldier), Henry, John, William, Mary, Elizabeth. His second marriage was to Susan Lee, and by this union there was one daughter, Margret.

Henry Bloodworth (1772-1856), son of John Bloodworth, married, first, Polly Temples. His second marriage, in 1818, was to Penelope Phillips (1796-1878). Among their children was John Bloodworth.

John Bloodworth was born May 28, 1827; died October 20, 1900; married Louie Anne Nalus, April 4, 1847. She was born July 3, 1831; died October 7, 1897. Among their children was Lydia Priscilla.

Lydia Priscilla was born July 28, 1850; died June 17, 1923; married Bartley Israel Stevens (Stephens), March 1, 1866. Bartley was born October 19, 1845. He served during the War Between the States (Company D, 57th Georgia Infantry). One of their children was Margie Ann Stevens.

Margie Ann Stevens was born February 1, 1872; died July 12, 1937; married first, Bascom M. Brown, March 25, 1888, and soon afterward moved to Laurens County. He was born June 19, 1858; died May 3, 1904. Of this union was born three children: Fred, Frank, and Maude.

Maude Brown married W. Alex Knight, December 15, 1917; they have one daughter, Bascom (see Knight genealogy).

Margie Ann Stevens Brown married, second, W. T. DuPree, in 1905, and they had one daughter, Ruth.

Ruth DuPree was married to Wm. Brooks Bryans, December 27, 1923. He is a Captain in 121st Infantry, 3rd Battalion, 30th Division of the United States Army. They have two children, Brooks (Billy) Jr., born May 19, 1925, and Margie Dell, born October 7, 1929.

Other grandchildren of Margie Ann and Bascom Brown are Edmond, Frank Jr., and Stanley Brown.

—*By Maude Brown Knight (Mrs. W. Alex)*
Bradenton, Florida.

BRIGHAM

The first Brigham who came to Laurens County was William Randall Brigham, in 1900. William Randall Brigham was born in Burke County, Georgia, January 17, 1874, the son of John Christopher and Julia Odum Brigham.

John Christopher Brigham was born in Burke County, June 16, 1846, and on October 17, 1872, married Julia Odum who was born August 8, 1853. To this union were born four sons and four daughters as follows: 1. William Randall, 2. Annie Beulah, 3. John Christopher, Jr., 4. Arthur Julian, 5. Jennie Freeland, 6. Savannah, 7. Ernest Talmadge (see Smith, J. D., genealogy), 8. Julia Pauline.

William Randall Brigham was educated in schools of Burke County; received degree in medicine from University of Georgia Medical School, in Augusta, in 1898; interned at University Hospital; began practice in Dublin, Laurens County, in 1900.

William Randall Brigham was not only interested in his profession but was alive to all public interests. He helped plan and build The First National Bank Building; was director of this bank; was a Mason and Shriner.

William Randall Brigham died July 29, 1826, and is buried in Northview Cemetery. He was a member of the Methodist Church.

William Randall Brigham married Charlotte Robertson Turner, the daughter of Elias James Robertson and Mary Ellen (Parker) Robertson. Elias James Robertson was born August 17, 1849, in Wicomico County, Maryland, the son of Samuel James Robertson and Ara Jane (Laramore) Robertson. Mary Ellen (Parker) Robertson was born January 22, 1852, in Baltimore, the daughter of James Henry Parker and Mary Jane (Williams) Parker.

Elias James Robertson and Mary Ellen (Parker) Robertson, parents of Charlotte Robertson Turner, were married May 29, 1873, in Baltimore, Maryland.

By the marriage of William Randall Brigham to Charlotte Robertson Turner there were born two daughters, Jean and Caroline Brigham. By her first marriage, to William Pitt Turner of Salisbury, Maryland, Charlotte Robertson had one daughter, Charlotte Robertson Turner, born March 30, 1915. This lovely girl passed away in Dublin, November 10, 1936, and her mother established and equipped a room in the Claxton Sanitarium as a memorial to her.

—*By Charlotte Robertson Turner Brigham (Mrs. W. R.)*

BUCHAN

In 1884, Dr. John Wesley Buchan and wife, Mary Ann Lancaster Buchan, moved from Eastman to Laurens County and settled at Reedy Springs, now known as Rentz. They had three children, William Hector, Robert Pickens, and Fannie Arlena.

Dr. Buchan, a graduate of the Georgia Eclectic Medical College, class of 1888, with post-graduate work in obstetrics at Johns Hopkins in Baltimore, was the second son of Dr. and Mrs. James Buchan, of Eastman, Georgia. He successfully combined his medical profession with farming and was a beloved "Country Doctor," who was untiring in his service to the people of this county, believing it more blessed to give than to receive. In 1896, he moved his family to McRae, Georgia, so that his children could attend South Georgia College. Dr. Buchan died in McRae and his family returned to Laurens County in 1899.

Mary A. Lancaster Buchan later married J. R. Baggett and moved to Dublin where she endeared herself to a wide circle of friends. She died in June, 1934, while visiting her son, W. H. Buchan, in Tallahassee, Florida.

William Hector Buchan married Miss Zalie Daughtery, of McRae, and they settled in Tallahassee, Florida.

Robert Pickens Buchan married Miss Olga McDuffie, of McRae, and they moved to Albany, Georgia. After his death, Olga McDuffie Buchan moved to Dublin with her three children, Josephine Louise, Mary Elizabeth, and Robert Pickens.

Josephine Louise Buchan is a graduate of G. S. C. W. She is

the first grade teacher of Calhoun Street School in Dublin, where she has served for a number of years.

Mary Elizabeth Buchan was graduated from G. S. C. W. in 1927. She taught school in Pavo, Georgia, and later married John T. Gilmore of that city. Their two children are John T., Jr., and Elizabeth Mae.

Robert Pickens Buchan is a successful young business man of Dublin, operating a wholesale candy business. He married Miss Gussie Bell Smith, of Dublin, in 1931. Their only child is Barbara Sue.

Fannie Arlena Buchan married Sylvester Woodard in 1900, and they moved to Blakely, Georgia. Mr. Woodard died in 1910, and Fannie A. Buchan Woodard moved to Dublin with her four children, Martha Estora, John Wilber, Dorothy May, and Frances Vesta. In 1916, she married Charles A. Hall and had one son, Hubert Hanson Hall. In 1924, she married B. F. Cochran (see Cochran genealogy).

Martha Estora Woodard attended Florida State College for Women where she specialized in music. She was married to Guy Vason Cochran, a wholesale grocer of Dublin, May 8, 1920. Their children are Martha Anne, Frances Nelle, Eleanor Faye, and Benjamin Guy. Anne is, at present, a student of Furman University, and Nelle attends Mars Hill Junior College in North Carolina.

John Wilber Woodard is a district manager for A. Nash Clothing Company with offices in Atlanta. In 1929, he married Miss Marjorie Ellen Tarrant of Lynchburg, South Carolina. They have two children, John W., Jr., and Carolyn Rutherford.

Dorothy May Woodard was accidentally killed during early childhood.

Frances Vesta Woodard attended G. S. C. W. in Milledgeville and received her A.B. degree from that institution in 1930. She taught in the Dublin Public Schools for several years. In 1938, she was married to Robert Frederick Driver, of Carroll County, who is, at present, principal of Dublin Senior High School. They have one son, Robert Frederick Driver, Jr.

Hubert Hanson Hall is employed by the Southern Pacific Steamship Lines and is located in Texas.

—*By Vesta Woodard Driver (Mrs. R. F.)*

BURCH

The Burch family is descended from Joseph Burch, who came from England and settled first in Richmond County, near Augusta, Georgia, later moving to Montgomery County, thence to Telfair County, which was Wilkinson County at that time. He settled at China Hill, near the Ocmulgee River.

Joseph Burch married first a Miss Hargrave, of Richmond County, and after her death, married a Miss Gillie. He was the father of twelve children; but we were not able either to learn which wife was the mother of the children or to obtain the names of all the children. (See Dodge County History—Burch Family.)

Alfred and Benjamin Burch, sons of Joseph Burch, settled in what is now known as Burch's District, Laurens County, near the present New Hope Church. This Church was organized as a Hardshell Church about the year 1820.

ALFRED BURCH FAMILY

Alfred Burch, son of Joseph Burch, the pioneer, married first a Miss Parish; they were the parents of five boys and seven girls. The boys were Henry, Mike L., Berry, John and Ben W. Burch. The writer was unable to obtain the names of the girls. Alfred Burch next married a Mrs. McLendon, who was formerly Annie McRae. They were the parents of one son, Daniel W. Burch.

JOHN BURCH FAMILY

John Burch, son of Alfred Burch and his first wife, whose maiden name was Parish, married Missouri Clemens; they had the following children: Henry Clayton, married Fannie Fuller; James A., married Nina Lee; Smith, died unmarried; Berry C., married Florence Parish; Jennie, married Virgil Taylor; Annie, married Owen Proctor; Lola, married W. T. Phelps.

John Edwin Burch, son of John and Missouri Clemens Burch, was one of Dublin's leading lawyers and held many positions of public trust. On November 30, 1904, he was married to Pauline Daley, daughter of Judge Alexander Ferdinand and Willie Howard Daley. They adopted two foster children: Joy, who married James Moore, and Marshall Burch.

DANIEL W. BURCH FAMILY

Daniel W. Burch, son of Benjamin Burch, son of Joseph Burch the pioneer, was born June 7, 1858, in what is now Burch's District of Laurens County, near New Hope Church. He became a member of this church when a young man, later moving his membership to the First Baptist Church, Dublin, Georgia. He was a devout Christian, and prominent member of this church for the remainder of his life. He married Sara Elizabeth Burch, daughter of William Burch, January 2, 1884. They spent their entire lives in Laurens County with the exception of a few years that were spent at Alamo, Georgia, prior to 1907, when they moved to Dublin. They lived happily together for fifty-three years, celebrating their golden wedding anniversary on January 2, 1934. They had extensive farming interests in Laurens County and owned much property in Dublin.

Daniel W. Burch and Sara Elizabeth Burch were the parents of nine children, two dying in infancy. Their other children are:

Hamilton Burch, born in Laurens County November 2, 1884. He married Emeline Coleman of Montgomery County; they are the parents of one child, Avrylea Elizabeth, who married A. J. McDaniel. They have one child, Jan Burch McDaniel. Hamilton is an attorney-at-law; he served as solicitor of city court at McRae, Georgia, from 1909 to 1911; he also served as solicitor of city court at Valdosta, Georgia, from 1933 to 1937.

Alexander Austin Burch was born in Laurens County November 28, 1886. He was admitted to the Bar of Georgia in 1909, after graduation from Mercer University. He practiced law in Dublin several years. During the World War, he served his country as Second Lieutenant with the Air Corps, from August 4, 1917, to December 26, 1918. Later he was commissioned Captain in the Judge Advocate General's Department. In 1935 he married Mary Durham, of Columbia, South Carolina; they are the parents of one child, Alexander Austin, II.

Julius Caesar Burch was born in Laurens County, January 11, 1890; after studying medicine he practiced in Laurens for a while. He married Dottie Meadows, of Helena, Georgia; they have no children. At this time, he is superintendent of Battle Hill Sanitorium, Atlanta, Georgia.

Nancy Bayne Burch was born in Dublin, Georgia, July 19, 1892. She married James B. Jones; they are the parents of one child, James Fleming, who married Sara Smith of Atlanta.

Daniel Fleming Burch was born November 21, 1895; died November 25, 1911.

Clarence Victor Burch was born March 28, 1898, in Alamo, Georgia. He graduated from Dublin High School and attended Mercer University. He is an active member of the Laurens Lodge, No. 75, F. & A. M., Dublin; a member of the Knights Templar and holds the office of Eminent Commander at this time. Clarence Burch married Cora Wilkes, of Emanuel County; they are the parents of one son, Clarence Victor Burch, Jr.

Birdie Estelle Burch was born at Alamo, Georgia, October 4, 1900. She married Oscar H. Duggan; they have one child, Elizabeth.

—*The foregoing records of the Burch family were compiled by Cora Wilkes Burch (Mrs. C. V.).*

BENJAMIN BURCH FAMILY

Benjamin, son of Joseph Burch the pioneer, married Sarah Hamilton, daughter of Stewart Hamilton, a Revolutionary soldier. They were parents of Cynthia Burch, who married Calphry Clark; Lottie Burch, who married Riley Sikes; Liza, who married first, a Calhoun, second, a Cadwell, third, a Clark; Mary Burch, who married first, William Hamilton, second Ephriam Mathews; Precious Burch, who married a Gauf; Pinkie Burch, who never married; Martha Burch, who married William Joiner; Benjamin Burch, II, who married Lydia Sanders; John H. Burch, who married a Miss Clark; and William Burch, who married Mary Emily Gay.

WILLIAM BURCH FAMILY

William Burch, son of Benjamin Burch, son of Joseph the pioneer, married Mary Emily Gay and they were parents of: William Gaulden Burch, who married Clifford Harville; Nathan Burch, who married Miss Emma Swailes; Sarah Elizabeth Burch, who married Daniel W. Burch, son of Alfred Burch; and John Benjamin Burch, who married Jennie Mathews.

JOHN BENJAMIN BURCH FAMILY

John Benjamin Burch, son of William Burch, son of Benjamin Burch who was a son of Joseph Burch the pioneer, was born in Laurens County, where he spent his entire life. He became a member of the New Hope Baptist Church at a very young age and remained a member of the same church all of his life. He was always interested in bettering conditions in the community in which he lived. Churches and schools could always depend on him for help. He gave the land and lumber to build two negro churches. J. B. Burch served several years on the finance committee of the Daniel Baptist Association, and when the Laurens County Baptist Association was organized, he served on its finance committee until his death. He was a leader in the Masonic Lodge and was several times Commander of the Knights Templar. John Benjamin Burch married Jennie Mathews, daughter of Ephriam Mathews, who was a Captain in the Confederate Army, and they were parents of: John Benjamin Burch, Jr., who died at the age of 24 years, William E. Burch, Harry Lee Burch, Roger Burch, Ilah Fay Burch, Emily Burch, Celestia Antonette Burch, Jessie Mae Burch, Sarah Clifford Burch who died at the age of five years.

William E. Burch married Annie Maud Clark and they were parents of: Margarete Burch, who married Clarence Locke; Benjamin Harlow (Jack) Burch, who married Ina May Smith and they are parents of one son, William Clark Burch, Mary Emily Burch, and Marian Evelyn Burch.

Harry Lee Burch, son of John Benjamin Burch, served over-seas as a lieutenant in a Motorized Machine Gun Battalion, during the first World War. He married Eileen Hobbs and they are the parents of a girl and a boy, Eileen Antonette Burch and Harry Lee Burch, Jr.

Roger Burch, son of John Benjamin Burch, married Jane Smith.

They are the parents of a boy and a girl, John Benjamin Burch, III, and Mary Selina Burch.

Ilah Fay Burch, daughter of John Benjamin Burch, became a member of the Baptist Church at an early age. She has always been a leader in the church in her community and a teacher in Sunday Schools, and has taught in the County Schools for several years.

Emily Burch was born in Laurens County and has taught in the County Schools for several years.

Celestia Antonette Burch was born in Laurens County. She has been a church worker and school teacher for several years.

Jessie Mae Burch, daughter of John Benjamin Burch, was born in Laurens County and joined the Baptist Church at an early age. She has always been a worker in the church.

NATHAN BURCH FAMILY

Nathan, son of William Burch, son of Benjamin who was a son of Joseph Burch the pioneer, married Miss Emma Swailes. They are the parents of (1) Mary Burch who married E. W. Watson, and they are parents of Ray Burch Watson, who married Sadie Forbes, and are parents of Mary Hilda Watson and Billie Roy Watson; (2) William Reese Burch who never married; (3) a daughter of Nathan Burch who married Carl H. Daniel and their children are Helen, who married J. L. Scoggins, Lucile who married R. L. Dawkins, and Mary Lizzie who married D. K. Mathews; (4) Coney J. Burch who served his country during the first World War. Coney J. Burch married Miss Ollie Holiday and they are parents of twins, a boy, Doris Burch, and a girl, Dorothy Burch.

WILLIAM GAULDEN BURCH FAMILY

William Gaulden Burch, son of William Burch who was a son of Benjamin, son of Joseph the pioneer, married Clifford Harvill and they were parents of: Nathan H. Burch, Alfred Burch, Essie Burch, Stewart Burch, Pearl Burch, Jewel Burch and Emmie Floy Burch.

CHARLTON O. BURCH FAMILY

Charlton O. Burch was a son of Benjamin, who was a son of Benjamin I. He married Rebecca Cadwell, and they were parents of: Charlton A., Matthew, and Bealer who married Nora Lowery. Bealer Burch and his wife are parents of Rebecca Burch, C. B. Burch, and Gus Burch.

—By Harry Lee Burch.

CAMP

Joseph Camp, the son of Orsamus and Margaret Camp, who came to Georgia from Virginia, was born in Floyd County, Georgia, September 12, 1837. He was an outstanding lawyer and educator, and was at one time on the staff of the Atlanta *Constitution*. His sons and grandsons later followed in his footsteps by also becoming editors and journalists. He and his first wife, Miss Collins, had four children: one child died in infancy; the other three were: Mary Elizabeth, Ida and Felix.

I. Mary Elizabeth Camp, born in Acworth, Georgia, married twice. Children by her first husband, Preston Moring, were: Nettie, Joe, Lillian (all deceased).

Nettie Moring (first wife of G. H. Williams, see Williams genealogy), spent the greater part of her married life in Dublin. She was an A.B. graduate of Monroe College (now Bessie Tift) and was an outstanding state Baptist worker. Her children were: (1) Gladstone Williams, who married Sara Orr. He lives in Washington, D. C., and is a distinguished journalist and Washington correspondent for the Atlanta *Constitution*. (2) Berner, a successful lawyer of Eastman, Georgia, married Frances Geeslin, daughter of Mr. and Mrs. J. W. Geeslin, of Dublin. They have one child, Frances. (3) Hershel (deceased). (4) Antoinnette married Lucius Fuller; one child, Lucius, Jr. Antoinnette later married Edgar Berry.

Mary Elizabeth Camp's children by her marriage to Robert James Williams (see Williams genealogy) were: (1) Ida Belle, who has won state and national recognition as a writer and educator. She is an A.B. graduate of Bessie Tift and A.M. graduate of Johns Hopkins University and University of Georgia, and has held professorships in Cox, Anderson, and Winthrop Colleges. (2) Robbie Jewel (deceased) married James Guyton Sanders of Dublin (see Guyton, Ramsay and Sanders genealogies). (3) Johnnie (deceased). (4) Roscoe (deceased). (5) Mary Leigh (Connell). (6) Felix Carlton, a lawyer, a former State Senator who is highly recognized in his profession. He married Louise Pierce and they have one child, Robert. (7) Louise (deceased). (8). Carolyn (Mrs. B. M. Creech).

II. Ida Camp (deceased), the second daughter of Josephus Camp and his first wife, was one of the earlier graduates of Shorter College. She married Thompson H. Berry of Rome, Georgia, and moved to Shebbyville, Tennessee. Their children were: Ailene, Edgar, and Ida Camp (Mrs. Claude Cunningham of Shebbyville, Tennessee).

III. Felix Camp, the only son by Josephus Camp and his first wife, was a graduate in law of Mercer University at the early age of seventeen, and for forty years practiced law in Atlanta, being recognized as one of the state's best authorities on title law. He married Bessie Barnes and their three children are Edith, Felix, and Harriet.

Colonel Josephus Camp's second wife was Sophronia Palestine Brown, they being married in Swainsboro, January 9, 1870. She was the daughter of Samuel and Nancy Dekle Brown, pioneer citizens of Emanuel County. There were three children by this marriage: Josephus, Ernest, and Robert Earl.

I. Josephus Camp, Jr., a journalist and editor, married Mrs. Eloise Sanders. Their children are: (1) Imogene (Mrs. Joe MaGhee), (2) Genevive (Mrs. Sam Luchese), (3) Joe. They are all residents of Atlanta.

II. Ernest Camp, for more than thirty years one of Georgia's best known newspaper editors and poets, was formerly a resident of Dublin, coming to this city in 1903 as editor of the Dublin *Times*. Here he married a descendant of three early Laurens County families, Irene Sanders, the daughter of Judge James Barnes and Alice Ramsay Sanders (see Sanders, Ramsay and Guyton genealogies). Irene Sanders Camp was a true helpmate to her husband in both his private and his public life and the inspiration of many of his poems. An ideal mother "whose heart was in her home and whose home was in her heart;" of a deeply spiritual nature, sincerity of purpose and exceptional personal charm, she was universally beloved by young and old, by those of high and low estate. Her untimely death on December 10, 1932, bereft the state of a rare and useful citizen. Three children were born to Ernest and Irene Sanders Camp: (1) Ernest Camp, Jr., a columnist of note, now (1941) in the advertising business in New York City; honor graduate and Phi Beta Kappa student of the University of Georgia; married Willie May Aycock of Monroe. (2) Martha Ramsay Camp, now (1941) holding a position with the Internal Revenue Department; Shorter College and University of Georgia; married Harry Power Burns. (3) Sanders Camp, business manager of his father's newspaper; graduate of the Georgia School of Technology; now (1941) First Lieutenant, Battery B, 214th Coast Artillery, Anti-Air Craft, Camp Stewart, Georgia; married Gladys Chambliss.

The second son of Josephus and Sophronia Brown Camp, Ernest Camp, was born in Swainsboro, Georgia, attended the local schools and at the age of 12, entered a Swainsboro printing office. He began writing and publishing his poems at an early age and soon became known as the "Wiregrass Poet." After leaving Dublin Mr. Camp went to Brunswick as editor of the Brunswick *Journal*. Thence to Monroe, Georgia, and in 1906 became editor and publisher of the Walton *Tribune*, which he later purchased. Ernest Camp served two terms, from 1925 to 1927, as President of the Georgia Press Association; was delegate to the National Democratic Conventions of 1912 and 1932; in 1928 and 1936 served as Presidential Elector for the state of Georgia. A number of times Mr. Camp served as a member of the State Democratic Executive Committee. From September, 1930 to 1931, he served as Secretary of the Georgia Tax Re-

JUDGE R. EARL CAMP

vision Association; and for the six years expiring January 1, 1932, was a member of the Board of Trustees of the Georgia State College for Women. He is a Mason, a Shriner, and a Deacon of the First Baptist Church of Monroe. Mr. Camp's poems, stories and sketches have been published in many newspapers and periodicals. In 1924 and 1933 he published brochures of his poems which were most favorably received; more ambitious books were published in 1938 and 1940, bringing him statewide and national commendation.

III. Robert Earl Camp, the youngest son of Josephus and Sophronia Camp, was born in Swainsboro, living there, in Shebbyville, Tennessee, where he attended preparatory school, and in Atlanta, before coming to Dublin to live. He studied law in the offices of the late R. J. Williams in Swainsboro and in the offices of G. H. Williams in Dublin. He was admitted to the Dublin Bar at the age of nineteen years and he achieved the front ranks of his profession at an early age and retained it with recognition throughout the state until he was elected to the bench. He married Augusta Smith, the daughter of Captain Hardy Smith and Ella Douglas Smith (see Douglas and Smith genealogies). Robert Earl Camp was Dublin City Attorney from 1906-1908; Assistant City Court Solicitor from 1908-1912; Lieutenant Colonel on Military Staff of Governor Thomas W. Hardwick, 1921-1925; Judge of Superior Court, Dublin Judicial Circuit, 1925-1933; delegate to National Democratic Convention in San Francisco; delegate to National Democratic Convention in Philadelphia, 1936; member State Democratic Committee 1936-1940; Presidential Elector 1940; recommissioned to Superior Court Bench in 1941.

The children of Judge and Mrs. Robert Earl Camp are: (1) Evelyn Douglas, born in Dublin; Shorter College; married Thomas Howard Newsome of Hawkinsville, Georgia. They have one daughter, Ann Camp Newsome. (2) Mary Adelaide Camp, Brenau College; married John Hightower Mahoney (see Hightower genealogy). (3) Sophie Frances, Georgia State Teachers College and Marsh's Business School; married Frederick Barksdale Gibbs of Washington, D. C. (4) Roselyn Earl, University of Georgia and Abbott School of Fine Arts in Washington, D. C.; married Benjamin Waggner of Wilmington, Delaware.

Sophronia Camp, after her husband, Josephus Camp's death, February 28, 1883, married Charles Smith. There were no children by this marriage. After his death she moved to Dublin, where she spent the remaining twenty-five years of her life with her youngest son, Judge Robert Earl Camp. She died November 7, 1939, at the age of ninety-one.

The compiler of the Camp genealogy is indebted to Henrietta Sanders Freeman (Mrs. E. B.) for the sketch of Ernest Camp and his family.

—By *Mary Camp Mahoney (Mrs. J. H.)*

CHAPPELL

Thomas Chappell, who sailed from Gravesend, England, June 23, 1635, for the colony of Virginia, became the progenitor of this family in America. He was born in 1612 and was the son of Captain John Chappell, master of the "Speedwell."

Thomas Chappell II, son of Thomas Chappell the immigrant, was born in Virginia about 1650. He married Elizabeth, daughter of James Jones, by whom he had four sons: Samuel, Thomas, James, Robert. He died between 1694 and 1700.

Samuel Chappell, son of Thomas Chappell II, and his wife Elizabeth, was born in Virginia about 1680. He married Elizabeth, daughter of John Scott. They had thirteen children.

The ancestor of the Georgia branch is John Chappell, son of Samuel and Elizabeth Scott Chappell. He was born in Virginia in 1738 and had four sons: Thomas, Joseph, John, Benjamin.

Thomas, eldest son of John and Nancy Chappell, was born in Virginia, January 23, 1761. In 1797 married Lavina (Cox) Wheelus, later moving to Twiggs County, Georgia, where he died September 1, 1836, at the age of seventy-five. He had five children: Nancy, Bethena, Mahala, Thomas Simmons, Joseph John.

Joseph John, youngest child of Thomas and Lavina Chappell, was born in Hancock County, Georgia, August 7, 1806; married Mary Hardin Lingo, July 6, 1826; died May 4, 1878. Children: Lucy Mahala, James Thomas, William Harrison, Roxie Saluda, Almedia, Benjamin Thomas, Varilla, Thomas, Allen Elijah, Joseph John.

James Thomas Chappell, second child of Joseph John and Lavina Chappell, was born in Twiggs County, Georgia, September 10, 1830; married Harriet Athalia Stanley (see Stanley history), October 18, 1855. He died December 22, 1899. Children were:

(1) Ira Stanley Chappell, born November 28, 1859; died August 8, 1931. Married Cora Elizabeth Mathis, June 12, 1900. Children: Ira Stanley II, Katharine, Robert, Athalia.

(2) Clifton Thomas Chappell, born October 30, 1862; died March 15, 1926. Married, first, Wilena Sherwood, October 17, 1888. Two sons, Cecil and Sherwood.

(3) Clarence Joseph Chappell, born August 27, 1864; died September 9, 1940. Married Lucia Hardeman, November 17, 1897. Children: Lucia, Clarence, Jr., Isaac, Logan.

(4) Roy James Chappell, born September 21, 1866; died November 22, 1932. Married Mary Warthen, September 18, 1890. Children: Maroy, Warthen, Joseph.

(5) Vance Lingo Chappell, born February 5, 1872. Married, first, Annie Poland. Children of this marriage were James Thomas II, Gladys, Elizabeth, Maggie, Karletta, Annie. Married, second, Mrs. Ida Lillian (Jackson) Spence, January 18, 1925.

—*By Katharine Chappell.*

CHIVERS

Laurens County is my home by adoption. I was born and reared at The Rock, Georgia. (See pages 880-884 Upson County History). With my father, the late Thomas Howard Black, my brother, Emmett Lee Black, I moved to Dublin in June of 1906.

On the 7th day of April, 1909, I was married to Otis Leaston Chivers, son of Mary and William Ramsom Chivers of Harrison, Georgia, Washington County, descendant of the Chivers family of Cambridge, England.

Our children—Otis Leaston, Jr., graduated from Dublin High School, continued his education at Teachers College, Statesboro, and the University of Georgia. Amelia Jeanelle, a graduate of Dublin High School, began her college work at Shorter, later transferred to the University of Georgia, is now Secretary and Treasurer of O. L. Chivers Produce Company. Bonita June finished Dublin High School, now a freshman at G. S. C. W., where she is actively identified with college and campus life. Clyde Black bears her mother's maiden name, is a junior in High School, special interest is music and dramatics, is vice-president of the Georgia Division, Children of Confederacy. Annolene Griffen (Anne Black) named for her great grandmother Black, is a well-rounded student at Dublin Junior High, where she carries an A record in all class work.

My husband, Otis L. Chivers, has been in business in Dublin since October, 1909, when the firm of Black-Chivers opened. On the death of my father, Thomas Black, his interest was bought by the members of the firm, Clyde Black Chivers and Otis L. Chivers, and is now operated as O. L. Chivers Produce Company, with Otis Chivers, Jr., and Jeanelle Chivers, members of the firm.

When the Legislature authorized the writing of County histories, I was appointed by Judge Earl Camp of Superior Court, to write the history of Laurens County. I became a member of the John Laurens D. A. R. Chapter and, learning that research work had been done toward writing a Laurens County history, I resigned my appointment in favor of the organization now publishing the history of Laurens County.

In 1922 Mayor B. Jones appointed me treasurer of the Carnegie Library. At the end of the year I made a financial report to the Council and suggested that each ward in Dublin be represented by a lady, thus creating a new library board of which I was president for a number of years.

I had the pleasure of organizing Dublin's first Parent-Teacher Association at Calhoun Street School in 1922.

Our entire family are members of the First Baptist Church of Dublin, where I teach a Sunday School class of 11-to-13-year-old girls, to which each of my four daughters has belonged.

I belong to the Womans Study Club, local and State U. D. C., and am an honorary life member of the Georgia Division of Children of the Confederacy.
—*By Clyde Black Chivers (Mrs. O. L.)*

CLARK

John Clark, born September 28, 1768, of Scotch descent, came from Ireland and settled in Burke County, Georgia. He married Amelia Sykes and moved to Laurens County. Their children are Nancy, Calfrey, John, Mary Amerinthe, Matthew, Elizabeth, Harlow, Emily, Flournoy, Francis Marion. Francis Marion, youngest son of John and Amelia Clark, married Eleanor Ingram, June 24, 1847. Their children are Eugene, David John, Seth E., Augustus Jenson, Julia, Mary, Luther M., Eleanor, Francis, Early.

Francis Marion Clark died in the Civil War and is buried in Oakland Cemetery, Atlanta, Georgia.

David John Clark served as a Laurens County Representative in the Georgia Legislature in 1905, 1906, 1907, and 1908.

Augustus Jenson Clark served as a Laurens County Representative in the Georgia Legislature in 1888, 1889.

Seth E. Clark married Eliza Crumpton. Their children: Arthur, Fannie, Oscar Eason, Seth Eva.

Arthur Clark married Lula Moye, December 1, 1898. Children: Floy, born August 19, 1899; Alta, born September 9, 1901; Ora, born October 10, 1903; Frank, born December 14, 1905; Clarence, born October 13, 1908; Olen, born January 22, 1917. Floy Clark, first married Griffin Heath, September 16, 1915. They had one child, Ralston, born December 17, 1916. Floy Clark Heath married Talmadge Lowery, February 3, 1922. Their children: Ruby, born September 23, 1923; Christine, born June 3, 1925, died November, 1934; Arthur, born March 23, 1926; Lymon, born October, 1930; Mary Lou, born March, 1932; Dorothy Ann, born January 6, 1936; Betty, born August 23, 1936; Eva Floy, born November 15, 1940. Talmadge Lowery died April 28, 1940. Alta married Charles Hutto, February 1, 1921. Children: Charles, born June 13, 1922; Cyril, born January 3, 1924; Arthur, born October 7, 1926. Frank Clark married Martha Purvis, November 5, 1938. Clarence Clark married Sevenna Brakave, March 21, 1940. Arthur Clark died December 29, 1936.

Fannie Clark married Edward David Ballard, August, 1900. Fannie Clark Ballard died October 5, 1934. Edward David Ballard died October 7, 1922. Their children: Martha Nell, born May 3, 1901; Seth Franklin, born January 14, 1903; Ellen Ingram, born June 17, 1905; Edward David, Jr., born August 16, 1907; Frances Elizabeth, born February 3, 1910; Mary Ann, born September 30,

1912; Ruth, born February 5, 1915; Sara Evelyn, born March 4, 1918. Martha Ballard married Morris Payne Webb, August 17, 1926. Their children: Morris Payne, Jr., born May 26, 1927; Nell, born September 2, 1930, died May 5, 1932; Mary Clark, born May 18, 1933; James David and William Allen, twins, born February 21, 1936. Franklin Ballard married Mauviree Kent Holmes, July 30, 1938. Their child: David Clark, born December 4, 1940. Ellen Ballard married Lucien Emerson Roberts, January 7, 1928. Their child: Lucien Edward, born January 29, 1935. Edward Ballard, Jr., married Evelyn Gay, December 25, 1932. Frances Ballard married William Buna Powell, Jr., June 5, 1933. Their child: William Ballard Powell, born June 21, 1938. Mary Ballard married Charles Pierce Gordon, Jr., June 10, 1938. Evelyn Ballard married Robert Jackson Webb, December 29, 1940.

Oscar Eason Clark married Nora Louisa Proctor, Nevember 23, 1902. Oscar Clark died June 29, 1928. Their children: Opal Eva, born March 23, 1904; Clyde Howard, born October 26, 1906; Ruby Nell, born July 5, 1910. Opal Clark married Joseph W. Thomas, October 1, 1922. Their children: Oscar Edwin, born August 14, 1924; Martha Louise, born January 26, 1927; Charles Wheeler, born September 12, 1939. Clyde Clark married Bessie Lou Posey, March 11, 1927. Their child: James Howard, born January 2, 1930. Ruby Clark married Marion Rogers Stover, December 25, 1927. Their child: Marjorie Nell, born January 1, 1936.

Seth Eva Clark, born February 14, 1880, married James Howard Proctor, June 21, 1905. Seth Eva died February 24, 1930. Their child: Grace, born January 11, 1907. Grace Proctor married Morris Dawson Kea, May 1, 1940.

—*By Grace Proctor Kea (Mrs. Dawson)*

CLARK-McQUAIG

Among the pioneers of Laurens County was John Clark (1768-1827), of Scotch-Irish descent, who came from Ireland to Burke County where he married Amelia Sikes (1785-1844). In early manhood he and his family moved to Laurens County and purchased three thousand acres of land along the Oconee River. On this land was a steamboat landing, Baughnaughclaughbaugh Bluff, famed in the history of Laurens County. One of the eleven children of this union was John Gias Nicholas Freeman Clark (1809-1894). He married Betsy McLendon (1817-1893), daughter of John McLendon and his wife who was a Miss Ward. One son of this union was Flournoy Tyson Clark (1850-1939), who married Sarah Elizabeth Currie (1854-1914), daughter of Malcolm Currie (1834-1906) and Amaryntha Miller (1836-1917), and the granddaughter of Samuel Miller and Amaryntha Cark. One daughter of Sarah Elizabeth Currie and Flournoy Tyson Clark is Emma Eudell Clark, who married Wiliam Thomas McQuaig (1870-1924) of Wheeler County. Their only children were

Nina McQuaig and Clark Menzo McQuaig. After William Thomas McQuaig's death, Emma Clark married Monroe Horace Smith. Nina McQuaig married James Frederick Nelson, son of Alfred Henry Nelson and Lallie Turner. Nina McQuaig and James Frederick Nelson, who is a lawyer, now reside in Dublin.
—By *Nina McQuaig Nelson* (Mrs. J. F.)

CLAXTON

The Claxton family came to Georgia from Edgefield County, South Carolina. The first Claxton who took up residence in Laurens County, Georgia, was Dr. Edward Burton Claxton, who came from Johnson County, Georgia, in 1912.

Edward Burton Claxton was born in Johnson County, Georgia, December 2, 1883, the son of Lorenzo Burton and Isable Allen Claxton.

Lorenzo Burton Claxton and Isable Allen Claxton had six sons and three daughters, viz.: (1) James Luther, (2) Edward Burton, (3) Manning Zachariah, (4) Minnie Bell, (5) Leslie E., (6) Arlie, (7) Ethel, (8) Nolan E., (9) Nell.

EDWARD BURTON CLAXTON, M. D.

Edward Burton Claxton was educated in the schools of Bartow, Georgia; attended the University of Georgia; received his M.D. degree from the Maryland Medical College located in Baltimore in 1905; did post-graduate work at Johns Hopkins University in Baltimore, Maryland, in 1909; at New York Medical College in New York City in 1914, and at Mayo Brothers, Rochester, Minnesota, in 1918. He is a member of the Phi Chi Medical Fraternity. During the World War he served as Medical Member of the Local Board; has served as President of the Laurens County Medical Association, as well as the Twelfth District Medical Society. He has been County Physician, and is Surgeon for the Macon, Dublin & Savannah and the Wrightsville & Tennille Railroads. He is also Federal Physician for the Dublin District.

Dr. Claxton helped to organize the Dublin Sanitarium, the Brigham-Claxton Hospital, and the Claxton Montford Hospital. In 1936-1937, he erected the Claxton Sanitarium, one of the most modern in this part of the country. Edward Burton Claxton also owns and directs extensive farm and dairy interests. He is a member of the First Baptist Church of Dublin, Georgia. He is a Mason, a Shriner and Woodman of the World.

Edward Burton Claxton married Irene Robertson of Nanticoke, Maryland, the daughter of Elias James Robertson and Mary Ellen (Parker) Robertson. Elias James Robertson was born August 17,

EDWARD BURTON CLAXTON, M.D.

1849, in Wicomico County, Maryland, the son of Samuel James Robertson and Ara Jane (Laramore) Robertson. Mary Ellen (Parker) Robertson was born January 22, 1852, in Baltimore, Maryland, the daughter of James Henry Parker and Mary Jane (Williams) Parker.

Elias James Robertson and Mary Ellen (Parker) Robertson, parents of Irene Robertson Claxton, were married May 29, 1873, in Baltimore, Maryland. By the marriage of Edward Burton Claxton to Irene Robertson there were born four children, as follows:

1. Charlotte Iris Claxton, who married Alfred Benjamin Eubanks on December 27, 1936. 2. Ellen Isabel Claxton, who married Dr. John Allen Bell, Jr., on October 25, 1939. 3. Edward Burton Claxton, Jr. 4. Irene Robertson Claxton.

—*By Irene Robertson Claxton (Mrs. E. B.)*

MANNING Z. CLAXTON

Manning Zachariah Claxton, son of Lorenzo Burton and Isabel Allen Claxton, was born in Johnson County, Georgia. In 1913 he came to Dublin and entered the drug business which he continued until entering World War No. 1, in which he served in General Hospital No. 6, Fort McPherson, Georgia.

Returning from the army, M. Z. Claxton resumed his drug business and has been owner and manager of the Claxton Drug Company since 1923. His success in this line of business is evidenced by the fact that in 1941 he was elected State President of the Pharmaceutical Association of Georgia.

M. Z. Claxton has held positions of importance in civic, religious, and fraternal organizations, both locally and in the state. He has served as Post Commander of American Legion, Laurens County Post No. 17; is Past Commander Knights Templar; at present (1941) is Captain General of this organization; Past Patron Eastern Star; Deacon, First Baptist Church of Dublin; Past Moderator Laurens County Baptist Association, now serving as chairman of this body's Executive Committee; for the past six years has been a member of the City Council of Dublin.

M. Z. Claxton married Georgia Lou Whitaker, daughter of James William and Nannie Vickers Whitaker, great-granddaughter of Joshua Walker and great-great-granddaughter of the Revolutionary soldier, Elisha Walker. Two children were born to this union: Georgia Nannette, who has the distinction of having served as mascot to the Eastern Star of Georgia in 1932-1933, and Manning Z. Claxton, Jr.

—*By Georgia Lou Whitaker Claxton (Mrs. M. Z.)*

COCHRAN

For more than half a century the Cochran family has been a prominent one in Laurens County, giving freely of their means and influence toward the upbuilding of the community in religious, educational and business affairs. This family is known far and near for its deeds of charity, and many are they who have been aided and given a start in life by the Cochran father and sons.

Benjamin Franklin Cochran was born in Baker County, Georgia, November 1, 1869, the son of Frank Cochran, Confederate veteran, and Mary Elizabeth Everingham. He attended the Hunter School for boys and later was sent to a military college in Cuthbert, Georgia, for further training.

Mr. Cochran has been engaged in various lines of business; bookkeeping, teaching and railroading being the most important.

In 1892 Mr. Cochran was married to Miss Rebecca Vason, the daughter of Dr. and Mrs. Marcellus E. Vason, of Albany, Georgia.

In December, 1894, Mr. Cochran, with his wife and an infant son, Guy Vason Cochran, moved to Laurens County.

Farming and the growing of livestock has been Mr. Cochran's chief interest. In addition to his homeplace four miles south of Dublin, he has owned and operated several extensive plantations in this state. In later years his interests have been more diversified, including the lumber business and wholesale grocery business. He served as president of Cochran Brothers Company for twenty years, resigning in 1940. His son, Guy Cochran, now holds this responsible position. The four sons of Mr. Cochran have had instilled into their lives, since childhood, the rudiments of this business, and are now carrying on the business with the same measure of success as did their father before them.

B. F. Cochran has served on the board of directors of the Citizens & Southern Bank of Dublin since its organization. He has always been especially interested in his church and has served as chairman of Board of Deacons of First Baptist Church of Dublin for the past ten years. He was also active on the charity committee of this church.

B. F. Cochran was thrice married; first to Rebecca Vason, second to Alberta Vason, third to Mrs. Frances Buchan Woodard.

Children of B. F. and Rebecca Vason Cochran:

I. Guy Vason Cochran, born in Atlanta, married Estoria Woodard, May 8, 1920, and has four children: (1) Martha Anne, born August 20, 1921; (2) Frances Nelle, born January 31, 1923; (3) Eleanor Faye, born January 23, 1931; (4) Benjamin Guy, born April 16, 1933.

II. Frank Cochran, born in Dublin, married Dorothy Perry, June 29, 1921. No children.

III. Louise Cochran, born in Dublin, married Maynard George Combs, June 14, 1922, has four children: (1) Jean Vason, born April 25, 1923; (2) Burke Cochran, born March 29, 1927; (3) Rebecca Adelaide, born January 10, 1929; (4) Doris Louise, born February 25, 1930.

IV. Marcellus Eugene Cochran, born in Dublin, married Hattie Mae Wade, December 26, 1923, and has one foster son, Robert Eugene Cochran, born November 10, 1935.

V. Ruth Cochran, born in Dublin.

VI. Carl Cochran, born in Dublin, married Doris Arnau, January 5, 1925, and has one daughter, Betty Rose Cochran, born June 10, 1934.

VII. Doris Cochran, born in Dublin and died at the age of nineteen.

VIII. Grace Cochran, born in Dublin, and married to Charles Birch Wray, Jr., December 19, 1939; no children.

There are no children of B. F. Cochran by later marriages.

I. Guy Vason Cochran, eldest son, educated in the Dublin Schools, now president of Cochran Brothers Company; chairman of Finance Committee and a deacon of the First Baptist Church; director of Baptist Training Union. Served as deacon in Olivet Baptist Church and instrumental in building the Sunday School rooms, and chairman of building committee of Olivet School. Guy V. Cochran served as Sergeant of 311 Supply Company, Q. M. C., in the World War, from August 1917 to July 5, 1919. He had thirteen months' foreign service and received the decoration for honorable service abroad from U. D. C.

II. Frank Cochran was educated in Dublin Schools; attended Moody Bible Institute in Chicago two years. He received an A.B. degree from Mercer University. After three years he received the T. H. M. degree from the Southern Baptist Theological Seminary in Louisville, Kentucky, and two years later he received the T. H. D. degree, majoring in Greek. He taught Senior Greek at Mercer University for two years. He has had many pastorates, among them being Cochran, Eatonton, and Chickamauga. At present he is serving in the U. S. Army as Chaplain with the rank of First Lieutenant, at Fort Bragg, Fayetteville, North Carolina. Frank Cochran also enlisted as Chaplain in the World War.

III. Marcellus Eugene Cochran, educated in Dublin Schools and attended Mercer University; former member of firm of Cochran Brothers Company; now owner and operator of Blue Ribbon Bakery; runs a chain of independent filling stations; owner of Dublin Live Stock and Commission Company; also operates many farms in this county.

IV. Carl Cochran, educated in Dublin Schools and attended Mercer University. He began his business career in 1920 with Cochran

Brothers Company and has served faithfully in every department for the past twenty years. He is at present an outstanding salesman and is the secretary and treasurer of this corporation.

V. Louise Cochran, eldest daughter, was educated in Dublin Schools and was graduated from Georgia State College for Women in Milledgeville. After teaching one year she was employed in the office of Cochran Brothers Company until she was married to Maynard George Combs, of Rockville Centre, New York. Mr. Combs served during the World War in the U. S. Navy, on the U. S. S. C. 54, Convoy duty, receiving honorable discharge in 1922.

VI. Ruth Cochran, educated in Dublin Schools and was graduated from Georgia State College for Women, Milledgeville. She received a B.S. degree from the University of Georgia, in Athens. She has proved herself an excellent teacher of unusual ability. She has taught in the county and Dublin schools, also in the Florida schools as instructor in Home Economics, History, Science, and Languages. She received her M.A. degree from the University of Georgia, majoring in English. At present she is teaching in West Palm Beach, Florida.

VII. Doris Cochran, educated in Dublin Schools, attended Bessie Tift College. She was graduated with distinction from the Louisville Conservatory of Music. Later, she completed a course in organ and in orchestration. While in Louisville, she also attended the University of Louisville. After teaching a few months, she passed away, the date of her death being November 6, 1926.

VIII. Grace Cochran, youngest daughter, was educated in Dublin Schools. She was graduated from Georgia State College for Women, Milledgeville, and attended University of Georgia. For many years she was employed in the office of Cochran Brothers Company where she proved herself both capable and efficient. She was married to Charles Birch Wray, Jr., of Baltimore, Maryland.

Cochran-Vason-Pearman Lineage

Rebecca Vason, first wife of B. F. Cochran, was born August 29, 1866; died March 29, 1910; daughter of Dr. Marcellus Eugene Vason, a graduate of Princeton University, Princeton, New Jersey, born November 27, 1828, and died December 11, 1896, and his wife, Martha Jane Pearman, a graduate of Bethel College, born January 10, 1847; died May 6, 1931. Dr. Vason was a Confederate veteran, acting as surgeon in General Lee's Division in Virginia.

Martha Jane Pearman was the daughter of Dr. James N. Pearman, born 1823, died January 22, 1847, and his wife, Martha Jane Nothington, born 1827, died January 10, 1847.

Dr. James N. Pearman was the son of Robert Pearman, born July 28, 1783, died after 1827, buried in Madison, Georgia, and his wife, Elizabeth Nothington, also buried in Madison, Georgia.

Robert Pearman was the eldest son of William Pearman, born 1760, died 1817, and his wife, Isabella Weakley, who died after 1817.

William Pearman, who was born in Virginia, lived in this state at the time of the Revolution. He moved to Wilkes County, Georgia, near Washington. He enlisted February 11, 1778, and served as Sergeant in Capt. Phillip Richard Francis Lee's Company, in Capt. John Peyton's Company, and Capt. Valentine Peyton's Company, 3rd Virginia Regiment, commanded by Col. William Heth. He was discharged in February, 1779. The proof of this cited by the Adjutant General in Washington, D. C.

—*By Louise Cochran Combs (Mrs. M. G.)*

COLEMAN

ALFRED TENNYSON COLEMAN

Alfred Tennyson Coleman, M.D., is a true Laurens Countian. Not only he, but his father and grandfather before him were numbered among the prominent and influential citizens of Laurens County. Born and educated in this county, later in 1910, graduating from the Emory Medical School, and in 1919 from the Post Graduate Medical School of New York, Alfred Tennyson Coleman has spent the greater part of his life alleviating the sufferings of humanity; and is today one of the most successful and widely known physicians and surgeons in the state. He is a member of the medical fraternity Chi Zeta Phi; Shriner, member of the American Medical Association, State Medical Association, Sixth District Medical Association, and is president of the Laurens County Medical Society.

Locating in Dublin in 1920, he was soon called to public service and for twenty years served as County Physician, and for four years as City Physician. In 1934 his first privately owned hospital was built; this in 1937 was greatly enlarged to accommodate the many patients from this entire section of the state who constantly sought admission. The Coleman Hospital is one of the handsomest buildings in the city and is recognized as one of the best equipped and most complete hospitals of its size in the state.

Not only along professional lines has Alfred Tennyson Coleman been an asset to his city and county, but he has also used his influence along educational lines, serving efficiently on the City Board of Education in 1939-1940. He, like his father before him, is a land owner on an extensive scale, and owns farms over the county, which he successfully operates. His latest acquisition is historic old "Valdosta," the 3,000 acre home estate of the late Governor George M. Troup, situated east of the Oconee River. The "Coleman Lake" estate, nearer the city, is a private pleasure resort where not only friends of the family, but also large gatherings are delightfully entertained. The lake was constructed in 1938, part of the water being well stocked with fish.

Alfred Tennyson Coleman was twice married; first, to Sarah Jessup, the daughter of Aaron M. Jessup and Matilda Kennington (1889-1921). To this union were born two sons: 1. Alfred Tennyson Coleman, Jr., born 1912, attended Dublin schools and University of Georgia System; journalist and editor of newspapers in Manchester, LaGrange, and Dublin; now (1941) First Lieutenant stationed at Fort Benning, Georgia; married Grace Fowler of Manchester, Georgia. 2. Fred Jessup Coleman, born 1915, B.S. degree from the University of Georgia, M.D. degree, class of 1941, University Medical School, Augusta. Following his interneship at the University Hospital, Augusta, Fred J. Coleman will be associated with his father in the Coleman Hospital, Dublin.

Alfred Tennyson Coleman married, second, on August 9, 1922, Blanche Anthony Davis, daughter of Augustus Swain Davis and Emily Anthony; granddaughter of William Anthony and Isabelle Samples; great granddaughter of James D. Anthony and Emily Baugh of South Carolina; great great granddaughter of Whitfield Anthony, son of Joel Anthony, son of John Anthony, the Revolutionary soldier.

One daughter, Blanche Davis Coleman, was born to Alfred T. and Blanche Davis Coleman, born 1924, now (1941) in her senior year in the Dublin High School; like her mother, she is a talented musician, and leader among the young social contingent of this city.

Previous to her marriage to Alfred T. Coleman, Blanche Anthony Davis was married to Joseph Alfred Rentz, son of Edward Pierce Rentz (see Rentz genealogy) and Katharine Wiles Gaston. There was one daughter by this marriage, Emily Katherine Rentz, who married Albert Flemming Geeslin of Dublin.

COLEMAN GENEALOGY

"The Colemans, a noted Southern family, came from Somersetshire and Gloucestershire, England, and were among the early settlers of Virginia. In Colonial days its members held the rank of gentlemen."

According to family tradition, the Georgia branch of the Coleman family is descended from the Virginia family of this name; members of which held positions of importance in Colonial and Revolutionary days, including one Robert Coleman who was Justice of the Peace in Essex County, Virginia, in 1708; John Coleman who represented Halifax County in 1779-1781; Henry E. Coleman who represented Halifax County, Virginia, in 1789-1790. Alfred Coleman, born 1802, son of Colonel Daniel Coleman (1768-1860) and Ann Page Harrison (1778-1853), was prominent among the early citizens of Virginia.

ALFRED TENNYSON COLEMAN, M.D.

Descendants of this Coleman family locating in Georgia have brought these same high qualities of citizenship which characterized their forefathers in the Old Dominion State. Extensive landholders, they have added to their agricultural interests many positions of public trust, including doctors, writers, statesmen and politicians.

Among the early settlers of Laurens County was William Coleman, who on January 14, 1847, was married to Emily L. Joiner, member of another pioneer county family. To this union were born six children: Henry Clayton, Alfred, William B., John W., Mary and Mamie.

William Coleman married a second time, and by this marriage had several children, but this genealogy will deal exclusively with the descendants of his first marriage, as follows:

Henry Clayton Coleman, eldest son of William and Emily Joiner Coleman, was born in Laurens County, in 1847. He was a large land owner and farmer in the western part of the county, near the Dodge County line. About 1869 he was married to Eucebia Knight, daughter of Greenbury Knight and Sarah M. (Ingram) Knight. Eucebia K. Coleman was born January 9, 1850, and died in 1918. Henry Coleman died in 1921. Children of Henry and Eucebia K. Coleman were William B. (1870-1932), John T. (1872-1896), Robert (1874-1932), Henry Clayton, Jr. (1880-1910), Reese Clinton, Alfred Tennyson, recorded above, Joel A., Isaac Francis, Alvin Alexander, Sara Emily, James M., two sons who died in infancy.

William B. Coleman was Representative from Laurens County from 1912 to 1916; married Latha Dominy. His children were Minnie, Baine, W. Randolph, John, Henry C., Ruth, Corine, Trallis, Zellie.

John T. Coleman died unmarried.

Robert Coleman was County Commissioner of Laurens County, 1914-1915, 1921-1922; married Sara Jane Bedingfield (1874-1917). To this union were born: Celeste, Otis Walter, Mayme, Alfred Henry, Gladys, Letty (Mrs. Walter Walker), Metty (Mrs. Jethro Grinstead), Rubye, and one grandchild, Barbara Jane Grinstead.

Henry Clayton Coleman, Jr., married Georgia Warren, daughter of D. T. Warren. To this union were born Lizzie, Thomas, David, Pauline, Bessie Lee, Offell.

Reese Clinton Coleman, sixth son, formerly a druggist in Dublin, now (1941) holds the responsible position of joint secretary to the State Examining Board in Atlanta. He was president of the Georgia Pharmaceutical Association in 1931 and 1932. While living in Rentz and Cadwell he served as mayor to each town. He married Pearl Moye of Johnson County, and has four children: Reese Clinton, Jr., Samuel Moye, Raeva, Rawson.

Joel A. Coleman is a prominent farmer and leader in the county; married Ella Grinstead; children are Thomas Clinton, Ritha Mae, Prentice, Marion, Roger.

Isaac F. Coleman, well known in political circles, served as Sheriff of Laurens County, 1936-1944; first married, Ada Grinstead, one child of this union, Della Mae; second wife, Winnifred Roache, to whom were born Hardwick, Wynelle, Camp, and Isaac, Jr.

Alvin Alexander Coleman left Dublin in 1918 and lived in Fulton County until 1933 when he returned to Dublin as wholesale distributor for Gulf Refining Company; married 1928, Eula Webb, daughter of Olive Cheney and Leon P. Webb, both descendants of old families in Jackson County, Georgia. Children: Alvin A., Jr., born 1934, Caroline Leon, born 1937. Eula Webb Coleman was the officia typist for the Laurens County history, giving her untiring services for this splendid work.

Sara Emily Coleman married Rufus M. Strozier; two children, Eucebia and Emily Strozier.

James M. Coleman, youngest son, married Pauline Blackshear (see Blackshear genealogy), one son, James M., Jr.

COLEMAN MATERNAL LINEAGE

On their maternal line the Coleman family is descended from another early settler of Laurens County, David Ingram, who married Margaret Rofs about 1816, probably in Jefferson County, Georgia, moving to Laurens County in 1817. They had three sons and three daughters: 1. Eliza, born May 19, 1817; died April 16, 1832. 2. Sarah M., born September 17, 1819. 3. John H., born April 22, 1822. 4. David B., born February 12, 1825. 5. Eleanor, born September 16, 1828. 6. Seth E., born June 16, 1831. Eleanor Ingram is the ancestress of the Clarke family of Laurens County, a member of which is Vallie Wilson, of this city, who has done valuable research on the Ingram and kindred families.

Sara M. Ingram, daughter of David and Margaret Rofs Ingram, married, first, A. H. Hudson and had one son named Hamilton, who was killed in the War Between the States. Sarah M. Ingram married, second, Green B. Knight and had the following children: 1. Mary E., born June 15, 1838. 2. Ferreis E., born March 8, 1840. 3. John S., born February 22, 1842. 4. Elizabeth, unmarried, birth not recorded. 5. Sara E. (Patsy), born March 5, 1944. 6. Robert, date of birth not recorded. 7. —————. 8. Rebecca, born April 9, 1854. 9. Eucebia A., born June 9, 1850. 10. Eugenia Hamilton, born September 5, 1860. 11. Nancy, birth not recorded.

David Ingram died August 9, 1831. Margaret Rofs died October 22, 1852. Both are buried in the old Ingram cemetery, near Dexter, Georgia.

Sarah Ingram and her husband, Green B. Knight, are buried in the Alligood Cemetery, near Dexter. Their tombstones read: "Sarah M., wife of G. B. Knight, born September 17, 1819, died March 11, 1892." "Green B. Knight born March 17, 1798, died October 17, 1904."

John H. and David B. Ingram died in the War Between the States. Eucebia Knight, daughter of Green and Sarah Ingram Knight, was married to Henry Coleman of this county and died in 1918. Henry Coleman, her husband, died in 1921. Both are buried in the Coleman cemetery in Laurens County.

Eleanor Ingram, daughter of David and Margaret Ingram, married Francis Marion Clark on June 24, 1847. They had the following children: 1. Eugenne Clark, born May 1, 1848. 2. David John Clark, born June 14, 1849. 3. Seth Cason Clark, born November 2, 1850. 4. Augustus Brinson Clark, born September 14, 1852. 5. Julia Clark, born March 19, 1854. 6. Luther Monroe Clark, born June 21, 1858. 7. Mary Lupino Clark, born April 8, 1856. 8. Eleanor, born September 21, 1859. 9. Francis Marion Clark, Jr., born June 18, 1861. 10. Early Clark, born April 5, 1864.

—By Blanche Davis Coleman (Mrs. A. T.)

CURRELL

Sarah Wallace, a descendant of Sir William Wallace of Scotland, married a Douglass of Virginia. Frederick Roberts (1757-1828), married Angelina Douglass. He fought in the Revolutionary War and received a grant of land in Burke County, Georgia, in 1784. He later moved to Dublin in 1804. Buried in Dublin.

Children: Angelina Roberts married Shadrack Dukes; Christiana married Hansell Harrison; Martha married, first, James Webb, second, Wright Sheffield; Sarah married Wm. Seward; Daniel married Elizabeth Carey; Mary married Alfred Thompson; Hansell never married.

Daniel Roberts was a member of one of the oldest school boards in Laurens County, was the father of Judge David Roberts of Eastman, and father of Fred Roberts for whom the Fred Roberts Hotel is named.

Martha Roberts married James Webb, an Englishman, in 1803. Their daughter, Elizabeth, married Henry Candler Fuqua, Sr., in 1824. Children: Mary Jane and Henry Candler, Jr.

Henry C. Fuqua, Sr., settled in Laurens County when Dublin was called Sand Bar. The home in which he reared most of his children is still standing. It is 112 years old, located on Bellevue Road. Five generations of this family are buried in the old cemetery.

Mary Jane Fuqua (1826-1889) married George Currell, Sr. (1819-1893) in 1841. Both are buried in old cemetery, Dublin. Children: Henry Currell, married Mollie Rogers; Margaret, married John Palmer; Thomas, unmarried; Mary Jane (Minkie), married W. B. F. Daniel; George, Jr., married Anna Rebecca Hamilton; William Lowther, married Evie Smith; James Andrew, married Belle Murray; Lula and Spencer died young.

George Currell, Sr., a pioneer citizen, merchant, planter, slave holder, Sheriff, one of the charter members of Masonic Lodge, was a leader in all things that helped in the growth of Dublin, socially, financially, religiously, as well as a promoter of educational activities.

Henry Currell, eldest son, fought in the Confederacy under General Lee and was with him when he surrendered at Appomatox Court House. He taught school in the rural districts.

Margaret Currell married John Palmer; children: Martha Luttrell, single; George Currell married Eva Moore; Samuel Bell married Elizabeth Harris.

Mary J. Currell married W. B. F. Daniel; children: Mary Jenny, married Rowell Manche Stanley; George Currell, married Nora Page.

George Currell, Jr., married Anna Rebecca Hamilton; children: Tinnie, Kathleen, Palmer, George II, all single.

William Lowther Currell married Evie Smith; children: Lula, married Francis Joiner; Ola, married Fisher Thomas; Jane, married Joe Harrison; Evaline, married Richard Travis; Ira, married Bertha Newton.

James A. Currell, married Belle Murray; children: Clara Belle, married Benjamin Buckner; Mabel, married W. T. Mixon; Lillie, Pearl, Randall, all single.

George Currell, Jr., and J. A. Currell, excellent bookkeepers, reared families in Dublin. W. L. Currell, merchant, reared family in Dexter, Georgia.

George Currell Palmer is Judge of Chattahoochee Circuit. Children: Wm. Randolph, married, first, Isabel Armour, second, Sarah Moore; Sue, married a Lieut.-Col., U. S. A., John B. Anderson.

Wm. Randolph Palmer, great grandson; children: George Currell, and Martin Armour Palmer, great, great grandsons of George Currell, Sr.

Youngest descendants living in Dublin are Wilbur Currell, Joseph Benjamin, Mary Jean, and Alice Reese Stanley, children of Mrs. Jennie Daniel Stanley.

—*By Jennie Daniel Stanley (Mrs. R. M.)*

DANIEL

Benjamin Daniel was a soldier in the Revolutionary War and received a certificate of service in the American Revolution, filed in the office of Secretary of State. His bounty surveys were 287½ acres of land in Washington County (1784), certified by Captain B. F. Johnson.

He (Benjamin) and Lucy Daniel were the parents of James (1818) who married Polly Armstrong; William (1823) married Tabithia Ricks; Polly married John McDaniel; Patsy married Benjamin

Brantley, grandparents of ex-Congressman William G. Brantley of Blackshear, Georgia.

John Daniel (1799-1883), married Elizabeth Hudson in 1828. Children: John B., married Fannie Scarborough; Lott M., married Jane Darsey; Eliza, married Leroy Hudson; James F., married Helen McGregor; Martha (Patsy), married Robert A. Robinson; Lucretia, married Thomas Scarborough; Rebecca, married Washington Thomas; William B. F., married, first, Edith Ryals McLendon, widow (1864), second, Martha E. (Mat) Robinson (1873), daughter of Honorable Robert Robinson and Rachel Fuqua, third, Mary J. Currell (1888), daughter of George Currell and Mary Fuqua.

All four of John Daniel's sons fought in the Civil War. Lott died on his way home and was buried at sea. William B. F. Daniel (1837-1916), buried in the Old Cemetery in Dublin, Georgia, served as First Lieutenant, Company B, 57th Georgia Regiment, during the Civil War and was in the siege of Vicksburg, Mississippi, was a prosperous planter and merchant, and also operated a cotton warehouse in Dublin for several years. He was a Mason, an upright, religious man and always stood for the growth and improvement of the community in which he lived. He reared twelve sons and daughters at his country home near Garretta and in Dublin. Children, first marriage: James Franklin (dec'd), married Lupiny Moore; John Ryals, married Emma Currie; Virgil Henry (dec'd), married first, Amanda Barron, second, Annie Jackson; Joseph Judson, married Margaret Dunham; William Childs, married Ophelia Harville. Children by second marriage: Belle Tallulah, married Michael Durward Burch; Sudie Machel (deceased), married Green William Beall. Sudie is buried at Bethel Baptist Church in Wilkinson County. Lota Urania, Erastus Stokes, and Mattie Elizabeth (all deceased) never married and are buried in Old Cemetery, Dublin, Georgia. Children by third marriage: Mary Jennie Daniel, married Rowell Manche Stanley; George Currell Daniel, married Nora Page.

There are twenty-seven grandchildren, a number of great grandchildren, and several great-great grandchildren. Only two grandchildren of the second marriage: Mattilu Burch, married Joseph Ernest Brown, Dublin, Georgia, and Mattie Will Beal, single, Wlikinson County, Georgia.

There are quite a number of descendants still living in Laurens County and elsewhere in Georgia who are prominent and prosperous citizens.

—*By Belle Daniel Burch (Mrs. M. D.)*

DANIELL

Robert Daniell, born in Scotland, 1646, sailed from Barbados on boat "Peggy Snow," 1697, was appointed Colonial Governor of South Carolina April 15, 1716. Married Martha Wainwright, died May 17,

1718; Issue, John, born March 29, 1717, married Sarah Raven, January 23, 1736; Issue, Stephen Beadon, Revolutionary soldier, born 1745, died 1820, married Rebecca Howe, 1769; Issue, George W., born April 5, 1782; died August 20, 1845; married Mary Gonto June 25, 1807, who died June 1, 1835.

George W. Daniell moved with his family from Onslow County, North Carolina to Laurens County in 1808, was a soldier of the War of 1812, drew land in Cherokee Land Lottery. His name appears in the 1820 Census of Laurens County as planter; buried three miles East of Dublin near Wrightsville & Tennille Railroad. Children: David Gonto, noted Baptist minister (Ref. Book on McCall-Tidwell Families); Nancy, married John Graham (see Graham genealogy); William, Amos Love, Samuel Hankins, Eliza D., Margaret, Benjamin Franklin, George M., Mary Jane, Fanny, and Robert Howe.

Samuel Hankins Daniell, born April 17, 1816; died 1881; married January 26, 1845, Elizabeth Gwinnette Swinson, born September 15, 1821. Children: George W., Starkey A., Samuel F., Margaret, David Judson, Mary, Joseph Blackshear, Sarah Elizabeth, Queen Leah and Jefferson Davis, twins.

Joseph Blackshear Daniell, born March 16, 1851; married September 9, 1886, Rachel Mae Duggan, born July 4, 1862; children: Lizzie Mae, born 1887; died 1905; married John A. Chaldler; Irene, born October 3, 1888; married December 27, 1910, Coleman D. Bailey; Joseph Barrett and Blanche, twins, born September 27, 1891. Blanche, married 1908, George Lee King; Samuel Duggan, born October 1, 1895; Katherine, born July 4, 1904, married R. D. Dill.

Jefferson Davis Daniell, born June 20, 1861; died August 18, 1935; married Emma V. Scarborough, daughter of S. F. and Martha Smith Scarborough; children: E. Talulah, Docia, Tommie Lee, Joseph, Nora Elizabeth, Estelle, William Jefferson, Walter, Lonnie Taylor.

E. Talulah Daniell, married, first, L. P. Lavender, children: Mamie Lee, married H. T. Coleman; Bessie Mae, married Robert L. Johnson; Lula, married Menzo Knight; Lewis Grady, married Ebbie Towson; Gladys, married James Rhodes. Tallulah Daniell, married, second, H. B. Bass; one child, Callie Mae Bass.

Tommie Lee Daniell married R. L. Collins; children: Cora Lee, married Fred White; Dewey, married Debby Evans; David, married Ida Mae McDaniel; Nettie, married Alfred Joiner; Emma Mae, married C. Kiser; Norene, married Ellis Davis; Alton, Edwin.

Nora Elizabeth Daniell married J. M. Warren; children: Max, Delmas, Harley, Hazel.

Estelle Daniell married B. F. Ridley; children: Avis, married Dr. C. R. Yeomans; Julia Grace, married J. N. Baker.

William Jefferson Daniell married Ethel Perkerson; children: Earl Lamar, married Jacquelyn Webb.

Walter Daniell, born April 16, 1896, volunteered in the World War, 1917, Army Serial No. 715759, Sgt. QMC, married April 3, 1921, Rubye Florence Burch, born October 3, 1896, daughter of Berry C. and Florence E. Parish Burch, granddaughter of Confederate veterans, John Burch and Henry Parish. Children: Emma Annette, born October 12, 1922; Jeff Walter, born June 29, 1924; Herman Burch, born May 25, 1929.

Lonnie Taylor Daniell, born 1900, died July 6, 1921, married Pearlie E. Bedingfield, born February 3, 1902; died March 13, 1922. Children: Dorothy, born May 11, 1919, married Talmadge Rawlins; Lonnie Pearl, born January 13, 1922.

—*By Walter Daniell.*

DEESE

In 1895 Dublin and Laurens County gained a valued citizen in the coming to this community of Reuben Frankk Deese. A man of highest integrity, with the courage of his convictions, of sound business judgment, he has given freely of his time and influence to the upbuilding of this locality in religious, educational, and civic affairs.

R. F. Deese has the distinction of having been in business in Dublin for a longer period of time than any Dublin merchant. For forty-five years the R. F. Deese Furniture Company has been in constant operation. His store on Jackson Street and his commodious warehouses carry the largest and most complete stock of furniture of any firm between Macon and Savannah.

An active and influential member of the First Methodist Church, he has served as Steward, Trustee, and Treasurer of the Sunday School for the past twenty-five years. He has also represented educational interests in serving on the City Board of Education for many terms.

Reuben Frank Deese, the son of James Ira and Elizabeth (Miller) Deese, was born in Toomsboro, Georgia, October 12, 1872. After attending the local schools he entered Gordon Institute, Barnesville, Georgia, and later attended the Georgia Military College, Milledgeville, Georgia. Following his completion of a business course at Lexington, Kentucky, in 1895, he came to Dublin to accept a position in the furniture department of the Sam Weichselbaum Company, and in 1896 bought an interest in the business. In December, 1898, this building was destroyed by fire; the following year Mr. Deese built his present store, and has been in business at this location for the past forty-two years. In 1940, when his third son, Thomas Madison Deese, entered into partnership with his father, the name of the firm was changed to R. F. Deese and Son.

On November 24, 1897, R. F. Deese was married to Attie May Freeman, daughter of Thomas Madison and Celia Van Landingham Freeman, of Wilkinson County, Georgia (see Freeman genealogy). To this union were born six children, all of whom were born in Dublin.

I. Attie Florine Deese, B.S. degree from Georgia State College for Women; member of the faculty of the Dublin Public Schools; married on June 11, 1924, George William Barbre (deceased) and has two children: George William and Clara May Barbre.

II. Robert Freeman Deese, A.B. and M.A. degrees from Emory University; Ph.D. degree from Johns Hopkins University; since 1930, Research Chemist with the E. I. duPont de Nemours & Company, Inc., Wilmington, Delaware.

III. James Ira Deese, manager of the Savannah branch of the Simmons Company; attended Georgia School of Technology; married Mary Helen Ivey, of Savannah, on January 2, 1937, and has one daughter, Helen Kay Deese.

IV. Thomas Madison Deese, business partner with his father in the firm, R. F. Deese & Son; married Dorothy Jackson, of Lovett, Georgia, August 27, 1939, and has one daughter, Barbara Jean Deese.

V. Ernest Frank Deese, A.B. and M.A. degrees from University of Georgia; now Research Chemist with the Tennessee Valley Authority; married Mary Keywood Julian, of Tuscumbia, Alabama, on November 13, 1940.

VI. Celia Elizabeth Deese, B.S. degree from Georgia State College for Women, in 1940; married William Tyndall Knox, Jr., March 12, 1941.

—*By Henrietta Sanders Freeman (Mrs. E. B.)*

DONALDSON

In the early Fifties, James Madison Donaldson (1816-1888) came with his wife, the former Sidney Elizabeth Fort, from Screven County, Georgia, settled in Laurens County and engaged in farming. Having been reared under Christian environment, he was converted in his boyhood and served as Chaplain in the Confederate War. In 1864 he was called to the work of the Baptist ministry, ordained at Shady Grove Church and served as its pastor until his death. His life was one of great usefulness. When not engaged in the work of his church he was busy helping organize churches throughout the Mount Vernon Association. The Lord greatly blessed his labors and where churches were instituted under brush arbors, there now stand comfortable buildings. He exemplified the Christian graces of love and humility. Goodness, in his estimation, was more important than greatness. At the time of his death he was serving four churches: New Bethel, where his portrait hangs as a memorial; Jackson, Pleasant Hill (all of Washington County), and Shady Grove near the village, Donaldson, which he settled. His wife, a monument of true Christian womanhood, survived him by a few years. Children: Elizabeth, married John L. Keen; Fanny, married John W. Jackson; Annie, married H. Troup Jones; Emma, died young; William H., married Martha Jane Bush; H. Judson, married Lydia Anne Spell.

William H. (1853-1919), elder son of James Madison and Sidney Elizabeth Donaldson, spent his entire life amidst the scenes and surroundings of his childhood. He engaged in farming on land inherited from his father and was always interested in the upbuilding of the church and community in which he lived. He served as Justice of the Peace for a number of years and at the time of his death was a Deacon and Sunday School teacher at Shady Grove Baptist Church. He is remembered for his kind deeds and thoughtfulness of others. His wife, Martha Jane Bush (1852-1927), was an ideal mother, a Christian character of noble attribute. She was loved by all who knew her and admired for her splendid disposition. Their home was one from which no friend or stranger was ever turned away. Children: Amma, married William J. Daley; Ella, married J. Wesley Hammock; Lizzie, married Davis Wicker; Minnie, never married; Jessie Leola, married William Andrew Brewer, and had one child, William Andrew, Jr.; Blanche, married Henry W. Thompson; Wilma, married David Addison Moorman (see Moorman genealogy); William Hyman, married Janie Pennington; James Henry, married Emma Robertson. Children: Lillian, Glenn, Sanford, Marjorie, Aline, Elaine.

H. Judson (1858-1937), younger son of James Madison and Sidney Elizabeth Donaldson, was a highly respected citizen and endeared himself to all who knew him by his genial manner. He and his wife were members of the Baptist Church. Children: Hattie, Gussie, Herschel, James J., Pink, Clyde, Annie Bell, Joe Benjamin, Evelyn.

—*By Jessie Donaldson Brewer (Mrs. W. A.)*

DREW

John Drew came from North Carolina, died before 1860, married Hulda Teiser Allen (1788-1884). John and Hulda Drew had two children: George Ann, married John N. Miller, and John Stephens (April 22, 1833-September 4, 1912), married Frances Elizabeth Iccles (May 10, 1836-May 8, 1888), in 1856. He volunteered for service during the War Between the States, was sent to make shoes for the Confederate Army. John and Elizabeth Drew had ten children: Laura Florence, married David Jordan Smith; George Ann, married Andrew L. Thigpen; Martha, married John A. Spivey; Elizabeth, married John W. Smith; John Stephens, Jr., married Nancy Elizabeth Smith; Ellavenia, married J. Ira Maddox; Hulda, married Calvin W. Davis; Amanda, married Charlie Wilkes; Kathryn, married Levi Spivey; William Harden (September 6, 1879-January 15, 1888).

John Stephens Drew, Jr. (December 7, 1865-December 21, 1917), married Nancy Eizabeth Smith (September 24, 1870-living), on November 28, 1886. Nancy Elizabeth Smith was the daughter of Joseph Curtis (October 25, 1884-November 1, 1900) and Elizabeth Mason Smith (May 10, 1836-February, 1922), married January 18, 1857. John Stephens Drew, Jr., was for thirty years a steward in the Mt. Zion Methodist Church, serving from the age of 21. He was Justice of the Peace for Oconee District for many years. He was also Road Commissioner for his district for two terms.

Nancy's father, Joseph Curtis Smith, fought as a private through the four years of the War Between the States. John and Nancy had five children: William Harden, married Elizabeth Smith; John Raiford, married Gertrude Harrison; Lollie Serepta, married R. Lanier Graham; Robert E., married Jennie Landrum; Pearl, marired Lelan Daniel Spivey (February 5, 1896-September 29, 1931), on December 7, 1919. There were three children: Alice Lorena, Reba Mazie, and Ellen Florence Spivey. Lelan Spivey was the son of John Jones (June 15, 1857-April 24, 1939) and Alice Sarchett Spivey (January 11, 1871-November 18, 1919), married in 1888; and grandson of Daniel (January 11, 1829-June 3, 1898) and Alsey Graham Spivey (March 8, 1828-1913), married April 30, 1824; also grandson of Thomas Peter (1830-February, 1895) and Margaret Holmes Sarchett; great grandson of Edwin (October 13, 1809-December 17, 1897) and Melinda Jones Holmes (June 13, 1814-October 9, 1897).

John Raiford Drew married Gertrude Harrison August 18, 1907. There were six children: William Stevens, married Dorothy Cloud; Robert Earl, married Rose Korenz; Raiford Lewis, married Gertrude Mooney; Myrtle Lucille, married Oliver Harris; James Richard and Charles Russell. Two granddaughters: Mary Stevens and Judith Ann Drew.

Gertrude Harrison Drew was the daughter of William Augustus (December 17, 1845-February 6, 1904) and Demaris Holmes Harrison (1852-June 22, 1931). William Agustus Harrison joined the church in 1859, at New Bethel; licensed to preach March 5, 1878, by Bethlehem Church, and ordained May 14, 1882. Gertrude was the granddaughter of Reverend L. J. Harrison (July 17, 1817- September 18, 1876) also of Edwin and Melinda Jones Holmes.

—*By Pearl Drew Spivey (Mrs. L. D.)*

DUGGAN

Isaac Jackson Duggan was the first of the Duggan family to make his home in Laurens County. He was born in Wilkinson County, November 17, 1859, the son of James Barnes and Nancy Jackson Duggan.

Dr. James Barnes Duggan (father of Isaac Jackson Duggan) was born in Washington County, Georgia, November 1, 1833, the son of Archelaus and Elizabeth Walker Duggan. He had four brothers, who were: 1. Ivey Walker, 2. Joseph Franklin, 3. Thomas Green, 4. Benjamin R.

James Barnes Duggan was graduated from the University Medical College in Knoxville, Tennessee. He then located in Wilkinson County. Here he built a home and here all of his children were born. As a physician, he had a large practice and became widely known throughout middle Georgia. He was also an extensive planter. Later, Dr. Duggan moved to Laurens County.

Dr. James Barnes Duggan was interested in all educational and cultural activities and helped to promote these in the county. He subscribed the first hundred dollars to a fund for the establishment of a free public library in Dublin. This offer from Dr. Duggan was the beginning of the movement for a public library and ended with Andrew Carnegie agreeing to donate ten thousand dollars for the erection of the present Carnegie Library Building. An account of this appeared in the Dublin *Courier-Dispatch* of Thursday, April 2, 1903.

Dr. Duggan's home in Laurens County was named "Elmwood" and was located about one-half mile from old Poplar Springs Church. He served as a Major in the Confederate Army, 1861-1865. He died September 29, 1915, and is buried in the Stanley Cemetery, better known as "The Ditch." (see Stanley genealogy).

Dr. James Barnes Duggan was three times married, first to Nancy Jackson, second to Miss Brown, and third to Emma Bass, sister of Elizabeth Bass Stanley, wife of Dr. Ben Stanley of Laurens County.

The last two wives of Dr. Duggan bore him no children, but his first wife, Nancy Jackson, was the mother of all four of his sons. James Barnes Duggan and Nancy Jackson were married at Chamberburg, Alabama, in 1858. Nancy Jackson was born in 1837, the daughter of Isaac and Elizabeth Perkins Jackson of Greene County, Georgia. Nancy Jackson Duggan's grandfather, Henry Jackson, was given 1,280 acres of land for his gallant conduct at Bunker Hill. Her only brother, Robert Houser, born 1829; married (1847) Mary E. Hall, the sister of the mother of Dr. William H. Kilpatrick of Columbia University.

James Barnes and Nancy Jackson Duggan's four sons were as follows: 1. Isaac Jackson, 2. William Lee, 3. James Henry, 4. Paul Franklin.

1. Isaac Jackson Duggan, eldest son of James Barnes and Nancy Jackson Duggan, was born November 17, 1859, and died July 15, 1937. He is buried in the cemetery at Dudley, Georgia, the land for this cemetery having been given to the town by him. When quite a young man Isaac Duggan came from Wilkinson County to Laurens County. Never has this county had a citizen more interested in

education than Isaac Jackson Duggan. He donated the land where the present school buildings of Dudley stand for school purposes. (see History of Dudley). For years he served on the Board of Education here.

Too, Isaac Jackson Duggan loved the church. For many years he served as clerk of old Laurens Hill Baptist Church, and he gave the land on which the Dudley Methodist Church stands. He served the town of Dudley as its first clerk and as mayor.

Isaac Jackson Duggan married Mary Joan Walker, daughter of Joshua Walker (see History of Laurens Hill) and Elsie Louise Dupree Walker. Mary Walker Duggan was born February 10, 1859. Their children are as follows: (1) Jerry Walker, (2) Nancy Pauline, (3) James Archelaus.

I. Jerry Walker Duggan, son of Isaac Jackson and Mary Walker Duggan, married Enda Ballard (see Ballard genealogy).

II. Nancy Pauline Duggan married James Jackson Weaver (deceased) and their children are: (1) James Jackson, who married Leone Pope; they have one son, James Jackson Weaver, Jr.; (2) Mary, who married Theron Arnau Jernigan (see Arnau genealogy), and have one daughter, Joan; (3) Duggan; (4) Jerry (deceased); (5) Palmer; (6) Martha; (7) Paul; (8) Sarah; (9) Alma.

III. James Archelaus Duggan, son of Isaac Jackson and Mary Walker Duggan, married ,first, Alma Stephenson (deceased) of Maplewood, New Jersey, and, second, Rosetta Taylor of South Bend, Indiana. By James Archelaus Duggan's first marriage to Alma Stephenson there were three sons, viz.: (1) George Stephenson, (2) James Jackson, (3) Donn Walker.

Jerry Walker Duggan has served the town of Dudley as clerk, mayor, and councilman, and was secretary-treasurer of the Board fo Education at the time the present school plant was erected. He was postmaster from 1914 to 1918, and from 1936 to present time.

Like his grandfather, James Barnes Duggan, and his uncle, James Henry Duggan, James Archelaus Duggan studied medicine and surgery. After graduating from the Medical College of the University of Maryland and interneing at the University Hospital at Baltimore, he practiced at Towson, Maryland. He later moved to South Bend, Indiana. When the United States entered the World War, he enlisted in the Navy and saw foreign service. At the close of the war he returned to South Bend, where he now resides.

II. William Lee Duggan, second son of James Barnes and Nancy Jackson Duggan, was born November 13, 1862, and died February 5, 1930; is buried in the Masonic Plot in Santa Anna, California, Cemetery. He held "Chair of Greek" at Mercer University, 1889 to 1892. In 1893 entered Life Insurance business in Santa Anna, California; member of $200,000 Club of New York Life Insurance Company; inspector of 8th Arch of Grand Council of Masons, of State of California; president of Board of Education, 1911-1915. He joined Sons of the Revolution, August 29, 1921.

In April, 1899, he married Clara Clyde and they have two daughters: (1) Clara, and (2) Dorothy. 1. Clara, married Roscoe Gulick Hewitt, son of William Lester and Lena Gulick Hewitt. Her children are (1) Helen Elizabeth, and (2) Richard Lee. 2. Dorothy Duggan lives in New York City, not married.

III. Dr. James Henry Duggan, third son of James Barnes and Nancy Jackson Duggan, was born December 14, 1864. He married Edda Stanley, daughter of Dr. Benjamin and Elizabeth Bass Stanley, and their children are: (1) Ivey Walker, (2) Edda Stanley, (3) Kathleen, (4) Nancy Elizabeth, (5) James Henry, (6) Sam McArthur, (7) Charles, (8) Lorenz. (For detailed account see Stanley genealogy). Both Dr. James Henry Duggan and his wife, Edda Stanley Duggan, are buried in the Stanley Cemetery.

IV. Paul Franklin Duggan, fourth son of James Barnes and Nancy Jackson Duggan, was born February 22, 1867. He married Jennie Roberts, daughter of Judge Roberts, of Linton, Georgia. Paul Franklin Duggan was County School Superintendent of Wilkinson County, later moving to Atlanta, where he has been engaged in the contracting and building business.

Nancy Jackson Duggan, wife of James Barnes Duggan, died 1882; buried in Ebenezer churchyard, Wilkinson County.

—*By Enda Ballard Duggan (Mrs. J. W.)*

DUNCAN

Judge John Thomas Duncan was born in Taliaferro County, Georgia, December 7, 1830.

Parents—James Duncan, born in Scotland, July 18, 1798, and Nancy Lancaster, born 1797. Married September 18, 1825. Nancy Lancaster previously married to James Lightfoot; one child, Catherine Lightfoot.

Born of James Duncan and Nancy Lancaster Lightfoot were five children: John, Julia, William, Henry Richard, Mary.

James Duncan died in 1840. Catherine Lightfoot married Francis Thomas of Dublin, Laurens County, May 14, 1846.

In 1849 Mrs. Nancy Lancaster Duncan came to live in Dublin. John, the eldest child, was nineteen years of age. The younger children died in early maturity. All buried in old cemetery in rear of Methodist Church, Dublin. Mrs. Duncan, a Real Daughter of the American Revolution, lies with them.

Richard Henry Duncan was a soldier in the Confederacy, Company H, 14th Georgia Regiment.

Judge Duncan was educated in Hancock County, attending Mount

Zion Academy and the famous school for boys, taught by Richard Malcolm Johnston, the writer. In 1849 he studied law and was admitted to the bar in Dublin. When twenty-one years of age he was elected High Sheriff in Laurens County. From that time until his death he was continuously in office as Judge of Inferior Court, Representative to State Legislature, Clerk of Court, and Ordinary for sixteen years preceding his death.

Of all his manifold fine qualities, Judge Duncan gave unstintingly in behalf of his belowed Laurens County.

It is a matter of interest that, though he presided over three different courts, a decision of his was never reversed in a higher court.

Judge Duncan was married three times.

I. First marriage July 3, 1854, to Sarah Amelia Fuqua, born November 1, 1836; died January 30, 1858. One child: Archibald Thomas, born October 2, 1856; died January 13, 1936. Archibald Thomas married twice, first, to Clara Arnau, 1885; second, to Mrs. Willie Lancaster Sharp Elliott of Warrenton. Children of first marriage: (1) Albert Thomas, born July 10, 1891; died May 7, 1936. Married Agnes Sharp Humphries of Warrenton. (2) Hazel, born August 8, 1894. Married Daniel Johnson, of Thomasville, Georgia. Two children: Albert and a little girl. Children of Albert Thomas and Agnes Humphries: (1) Alice Joan, degree in Home Economics from Georgia State College for Women; finished as dietitian in New York Hospital; is dietitian at hospital in Winston-Salem, North Carolina. (2) William Thomas (Bill) graduated with honors from college at Dahlonega, captain of his company, president of his class; now operates a Dunlop Tire Store.

II. Second marriage, August 21, 1861, to Sarah Elizabeth Stokes, born in Houston County, October 25, 1838, died near Dublin March 7, 1875. One child, Jennie Goulding, born October 30, 1862; died July, 1900. Married Theophilus Henry Overby, February, 1880. Children: Jennie, Duncan, James, Thee, and Robert.

III. Third marriage, November 27, 1875, to Nancy Stokes, born May 15, 1849, in Houston County, died February 21, 1913, in Cordele, Georgia. Children: (1) Mary Elizabeth (called Lizzie May); (2) John Thomas, Jr.

Mary Elizabeth Duncan was graduated from the Dublin High School and the Georgia Normal and Industrial College at Milledgeville. She has taught at intervals in the Dublin Public School system as primary teacher and as teacher of high school English.

On December 18, 1902, she married Wiliam Rufus Lanier, B.S. from Mercer University, Superintendent of Schools in Dublin, Jackson, Cordele and Sparta; now real estate dealer in Dublin and farms in Laurens County. Rufus Lanier is an ordained minister, and though his health does not permit him to accept a regular charge, his efforts for the betterment of Dublin and Laurens County have accomplished great good.

JUDGE JOHN THOMAS DUNCAN

Born of the last named marriage, that of Lizzie May Duncan and Rufus Lanier, are four daughters: Clara Duncan, Elizabeth Lewis, Frances Etheridge, and Virginia Ramsay. All have graduated from the Dublin High School and from the Georgia State College for Women at Milledgeville.

(2) John Thomas Duncan, Jr., married Alice McGehee of Dahlonega. No children. Of brilliant intellect and strong qualifications, John Duncan was head bookkeeper in a large department store when but twenty-one years of age; Superintendent of Dalton Schools for a decade; Superintendent of the large Jones Manufacturing Plant at Canton. His greatest work has been as teacher of a very large Sunday School class for men.

In early married life, Judge Duncan lived in a house which stood on the corner of Jackson and Monroe Streets. During the Civil War near-sightedness incapacitated him for fighting, and he was Clerk of Court and head of Department of Supplies in Laurens County.

After the war, he bought the old Warren-Rowe home about two miles west of Dublin, said to be oldest house of pretentions in or near Dublin. Old and quaint, with eleven rooms, an avenue of elms; a grove of giant oaks; surrounded by vegetable gardens; orchards, a vineyard, and a most beautiful flower garden; this old home was a place of great charm and attractiveness. Here Judge and Mrs. Duncan kept "open house" for many years.

The acres of land were brought to a state of high cultivation. The owner is said to have been far in advance of his times in cultivating his farm lands, experimenting in many modern methods of farming.

He was possibly the first to introduce thorough bred cattle and hogs and to help in their development in the county. He was a large landowner, most of Bellevue Avenue on the south and hundreds of acres toward the south and west being in his possession.

The colored people called him "friend." The lot upon which now stands the First Baptist Church for Negroes was donated by this generous citizen.

That the two children might attend Dublin schools, Judge Duncan built the home on the corner of Bellevue and Duncan Streets. This home is now occupied by his daughter, Elizabeth Duncan Lanier, and family. Mrs. Lanier came here as a child, was married here, and has spent most of her life in the home that was built by her father nearly half a century ago.

The builder of the "new home" spent but one year under its roof. During this year the responsibilities of the Ordinary's office were heavy; the building of County bridge over the Oconee River; building of the new County Jail and other activities. In July, when court was in session, while seemingly well, Judge Duncan was stricken with paralysis. He died within a week, death coming August 3, 1891.

The court house was draped in mourning and resolutions from the Grand Jury declared that "Laurens County had lost her best friend."

The loyal citizen and Christian gentleman was a Mason and a member of the Baptist Church. The funeral was conducted by his life-long friend, Col. W. S. Ramsay, and he was interred with Masonic honors. He is buried in the Old Cemetery under a live oak with his wife, Nancy, and his daughter, Jennie, buried beside him.

—*By Elizabeth Duncan Lanier (Mrs. W. R.)*

ELLINGTON

Joel Franklin Ellington (1846-1916) came to Laurens from Wilkinson County about fifty-five years ago; in 1886, he settled near Blackshear's Ferry, on the Oconee River. He was engaged in the timber business, and although farming was his main interest, he owned and operated a large farm.

He was the son of Simeon Walter Ellington and Asha Jane Fordham; grandson of Benjamin Fordham, Jr., and Elsie Miller; great-grandson of Benjamin Fordham, Sr., of Jones County, North Carolina.

Joel Ellington married Leandie Braswell (Dolly) Duncan; both were devout members of Marvin Methodist Church. They meant much to the community in which they lived; it has been said that Joel Ellington never turned a stranger away from his door, and when there was illness in a family miles around they always sent for "Miss Dolly." He served in the Civil War, Company F, 2nd Georgia Infantry, State Troops Regiment.

Dolly was the daughter of John E. Duncan and Lucinda Wynn. Both Joel and Dolly are buried in Northview Cemetery, Dublin. They reared twelve children to maturity, namely: Anna, married R. A. Johnson; Sally, married Louis Lovick Prescott; John Simeon, married Willie Lee Evans; Beatrice, married D. P. Attaway; Joel Perry, married Dolly Thomas; Celia, married James Albert Attaway; Thomas Cleveland, never married; Ida Lee, married A. W. Dominy; Gussie, married Hendricks Walters; twins, Lillie and Willie, Lillie marrying Zenas Fordham, Willie marrying Joe Kennedy; Flossie Mae, married V. J. Wyatt.

Celia Ellington married James Albert Attaway in 1898, a woman of high Christian character, both were members of Methodist Church. Mr. Attaway, son of Daniel Pervin Attaway, Sr., and Annie Matthews of Burke County, Georgia, was influential in civic and business life of Laurens County, engaged in farming and livestock, dealer in livestock in Dublin the past forty years.

Children: (1) Viola, married Theodore Neal (deceased) in 1922; graduated from Dublin High School; attended Brenau College; Past President Johnson Street P.-T. A.; Past Worthy Matron O. E. S.;

present President of Woman's Society Christian Service, of First Methodist Church, Dublin, and U. D. C. (2) Frances, educated in Dublin Public School, married Theo Parkerson in 1925; an accomiplshed musician; owner and operator of Modern Beauty Shop. Has one daughter, Fay Celia Parkerson. (3) Lloyd, born 1911, died 1940; graduate of Dublin High School and attended G. M. C., Milledgeville. Buried in Northview Cemetery. (4) Ralph, married Elizabeth Kent in 1932; educated in Dublin, attended G. M. C., engaged as agent for the National Life and Accident Insurance Company for years. Elizabeth, his wife, is daughter of Louie Kent and Lillie Culver, granddaughter of Judge J. L. Kent. They have one daughter, Elizabeth Gayle Attaway.

—By Viola Attaway Neal (Mrs. E. T.)

FELDER

Thomas Brailsford Felder, Jr., came to Dublin in 1884, after graduating from University of Georgia Law School. Entering the law office of Colonel John M. Stubbs, as junior partner, he soon was a civic leader serving as mayor of Dublin when a very young man.

He brought his father, his stepmother and their three young children from Burke County, Georgia, to reside in Dublin. Father and son practiced law together.

Thomas, the only child of Thomas Brailsford Felder, Sr., and Clara Lanier Corker, was born October 6, 1865, in Burke County, Georgia. His mother, the daughter of Selena Lanier and Drury Corker, was the granddaughter of Benjamin J. Lanier and "Puggie" Mills Lanier, of Bulloch County, Georgia. His paternal grandparents were Doctor William Felder and Julia Brailsford, of Sumter, South Carolina.

He was married twice, his first wife being Charlotte Johnson, of Greenwood County, Indiana. She died in 1904. There were no children. His second marriage was to Wilson Norfleet, of Memphis, Tennessee. They had one son, Thomas Brailsford Felder, III, who married Betty Rice, of New York State. Thomas Felder, Jr., died March 12, 1926, in Savannah, Georgia, and is buried in Dublin.

Thomas Brailsford Felder, Sr., married twice, his second marriage being to Mary Elizabeth Jones, daughter of Mary Temperance Francis, of Washington County, and Francis Allen Jones, of Burke County, Georgia. Elizabeth was the great granddaughter of Elizabeth Mills, sister of "Puggie" Mills, and James Jones, for whom Jones County is named. James Jones was the son of Francis Jones, of Virginia.

Children of Thomas and Elizabeth Felder are: Mary Elizabeth Felder, who married Andrew William Garrett (see Garrett genealogy); Lula Jones Felder, who married Samuel Harrison Fuller;

William Corker Felder, who married Eleanor Williams, of Texas; Lula Felder Fuller died September 13, 1924, and is buried in Dublin.

Grandchildren of Thomas and Elizabeth Felder are: Charlotte Felder Fuller, wife of Elliott B. Gregory, of New York State; William Harrison (Steve) Fuller, who married Jeanctte Meaders, of Toccoa, Georgia.

Great grandchildren are: Jean Fuller Gregory, Mary Eliabeth Gregory, William Harrison (Steve) Fuller, Jr.

Thomas Felder, Sr., born April 22, 1841; died June 1, 1897, is buried in Augusta, Georgia. Elizabeth, his wife, born November 8, 1849, died October 30, 1912, is buried in Dublin.

The Felders are lineal descendants of Daniel Inman, of Burke County; William Gaynor, William Francis, of Washington County, Georgia; Henry Stroman Felder, Moultries, Brailsfords, Ransoms, and Lawsons, of South Carolina.

For references see International History Great Men of Georgia; Sally's History of South Carolina; Marquis "Who's Who of America," Hardin's History of South Georgia.

—*By Mamie Felder Garrett (Mrs. A. W.)*

FLANDERS

John Flanders, a native of Virginia, a soldier of the Revolution, and a pioneer settler of Georgia, is the progenitor of many of the Johnson and Laurens Counties Flanders families. He was among the earliest settlers of Emanuel County, and while nothing is preserved of his personal history, it is certain that he was a typical pioneer, a man of great courage, great endurance and great strength of character, formed by nature to conquer the savage of the forest and bring under the reign of civilization the inhospitable wildness.

His eldest son, Francis E. Flanders, was born in Emanuel County before that county was divided and the old Flanders homestead was thrown into Johnson County, as was subsequently done. The date of his birth was October 4, 1800. For eighty-five years he lived in the same locality and followed the business of a planter. For many years he was also a prominent minister of the Methodist Church. His first marriage was to Delila Beasley, August 21, 1821. She died shortly and he married Elizabeth Mason, August 26, 1824, daughter of Reverend James Mason of Laurens County (now Johnson) by whom he had six children; namely: Mary Ann, Nancy, Jefferson Tucker, James Washington, Martha C., and John Mason.

The above was taken from the Biographical Souvenir of Georgia and Florida.

Jefferson Tucker Flanders (1837-1903), married November 25, 1858, to Sarah Jane Elizabeth Montford (1840-1916). Children were

Ida (died young); Ella (1864-1897); John, (died young); James Joseph (1869-living); Cornelius, (died unmarried); Thomas Edgar, (1876-1934); Henry Bascom, (died unmarried); and Charles Leven, (1882-1933).

James Joseph Flanders married March 31, 1895, to Florence Leona Deen, (1877-living). Children: Robert Luther, Ella Louise, Norwood Bascom, Annie Elizabeth, James William, Walter Bennett (died in infancy), and Florence Margaret (died at ten years).

Robert Luther Flanders married Elizabeth Boyd. They have two sons, James and Thomas.

Ella Louise Flanders married Clyde Inman Hilburn, son of Octavus Inman and Callendonia Jackson Hilburn, November 8, 1916. They have one son, James Eugene.

Norwood Bascom Flanders married, first, Louise Wilson, March 31, 1924. They have one daughter, Carolyn; married, second, Nettie Hawkinson, February 12, 1938.

Annie Elizabeth Flanders married William Oscar Cate, May 25, 1923.

James William Flanders married Helen Lane Smith, November 6, 1931. They have two children, James William and Betty Lane.

—*The foregoing records of the Hilburn family were compiled by Louise Flanders Hilburn (Mrs. C. I.).*

JAMES WASHINGTON FLANDERS, M.D.

James Washington Flanders, M.D., was born in Laurens County (now Johnson County), July 4, 1839. He was youngest son of Francis E. Flanders, son of John Flanders of Virginia and later of Northampton County, North Carolina, who was a soldier of the Revolutionary War. This family migrated to Burke County, Georgia, a short time after the close of this war, sojourning there for a few months; thence to Jefferson County, Georgia, and from there to what is now the northwestern section of Emanuel County, where a permanent home was established. From that point these descendents spread over this section of Wiregrass Georgia.

Dr. J. W. Flanders, youngest son of Francis E. Flanders, took a pre-medical and practical course under Dr. Lucien Tucker, a prominent physician of the Buckeye District of Laurens, and in 1859 graduated from Oglethorpe Medical College, Savannah, Georgia. After returning to his native county (then a portion of Laurens) he settled down to the practice of his profession. At the outbreak of the War Between the States he enlisted as a surgeon in the Confederate Army for the duration of the war.

On December 8, 1864, Dr. Flanders was married to Sarah Hightower (born September 14, 1848), daughter of Joshua Hightower. After the close of the war he returned to Johnson County and thence after a short period of time to Dublin, Georgia, and back to his native section; thence in 1874 to Wrightsville, Georgia, where he spent the remainder of his life, which came to a close in 1913.

From this marriage were born Eugenia Flanders Perkins, now of Claxton, Georgia; Augustus D. Flanders, deceased; Mary E. Flanders Butterly, of Cochran, Georgia, deceased; Maud Flanders Birch, Atlanta, Georgia; John Wesley Flanders, Laurens County; James Frank Flanders, Dublin, Georgia; Austin Flint Flanders, Wrightsville, Georgia, and Richard N. Flanders, deceased.

As indicated, two of these descendants are now residents of Laurens County: John W. Flanders, who married Mamie Carter, daughter of George W. Carter of this county, whose only son is Fred Flanders. James F. Flanders, a resident of Dublin, Georgia, married Irene Dominick, daughter of George J. Dominick, native of Greensboro, Alabama. To this union were born Dorothy Flanders, James Frank Flanders, Jr., and Marvin Jackson Flanders, all born and reared in Dublin, Georgia.

—By James Frank Flanders.

FORDHAM

The first member of the Fordham family of whom we have record is Benjamin Fordham, I., who was born on November 27, 1743. The name of his wife is unknown; he lived on Great Chinquapin Creek in Jones County, North Carolina, and he and his wife are buried at their old home on or near this creek. They had twelve children, namely: Elizabeth, Tenah, John, Mary, Ann, Leah, Susannah, Martha, Benjamin, Alcy, Caty, and William. Two of these daughters, Mary and Leah, married Stanleys (see Stanley history) and lived in Laurens County.

Benjamin Fordham, II., son of Benjamin Fordham, I., was born May 10, 1784, and died March 19, 1864; his wife, Elsie Miller, was born April 11, 1785, and died July 27, 1863. They were married February 17, 1805. There is a tradition in the family that this Benjamin Fordham crossed the Oconee River on his way to settle in Georgia on January 12, 1812. He settled in Wilkinson County, Georgia. They are buried in the old Fordham cemetery in Wilkinson County. They had twelve children, namely: Frank, Robert, Wiley, Zenus, Selathiel, Benjamin, Olive, Elizabeth, Martha, Elsie, Mary Ann, and Jane.

Benjamin Fordham, III., son of Benjamin Fordham, II., and Elsie Miller Fordham, was born on February 22, 1818, and died February 14, 1900. His wife, Rosa Minton Lord, was born January 17, 1820, and died June 15, 1885. They were married January 22, 1846. This Benjamin Fordham served in the War Between the States and in the Georgia Legislature. They are buried in the old Fordham cemetery in Wilkinson County. They had four children, namely: Robert M., Benjamin H., Joseph M., and Nancy E. Fordham.

Nancy E. Fordham, daughter of Benjamin and Rosa Lord Fordham, married Ira B. Stanley, April, 1883 (see Stanley genealogy), and had four children, namely: Rosa, Roberta, Mala, and Ira B. Stanley.

—*By Rosa Stanley Kellam (Mrs. T. E.)*

DESCENDANTS OF WILLIAM FORDHAM (1791-1874)

William (1791-1874), youngest son of Benjamin Fordham, I., came to Laurens County and bought what is now known as the Knight place, near Poplar Spring Church. He had six children of whom anything is known: Nancy (1809-1884), Penelope, married William Perrien Scarborough; Martin, Hannah, John, Benjamin III (1815-1853), married Caroline Howard.

Benjamin III's children: Matilda, James Martin (1846-1930), married Sarah F. Taylor; William, married Kate Hall; Joseph, married Mollie Perry; Jefferson, married Lucy Pierce.

James Martin Fordham, affectionately known to many as "Cousin Jim," was a man of exemplary character whose influence cannot be estimated. He was a deacon in the Poplar Spring Baptist Church and was superintendent of the Sunday School until his death. His children are: Carrie, married John Anderson Wolfe, son of Judge John B. Wolfe (1892); Anna (1873-1915), married Morgan H. Hobbs (1891); Jennie (1875-1941), married James S. Montford (1898); James Ramsay, married Bessie Lee Cook (1905); Theodosia; Mamie Esther, married Robert H. Roach (1911).

Children of John Anderson and Carrie Fordham Wolfe: Mamie, married John Nathan Cannon; John, married Myrtie Lou Moorman; Arthur, married Mary Brown; Ruth, married Bryant Garner. Grandchildren: Mary Cannon, teacher in Laurens County, married Prof. O. K. Jolly, superintendent of Dexter School for many years; Gussie, married, first, Curtis Chambers, second, James Canady; Miles Anderson Cannon, married Margaret Brown; Claxton Cannon; Oscar Anderson Wolfe, married Mildred Scarborough; James Wolfe, married Alma Register; Myrtie, Esther, Martha, Emory, Charles and Mary Helen Wolfe; Baynard, Rose Ellen, Wendell and James Douglas Garner. Great grandchildren: Dorothy Jolley, William Harold and Miriam Cannon.

For children of Morgan H. and Jennie Fordham Hobbs, see Hobbs genealogy.

Children of James S. and Jennie Fordham Montford· James Henry, married Ruth Colley (191), who has a normal diploma and taught in Laurens County; Clarence Bennett, married Myrtle Green, a teacher in Laurens County; Sallie, who attended Georgia State College for

Women and taught in Laurens County, married Hansley Horne. Grandchildren: Miriam and Nell Montford.

John Fordham served on the County Board of Education for several years, served as Sunday School superintendent, church clerk, and is a deacon in the Poplar Spring Baptist Church. His wife, Emma Hobbs, taught in Laurens County thirteen years before her marriage. Her personality and ability as a teacher have made her a remarkable influence in her community. Their children are: James Abner, graduate of Mercer University, married Carrie Horne; Dorothy, graduate of Bessie Tift and University of Georgia, married Carl K. Nelson, A.B. and LL.B., University of Georgia, city attorney, former county attorney and legislator; John B., B.S. and A.M., University of Georgia, married Rebecca Jones, graduate of Judson; Frances, A.B. Georgia State College for Women, and teacher in Dublin High School.

Children of James Ramsay and Bessie Lee Cook Fordham: Edith, normal diploma from Teacher's College and teacher in County; Charles Eugene, married Clyde Lowery, teacher in Laurens County; Martha, married Mack Strickland; Benjamin Hugh, married Katherine Harper, who attended Wesleyan College; Joel Marcus.

Mamie Esther Fordham married Robert Henry Roach, clerk of Poplar Spring Baptist Church and former Sunday School superintendent. Their children: Robert Henry, Jr., married Corine Minton; Abner Earl, married Minnie Parker. Grandchild: Anne Roach.

William B., third child of Benjamin Fordham III, married Mollie Perry. Children: Agnes, married John Stinson; Elizabeth; Mattie, married West Bennett; Louise, Lee, Clarence D., soldier in Rainbow Division of Expeditionary Army in France during World War where he gave his life.

Jefferson I, fifth child of Benjamin III, married Lucy Pierce. Children: Genia, married Luther Strickland; Bessie, married Walter Burgess; Lonnie; James Ira; Georgia, married Cornelius Jones.

Source of information for the above was largely the Fordham family history, compiled by the late Judge I. S. Chappell and presented by him to James M. Fordham on his eighty-third birthday, May 16, 1929.

—*By Dorothy Fordham Nelson (Mrs. Carl K.)*

FREEMAN

For four generations the Freeman family has been numbered among the influential residents of Wilkinson County, standing prominently in their communities as leaders in the church, the schools and in both agricultural and business pursuits. Members of this family located in Dublin slightly more than forty years ago, bringing these same high qualities of citizenship which have made them valuable assets to the county of Laurens.

On November 24, 1897, Attie May Freeman, daughter of Thomas Madison and Celia Van Landingham Freeman, was married to Reuben Frank Deese, of Dublin, a native of Wilkinson County (see Deese genealogy), and came to make her home in this city, where she has been prominently identified with the civic and religious life of this community. Four sons and two daughters were born to Reuben Frank and Attie Freeman Deese, all of whom are leaders in their various professions:

I. Attie Florine Deese, married George William Barbre (deceased) and has two children: George William Barbre, Jr., and Clara May Barbre.

II. Robert Freeman Deese, of Wilmington, Delaware.

III. James Ira Deese, of Savannah, Georgia, married Helen Ivey and has one daughter, Helen Kay Deese.

IV. Thomas Madison Deese, of Dublin, Georgia, married Dorothy Jackson, and has one daughter, Barbara Jean Deese.

V. Ernest Frank Deese, of Tuscumbia, Alabama, married Mary Keywood Julian.

VI. Celia Elizabeth Deese, married William Tyndall Knox, Jr.

In 1900, Elliott Blount Freeman, son of Thomas Madison and Celia Van Landingham Freeman, located in Dublin, following several years attendance at the Georgia Military College, at Milledgeville, Georgia, and at Gordon Institute at Barnesville, Georgia. Blount Freeman was connected first with the Sam Weichselbaum Company. In 1911 he went into business for himself as senior partner and president of the mercantile firm of Freeman and Walker Company. He is a Methodist and was a charter member of the local Elk Lodge and of the Dublin Country Club. On January 22, 1913, Elliott Blount Freeman was united in marriage to Henrietta Marion Sanders, daughter of Judge James Barnes and Alice Ramsay Sanders, a member of three early county families. (see Sanders, Ramsay and Guyton genealogies). After 1922 Mr. Freeman discontinued his mercantile business and became a traveling salesman.

Henrietta Sanders Freeman (Mrs. E. B.) was born in Dublin and has been a life-long resident of this city, as have been her forefathers for many generations. She is a graduate of the Dublin High School, also a graduate of the Georgia State College for Women, at Milledgeville, Georgia. For five years she was a member of the faculty of the Dublin Public Schools; since 1930 has held the position of Night Librarian of the Dublin Carnegie Library; is active in the work of patriotic societies, both locally and in the state. She is a charter member, ex-Chaper Regent, and Honorary Regent of the John Laurens Chapter D. A. R. and has held three state offices in the D. A. R. organization; is also a member of the Georgia Society of the Colonial

Dames of America. Locally, she is a member of the Oconee Chapter U. D. C., charter member of the Thomas McCall Chapter U. S. D. 1812; member of the Woman's Study Club.

In 1901, Mrs. Thomas Madison Freeman and her youngest son, John Ernest Freeman, came to make their home in Dublin, Mrs. Freeman residing here with her daughter, Mrs. R. F. Deese, until her death in this city, April 17, 1925. Ernest Freeman attended the Dublin High School and later the Southern Business College, at Atlanta. Upon his graduation from the latter he was connected continuously with the First National Bank, of Dublin, for twenty years, as bookkeeper, assistant cashier, and cashier. Ernest Freeman was also secretary and treasurer of the mercantile firm of Freeman and Walker Company.

On October 18, 1917, John Ernest Freeman was married to Gradye Irene Thigpen, daughter of Judge Charles DuBose and Leila Clarke Thigpen, of Sandersville, Georgia. Two children were born to this union: John Ernest Freeman, Jr., and Louise Irene Freeman. Gradye Thigpen Freeman (Mrs. J. E.) is a graduate of the Georgia State College for Woman, at Milledgeville, Georgia, and for several years was a teacher in the Dublin Public Schools. The Ernest Freeman family now (1941) reside in Milledgeville, Georgia, where Mr. Freeman represents the Federal Seed and Loan Company.

Freeman Genealogy

The Freemans were early settlers in Virginia and North Carolina, appearing first in the coastal regions of these states, whither they went from New England. Just when they first came to this country is not definitely known, but it was before 1669, for in that year, in New England, Elizabeth Freeman, sister to William and John Freeman, was married to Robert Harmon.

As time advanced sons of the Freeman family followed the trend southward, first to Virginia, later to the frontier of North Carolina; afterward to other states, until descendants of the brothers, William and John, especially William, are to be found from coast to coast and from the Canadian border to the Rio Grande.

I. William Freeman. First of the Freeman family in North Carolina of whom we have record is William Freeman, who made a will, February 7, 1736, in Chowan County, North Carolina, naming the following heirs: wife, Mary; son, John, married Tabitha ———; son, William, married Miss Christian; son, Thomas; son, Richard, married Ruth ———; son, Aaron; son, Samuel, married Elizabeth Alexander.

II. John Freeman, son of William and Mary Freeman (above), was Justice of the Peace for Bertie County, North Carolina. His will, signed March 30, 1776, probated in that county after 1778, names as heirs: wife, Tabitha; son, William, married Sarah ———;

son, Jacob; son, John; son, Richard; daughter, Zilpha, married ---
Outlaw; daughter, Tabitha married —— Mansfield; daughter, Priscilla, married —— Hinton; daughter, Catharine.

III. William Freeman, son of John and Tabitha Freeman (above), was born in North Carolina, about 1744; enlisted from Surry County, North Carolina, July 20, 1778, in Child's Company, 10th North Carolina Regiment, and thus rendered active service in the American Revolution. William Freeman was a nephew of Samuel Freeman, prominent in Surry County, North Carolina, as member of the General Assembly and incumbent of other offices of trust; who also marched as a private in the ranks.

The will of William Freeman, made in May, 1802, in Surry County, North Carolina, names the following heirs: wife, Sarah; son, Josiah; daughter, Mary (Polly), married Elijah Beverly; daughter, Penelope, married Nathan Hayes; six sons: Tyre, Noah, David, William, born March 10, 1790, married Martha Cole; Richard; John, married Elizabeth Cawley, a native of Lenoir County, North Caroilna.

William Freeman died in 1802, and is buried in Surry County, North Carolina.

IV. John Freeman, son of William and Sarah Freeman (above), was born in North Carolina, March 20, 1796; came to Wilkinson County, Georgia, and there, on July 3, 1822, was married to Elizabeth Cawley, a native of Lenoir County, North Carolina. John Freeman died August 6, 1867, and Elizabeth, his wife, preceded him five years, dying May 25, 1862. Both are buried in the Freeman burial graund, near Ball's Ferry, Wilkinson County, Georgia. Children: John D.; Jacob M.; James H.; Harvey M.; Thomas Madison; Polly, married her cousin, John Freeman; Ann, married Enoch Miller; Miriam, married Ivey L. Davis.

V. Thomas Madison Freeman, son of John and Elizabeth Cawley Freeman (above), was born in Wilkinson County, Georgia, December 9, 1833; became one of the most influential and highly esteemed citizens in his community and one of the largest land owners in this section of the state. A man of highest integrity, and so given to deeds of philanthropy that he won for himself the title, "The Poor Man's Friend." During the War Between the States, Thomas Madison Freeman served as First Lieutenant, Company D, 57th Regiment Georgia Volunteers Infantry, C. S. A.; was captured and exchanged at Vicksburg, Mississippi, 1863; was wounded at New Hope Church, Georgia, May 25, 1864, and was unable to render further service.

Thomas Madison Freeman was twice married, first, on November 12, 1856, to Eliza Nancy Davis (1835-1864), daughter of Oren Davis, and had three children:

I. Leonard Haschal Freeman.

II. Temperance Elizabeth Freeman, died young.

III. Emma Missouri Freeman, married Lawrence A. Duggan and had five children: 1. Joe Duggan, who has a son Roy Duggan; 2. Annie Duggan, who married Homer Hammock and has four children, viz.: Dan, Susie, Earline and Eugenia Hammock; 3. Hugh Duggan married Ruby McLean and has a daughter, Kathryn Duggan, now Mrs. Irvin Mimms; 4. Roy Duggan.

IV. Thomas Elbert Freeman, married Ida Johnson, and had five children: Leonard, Alice, Anne, Ruth, and Kathleen Freeman.

Thomas Madison Freeman married, second, on March 16, 1865, Celia Van Landingham (born September 7, 1842; died April 17, 1925), daughter of William and Elizabeth Dean Van Landingham. Eight children were born to this union:

I. James Lee Freeman married Lada Hooks and had four children: 1. Gertrude Freeman, married Thomas Finney and has one daughter, Eugenia Finney; 2. Lance Freeman, who has one son, J. Lance Freeman, Jr.; 3. Charles T. Freeman; 4. John William Freeman.

II. Loomin Oscar Freeman married Emmie Castellow and has two children: 1. Loomin Oscar Freeman, Jr., of Richmond, Virginia, married Virginia Oliver of Georgetown, South Carolina, and has one son, Bryant Castellow Freeman; 2. Mary Freeman, married Dr. Walker Lewis Curtis, and has one daughter, Mary Emmye Curtis.

III. Lillie Elizabeth Freeman married William Alfred Hall and has four children: 1. Willie May Hall; 2. Murray Hall, married Geraldine Collins and has two children, Clara May and Murray Hall, Jr.; 3. Mary Hall, married Lamar M. Ware and has three children, Lamar, Jr., Betty and Jeannette Ware; 4. Lillie Hall, married John Cottier and has one son, John Cottier, Jr.

IV. William Harvey Freeman married Lorah Branan and has three children: 1. Thomas M. Freeman, married Charlotte Page; 2. Willorene Freeman, married Ross Brock and has one son, Ross Brock, Jr.; 3. Celia Freeman.

V. Attie May Freeman married R. Frank Deese and has six children. (Recorded above).

VI. Clara Freeman married, first, Isaac Oliver Hall and had two children, both of whom died young, Celia Frances and William Hall; married, second, John T. Bush.

VII. Elliott Blount Freeman married Henrietta Marion Sanders. (Recorded above).

VIII. John Ernest Freeman married Gradye Irene Thigpen and has two childred. (Recorded above).

Thomas Madison Freeman died January 26, 1895. He and his second wife, Celia Van Landingham Freeman, are buried in Poplar Springs cemetery, Wilkinson County, Georgia.

The compiler of the Freeman genealogy, Henrietta Sanders Freeman (Mrs. E. B.), is indebted to the late Lily Doyle Dunlap (Mrs. J. M.), State Chairman Genealogical Research Committee, N. C., D. A. R., for the early records of the Freeman family in North Carolina. Other data was obtained from the "History of Wilkinson County, Georgia," by Victor Davidson, and from old Freeman and Deese Bibles in the possession of Mr. and Mrs. R. F. Deese of Dublin, Georgia.

GARRETT

Andrew William Garrett, native of Hancock County, Georgia, chose Dublin and Laurens County as his home when he reached manhood. He began his first business venture with the McRae mercantile establishment.

The son of Herbert Ellison Garrett and Mary Elizabeth Hood, Andrew was born November 10, 1870, at the ancestral Garrett home in Hancock County, near historic Knowles Chapel and Sparta Camp Ground, so famous in Georgia Methodism. He was educated in the Sparta schools and Macon Business College. Reaching the age of twenty-one he came to Laurens County and became a civic and church leader.

He served his banking apprenticeship with the Dublin and Laurens Bank and was active in the organization of the First National Bank of Dublin, serving as its first cashier and later as vice-president. He was a superintendent of the First Methodist Church and a member of the Board of Stewards, organized the Leaders Class of the church school and was the first teacher of the class. He also served as an alderman of the city.

Garretta, a small town near Dublin, bears the Garrett name. The railroad station was located there through Andrew Garrett's efforts and interest.

Andrew Garrett was married to Mamie Lou Culver, daughter of John P. Culver and Martha Frances Strozier, of Sparta, Georgia, January 22, 1902. She was born March 30, 1877, in Hancock County, died November 26, 1906, in Dublin, and is buuried in parta.

Two daughters were born of this union, Mary Elizabeth Garrett and Martha Frances Garrett.

Elizabeth Garrett married Bluford Blount Page (see Page genealogy), of Dublin, December 19, 1923. They have four children: Elizabeth Garrett Page, Bluford Blount Page, Jr., William Garrett Page, Mary Frances Page. They reside in Dublin.

Martha Garrett married Lewis William Turner, son of Fannie Ledbetter Turner and Paul R. Turner, of Cedartown, Polk County, Georgia, May 18, 1930. They reside in Cedartown, where Mr. Turner is May 18, 1930. They reside in Cedartown, where Mr. Turner is resident engineer for the Georgia Highway Department. Mrs. Turner is owner and operator of the Cedartown Credit Exchange, which she organized in January, 1937.

Andrew Garrett married Mary Elizabeth Felder (see Felder genealogy), daughter of Thomas Brailsford Felder and Mary Elizabeth Jones, July 16, 1908, who survives him. She resides at the Garrett home in Dublin.

A sister, Addie Garrett, came from Hancock County to live with her brother, Andrew, in 1906. She married Thomas Benjamin Brantley of Dublin, July 12, 1911. She lives at the Brantley home in Dublin. Andrew Garrett died January 23, 1939, and is buried in Dublin.

—*By Elizabeth Garrett Page (Mrs. B. B.)*

GRAHAM

John Miller Graham was born January 31, 1844, died December 14, 1909. He was a direct descendant of General Robert Howe of Revolutionary fame, and of General Robert Daniell, Colonial Governor of South Carolina, being a great grandson of both these illustrious men.

The family Graham date their lineage to the eighth century, their coat of arms being a cross of the Scotch and English Graham and the Montrose of the nobility at that time.

John Miller Graham was the son of John Graham and Nancy Daniell, the latter the daughter of George W. Daniell, who came from North Carolina to Laurens County, Georgia, the latter part of the 17th century (see Daniell genealogy). David G. Daniell, a son of George and an uncle of John Miller Graham, was a noted Baptist minister of Georgia. He instituted the first Baptist church in Atlanta. He, his wife and daughter constituted three of the seventeen members.

John Miller Graham was reared on a farm and at an early age his father died. At the age of sixteen, with his brother, William, then fourteen, he enlisted in the Confederate Army in the regiment of Colonel Guyton. John M. Graham and his brother "Bill" were in Company "C" of the 57th Georgia Regiment. They both served valiantly and bravely the four years of the War Between the States, both were mustered out at Greensboro, North Carolina, in 1865 after the surrender of Johnson. They returned to their home foot sore and weary, having walked all the way, coming by way of Savannah, where they rested a few days at uncle "David's" who was pastor in Savannah at that time. Upon arriving at their home here, they learned their mother had died only a short time before.

John M. Graham was married to Mary Linder Moorman in 1868. Mary Moorman was a descendant of the Linder and Moorman families, pioneers of Laurens County. These two families were outstanding in the development of Laurens County. Their names will be found as active, progressive citizens in the making of the county in civic, political and religious activities.

Mary Moorman was born November 22, 1844, died October 18, 1916. She was a lady by instinct, something engraved within her, repelled that which even whispered of the ugly and unrefined. A woman of high ideals and strong character, whose influence was far eraching, a lovely Christian.

This couple lived their years, with honor and usefulness, with leadership and distinction. They erected the only monument that will be required to mark the spot on which they were allowed to light for a while, fulfill their mission and be gone again, to be gathered to the Father. Of this couple four daughters survive: Annie, (Mrs. William W. Ward); Ella, (Mrs. Joseph B. Anchors); Daisy, (Mrs. Lester V. Stone); Mary, (Mrs. William T. Simmons). There are six grandchildren: L. V. Stone, Jr. (deceased), John E. Stone, Mary Stone (Mrs. Clifford Welton), Ward Stone, Florence Simmons (Mrs. W. F. Isom), William Simmons. Six great grandchildren: Loyd V. Stone (Pete), son of L. V., Jr.; David Heaton Isom, son of Florence; Mary Jane, Billie, and Florence Ann Simmons, daughters of William; Graham Stone and Virginia Stone, daughters of John.

—*By Annie Graham Ward (Mrs. W. W.)*

GREEN

Jesse Green, private in North Carolina Militia, lost his life for the cause of liberty, in the Revolutionary War. (His name and service can be found in the Roster of Revolutionary Soldiers of North Caroilna by the N. C. D. A. R.). His wife was a Miss Culpepper.

Jesse J. Green, son of Jesse Green of North Carolina, immigrated to Georgia when a lad in his teens, coming in company of an uncle, Henry Culpepper, from South Carolina. Jesse J. Green located on the frontier along the Oconee River and in time grew to be a wealthy planter.

Eason Green, son of Jesse J. Green, was born in Laurens County and spent his life here, as a planter, proving very successful in agriculture. He died in 1878 at the age of 74 years. He married on November 17, 1825, Eliza Weaver, daughter of Jethro Judson Weaver, one of the pioneer settlers of Laurens County, and his first wife, Ann Albritton. (see Weaver History). Eason and Eliza Weaver Green had thirteen children, nine boys and four girls. This family furnished seven volunteers to the Confederate Army, three of whom died in service.

Children of Eason and Eliza Weaver Green:

I. Wade Hampton Green, married Nannie Holliman. Children: 1. Jule, married Bett O'Neal, two sons, Jule and James; 2. Hattie, married Oscar Register, five sons, Otto, Vivian, married Myrtle Smith, two daughters, Betty Anne and Helen; Holt, married Sara Souther; Edgar; Charles; 3. Nannie, married R. B. Register, six children, Thelma, John H., Bernice, Roy, Virginia, Dorothy; 4. Stella, married ——; 5. Edgar, married Elo Taylor, two daughters, Lucile and Myrtle; 6. Custus, married Babe Stuckey.

II. John R. Green, married, first, Clara Perry, second, Mattie Smith; children: Walter, married Mattie Perry; Mae, married Oscar Wright; Ernest, married Mamie Albritton; Joe Brown, married Mattie Belle Gibbs.

III. Jesse J. Green married, first, Susan Stanley, second, Rachel Roach; children: 1. Marion Stanley, married Emma Brack and they had eleven children: Ethel, married Woodfin Ashley; Arthur, married Iris Dixon; Mary; Ruth, married Arthur Hillard; Eugene, married, first, Mira Hanley; Clarence, married Frances Weaver; Prentice, married Mary Lord; Cordie, married Elizabeth Shelnutt; Curtice, married Nina Howell; George, married Lady Mae Lamb; Susie, married Doctor Green Adams, their children are Lois, married Rollin Collie Sheffield, one son Henry Collie Sheffield; Charles Emory; James Cecil; Sidney Claxton, and Willa Jean; 2. Laura, married Robert Rozier, Sr.; 3. Mildred, married William N. Watson; 4. Luther, married Mary Jane Payne; 5. Jefferson, married Dora Carr; 6. Molly, married James Cannon; 7. Marshall, married Sally Cook and their children are: Bernard, married Laura Sanders; Gordon, married Ann Davidson; Felton, married Pearl Ellington; Myrtice, married Homer Stucky; Louise, married Troy Connell; Blanco, married Lovie Arnold; Jesse, married Martha Christian.

IV. Thomas Green.

V. Benjamin C. Green married, first, Polly Cone, no children; married, second, Mattie Harrell, five children: Hezzie, Mary Frances, Mattie Lee, Willie May, Elgie.

VI. Marshall Green married Mary Cannon.

VII. Elliott Green.

VIII. Hassie Green married Joel Smith.

IX. Millie Ann Green married Wylie Lewis Cannon.

X. Laura Green.

XI. Jane Green.

XII. William Eason Green.

XIII. George Franklin Green (1856-1915) was a prominent physician, coming from Wilkinson County to Laurens in 1883, and was an influential citizen until his death here in 1915. In addition to his medical profession he had large farming interests. In 1872 he married Mildred M. Holliman, daughter of Thomas Jefferson and Nancy Spivey Holliman. Six children were born to this union:

1. Bessie Green, married Thomas Davis, two sons: George and Thomas Davis.

2. Thomas H. Green, married Florence McCoy, four children: Mildred, married Robert Pittman Rasberry, one son, Robert P. Rasberry, Jr.; Bertie; Clarence Welborn, married Inez Rountree, two children: Grace and Clarence W. Green, Jr.; Ethel, married Leland Charles Murphree, two children: Leland Jr., and Mary Margaret Murphree.

3. Clarence Green, died in young manhood.

4. Annie Green, married William Wallace Brandon, two daughters, Annie Reid and Agnes Brandon.

5. Agnes Green, married T. S. Martin, four daughters, Mildred, Ann, Bessie and Agnes Martin.

6. Minnie Mae Green, married Newell Green Bartlett, one daughter, Minnetta Bartlett.

—*By Thomas H. Green.*

GUYTON

For more than a century the Guyton family has been a prominent one in Laurens County. In the early 1800's three brothers, natives of Spartanburg District, South Carolina, John, Charles, and Moses Guyton, located here and purchased large holdings in the Buckeye neighborhood. So extensive were the plantations owned by these Guyton brothers that it was necessary for them to own hundreds of slaves for their cultivation; yet so well cared for were the Guyton negroes that even after the Emancipation Proclamation many refused to leave their homes and remained faithful retainers to the Guyton family.

GUYTONS IN FRANCE

(Giton, Guiton, Guton, Guyton)

Of French Huguenot lineage, the Guytons were among the French Protestants who left France seeking religious and political freedom, first in England, later in America.

In Maithol's "Directory of the French Nobility" we find that "the Guyton family originated in Normandie, with one branch establishing its residence in Brittany. The family bore the title of count."

The "Concise History of France"—Guizot-Gustave Masson, records the fact that John Guiton was Burgess of La Rochelle at the time of the siege by Louis XIII, A. D. 1625. On page 353: "The siege of La Rochelle has become famous in history; it lasted thirteen years and the brave Huguenots had to surrender in spite of the heroism of Guiton, the mayor of the town, assisted by the energy of the old Duchess of Robou."

French history also records the fact that one John W. Guiton was one of the Generals who fought in the Battle of Waterloo.

Early Guytons in America

As early as 1669 we find members of the Guyton family living in South Carolina, as in this year the records of the Huguenot Society in Charleston show that Judith Guiton (the widow Royer), was married to Pierre Manigault.

In the first census of the United States of America, 1790, the following are listed as heads of families in 96th District, Union County, South Carolina: Moses Guyton, family of eight; Joseph Guyton, family of seven; Nathaniel Guyton, family of six.

Joseph and Nathaniel Guyton were French Huguenot refugees. The original Nathaniel had four sons: Jacob, Isaac, Nathaniel, and John. This genealogy, however, will deal exclusively with the original Joseph and his descendants. Some say Joseph and Nathaniel landed first in Charleston; other say Baltimore. However as that may be, Joseph and Hannah, his wife, lived at one time in Baltimore, for their son Aaron was born there, October 26, 1761. Soon after his birth the family came to York County, South Carolina, and settled in that part which is now Union County. During the War for American Independence Joseph Guyton, the patriot, furnished horses and supplies for the Continental troops; his sons Aaron and Moses were officers in the Revolutionary War.

Nine children were born to Joseph and Hannah Guyton:

I. Moses Guyton I, born October 27, 1758; died February 18, 1817; married, first, Tabitha Saxon, second, Nancy Cole. Detailed record later.

II. Aaron Guyton, born in Baltimore County, Maryland, October 26, 1761; died June 30, 1841, in Anderson District, South Carolina; soldier in the American Revolution, volunteered in 1779 and served in several companies until "peace was made," for three months as private in Captain Moses Guyton's Company. (Record on file in Veterans Administration, Washington, D. C.). Married in 1789 to Margaret McCurdy, daughter of Robert and Mary Watson McCurdy, and had twelve children: Mary, Hannah, Elizabeth, Katherine, Jane, Robert McCurdy, Joseph, Margaret Watson, Aaron W., Sarah M., John W., and Gite. Joseph (1805-1880), son of Aaron and Margaret McCurdy Guyton, married in 1828, Zemuly Coats McClesky (1811-1882) and had ten children: Martha Margaret, Mary Jane, Aaron Steele, John Whitaker, David Thomas, Harriet Louise, Robert Alfred, Sarah Elizabeth, Zemuly Matilda, Joseph William Southerland. David Thomas Guyton, son of Joseph and Zemuly McClesky Guyton, was born near Gainesville, Georgia, January 29, 1838; moved with his father and family to Mississippi in 1844 and settled in Attala County; married, on November 14, 1867, Sarah Susannah Ellington, and had nine children: Mary Lura, Zemuly Harriet, Robert Steele, Alice Dent, Thomas Percy, Joseph Daniel, Whitaker Fleming, Sarah Josephine Pearle, and Grady. David Thomas Guyton died in Kusciusko,

Mississippi, January 20, 1911. Thomas Percy Guyton, son of David Thomas and Sarah Ellington Guyton, was born in Attala County, Mississippi, January 11, 1877, has held many eminent positions of public trust in his state, and is one of Mississippi's most honored and influential citizens and jurists; at present (1941) he is Chancellor, Sixth District, Mississippi. In the Spanish-American War he served as Sergeant, Company K, 1st Mississippi Volunteer Infantry. On June 18, 1902, he was married to Annie Dicie Love, daughter of David F. and Callie Fleming Love, and has six children: David Thomas, Percy Love, Earl Ellington, Fred Fleming, Annie Ruth, and Sarah Dicie.

II. Abraham Guyton, born 1765; died February, 1815; married Patsy Ellis and had a large family of boys and girls. His descendants are scattered, some of whom live in north Mississippi, near Blue Mountain. They are highly educated and very superior citizens. One of these, Dr. David E. Guyton has been blind for years but graduated at Columbia University after losing his sight and is now Professor of History and Economics at Blue Mountain College, Mississippi. *The New York Sun* gave a full page write up of Dr. David E. Guyton and Helen Keller, the blind girl. Dr. David E. Guyton has gained a wide reputation as a scholar, educator, poet, orator, journalist, financier and economist. He is at present president of the Blue Mountain Bank. Another descendant is Dr. B. S. Guyton, of Oxford, Mississippi, a prominent doctor, surgeon, and Dean of the Medical College at the University of Mississippi.

IV. Joseph Guyton, born 1776, died 1865; had eight children: Isaac, who died in Texas; Abraham and Isaiah, who died in Pickens County, Alabama; Whitaker and John, who died probably in Alabama; three girls.

V. John Guyton, killed in the Indian Wars.

VI. Mary Guyton married Jonathan Smith.

VII. Hannah Guyton married Alexander Martin.

VIII. Elizabeth Guyton married Isaac Parker.

IX. A daughter married Abraham Smith.

Joseph Guyton I and Hannah, his wife, died and are buried in Union County, South Carolina. Joseph died in 1818, his wife's death evidently preceding his since she is not mentioned in his will.

The will of Joseph Guyton, recorded in Will Book D, Union County, South Carolina, signed May 26, 1818, probated August 3, 1818, names the following heirs: son, Joseph; son, Aaron; children of son, Moses, deceased; three daughters of son, Moses, deceased, viz.: Hannah Fondrin, Sallie Guyton, Tabitha Guyton; children of daughter, Betsy Parker, deceased; two daughters, Molly Smith and Hannah Martin; grandson Abraham Guyton, son of Joseph; executors: son, Joseph Guyton and son-in-law, Alexander Martin.

DESCENDANTS OF MOSES GUYTON I. (1758-1817)

Moses Guyton I, eldest son of Joseph and Hannah Guyton, was born October 27, 1758. In 1782 he married Tabitha Saxon, of Spartanburg, South Carolina, daughter of Captain Charles Saxon (1743-1808) and his wife, Mary. Charles Saxon held the rank of Captain in the Continental Army during the American Revolution. Tabitha Saxon, wife of Moses Guyton I, was born in Spartanburg, December 10, 1764; died in Charleston, February 10, 1811. Moses Guyton I, died in Charleston, February 18, 1817. (National Archives R-4-400). Moses Guyton was a Revolutionary soldier with rank of Lieutenant of Cavalry, in Captain Robert Montgomery's Company. Colonel Thomas Brandon's Regiment.

The children of Moses Guyton I, and Tabitha Saxon Guyton were:

I. John, born February 5, 1784, married Henrietta Bostwick, December 12, 1810.

II. Judith, born March 22, 1786, married —— Jewett.

III. Hannah, born June 29, 1788, married Matthew Fondrin.

IV. Mary, born April 4, 1791.

V. Charles Saxon, born September 6, 1793, married Elmina Horn.

VI. Joseph, born September 12, 1795.

VII. Sarah, born August 21, 1797.

VIII. Moses II, born September 4, 1799, married Mary Ann Love.

IX. Tabitha, born August 11, 1801, married —— Coleman.

X. Elizabeth, born November 22, 1804.

Moses Guyton married, second, Nancy Cole, daughter of Thomas Cole, December 1814, in Spartanburg District, South Carolina. Nancy Cole Guyton died in March, 1856. (National Archives R-4-400).

JOHN GUYTON (1784-1826)

John, eldest son of Moses I, and Tabitha Saxon Guyton, was born in Spartanburg District, South Carolina, February 5, 1784, came to Laurens County, Georgia, in early manhood, and acquired considerable wealth, some of which came through his first marriage (December 12, 1810) to Henrietta Jane Bostwick, daughter of the illustrious statesman and patriot, Chesley Bostwick, Esq., and wife, Jane Gervais (Jarvis) Bostwick of Augusta.

Chesley Bostwick (1741-1806), father of Henrietta Bostwick Guyton, was appointed Captain 1st Georgia Regiment, January 7, 1776, and rendered distinguished service both in the Colonial Army, and in the Continental Army during the American Revolution. Henrietta Bostwick's grandparents were John (1720-after 1795) and Elizabeth (Chesley) Bostwick, natives of Virginia. John Guyton also held the rank of Captain of a North Carolina Regiment in 1783.

John Guyton served as Justice of the Inferior Court, Laurens

County, February 26, 1821-January 15, 1825. He died in Macon, Georgia, October 22, 1826.

John and Henrietta Bostwick Guyton had two sons:

I. Charles Brutus Guyton, M.D., born November 17, 1812; died May 16, 1857; married Lupina Horn (see Horn genealogy) and had one child who died in infancy; postmaster, Dublin, 1836; member of the House of Representatives from Laurens County, 1841-1843, 1855-1856; represented Laurens County in the State Convention, 1850; Senator from Laurens County, 1853-1854; charter member Laurens County Masonic Lodge, served as Worshipful Master from 1850 to 1857.

II. Thomas Northrop Guyton, born February 12, 1814; married Elvira Leonora Dasher; died November 9, 1857. (Detailed record later).

Henrietta Bostwick, first wife of John Guyton, was born in Augusta December 26, 1791; died in Dublin, April 17, 1822. John Guyton later married Ann Davis and had one daughter, Tabitha Ann Guyton, born November 5, 1825, who married Sidney Pughsley, and had one daughter, Ella Pughsley, who married Frank Hopkins and had two children, viz.: Frank Hopkins, Jr., and Nora Hopkins, who married Thomas A. Wicker, of Washington County, Georgia.

THOMAS NORTHROP GUYTON (1814-1857)

Thomas Northrop Guyton, son of John and Henrietta Bostwick Guyton, was born in Laurens County, February 12, 1814, and was married on October 17, 1837, to Elvira Leonora Dasher (born November 4, 1823-died November 6, 1869), of Savannah, daughter of Solomon (1791-1854) and Maria Wylly Dasher (born 1796-died 1851-married February 8, 1813); and granddaughter of Captain John Martin Dasher (1738-1812) and his first wife Elizabeth (born 1750-died 1791-married 1772). John Martin Dasher served as Second Lieutenant in the American Revolution. Elvira Dasher Guyton's maternal grandparents were Captain Thomas Wylly (1762-1846) and his wife, Naomi Rosenburg (born September 13, 1770). Thomas Wylly served as Lieutenant, Assistant Quartermaster and Captain in the American Revolution. Elvira Dasher Guyton's maternal great-grandparents were William and Mary Wylly of Savannah; William Wylly received the Colonial appointment of Commissioner of Roads in the first N. W. District, September 29, 1773.

The spacious Colonial residence of Thomas N. Guyton stood on the present site of the old Dublin Post Office building and here many prominent guests were entertained. In addition to his plantations on the east side of the Oconee River he owned a large sheep ranch and a mercantile establishment. He was a charter member of the Masonic Lodge of Laurens County; for six years, from 1849 to 1855, was Senior Warden.

Thomas N. and his wife, Elvira Guyton, are buried in the Guyton lot in the "Old Cemetery" at Dublin. Thomas N. Guyton died November 9, 1857, and his wife, Elvira, died November 6, 1869.

Thomas N. and Elvira Dasher Guyton had five children:

I. Thornton Wylly, born August 31, 1840; died November 27, 1840.

II. Henrietta Jane, born December 3, 1841, married Whiteford S. Ramsay (1839-1900) (see Ramsay genealogy); died in Dublin, August 10, 1916; buried in "Old Cemetery," Dublin.

III. Mary Ann, born October 1, 1843; died July 16, 1846.

IV. John, born May 18, 1846; died October 30, 1851.

V. Clara, born August 10, 1848, married Edwin J. Williams of Atlanta; no children; died November 1, 1918, and is buried in the "Old Cemetery," Dublin. No member of the Guyton family has ever been more generally beloved than Clara Guyton Williams; of magnetic personality, she numbered her friends by her acquaintances.

HENRIETTA GUYTON RAMSAY (1841-1916)

Henrietta Jane, daughter of Thomas N. and Elvira Dasher Guyton, was born in Dublin December 3, 1841, and spent her entire life in this city, with the exception of three years' residence in Cave Springs, Georgia. Henrietta Guyton Ramsay was a woman of rare beauty, culture and accomplishment, receiving her education through private tutors and at the old Masonic College for Young Ladies at Covington, Georgia. On December 15, 1858, she was married to Whiteford S. Ramsay (see Ramsay genealogy) and reared a family who have lived up to the traditions bequeathed them by a long line of distinguished ancestors.

Whiteford S. Ramsay died March 4, 1900; Henrietta Guyton Ramsay died August 10, 1916. Both are buried in the "Old Cemetery," Dublin.

Children of Whiteford S. and Henrietta Guyton Ramsay:

I. and II. Ida and Elbert Ramsay died young.

III. Martha Bass Ramsay.

IV. Alice Viola Ramsay, married James Barnes Sanders (see Sanders genealogy) and had four children: 1. Henrietta Marion Sanders, married Elliott Blount Freeman; 2. Irene Natalie Sanders, married Ernest Camp and had three children: (1) Ernest Camp, Jr., married Willie May Aycock, (2) Martha Ramsay Camp, married Harry Power Burns, (3) Lieut. Sanders Camp, married Gladys Chambliss; 3. James Guyton Sanders, married Robbie Jewel Williams (see Williams genealogy); 4. Randolph Ramsay Sanders, married, first, May Corker, second, Jean Mason.

V. Tallulah Corinne Ramsay, married Lucien Quincy Stubbs (see Stubbs genealogy) and had six children, the first three of whom died young; 1. Clara Guyton Stubbs; 2. John Madison Stubbs; 3. Ella Ophelia Stubbs; 4. Jeannette Ramsay Stubbs, married James Davis Glover and has four children: (1) Corinne Ramsay Glover, (2) James Glover, Jr., (3) Marthalu Glover, (4) Julia Allaphair Glover; 5. Robert Flournoy Stubbs; 6. Lucien Quincy Stubbs, Jr.

VI. Mary Guyton Ramsay.

VII. Thomas Randolph Ramsay, married Lil Frances Hightower (see Hightower genealogy).

VIII. Virginia Augusta Ramsay, married John Middleton Simmons (see Simmons genealogy) and has four sons: 1. Jack Whiteford Simmons, married Sarah Scott and has four children, viz.: (1) Virginia Simmons, (2) Jack Whiteford Simmons, Jr., (3) Mary Edna Simmons, (4) Sarah Marie Simmons; 2. David Ramsay Simmons, married Ellen Carswell and has three children, viz.: (1) Virginia Claire Simmons, (2) David Ramsay Simmons, Jr., (3) John Middleton Simmons III.; 3. Thomas Randolph Simmons, married Elizabeth Burney and has two daughters, Sara Elizabeth and Virginia Ruth Simmons; 4. William Pinckney Simmons, married Betty Sweet Smith and has one son, William Pinckney Simmons, Jr.

DESCENDANTS OF CHARLES SAXON GUYTON (1793-1848)

Charles Saxon Guyton, second son of Moses I. and Tabitha Saxon Guyton, was born in Spartanburg District, South Carolina, September 6, 1793; located in Laurens County, Georgia, in 1815, and was an honored resident of this county, where he died December 3, 1848. A man of highest integrity and ability, he acquired wealth and owned large plantations in the Buckeye settlement, some of which are still in the possession of his grandchildren. Charles Saxon Guyton was a member of the House of Representatives from Laurens County in 1838 and represented his county in the State Convention of 1839. On June 29, 1830, he married Elmina Horn, daughter of Josiah and Rebecca Young Horn, of another pioneer county family (see Horn genealogy) and had four children:

I. Cincinnatus Saxon Guyton, born December 2, 1834. (Detailed record later).

II. Moses Josiah Guyton, born March 31, 1845; died August 31, 1879; married Babe Fisher; no children.

III. Louise Guyton, married Seaborn Jones, Rockmart, Georgia.

IV. Annie Eliza Guyton, born November 6, 1831; died August 10, 1856, is buried in the family burial ground in Buckeye District.

CINCINNATUS SAXON GUYTON (1834-1884)

Cincinnatus Saxon, son of Charles and Elmina Horn Guyton, was born in Laurens County, December 2, 1834, and was a distinguished, honored and revered citizen; died August 14, 1884. A detailed sketch of his life appears on page 391.

Cincinnatus Saxon Guyton married, first, Mary P. Blackshear of a prominent pioneer county family (see Blackshear genealogy), and had five children, all of whom died young; married, second, on January 4, 1876, in Macon, Georgia, Caroline Elizabeth Boisfeuillet, of distinguished lineage, being the daughter of John Theodore Boisfeuillet (1821-1878) and Anne McKinnon (1823-1901); granddaughter of John James Penfield Boisfeuillet (1794-1363) and Elizabeth Cecil Virginia Arnaud (1801-1839); great granddaughter of the Revolutionary soldier, Jean Pierre Arnaud (1751-1833) and Elizabeth Leland (1760-1853). Caroline Boisfeuillet Guyton married, second, Reverend George C. Thompson. She died March 10, 1916.

Children of Cincinnatus Saxon and Caroline Elizabeth Boisfeuillet Guyton:

I. John Saxon Guyton, born in Laurens County, October 15, 1876; died at Dublin, March 5, 1921; married, first, Lee Brantley; married, second, Mrs. Mary Lizzie Sessuons Scarborough; no children by either marriage.

II. Katie May Guyton, born in Laurens County, August 23, 1878; graduate of Wesleyan College; married Dr. Oliver Hyde, of Albuquerque, New Mexico, and is buried in Perpetual Care Section, Fairview Cemetery, Albuquerque, New Mexico.

III. Cincinnatus Saxon Guyton, born in Laurens County, December 14, 1881; died February 28, 1918; married Leoline Blackshear. (detailed record later).

IV. Moses Josiah Guyton, born in Laurens County, May 24, 1880, is the only remaining male representative of this illustrious name in this county. Like his distinguished forebears, he too, is a man of highest integrity and is held in highest esteem in this community where those of his name and blood have been prominent citizens for four generations. Moses Josiah Guyton married Leila Crawford Vinson, daughter of the late Edward Story and Annie Morris Vinson, of Milledgeville, Georgia, and sister of the Honorable Carl Vinson, Congressman from this district and one of the most influential figures at the nation's Capitol. Mrs. Guyton is a prominent clubwoman, a charter member and ex-Regent of the John Laurens Chapter D. A. R.; charter member of the Woman's Study Club; member of the Georgia Society, Colonial Dames of America. A biographical sketch of Moses Josiah Guyton appears on page 392.

V. Eloise Guyton, born in Laurens County, January 31, 1884; graduate of Wesleyan College; married Dr. Walter Edward Clark; is a prominent clubwoman of Augusta, Georgia. Dr. and Mrs. Clark have a foster daughter, Caroline Elizabeth Clark, born March 19, 1921, married on November 2, 1940, to Frank Durst of Augusta, Georgia.

CINCINNATUS SAXON GUYTON II. (1881-1918)

Cincinnatus Saxon, son of Cincinnatus Saxon I, and Caroline Boisfeuillet Guyton, was a graduate of Emory University, member of Sigma Nu fraternity. Though only 37 years of age at the time of his death, he was an outstanding citizen of this county. He married into one of the most prominent of the pioneer county families, Leoline Blackshear (see Blackshear genealogy), daughter of John M. and Carrie Reeves Blackshear, and great great granddaughter of the noted General David Blackshear. Five children were born to this union:

I. Cincie Marmaduke, died young.

II. Caroline Boisfeuillet Guyton, married Joseph Wilton Jolly and has one daughter, Frances Rosemary Jolly.

III. Mary Kate Guyton, married Henry Neilson Wilkinson and has one son, William Guyton Wilkinson.

IV. Frances Evelyn Guyton, married William Comer Cherry and has one son, William Comer Cherry, Jr.

V. Rose Blackshear Guyton, married James Raymond Edmondson.

Cincinnatus Saxon Guyton II., died February 28, 1918, and is buried in Northview Cemetery, Dublin.

DESCENDANTS OF MOSES GUYTON II (1799-1870)

Moses Guyton II., son of Moses I. and Tabitha Saxon Guyton, was born in Spartanburg District, South Carolina, September 4, 1799; located in Laurens County in the early 1800's and became one of its largest land holders and most influential citizens. His hospitable home was in the Buckeye settlement near those of his brothers, John and Charles. After the death of his brother, John, he became guardian for his two minor sons, Charles Brutus and Thomas Northrop, and thus had combined under his management two of the largest estates in the county. In the Indian Wars Moses Guyton II. served with honor and distinction, holding the rank of Major.

On October 29, 1829, Moses Guyton II, married Mary Ann Love (born February 18, 1811-died May 3, 1895), daughter of the Revolutionary soldier, Amos Love and his wife, Margaret James .(see Love genealogy). Ten children were born to this union:

I. Tabitha Jane, born December 6, 1830; married Wiley G. Parks, May 25, 1852.

II. Mary Elizabeth, born July 7, 1833, married James Bishop of Eastman, December 1, 1853.

III. Margaret Love, born February 7, 1839, married W. C. Bryan, February 11, 1857.

IV. Augusta Helen, born May 7, 1841, married James L. Wimberly of Macon, July 15, 1857.

V. Emma Saxon, born August 24, 1843, married Thomas H. Rowe, May 11, 1865 (see Rowe genealogy). (Detailed record later).

VI. Moses III., born August 30, 1846, died April 2, 1911, married Anna B. Russ, November 29, 1870. (Detailed record later).

VII. Julia Elmira, born October 17, 1849, married Dr. Harris Fisher, of Eastman, October 7, 1869.

VIII. Charles Amos, born September 3, 1852, married Ella Reynolds, June 15, 1874.

IX. Sarah Caroline, born May 4, 1836, died July 27, 1849.

X. John, born March 31, 1855; died young.

Moses Guyton II., died December 12, 1870; his wife, Mary Ann Love Guyton, died May 3, 1895, aged 84 years; both are buried in the family burial ground, Buckeye, Laurens County.

EMMA SAXON GUYTON ROWE (1843-1904)

Emma Saxon Guyton, daughter of Moses II, and Mary Ann Love Guyton, on May 11, 1865, married Thomas Hugh Rowe (see Rowe genealogy); was one of the most beloved and esteemed matrons of this community. A talented musician and of high intellectual attainments, her home was a center of cultural and social gatherings where many distinguished visitors were entertained. Emma Saxon Rowe died September 17, 1904; Thomas Hugh Rowe died October 4, 1915. Both are buried in Northview Cemetery, Dublin.

Eight children were born to Thomas H. and Emma Guyton Rowe:

I. Margaret Jane Rowe married Thomas B. Hicks and had four children: 1. Rowe G. Hicks married, first, Jennie Grier, three daughters: (1). Margaret Janet Hicks, married Paul Christian Huelsenbeck, (2) Rosemary Hicks, married James K. Pace, (3) Dorothy Amelia Hicks, married John Nairn Ross. Rowe Gainer Hicks marierd, second, Louise Esther Burnley, no children. 2. Mary Jane Hicks, married Dr. William Calhoun Thompson, three children: (1) William Calhoun Thompson, Jr., married Beatrice Spain of Richmond, Virginia, (2) Margaret Hicks Thompson, (3) Robert Hicks Thompson, 3. Ruth Guyton Hicks, married Lester Lee Porter, two children: (1) Ruth Hicks Porter, (2) Lester Lee Porter, Jr.; 4. Henry Hicks, married Grace Pryor, three children: (1) Mary Grace Hicks, (2) Amelia Ruth Hicks, (3) Henry Hicks, Jr.; 5. Charles L. Hicks, married Elizabeth Carerre, one son, Charles L. Hicks, Jr.

II. Josephine Augusta Rowe, married Judge Henry F. Carswell, no children.

III. Mary Guyton Rowe, married Reverend William Ellis Harville and had four children: 1. William Edgar Harville, married Julia Heard Leonard; 2. Thomas Rowe Harville, married Elizabeth Hobbs (see Hobbs genealogy); 3. Margaret Janet Harville, married Henry Cooper Standard and has one son, Henry Cooper Standard, Jr.; 4. Harris Harville, married Opal Sutherland.

IV. Freeman Hugh Rowe married, first, Jennie Pate Robinson, second, Mrs. Katherine Smith Walton.

V. Twins: Thomas Harris Rowe, died young, and Charles Saxon Rowe, married Alma Burney, four children: 1. Thomas Hugh Rowe, 2. Estelle Rowe, 3. Ruth McCall Rowe, married Edward Moses, 4. Helen Rowe, married Crawford Bickford.

VI. Emma Love Rowe, married Wiliam T. Smith, three children: Walter Guyton Smith, 2. James Lawrence Smith, 3. Margaret Love Smith.

VII. George Thomas Rowe, married Mamie Lee Rogers, one daughter, Emma Saxon Rowe, who married George Carver, a missionary in Shanghai, China.

VIII. John Ludington Rowe, died young.

Moses Guyton III.

Moses Guyton III., son of Moses Guyton II., and his wife, Mary Ann Love, was born in Laurens County, Georgia, August 30, 1846; graduated from University of Georgia with A.B. degree in 1869; private, 5th Georgia Regiment, C. S. A.; Clerk of Court, Jackson County, Florida; Steward in Methodist Episcopal Church, Marianna, Florida; treasurer, Jackson County, Florida, at the time of his death, April 2, 1911.

Moses Guyton III., was married on November 29, 1870, to Anna Beman Russ (1849-1927), daughter of Joseph W. Russ and his wife, Mary Williams Beman, and granddaughter of Henry D. Beman and Caroline Frances Myrick Beman.

Issue:

I. Moses Guyton, IV., born in Dublin, Georgia, November 30, 1871. Detailed record later.

II. Mary (Marie) Beman Guyton, born in Marianna, Florida, November 12, 1874; married on December 27, 1898, Dr. William Heard Kilpatrick, born November 20, 1871, son of Reverend James H. Kilpatrick, D.D., of White Plains, Georgia, and has wife, Edna Perrin Heard. Dr. Kilpatrick, "America's Number One Educator," also an author of note, is now Professor Emeritus of Education at Columbia University, New York. Two children were born to this union, the younger of whom, William Heard Kilpatrick, Jr., died young. Their daughter, Margaret Louise Kilpatrick, was born in Marianna, Florida, January 13, 1901, graduated from Teachers College, Columbia University in 1922; married on January 23, 1925, to Theodore Baumister, II., son of Theodore Baumister I. and his wife, Mary Louise Wilson. Theodore Baumister II. is (1941) associcate professor of engineering in Columbia University; he and his wife, Margaret Kilpatrick Baumister, reside in New York City, and have two sons: Theodore Baumister III., born February 1, 1926, and Heard Kilpatrick Baumister, born January 20, 1929.

III. Annie Louise Guyton, born in Marianna, Florida, October 4, 1878; married on February 27, 1901, William DeLacy Doughtie of Columbus, Georgia, and has three children: (1) Annie Louise Doughtie, born January 31, 1903, married on March 23, 1923, to Liddon Solomon; (2) William DeLacy Doughtie, Jr., born July 4, 1905; (3) Marie Guyton Doughtie, born October 2, 1910, married on December 26, 1936, C. J. Butler.

IV. Margaret McClellan Guyton, born November 13, 1880; married Paul J. Christopher, son of William H. and Martha Johnson Christopher, of White Plains, Georgia; now (1941) living in Decatur, Georgia; one son, Moses Guyton Christopher, who was born in White Plains, Georgia, September 17, 1917.

Moses Guyton IV.

Moses Guyton IV., son of Moses Guyton III. and his wife Anna Russ, was born in Dublin, Georgia, November 30, 1871. Dublin and Laurens County claim with pride this native son, who is a worthy bearer of this distinguished name, being the 4th Moses Guyton in direct succession from the Revolutionary soldier Moses Guyton I., of French Huguenot parentage. Moses Guyton IV. received A.B. degree with honors from the University of Georgia; member Chi Phi fraternity; for many years a prominent lawyer of Marianna, Florida. On January 29, 1902, he married Lucy Hall Milton, daughter of Major William Henry Milton and his wife, Lucy Hall Hearn, of Marianna, Florida. Two sons were born to this union, the younger, William Milton Guyton, dying in infancy. The elder son, Moses Guyton V., was born November 16, 1903, in Marianna, Florida; graduate of University of Florida; member Kappa Alpha fraternity; now (1941) in partnership with his father in a prominent law firm of Marianna, Florida; married on November 12, 1935, Margaret Almeria McKay (born January 18, 1903), of Tampa, Florida, and has one daughter, Lucy Jane Guyton, who was born in Lake Wales, Florida, January 17, 1939.

The compiler of the foregoing records of the Guyton family, Henrietta Sanders Freeman (Mrs. E. B.), is indebted to the late Lily Doyle Dunlap (Mrs. J. M.), State Chairman of the Genealogical Research Committee of the North Carolina D. A. R., for much of the early history of the Guyton family. Judge Thomas P. Guyton, of Kosciusko, Mississippi, Col. Moses Guyton, of Marianna, Florida, Dr. William H. Kilpatrick, of Columbia University, New York, and the late Josephine Rowe Carswell, of Dublin, Georgia, also contributed valuable data. Dates of birth, death and marriage were obtained from old family Bibles of Moses Guyton I. and II., John Guyton, Charles Guyton, Thomas Northrop Guyton, and Aaron Guyton.

COLONEL CINCINNATUS SAXON GUYTON

CINCINNATUS SAXON GUYTON (1834-1884)

Cincinnatus Saxon, son of Charles and Elmina Horn Guyton, was born December 2, 1834, in Laurens County, of which he was a lifelong resident. Like his father, he was a planter on an extensive scale, owning many slaves, in whose welfare he always took great pride. In his early manhood, and prior to 1861, aside from persuing the quiet pleasures of agriculture, his interest in all matters of public character was highly dominant, and his activities in protecting and preserving the cultural heritage of his people were not only large, but always of a constructive nature. When the war clouds lowered over the land in 1861, and the tocsin called to arms, his sword was one of the first to be laid upon the altar of his country; elected Captain of Company C, 2nd Regiment, 1st Brigade Georgia State Troops, October 12, 1861, and promomted to Major, February 12, 1862. Elected Lieut.-Colonel 57th Regiment, Georgia Volunteers, Ledbetter Brigade, Army of Tennessee. May 24, 1862. Captured Vicksburg, Mississippi, July 4, 1863. Member of Board of Examiners near Tupelo, Mississippi, January 22, 1865, in which year he surrendered in North Carolina. Though the army was captured, the Confederate Flag did not fall into the hands of the enemy, for Colonel Guyton concealed it in his saddle bags and thus brought it safely home. It is a prized possession of the Guyton family, now owned by Eloise Guyton Clarke, of Augusta, daughter of Colonel Guyton. As Commander of the gallant 57th Regiment, Colonel Guyton rendered distinguished service in the War Between the States, in which he received numerous citations for exceptional bravery and leadership.

Returning to civil life in 1865, he assumed unflinchingly the responsibilities imposed by the ravages of war upon his once happy and contented people; now dominated by radical advocates of anarchy and plunder, and controlled by tyrants, knaves, and negroes. Although actively engaged in the war during its entire duration, the Georgia Department of Archives records Colonel Guyton as Senator from the 16th District in 1863, and as Senator in both extra sessions of 1864 and 1865. He was again Senator in 1882 and 1883, and Representative in 1877. His service in the Senate was terminated in 1884, the year of his death. The challenge of the carpetbagger always found him eager for battle, and uncompromising in principle. Colonel Guyton was a life-long member of the Executive Committee of Laurens County, and from whom the family now possesses a highly cherished Testimonial presented upon the occasion of his death. He was also very active in Masonic circles; being a member of Anderson Lodge No. 243, Wrightsville, Georgia, and from whom a beautiful memorial, attesting his high integrity, honor, and value as to citizenship to the entire community, was presented the family and which is preserved as a priceless reminder of his life. Colonel Guyton died August 14, 1884, and was buried in the family cemetery, Buckeye District, with full Masonic ceremonies conducted by the Anderson

Lodge. *The Dublin Post,* August 21, 1884, editorially carried this summation of his life upon the occasion of his death: "In the dark days of Reconstruction and radical misrule, his name is the brightest on our history's page. Whether at the head of his regiment on the battlefields at Vicksburg, or breasting the tide of mad legislation in the House of Representatives and the Senate, leading the forlorn hopes of the beaten and demoralized Democracy against the tyranny of the carpetbaggers, his virtues shine with equal lustre. It is universally admitted that Colonel Guyton was one of Laurens County's most distinguished sons, and who was loved by every one for his genial nature, liberal heartedness, unbending integrity and practical intelligence. In all the relations of life he was a man fashioned in the mould of honesty, kindness and charity, and crowned it all with the beauty of holiness and the bright halo of professed Christianity. It was indeed fitting, that upon the news of his death, all the stores on last Saturday closed and all business suspended; not by any concert of action, but by promptings of sincere deep sorrow over the death of our most honored, useful and dearly beloved citizen. In his death Laurens County, the state and the church lost irreparably, a wise counselor, warm friend, fearless foe, liberal benefactor and safe arbitrator. A devoted husband and loving father . . . "

MOSES JOSIAH GUYTON

Moses Josiah Guyton, born May 24, 1880, at the old Guyton homestead, Laurens County, Georgia, is the son of Cincinnatus Saxon and Caroline Boisfeuillet Guyton. His early childhood was spent on the plantation. In 1889 his mother, Caroline Boisfeuillet Guyton, was married to Reverend George Calvert Thompson, and the family moved to Louisville, Georgia, where he lived for several years, returning to their Laurens County home in 1892. The years intervening, and until 1896, his boyhood activities were concerned mostly with the usual chores incident to life on a large busy plantation, teaming with many loyal, but dependent old slaves, who with characteristic faithfulness refused to be reconstructed. True to the traditions of his family, that kindly interest in the welfare and protection of the old slaves was manifest in his early years; partly as an inherent duty in perpetuating the life and practices of his family, but also as an outcry of that fidelity to a happy civilization which passed out with the emancipation period, and which will always have its abode as a shrine in the lives and hearts of descendants of all the old antebellum families.

Having completed his elementary schooling in Laurens County and at Louisville, Georgia, he was given preparatory college training at N. L. W. Institute, Wrightsville, Georgia, from which institution he entered Emory College in 1898, graduating with Ph.B. degree in 1902, specializing in applied mathematics. In 1903 received special training in chemistry at Philadelphia College of Pharmacy, Philadelphia, Pennsylvania, in preparation for field work in the engineering profession.

Mr. Guyton engaged in private practice as construction engineer until his appointment as City Engineer of the City of Dublin in 1907, which position he held until 1925. His activities as City Engineer extended for period of 18 years, covering all branches of municipal engineering, including design, construction and responsible charge of paving, sewerage, hydraulic, drainage, bridge construction, and operation and maintenance of the city's public utilities system. Most of the city's public improvements and records were made during his administration.

Member of American Society of Civil Engineers, 1916, which position he still holds.

Resigning the position of City Engineer in 1925, he engaged in the wholesale petroleum business until 1933.

Assuming the postmastership of Dublin, Georgia, in 1934, he was reappointed at the expiration of his first term in 1939, and to the status of permanent postmaster.

Member of the Sigma Nu fraternity at Emory, and of the Phi Chi fraternity at Philadelphia. Has served on the Board of Stewards of the First Methodist Church for many years; member of City Council as alderman from the city at large, 1931-1933. In addition to his many years in public service work, has always shown a special interest in all local civic organization in which he has served in various capacities; being a charter member of the Kiwanis, and Exchange clubs, and serving as president of the latter in 1927-28 when first organized. His civic activities also extended to the Chamber of Commerce, serving as a director of that institution at various periods.

HAINES

Dr. Alfred I. Haines was born November 18, 1848, in Washington County, Georgia, above Sandersville. He was the son of Alvin O. Haines and Eliza M. McCulers, who were married September 16, 1845.

Dr. Alfred I. Haines received his early education in a private school. He finished in medicine at the Medical College in Savannah, Georgia, in the class of 1870. After finishing college he came to Laurens County (Buckeye District), Georgia, and started his practicing and took over the practice of Dr. Tucker, of Tucker's Cross Roads. On November 21, 1872, he was married to Mourning W. Wright, daughter of Colonel John B. Wright and Mourning Smith Wright, Colonel Wright at that time being an outstanding figure in State affairs and one of the largest land owners in the state. Colonel John B. Wright was born in Laurens County, Georgia, November 20, 1808. He was a member of the Masonic Order, Anderson Lodge, F. & A. M.

To this union were born six children, two sons, both having died while attending college, and four daughters: Fannie, wife of Dr. Henry Hicks; Nannie, second wife of Dr. Henry Hicks; Lizzie, wife of Captain John L. Martin; Mourning, wife of Dr. Alfred I. Haines.

Colonel Wright served in the Georgia Legislature and was the first Senator from Johnson County after that county was created from a part of Laurens. During this time he was very instrumental in the passing of the bill for a woman to control her property after marriage. The town of Wrightsville was named for Colonel Wright. He was one of the most successful farmers in Georgia, being one of the five largest slave owners in the state. He was not in active duty during the War Between the States but remained at home to help provide food for the armies of Lee and Jackson. John B. Wright died August 9, 1874. Dr. Haines was made administrator of Colonel Wright's estate.

Dr. and Mrs. Haines were outstanding in religious and educational activities, having given the land for several churches and schools. They were members of the Christian Church at Buckeye, in Laurens County.

To this union were born seven children, four dying in early life. M. Helen Haines was born February 15, 1875. She married Oscar A. Kennedy, of Wrightsville, Georgia. To them were born eight children. The surviving ones are: Mrs. B. B. Tanner, of Dublin; Mrs. George East, Mrs. D. H. Mayo, and Beverly Kennedy of Wrightsville, and Harold Kennedy of Fort Jackson, South Carolina.

E. Maggie Haines was born February 12, 1877, and married Beverly Hayes of Wrightsville.

John B. Haines married Essie Keen.

Dr. and Mrs. Haines moved to Wrightsville, Mrs. Haines dying there in 1905. Dr. Haines died in 1916.

—*By Mrs. B. B. Tanner.*

HARRISON

The Reverend Gainor Green Harrison is head of one branch of the Harrison family in Laurens. The county is his by adoption, but his son, William Macon Harrison, is a native, having been born at Laurens Hill, November 6, 1902.

The Reverend Mr. Harrison is the son of the late William Henry and Annie Burns Harrison. He was born June 17, 1879, at Wrightsville, and attended school at Beulah, Nannie Lou Warthen College, and Georgia Alabama Business College.

On January 16, 1901, Mr. Harrison married Sadie Gertrude Whitaker, daughter of James Macon and Georgia Walker Whitaker, Harrison, Georgia. They lived at Laurens Hill four years and then Mr. Harrison, feeling the urge to preach, attended Southern Baptist Theological College, Louisville, Kentucky. Returning to Georgia he began a career of preaching in country churches which has lasted thirty years. During this period he also taught school in Johnson, Montgomery, Toombs, Wheeler, and Telfair counties.

Nineteen hundred sixteen marked the end of one period in his life, as his wife died, leaving him and his son. There two were unusually close, and have remained the same throughout the years, father and son extending a helping hand to each other when necessary.

Thus it came about that on September 18, 1917, Mr. Harrison and his son drove to the Garnto home near Dublin, and were joined by Rosa Pearl Garnto, daughter of the late William David and Florence May Garnto, who became his second wife. They have one child, Rosa Pearl Harrison, born February 27, 1921. She attended school in Scotland and Dublin, graduating with the Dublin Seniors of 1938. She completed a business course and began a journalistic career with her brother, editor of the *Dublin Courier-Herald* since July 2, 1929.

Macon Harrison attended school in Harrison, Brewton-Parker Institute, and Georgia-Alabama Business College. In 1924, he went to the Swainsboro newspaper and met Grace Rountree, daughter of Robert Ebb and Lexie Brown Rountree.

Thus it came about that on May 1, 1925, Mr. Harrison and his father drove to Augusta and were joined by Miss Rountree, who became his wife. His father was the officiating minister.

Mr. and Mrs. Harrison spent the next two years in Valdosta, Mr. Harrison joining the *Valdosta Daily Times*. In 1927, they moved to Moultrie and Mr. Harrison was with the *Moultrie Observer*.

In 1929, after a few months with the Steubenville, Ohio, *Times*, Mr. Harrison became editor of the *Dublin Courier-Herald*, and in 1934 became part owner with W. H. Lovett after the paper was bought from a Texas owner.

—By *Grace Rountree Harrison (Mrs. W. M.)*

HARVARD

David Harvard (1809-1865) was born in Washington County, May 7, 1809. In 1833 he, with his bride, Mary Ann Fish (1814-1877), came to Laurens County. Here in the District which bears his name, "Harvard," was spent the entire life of this couple. David Harvard and his cultured wife contributed much to the development of the community (see Laurens Hill) and left behind a rich heritage for their descendants. Five children born to this couple came to their maturity: Quintillian Lamar, David John, William Clay, Sarah, and Mary.

David John Harvard was never married. William Clay married Ella Toler and had four children: Guy, Lewis, John (all deceased), and Leila Bell (Haynes). Mary married Dr. John Barkwell and had no children. Sarah married Dr. Thomas Barkwell and bore one son, David Harvard, and a daughter Tommie (Mrs. Melton Wall).

Quintillian Lamar Harvard was a Lieutenant in the Fifth Georgia Cavalry, enlisted in 1861, was imprisoned at Johnston Island and discharged in 1865. He reared his family in the community in which he was born, but later moved to Cochran, Georgia, where he served as postmaster up to the time of his death. Quintillian Lamar (1834-1893) married, first, Laura Virginia Booth (1836-1888), and, second, Viola Reynolds. From the first marriage came five children who reached maturity: Eugene Lamar, William Fish, James Quinn, David, and Mary Elizabeth.

James Quinn Harvard (1861-1882) was killed by a colored mob in Eastman, when he was mistaken for an officer of the law.

Mary Elizabeth Harvard (1876) married Mance Singletary, of Dooly County, and had no children.

David Harvard (1867-1922), married Lina O'Berry and had six children: Ralph, Raymond, David, Juanita, Sarah, and Gladys—none of these are living except Gladys, who is Mrs. R. L. Whipple, of Cochran, Georgia.

Eugene Lamar and William Fish Harvard married sisters, Laverna and Clara Summers, daughters of Joseph W. and Harriett Bates Summers. Harriett Bates came from Maine in 1847 to teach in Georgia and rendered valuable service over a period of many years to the cause of education.

To Eugene (1855-1881) and Laverna Harvard were born two sons, Quinn Lamar and Eugene Lamar. Quinn Lamar married Pennie Payne and had one daughter, Louis Rostine. By his second marriage with Lena Rowland he had a daughter, Marguerite, and a son, Quinn Lamar. Eugene had no children.

William Fish (1858-1919) and Clara Harvard (1856-1930) lived for many years in the original Laurens Hill community. All of their children were born there. They were influential citizens, friends of all who knew them and hospitable to every one. They were always alert to everything that was for the betterment of their neighbors. In 1899 they moved to Dublin.

To William Fish and Clara Harvard were born two children who died in infancy, Laura Virginia and William Summers. They had six other children who lived to maturity: Alice May married Simeon Russell Brinson and had one daughter, Marguerite Russell Brinson; Mabel Claire who married Charles C. Youmans of Miami, Florida, no children, she served Everglades Chapter D. A. R., Miami, Florida, as Regent in the year 1941; Harriett Bates who died January 29, 1924; Laverna who is a registered nurse; Halbert who married Dorothy Kreuger, of San Jose, California, they have no children; Clara Ursula who married Trammell C. Keen (see Keen and Linder genealogies), and has four children: Trammell Colwell, William Harvard, James Lemuel, and Susan Ward. This branch of the Harvard family has lived in Laurens County from 1833 to the present time.

—By Alice Harvard Brinson (Mrs. S. R.)

HAYNES

Mercer Haynes, son of Zachariah Taylor Haynes and Maria Cooper Haynes, was born February 21, 1845, in Chatham County, Georgia.

His early life was spent in South Carolina. In the Barnwell County schools of that State he received his education and later attended school at Griffin, Georgia. At the age of sixteen he began the study of law in the office of his brother-in-law, the late Colonel Fred Dismuke of Griffin, but when the last call came from the Southern Army for volunteers, though but a youth, he enlisted and entered the army in 1862. He was a member of Wheeler's Cavalry, was captured and put in prison during the year of 1864 where he remained until he was released in 1865. He then returned to his home at Griffin where he again took up the study of law.

On April 9, 1867, he was married to Rosamond Parmeter Warren, the daughter of Remeliah Thompson Warren and William B. Warren, of Barnwell County, South Carolina.

His maternal grandfather and grandmother were Thomas Cooper and Stephanie Cooper, coming from England to New York and later settling in Savannah, Georgia. In the spring of 1870 he, with his wife and small son, William Rowell, who was born in Griffin, Georgia, on May 31, 1869, moved to Brunswick, Georgia, where they resided four years. It was there a daughter, Anna Maria, was born on January 27, 1872. During the fall of 1874 he and his little family moved to Dublin, Laurens County, Georgia, where he spent the remainder of his life.

Six children came to bless this union: Augusta Rowe, who died at the age of two and one-half years; Martha Savannah, at the age of twenty-one years. Those remaining are William Rowell Haynes, now of Macon, Georgia; Anna Maria Haynes (Mrs. J. Tom White), of Dublin, Georgia; Baker Warren Haynes, of Akron, Ohio, and Jennie Thompson Haynes (Mrs. W. A. Dial), of Columbus, Georgia.

When but a child Mercer Haynes united with the Missionary Baptist Church and soon after coming to Dublin he was ordained as Deacon of the First Baptist Church, at its present site, and for many years was a faithful teacher in the Sunday School. He was also director of music and was always to be found in his place in the choir. As a singer he possessed a bass voice of unusual volume and sweetness. For a long period of time he served as a member of the Executive Board of the Ebenezer Association.

In 1874 he was admitted to the bar and practiced law in all the courts of the county until the close of his life. He was elected Mayor of Dublin in 1877 and served four successive terms. He was then appointed postmaster, holding that position for four years. County Court was established in Laurens County in 1885 and Mercer Haynes was appointed Judge of this court by Governor John B. Gordon and served in that capacity until the court was abolished some years later.

He was a member of the Board of Education. His library, one of the largest and best in his town, was always a source of inspiration and pleasure not only to his own family but to friends and neighbors far and near.

He died at the age of 55 years on September 11, 1901.

The grandchildren are: Stanley Haynes of Columbus, Ohio; Helen Haynes Burns, Williston, Florida; William Russell Haynes, of Texas; Rosamond Haynes (deceased); Margaret Haynes Owens, Macon, Georgia; Janet Haynes Kelley, Americus, Georgia, the children of William Rowell Haynes and Florence Stanley Haynes Rosamond White Moffett, Macon, Georgia; Anna Pearl White Waldron, Dublin, Georgia; Thomas Haynes White, Dublin, Georgia; Martha White Pinkston, Dublin, Georgia, children of Anna Haynes White and John Thomas White. William Albert Dial and Anna Jennelle Dial, of Columbus, Georgia, children of Jennie Haynes Dial and William Albert Dial, of Columbus, Georgia.

—*By Anna Haynes White (Mrs. J. Tom)*

HERNDON

James Herndon's father came from South Carolina to Georgia in 1814, with his wife and five sons, and settled in Laurens County. James, the youngest, was four years old. His four brothers were Henry, Richard, Phillip, and Wesley.

James Herndon (April 26, 1810-July 25, 1886) first married Miss Wolfe. There were seven children: Bryant Alexander (November 29, 1829-December 22, 1881); Warren, birth date not known, mar-

JUDGE MERCER HAYNES

ried Piety Williams; Jane, born January 15, 1837, married Thomas Moore; Queen, born August 20, 1838, married Noah Rowe; Harriet, born March 26, 1841, married Alex Maddox; Hollie Anne, born February 8, 1843, married Wallace Rowe; Matthew, born March 12, 1845, married Liza Hobbs.

James Herndon's second wife was Mrs. Fountain, the former Sara Anne Hester. There were four children: George (January 21, 1867-May 3, 1893); Columbia, born March 28, 1869, married John Joiner; William Meredith (September 2, 1872——), married Georgia Harden; Sallie, born May 28, 1874, married Freeman Harden.

Bryant Alexander (November 29, 1829-December 22, 1881), son of James Herndon, married Jane Murphy (May 10, 1839-April 21, 1896), of Washington County, daughter of Cullen and Caroline Malpass Murphy, on June 18, 1868. Bryant A. Herndon served from 1861 to 1865 as a private in Company A, Second Georgia Regimnet, under Captain R. A. Stanley. After the war he was for a time a Revenue Officer. He was appointed census enumerator in 1880 for District 63, and during 1880-1881 served as postmaster for Dublin. He died on December 22, 1881. There were three children: Louis Alexander, Celestia Lessie, born October 15, 1869; and Julia Irene, born August 28, 1871. Louis died June 17, 1872.

Celestia Herndon (October 15, 1869-December 19, 1933), married Daniel Anderson Smith (September 9, 1851-January 7, 1919) on March 4, 1885. Daniel A. was the son of Hardy Smith (October 17, 1801-March 27, 1864), and Ann Anderson (August 11, 1819-November 24, 1907), and grandson of Hardy Smith (February, 1757-August, 1852), Revolutionary soldier. Ann Anderson's grandfather, John Gaillard Anderson, was also a soldier of the American Revolution. (see Hardy Smith genealogy). Daniel A. Smith, farmer and cottonseed buyer, was a gentle, kindly man, and a faithful member of the Baptist Church. Celestia was a leader among the women of the Methodist Church for many years. A charter member of the local Woman's Missionary Society, she was its president for many years, and an honorary life member. Much loved, the Celestia Smith Bible Class for Women is named for her. The children of Daniel and Celestia Herndon Smith were: Jane Roberta, Lee Edward and Robert Murphy.

Jane Roberta Smith, A.B. Wesleyan College, student Emory University Library School, and first recipient of the Mary McCants Memorial Award for Librarians, 1940, has been City Librarian since January, 1934.

Lee E. Smith (May 9, 1890——), a graduate of Emory University Medical School, and a surgeon in the Naval Reserves during 1917-1918, married Alma Louise, daughter of Harry L. and Maude Gooby Boyle, of Oakland, California, on October 17, 1918. Their daughter, Celestia Louise, married Wayne Petersen, of Oakland, on September 5, 1937. They have one daughter, Karen Lee.

R. Murphy Smith (June 20, 1893—), a graduate of Meridian Military College, Mississippi, married Lois Polhill, daughter of James B. and Lois Phillips Polhill, of Louisville, Georgia, on April 6, 1927. They have one daughter, Lois Polhill. Murphy enlisted as a volunteer in the United States Army on December 13, 1917, was commissioned Second Lieutenant from the ranks in 1918, in the Motor Transport Corps, and served until March 15, 1919. After his discharge, he was for several months Commanding Officer, Headquarters Company, of the Third Battalion of the 121st Infantry, Georgia National Guard.

Bryant Herndon's second daughter, Julia Irene (August 28, 1871- —), married Otis Hazard Perry Rawls (February 23, 1869-November 18, 1919) on November 10, 1892. Otis was the son of Oliver Hazard Perry (1820-1873) and Martha Fordham Rawls (1828-1910). Oliver Howard Perry was the son of Willis and Elizabeth Skipper Rawls, married about 1818. (see Rawls genealogy). For many years Otis Rawls and his brother Ben H., were prominent merchants, their firm being known as The Farmers' Supply Company. From July, 1901, to July, 1904, Otis Rawls was a member of the Dublin City Council. It was during this period that the High School building and the Carnegie Library were built. The children of Otis and Julia Herndon Rawls were: Wendell Lytton, Otis Bryant, James Julian, Grace Elizabeth, and Martha Jane.

Wendell Rawls (February 17, 1895-July 19, 1934), married Lenora Verner, of Denver, Colorado, in 1919. He enlisted in the regular army as a volunteer June 1, 1917, at Akron, Ohio, and was honorably discharged in 1919. He was given a position as city salesman for E. S. Street and Company, and was manager of the Vidalia branch. When Werden and Company succeeded E. S. Street and Company, he was made traveling salesman, which position he held until his death.

Otis Bryant Rawls (June 20, 1897——) first married Lucile Irwin. Their son, Otis Bryant, Jr., (October 11, 1921—), is radio operator on the steamship M. S. Norden, running between Jacksonville and Cuba. Otis' second marriage was to Gladys Tindol, daughter of F. Cordy and Mamie Burke Tindol. Their son is Jackie Bryant (September 12, 1939—). Otis Rawls enlisted in Battery A, First Field Artillery, Alabama National Guard, June 24, 1916 to July 27, 1917, serving for several months on the Mexican Border. He also served as private in the World War from October 25 to December 5, 1918; is owner of the Rawls Garage, and instructor in acetylene and electric welding for government classes for national defense.

James Julian Rawls (April 20, 1901-February 2, 1938), married Mrs. Evelyn Prince Watson, daughter of Sam M. and Elizabeth Chapman Prince, on November 2, 1935. Julian served two years in the United States Army and fifteen years in the Navy. He was radio operator in the bombing squadron V. P. I., of the Pacific Fleet, this squadron distinguishing itself in 1937, when it carried twenty-six giant bombers to Honolulu without accident. He lost his life with his squadron in sham battle maneuvers of the Pacific Fleet on the night of February 2, 1938.

Grace Elizabeth Rawls is a B.S. graduate of Georgia State College for Women at Milledgeville, and is a member of the facuty of the schools of Bainbridge, Georgia.

Martha Jane Rawls was first married to Ernest L. Freeman (August 2, 1889-May 11, 1931), son of C. E. and Sallie Moye Freeman, of Laurens County. Ernest Freeman was drowned in May, 1931, while swimming at Bradenton, Florida. There was one daughter from this marriage, Sara Irene Freeman. On May 23, 1936, Martha married Roy Meadows, son of Reverend Meadows, of Winder, Georgia.

William Meredith (September 2, 1872—), youngest son of James and Sara Hester Herndon, has for twenty years served on the Laurens County Board of Education, and was County Commissioner from 1912-1916. Meredith married Georgia Harden in 1901. Their five children are: Barton (January 1, 1903—), married Berlin Warren, is cashier of Farmers and Merchants Bank of Dublin; Eunice, married Felton Moore; Lorene, unmarried; Gladys, married Arthur Ballard; Lois, married Randolph Clarke.

—*By Julia Herndon Rawls (Mrs. O. H. P.)*

HICKS

Nathaniel Hicks, courier on the staff of Generals Greene and Whittaker, located on the Great Ohoopee. He had three children. A son, James, represented Johnson County in the State Legislature; wrote a textbook on Geometry; built and gave the first Academy to Wrightsville, Georgia; married, first, Mabel Pullen; children: Willie, Henry, Elizabeth, and Jane; married, second, Mary Hightower, daughter of Josiah Hightower; children: Mattie, Captain Jimmie, Sara Joyce, Reuben, Nancy Ellen, Richard Lowery (Dick), Eugene (Sawnie), and Dr. Charles.

Willie Hicks married Jane Outler; children: Maymie, Tobe, Bill, Dan, E. E. (Pomp), Big Fort Tom, and Ida. E. E. Hicks, of Cadwell, son of Tobe, married Belle Brown; children: Lieut. James Everett, Redding. E. E. (Pomp) Hicks, Sheriff of Laurens County, married Winnie Thomas, daughter of Frank and Victoria Whitehead Thomas; children: Palmer Whitehead, World War veteran now (1941) Judge of Dublin City Court; Carrie Jane, Guy Lowery, Winnifred.

Dr. Henry Hicks, graduate of Medical College, Atlanta, practiced in Johnson and Laurens counties, served in the War Between the States, member of the firm of H. Hicks and Company; married, first,

Mary Wright, daughter of a wealthy landowner John B. Wright, of Buckeye; children: Thomas Benjamin, Fannie, and John. Henry Hicks married, second, Nancy Wright, sister of his first wife; children: James B., Leslie, Mabel, Talmadge, Richard Pullen (Jupe), and Gainer.

Thomas Benjamin Hicks, son of Henry and Mary Wright Hicks, Mercer University, A.T.O. fraternity, member of the firm of H. Hicks and Company, operated Hicks Drug Company, a boat line, and *The Dublin Post;* fought for prohibition in Dublin, in 1885; owned many horses and stables; married Margaret Janet Rowe (see Rowe, Guyton, and McCall genealogies), daughter of Thomas H. and Emma Guyton Rowe; children: Rowe Gainer, Mary Jane, Ruth Guyton, Henry, and Dr. Charles L. Hicks.

Rowe Gainer Hicks married, first, Jennie Grier; children: Margaret Janet, married Paul C. Hulsenbeck, of Newark, New Jersey, one son, Paul C., Jr.; Rosemary, married James K. Pace, of Pace, Mississippi; Dorothy Amelia, married John Nairn Ross, of Savannah, Georgia, one daughter, Dorothy Rose. Rowe G. Hicks married, second, Louise Burnley, A.B. degree Wesleyan College, now serving in the Welfare Department of the State of Georgia.

Mary Jane Hicks, pianist of note, Randolph-Macon and New England Conservatory, charter member of the Woman's Study Club and the John Laurens Chapter D. A. R., married Dr. Wiliam Calhoun Thompson, of Anderson, South Carolina, graduate of Atlanta School of Medicine, operated the first successful hospital in Dublin; children: William Calhoun Thompson, Jr., graduate U. S. Naval Academy, 1935, Lieut. (j. g.) U. S. S. Sealion, married Beatrice Spain, of Richmond, Virginia; Margaret Hicks Thompson, graduate of Shorter College; Robert Hicks Thompson, an aviation enthusiast.

Ruth Guyton Hicks, B.A., Agnes Scott College, married Lester Lee Porter, of Danville, Georgia, attorney, Mercer University (see D. A. R. records of William Mitchell, Preserved Whipple, and Timothy Bennett); children: Ruth Hicks Porter, graduate University of Georgia, and Lester Lee Porter, Jr.

Henry Hicks, Mercer University, A.T.O. fraternity, married Grace Prior: children: Mary Grace, Amelia Ruth, and Henry Hicks, Jr.

Dr. Charles L. Hicks, University of Georgia, Medical College in Augusta, Georgia, member International College of Surgeons, Sigma Nu fraternity, owns and operates Hicks Hospital, Dublin; married Elizabeth Calhoun Carerre, daughter of Henry M. and Anna Huger Carerre, of French Huguenot lineage, Agnes Scott College, one son, Charles L. Hicks, Jr.

Judge James B. Hicks, son of Dr. Henry Hicks and his second wife, Nancy Wright, graduate of Mercer University, Kappa Alpha fraternity, noted lawyer, former mayor of Dublin, represented Laurens County in the State Legislature, former Judge of the City Court of Dublin.

JUDGE JAMES B. HICKS

Leslie Hicks, daughter of Henry and Nancy Wright Hicks, married Lee Kennedy; two children: Elizabeth Kennedy married, first, Sheppard Page, second, George Brown. Madge Kennedy, Shorter College, married Lloyd Alexander, Guilford College, two sons, Lloyd Alexander, Jr., and James Hicks Alexander.

Talmadge Hicks, son of Henry and Nancy Wright Hicks, University of Georgia, County School Superintendent for eight years, married Clara Fields, of Vincennes, Indiana, and has one daughter, Nannie Claire Hicks, Wesleyan College and University of Georgia, Kappa Delta Phi fraternity, married Henry Lord, University of the South, National Law School, Doctor Jurisprudence.

Richard Pullen (Jupe) Hicks, son of Dr. Henry and Nancy Wright Hicks, Gordon Institute, Barnesville, and University of Georgia; married Mary Lee Marshall of Grovania, Georgia.

Elizabeth Hicks, daughter of James Hicks, married Robert J. Hightower; children: James E. Hightower, Dr. Robert H. Hightower, William Joshua Hightower, and T. Marion (Cone) Hightower. (see "Descendants of Joshua Hightower").

Richard Lowery Hicks (Dick), son of James Hicks, graduate of Washington and Lee University, taught a school for boys in Dublin, member of the firm of H. Hicks and Company, operated a freight boat, drug store and newspaper; married Sara Daniels and had two daughters, Mary and Mildred Hicks.

Dr. Charles Hicks, son of James Hicks, University of Maryland, 1877, New York Polyclinic, President Georgia Medical Association; author of a notable treatice on malaria which was read in Paris; was instrumental in bringing the Wrightsville and Tennille Railroad to Dublin; married Alice McRae, of Scotch descent; children: Seward, Emmett, Arpad, and Charles McRae (Pat).

Sara Joyce Hicks (Sallie), daughter of James Hicks, married John Peacock; children: Tullie Peacock, and John Asa Peacock, married Anne Boisfeuillet Todd (Mrs.), and had six children: John Asa, Jr., Kathleen, Annelie, Roderick, Marion, and Saralyn. (see Peacock Family).

Nancy Hicks, daughter of James Hicks, married Reverend Charles Moore; children: Rawlston, Sallie, Ira, Richard, Homer, and Mary Moore. Rawlston Moore married, first, Minnie Taper; second, Maxie Freeman, children by second marriage, Freeman M., Mary Ellen, Harold, Martha, and Thomas. Ira Moore, married Virginia Kea; children:Reverend Leland Moore, Lyman Moore, and Annie Moore. Sallie Moore married William Elbert Arnold; children: Patsie, Bessie, Belle, Hinton (Lieut.-Col.), Mary Moore and Ruth Moore Arnold. (Lieut.-Col.), Mary Moore and Ruth Moore.

—*By Ruth Hicks Porter (Mrs. L. L.)*

HIGHTOWER

JAMES RICHARD HIGHTOWER

In 1894 the family of James Richard and Amarinth Sims Hightower came to make their home in Dublin and have been prominently identified with the civic, religious and social life of this community. Mrs. Hightower, a woman of high intellectual attainments, was especially active in church work, was president of the Woman's Missionary Union of the First Baptist Church for many years, during which time she laid the first brick when the corner stone of this handsome edifice was placed in 1907.

The two younger daughters, Lil Frances and Ruby Usher, came to Dublin with their parents and were leaders in educational and social circles. Lil Frances, now Mrs. Thomas Randolph Ramsay (see Ramsay and Guyton genealogies), was librarian of the Dublin Carnegie Library and held this position continuously from 1904 until her marriage in 1922. Her lovely soprano voice was in constant demand, both as a member of the choir of the First Baptist Church and at gatherings of all kinds.

Dr. Ruby Usher Hightower was a member of the faculty of the Dublin High School, as teacher of mathematics and Latin, later going to Shorter College, Rome, Georgia, where she has held the chair of mathematics since 1919. In 1927 Dr. Hightower received the degree of Ph.D. in mathematics from the University of Missouri, and is recognized as one of the foremost authorities on this subject in the United States. Many honors have been accorded Dr. Hightower, among them election to the honorary scientific society Sigma Xi (called the Phi Beta Kappa of science); membership in the Pi Lambda Theta, Pi Mu Epsilon, Sigma Delta Epsilon, all of these being national honorary fraternities.

Minnie, the eldest daughter, married Hon. Stanley Bennett of Quitman, Georgia, one of Georgia's most prominent lawyers and statesmen. Four children were born to this union: 1. Louise Bennett, member faculty of Shorter College; 2. Spencer Bennett, married Merle Kitchings; 3. Paul Bennett, married May Bec Bowman and has two daughters, Mary Ann and Jane Bennett; 4. Mildred Bennett.

Alma, the second daughter, married James D. Kilpatrick, of Monticello, Georgia, who at the time of his death in 1913 was president of the Georgia Bar Association. There are two living sons: Louis, who married Betty Marechal, and Donald, who married Rebecca Childs. Three other children died young.

James Richard Hightower, the subject of this sketch, was born in Henry County, Georgia, February 16, 1846, and spent his boyhood around Atlanta when that metropolis was in the small town class. At the age of 16 he volunteered in Company E, 13th Georgia Regiment and was soon made a messenger of the Confederate Govern-

JAMES RICHARD HIGHTOWER

ment, a post he held until imprisoned in Atlanta by Sherman. He saw the greater part of the Battle of Atlanta and in this battle had two horses shot from under him in a single day. His discharge was signed May 15, 1865.

In March, 1869, James Richard Hightower married Amarinth Sims who was born at Island Shoals, Henry County, Georgia, March 27, 1844, and died in Dublin, Georgia, April 8, 1908. She was the daughter of Thomas Washington Sims (1818-1878) and Nancy Amelia Clark Simms (1822-1899); granddaughter of William Simms (1796-1866) and Sara Hull Sims (1800-1852); and great granddaughter of the Revolutionary soldier, John Sims, of South Carolina (died after 1796), and his wife, Fannie Tucker Sims. Other Revolutionary ancestors of Amarinth Sims Hightower were: Captain Thomas Clark (1753-1837) of Virginia and Georgia; Thomas Parks (1750-1831) of Virginia, South Carolina and North Carolina; John Brockman (1735-1825) of Virginia and South Carolina. John Clark (1780-1870), father of Nancy Amelia Clark Sims, was a soldier in the War of 1812, and was married in 1816 to Susan Parks (1796-1880), daughter of the Revolutionary soldier, Captain Thomas Parks (1750-1831) of Virginia and North Carolina, and his third wife, Annie Brockman.

While in Dublin, James Richard Hightower was Chief Inspector for the state of Georgia on farm lands for Forman and Company until he retired from active life during his declining years. The last three years of his life were spent in Bainbridge, at "Rose Arbor Cottage," the home of his daughter and son, Mr. and Mrs. Thomas Randolph Ramsay, whose beautiful gardens are the mecca for visitors from many states. Here he died February 17, 1933. In all his dealings Mr. Hightower was considered the highest type of an honorable gentleman. He was a member of the Baptist Church.

HIGHTOWER GENEALOGY

The Hightower family is of English origin, settling first in this country in Virginia and the Carolinas. The first of this line of whom we have record in Georgia was William Hightower, one of the original settlers of Campbell County, which was formed in 1828 from parts of Fayette, DeKalb, Carroll, and Coweta counties, and which has since been absorbed into Fulton. Lucian Lamar Knight in his Roster of the Revolution for Georgia records the fact that William Hightower was a Revolutionary soldier from this state.

William Hightower married Miss Fann of Fayette County, Georgia, and had six children: 1. James Calhoun Hightower, 2. Raleigh Hightower, married Elizabeth House, 3. Isaac Hightower, 4. Carroll Hightower, 5. Fannie Hightower, married —— Couch, 6. Sallie Hightower, married Jonathan Mitchell.

William Hightower died after 1830 and is buried in Bishop Cemetery, Fayette County, Georgia.

Raleigh Hightower, second son of William Hightower, was married to Elizabeth (Betsy) House of Clarke County, Georgia, in 1819, and this marriage is on record in the Ordinary's office of that county. Children of this couple were: 1. Dr. Richard House Hightower, married, first, Anne Chapman, second, Miss Brown, 2. William Hightower, 3. Paschal Hightower, 4. John Nelson Hightower, married Miss Chapman, 5. James Cook Hightower, married first, Lucinda Elizabeth Johnson, second, Sarah Patillo, 6. Dr. Raleigh Hightower II, 7. Caroline Hightower, married Johnson H. Turner, 8. Winnifred Hightower, 9. Martha Hightower, married Richard Carroll.

Raleigh Hightower is buried in Henry County, near Stockbridge.

James Cook Hightower, fourth son of Raleigh and Elizabeth House Hightower, was a prominent citizen of Henry County, Georgia, where he died about 1890. He married Lucinda Elizabeth Johnson, daughter of Moore and Charity Couch Johnson, and first cousin to Governor Herschel V. Johnson of Georgia. Moore Johnson was the son of Captain Richard Johnson, of Virginia, who married the widow, Mrs. Charity Willis. The following reference shows Captain Richard Johnson to have served in the Colonial Army: Burgess, "Virginia Soldiers of 1776," Vol. III., p. 1241: "Captain Richard Johnson's roll call given in full, 5th October, 1774."

Children of James Cook and Lucinda Elizabeth Johnson Hightower were: 1. Bartholomew Hightower, born 1842, married Nancy Owens; 2. John Wesley Hightower, born November 4, 1844, married, first, Mary Lora Cherry, second, Ada Bean; 3. James Richard Hightower, the subject of this sketch, recorded above; 4. Jordan Ogburn Hightower, born 1848, married Mary Lummus; 5. Willis Weaver Hightower, born 1850, married, first, Penelope Glass, second, sister to his first wife.

Children of James Cook and his second wife, Sarah Patillo Hightower: 1. Berry Hightower, married Minnie Buckaloo; 2. Barbara Hightower, married Robert Austin.

JOHN WESLEY HIGHTOWER

John Wesley Hightower, second son of James Cook and Lucinda Elizabeth Johnson Hightower, was born in Henry County, Georgia, November 4, 1844; married, first, May, 1873, Mary Lora Cherry (born February 11, 1857- died August 10, 1900), and had two daughters: 1. Lynnette Hightower, married Michael Vincent Mahoney; 2. May Hightower, married Frank Brown Waterman, and has two children: (1) Lora Waterman, married Edward Walter Burke, of Macon, Georgia, and has one son, Edward Walter Burke, Jr.; (2) John Thomas Waterman, married Eleanor Freeman of Birmingham, Alabama, and has three children, viz.: Eleanor Louise Waterman, John Thomas Waterman Jr., and Frank Brown Waterman.

LYNNETTE HIGHTOWER MAHONEY

Lynnette Hightower Mahoney, daughter of John Wesley and Lora Cherry Hightower, was born in Griffin, Georgia; married on May 17, 1899, to Michael Vincent Mahoney I. and resided first in Hawkinsville, Georgia, where their eldest son, John Hightower Mahoney, was born. In 1901 the Mahoney family located in Dublin and have given this community the highest type of citizens, both in business and in cultural circles. M. V. Mahoney I. was a prominent railroad official, holding the position of General Freight and Passenger Agent for the Wrightsville and Tennille Railroad for 25 years, which post he was filling at the time of his death, April 21, 1924. No more highly esteemed matron has ever resided in Dublin than that gracious gentle woman, Lynnette Hightower Mahoney, whose sudden passing on January 3, 1941, cast a pall of sadness over the entire city, where she was admired and revered for her genuineness and true nobility of character.

Three sons and one daughter were born to Michael Vincent and Lynnette Hightower Mahoney:

I. John Hightower Mahoney, a prominent financier and insurance agent of this city, who married Mary Camp (see Camp genealogy).

II. Michael Vincent Mahoney II., a prominent journalist of Los Angeles, California, who married Virginia Nisson and has one son, Michael Vincent Mahoney III., born in London, England, September, 1937.

III. Joseph Aloyisius Mahoney, also a journalist of note of Los Angeles.

IV. Lynnette Hightower Mahoney, who married Charles Jacques Warner, Jr., of Rome, Georgia.

—*By Henrietta Sanders Freeman (Mrs. E. B.)*

HIGHTOWER

DESCENDANTS OF JOSHUA HIGHTOWER

In the early days of Laurens County Joshua Hightower, a native of Virginia, a young man with an ambition to become a large landlord proprietor, made his way into middle Georgia. Here he survived all hardships of the frontier and all encounters with the Red men. When he died in 1847, he had achieved the aim of his life. He left a good estate to be enjoyed by a large family. His will signed April 19, 1847, probated January, 1849, in Laurens County, names the following sons and daughters: (1) Raleigh, (2) Rebecca, married James Underwood, (3) Gregory D., (4) Winfield, (5) Mary, married James Hicks, (6) Josiah Warren, (7) Frederic, (8) Sarah, (9) Joshua E.

Gregory D. Hightower, son of Joshua, was born in Laurens County and when he reached maturity migrated to Alabama, and there became an extensive planter, reared a large family and died at the good old age of 85. His eldest son, Robert J. Hightower, returned to Laurens County and became an esteemed citizen and a highly successful farmer. He married Elizabeth Hicks, daughter of Nathaniel Hicks, and reared and educated four sons: (1) James E. Hightower, (2) Robert Henry Hightower, (3) William Joshua Hightower, (4) T. Marion (Cone) Hightower.

Dr. Robert Henry Hightower, son of Robert and Elizabeth Hicks Hightower, was born July 22, 1851; died July 23, 1905; married Eugenia Williams of Montgomery County, Georgia, daughter of Captain T. F. Williams on June 3, 1878. Eugenia Williams Hightower died in Dublin, January 25, 1938.

Dr. Robert Henry Hightower was born in Laurens County, now Johnson County, at the Hightower plantation, where he spent his childhood. Upon graduation from medical school at Washington College, now Washington and Lee University, General Robert E. Lee, president of the University, presented him with an autographed book.

After graduating from medical school, he located in Dublin and started practicing medicine. His office was the first brick building to be erected in Dublin and he built the first bridge to cross the muddy Oconee River. He owned the first library in Dublin and gave the land for the First Episcopal Church, of which he was a member. The church is still in use. Dr. Hightower had a large practice and was very prosperous during his lifetime. He was a true sportsman. His favorite sports were hunting, fishing and horseback riding. His sense of humor and pleasant personality were well known to everyone that knew and came in contact with him.

Eugenia Williams Hightower was a charter member and helped to organize the first Missionary Society of the First Methodist Church. After the death of her husband, Dr. Robert Henry Hightower, she became a very successful business woman. During her lifetime she owned and operated music store, drug store, farms, and to her goes the credit of erecting the first picture show ever to operate in Dublin.

Two haughters and one son were born to Dr. Robert H. and Eugenia Williams Hightower: (1) Caroline Hightower, who married Davis Dakota Hankkins and they have one son, D. D. Hankins, Jr., and a grandson, D. D. Hankins, III.

(2) Vera Hightower, married Lipscomb Simpson and has one daughter, Vera Simpson.

(3) Robert Henry Hightower II., was born September 13, 1895, married Jewette Ashley on November 28, 1920. They have two children, Robert H. III., and May Dorothy Hightower. Robert H. Hightower, II., served his country in the first World War by enlisting in the U. S. Navy. He is past Exalted Ruler of B. P. O. E., Legionnaire, member of the Lion's Club and a Mason. His work in civic affairs has been outstanding. He has been in the show business

practically all of his life and at the present time is manager of the two theatres in Dublin.

Robert H. Hightower, III., is now (1941) a junior at Georgia School of Technology, where he was awarded a scholarship for his athletic ability. He is a member of Sigma Alpha Epsilon fraternity.

William Joshua Hightower, son of Robert and Elizabeth Hicks Hightower, born September 5, 1854, died March 21, 1909, was a prominent official, serving as Clerk of Superior Court from 1893 to 1909. He married Alice G. Hall, a native of Portland, Maine. Both are buried in Northview Cemetery. Children: 1. Foye; 2. Elisabeth, married Walter Prescott, one daughter, Audie; 3. Willie Cone, married, first, Paul Q. McCreary, second, Hill G. Thomas, and has one daughter, Margie Thomas. Hill is the son of James Archibald Thomas and Josephine Augustus Corbett. J. A. Thomas served four years in the Confederate Army, joining at sixteen years of age, was also Commander-in-Chief of the United Confederate Veterans. Josephine Corbett Thomas was the daughter of Colonel Edmund C. Corbett, of the Confederate Army. J. A. and Josephine's children: Cumming Francis; Colonel James A., Jr., who died in France in World War No. 1; Hansel Provost; Hill G.; and Daisy (Thomas) Brannon. 4. Louise, married Morris Q. Waddell, one daughter, Evelyn; 5. Margie, married Jep Cloude, their daughter Elizabeth married H. W. Bailey, and they have twin sons, Billy and Bobby Bailey; 6. Ruth, married S. Parker New, children: Parker, Jr. (died young), Jane and William (see New Family); 7. Darte, married J. A. Aldred, one daughter, Dorothy.

Thomas Everett Hightower, son of Thomas (Cone) Hightower, married Lil Salter, daughter of Z. B. Salter and Molly Smith Salter, of Bartow, Georgia. Children: 1. Charlotte, married John Harwell, one son, John, Jr.; 2. Carolyn, married George Garrett, one daughter, Carol; 3. William J., married Patsy Fordham; 4. Betty Rose. Thomas E. Hightower held important positions, was City Solicitor and Mayor of Dublin, 1928-29.

—*By Robert H. Hightower.*

HOBBS

When Laurens County was in its infancy two brothers, J. Larry and Boling Hobbs, came to settle within her bounds. Both received land in the lottery of 1819. Part of this same land is still owned and tilled by descendants of these two men.

It has been said of these men: "Their educational advantages were scant but rugged constitutions, strong minds and an unconquerable ambition to learn was equipment in itself which helped them along the road of life." They began their careers as farmers, took up the study of the Bible, Greek, and Hebrew, as students of Jesse Mercer, were real Christians and leaders of men to Christ.

J. Larry Hobbs (1798-1868) married Mary (Polly) Keen (1800-1870) in 1820. (See Keen History.) Children: John, married Mary Faircloth; Berry, married Harriett Witherington; Elizabeth, married Thomas Alligood; Mary; Martha; Sarah, married Hardy Alligood; Nancy, married George McDaniel; Larry, married, first, Eliza Nobles, second, Unity Scarborough. Larry and Mary Hobbs are buried in the Hobbs family cemetery near Dexter.

John Hobbs (1824-1893), married Mary Faircloth (1830-1913) in 1841. He served four years in the Civil War, Company "C," 57th Georgia Regiment. Both are buried in the Hobbs cemetery near Dexter. Children: Frank, married Charlotte Bryans; Eugenia, married Tom Bryant; Allen Lemuel, married Annie Elizabeth Graham. John and William never married. Augustus, married Mamie Charters; Early, married Hattie Maddox; Eliza, married, first, W. B. Scarborough, second, Bill Singleton.

Franklyn's children: Lantie, Roene, Yuntie, Winnie, Stella, John, Lemuel, and Frank.

Augustus Hobbs moved to Texas in 1890 where the family still resides. Children: Effie, Eula, Vera, Lavisher, Mary, and Burnace.

Eliza's children: Parl and Billy Scarborough; Dora, Orene, May, Alice, Lena, and Clifton Singleton.

Early Hobbs (1868), married Hattie Maddox (1869) in 1892, is a progressive farmer, owns and operates a large farm three miles from Dublin, a Christian gentleman and is the only living child of John Hobbs. Children: Lila, married William Lee; Estoria, married John Brown. Grandchildren: Mavis, married J. B. Mathis; Carl, married Sarah McCoy; Verlie, Robert Lee, E. W., Francis, Rosalynd, John and Edward Brown. Great-grandchildren: William, Reba, Grace, and Wendell Mathis, and William Lee.

Allen Lemuel Hobbs (1856-1914), married Annie Elizabeth Graham (1855-1927) in 1880, daughter of Archibald Hugh Graham and Sara Rebecca Dopson of Telfair County, Georgia. Beulah, a sister of Annie, married John Henry Thomas of Laurens County, both prominent citizens who contributed much to the social, business and religious life of Dublin. Their children are: Dr. Hugh Graham Thomas and Mrs. Ethel Linder, Macon, Georgia; Mrs. Ruby Tye, Ellaville, Georgia; Mrs. Bernice Hansard, Tuscaloosa, Alabama. Mrs. Lemuel Hobbs was a woman of high Christian character whose life of good deeds are still remembered. She and Judge Hobbs are buried, as are the Thomas', in Northview Cemetery of Dublin. Judge Hobbs was a deacon of Dexter Baptist Church, Mason, Woodman of the World, known and loved for his splendid traits of character and his helpfulness to his fellowman. Children: James Duncan, married Esther Hall; Maude, married Kilpatrick

Carswell; Willie, married, first, Augustus Joiner, second, Ralph Johnston, third, Abner Camp; Mable, married James Goodson; Walter Allen, married Mary Lucile Arnold. The daughters are residents of Atlanta, Georgia.

James Duncan Hobbs (1883-1928), married Esther Hall (1881-1941) in 1901, daughter of Dr. Thomas Hartley Hall, a leading physician of Dublin and Laurens County for fifty years. James served as Deputy Clerk of the Superior and City Courts. Both were charter members of Jefferson Street Baptist Church and are buried in Northview Cemetery. Children: James, married, first, Gladys Fuqua, second, Ruby Carlisle; Rupert, married Wilhelmina Faulk; Allen, married Gertrude Tarpley; Hartley, married Julia Coley; Edwin. Grandchildren: Betty, married Reginald Seymour, Jimmy, Ellen and Julia Hobbs.

Walter Allen Hobbs, married Lucille Arnold in 1915. A highly respected citizen, associate deacon of First Baptist Church, Dublin, officer in the Citizens & Southern Bank, treasurer City of Dublin, Woodman of the World, Mason and charter member of Rotary Club. Children: (1) Marjorie Alvina Hobbs, Georgia State College for Women, Milledgeville, Georgia, married Robert Lee Wilson, University of Georgia, now (1941) residents of Hololulu, Hawaii, where Mr. Wilson is Sergeant-Major, U. S. Marine Corps; (2) Walter Allen Hobbs, Jr., Georgia Military College, Milledgeville, and North Georgia College, Dahlonega.

Other grandchildren and great-grandchildren of Allen Lemuel Hobbs, besides those already mentioned of James and Walter, are: Lucille Carswell, married Virgil Baker, Jr.; Harry Carswell, married Harriett Edwards; Ralph Johnston, married Virginia Miller; Malcolm Johnston, married Frances Wiley; Abner Camp; Clyde Goodson, married Sara Hall; Dorothy Goodson; Virgil Baker, III.; Harry, Catherine, Carol and Edward Carswell; Richard, Peggy, and Diane Johnston; David and Carol Goodson.

Boling Hobbs, married Sally Clemants in 1820. Children: Drury, married, first, Annie Roach, second, Sarah Kennedy; Lucretia, married James Wyatt; Nancy, married James Wright; Sarah, married William Perry; Berry, died young; Andrew Jackson, married Mary Scarborough.

Drury's children: John Boling, married Clem Scarborough; Andrew, married Anna Robinson; Charlie, married Fannie ——; Frances, married Webb Wyatt; Drury E., married Mattie Rozier. Drury and Sarah are buried in Wells Cemetery near Marie Baptist Church.

Andrew Jackson Hobbs (1828-1894), married Mary Scarborough in 1856, was a gentleman of splendid character, land owner and farmer of the Poplar Springs community, joined that church in 1857, is buried in the church cemetery. Children: Fannie, Augustus, Alfred, Alonza never married; Morgan, married Anna Fordham; Emma, married John Benjamin Fordham.

Drury E. Hobbs, land owner and member of Marie Baptist Church, buried in Wells cemetery. Children: Horace, married Inez Jones; Robert, married Ellen Jones; Herschel, married Annie Perry; Sarah, married Jim Hobbs; Mattie Lou, married Robert Orr. Grandchildren: Ann, Earl, Edsel, Robert, Eldee, Virginia and H. D. Hobbs.

Morgan's children: James Andrew, married Mary Jim Morgan; Albert; Elizabeth, married Thomas Harville; Robert, married Mrs. Annabel Humphries; Joseph, married Nell Jones. Grandchildren: Rebecca Hobbs, married J. D. Hogan; Charles, James, Patsy, and Joan Freeman, Thomas, Morgan, and Betty Harville.

Emma Hobbs Fordham (see Fordham genealogy).

HOBBS-ARNOLD-GAINES BRAWNER LINEAGE

Lucille Arnold Hobbs (Mrs. W. A.) is the daughter of Willis Roberson Arnold (1866-living) who married, first, Jennie Gaines, 1887, deceased; second, Mary Agnes Heeden, 1899. Children by first wife: Maggie Fredonia, married Otis Benjamin Dixon; Annie; twins, William Alfred, soldier in World War No 1, Headquarters 5th F. A. Brigade, 5th Division, in France one year, two Divisional Citations, married Lucille Hall; John Allen, twin to William, married Wilibel Buchanan; Mary Lucille and Lois. Children by second wife: Henry Ormand, married Noel Bufford; Robert Wiley; Willie; Oliver Chester, married Louise Bruorton; Julia Lillian, married Max W. Bryant. Grandchildren: Arnold Dixon; William Alfred, James Allen, and Tommie Arnold. John Allen Arnold, married Jean Rawls; Eleanor Ruth Arnold, married Bernice W. Hailey; Marjorie A. Hobbs, married Robert Lee Wilson; Walter Allen Hobbs, Ormand Arnold, Jr., Chester Arnold, Jr.; Max W. and Lillian Kirk Bryant. Great-grandchildren: David Allen Arnold, and Bernice Arnold Hailey.

Willis Roberson Arnold was the only son of James J. Arnold, born 1838, Confederate soldier, Company F, 4th Alabama Infantry, and Aminda Clemantine Brawner (1843-1886), married 1862; two daughters, Sarah Permelia (1865-1931), married Winston Barnett; Annie C. (1869-living), married William A. Wethington. Aminda C. Brawner Arnold, daughter of Jesse Brawner (1806-1844) and Sarah Coffee (1812-1893), married 1833; their children: Loney Charlotte, born 1836, married Thomas McLain; Selena Elizabeth, born 1834, married ——; Sarah Milinda (1838-1893), married Charles Westley Elliott (1824-1901); Mary Melissa (1841-1918), married George W. Elliott (1839-1906), and Aminda Clemantine. Sarah Coffee Brawner, married, second, Willis Kirby (1808-1879), married 1852, one son Lewis Kirby, born 1856, married Mrs. Hattie Snelling.

Jennie Gaines (1868-1898) was the daughter of Reverend John

Richard Gaines (1830-1869) of the North Georgia Methodist Conference, who married Sarah Elizabeth Baxter, 1851. Children: John Richard, married Irene Tumlin; Fannie (1854-1940), married, first, Lum Dowdy, second, D. A. McNabb; Viola (1865-1930), married Robert C. Finch (1851-1916); George, married Salley English; Amanda, married D. A. McNabb; Mary (1856-living), married Young A. Murphy (1850-1912); and Jennie.

Reverend John Richard Gaines was the son of William Richard Gaines (1781-1884 or 85) and Mary Smith. Children: Ransom C., Calvin, Elizabeth, Nancy, Louranie, married W. L. Johns; John Richard, married Sarah E. Baxter, and perhaps others.

William Richard Gaines was the son of Richard Gaines (1752-1837), soldier in Revolutionary War, Sergeant in 5th Virginia Regiment, buried at Poplar Springs Church, Laurens District, South Carolina, married Frances Jolly. Children: Mary Ellen, married George Tierce; William Richard, married Mary Smith; Stephen, Henry, James, and perhaps others.

Richard Gaines was the son of Henry Gaines (1731-33-1796) who married Maria Woods; Henry Gaines, charter member of Poplar Springs Church, South Carolina, organized 1794, moved from Virginia to South Carolina about 1790, was the son of Richard Gaines, Culpepper County, South Carolina, who died about 1756, married Dorothy ———.

Sarah Elizabeth Baxter Gaines (1834-1908) was the daughter of James W. Baxter (1805-1892) and Elizabeth (Betty) Isom (1806-1887) who married in 1825 or 1827. Children: Joseph W., born 1828; Charles William, born 1837; Jasper, born 1842; Melissa Ann (1844-1907), married J. Thomas Wethington; Parthena, born 1830, married a Wilson, and Sarah E.

James Baxter, called "Uncle Jimmy," leader of same Sunday School class in Level Creek Methodist Church for over 50 years, a resident of Gwinnett County, Georgia, at time of death, was the son of Andrew Baxter, Jr., born in South Carolina December 21, 1750, died in Wilkes County (now Greene), Georgia, 1816, served in Continental Army in the American Revolution. Received bounty grant of land in Georgia for his service. Married, 1784, Elizabeth Harris (1764-1844), daughter of Charles Harris, born in Mecklinburg County, North Carolina in 1740, died in Greene County, 1791. Charles Harris, a Revolutionary soldier, received land in Georgia for his services, married Elizabeth Thompson Baker. Children: Thomas W. (1784-1844), married Mary Wiley; Eli H., married Julia Richardson; Andrew, John, Cynthia, Eliza T., James, born May 5, 1805; died 1892, married Elizabeth Isom; Richard; Mary, married Wm. Green Springer. Andrew Baxter married Martha Williams and they were the parents of Alice Baxter, prominent member of the D. A. R. and U. D. C. Societies.

Andrew Baxter, Jr. (1750-1816) was the son of Andrew Baxter

(1725-1781), Revolutionary soldier of South Carolina, Lieutenant and Major, killed by the Tories and his wife, Frances.

Dates of birth, death and marriage in the foregoing records of the Hobbs and kindred families were obtained from old Bibles in the possession of Walter A. Hobbs, of Dublin, Georgia, from tombstone inscriptions, and Court records, and from "Roster of Revolutionary Soldiers in Georgia" by McCall.
—By Lucile Arnold Hobbs (Mrs. W. A.)

HORN

Pioneer families came to this section of Georgia from other states, making their homes in the fertile valley following the course of the Oconee River. Such a family were the Horns, for in the early 1800's, Josiah Horn and his wife, Rebecca Young Horn, with two of their children came from North Carolina and settled in Laurens County. The old home place was on the Dexter road five miles from where the city of Dublin now stands; the house stood opposite the New Bethel Baptist Church.

Two brothers came from North Carolina with Josiah Horn as far as Toomsboro, Georgia, where they left him to go to California and were never heard from since.

Josiah Horn owned tracts of land extending from the original Shewmake property to Turkey Creek; records show that he also owned lands lying outside Laurens.

The early county families often intermarried with others of their community and the sons and daughters of the Horn family intermarried with the Bender, Davis, Corbett, Fullwood, Guyton, Mizell, O'Neal, Roberts, Tucker, Yopp and other prominent families and thus were related to many of the earliest county families. Josiah Horn was an ancestor of M. J. Guyton, present postmaster of Dublin. (see Guyton genealogy).

Records from Department of State, Atlanta, read thus:

Josiah Horn, member, House of Representatives, Laurens County, 1821, 1822, 1823, 1824-25 Extra, 1825; Senator, Laurens County, 1826; Justice Inferior Court, Laurens County, February 10, 1824-1830.

Josiah Horn died in 1830; his wife, Rebecca Young, some years later; they are buried on the original home site near New Bethel Baptist Church.

Josiah and Rebecca Young Horn had four sons and four daughters:

I. Charles Washington Horn, married Laura Ann Hampton, April 7, 1836; six children.

II. Josiah Horn, married Susan Roberts; one child.

III. Crosby J. Horn (died 1866), charter member Laurens Lodge No. 75, F. & A. M., Dublin; married Mary Jane Roberts, April 3, 1845; four children. A son, Guyton Fondren Horn (born September 29, 1862), married Emilie Harrell, of Dodge County, in January, 1896; three daughters, Mary Lee, who married L. R. Lanier, with children (a) Mary Emilie, (b) Dick; Louise, who married R. M. Fletcher; Carrie, who married Abner Fordham. (This oldest known living Horn gave valuable information for Horn history).

IV. Benjamin Hunter Horn, born January 10, 1822; died December 5, 1856. (Detailed record later).

V. Lupina Horn (died 1870), married, first, Dr. Charles Brutus Guyton, January 27, 1836 (see Guyton genealogy); married, second, Mr. Davis.

VI. Louisa Horn (died 1878), married, first, William L. Hampton, February 8, 1838; married, second, Benjamin R. Smith. No children.

VII. Elmina Horn (died 1882), married Charles S. Guyton, June 29, 1830; four children (see Guyton genealogy).

VIII. Anne Horn (born October 5, 1810; died 1892), married Dr. Nathan Tucker, October 14, 1830; seven children. (see Tucker History).

HORN GENEALOGY (HORNE)

Benjamin Hunter Horn, born January 10, 1822; charter member Laurens Lodge No. 75, F. & A. M., Dublin; married June 6, 1848 Winneford E. A. Yopp; died December 5, 1856.

Winneford E. A. Yopp, born March 22, 1833; died February 28, 1889; married, first, Benjamin H. Horn; second, Cullen O'Neal. Children of Benjamin Hunter and Winneford Yopp Horn are:

I. Josiah Samuel Horn, son of Benjamin H. and Winneford Horn, born December 28, 1849; died July 4, 1892; married March 27, 1872, Anna Corbett (born September 12, 1851; died July 10, 1933); no children.

II. Washington Hansley Horn, son of Benjamin H. and Winneford Horn, born July 31, 1851; died December 6, 1851.

III. John William Horn, son of Benjamin H. and Winneford Horn, born April 26, 1853; died July 23, 1936. (Detailed record later).

IV. An infant son, died in infancy.

John William Horn, born April 26, 1853; died July 23, 1936. Married, first, on December 23, 1874, to Brancie Bender, daughter of Wiley J. and Sarah Jane Adams Bender; second, to Susan Bonner Hampton, daughter of George W. and Susan Fox Hampton, on June 11, 1897.

Bracie Bender, born September 20, 1850; died October 15, 1896. Children of John William and Brancie Bender Horn are:

I. Anna Tallulah Horn, daughter of John W. and Brancie Horn, born February 28, 1876; died October 17, 1896.

II. Benny Ola Horn, son of John W. and Brancie Horn, born January 21, 1878; died September 5, 1879.

III. Anton Bender Horne, son of John W. and Brancie Horn, born December 9, 1879; died May 24, 1941.

IV. Josiah Hansley Horne, son of John W. and Brancie Horn, born October 3, 1882; died March 25, 1938.

V. Lena May Horn, daughter of John W. and Brancie Horn, born November 28, 1888.

Anton Bender Horne (1879-1941) was a member of Laurens Lodge No. 75, F. & A. M., Dublin, also member Harmony Chapter No. 56, R. A. M.; married, first, Alice Inez Crowder (deceased), daughter of Dr. C. R. and Ella Flanders Crowder, on January 12, 1908; married, second, Nancy Jackson (born March 27, 1896), daughter of Wiley and Elizabeth Childs Jackson, of Monroe County, Georgia, on June 17, 1914. Children of Anton Bender and Nancy Jackson Horne are:

I. Anna Elizabeth Horne, born April 1, 1915; married Thomas Ralph Fountain, son of I. H. and Mary Pharis Fountain, on December 7, 1935; one son, Thomas Ralph Fountain, Jr.

II. Anton Bender Horne, Jr., born February 2, 1919. U. S. Navy, Gunner's Mate, 3rd class, U. S. S. Philadelphia, Hawaii.

III. Clarence Jackson Horne, born May 9, 1921.

IV. Emily Nankit Horne, born January 14, 1923.

Josiah Hansley Horne, born October 3, 1882; married Maude Dell Crowder (born February 27, 1885), daughter of Dr. C. R. and Ella Flanders Crowder, on March 5, 1908; died March 25, 1938. Children of Josiah Hansley and Maude Crowder Horne are:

I. Alice Florence Horne, born September 26, 1909; died April 18, 1924.

II. Josiah Hansley Horne, Jr., born December 14, 1910; in April, 1937, married Sally Montford, daughter of J. S. and the late Jennie Montford.

III. Kelso Crowder Horne, born November 12, 1912.

IV. Brancy Hannah Horne, born October 16, 1914.

V. Ella Dell Horne, born December 29, 1916.

Lena May Horn, born November 28, 1888; received her education in Dublin Public Schools and State Normal School of Athens; taught in various parts of the state; married, first, on January 7, 1914, to George Thomas Daniel (born March 29, 1888; died November, 1921), son of James Wright and Martha Davis Daniel; married, second, to

Benjamin A. Hurley (born October 6, 1870), on December 7, 1924. Children of George Thomas and Lena Horn Daniel are:

I. George Thomas Daniel, Jr., born April 1, 1915. U. S. Navy, Baker 1st class, U. S. S. Honolulu, Hawaii.

II. William Wright Daniel, born August 16, 1917; died January, 1918.

III. James Wesley Daniel, born December 7, 1919. U. S. Army, 6th Cavalry, Fort Oglethorpe, Georgia.

One son was born to Benjamin A. and Lena Daniel Hurley (nee Horn): Bernard Horn Hurley, born March 25, 1926.

John William Horn, married, second, Susan Bonner Hampton (born February 11, 1875), in June, 1897). Children of John W. and Susan Bonner Hampton Horn are: John William Horn, Jr., born March 18, 1907; and George Hunter Horn, born July 1, 1912. U. S. Army, Corporal, Battery "A," Second Field Artillery, Fort Clayton, Canal Zone.

Reference: Bible owned by Anton Bender Horne.

—*By Nancy Jackson Horne (Mrs. A. B.)*

JOHNSON

Pinckney (Pink) McDonald Johnson, M.D., son of William L. Johnson and Sara McGraw, was born March 9, 1856, in Washington County, Georgia; died January 19, 1907, in Lovett, Georgia; buried in Lovett cemetery. Married, October 1, 1893, at Lovett, Georgia, Mary Cornelia Marchman, born November 14, 1872, daughter of Cicero Abner Marchman and Mary Askew Marchman. They were natives of Greene County, later making their home in Laurens County. Cicero Abner Marchman served four years in the Confederate War as a member of the 8th Georgia Regiment, Company I, Stephens Lightguards "B" of Greene County. Was severely wounded in battle.

"Pink" Johnson was widely known for his civic leadership and had one of the largest practices ever known in this County, during the era of the horse and buggy county doctor. He acquired considerable land holdings and other interests in the county.

He was a learned man and one of the foremost men of this section. He took an interest in the advancement of his county and state, and was a moving spirit in all laudable enterprises. He was a member of the Shady Grove Baptist Church, but realized the need of a church in Lovett, Georgia; so gave the land, time and money to help build the Methodist Church there.

Seven children were born to Pinckney McDonald and Mary Cornelia Johnson: Nina, born August 17, 1894; Rubye, born October 27, 1896; Wade Hampton, born November 10, 1897; Vera, born June

3, 1899; Joseph McDonald, born July 19, 1901; Ralph Lamar, born December 3, 1904; Mary, born January 19, 1906.

Nina married Charles Douglas LaFrage, of Wilmington, North Carolina, February 5, 1912. Their children and grandchildren are: Charles Brigham LaFrage, born October 27, 1912; Lutrelle, born March 3, 1914, married James Griffin, Raleigh, North Carolina, August 9, 1939. Their daughter, Sara Lutrelle, born March 12, 1940. Rubye married Roy Watson Jackson, of Lovett, Georgia, November 6, 1911. Their children: Rex Leonard, born October 3, 1912, a member of First National Guards, 121st Infantry, Division 30, Company K, Fort Jackson, South Carolina; Jean Claire, born October 8, 1914, married Albert John Chaney, February 12, 1939, of Marion, Ohio, and Washington, D. C. Wade Hampton, married Florence Marland Daniels, November, 1918, of Minneapolis, Minnesota. He is a World War veteran and a Reserve Officer of the regular army. He was a Major in the 122nd Infantry of the regular army during the World War. Now lives in Los Angeles, California.

Vera married Marcus Daley, August 29, 1914, of Lovett; their children: Hugh Marcus Daley, born August 15, 1915, married Carlton Thorpe, August, 1938, of Rocky Mountain, North Carolina. Their child, Gerald Thorpe, born December 1, 1940, and lives in Rocky Mountain, North Carolina.

Joseph McDonald married Hazel Quincy, September 3, 1924, of Jacksonville, Florida. Their child: Joseph McDonald, Jr., born March, 1927, now living in Birmingham, Alabama.

Ralph Lamar died in infancy.

Mary married Matt Freeman Young, November 8, 1923, of Macon, Georgia. Their children: William Freeman, born 1926; Wade Hampton, born July 4, 1929.

Seaborn Johnson, with his wife, Barbara McGraw White, moved from Edgefield, South Carolina, to Washington County, Georgia, in 1849. He acquired large land holdings in what was Washington County, but due to the size of the county, a portion was cut off and Johnson County was established, changing his holdings to Johnson County. Their children: William L. Johnson, Captain in Civil War, married, first, Sarah McGraw, of Edgefield, South Carolina, married, second, Fannie Page; Eldridge A. Johnson, the first, married Elizabeth Massey; John Johnson, Captain in Civil War, married Fannie Clegg; Sampson Johnson died in Civil War, unmarried; Mary Johnson, married Eldridge Williamson and moved to Texas; Emily Johnson, married Wilson Shealey; Missouri Johnson, married Thomas B. Smith; Martha Johnson, married A. William Guinn; Amanda Johnson, married David Smith; Margaret Johnson, married, first, George Massey, killed in Civil War; married, second, William Jenkins; Sarah Johnson, married Samuel Page.

William L. Johnson, son of Seaborn, held large land interests and slaves before the Confederate War. He served as Captain in the War. First married Sara McGraw, who died during Civil War; later he married Fannie Page, mother of Dan Page, of Eastman, Georgia, and grandmother of the very talented and capable Bertha Sheppard Hart, of Dublin, Georgia, author of several text books, a writer and teacher of note.

Two of his sons, Pinckney McDonald and Seaborn Monroe Johnson, graduated from Augusta School of Medicine, Augusta, Georgia, did post graduate work in Philadelphia, and were practicing physicians in Laurens County; later Seaborn moved to Wrightsville, Georgia, and continued his practice until his death in 1933. "Pink" lived in Lovett until his death.

Nina Johnson LaFrage taught school in Laurens County before moving to North Carolina, where she now teaches in the city of Raleigh.

—By Rubye Johnson Jackson (Mrs. Roy)

KEEN

Among the early settlers of Laurens County was the Keen family, members of which have been prominently identified with the County's progress for six generations. First of this family to locate here were Elizabeth Keen, widow of a Revolutionary soldier of North Carolina, her two daughters, Mary (Polly) and Nancy Jane, her son Young and his wife, Lydia Dudley Keen. In the early 1800's they left their home, some distance from Goldsboro, North Carolina, and made the long and arduous journey to seek a new abode in this section of Georgia.

Elizabeth Keen, whose maiden name was Elizabeth Curlee, and her husband, John Keen, had five children: John Jr., William, Young, Nancy Jane, and Mary (Polly). The will of John Keen, written by him December 7, 1803, is on record in Sampson County, North Carolina. (Sampson County is adjoining county of Wayne, of which Goldsboro is county seat and near which the Keen family originally lived.) John Keen named as heirs his wife Elizabeth and his son William; his son John, Jr., was executor. His daughters and his son Young (then a minor of 13 years) are not named.

It is an established fact that Elizabeth Keen's husband was a soldier in the American Revolution, for her name is recorded as the widow of a Revolutionary soldier living in Laurens County, Georgia, in the "List of 600 Revolutionary soldiers living in Georgia, 1827-1828," compiled by Martha Lou Houston from original records in the National Capitol. His service is further established by the fact that Elizabeth Keen drew land in the Cherokee Land Lottery of 1838, as the widow of a Revolutionary soldier. This land was located in Laurens County, District 9, Section 1, Lot 205. ("Georgia Roster of the Revolution" by L. L. Knight.)

Elizabeth Keen continued to live in this County until her death, and is buried in the old Ballard family burial ground, near Brewton.

The two daughters of Elizabeth and John Keen married and reared families in the County. Mary (Polly) Keen married J. Larry Hobbs, September 7, 1820 (see Hobbs History); Nancy Jane Keen married James Witherington, in Pulaski County, September 25, 1831.

Young Keen, son of John and Elizabeth Keen, was born in North Carolina, March 27, 1790, and in his native state married his first wife, his cousin Lydia Dudley, daughter of Levi Dudley. The will of Levi Dudley was recorded in Clinton, Sampson County, North Carolina, in 1808, and in his will he named "my daughter Lydia Dudley" as an heir. Young Keen, who later married Lydia, signed this will as witness.

Young Keen was thrice married. By his first marriage to Lydia Dudley there were four children: Green L., Young Bright, Anna Leah, and Sinah. He married, second, on April 15, 1827, Rebecca Hester, and to this union were also born four children: John, Eli, William, and Rebecca. He married, third, on April 20, 1834, Mary Ann (Polly) Jones, and they had eight children: Lawrence, Henry, George, Elizabeth, Jane, Nancy, Almeda, and Dililah.

Young Keen died February 23, 1875, and is buried in the Fuller burial ground in this County.

Young Bright Keen, son of Young Keen and his first wife, Lydia Dudley, was born in Laurens County, December 7, 1821; married Malvina Todd, March 25, 1841; died in Dodge County, Georgia, August 3, 1886, and is buried there. Malvina Todd Keen was born in Laurens County, April 29, 1824; died May 10, 1887.

To Young Bright Keen and Malvina Todd Keen were born the following children: 1. Margie Ann; 2. John Lawrence; 3. Joseph Eldridge; 4. William David; 5. James Lemuel.

1. Margie Ann Keen (1842-1937) married James E. Jackson on May 4, 1862. Children: (1) James Allen Jackson married Maggie Moody Bland, seven children, viz., Ferrell Dee, Nina, Ralph Allen, Loren, Ruby Malone, Margaret, and Fletcher Jackson. (2) Malvina Cornelia Jackson married, first, Ira Hilbun, one son, Ira Hilbun, Jr., married, second, John William Cheek, five children, viz., Dr. Ovid Hugh, Claudia (Mrs. C. R. Carter), Lyman and Trellie (deceased). (3) Fannie Jackson married James B. Jones, ten children, viz., Gussie, Lamar, Pearl, Idus, Thurston, Bernice, Herbert, Gladys, Evelyn, and Jessie. (4) Melissa Jackson married James E. Page (see Page History), six children, viz., Pearl, Marvin, Landrum, Bluford Blount, Ruby, and Jackson. (5) Caledonia Jackson married O. I. Hilburn, six children, viz., Carl, Annie Maude, Clyde, James, Lucile, and Earl. (6) Sula Jackson married George Elbert,

five children, viz., Louis, Pauline, Gretchen, Hortense, and Solomon. (7) Rachel Stella Jackson married, first, Charlie L. Orr, two children, Freeman Roy married Addie Kellam (see Kellam History), and Ethel Orr married J. Felton Pierce (see Pierce History); married, second, I. E. Thigpen, two children, Hugh Isaac and Frances Elizabeth Thigpen. (8) Carrie Lee Jackson died young. (9) Willie Felder Jackson married Ida Braddy, twelve children, viz., Loren Felder, James DeWitt, Dorothy Clyde, Margie Lucile, Wilmon David, Wyman, Douglas Harold, Travis Eugene, Edwin Meldrom, Cecil Ray, Berdie Christine, and Annette.

2. John Lawrence Keen (1845-1910) married Elizabeth Donaldson; three children. (1) James Young Keen married Bessie Vickers, two children, viz., James Aurice and Bessie Lee Keen who married, first, J. Hughes Lord, second, Walker S. Reese. (2) Emma Keen married W. H. Tyre, three children, viz., Charles Craig, Jimmie Lee, and Ruby Dell Tyre. (3) Charley Keen married Sue Brown.

3. Joseph Eldridge Keen (born 1848) married, first, Mandy ———; four children, viz., Gussie, Carrie, Fannie, and Georgie; married, second, Nancy Maddox, five children, viz., Nellie, Sallie Nettie, Y. B., Josie, and Hattie; married, third, Mrs. Chambers, one son, J. B.; married, fourth, Mrs. Waver Barnett, no children.

4. William David Keen (1850-1925) married, first, on December 16, 1869, Zinphrey Holmes (1840-1893), daughter of Edwin Holmes (1808-1893) and his wife Melinda (1816-1870); seven children: (1) Demaris; (2) William Albert; (3) James Henry; (4) Lemuel McGee; (5) David Lanier; (6) Clara Melvina Melinda; (7) Young Cleveland. William David Keen married, second, Mrs. Mary Haskins Renfroe, one son, T. B.

William Albert Keen (1872-1934), eldest son of William David and Zinphrey Holmes Keen, married, first, on December 29, 1895, Bashaby Nell Guest (1879-1920). Children: (1) Zinnie Lee married Luther Burns Word, two children: Luther Burns, Jr., and Saralyn Word; (2) J. C. died in infancy; (3) Evie Dell married Julian A. Rachels, three children, Mary Nell, Evie Jean, and Julian A. Rachels, Jr.; (4) Willie Nell married Alexander Newton Moye, three children: Ruth Keen, Alexander Newton, Jr., and Thomas Floyd Moye; (5) Iris Guest married James H. Burns; (6) Demaris married John David Humphries, Jr. William Albert Keen married, second, Clara Gilbert, no children.

5. James Lemuel Keen was born May 11, 1853, and has lived to serve the County for many years. Perhaps no man, who has ever lived in Laurens County, has given public service over a longer period of years. In 1894, James Lemuel Keen was elected to serve the 16th Senatorial District in the State Legislature, and it was he who introduced the bill in the Senate to change the name of the town

Bruton to Brewton. Thus the spelling of the name but not the name itself was changed.

For over fifteen years James Lemuel Keen served as Chairman of the County Board of Education. When the present bridge, which spans the Oconee River was built, he was one of three men (J. M. Finn and F. M. Daniel were the other two) who served on the Bond Commission for the erection of this first concrete bridge in the county. He was Superintendent of the Sunday School of old Shady Grove Baptist Church for over thirty-eight years. It was James Lemuel Keen who was one of the organizers of the Farmers and Merchants Bank in 1910, and served as president of this bank until 1938. He then became, and is still, the chairman of the Board of Directors of this bank. This bank has been in continuous operation for thirty-one years. James Lemuel Keen also does extensive farming and has proved that he is as successful a planter as he is banker.

On January 25, 1877, James Lemuel Keen married Leona Jane Linder (see Linder genealogy) and had thirteen children, as follows:

1. Omar Wilder Keen married Zemmie Rogers and their children are: 1. Lennie, who married Dan Baker; 2. Ruth, who married M. A. Garrard; 3. Carl; 4. Margaret, married Cecil Carter and has one son, Pratt; 5. Lala.

2. Freeman Hill Keen married Jennie Jordon and their children are: 1. Grady Clinton; 2. Ammie, who married Fred Terrell and have (a) Fred, Jr., (b) Nancy; 3. Fay, who married Herman Rogers and have one child, Fay Catherine; 4. Youman Hill Keen.

3. Rebecca died in infancy.

4. Lennie Leona Keen married Walter C. Wilson (deceased), and had four children as follows: 1. James Keen Wilson, who married Julia McArthur, and has one son, viz., James Keen Wilson, Jr.; 2. Nannie, who married Kenneth Matthews; 3. Sybil, who married Roy Powell; 4. Gladys, married Tom Spight.

5. Mamie Willie died in infancy.

6. Ola L. Keen.

7. Essie Laffel Keen married John B. Haynes; no children.

8. James B. died in infancy.

9. Osee Fulton Keen married Margaret Foulks, of Amite, Louisiana, and they have three children, viz., 1. Ann, 2. Marshall Fulton, 3. Cary.

10. Lehman Pratt Keen married Mildred Elizabeth Arnau (see Arnau genealogy), and they have one son, Lehman McGrath Keen.

11. Trammell Colwell Keen married Ursula (Sula) Harvard (see Harvard genealogy), and their children are as follows: 1. Trammell Colwell, 2. William Harvard, 3. James Lemuel, and 4. Susan Ward.

12. Beeman Chandler Keen married Mary Elizabeth Bryans, of Riddleville, Washington County, Georgia, and they have one son, Beeman Chandler.

13. James Lemuel Keen, Jr., married Lila Moore, of Winder, Georgia, and their children are: 1. Jane Virginia, and 2. James Lemuel the third.

It seems that every generation of Linders must have at least one doctor among its number. The doctor in the present generation is Osee Fulton Keen. He was graduated from the Atlanta Medical College; interned at Georgia Baptist Hospital; practiced medicine in Mississippi; served as Captain in 39th Infantry, 4th Division; three years in service and fifteen months in France and Germany; was given citation for bravery during the Meuse-Argonne Drive. He was one of the organizers and is one of the owners and directors of Oglethorpe Infirmary in Macon, Georgia.

Lehman Pratt Keen was cashier of the Farmers and Merchants Bank (first located in Brewton, but now in Dublin) for twenty-six years. At the end of that time, his father, James Lemuel Keen, retired as president and he succeeded his father to that office.

Trammell Colwell Keen has served two consecutive terms, 1930-1934, as mayor of the city of Dublin, Georgia; served as member of the Board of Alderman, 1923-1928; on City Board of Education as Treasurer, 1929, and has held the office of Tax Collector for Laurens County from 1935 to present time. Trammell Colwell Keen held the commission of Commander of Company K, 121st Infantry of the National Guards from 1922 to 1935.

Beeman Chandler Keen served in Company 6, Replacement Group, as a secretary at Fort McPherson, Georgia, during the World War. He is a member of the Jury Commission of Laurens County and has served for ten consecutive years as Secretary of the Laurens County Baptist Association. He resides at the original home of his father, James Lemuel Keen.

James Lemuel Keen, Jr., is the present Clerk of the Laurens County Commissioners and held the same position during the term, 1932-1936. He is a member of the present Board of Education for the city of Dublin and for a number of years was the superintendent of the Sunday School of the First Baptist Church of Dublin.

The early records of the Keen family in North Carolina and in Laurens County, Georgia, were obtained from the following sources: (1) Will of John Keen recorded in Sampson County, North Carolina; (2) Certified statement made by Margie Ann Keen Jackson (deceased), grand-daughter of Young Keen; (3) Information given by Delilah Autry (deceased), daughter of Young Keen; (4) Family Bibles. John D. Humphries, Jr., has done extensive research on the Keen family, and has furnished valuable information.

—*By Lehman Pratt Keen.*

KELLAM

The Kellam family is of English descent, settling first in this country in Virginia; later, sons of the family emmigrated southward and located in Georgia. Russell Kellam settled in Laurens County, and the home he built, over one hundred years ago, is still standing —a large two-story structure, typical of the early Southern homes of this section.

Russell Kellam, born September 4, 1795, was married January 1, 1820, to Temperance B. Jordon, of Washington County, Georgia, who was born December 24, 1802. He served in the Legislature when the capital was Milledgeville. His brother, Gideon Kellam, served in the War of 1812, as Captain under General Blackshear. Russell Kellam's children are:

I. James Gideon Kellam, born November 12, 1820; married Mary S. Howard, April 5, 1849.

II. A. Russell Kellam, born May 4, 1823; married Zoe Love Buffington, November 24, 1846. He moved to Missouri and became Governor of that state.

III. Green Troup Kellam, born March 13, 1825, served in the War Between the States; married N. F. Buffington, September 14, 1851. He was Ordinary of Johnson County, Georgia, in 1860. Was appointed by Governor Brown as one of his staff, with the rank of Colonel.

IV. Elizabeth Susannah Kellam, born April 17, 1827; married Thomas C. Howard, May 16, 1849. Children: 1. Thomas Coke Howard, married Annie Lee; their children: Coke, Lee, Lizzie Mae, Pauline, Robert. 2. Pauline Howard, married David S. Blackshear (see Blackshear History); their children: (1) Howard Blackshear, unmarried; (2) Carrie Belle Blackshear, married J. E. Smith, Jr., two children, Eldridge and Clyde Smith; (3) Marmaduke H. Blackshear, married Annie Hardeman, two children, Hardeman and Carolyn B. Wilson; (4) Alex D. Blackshear, unmarried; (5) Robert H. Blackshear, married Rebecca Branham, three children, Hamilton, Robert, Jr., and David; (6) Pauline Blackshear, married C. D. Greenway, two children, Alex and Carlos Greenway. 3. Willie Howard, married Alex Daley, their children: (1) Pauline, married J. E. Burch; (2) Julian, died in infancy; (3) Clifford, died in infancy; (4) Inez, died in infancy; (5) Russell, married Lois Walton, four children, Lois, Alexa, Russell, Trabue; (5) Millard, married Frances Wooten, two children, Alex and June, (6) Rowena, married Will Burford, minister, two daughters, Rowena and Wilma Burford, lost a son, Billy; (7) Elmer, married May Ware, one daughter, May Ware Tyson; (8) Myra, married Edison Varner, one son, James Varner; (9) Fred, died unmarried; (10) Albert, died in infancy; (11) Comer, married Josephine Whitmire, no children. 4. Mattie Howard, married Frank Bilbor, six children: Maude, Frank, Bessie, Lee, Howard, Ida Bilbor.

V. Mary Ann Jane Kellam, born October 12, 1829, married James H. Oliver December 2, 1850. She died February, 1913.

VI. Seth Jordon Kellam, born October 20, 1832, fought in the War Between the States. Married A. Victoria Ellington, May 8, 1862. Children: 1. Seth Monte Kellam, born April 25, 1871, died June 28, 1936; married Wilhelmina Blackshear (see Blackshear history); six children: Monte (died in infancy), Thomas Blackshear, Seth Hamilton, Wilhelmina Blackshear, Eva Elizabeth, and Paul David. 2. William E. Kellam, born 1872; died October 23, 1898. 3. Talley E. Kellam, born September 16, 1876, married Rosa Stanley. (see Stanley history). Their children: (1) Addie, married F. Roy Orr, two sons, Freeman and Tal Orr; (2) Nannette, married John coggins of South Carolina, one child, Anne Scoggins. (3) Victoria, unmarried. (4) William Eustace, married Julia Thomas, two daughters, Caroline and Rosalind Kellam. (5) S. M., married May Proctor, one child, Seth Monte Kellam. 4. Jesse Kellam, born 1879; died September, 1936; married E. E. Swinson, February 5, 1907. Their children: (1) Sam, married Frances Crawford; (2) Edward, married Frances Jones; (3) Mary Will, unmarried; (4) Warren Starkey, married Edna Ard. 5. Bettie Kellam, born October 17, 1866; died February 22, 1875. 6. Callie Kellam, born 1868; died September 15, 1876.

VII. Carolina Kellam, born May 1, 1836.

VIII. Adrian Florida Kellam, born June 1, 1838: died July 8, 1912.

IX. Richard Amasa ("Tobe") Kellam, born October 14, 1840, fought in the War Between the States; married E. B. Blackshear, December 17, 1874; died May 29, 1876. Their son, R. A. Kellam, lives in Baltimore, Maryland.

X. Zoe B. Kellam, born August 14, 1843, married Josiah Ellington, June 18, 1861.

—By *Wilhelmina Blackshear Kellam (Mrs. S. M.)*

KITTRELL

Dr. Charles H. Kittrell, optometrist, was born in Washington County, Georgia, February 22, 1876. At the age of seven he moved with his parents, the late Baldwin S. Kittrell and the late Sara Harrison Kittrell, to the Parson's lands in Laurens and Johnson counties. There "Baldy" Kittrell, as the father was known, rose from a tenant farmer of modest means to one of the foremost planters and business men of this section. His farming methods were copied by the community and he was soon operating a gin and commissary for the surrounding plantations. In 1889, the elder Mr. Kittrell died and the family moved to the town of Wrightsville.

In 1897, after studying in Peoria, Illinois, Dr. C. H. Kittrell came to Dublin and established a jewelry store and optical offices. He has served as president of the Georgia Optical Association which he helped found. The National Association of Optometry granted him a fellowship for research work done in special fields of optometry. He was the first optometrist in a small city in the south-east to install a laboratory for the manufacture of lenses. Dr. Kittrell has always been interested in educational advantages for the young and in improved marketing facilities for the farmers. In the educational field one of his first efforts was through the Dublin Chautauqua and Lyceum Bureau, a locally formed organization, which constructed its own theatre and booked some of the best talent available for appearances here.

In 1917, Dr. Kittrell served on the city Board of Education and took a leading part in establishing the department of Home Economics in the Dublin High School. His support, coupled with the work of the women of the Laurens School Improvement Club, of which the late Mrs. T. B. Hicks was president, and the late Mrs. C. H. Kittrell vice-president, caused the construction of quarters and the purchase of equipment for this department.

In 1916, Dr. Kittrell paid half the salary for a County Home Demonstration Agent in order to induce the County Commissioners to establish this work in Laurens County. About 1923, Dr. Kittrell cooperated with representatives of the Rosenwald Fund to help the negro citizens establish Home Demonstration work for their people. In 1921-22, Dr. Kittrell served as Representative in the Georgia Legislature from Laurens, his chief interest as a legislator being improved markets and vocational education. As chairman of the agricultural committee of the House he aided in expanding activities of the State Bureau of Markets. He also introduced a bill to establish a state owned terminal at the port of Savannah, a movement that attracted wide-spread attention, but failed to pass, due to the fight waged by other port cities to prevent Savannah from getting the project.

Dr. Kittrell aided in establishing the first Federal Farm Loan Association in this county and later served as president of this organization. The Federal Intermediate Credit Bank was also created because of his efforts, as he arranged with Washington to send a representative here to meet with a group of farmers and bankers called together by him for the purpose of creating this service. He has also served as president of the Dublin Lions Club and chairman of the Dublin-Laurens County Chapter Red Cross.

In the past few years Dr. Kittrell has created a country home which is one of the most unique places in this section. This rock house and picturesque lake are located on a section of the historic "Valombrosa" estate of Georgia's famous Governor George M. Troup. In naming his place Dr. Kittrell translated "Valombrosia," which means valley of shade, and named his farm "Shady Valley," thus, in a measure, keeping the original name.

SHADY VALLEY—COUNTRY HOME OF DR. C. H. KITTRELL

Leila Brinson Kittrell (Mrs. C. H.) was born in Wrightsville, Georgia, October 8, 1877, and died in Dublin, Georgia, March 2, 1927. Mrs. Kittrell was the daughter of the late Jeremiah Wesley Brinson and the late Ida Sykes Brinson, of Wrightsville. Coming to Dublin with her husband, in 1897, Mrs. Kittrell lived a life of great service to her community. A member of the First Methodist Church she was active in affairs of the Missionary Society and served for several years as its president. A charter member of the Woman's Study Club, she took keen interest in the organization and served three terms as its head. Mrs. Kittrell was also president of the Carnegie Library Board and filled the office of president of the Twelfth District Georgia Federation of Women's Clubs for five years. She aided in founding the Laurens School Improvement Club, an organization which preceeded the present P.-T. A., and served as its president. As head of this work she aided in establishing similar clubs throughout the county and worked to help organize Home Demonstration Clubs among the women and girls of the county. Other organizations which she helped to direct were the Associated Charities and the Red Cross.

Three children were born to Dr. Charles H. and Leila Brinson Kittrell: Marie, who died in infancy; Carl, who died at the age of four; and Leah Kittrell, now associated in business with her father, former president of the Woman's Study Club, member of the John Laurens Chapter D. A. R., and Oconee Chapter U. D. C.

Two other grandchildren of Dr. Jeremiah Wesley Brinson, of Wrightsville, now reside in Dublin: (1) William Wesley Brinson, son of Dr. J. W. Brinson, Jr., and Mary Lovett Brinson, who married Elizabeth Reese, daughter of Walker Shields Reese and Mamie Stanley Reese, and has one daughter, Barbara Lynn Brinson; (2) J. Edison Brinson, son of Dr. Robert Earl Brinson and Sarah Lovett Brinson, who married Martha Frances Adams (see Adams History), daughter of Wiley Horry Adams and Martha Atwater Adams.

—*By Leah Kittrell.*

KNIGHT

William Alexander Knight came from Bulloch County, Georgia, to Laurens County. He was born April 26, 1832; died September 1, 1867; married Margaret Rawls (nee Mikell), born July 18, 1833, died November 25, 1898. His father was Alexander Knight, whose will is on file in Bulloch County. He married a Miss Lowther. We have good reason to believe that Thomas Knight was the father of Alexander Knight. He is said to have come from North Carolina to Bulloch County, Georgia. The Lowthers are said to have come from South Carolina. Among William Alexander Knight's children was a son, Horace Alexander.

Horace Alexander Knight was born January 28, 1861; died November 20, 1934. He married Mary Ellen Metts on January 27, 1891 (see Metts genealogy). They had two children: W. Alex Knight, who married Maude Brown December 15, 1917, and has one daughter, Bascom (see Bloodworth genealogy).

Louise Knight married S. Martin Alsup, October 28, 1918, and by this union are three daughters: (1) Mary Ellen, married Travis Taylor October 28, 1939, and has one daughter, Ellen Meriwether Taylor; (2) Janice Dillard; (3) Alexa Louise Alsup.

—*By Louise Knight Alsup (Mrs. S. M.)*

LINDER

There were three Linder brothers who came from Scotland to Georgia and South Carolina. One brother settled in South Carolina just across the river from what is now Hart County, Georgia. One brother settled on the Altamaha River at a place known as "Linder's Bluff," and his descendants are the Hines family of Liberty and adjacent counties. The third brother, Lewis Linder, settled in Washington County and his two sons, Jacob Thomas and Lewis, moved to Laurens County in the 1830's.

Dr. Jacob Thomas Linder purchased a large tract of land on the east side of the Oconee River from Big Creek to Shaddocks Creek, bounded on the west by the old Milledgeville and Darien stage road, over which stage coaches operated from Milledgeville to Darien and Savannah. This old stage road followed the route of an old Indian trail from St. Augustine, Florida, up through the mountains of North Georgia into Tennessee. The home of Mrs. Nannie J. Linder faces this old stage route, and this farm, together with the G. M. Linder farm and the "Doc" Linder farm (this latter now owned by Mr. W. H. Lovett), both of latter lying along highway to Wrightsville, are all parts of this large tract of land owned by Dr. Jacob Thomas Linder.

Dr. Jacob Thomas Linder was a large slave-holder and an extensive planter. He was also a typical country doctor of his day. He practiced medicine in Laurens and adjoining counties, riding on horseback and carrying his medicine and surgical instruments in saddlebags. He died about 1890.

Dr. Jacob Thomas Linder married Martha Jane Askew and they had seven sons and three daughters to live to maturity, viz.: 1. Berrien Belt, 2. Lumpkin, 3. Lewis Brothers, 4. Osee Wilder, 5. James L., 6. Jacob Thomas, 7. Knox Hill, 8. Lavenia, 9. Leona Jane, 10. Rebecca.

The oldest son, Berrien Belt, for many years owned and operated a large farm on the original tract of land purchased by his father, Dr. Jacob Thomas Linder. Berrien Belt or "Doc," as he was nicknamed, was one of the best farmers in Laurens County and his farm was known for miles around. He served as Tax Collector of Laurens County. He volunteered as a private at the beginning of the War Between the States and was in some of the fiercest battles of the war.

Lumpkin Linder volunteered and served in the Confederate Army about two years before he died with typhoid fever at Milam Bottom on Green Brier River in Virginia (now West Virginia), in August, 1862. "Ten Cent Bill" (Yopp) was with him when he died and helped to bury him.

Lewis Brothers Linder volunteered as a private in Company K, Fifth Georgia Reserves, and served under General Joseph E. Johnston until the close of the war and the surrender at Greensboro, North Carolina. At the close of the war he settled on the east side of the old Darien and Milledgeville road and on a part of the land purchased by his father (Dr. J. T.). He was one of the best and most progressive farmers of his day. He was one of the first in Laurens County to apply scientific ideas to practical purposes on the farm in the way of balanced fertilizers, crop rotation, etc. His advice was sought by other farmers all over the county. Lewis Brothers Linder was County Surveyor and surveyed much of the land in Laurens County. He was also Justice of the Peace for many years and was known for his efforts and success in getting neighbors to settle their differences out of court and for keeping them from having law suits with each other.

Osee Wilder Linder was for many years Tax Collector of Laurens County but lost his eyesight and was blind during his latter years. He died in 1920.

Dr. James L. Linder studied medicine at University of Louisville, Kentucky, as his father had done, and for many years had a wide practice not only in Laurens but adjacent counties, especially on the west side of the Oconee River.

Jacob Thomas Linder died in early manhood.

Knox Hill Linder lived at the original ancestral home of the Laurens County Linders. He lived here throughout his entire life and died about 1923; married Maggie Burke and had three children, viz., (1) Ferrell H. married Ethel Thomas; (2) Glenn M. married Annie May Graham; (3) Thurla married Melvin York.

The eldest daughter of Dr. Jacob Thomas and Martha Jane Linder was Lavenia, who was born June 14, 1845, and died October 22, 1881. She married Nathaniel B. Bostwick.

The second daughter, Leona Jane, married James Lemuel Keen; the youngest daughter, Rebecca, married Benjamin Franklin Ballard. (see Ballard genealogy).

Jacob Thomas Linder was born in Washington County, Georgia, September 22, 1810, and died at his home in Laurens County in

1890. Martha Jane (Askew) Linder, his wife, was born May 23, 1820, and died in 1891. Both are buried near the original home of Jacob Thomas Linder.

BRANCH OF LEWIS BROTHERS LINDER

Lewis Brothers Linder, son of Jacob Thomas and Martha Jane Askew Linder, was born September 26, 1846. He married Nancy Jane Beall, daughter of Captain W. O. Beall and Ella Fair Hicks Beall, of Irwinton, Georgia, who was born May 16, 1850. Their children are as follows: 1. Mary Ella, 2. Lillian Hicks, 3. Nannie Beall, 4. Lewis James, 5. Thomas Mercer, 6. Alma Lavenia, 7. Harriet Leona (Hattie Lee).

1. Mary Ella Linder died at age of 22.

2. Lillian Hicks Linder married John L. Bush, and had one daughter, Agnes, who married Homer Champion; their children are: (a) Charles Jonathan, and, (b) Mygnon Champion.

3. Nannie Beall Linder married Joseph W. McDaniel (deceased) and their children are: (a) Mildred, who married J. J. Walker, and they have one daughter, Gwendolyn. (b) Alma Lee, who married John Register, and they have two daughters, viz.: Mary and Carolyn. (c) James (Jimmie) McDaniel (not married).

4. Lewis James Linder was twice married, first, to Dolly Kea, and, second, to Mary Brown. By his first marriage to Dolly Kea there were born two sons, viz.: (a) Herbert D. Linder, who married Odie Allen, and they have one daughter, Janice. (b) James W. Linder (unmarried). Lewis James Linder has no children by his second marriage.

5. Thomas M. Linder married Hazel Carter and their children are as follows: (a) Thomas Malcolm, who married Mary Ella Tidwell, of Meriwether County, and they have one son, Thomas Mercer. (b) Raymond, who married Mary Crow. (c) Hazel Mae, who married Earl Wingo, and they have one son, viz.: Linder Earl.

6. Alma Lavenia Linder married Luther P. Greer (deceased), and by this marriage there is one daughter, Louise.

7. Hattie Lee Linder (deceased), married Peter Bivins, and their children are: (a) Janie Frances, and (b) Steven Thomas.

Lewis Brothers Linder died November 8, 1914, and is buried in the churchyard of old Bethlehem Church.

Thomas Mercer Linder, second son of Lewis Brothers and Nancy Beall Linder, has a long record of public service. When quite a young man, he moved to Jeff Davis County. Here he served as County Surveyor. Next we find him in the state legislature, where he represented Jeff Davis County for four years (1923-1927). For five years (1927-1932), he served as Assistant Commissioner of Agriculture to Hon. Eugene Talmadge. Here, his services were such, that, when Mr. Talmadge was elected governor of the state, he chose

Tom Linder for his Executive Secretary and he served in this capacity during 1933-34. At the end of Governor Talmadge's first administration as governor, Thomas Linder was elected Commissioner of Agriculture (1934-1936).

Perhaps at no time in its history has the state's Department of Agriculture done more for its farmers than during Tom Linder's first administration. Without any appropriation whatsoever he built farm markets at centers throughout the state where farmers can take their produce and find a sale for it. If Tom Linder had achieved no accomplishment other than the creation of these markets, he would have rendered the people of the state a great and outstanding service.

Thomas Linder was defeated for re-election in 1936; but in the meanwhile, the voters of the state, realizing what his services had meant to the people, voted him back into office in 1940. This is unique for he is the only man in the history of Georgia ever to have been elected to this office after having been defeated.

During his scond administration of this office, Tom Linder has built a farm market in the city of Atlanta that is a marvel to all who see it. It covers 16 acres of ground and is so modernly equipped and so conveniently arranged that there is nothing like it in the United States. Governors, Commissioners of Agriculture, and other officials from many of the southeastern states have visited this market in order to model markets in their respective states from it. Too, in 1935, Tom Linder sent a Market Bulletin of the Agriculture Department which he had edited to the World's Fair in Peru and it won the world's prize.

Today, Tom Linder is an outstanding political figure in Georgia.

LINDER - KEEN

Leona Jane Linder, second daughter of Jacob Thomas and Martha Jane (Askew) Linder, was born March 23, 1853, and died June 17, 1930. She is buried in the church yard of old Shady Grove Church, where she worshipped for over fifty years

On January 25, 1877, she married James Lemuel Keen, the son of Young Bright and Melvina Manson (Todd) Keen. To this union were born 13 children: 1. Omar Wilder Keen; 2. Freeman Hill Keen; 3. Rebecca Keen (died in infancy); 4. Lennie Leona Keen; 5. Mamie Willie Keen (died in infancy); 6. Ola L Keen; 7. Essie Laffel Keen; 8. James B. Keen (died in infancy); 9. Osee Fulton Keen, M.D.; 10. Lehman Pratt Keen; 11. Trammell Colwell Keen; 12. Beeman Chandler Keen; 13. James Lemuel Keen, Jr.

A detailed record of the marriages and children of the above named sons and daughters of James Lemuel and Leona Jane (Linder) Keen will be found in the history of the Keen family, which see.

Rebecca, the youngest daughter of Jacob Thomas and Martha Jane Linder, married Benjamin Franklin Ballard and had children as follows:

1. Frankie Folsom Ballard, married John Louis Veal (deceased), and has three sons, viz., (1) Floyd Thomas, (2) John Louis, (3) James McGruder Veal.

2. Enda Ballard, married Jerry Walker Duggan (see Duggan genealogy).

3. Kellie Hinton Ballard.

4. Cummie Lin Ballard.

5. Benjamin Franklin Ballard (died in infancy).

Rebecca Linder Ballard was born August 31, 1854, and died November 7, 1931.

(Detailed account found in Ballard genealogy).

—By Enda Ballard Duggan (Mrs. J. W.)

LOVE

Amos Love, with his brothers John and Charles, shortly after the death of his father in Onslow County, North Carolina, in 1798, moved to that part of Wilkinson County, which afterwards became Laurens County. He was the third of the same name in a direct line. The will of the first Amos is shown in the North Carolina Historical and Geneological Register for April, 1900 His wife was Mary. Salisbury District, North Carolina, was their home. Their son, the second Amos, served as a Captain in a regiment during the Revolution. Wheeler's History of North Carolina, Vol. XVII, p. 915. He afterwards moved to Onslow County, where he served as Judge of the Common Pleas and Quarter Sessions. The minutes of the judgments of that court bearing his signature are still preserved. He was possessed of many acres and many slaves as indicated by his will, for besides providing for his wife, Mary, and daughters, he gave a plantation and negroes to each of his three sons, Amos, John and Charles. Records of Onslow County Wills, published by the North Carolina Historical Society. The third Amos, to which this sketch relates, likewise acquired large land holdings. He resided a few miles north of Dublin on the west side of the Oconee River, near Hunger and Hardship Creek.

Amos Love married Margaret James. He became a leading merchant of Dublin, A. Love & Company, being for years a well-known house. He was one of those selected by the General Assembly as commissioners of the court house and jail of the county upon the passage of the Act to make permanent the site of the public buildings in Laurens. Lamar's Digest, p. 232. It may be declared, therefore, that he was one of the fathers of Dublin—one of the founders —for he was one of those to decide just where the public buildings should be fixed definitely—the precise location of the county site that afterwards became the city of Dublin. He was the first Clerk of the Superior Court of the county, and afterwards a Justice of the Inferior Court, a tribunal that performed not only the duties at present exercised by the Commissioners of Roads and Revenues, but those also of the present Court of Ordinary, as well as having civil and criminal jurisdiction as large as that now conferred on the City Court of Dublin. In 1819, he was elected to represent the county in the General Assembly and served for three sessions. He died shortly thereafter, leaving besides his widow, three children, to wit: Jane, the eldest, who became the wife of General Eli Warren; Mary Ann, who married Moses Guyton, Esq. (see Guyton genealogy), and Peter Early Love, the youngest, all having been born in Laurens County. The last named became Legislator, Solicitor-General, Judge and Member of Congress. He was one of the seven Representatives from Georgia who withdrew when the State passed the Ordinance of Secession. He had an only son, Captain Amos Love, a handsome and dashing cavalry officer in the Confederate States Army, who died without having married. Thus, there are none of Amos Love's offspring now living who bear the name of Love, although each of his three children have living descendants. There still reside in the county grandchildren and great-grandchildren of the late Emma Saxon Guyton Rowe (Mrs. Thomas H.), who was a daughter of Mary Ann Love and Moses Guyton, Esq. The late Margaret Landrum Watkins (Mrs. Frank N.) and Dr. Grace Warren Landrum, Dean of Women at William and Mary College, Williamsburg, Virginia, are descendants of Jane Love, who married General Eli Warren. (see Warren genealogy). Amos Love was the great-grandfather of the late Dr. William W. Landrum, father of the above, formerly of Atlanta, the late Eli W. Goode, former Mayor of Hawkinsville, the late James Bishop, Jr., of Eastman, the late Judge James G. Parks, of Dawson, the late Lloyd B. Parks, of Atlanta, the late Charles R. Blount, of Blountsville, Florida. The late Olin Wimberly of Macon, Warren Grice, Associate Justice of the Supreme Court of Georgia, Col. Moses Guyton, IV., a native of Dublin, now of Marianna, Florida, his son, Moses Guyton, V., are also lineal descendants of Amos Love.

Amos Love was an active Baptist and gave the land on which Poplar Springs Church was built. He was a deacon of that church. He was a subscriber to the first issue of *The Columbia Star*, afterwards *The Christian Index*. The returns made by his administrators to the Court of Ordinary, their vouchers, and the appraisement of his estate are on file in the county court house. It shows him to have possessed those things with which a gentleman of breeding and culture was accustomed to surround himself in the period in which he lived. He sleeps under the sod of the county with which he

identified himself in his youth, where his children were born, where he became a useful and honored citizen, and where he died.
—*By a descendant of Amos Love.*

METTS

George Metts, Sr., was a Palatine and came with De Graffenreid to North Carolina, where he died in 1727, leaving a wife, Susana, and two children, George, Jr., and Anna Curtice. He was a high German.

George Metts, Jr., died 1794, served in the Colonial Wars, as given in North Carolina records, Volume No. 22, page 233: "Craven County. A list of soldiers commanded by Capt. Thomas Graves, bearing date January, 1751, for the lower side of Southwest Crick of Town Bounds. George Metts (among those listed) a true list taken the 15th of October, 1754, by me, Farmfold Green, Clerk." George Metts, Jr., married about 1751 to Amy, a widow, and had at least three children, Frederick, George, and Trusar.

Frederick Metts was born October 6, 1751; died after 1800. He served in Revolutionary War under General Marion, of South Carolina, and was given a grant of land in Washington County, Georgia, for his services in Revolution. Frederick Metts married about 1775, Ann Askew, born April, 1760. They had fourteen children, one of whom was Nathan Metts, born January 1, 1784, in North Carolina, who married Sarah Dixon, born 1805, in Georgia Nathan Metts, died in 1850. They had four children, Susan, Polly, Thomas, and Lewis.

Lewis Metts was born March 25, 1838; died December 13, 1924. He married Rachel Fordham, February 2, 1869. She was born October 20, 1849; died May 3, 1922. Lewis Metts served in the War Between the States, 57 Georgia Volunteers, Sergeant. Rachel Fordham was the daughter of Wiley Fordham, born April 7, 1816; died November 8, 1900; married Lucretia Cannon, March 14, 1845. Wiley Fordham was the son of Benjamin Fordham, II., born May 10, 1784; died March 19, 1864; married Elsie Miller, born April 11, 1784; died July 27, 1863, about 1805. Elsie Miller was the daughter of William Miller, born 1759; died 1837, and Amy Barker, born 1757; died 1831; married in 1783. William Miller was a Revolutionary soldier and is buried in Ware County, Georgia. Lewis Metts and Rachel Fordham Metts had eight children: Nathan, Mary Ellen, Frances, Zenie, Virginia Byrd (see Walker genealogy); Blanch, Iva, and Marshall. Mary Ellen married Horace A. Knight (see Knight genealogy).
—*By Louise Knight Alsup (Mrs. S. M.)*

MOFFETT

For fifty years the Moffett family has helped build Laurens County. They are of Scotch descent, from Dunse, Scotland.

Alexander Moffett (1832-1899), born in Charleston, South Carolina, came to Laurens County in 1891, son of Andrew and Anna Reed Moffett; married, 1854, Sarah Nesbet (1834-1911), of Athens, Georgia, daughter of Alfred Nesbet (1797-1866) and Sarah Stillwell (1795—). Children: Anna, Morton, Lewis, Margret and Carrie.

Louis Moffett, Milledgeville, Georgia, born February 12, 1862, married, first, Nancy Estelle Kendrick, Hancock County, April 19, 1893 (born May 9, 1864, died April 12, 1923, buried Northview Cemetery), daughter of Green Marshall Kendrick (1834—) and Olivia Stovall (1832-1897); buried at Augusta, Georgia. Children: Kendrick, Nannie Louis, Eileen, Alfred and Annie Margret. Kendrick, married Rosamond White, January 5, 1918, one son, Kendrick, Jr., born October 14, 1924. Nannie Louis, married Paul Ward Alexander, July 3, 1918; children: Paul Ward (1919-1937), buried Northview Cemetery. Louis Moffett, born March 22, 1923; Charles Turner, born March 10, 1925.

Eileen (1899-1937), married Elbert Brunson, March 29, 1922; children: Elbert Bradford, born April 27, 1923; Sandifer, born October 9, 1926; Nannelyn, born August 4, 1928; Ronald, born July 17, 1936.

Alfred Nesbet married Elizabeth McLean, November 5, 1929, Presbyterian preacher, Memphis, Tennessee; children: William Andrew, born January 25, 1932; Mary Ann, born April 5, 1937; Annie Margret Moffett 1905-1907).

—*By Nannie Moffett Alexander (Mrs. Paul).*

MOORMAN

Among the earliest settlers of Laurens County was William B. Moorman (1800-1864), who owned and operated extensive farming interest in the eastern part of the county, known as Buckeye District. He was a Methodist minister, charter member and second Worshipful Master of the first Masonic Order chartered in Dublin, Georgia, also, a charter member of Boiling Springs Methodist Church. He married Susan Ellington; children: Simeon Josiah, married Louisa Snell; Jane, married Isaac Hartley; Eliza, married Jasper Hartley; David J., married Clara Duggan; William B., Jr., married Amanda ——; Emma never married; Henry Ellington, married Sarah Elizabeth Moye (1873).

Simeon Josiah Moorman (1838-1897) was a Confederate soldier, later engaged in farming, was a Mason and member of Methodist Church; children: Everett, married Nannie Wood; William B., married Amanda Johnson; Catherine, married Jordan Wombles; Georgia, married J. S. Graham; Osee, married Ruth Smith; Benzie, married E. G. Blankenship; Homer, married Alice Moye.

David J. Moorman (1842-1888), served with distinction as a Confederate soldier in the 57th Georgia Regiment. After the war, he engaged in farming on land inherited from his father. He was a Mason, devoted to the Order, and served as Justice of the Peace of his district for twenty years; children: Ivy W. (1868-1938), prominent physician of Douglas, Georgia, married Eliza Vickers; Oscar L., married Dora Evans, had one child, Myrtie Lou, who married James M. Wolfe; James Rushin, married Bessie Patterson; Myrtie, married T. Johnson.

Henry Ellington Moorman (1848-1921), entered the Confederate War, Company K, 5th Georgia Regiment, at sixteen years of age. Faithful to the inherited principles of his ancestors, he placed duty ahead of all other interests. Duty well done was his aim in life. He often quoted David Crockett: "Be sure you are right and then go ahead." After giving faithful service to his country, he engaged in farming and was a successful planter. His wife, Sara Elizabeth Moorman, was a true helpmate, an ideal mother, a consecrated Christion, widely known and loved for her deeds of kindness. They were faithful members of the Methodist Church; children: Edgar Stout, died young; Minnie, married John J. McAffee; John William, married Arlena Hogan; Verna, married J. David Hogan; David Addison, married Wilma Donaldson; Winifred, married Charles Homer Lovett; Henry McDonald, married Earnest Wicker.

John William and Arlena Moorman's children: David, Ailene, Rufus, Vivian, Joseph, Joyce.

David Addison Moorman received his preparatory education at Georgia Normal College and Business Institute, Abbeville, Georgia. He then engaged in the mercantile business until his appointment as postmaster, at Lovett, Georgia, where he served six years, resigning to accept an appointment as rural carrier at the Dublin, Georgia, postoffice, the position he now fills. He owns and operates the plantation formerly owned by his father. His wife, Wilma Donaldson Moorman, is a daughter of the late William H. and Martha Bush Donaldson, granddaughter of James M. and Sidney Fort Donaldson. James M. Donaldson was a prominent and beloved Baptist minister of this county. Children: Wilma Saralyn, married Clayton West Cordell; Mary Donaldson; Banks Addison; Billy Fred.

Henry McDonald and Earnest Moorman's children: Nell, married Robert L. Jernigan; Don died at thirteen years of age; Janice.

—*By Wilma Donaldson Moorman (Mrs. D. A.)*

NEW

Prominent among the earliest families of Laurens County, who have held positions of importance in agricultural, educational, political, and financial pursuits, are the New family, who came to this county in the early 1800's.

The paternal ancestor of the New family was Daniel Mack Quira New, who was the father of John New, who married Nancy Harrison.

The maternal ancestor of this family was Thomas Wood, of Virginia, who moved to North Carolina, thence to, and permanently settled at a point near Harrison, in Washington County, Georgia. He was of English descent. By occupation he was an educator and Justice of the Peace. He married Annie Smith, daughter of Colby Smith, a soldier of the Revolutionary War, whose wife was Annie Henry. Among those born to this union was James Raiford Wood, who was born in Washington County, Georgia, on June 30, 1809, and there died December 31, 1882. He was a farmer but spent the greater portion of his time as a Baptist preacher. He organized and served as pastor of a large number of churches in the counties of Washington, Jefferson, Emanuel, Montgomery, and Laurens, each in Georgia. In its early days he was Clerk and Moderator of the Mount Vernon Association. On December 13, 1837, James Raiford Wood married Martha Chester, daughter of Absolom Chester and Rebecca Barbour. The Chester and Barbour families were other pioneer Carolina and Georgia stock. From this marriage ten children were born, namely, Thomas Jefferson, Isaac Smith, Joseph Madison, Mary Ann Rebecca, Martha Elizabeth, James Solomon, Absolom William Jordan, George Washington, Charles Spurgeon, Sarah E.

In 1866, following the War Between the States, Stephen Florence New, before mentioned, who had served therein under General Robert E. Lee in Virginia, Maryland, and Pennsylvania, was married to Martha Elizabeth Wood, before mentioned. To this union twelve children were born, namely: Mary Victoria, John Florence, Martha Jennie, Nancy Ann Elizabeth, Edna Earle, Benjamin Thomas, James Ezra, M. D., Charles Spurgeon, Minnie Lee, Susan Bell, David Mack Quira, and Stephen Parker, five of whom settled in this county, and have been prominent among its leaders.

(1) Edna Earle New, married William Braxton Taylor, M.D., a prominent physician and large land owner in Laurens County. Seven children were born to this union, namely: Mae, Loomis, Flovilla, Florence, Alma, Ruth, and Edna Earle.

(2) James Ezra New, M.D., was born in Washington County, Georgia, in 1878, and spent his boyhood there. In 1901, he was graduated with honors from the University of Georgia Medical College. After interning in New York City Hospital, and completing post-graduate courses in Chicago and New York City, he came to Dexter, Georgia,

where he has been active and prominent in his profession, serving several times as president of the Twelfth and Sixth District Medical Societies, as well as president of Laurens County Medical Society for several terms. In addition to his medical profession, he has extensive farming and real estate interests, and is prominent in civic affairs. He has served several terms as mayor of the city of Dexter, Georgia, and has been chairman of the Board of Education of the Dexter Public Schools for thirty years. He was the first and only president of the Dexter Banking Company, until it liquidated, a position he held for thirty-one years. He is, at present, a director of the Citizens & Southern Bank, of Dublin, Georgia, and chairman of the Laurens County Welfare Board.

In 1905, he was married to Julia Maude Brantley, daughter of Charles W. Brantley and Robbie Ashley, both of whom were members of prominent agricultural, educational, and financial families. To this union five children were born: Anne Marie New, who married John Merritt Fisher, and resides in Washington, D. C.; Robiclair New, who married Arthur Adams (see Adams genealogy); James Stephen New, M.D.; Charles Brantley New; Jacob New.

(3) Charles Spurgeon New, married Lucille Malone Digby. He is a druggist by profession, and associated with his brother, in the firm of J. E. & C. S. New, Druggists. They have no children.

(4) Minnie Lee, married Charles Alfred Sheppard and had six children, namely: Amantine Lee Roy, Mary Gladys, Martha Elizabeth, who married Crumbley Marshall, Charles Alfred, Jr., James Rayford, and Maud New.

(5) Stephen Parker New, born March 11, 1888, in Laurens County. He attended the public schools at Harrison, later graduating from High School in Richmond County, near Augusta, in 1907. He taught for a short time as principal and superintendent of New Home High School, in Johnson County. In 1910, he was graduated from Mercer University Law School, and immediately came to Dublin, Georgia, where he became one of the county's most prominent lawyers. He has served his county, state, and nation with ability and distinction as Solicitor of the City Court of Dublin for four years, resigning to volunteer as Yeoman in the United States Navy, where he served until 1919. He represented Laurens County in the State Legislature for four consecutive terms; was attorney for Laurens County for four years; also served from time to time as Special Attorney for the State Department of Banking. He is a Baptist, Mason, Shriner, and member of the American Legion. In 1936, he was appointed attorney for the Interstate Commerce Commission, and moved to Washington, D. C., where he has since resided.

In 1922, he was married to Ruth Hightower, daughter of William J. Hightower and Alice Gertrude Hall, who were members of prominent Laurens County families. Three children were born to this union, namely: Jane Carl, Stephen Parker, and William Hightower New.

—By Robiclair New Adams (Mrs. A. A.)

PAGE

Doctor Joseph Morgan Page was not only a leading physician of Dublin and Laurens County, but also a worthy citizen. He was descended from a notable and old Virginia family.

Descendants of Henry Page, of Middlesex, England, who was born in 1500, immigrated to Virginia in 1650 and were founders of the Page family of Virginia. This clan furnished members of the Federal Congress, American Revolutionary patriots, and a Governor of the State of Virginia, in 1802.

Allen A. Page and Elizabeth Webb Page moved from Virginia to Washington County, Georgia, and later to Johnson County, where Joseph Morgan Page was born, November 26, 1860.

After attending Wrightsville, Georgia, High School, Joseph Page enrolled at Augusta Medical College, was graduated there in 1882 with a medical degree, and later took post-graduate courses in the New York Polyclinic. He began the practice of medicine in Johnson County, Georgia.

On January 10, 1886, he was married to Melissa Jackson, daughter of James Erwin Jackson and Margie Ann Keen, members of leading Laurens County families.

In 1903, Doctor Page moved to Laurens County, Georgia, and continued practice of the medical profession. He acquired extensive farming interests; owned and operated a drug business; also assisted in organizing the Commercial Bank of Dublin, of which bank he was a president and stockholder. He was interested in building and erected many homes and business houses here.

Completing almost half a century in the practice of medicine, Dr. Page retired in 1923. In 1927 and 1928, he represented the Sixteenth Senatorial District in the Georgia Legislature. He was a member of the Christian Church, of Dublin, the Masonic Order, and the Laurens County Medical Association.

Joseph Morgan Page died December 14, 1934, and is buried in the Northview Cemetery Masoleum, in Dublin.

Seven children were born to Joseph Page and Melissa Jackson Page, viz., Maude Page (died in infancy); Pearl Page, wife of Edgar G. Simmons (see Simmons genealogy); Joseph Marvin Page; Landrum J. Page; Bluford Blount Page; Ruby Page, wife of Harry Honeywell; Jackson Keen Page.

Grandchildren are: Pearl Page Simmons, wife of Richard Zantzinger Graves; Frances Page Simmons; Marjorie Beacham Page (deceased in 1940), daughter of Joseph Marvin Page and Reba Beacham Page (deceased); Patricia Page Shepper (deceased in infancy), daughter of Ruby Page Honeywell and F. W. Shepper; Elizabeth Garrett Page; Bluford Blount Page, Jr.; William Garrett Page; Mary Frances Page.

The latter four are children of Bluford Blount Page and Mary Elizabeth Garrett Page (see Garrett genealogy).

—*By Frances Page Simmons.*

PARKER

In 1884, George Washington and Louis Hill Parker came to Laurens County from Houston County, Georgia; a year later a brother, Benjamin Franklin, joined them. They were influential citizens of the communities in which they lived, were engaged in farming. They were the sons of Weeks Parker, born December 22, 1824; died July 1, 1884. He married Nancy Elizabeth Ivy of Dooly County, Georgia, born February 20, 1829; died March 30, 1903. She lived to see her eldest son, Benjamin Franklin, seventy-five years old. Other children than the three who settled in Laurens County were: Francis Marion, Lucinda Anna, Laura Emma, Sarah Frances, Joseph Weeks, Sylvester and James Myrick. Weeks and Nancy are buried in "Parker Family Cemetery," near Perry, Georgia.

George Washington Parker, born December 5, 1849; died June 3, 1922, settled in Dublin District about one mile from the Dexter Highway, on the road between the Dexter and McRae highways. He was married four times, first, to Frances Susan Blasingame in 1875; to them were born two children, Oliver, who married Pearl Boatright and Nancy Susan (Nanny). Nancy Susan married Benjamin Augustus Moye in 1898. They have five daughters: Gussie Pauline, married J. B. Bedingfield (present Clerk of Superior and City Courts); Essie Marie, married S. H. Riley, of Houston County; Georgia; Fannie Flovilla, married M. L. Criswell, of this county; Nannie Lou, married Frank E. Waldrep (son of Cliff and Bessie Evans Waldrep, of Laurens County); Florrie, secretary to Baldwin County, Georgia, Clerk; Audie Lee, co-owner and operator of "Au-nelle Beauty Shoppe." Married, second, Mollie Smith, and they had one daughter, Emma Claude, who married James S. Kight. Married, third, Mrs. Frances Weaver Sims; to this union were born two daughters: Lula Mae, who married L. M. Barron, and Alma, married W. A. Scarborough. Married, fourth, Annie Burch.

Benjamin Franklin Parker settled at Lovett, Georgia, born September 27, 1846; died May 13, 1921; married twice, first, Roxie Ann Daughtry, November 18, 1869; married, second, Georgia Elizabeth Holly, October 15, 1874. Benjamin Parker volunteered at the age of sixteen for service in the Civil War in his father's place, as he was sent home ill on furlough. He was in 14th Battalion of Georgia Light Artillery. Children: Ida, C. W., Lena Rivers, Ella Mae, Maude, Bennett Durward, Gordan, Holly, D. R., Lucille, and Cecil. Ella Mae and Maude reside at the Benjamin Parker home at Lovett.

Louis Hill Parker was born June 24, 1860; died March 17, 1918;

settled in Dublin District about two miles north of the city. He was a prominent farmer and business man, life-long member of First Baptist Church, lived strictly in accord with his religious vows. He is buried in Northview Cemetery. Married Josiephine Swinson August 3, 1887, daughter of Thomas Elliott Swinson and Nancy Williams Swinson. Thomas died 1863, in General Hospital, No. 7, Raleigh, North Carolina. He enlisted December 17, 1862, at Macon, Georgia, as private in Captain Slaton's Company, Macon Light Artillery, Georgia Artillery Confederate States. Josephine, born and reared in Laurens County, still lives (at age of 79) in the home she went to as a bride, member of First Baptist Church. Children: Ernest, Eloise, Mamie, Oma Louis, Pearl, and Duren.

Pearl and Duren Parker are the only living children of their parents; with their mother they own and operate "Parker's Guernsey Farm." Duren, married Georgia Lucille Prescott, October 12, 1927, daughter of Oliver Perry Prescott and Maggie Flanders Prescott, granddaughter of Reverend George M. Prescott and Hannah Lucendia Webb and Reverend George Flanders and Mary Stokes. Pearl, Duren and his wife are members of First Baptist Church. He is vice-president and director of "Guernsey Breeders of Georgia," also a Rotarian. Children: Louis Hill Parker, born February 1, 1929; Duren Ivy Parker, Jr., born December 11, 1934.

Cecil Embree Parker, son of Bennett Durwood Parker, also resides with the Duren Parker family.

—*By Pearl Parker.*

PEACOCK

John Asa Peacock (1859-1937).

Anne Boisfeuillet Peacock (1861-1928).

John Asa Peacock (son of John A. J. and Sarah J. Hicks Peacock) and Anne Boisfeuillet (daughter of John Theodore and Anne McKinnon Boisfeuillet) were married in Wrightsville, Georgia, December 30, 1885, at the home of Mr. and Mrs. D. S. Blackshear, and later became prominent citizens of Dublin.

Their children are: John Asa, Jr., Roderick Theodore, James Marion, Sarahlyn Peacock White and Annelie Peacock Brown, of Dublin, Georgia, and Kathleen Peacock Roberson, of Greenville, South Carolina.

Their grandchildren are: Edmund F. Brown, Jr., Christopher G. White, Jr., Roderock T. Peacock, Jr., and Annah Carrere Peacock, of Dublin, Georgia, and Kathleen Peacock Roberson, of Greenville, South Carolina.

John Asa Peacock, native of Washington County, Georgia, reared in Johnson County, Georgia, moved to Dublin in 1885. A pioneer in the newspaper business he enjoyed a long career as publisher and editor. His public service was very large and varied; he served as Chief of Police of the City of Dublin in 1899, and again in 1932 and 1933; he was elected Sheriff of the City Court of Dublin in 1900 and served several terms; he served as a member of the staff of Governor Joseph M. Terrell; was a member of the Board of Stewards of the First Methodist Church of Dublin for years, and for several years was chairman of the Democratic Executive Committee; was Grand Regent of the Royal Arcanum Lodge, and an active member of the Knights of Pythias, Elks, and Odd Fellows, and held important offices in each.

Anne Boisfeuillet Peacock, a graduate of Wesleyan College at Macon in the class of 1878, was organist of the First Methodist Church for thirty years, and while organist was instrumental in securing a gift from Andrew Carnegie that enabled the Church to install the pipe organ. She was the first Society Editor Dublin ever had. She was Organizing Regent of the John Laurens Chapter D. A. R., and served as State Historian, and State Chaplain, two years each. A chair was placed in Constitution Hall in Washington, D. C., by the D. A. R. in her honor. It was her thought and planning that made the Community Christmas Tree on the Court House lawn possible in 1912, this being the second Municipal Christmas Tree in the United States, Philadelphia erecting the first. This evaluation of her accomplishments and public service was contributed to the local Press by a friend: "Mrs. Peacock helped to lead church, social and club matters, helped to shape civic policies for a city that was growing from its village stage into a town, and then into the present city. She left the impress of a strong and wonderful character and personality on the city as no other has done. She was a musician of more than usual attainments, and as such was a leader in musical circles for years. As a community and civic worker she was one of the most active Dublin ever knew. She led many movements for civic improvements that have resulted in better things for Dublin."

—By Annelie Peacock Brown.

PETERS

William Peters came to Philadelphia, Pennsylvania, from England as representative of the English Crown in the American Colonies; bought an estate on the Schuylkill River and built a home which he called Belmont Mansion. He married Mary Brientnall, of Pennsylvania, and they had three children: Richard, who for a number of years was Judge of Philadelphia; Thomas and Mary, all born at Belmont. When war was declared between the Colonies and England, William was called, and Belmont Mansion sold for what is now Fairmont Park. The Peters' coat of arms is in the ceiling of this mansion, which is still in the Park.

Thomas, the younger son, was a member of the Philadelphia Troop of Horse, who volunteered their services to Washington at the beginning of the Revolutionary War, and served for a time as his body guard, crossed the Delaware with him and gave distinguished service at the Battle of Trenton. After the war they became quite intimate friends and bought adjacent farms; many letters from General Washington to Thomas are still in the Peters family. Thomas married Rebecca Johnson, they had a large family of which Thomas was the oldest son.

Thomas Peters was born in 1797 in Baltimore, Maryland, and was with the United States Census Bureau in Washington, D. C., at which time he married Hester Ann Cohen, granddaughter of the Earl of Windham. Six children were born to them, of whom Thomas was the oldest. Thomas was born in Washington, D. C., in 1840, and served as Page in the U. S. Senate when Daniel Webster made his memorable speech on the Missouri Compromise. When war was declared between the States he went to Richmond, Virginia, and enlisted in the Confederate Army, being the only member of his family whose sympathy was with the South. He served with distinction under General James E. Johnson at the "Battle of Gettysburg." After peace was declared he moved to Selma, Alabama, and was prominent in the banking and insurance world. He helped revise the Standard Dictionary and was an authority on Astronomy. Thomas Peters married Kate Lendsay, of Selma, in 1867, moved to Atlanta in 1879. They had seven children of whom Thomas was the oldest.

Thomas Peters, born in Selma, Alabama, 1873, married Kate Lewis, of Hawkinsville, Georgia, June 7, 1899. Thomas followed the line of his father, being prominently identified in the life insurance world, moved to Dublin in 1902. To this union five children were born: 1. Kate, married Lieut.-Col. Chas. Johnson, U. S. A., in 1914, two children, Charles and Kate Johnson. 2. John, married Helen DeLamar, June 16, 1931, two children, John and Emily Peters. 3. Margaret, married George Powell (deceased) March 27, 1926, two children, George and Thomas Powell; married, second, Robert Dudley West. 4. Thomas, married Gladys Hodges, June 4, 1933, one son, Thomas Hodges, who is the 6th direct descendant of the Philadelphia Thomas Peters. 5. Wilmer, married Fay Strickland, August 31, 1940.

—*By Margaret Peters Powell West (Mrs. R. D.)*

PHILLIPS

William Spencer Phillips, son of Benjamin Franklin Phillips and Elizabeth Dillon, was born July 31, 1862, in Las Cassas, Tennessee, and died January 19, 1919.

In 1884, William Spencer Phillips, who was then twenty-two years old, and his eighteen-year-old brother, L. A. Phillips, came to Laurens County from Tennessee. L. A. Phillips returned to Tennessee. In 1892, after William Spencer Phillips married Ada Owen, also of Tennessee (born February 18, 1868; died March 28, 1940), daughter of Stephen Owen and Judith Robertson, he considered Laurens County his home.

During his life he was actively engaged in selling horses, mules, and fertilizer. He helped to organize the First National Bank and was a director and vice-president. This institution served the county for many years.

He was an active member of the First Baptist Church. He served as Mayor of Dublin and it was during his administration that the first paving was laid.

William Spencer Phillips and Ada Owen had one daughter, Vera Phillips, born March 9, 1894; married June 27, 1919, to George Blue Hollemon, born January 26, 1897, son of Nath Hollemon and Harriet Blue; a daughter, Jane, was born June 6, 1932.

L. A. Phillips was married December 25, 1895, to Lula McAdoo, born April 7, 1873, daughter of Jim and Angie McAdoo, and has one daughter, Hazel Phillips, born January 8, 1898, married November 26, 1919, to T. Coke Brown, born January 5, 1896, son of Gaston and Georgia Brown; a daughter, Hazel Phillips Brown, was born December 6, 1922. L. A. Phillips moved to Laurens County in 1912, to be associated with his brother, William Spencer Phillips, in business.

The Phillips family traces its ancestry back to Joseph Phillips, born in Wales, in 1716, married to Mary, born in 1710. He had four sons: David, born March 26, 1742; John, born 1745; and Joshua, born 1751. Joseph Phillips, his wife Mary, and three sons, immigrated to America in 1755 and a fourth son, Joseph. Jr., was born November 1, 1756. Joseph Phillips settled in Westchester, Chester County, Pennsylvania. Joseph and his sons used only one "l" in spelling their name. An extra "l" crept in the Tennessee branch.

All four of Joseph's sons were active in organizing the Seventh Battalion, Chester County Militia, in the American Revolution. David was Caputain of Company 2 in the militia. All four brothers distinguished themselves for bravery in the Revolutionary War. Reverend David Phillips, born March 26, 1742, died March 5, 1829, married in Chester County, Pennsylvania, Mary Thomas who died October 31, 1804.

John Phillips was born April 6, 1768, in Chester County, Pennsylvania. He was the son of David and Mary Thomas Phillips.

David Phillips, son of John and Mary, was born December 11, 1794, in Washington County, Pennsylvania, three years before his parents migrated to Tennessee. He married Mary Waters, born May 4, 1802, and died December 14, 1820. She was the daughter of Shelor Waters and Nancy Turner Waters. David Phillips was a soldier in the War of 1812.

Benjamin Franklin Phillips, father of William Spencer Phillips, was born January 28, 1834. He saw active service in the War Between the States; he died January 20, 1890.
—*By Vera Phillips Holleman (Mrs. G. B.)*

PIERCE

Edward Clifton Pierce came to Dublin, Georgia, about 1912. He formerly lived in Wilkinson County, owned and operated a farm there and also served as Sheriff. Upon taking up his residence in Dublin, he served with the Federal Government as Revenue Officer from 1913-1928, and as Dublin's Chief of Police and Deputy Marshal for a number of years. He is the son of Joel T. Pierce and Elizabeth Ogburn, who were representative citizens of Wilkinson County. They are buried at Big Sandy Church Cemetery.

Edward Clifton Pierce married Rachel Elizabeth Fordham, December 19, 1892, daughter of Joel M. Fordham and Sallie Elizabeth Duncan, granddaughter of Benjamin Fordham, III, and Rosa Lord, and of John Duncan and Cinthia Wynn. All were prominently identified with the building of Laurens County. Benjamin, III, son of Benjamin, II., of Wilkinson County, Georgia, married Elsie Miller, daughter of William Miller, a Revolutionary soldier. Benjamin, II., was the son of Benjamin Fordham, I., of Jones County, North Carolina. Edward Clifton and Rachel Elizabeth Fordham Pierce's children are: Vera, Joel Felton, and Gertrude.

Joel Felton Pierce, born in Wilkinson County, came to Dublin as a small boy with his parents, was educated in Dublin Public Schools, served in World War No. 1, spent ten months in France with 31st Division, Ordnance Detachment of A. E. F. After the war Felton returned to Dublin, was connected with Hicks Drug Company and Laurens Hardware for a number of years. In 1921, Pierce and Orr Grocery Company was formed of which he is co-owner and operator; member of First Methodist Church, secretary and treasurer of its Board of Stewards; charter member of Rotary Club, W. O. W., Mason, and member of Laurens Lodge No. 75, Harmon Chapter No. 56, and Olivet Commandry No. 27, of which he has served as Commander. Felton Pierce married Mary Ethel Orr on December 16, 1920.

Ethel Orr Pierce, is the daughter of Rachel Stella Jackson and Charles Lofton Orr, granddaughter of James Erwin Jackson, a soldier of the Confederate Army, and Margie Ann Keen, prominent planters of Jackson District. Margie Ann Jackson was known for her business ability (operating her large farm after the death of her husband) and loved for her splendid traits of character. She reared a large family of her own children and helped rear two grandchildren, Roy and Ethel Orr, after the death of their father. She died at the age of ninety-five, in the home of her daughter, Mrs. J. W. Cheek, at Dublin. It has been said of Grandmother Jackson, "She knew and loved Laurens County." Mr. and Mrs. Jackson are buried in Brewton Cemetery.

Children of Ethel and Felton Pierce are: Ethel Orr, born March 29, 1922, a graduate of Dublin High School and now a sophomore at Wesleyan College, Macon, Georgia; Rose Elizabeth, born February 13, 1927, a student in Dublin Junior High; Joel Felton, Jr., born January 19, 1934, a student in Calhoun Street School.

—*By Joel Felton Pierce.*

POWELL

John C. and William C. Powell came to Laurens County about 1885, engaged in Naval Stores business at Grimsley, ten miles south of Dublin. In 1889, a nephew, Frank Wooten Powell, came to Leurens and purchased their business.

Frank Wooten Powell was born June 24, 1868, in Grists, North Carolina, son of James William and Columbia E. (Grisette) Powell, descendants of the pioneer Carolina families of Wooten and Powell. Business interest carried him to other counties and states but faith and interest in Laurens County brought him back, so in 1900, he returned to Dublin where he spent the remainder of his life. He died July 23, 1903; is buried in Northview Cemetery. It was said of him at death: "He was the soul of honor, courteous to everyone, respected everybody's opinions and rights, and all of his acts were on the high plane of do unto others as you would have them do unto you."

November 26, 1890, Mr. Powell married Linnie Elizabeth Rogers, of North Carolina, daughter of John Dew Rogers and Catherine (Grantham) Rogers, descendants of the Carolina Gaddy and Skeeter families. Linnie is a devout Christian, member, as was her husband, of the First Baptist Church; has held the offices of Worthy Matron of O. E. S., and president of W. M. U.; is known for her unselfishness and kindness. Children born of this marriage are: Albert Rogers, Maude, Robert Henry, Grace, Frank Rogers, George Edwin, and Evelyn. Albert died in 1900, buried at Fair Bluff, North Carolina. Maude, married Turner F. Schaufele, no children. Robert Henry, married Irene Thomas, October 22, 1916; one child, Nancy Grace, was born of this union, June 13, 1918. Nancy married Marshall Webster Henry, June 20, 1938, now living in Rocky Mount, North Carolina.

Grace married Benjamin Franklin (Dee) Sessions November 26, 1927, no children. "Dee" is the son of B. F. and Sarah (Robison) Sessions, who came to Dublin in 1902. They are descendants of the representative Washington and Emanuel County families of Lewis and Tarbutton. "Dee," a World War veteran, served on City Council seven years, and is the present Mayor of Dublin.

Rogers married Gladys Bradford, no children, residents of Macon, Georgia. George Edwin, born April 18, 1900, married Margret Peters, March 27, 1926, daughter of Thomas Peters and Kate (Lewis) Peters. George's life was well rounded, marked for its simplicity and characterized by strong convictions of right and duty, both to His Maker and fellowman. He died January 17, 1935, is buried in Northview Cemetery. Children: George Edwin, Jr., born December 27, 1926; Thomas Wooten, born August 9, 1932. Tommy was named for Dr. Thomas Wooten, one of the first doctors of medicine in America, (see books "Relations of Virginia" by Captain John Smith, and "First Republic of America" by Albeert Brown). Evelyn died in infancy, and is buried in Northview Cemetery.

—By Grace Powell Sessions (Mrs. Dee)

PRESCOTT

George M. Prescott (1840-1898), son of Benjamin Prescott, Sr., who died in Screven County, Georgia, July 31, 1867. Benjamin Prescott, Sr., represented his county in the Georgia Legislature for several years.

George M. Prescott enlisted in Company G, 25th Regiment, Georgia Infantry, August 8, 1861; paroled at Augusta, Georgia, May 18, 1865. After the war, he studied at home with his sister's help and became a teacher and preacher. Bascom Church, Burke County, was his first pastorate; coming to Laurens about 1869. He served other churches, Salem (Wilkinson County), Evergreen and Marvin (Laurens County). He was a teacher in Johnson County when he married Lucinda Webb (1850-1929), September 27, 1866; both are buried in Marvin Church Cemetery.

Children: Louis Lovick, married Sallie Jane Ellington; George Maurice, never married; William Osgood Andrew, married Annie Lou Webster; Oliver Perry, married Leila Flanders; Mary Elizabeth, married J. Tom Flanders; Esther Alma Saxon, married Alfonzo Wood; Benjamin Z., died young; Walter Toplady, married, first, Victoria King; Sara Mattie Lou, married Henry McCord Watson.

Louis Lovick Prescott (1867-1920), eldest son of Reverend George M. Prescott and Lucinda Webb Prescott, owned and operated a farm in Buckeye District and became a Rural Carrier of the Dublin post office serving for about sixteen years. Member of the First Methodist Church, buried in Northview Cemetery. March 6. 1892, he married Sallie Jane Ellington, daughter of Joel F. Ellington and Leandie Braswell (Dolly) Duncan. (see Ellington genealogy).

Children: Excell Ellington, married Jewel Horn, twin daughters died in infancy. Excell served more than twenty-nine years as Rural

Mail Carrier of which fourteen months were served in Company C, 52nd Infantry, 6th Division (May 3, 1918 to June 20, 1919); eleven months overseas in the American Expeditionary Forces.

Picciola, taught school in Laurens County and during World War served, by appointment, as temporary carrier for Excell; is now connected with Southern Bell Telephone and Telegraph Company as Chief Operator, since December 6, 1920.

George M. Prescott, married Nina Carter, interested in farmnig and business activities in Laurens County.

John Reubin (Joe) Prescott, married Callie Graham, interested in farming and business activities; three children: Helen, Louis Calvin, and Ann.

—*By Picciola Prescott.*

PRINCE

The Prince family came to Laurens County from Washington County. Syl P. Prince, father of the Laurens County branch, lived in Washington County and is buried in the Poplar Springs Christian Church cemetery. He married Annie Melinda Armstrong, of Washington County, and after the death of her husband she came to Laurens County to reside with her children. She died in the home of her daughter, Lidie Bailey (Mrs. E. F.), and is buried in Northview Cemetery. Among their children are: John D.; Mollie Tucker (Mrs. M. R.); twins, Willie and Syl; Callie Summerlyn (Mrs. A. T.); Annie Lou Hodges (Mrs. J. C.); Lidie Bailey; Sherman Smith (Mrs. J. T.); Samuel Miles; and Tom.

Samuel Miles Prince, ninth child of Syl and Annie Melinda Prince, a man of high Christian character, member of the First Baptist Church, Assistant Postmaster of Dublin office for about thirty years, married Elizabeth Chapman, daughter of L. A. Chapman and Elizabeth Headden, pioneer citizens of Laurens County Samuel and Elizabeth Prince's children are: Lyman, Clifford Haynes, and Evelyn.

Clifford Haynes Prince, at present, is Captain of Company K, 121st Infantry of 30th Division, United States Army. He served in the local post office as Clerk, for about fifteen years, and was appointed Assistant Postmaster at the death of his father. He held that office for five years, or until he was called in Defense Work. He is a member of the First Methodist Church, a Mason, W. O. W., and a member of the Exchange Club.

Clifford Haynes Prince married Lula Massey King, August 15, 1922, daughter of Clifford Morrel King and Lula Georgia Massey, granddaughter (on paternal side) of Sara Jane Morrell and Francis King, on maternal side of John Andrew Massey and Georgia Keefe, prominent Cobb County citizens. (Ref.: Cobb County History).

Clifford Morrell and Lula Georgia Massey King's children are:

(1) Andrew; (2) Fannie, married Henry Blinn, two children, Billy and Jane Blinn; (3) Sara, married Tracy W. Hill and they have one son, Tracy W. Hill, Jr.; (4) Lula, married Clifford Haynes Prince, and they have two children, viz., Clifford Haynes Prince, Jr., born October 26, 1924, senior in Dublin High School, and Mary Massey Prince, born March 10, 1929, student in Calhoun Street School, Dublin.

—By Lula King Prince (Mrs. C. H.)

PRITCHETT

In the early 1900's the four brothers, William, Thomas Jordan, Henry Ellison, and George Ellison Pritchett, located in Dublin and were important factors in the business, educational and religious life of this city and county.

The first of these to locate in Dublin was Thomas Jordan Pritchett, who was born in Pitt County, North Carolina, August 23, 1855, and moved to Montgomery County, Georgia, in 1880. On March 19, 1884, he was married to Willie MacLeod of Mt. Vernon, Georgia. He was engaged in the naval stores business; was president of the Dublin Banking Company, the Georgia Warehouse and Compress Company, also on the Board of Education during the erection of the present Dublin High School building. He was one of the organizers of the first wholesale grocery and senior partner of the firm Pritchett and Hooks, which also operated an undertaking establishment. He was one of the outstanding contributors of the Dublin Episcopal Church and was active in many other enterprises for the upbuilding of the city and county.

He was a member of the Methodist Church. He died September 26, 1910, leaving his widow, Willie MacLeod Pritchett, and four children: Lida, Margaret, Thomas Jordan, Jr., and Ellison MacLeod, who married Paulette Leduc of Paris, France. The second child of Thomas Jordan and Willie MacLeod Pritchett was a son, William Howard, who died young.

William Pritchett, eldest son of James Henry Pritchett and his wife, Mary Elizabeth Jordan, was born in Robinson County, North Carolina, February 24, 1853, and located in Dublin shortly after his brother, T. J. Pritchett. He was one of Laurens County's most prominent and successful business men. His main business interests were in the naval stores; he was also the organizer of the Dublin Telephone Exchange and president of the Dublin Cotton Mills. He died September 12, 1916, in Dublin.

William Pritchett was twice married, first, to Laura Emily MacLeod, and had one son, James Henry Pritchett; married, second, to Maude Lillian Stubbs (see Stubbs genealogy), and had two daughters: (1) Ethel Inez Pritchett, married John Frederick Thigpen, no children; (2) Laura Emily Pritchett, married Henry Strickland Morgan, and has two sons, William Pritchett Morgan and John Beaumont Morgan.

PRITCHETT - ELLISON GENEALOGY

James Ellison came from the Isle of Man to America in 1732, and settled in Bath, Beaufort County, North Carolina; served as High Sheriff of that county. (See Book 3, page 279, Register of Deeds, Washington, North Carolina). His commission from King George was in the possession of the family until the War Between the States. He was a member of the General Assembly, 1764— (see Colonial Records of North Carolina, Vol. VI., page 1150).

James Ellison married Sarah Alderson, daughter of Simon Alderson, Jr.; to this union was born a son:

Alderson Ellison, Sr., who was born in 1743, married Lucretia Smaw, and had five children: (1) Henry Ellison, married Sarah Bonner; (2) Thomas Ellison, married, first, Julia Trippe, married, second, Elizabeth Pritchett; (3) William Ellison, married Lois Barlow; (4) Alderson Ellsion, Jr., married, first, Lucretia Palmer, married, second, Clarissa Bryan; (5) James Ellison, married Mary Ann Woodward.

Alderson Ellison, Sr., was High Sheriff of Beaufort County, North Carolina. (See Book 4, page 324, Register of Deeds, Washington, North Carolina). Through him his descendants are eligible to membership in the Colonial Dames and Daughters of the American Revolution.

Thomas Ellison, second son of Alderson Ellison. Sr., and his wife, Lucretia Smaw, was married to Julia Trippe May 16, 1793. Julia Trippe was the daughter of William Trippe (son of John Trippe, a planter of Nanesmond County, Virginia) and his wife, Eleanor Peyton, daughter of Benjamin Peyton and granddaughter of Sir Robert Peyton, who succeeded to the Baronetcy upon the death of Sir William Peyton, who was the first to live in Pamlico, in "Ye Old Bath Town." The ancestral lines of the Peytons residing in America came from Major Robert Peyton, who was born in Isleherne, England, in 1610, and came with his brother, Sir John Peyton, to Gloucester County, Virginia, in 1670. Their descendants moved to Currituck County, North Carolina, in 1723. This family was one of the most prominent and wealthy families in Virginia and North Carolina. Sir William Peyton was appointed one of His Majesty's Justices, August 1, 1726 (see Vol. II, page 636). Robert Peyton's will is found in North Carolina History and General Register, Vol. 141, page 65. William Trippe, the father of Julia (who was the wife of Thomas Ellison), published his will February 19, 1780, recorded in "Old Wills," page 153, Beaufort County, North Carolina, and mentions, among other children, his daughter, Juliet, afterward called Julia. His second wife was Elizabeth Pritchett. He was High Sheriff, Clerk of Court, and for many years a member of the Legislature from Beaufort County. His home was called "Welcome Hall" and was the scene of unstinted hospitality. He lies buried at what is known as "Grey's Place" near the mouth of Durham's Creek.

From the record of the old Family Bible, Thomas Ellison and his first wife, Julia Trippe, had ten children: Lucretia, died unmarried; Charlotte Corday Ellison, married William Pritchett: William Ellison, married Olivia Brickle; Henry Ellison, died young; Ellen Ellison, married John Braddy; Harriet Ellison, died at 84 years, unmarried; Henry A. Ellison, married, first, Caroline Telfair, married, second, Eliza Ann Trippe; Edward Ellison, died young; Mary Bonner Ellison, married Patrick Maul Bryan; Julia Ellison, died young.

Thomas Ellison and his second wife, Elizabeth Pritchett, had two children: Sarah Freeman Ellison, died unmarried; Julia Trippe Ellison, married Charles Latham.

Charlotte Corday Ellison, daughter of Thomas Ellison and his first wife, Julia Trippe, married William Pritchett and had six children: James Henry Pritchett, married Mary Elizabeth Jordan; Thomas Pritchett; Harriet Pritchett, died unmarried; Edward Pritchett; Olivia Pritchett; George Pritchett, died unmarried.

James Henry Pritchett, eldest son of William Pritchett and his wife, Charlotte Corday Ellison, married Mary Elizabeth Jordan, and had eight children: William, married, first, Laura Emily MacLeod, married, second, Maude Lillian Stubbs (detailed record above); Thomas Jordan Pritchett, married Willie MacLeod (detailed record above); Howard Bogey Pritchett, died unmarried; Olivia Pritchett, married Nathaniel Quince; Henry Ellison Pritchett, married Effie Flora MacRae; George Ellison Pritchett, married Leila Gay; Harriet Ellison Pritchett, unmarried.

—*By Willie MacLeod Pritchett (Mrs. T. J.)*

PROCTOR

Joseph Lindsey Proctor, born December 15, 1849, died November 25, 1935, married Eugenia Ann Tolleson, July 27, 1875, in Monroe County, Georgia. Moved to Laurens County November, 1896. Eugenia, born August 14, 1855, died May 8, 1936. Children: John Owen, born May 31, 1876; Martha Beatrice, born November 24, 1877, died April 8, 1937; James Howard, born March 24, 1880; Nora Louisa, born October 28, 1882; Iddie, born July 24, 1885; Florrie Eugenia, born November 5, 1890; William Jefferson, born November 3, 1892. Owen Proctor, married Annie M. Burch, January 20, 1907; children: Kate, born December 15, 1907; Gertrude Eugenia, born August 4, 1912; Jeannette, born June 18, 1919. Kate, married Jesse Ralph

Chambliss, December 31, 1925; children: Ralph Proctor, born April 10, 1928; Fred Parker, born February 7, 1933; Sylvia Nell, born January 28, 1940. Gertrude, married Francis Ray Phelps, March 25, 1933.

Beatrice Proctor, married Harlow M. Register, December 23, 1900; children: Bevis, born October 25, 1902; Jewell, born April 25, 1903. Bevis, married Annie Lizzie Flournoy, September, 1926; children: Bevis Flournoy, born March 31, 1930; Peggy Jewel, born October, 1932. Jewell, married Leo Grinstead, August 21, 1927. Their child: Janice, born June 25, 1934.

James Howard Proctor, married Seth Eva Clark, June 21, 1905. Eva Proctor died February 24, 1930. Their child: Grace, born January 11, 1907. Grace Proctor, married Morris Dawson Kea, May 1, 1940.

Nora Proctor, married Oscar Eason Clark, November 23, 1902. Oscar died June 29, 1928. Children: Opal Eva, born March 23, 1904; Clyde Howard, born October 26, 1906; Ruby Nell, born July 5, 1910. Opal, married Joseph W. Thomas, October 1, 1922; children: Oscar Edwin, born August 14, 1924; Martha Louise, born January 26, 1927; Charles Wheeler, born September 12, 1930. Clyde, married Bessie Lou Posey, March 11, 1927. Child: James Howard, born January 2, 1930. Ruby, married Marion Rogers Stover, December 25, 1927. Their child: Marjorie Nell, born January 1, 1936.

Iddie Proctor, married Thomas Fuqua, November 29, 1903; children: Gladys, born October 21, 1904, died January 28, 1928; Proctor, born November 24, 1908. Gladys, married James Hobbs, July 18, 1921. Child: Betty, born April 4, 1923, married Reginald Seymour, June 14, 1940.

Florrie Proctor, married Rezin Andrew Bedingfield, June 28, 1911; children: Ralph Proctor, born July 23, 1912; Fannie Joe, born May 3, 1916; James Andrew, born March 8, 1921; Edna Elizabeth, born August 30, 1923. Ralph, married Beatrice Barrs, December 25, 1936; child: Ralph Lindsey, born February 25, 1938.

Jefferson Proctor, married Roberta Jordan, November 28, 1917; children: Camille, born August 24, 1920; Jefferson, born September 21, 1925.

—*By Grace Proctor Kea (Mrs. M. D.)*

RAMSAY

Col. Whiteford S. Ramsay

In 1858, Dublin and Laurens County gained a distinguished, valued and revered citizen in the coming to this county of Col. Whiteford S. Ramsay—a citizen who played a prominent and beneficent role in shaping the religious, educational and civic life of this com-

COLONEL WHITEFORD S. RAMSAY

munity. Excerpts from tributes paid to Col. Ramsay at the time of his death, March 16, 1900, bear testimony to the universal love and esteem in which he was held:

"Col. Whiteford S. Ramsay was perhaps the best known and most universally beloved man in Middle Georgia. He was born at Milledgeville, Georgia, June 8, 1839, and came from a distinguished Scotch family. His father was Professor Randolph H. Ramsay, one of the noted educators in Georgia in his time. Col. W. S. Ramsay was educated at Oglethorpe University under his father and graduated in 1857. The following year he took a course at Princeton; later he located in Dublin and opened a school. For more than twenty years he was one of Laurens County's most zealous educators. There was a temporary suspension of his services in this direction during the War Between the States, as he went on the battlefield at the opening of the conflict. He raised a Company in Laurens County known as the Blackshear Guards, which was mustered into the 14th Georgia Regiment, Confederate Service, of which he was elected Captain and was later promoted to the rank of Lieutenant Colonel. His regiment was ordered to Virginia and that was the scene of his services.

"Immediately after the war he resumed teaching and a few years later was ordained a minister of the Baptist Church. On August 14, 1874, Colonel Ramsay was made a Master Mason; in June, 1891, he joined a chapter of the Royal Arch Masons; later connected himself with the St. Omer Commandery Knights Templar and other Masonic bodies, being considered at the time of his death one of the most brilliant Masons in the State. For several years he served as chairman of the Foreign Correspondence Committee of the Grand Lodge, Grand Chaplain of the Grand Chapter of Royal Arch Masons, Grand Chaplain of the Royal and Silent Masters, and Grand Chaplain of the Order of the High Priesthood.

"But it is as a minister and as an educator that the people knew him best. For twenty-two years Colonel Ramsay was pastor of the First Baptist Church, of Dublin, and at the time of his death was pastor of Poplar Springs Church, Ohoopee Church, Bethlehem Church and the Church at Jeffersonville. As a pulpit orator he had few equals in the state. Some of the most eloquent sermons ever delivered in Georgia were by him. During his ministry he perhaps married more people and buried more people than any minister in Middle Georgia."

Colonel Ramsay was a born educator, not only as a teacher but also as an able director of the educational life of this county. For twenty years he served as County School Commissioner and a few days before his death was re-elected for another term of four years.

Colonel Ramsay died at his home in Dublin, March 16, 1900. His funeral is said to have been the largest ever held here. So vast was the crowd which came from all parts of the state to pay a last tribute of respect to this honored Georgian that the portico of the old Baptist Church was used as a pulpit, and the assembly overflowed the Church grounds and extended into the school campus across the street.

On December 15, 1858, Whiteford S. Ramsay was united in marriage to Henrietta Jane Guyton, member of one of the oldest County families. (See Guyton genealogy.) Through a long line of patriot ancestors Henrietta Guyton Ramsay had a background concurrent with the beginnings of this nation, being a lineal descendant of five Revolutionary officers: Lieut. Moses Guyton, Lieut. John Martin Dasher, Capt. Thomas Wylly, Capt. Chesley Bostwick, and Capt. John Bostwick. Capt. Chesley Bostwick also held the rank of Captain in the Colonial Army of Georgia. William Wylly, father of Capt. Thomas Wylly, held the Colonial appointment of Commissioner of Roads in Georgia in 1773.

Eight children were born to Whiteford S. and Henrietta Guyton Ramsay:

I. and II. Ida and Elbert, died young.

III. Martha Bass Ramsay, born in Dublin and a life-long resident of this city, was educated in the Dublin schools and in Midway, Georgia., where she spent some time in the home of her grandfather, Randolph H. Ramsay, M.A., Rector of the Preparatory School of Oglethorpe University; a charter and honorary member of the Oconee Chapter U. D. C.; charter member of John Laurens Chapter D. A. R.

IV. Alice Viola Ramsay, born in Dublin, married James Barnes Sanders (see Sanders genealogy) and had four children: 1. Henrietta Marion Sanders, married Elliott Blount Freeman (see Freeman genealogy); 2. Irene Natalie Sanders, married Ernest Camp (see Camp genealogy) and had three children, viz., (1) Ernest Camp, Jr., married Willie May Aycock, (2) Martha Ramsay Camp, married Harry Power Burns, (3) Lieut. Sanders Camp, married Gladys Chambliss; 3. James Guyton Sanders, married Robbie Jewel Williams (see Williams genealogy); 4. Randolph Ramsay Sanders, married, first, May Corker, married, second, Jean Mason.

V. Tallulah Corinne Ramsay, born in Cave Springs, Georgia, a talented musician, married Lucien Quincy Stubbs (see Stubbs and Tucker sketches) and had six children, the first three of whom died young: 1. Clara Guyton Stubbs; 2. John Madison Stubbs; 3. Ella Ophelia Stubbs; 4. Jeannette Ramsay Stubbs, married James Davis Glover and has four children, viz., (1) Corinne Ramsay Glover, (2) James Davis Glover, Jr., (3) Marthalu Glover, (4) Julia Allaphair Glover; 5. Robert Flournoy Stubbs; 6. Lucien Quincy Stubbs, Jr.

VI. Mary Guyton Ramsay, a native of Dublin and a life-long resident of this city; educated in the Dublin schools, also studied at the University of Georgia, Emory University, Knoxville (Tenn.) University, and Asheville (N. C.) Normal College; in 1940, took an extensive Piedmont Educational Tour; has been a member of the faculty of the Dublin Public Schools for a number of years; since 1934, has served as Assistant Principal of the Calhoun Street School; charter member and ex-Regent of the John Laurens Chapter D. A. R.; member of the Oconee Chapter U. D. C.; charter member of the Woman's Study Club; has served on the Board of Directors of the Dublin Carnegie Library.

VII. Thomas Randolph Ramsay (biographical sketch later), married Lil Frances Hightower. (See Hightower genealogy).

VIII. Virginia Augusta Ramsay, born in Dublin, now a prominent clubwoman of Bainbridge, Georgia, married John Middleton Simmons (see Simmons genealogy) and has four sons: 1. Jack Whiteford Simmons, married Sarah Scott and has four children, viz., (1) Virginia, (2) Jack Whiteford, Jr., (3) Mary Edna, (4) Sarah Marie; 2. David Ramsay Simmons, married Ellen Carswell and has three children, viz., (1) Virginia Claire, (2) David Ramsay, Jr., (3) John Middleton, III.; 3. Thomas Randolph Simmons, married Elizabeth Burney and has two daughters, Sara Elizabeth and Virginia Ruth; 4. William Pinckney Simmons, married Betty Sweet Smith and has one son, William Pinckney, Jr.

THOMAS RANDOLPH RAMSAY

Thomas Randolph Ramsay, only surviving son of Colonel Whiteford S. and Henrietta Guyton Ramsay, is a worthy bearer of the Randolph-Ramsay names, also of the French Huguenot lineage which comes to him through his mother (see Guyton genealogy). Born in Dublin, in the Ramsay residence on Bellevue Avenue, he spent his boyhood days in this city; here he received his education at the Dublin schools, supplemented with private instruction from his father, who was recognized as one of the leading educators of his time.

In Dublin, Thomas R. Ramsay was affiliated with many fraternal organizations: Masons, Knights of Pythias, Odd Fellows, Elks, Kiwanis, and was a charter member of the Dublin Country Club. He is Past Eminent Commander of the Olivet Commandery Knights Templar, of Dublin; he was District Inspector for the Elks; he is a Shriner, belonging to the Alee Temple of Savannah, Georgia.

In 1914, Thomas R. Ramsay located in Atlanta and was engaged in the automobile business; while there he became a member of the Capitol City Club. After a few years residence in Atlanta, he spent a short time in Jacksonville, Florida, also in the automobile business; returning to Dublin in 1917, he became partner with S. M. Kellam, in the firm of Kellam and Ramsay, distributors of Dodge cars, equipment and accessories.

In 1921, Mr. Ramsay went to Bainbridge to take charge of the commissary in connection with the Elberta Crate and Box Company, this plant being owned and operated by his brother-in-law, John M.

Simmons. In 1922, Thomas R. Ramsay was united in marriage to Lil Frances Hightower, of Dublin (see Hightower genealogy), and Mr. and Mrs. Ramsay have resided in Bainbridge continuously since that time. Not only has Mr. Ramsay been highly successful in the commissary business but he also owns a large nursery and florist business, specializing in camellias and azaleas. Of camellias alone the Ramsay Nurseries have nearly one hundred named varieties. Many "blue ribbons" have been awarded them, in various flower shows over the state, for artistic exhibits and individual specimens of flowers. Many Georgia and Florida gardens owe their beauty to the landscaping department of the Ramsay Nurseries. "Rose Arbor Cottage," the lovely home of the Ramsays, in Bainbridge, is famed for its gracious Southern hospitality, and their beautifully landscaped gardens draw visitors and sightseers from many states.

In Bainbridge, Mr. Ramsay is a Rotarian and a member of the Sportsman's Club; he and Mrs. Ramsay are prominently identified with the religious, civic, patriotic, and social organizations of their locality. As were their parents before them, Mr. and Mrs. Ramsay are members of the Baptist Church.

—*By Henrietta Sanders Freeman (Mrs. E. B.)*

RAMSAY GENEALOGY

Those familiar with Scotch history need not be told that the Ramsays are of Scotch extraction. Scottish histories, novels and old songs are full of allusions to the name. Just when William Ramsay came to Virginia is not definitely known, but in Albermarle County, Virginia, in 1741, William Ramsay married Caroline Randolph—and it is of them and their descendants that this story deals.

William Randolph was the first of that name in Virginia. He came from Yorkshire, England, in 1673. He married Mary Isham and they lived on their estate, "Turkey Island," on the James River. The house was built of bricks brought from England. He was a member of the Assembly in 1684 and a founder and a trustee of William and Mary College. There is at Henrico County Court House a paper dated 1698 bearing his signature and a fine impression of his coat of arms. Among his descendants are John Marshall, Thomas Jefferson, and Robert E. Lee. He had seven sons and three daughters, and settled his children on other estates, building excellent homes for all of them. By 1705 he owned 10,000 acres of land in Henrico County alone.

One of his sons, Isham Randolph, lived in baronial style on his estate, "Dungeness," with his wife, Jane Rogers Randolph, whom he met and married while on a trip to England in 1717. He was a member of the House of Burgesses from Goochland County and Adjutant General of the Colony.

THOMAS RANDOLPH RAMSAY

Peter Jefferson, in 1739, married Jane Randolph, oldest child of Isham Randolph of "Dungeness," who connected her husband with perhaps the most distinguished family in the province, assuring the social standing of his children.

It was in this home, "Dungeness," in 1741, that another daughter of Isham Randolph, Caroline, married William Ramsay. Their son, Randolph Ramsay, was born in 1742 in Albermarle County, Virginia. He was first cousin to Thomas Jefferson. In a cabinet of family relics in "Monticello," the home of Thomas Jefferson, reposes an old breast-pin which bears a label: "Owned by Caroline Randolph Ramsay," who was the aunt of Thomas Jefferson.

Though accustomed to luxury in Virginia, by the time he was thirty Randolph Ramsay was seeking his fortune in Georgia. Georgia Council, Savannah, January 7, 1772: "Granted a petition of Randolph Ramsay setting forth that he had been some time in the province, that he had a wife, seven children and two negroes and desired 600 acres of land on the Little Kioka." At the beginning of the Revolutionary War there were about 200 families in the settlement of the Little Kioka, which was about 35 miles northwest of Augusta. The leading families were: The Reverend Abraham Marshall, the Fews, Ramsays, Candlers, Crawfords, and Applings.

John Ramsay, son of Randolph Ramsay and wife, Caroline Randolph Ramsay, was born in Virginia in 1764 and was only a small boy when his parents moved to Georgia at the beginning of the Revolutionary War; nevertheless, he joined Col. James Jackson's Georgia Light Dragoons and was wounded in the left arm by a broad sword, July 6, 1791, near Long Cane Mills. In 1783, John Ramsay married Sarah Allen, who was born in 1764 in Wilkes County, Georgia, the daughter of James Allen, who was born in Martha's Vineyard, Massachusetts, in 1716. James Allen's great grandfather, George Allen, was born in 1568 in Essex, England, and in 1636 settled in Sandwich, Massachusetts, where he was chosen Deputy General, the first office in the town; and served as Representative, 1641-42, at Plymouth.

John Ramsay and wife, Sarah Allen Ramsay, had five children: William, Randolph, John, James Allen, and David. The fourth son, James Allen Ramsay, was born in 1785 in Wilkes County, Georgia, but moved to Mecklenburg County, North Carolina, and was always active in state politics. He was State Congressman several years and candidate for governor. He wrote a very useful history of North Carolina. James Allen Ramsay and wife, Eliza Hassell Ramsay, had several children. Their son, Randolph Hassell Ramsay, was born in 1814, in Mecklenberg County, North Carolina. He married Mary Anne Monroe Cleghorn, the daughter of Dr. George Elbert Cleghorn, an eminent physician and scientist from Edenburg, Scotland, and his wife, Martha Moss Cleghorn. She was the daughter of Henry Moss, a Revolutionary soldier of Virginia, and wife,

Sallie Scott Mimms Moss, whose great grandfather, Samuel "Ready Money" Scott, of Scott's Ferry, South Carolina, was too old to fight in the Revolutionary War, but he aided South Carolina in 1781 by having "ready money" which he loaned the militia for provisions.

Randolph H. Ramsay was listed in the Cherokee Land Lottery published in 1838; address, 119th Richmond County, Section 2, District 14. He died in Midway, Georgia, 1877.

Dr. Samuel K. Talmadge was pastor of the Presbyterian Church in Augusta, Georgia, from 1826-1837. The older children of Randolph H. Ramsay were born in Augusta and the Ramsays were Presbyterians. Dr. Talmadge went to Midway, near Milledgeville, the capital of the state, to be president of Oglethorpe University when it was established by the Hopewell Presbytery in 1838. Randolph Ramsay went soon after he graduated from Yale in 1839. The Talmadges lived in the beautiful President's home at the University and the Ramsays lived nearby. Ruth, wife of Dr. Talmadge, was a close relative of Mary Ann Cleghorn Ramsay. Both families are buried in family burying grounds at old Midway, their slaves being buried there also. Oglethorpe University was at Midway, near Milledgeville, from 1838-1862, when the endowment, which was in Confederate bonds, became valueless. The facilities were adequate to needs of the period. It contained the finest college chapel in the United States, not excepting Yale, Harvard, or Princeton. Nearby was the academy for boys preparing for Oglethorpe, of which Randolph Hassell Ramsay, M.A., was Rector. Neighbors were the Honorable Alfred Nesbit, Dr. Thomas Hall, Col. David C. Campbell, Sherwood Thomas, Dr. Thomas Lamar, and Dr. Thomas F. Green, Superintendent of the State Sanitarium. In 1847 the trustees of the Sanitarium were: Dr. Benjamin White, Randolph H. Ramsay, B. F. Stubbs.

Mrs. Randolph H. Ramsay's mother was Martha Moss Cleghorn and, after the death of her husband, Dr. Cleghorn, she married Capt. Hamlin Bass. Her will as Martha Bass is on file in Milledgeville, under date of July 25, 1862. Bequests of money, slaves, stock in the South Western Railroad, in the Georgia Railroad and in the Georgia Banking Company were made to her children and grandchildren. Stock in the Georgia Railroad and substantial sums of money were bequeathed to each of the children of her daughter, Mary (Cleghorn) Ramsay: George R. Ramsay, Elbert C. Ramsay, Robert H. Ramsay, Whiteford S. Ramsay, H. Clay Ramsay, and Mary Ann Ramsay.

The children of Randolph Hassell Ramsay and wife, Mary Ann Cleghorn Ramsay, were:

I. Elbert Cleghorn Ramsay was born in Augusta, Georgia, March 6, 1833, and died at his home at Midway December 23, 1890. He married Mary Screven, daughter of Dr. James Odginsell Screven of LaGrange, Georgia, a Baptist minister, who was the grandson of

General James Screven of Revolutionary fame. Elbert Ramsay brought his bride to his parents' home at Midway and they lived there until his death. He was a graduate of Oglethorpe University, Judge of the County Court of Baldwin County, a successful farmer and superintendent of "the Little Church Under the Pines," at Midway, for many years.

II. George Randolph Ramsay graduated at Oglethorpe University. He became a practicing physician and lived at Lawtonville, South Carolina. He married Esther Ann Solomon and they had two children: 1. Ettie Ramsay, married John Lawton Morrison. 2. Elbert S. Ramsay, married Rubye Rhodes; their children are: (1) Dorothy Adelaide Ramsay, married Harry Clay Canady; (2) Rupert Solomon Ramsay, married Thelma Herndon; (3) Kenneth Ramsay, married Lessie Fitts; (4) Annie Dasher Ramsay; (5) Ernest Ramsay, married Miriam Canady; (6) Mildred Hope Ramsay.

III. Robert Hassell Ramsay was born in 1838 in Augusta, Georgia. He graduated from Oglethorpe University in 1857. On May 5, 1858, in Macon County, Alabama, he married Alice Ware Howard, daughter of William John Howard and wife, Anne Flewellen Billingslea Howard. They with a colony of Georgians had settled in Alabama after their marriage at "Lowther Hall" in Clinton, Jones County, Georgia, in 1838. William John Howard's home was what is now 914 Milledge Road, Augusta, Georgia, where today still hangs the beautiful portrait of his grandmother, Hannah Few Howard, which was painted by Gilbert Stuart. She was a sister of Col. William Few, Georgia's first U. S. Senator and signer of the Constitution. Her father, William Few, Sr., was a Revolutionary soldier, as was her husband, Rhesa Howard. Alice Ware Howard attended Nashville Female Academy in Nashville, Tennessee. She painted beautifully and was an accomplished musician. In 1862 Professor Robert H. Ramsay was made head of the Bolivar Seminary near Madisonville, Tennessee. He and his wife and a few slaves moved to Madisonville and made that their home. His grandfather, Dr. George Elbert Cleghorn, had left to Robert his silver headed cane and Professor Ramsay was the typical old schoolmaster, always wearing a high silk hat and carrying this cane. He was later principal of Union Institute at Sweetwater, Tennessee, which became Sweetwater College. W. B. Lenoir in his history of Sweetwater Valley said of Professor Ramsay: "He was a very brilliant man and made quite a reputation as an educator. And I never knew a man more conversant with the best books in English Literature."

Robert Hassell Ramsay and wife, Alice Howard Ramsay, had six children: 1. Howard Hassell Ramsay, born January 21, 1861; 2. Randolph Ramsay, born March 11, 1863; 3. Whiteford Clay Ramsay, born February 21, 1866; 4. Robert Lee Ramsay, born May 5, 1868; 5. Marian Ramsay; 6. Walter Ramsay.

Robert Lee Ramsay, son of Robert Hassell and Alice Howard Ramsay, was born in Madisonville, Tennessee, May 5, 1868. And the worthwhileness of the Ramsays was in this man. He married, November 6, 1889, Eleanor Gault, of Rogersville, Tennessee, daughter of Dr. Samuel Henry Gault and wife, Sarah Eliza Henry Gault. She was a great granddaughter of James Henry, a Revolutionary soldier of Virginia. Robert Lee Ramsay and wife, Eleanor, moved to Chattanooga, Tennessee, and made that their home. They were members of the First Presbyterian Church. They had two children: 1. Robert Gault Ramsay, born April 12, 1895, died October 4, 1918; 2. Eloise Ramsay, born February 20, 1898, married July 5, 1919, to James Ryan Maddock, of Savannah, Georgia. They have one daughter, Eleanor Ramsay Maddock, born April 21, 1920. She is now (1941) a senior of the University of Georgia, a Phi Beta Kappa, and president of Kappa Alpha Theta.

IV. Whiteford Smith Ramsay, born in Milledgeville, Georgia, June 8, 1839. Full record appears on preceding pages.

V. H. Clay Ramsay, born in Milledgeville, Georgia, graduate of Oglethorpe University; died in early manhood.

VI. Mary Ann Ramsay.

BIBLIOGRAPHY:

Dictionary of American Biography, Vol. X, p. 17; Vol. XV, p. 371.
Appleton's Cyclopedia of American Biography, Vol. IX.
National Cyclopedia of American Biography, Vol. VIII.
Colonial Records of Georgia, Candler, Vol. XII, 1711-1782.
Statistics of Georgia, White, Pub. 1849.
Ab. Comp. Amer. Gen. 1st Families of America, Vol. III, p. 645.
Biographical Souvenir of the States of Georgia and Florida, Pub. 1889, p. 677.
History of Georgia, White, Pub. 1849.
History of Baldwin County, Green.
History of Baldwin County, Georgia, Cooke.
Garden History of Georgia.

—By *Eloise Ramsay Maddock (Mrs. J. R.)*
Savannah, Georgia

RAWLS

Willis Rawls, native of North Carolina, married Elizabeth Skipper about 1818, and with their three children, Oliver Hazard Perry, Alec and Margaret, traveled to Georgia, via ex-cart, first settling in Wilkinson County, Georgia, and later in Laurens County. They established a home on land received in a land grant. Elizabeth was the daughter of Nathan Skipper, a Revolutionary soldier, who enlisted in 1777, and served through 1780, under Captain Flangett and Colonel Armstrong, in North Carolina. He engaged in the battles in Brandywine, Germantown, and Monmouth. He served in North Carolina and was a pensioner in Maury County, Tennessee—probably being paid for his services in Tennessee land. He stated he had nine children at the time of his application, June 30, 1826.

Oliver Hazard Perry Rawls (1820-1873) married, in 1845, Martha Fordham (1827-1910), daughter of Benjamin (1784-1864) and Elsie Miller Fordham (1785-1863). Martha Fordham's sisters and brothers were: Frank, Robert, Wiley, Zenus, Selathiel, Benjamin, Olive, Elizabeth, Elsie, Mary Ann, and Jane. Martha was the granddaughter of William (1759-1837) and Amy Barker Miller (1757-1831), married February 17, 1805. William Miller, an Englishman, who came to America prior to the war of the Revolution, and his wife, Amy (Barker), a native of Ireland, had nine children. On his tombstone in Kettle Creek Cemetery, Ware County, Georgia, is the following inscription: "Sacred to the memory of William Miller who served his country in the Revolutionary War and departed this life 27th day of November, 1837. Age 79 years, 7 months, 19 days." (Services of William Miller found in Smith's "History of Georgia and Georgia People").

Alec Rawls, son of Willis and Elizabeth Rawls, settled in Mississippi after coming to Georgia, acording to the Census of 1790.

Margaret, daughter of Willis and Elizabeth Rawls, married John Dominy.

The children of Oliver Hazard Perry and Martha Fordham Rawls were: James R. Rawls (1847), Benjamin Haywood (1848), Olive Jane (1850), Oliver Marshall (1851), Letha Sara (1853), Napoleon Bonaparte (1855), Martha Etta (1857), Joel Ira (1859-1879), Robert L. C. (1860), Mary Civilia (1862), Otis H. P. (1870).

James Roy Rawls married Laura T. Mitchell. Their children were: James Roy, Jr., Polhill, and Mateel (deceased). James Roy, married Nette Lord and to this union were born: Allen, Albert, Mildred, Carolyn, Katherine, and J. R.; Polhill Rawls married Grace—and they have one daughter, Annie Laurie.

Latha Sara Rawls, married Dr. Linder and had two children: Lee (deceased), and Oliver (deceased).

Napoleon Bonaparte Rawls (1855-1933), married Mrs. Louisa Sabelia Evans Bruner (1862-1934), widow of Nathaniel Alec Bruner (1850-1887). Louisa Sabelia, daughter of Julius Wright (1819-1905) and Nancy Mariam Garrett Evans (1831-1915), had two sons by her marriage in 1879 to Nathaniel Alec Bruner: Charles Nathaniel and Warren Evans Bruner. By her marriage in 1890, to Napoleon Bonaparte Rawls, there were two children: Martha Pauline and Robbie Louisa. Charles Nathaniel Bruner, married, in 1919, Pearl Freeman and their children are: Nathaniel Alec, Thomas Freeman, Julius Wright, and Emily Louise. Warren Evans Bruner married (1911) (1) Fannie Elizabeth Wyche and they had one son, Wyche Evans, who married Benie Phillips (1934). He resides in Spartanburg,

South Carolina. Martha Pauline Rawls married (1914) Ivan Gray Prim, of Jackson, Alabama, son of Doctor Thomas Jefferson and Clara Williams Prim. Ivan Gray Prim, Jr., is the only son of Pauline Rawls and Ivan Gray Prim. Robbie Louise Rawls, married Paul Shiver. Their children are: Paul (deceased), Robert Vernan, and Leitha Joyce.

Robert L. C. Rawls, married Emma Cooper. Their children are: Floy T., Tom, and Martha (deceased).

Otis H. P. Rawls, married Julia Irene Herndon. Their children are: Wendell Lyton (deceased), Otis Bryant, James Julian (deceased), Grace Elizabeth, and Martha Jane. (See Herndon genealogy).

—*By Pauline Rawls Prim (Mrs. I. G.)*

RENTZ

The Rentz and allied families were prominent among the early families of Laurens County. They numbered among their group, leaders in finance, ministry, education and general business affairs.

First of the name in the county was Joseph Rentz and wife, Martha McGehee. He was a Methodist minister and was one of the first Presiding Elders in the Methodist denomination in the county. He was a direct descendant of John Von Rentz and wife, Barbara (Unseldt), Salzburgers, who came to this country from Germany because of religious persecution; they were numbered among the earliest settlers of old Ebenezer, and were members of old Ebenezer Church. The marriage of John Von Rentz and Barbara Unseldt, November 26, 1754, and the baptism of their eight children are recorded in the history of this church, by A. G. Voight.

Edward Pierce Rentz, born 1862, was the son of Joseph Rentz and Martha McGehee Rentz. Martha McGehee and her brothers, John and Howard, were descended from a family prominent in Methodism and in Georgia history. Edward Pierce Rentz built the railroad from Dublin to Eastman in 1903. He was the founder of the town in Laurens County which bears his name, Rentz. He was an extensive sawmill operator and lumberman, operating many turpentine stills in Laurens County. He was a leading financier of his day and owned much property in the county. He died in Florida in 1920. He married Katherine Wiles Gaston, of Eufala, Alabama, in 1883. Through Kate Gaston, the family traces its ancestry through the Pierce family to Lovick Pierce, noted Methodist Bishop, and to George F. Pierce, first president of Wesleyan College in Macon, Georgia. To this Rentz-Gaston union was born eight children. Four died in infancy. The other four spent their early years in Dublin, Laurens County.

Joseph Alfred Rentz, oldest son of Edward Pierce and Katherine Rentz, was born in 1888, and died in October, 1918. He married

Blanche Anthony Davis (see Coleman genealogy), in December, 1907. His business interests carried him to Ocala, Florida, and there the one child of this union was born, a daughter, Emily Katherine Rentz. Emily Rentz married Albert Fleming Geeslin, in 1927. They now reside in Dublin, Laurens County, Georgia.

James Tanner Rentz, second son, was born in 1893.

Martha Kate Rentz married Homer Lee Oliver, of Apalachicola, Florida, and to this union was born one daughter, Mercia Louise Oliver.

Addie Louise Rentz married James King, of Louisburg, North Carolina. To this union was born three children, Martha Grey, James, and a younger son.

—By Emily Rentz Geeslin (Mrs. A. F.)

RICE

William Brooks Rice was born in Edisto Island, South Carolina, in 1856. His mother died when he was two years of age and he was reared by a devoted aunt, Mrs. Jack Rice, until twelve years of age.

When quite a young man he moved to South Georgia, where he became interested in Naval Stores, later becoming one of the most successful operators in this section of the State, also in Florida. In 1886, he married Miss Maud Halcyone Bradley, of St. Louis, Missouri. In 1904, he purchased the Dan Smith estate in the suburbs of Dublin, Georgia, later known as Brookwood, and that same year moved his family there, where he owned and operated one of the largest dairies and farms in Laurens County. Captain Rice, as he was called, was a leader and benefactor in all public enterprises for the development of his community. He was a consistent member of the Baptist Church, but never failed to help in the building and support of all churches and schools in the different communities where he lived. Captain Rice was never known to turn away anyone in distress or fail to help a worthy cause. He was looked upon as the foster father of two sets of half brothers and sisters and helped educate and start in life many young men and women. He had varied interests, but Naval Stores was his main and cherished business. Captain Rice lived a long and useful life and died on his estate, Brookwood, December 9, 1929.

RICE FAMILY IN AMERICA

PEDIGREE NO. 1

I. DEACON EDMUND RICE, first ancestor in America, came from Barkhomstead, England, in 1638. He was born in 1594, died May 3, 1663, in Marlboro, Massachusetts; lived for over 20 years in Sudbury, Massachusetts (now Wayland, Massachusetts). He married

Tamazine Hosmer and they had ten children; married, second, Dame Mercie Brigham, and had two children by her. There were nine sons, and three daughters.

II. EDWARD RICE, second son of Deacon Edmund Rice, was born in Barkhomstead, England, in 1619; died August 15, 1712, in Marlboro, Massachusetts. He married Agnes Bent and there were eleven children, nine born in Sudbury, and two in Marlboro.

III. DANIEL RICE, SR., fifth child of Edward and Agnes Rice, born November 8, 1655; married Bertha Ward in Massachusetts; died in Marlboro, July, 1717.

IV. DANIEL RICE, JR., the first child of Daniel and Bertha Ward Rice, was born June 3, 1684; died in Orangeburg, South Carolina, in 1734; married Elizabeth Taylor.

V. DAVID RICE, SR., third child of Daniel and Elizabeth Taylor Rice, was born September 16, 1717; died in Massachusetts in 1801; married Love Moore in Massachusetts; member Massachusetts Militia, Revolutionary War.

VI. DAVID RICE, JR., first child of David, Sr., and Love Moore Rice, was born in Massachusetts, February 18, 1759; died in South Carolina in 1825; married Abigail Reed in 1785, and had eight children: Hannah, born 1787; John, born 1789; David (dead at birth), 1791; Aaron, born 1793; David F., born 1795; Reuben, born 1797; Nathan, born 1800; William.

David Rice, Jr., was a member of South Carolina Militia in the American Revolution and the record of his service may be found in Book N, page 294, and Book L, "Stub Entries to Indents Issued in Payment of Claims Against South Carolina Growing Out of the Revolution," by A. S. Sally, No. 273.

VII. DAVID F. RICE, fifth child of David, Jr., and Abigail Reed Rice, was born August 16, 1795, married Rebecca Simmons, of Charleston, South Carolina. Both died in South Carolina.

VIII. BENJAMIN F. RICE, son of David F. and Rebecca Simmons Rice, was born in South Carolina, September 28, 1830; died April 4, 1884. Benjamin F. Rice was thrice married, first, to Rebecca Sauls, of Walterboro, South Carolina. They had one son, William Brooks Rice, who married Maud Halcyone Bradley, of St. Louis, Missouri (Recorded above). Married, second, to Rachel King, of South Carolina, and had five children: (1) Ellen Rice, who married James W. Wood; (2) Benjamin Rice; (3) Florence Irene Rice, married Edward Bryan; (4) Minna Earl Rice, married Willie Bennett; (5) Daniel Guess Rice, married Bertha Williams. Married, third, Ellen Frances Reed, of Blackwell, South Carolina, and had three children: (1) William Capers Rice, died at age of 16; (2) Samuel Percy Rice, married Claudia McLemore, of Swainsboro, Georgia; (3) Evie Delle Rice, of Blackville, South Carolina married Edgar Thompson Barnes, of Jasper County, Georgia.. Evie Rice Barnes' mother (Ellen Frances Reed Rice) was the daughter of Samuel Reed, Jr., (1810-1887) and Matilda Reed (1815-1865); granddaughter of Hugh Reed (1783-1854) and Jane McFadden(1794-1839); great granddaughter of Samuel Reed, Sr., (1751-1823), Revolutionary soldier, and Mary Clark (1752-1846); great great granddaughter of Malcom Clark (1739-1786), Revolutionary soldier, and Mary Clark, Sr. (1741-1774); also a granddaughter of Robert Willis (1772-1844) and Kesiah Watson (1780-1846); great granddaughter of Captain Michael Watson (1726-1782), Revolutionary soldier, and Martha Watson, died 1817. Her grandfather, Hugh Reed, rendered efficient service in the War of 1812.

GENEALOGY OF THE RICE FAMILY IN ENGLAND

PEDIGREE No. 2

Direct line of descent from Coel Codevog, King of the Britons, to Deacon Edmund Rice, the immigrant ancestor (1594-1663), recorded in Pedigrees 1 and 3.

Generations:
1. Coel Codevog, King of the Britons.
2. A son (and daughter Helena, mother of Constantine the Great).
3. Mierchion Gul, grandson of King Codevog.
4. Cynvarch Oer ap-Mierchion Gul. (Had three sons).
5. Vryan Reged, (also spelled Uryan Rheged and Urien Rheged) by birth a Cambre Briton, who, in the sixth century, was Prince of North Briton, but was expelled by the Saxons, and fled to Wales, married Margaret La-Faye, daughter of Gerlois, Duke of Cornwall, and was Prince of Rheged in Wales, Lord of Kidwelly, Carunllon, and Iskennen in South Wales. He built the Castle Carrey Cermin in Carmanthenshire.
6. Pafgen, (also spelled Pasgen)..................................Lord of Kidwelly
7. Mori, (also spelled Mott).......................................Lord of Kidwelly
8. Liarch, (also spelled Larch)...................................Lord of Kidwelly
9. Rhyne, ...Lord of Kidwelly
10. Cecil, (also spelled Cecilt)...................................Lord of Kidwelly
11. Gurwared, ...Lord of Kidwelly
12. Kynbatywe, (also spelled Kynbatwye)..............Lord of Kidwelly
13. Liarch, (also spelled Licarch)..............................Lord of Kidwelly
14. Enyion, (also spelled Eynion)..............................Lord of Kidwelly
15. Granwey, (also spelled Gronwey).......................Lord of Kidwelly
16. Voed (in Burke's Peerage 1914, caled Rice of Iskennen), married Margaret, daughter of co-heir of Griffith of Kiddz, Lord of Cwynav.
17. Elider ap-Rhys of Iskennen, Esquire, married Glafis (also spelled Gwadlys), daughter of Phillip, son of Bah.
18. Sir Elider Dhu, Knight of the Holy Sepulchre, married Cicily, daughter of Siscilite ap-Hyn.

19. Phillip ap-Elider FitzUryan, married Gladis (spelled Gwadlys), daughter of David Uras.
20. Gwylliam Nicholas, (in Burke's Peerage 1914, called Nicholas ap-Phillip FitzUryan), married Joan, daughter of Llwellin Veythes.
21. Griffith ap-Nicholas, was slain at Wakefield on the side of York.
22. Thomas ap-Griffith Fitz-Uryan, married Elizabeth, daughter of Sir John Griffith, of Abermarlais.
23. Sir Rhys ap-Thomas Fitz-Uryan made a Knight Banneret, by Henry VII, Knight of the Garter in the 21st year of same reign (1506). He married, first, Eve, daughter and heir of Henry ap-Gwylliam, married, second, Joan, daughter of Thos. Matthew, and widow of Thos. Stradling.
24. Sir Griffith Rice, made Knight of the Bath at the marriage of Prince Arthur, November 14, 1501. Married Katherine, daughter of John St. John, and by her had two daughters and a son.
25. Rice ap-Griffith Fitz Uryan married Katherine, daughter of Thomas Howard (see pedigree of the Howard family), Duke of Norfolk and by her had issue a son and daughter, Agnes and Griffith ap-Rice, born 1500, beheaded by Henry VIII from whom the present Lord Dynevor is descended, and
26. William Rice, brother of the above Griffith ap-Rice, called Wm. of Boemer, of Bucks or Buckinghamshire, granted arms in 1555, (born 1522) and was the grandfather of Deacon Edmund Rice.
27. Thomas Rice, son of William, of Boemer, and father of Deacon Edmund and Robert Rice (twins).
28. Edmund Rice and Robert Rice, born 1594. Edmund came to Massachusetts in 1638. Robert Rice came in 1631.

Deacon Edmund Rice, our first Rice ancestor in America came from Barkhomstead, England, in 1638. He was born in 1594; died 1663, May 3rd, in Marlboro, Massachusetts. Lived for over 20 years in Sudbury, Massachusetts (now "Wayland," Massachusetts). He married Tamazine Hosmer and they had ten children. Married, second, Dame Mercie Brigham, and had two children by her. There were nine sons and three daughters.

PEDIGREE NO. 3

ROYAL LINE OF THE RICE FAMILY

Direct line of descent from Egbert (802-839) to Deacon Edmund Rice (1594-1663) recorded in Pedigrees 1 and 2.

SAXON PRINCES
1. Egbert, 802-839.
2. Ethelwulf.
3. Alfred, the Great.
4. Edward, the Elder.
5. Edmund.
6. Edgar.
7. Ethelred, the Redeless.
8. Edmund, Ironside.
9. Edward, the Outlaw.
10. Margaret married

SCOTTISH PRINCES

Kenneth III, Malcolm II, Beatrix Grimus, Duncan I, Malcolm III, of Scotland.

DUKES OF NORMANDY

Rolf, the Walker; William Longsword, Richard I, the Fearless; Richard II, the Good; Robert, the Devil; William, the Conqueror; Henry I, of Engand.

11. Maud or Matilda married
12. Matilda Geoffrey Plantagenet.
13. Henry II.
14. John Lackland (King of England).
15. Henry III.
16. Edward I.
17. Thos. of Brotherton.
18. Margaret John, Lord Segrave.
19. Elizabeth John, Lord Mowbray.
20. Thomas de Mowbray.
21. Margaret, Sir Robert Howard.
22. John Howard, 1st Duke of Norfolk.
23. Thos. Howard, 2nd Duke of Norfolk.
24. Katherine Howard Rice ap-Griffith.
25. Wm. Rice, of Boemar.
26. Thos. Rice.
27. Deacon Edmund Rice.

BIBLIOGRAPHY

1. Charles Elmer Rice. Record of the Rice Family of England. As abstracted from various authentic sources, including an illuminated Pedigree of the Family of Rice, in the possession of Lord Dynever, drawn and attested in the year 1600, by Ralph Brooks, York Herald, and continued to the present time by Dr. Charles Elmer Rice.
2. The Peerage of Great Britain and Ireland, by Sir Howard Burke, 1914. (Lord Dynevor-See).
3. Dictionary of the Landed Gentry of Great Britain and Ireland, Burke 1851.
4. Dr. Charles Elmer Rice, of Alliance, Ohio, through his admirable book, "By the Name of Rice," and through an extremely courteous correspondence for all references and information which made it possible for me to compile these, viz. "A" Record of the Rice Family of England, Descent of Lord Dynevor from Rice ap-Griffith Fitz-Uryan and of the American Rices through Sir William Rice of Boemer and Deacon Edmund the Pilgrim.
5. Credit is due the late Claudia McLemore Rice (Mrs. S. P.) for extensive research on the Rice genealogy.

—*By Evie Rice Barnes (Mrs. E. T.)*

ROWE

John Rowe, of Landseng, England, settled in Fairhaven, Connecticut; married Miss Ludington; children: Willie; Miles; Freeman Hugh, merchant, engaged in shipping. At eighteen, Freeman Hugh Rowe (1816-1890) went to Cuba, returning by Florida and Dublin. In 1834, he returned to Dublin, and became a merchant and manager of the Dublin branch of the Bank of Savannah; built the "*Gov.*

Troupe," first freight boat on the Oconee River, operating as "Rowe, Wright, and Robinson;" Judge of Old Superior Court; married Margaret Janet Moore (1820-1904), daughter of Dr. Thomas Moore, noted physician and Revolutionary soldier; children: Thomas Hugh and Augusta Rowe. Jefferson Davis was invited to their home on Rowe and Academy Streets.

Thomas Hugh Rowe (born September 7, 1840; died October 4, 1915), planter, merchant, Captain in War Between States, served in Legislature; married, first, Winnifred Whitehead: married, second, Emma Saxon Guyton (born August 24, 1843; died September 17, 1904) (see Guyton genealogy), graduate of Wesleyan College, also attended school in Washington, D. C.; a finished musician; children: Margaret Janet, Josephine Augusta, Mary Guyton, Freeman Hugh, twins, Charles Saxon and Thomas Harris, Emma Love, George T., John Ludington.

"Maggie" (born April 28, 1867; died July 29, 1916), honor graduate Wesleyan College, teacher, charter member D. A. R. Chapter, Woman's Study Club, and P.-T. A.; married Thos. B. Hicks (see Hicks genealogy); children: Rowe Gainer, Mary Jane, Ruth Guyton, Henry, Charles L.

"Josie," beloved Sunday School teacher, efficient librarian, charter member of local D. A. R. Chapter and Woman's Study Club; married Henry Carswell, of Irwinton, Georgia.

Freeman Hugh Rowe (1874-1934), Georgia Tech, Deacon First Baptist Church, Chairman Board of Education for 21 years, President City National Bank, owner of Hicks Drug Store; married, first, Jennie Pate Robinson, married, second, Mrs. Katherine Walton, M.A. degree, Emory University; teacher of science in Dublin schools, President of Woman's Study Club, 1940-41.

Mary Guyton Rowe, artist, versatile writer, and speaker; married Reverend William Ellis Harville, Mercer University, beloved pastor of many county churches, for years Moderator of Laurens County Baptist Association; children: William Edgar, Thomas Hugh, Margaret Janet, Harris.

Charlie Rowe, University of Kentucky, World War veteran, employee in post office for 25 years; married Alma Burney; children: Thomas Hugh, Estelle, Ruth McCall, Helen.

Emma Love Rowe, accomplished pianist, teacher; married William T. Smith, of Duke, North Carolina, Civil Engineer; children: Walter Guyton, James Lawrence, Margaret Love, of North Carolina.

George T. Rowe, World War Chaplain; married, first, Mamie Rowe; one child: Emma Saxon, married George Carver, both missionaries to China; recalled in 1941.

—By Ruth Hicks Porter (Mrs. L. L.)

JUDGE THOMAS H. ROWE

SANDERS

JAMES BARNES SANDERS

James Barnes Sanders, a native of Penfield, Greene County, Georgia, located in Dublin, Georgia, in 1883. After graduation with honors from the University of Georgia in 1881, he followed the profession of teaching—first, in Hawkinsville, later, in Dublin. In the meantime he studied law and was admitted to the bar in Dublin in July, 1886, immediately entering into partnership with Thomas B. Felder in the well known firm of Felder and Sanders. Mr. Sanders was soon recognized as one of the leading lawyers in this section of the State; served as Judge of the City Court of Dublin, and as Mayor, 1895-1896. He was a deacon in the Baptist Church and a Mason.

James Barnes Sanders, youngest son of James Rabun and Cordelia Janes Sanders, was born in Penfield, Georgia, July 4, 1861; died in Dublin, March 6, 1915; married, first, Alice Ramsay, daughter of Whiteford S. and Henrietta Guyton Ramsay (see Ramsay and Guyton genealogies) and had four children:

I. Henrietta Marion Sanders, married Elliott Blount Freeman (see Freeman genealogy).

II. Irene Natalie Sanders, married Ernest Camp (see Camp genealogy) and had three children: (1) Ernest Camp, Jr., prominent journalist of New York City, married Willie May Aycock; (2) Martha Ramsay Camp, married Harry Power Burns; (3) Lieut. Sanders Camp, married Gladys Chambliss.

III. James Guyton Sanders, of Dublin, married Robbie Jewel Williams, daughter of Robert J. and Mollie Camp Williams, of Swainsboro, Georgia (see Williams and Camp genealogies).

IV. Randolph Ramsay Sanders, of San Antonio, Texas, Lieutenant in the Air Service, World War, married, first, May Corker, second, Jean Mason.

James Barnes Sanders married, second, Julia Boyd Ramsay, of Union Springs, Alabama, (no relation to first wife) and had one daughter, Emily, who died in infancy.

In each generation, sons of the Sanders family have rendered active service in the major wars of their country. Joshua Sanders, great grandfather of James Barnes Sanders, was a soldier in the American Revolution. Jeremiah Sanders, son of Joshua Sanders, held the rank of Captain, Georgia Militia, in the War of 1812. James Rabun Sanders, son of Jeremiah Sanders, served as Lieutenant and later as Captain in the Confederate Army. Hervey Hall Woods, of Bowling Green, Kentucky, great grandson of Jeremiah Sanders, was Captain in the Spanish-American War, and later rose to the rank of Brigadier General. Randolph Ramsay Sanders, son of James Barnes Sanders, was commissioned Second Lieutenant,

Air Service, Military Aeronautics Branch of the United States Army, November 7, 1918; enlisted September 27, 1917; honorably discharged January 19, 1919, by reason of the demobilization of the Emergency Forces in the World War. Sanders Camp, grandson of James Barnes Sanders, is now (1941) First Lieutenant, Battery B, 214th Coast Artillery, Anti-Aircraft, Camp Stewart, Georgia.

SANDERS (SAUNDERS) GENEALOGY

The Sanders family is of English descent; they settled first in Virginia, later, in the Carolinas and Georgia. First of this family of whom we have record in Georgia is Joshua Sanders, the Revolutionary soldier, who settled in the Province of Georgia in 1751. Volume 7, pp. 605-606, "Colonial Records of Georgia," by Candler, shows that in July, 1757, Joshua Sanders was granted 100 acres of land about 40 miles north of Augusta, and on March 28, 1758, was granted an additional 100 acres. Volume 9, pp. 447-448, carries the following entry, under date of December, 1765: "Read a petition of Joshua Sanders setting forth that he had been 14 years in the Province, had had tracts of 100 acres of land previously granted him, and was desirous to obtain an additional tract, having a wife and two children. Therefore praying for 150 acres on a creek of Little River about 40 miles above Augusta, joining the land heretofore laid out for Thomas Williams, who was since dead, and he had married the said Williams' eldest daughter." The Thomas Williams referred to was a resident of old Aldgate (now a dead town). Volume 3, p. 13, "Colonial Records of Georgia," carries a list of "monies received from several persons to be applied to establishing the colony," and under date of April 16, 1732, is found the entry that Thomas Williams, Church Warden of the Parish of St. Botolph, Aldgate, contributed £33:7. The service of Joshua Sanders in the American Revolution is recorded in Knight's "Roster of the Revolution for Georgia."

Joshua Sanders was married, about 1754, to Patience Williams, eldest daughter of Thomas Williams, of old Aldgate, Georgia. The will of Joshua Sanders is recorded in the First Book of Wills (1790-1814) Columbia, County, Georgia, and names the following heirs: wife, Patience; sons, Nathan, Mark, Reuben and Jeremiah; daughter, Patience Tripp; grandchildren, Polly Case, Patience Sanders and William Sanders; executors, wife, Patience Sanders, and Robert John. This will was signed December 3, 1799, and recorded June 23, 1800.

Jeremiah Sanders, youngest son of Joshua and Patience Williams Sanders, was born in Columbia County, Georgia, January 11, 1782; died in Kemper County, Mississippi, November 9, 1840; married, first, on December 23, 1802, Mary Barnes (born August 30, 1785, died November 27, 1829); married, second, on May 9, 1830, Lucy Comer Griggs.

Children of Jeremiah Sanders and his first wife, Mary Barnes: 1. Willis Sanders (born November 1, 1803, died September 1, 1862) married on March 16, 1824, Matilda Callaway. 2. Missouri Williams Sanders (1805-1813). 3. Eliza Thoma Sanders (born September 8, 1806). 4. Permelia James Sanders (born March 7, 1808) married on May 15, 1833, James B. Gage. 5. Joshua Lewis Sanders (born August 30, 1809). 6. William Washington Sanders born February 10, 1811). 7. Mark Sanders (1813-1827). 8. Patience William Sanders (born May 8, 1815) married on July 12, 1833, Matthew Gage. 9. Elizabeth Catherine Sanders (born April 17, 1817) married on December 26, 1833, William S. Harrison. 10. James Rabun Sanders (born February 29, 1820; died July 2, 1890) married on January 4, 1842, Cornelia Marion Janes. (Detailed record will appear later). 11. Jeremiah LaFayette Sanders (1824-1850). 12. Mary Ann Sanders (born July 30, 1827) married on August 26, 1845, Edward Jones. 13. John Thomas Sanders (1829-1831).

Children of Jeremiah Sanders and his second wife, Lucy Comer Griggs: 1. Polly Barnes Sanders (born March 12, 1834; died April 5, 1851). 2. Lucy Comer Sanders, died in infancy. 3. Rebecca Sanders, died young. 4. Victoria Comer Sanders (born May 27, 1838; died July 3, 1910) married on October 5, 1855, David Beatty.

The records in the office of the Adjutant General, War Department, Washington, D.C., show that Jeremiah Sanders served in the War of 1812 as Captain of a Company designated as Captain Jeremiah Sanders' Company, First Regiment (Chambers) Georgia Militia. His service commenced October 9, 1812, and ended April 12, 1813. Previous to his service in the War of 1812, Jeremiah Sanders was, on April 14, 1808, appointed Captain of a Volunteer Company of Riflemen attached to the 29th Battalion, Georgia Militia.

When the vast territory of Indian lands was opened for settlement in Mississippi, Jeremiah Sanders purchased extensive holdings, located in old Wahalak, Kemper County, and became one of the largest land owners in that State; was an outstanding man in his section, both in civic and religious affairs. He also had extensive business interests in Mobile, Alabama, where he owned and operated a banking establishment under the joint management of himself and his eldest son, Willis Sanders.

The parents of Mary Barnes, first wife of Jeremiah Sanders, were Virginians. Mary Barnes had four brothers: James Barnes (for whom the subject of this sketch was named), Bryant Barnes, Lewis Barnes, and Burwell Barnes, a Baptist preacher.

James Rabun Sanders, son of Jeremiah Sanders and his first wife, Mary Barnes, was born in Kemper County, Mississippi, February 29, 1820; attended the University of Virginia; after graduation, located in Penfield, Greene County, Georgia, where he died, July

2, 1890. James Rabun Sanders was married on January 4, 1842, to Cornelia Marion Janes (born September 28, 1820; died September 1, 1901), eldest daughter of Absolom and Cordelia Callaway Janes, of Greene County, Georgia. The stately Colonial residence of James Rabun Sanders, in Penfield, Georgia, is still standing. Here, during the days when old Mercer University was located in Penfield, gathered the literati of the State, James Rabun Sanders being a liberal patron of this institution and a trustee for many years. The large plantations owned by James Rabun Sanders, together with the Janes property, inherited by his wife, constituted a vast estate.

Soon after Georgia joined the ranks of the Confederate States, James Rabun Sanders was appointed First Lieutenant, Dawson Grays, a Company that was organized around Penfield, and mustered out near the beginning of the War. Robert L. McWhorter, a brother-in-law of James Rabun Sanders, was Captain of the Dawson Grays and when McWhorter rose to the rank of Major, James Rabun Sanders succeeded him as Captain.

Eight children were born to James Rabun and Cordelia Janes Sanders:

I. Marion Cordelia Sanders (born August 4, 1844).

II. Jeremiah Janes Sanders married, first, Mary Willis, had twin children, a boy, who died in infancy, and Annie Willis Sanders, who married Thomas Raiford; married, second, Susie Willis, and had seven children: (1) C. Boyce Sanders, married Marcella Callaway, two sons, Willis W. and Robert C. Sanders; (2) Cecil Sanders, married R. L. DuBose; (3) Marion Sanders; (4) Francis Sanders; (5) James Rabun Sanders; (6) Cornelia Sanders; (7) Caroline Sanders.

III. Rabun Clifford Sanders (born December 25, 1848; died February 16, 1924) married on December 8, 1902, Birdie Barkesdale. Record later.

IV. Annie Henrietta Sanders (born January 8, 1853; died February 13, 1862).

V. William Olin Sanders (born March 4, 1855; died June 3, 1909) married on August 3, 1892, Emeline Tallulah Mashburn, and had seven children: (1) Cornelia Ollie Sanders, married George Monroe Bazemore, four children, viz., George Monroe Bazemore, Jr., William Sanders Bazemore, Frances Elizabeth Bazemore, and Charles Bernard Bazemore; (2) Marie Frances Sanders; (3) William Clifford Sanders, married Lillian McKenzie, of Cordele, Georgia, and has two children, William and Barbara Sanders; (4) James Hamilton Sanders, died in infancy; (5) Franklin Sanders, died in infancy; (6) John Loomis Sanders, of Miami, Florida; (7) Bivins Sanders, died young.

VI. Preston Wilmot Sanders (born December 14, 1857; died July 24, 1859).

JUDGE JAMES BARNES SANDERS

VII. Helen Agnes Sanders (born October 19, 1859; died May 5, 1883).

VIII. James Barnes Sanders (born July 4, 1861; died March 6, 1915) married Alice Ramsay. Detailed record on preceding pages.

RABUN CLIFFORD SANDERS I

Following his graduation from Mercer University, in June, 1868, with A.B. Degree, Rabun Clifford Sanders I came to Dublin and taught in the Dublin Academy for several years; later, taught in Twiggs and Pulaski counties, and served as County School Commissioner of the latter from 1902 to 1910. Rabun Clifford Sanders was also a Baptitst preacher of note.

On December 8, 1902, he married Birdie Barkesdale, of Longstreet, Bleckley County, Georgia, and had three children:

I. Beverly Barkesdale Sanders, born June 17, 1905, married Myrtle Hunt and has two children, viz., Beverly Barkesdale Sanders, Jr., and Floyd Hunt Sanders.

II. Rabun Clifford Sanders II, born August 6, 1908, married Edith Califf, and has one son, Rabun Clifford Sanders III.

III. Marion Austelle Sanders, born December 7, 1910, married John Wimberly Faulk, and has two children, viz., Austelle Sanders Faulk, and John Gordon Faulk.

SANDERS MATERNAL LINEAGE

Cornelia Jones was born in Greene County, Georgia, Septetmber 28, 1820; died in Greene County, Georgia, September 1, 1901; was married to James Rabun Sanders, January 4, 1842. Cornelia Janes was the daughter of Absolom Janes (born June 8, 1796; died September 25, 1847) and Cordelia Callaway (born October 3, 1801; died July 1, 1846; married July 16, 1817). Absolom Janes was treasurer of the Georgia State Baptist Convention for eleven years; trustee of Mercer Institute from its beginning in 1833 to 1838, when it was changed to Mercer University, and was trustee of Mercer University until his death in 1847; represented Taliaferro County several terms as Senator to the State Legislature. His son, Thomas P. Janes, was the first Commissioner of Agriculture for the State of Georgia.

Cordelia Callaway, wife of Absolom Janes, was the daughter of Isaac Callaway (1775-1820) and Winnifred Ragan (married 1796). Isaac Callaway was the son of Job Callaway (1741-1804) and his wife, Mary; grandson of John Callaway and Bethany Arnold; great grandson of Captain Thomas Callaway, who married Miss Anderson, of Virginia. Both Job and John Callaway were Revolutionary soldiers. Captain Thomas Callaway was an officer in the Colonial Army of Virginia in the French and Indian Wars. He emigrated to North Carolina, and later, with four sons, settled in Wilkes County, Georgia, at the close of the Revolutionary War. Winnifred Ragan, wife of Isaac Callaway, was the daughter of the Revolutionary soldier, Jonathan Ragan (1744-1815) and his wife Ann (married 1770).

Absolom Janes was the son of William Janes (born December 9, 1771; died July 9, 1827) and Selah Gresham (married January 31, 1793). Selah Gresham was the daughter of Edward Gresham, of Greene County, Georgia; granddaughter of Edward Gresham and Mary Leonard, of England and Virginia; great-granddaughter of Sir Thomas Gresham, Kt., of England, who married the widow of William Read, a London merchant. (Abridged Compendium of American Genealogy).

The Janes genealogy is as follows:

I. Absolom Janes, born June 8, 1796; died September 25, 1847; married Cordelia Callaway, July 16, 1817; son of

II. William Janes, of Virginia and Georgia, born December 12, 1771; died July 9, 1827; married Selah Gresham, January 31, 1793; son of

III. Thomas Janes, of Richmond, Virginia, born 1752; died "in the prime of manhood"; married Miss Reames, of Virginia; son of

IV. William Janes, of Massachusetts and Connecticut, born 1732; married Miss Paine; son of

V. Michael Janes, born September 29, 1686; son of

VI. William Janes, of Massachusetts and Connecticut, born 1654; married Sarah Clarke; son of

VII. Elder William Janes I, the emigrant ancestor, born in Sussex, England, in 1610; died in Northampton, Massachusetts, September 20, 1690; married his first wife, Mary, in Essex, England; she died April 4, 1662. Elder William Janes I was Deputy of the General Court of New Haven, Connecticut, 1648; Deputy General Court, Northampton, Massachusetts, 1657; was a liberal subscriber to Harvard College. References: Volume I, "History of Northampton, Massachusetts," by Trumbull; "Janes Genealogy," by Rev. Edward Janes, with revisions by Frederick Janes.

—*By Henrietta Sanders Freeman (Mrs. E. B.)*

SIMMONS

Dublin and Laurens County have just cause for pride in their sons and daughters whom they claim by right of adoption. Such is the case with the Simmons family, for descendants of the Revolutionary soldier, William Simmons I, have brought honor not only to the immediate communities in which they have lived but to their State and Nation as well.

John Middleton Simmons II

The State of Georgia has today (1941) no more honored and influential citizen than the financier, philanthropist and statesman, John Middleton Simmons II, son of Dr. John Middleton Simmons I and Mary Elizabeth Slappey Simmons, who was born in Houston County, Georgia, March 19, 1871. After attending the schools at Perry and Fort Valley, John M. Simmons II entered upon a business career and, in 1898, located in Dublin where he established the Simmons Lumber Company, manufacturing commercial veneer and household furniture.

On June 20, 1900, John M. Simmons was united in marriage to a descendant of two of the early Laurens County families, Virginia Ramsay, daughter of Col. Whiteford S. and Henrietta Guyton Ramsay (see Ramsay and Guyton genealogies). It was here that their two eldest sons, Jack Whiteford and David Ramsay, were born.

After leaving Dublin, Mr. Simmons located in Marshallville, Georgia, where he changed the name of his business corporation to the Elberta Crate and Box Company; in 1914, the mills were transferred to Bainbridge, and there they have been in constant operation for the past twenty-seven years. In addition to the original plant in Bainbridge, the Simmons family have extended their business operations widely, and now own and operate large mills in Macon and Tennille, Georgia, Tallahassee, Cottondale, and Plant City, Florida, also a plant in Barranquilla, Columbia, South America. The Elberta Crate and Box Company ranks among the largest crate factories in the world, shipping their products to practically every State in the Union and carrying on an extensive export business to Cuba, Trinidad, the Bahama Islands and even to continental Europe.

John M. Simmon II has not confined his unusual business ability to his family's personal interests, but is an active and prominent figure in local, State and National affairs; has served as mayor of the City of Bainbridge; represented Decatur County in both the State Senate and House of Representatives; and was elected councilman in the National Chamber of Commerce, United States of America, in which he represented the fruit and vegetable crate manufacturers of the entire United States.

Virginia Ramsay, wife of John M. Simmons II, like her husband, has held positions of importance in the civic, religious and patriotic organizations of the State, with State offices in the Colonial Dames of the 17th Century, Daughters of the American Revolution, United States Daughters of 1812, United Daughters of the Confederacy and Georgia Federation of Women's Clubs.

Four sons were born to John M. and Virginia Ramsay Simmons, who have inherited both their mother's charm and their father's business acumen and ability. These four sons are now at the heads of the various branches of this mammoth manufacturing company. The Simmons family are Methodists.

I. Jack Whiteford Simmons, of Tallahassee, Florida, born in Dublin, Georgia; attended the Georgia School of Technology; member Sigma Nu Fraternity; married Sarah Scott, daughter of Blanchard Killis and Lavonia Story Scott, and has four children: 1. Virginia, 2. Jack Whiteford, Jr., 3. Mary Edna, 4. Sarah Marie.

II. David Ramsay Simmons, of Bainbridge, Georgia; born in Dublin, Georgia; attended the Georgia School of Technology and Emory University; member of Sigma Nu Fraternity; married Ellen Carswell, daughter of Hon. George S. and Ethel Wood Carswell, and has three children: 1. Virginia Claire, 2. David Ramsay, Jr., 3. John Middleton III.

III. Thomas Randolph Simmons, of Tennille, Georgia, born in Marshallville, Georgia; attended the V. M. I., Lexington, Virginia; married Elizabeth Burney, daughter of Glover McCall and Ruth Taylor Burney, and has two daughters, Sara Elizabeth and Virginia Ruth.

IV. William Pinckney Simmons, of Macon, Georgia, born in Bainbridge, Georgia; graduated from Duke University, at which institution many high honors were accorded him; member Sigma Nu Fraternity; married Betty Sweet Smith, daughter of Charles Sweet and Grace Hines Smith, of Cocoa, Florida, and has one son, William Pinckney, Jr.

John M. Simmons II, and his four sons hold many positions of importance in the states of Georgia and Florida. John M. Simmons is Chairman of Board of Elberta Crate Company and subsidiary branches; Past President Standard Container Manufacturers Association; Chairman of the Board of Southern Life Insurance Company and Southern Fire and Marine Insurance of Atlanta, Georgia; on Governor's staff under Governor Rivers; operates a farm near Bainbridge, where he raises thoroughbred stock. He is a Mason and Rotarian.

Jack Whiteford Simmons, of Tallahassee, Florida, is a Mason, Rotarian, Elk; member Tallahassee City Commission, Mayor Pro Tem, and Past President Tallahassee Chamber of Commerce; Past President Tallahassee Rotary Club; Past President Standard Container Manufacturers Association; Representative Southeastern District Fruit Package Industry, under NYA; Secretary and Treasurer Employees Benefit Insurance Company; State Chairman of the Conservation of Man Power in Defense Industries, under United States Department of Labor; Member District Drafts Appeal Board; Past President Federal Wooden Package Association; Vice-President and Director of Industrial Bank of Tallahassee, Florida; Past President and Director of Tallahassee Federal Savings and Loan Association; President of Developers, Inc.; Secretary and Treasurer of Travel Chair Company, of Thomasville, Georgia; Secretary and

Treasurer of Florida Centennial Commission Committee; Director in Florida Tax Survey; Director in Southern Fire and Marine Insurance Company; Past President Tallahassee Country Club; on Governor's staff under Governor Holland of Florida; President Elberta Crate and Box Company; Vice-President Southern Crate and Veneer Company, of Macon, Georgia.

David Ramsay Simmons, of Bainbridge, Georgia, is a Mason; Organizing President of Bainbridge Rotary Club; Member Board of Education; Director First State National Bank; President Southern Crate and Veneer Company; Vice-President, Secretary, and Treasurer Elberta Crate and Box Company; President Employees Benefit Insurance Company; Secretary and Treasurer Developers, Inc.; on Governor's staff under Governor Eugene Talmadge, 1941; Past District Chairman Boy Scouts of America; Director in Southern Life Insurance Company.

Thomas Randolph Simmons, of Tennille, Georgia, is a Mason; President Tennille Rotary Club; Vice-President Elberta Crate and Box Company; Manager of Simmons Company; Vice-President Southern Crate and Veneer Company; Past President Junior Chamber of Commerce, Bainbridge, Georgia.

William Pinckney Simmons, of Macon, Georgia, held the following positions at Duke University: President Sigma Nu Fraternity; Omicron Delta Kappa; President Alpha Kappa Psi; Red Friars Student Council; Pan-Hellenic Council; Honors Student; Board of Trustees of Y. M. C. A.. He is now (1941) Director of Georgia Southern and Florida Railway; Vice-President, Secretary and Treasurer of Southern Crate and Veneer Company; Vice-President Elberta Crate and Box Company.

Dr. John Middleton Simmons I

Dr. John Middleton Simmons I located in Dublin in 1899 and until his death in this city, May 29, 1904, made his home with his son, John M. Simmons II. Dr. Simmons was the son of William Pinckney Simmons and his first wife, Sarah Bethea Middlebrooks. He was born in Crawford County, Georgia, October 15, 1839; graduated from the Philadelphia Medical School; served for four years as a Confederate soldier, being wounded in the knee; practiced medicine and farming in Houston County, Georgia; on December 12, 1865, married Mary Elizabeth Slappey (born November 28, 1843; died February 11, 1895), and had four children:

I. David Turner Simmons (1867-1921) married Gussie B. Smith, of Asheville, North Carolina; no children.

II. Mary Slappey Simmons (1869-1911), an artist of note.

III. John Middleton Simmons II, born March 19, 1871; married Virginia Ramsay (see Ramsay and Guyton genealogies), and has four sons, recorded above.

IV. Susie Elizabeth Simmons, born December 11, 1877; married Thomas Jefferson Dykes, of Montezuma, Georgia (1876-1932) and has three children: 1. Thomas Jefferson Dykes II, married Edith Estelle Satterfield, two children: (1) Mary Ann Dykes and (2) Thomas Jefferson Dykes III; 2. Mary Claudia Dykes; 3. James Robert Dykes.

WILLIAM THOMAS SIMMONS I

William Thomas Simmons I, son of William Wright and Alice Dennis Simmons, located in Dublin in 1899 and was engaged in the wholesale grocery business for many years, first, with the D. S. Brandon Company, and later, as senior partner of the firm, Dublin Fruit and Produce Company. On August 6, 1902, he married into an early county family, Mary, daughter of John M. and Mary Moorman Graham (see Graham genealogy), and has two children:

I. Florence Graham Simmons, married first, W. D. Heaton, one son, David Heaton; married second, W. F. Isom.

II. William Thomas Simmons II, married Irene Ormond; three daughters, Mary Jane, Billy and Florence Ann Simmons.

William Wright Simmons, father of William Thomas Simmons I, spent the greater part of his later years in Dublin, making his home here with his son. He married Alice Dennis and had four children: 1. Mary Augusta Simmons, married Herbert Eugene Adams; 2. William Thomas Simmons, married Mary Graham (recorded above); 3. Missouri Alberta Simmons, married E. A. Richards; 4. Sallie Eugenia Simmons, married Gordon Walters.

ELGAR G. SIMMONS II

Edgar G. Simmons II located in Dublin in 1908 and for the past thirty-three years has been highly successful in the real estate business in this section of the State; is a leader in all civic affairs; was Organizing President of the Rotary Club of Dublin; member First Baptist Church. The Simmons residence on Bellevue Avenue, with its spacious grounds, is one of the handsomest of the city's many handsome homes and is noted for its gracious Southern hospitality.

Edgar G. Simmons II is the son of Hon. Edgar G. Simmons I and Lucy Hollis Simmons; was born in Americus, Sumter County, Georgia; was married in 1909, in Dublin, to Pearl Page, daughter of Dr. John Morgan and Melissa Jackson Page (see Page genealogy). To this union were born two daughters, both attended Shorter College, Rome, Georgia, and are leaders among the young social contingent of this city: (1) Pearl Page Simmons, who married Richard Zantzinger Graves, son of Clarence D. Graves, D.D., and Octavia Bates Graves; (2) Frances Page Simmons.

Edgar G. Simmons I, of Americus, Georgia, (father of Edgar G.

Simmons II, of Dublin) was the son of James Marion Simmons, (born May 29, 1828; died November 25, 1883) and Frances E. Hollis Simmons (born May 25, 1832); was born in Crawford County, Georgia, on May 18, 1852; graduated with honors from the University of Georgia and became one of his city's foremost jurists and statesmen; represented Sumter County in 1886 in the State Legislature. He died in Americus at the early age of 39.

Five children were born to Edgar G. Simmons I and his wife, Frances E. Hollis, who were married on October 15, 1873:

I. Howell R. Simmons, married Jose Putnam and had three children: 1. Josephine Putnam Simmons, 2. Lucy Putnam Simmons, 3. Charles Putnam Simmons.

II. Floyd Simmons died young.

III. Susanne Simmons, married Benjamin G. Statham and has three children: 1. Benjamin G. Statham, Jr., 2. Lucy Statham, 3. Susanne Statham.

IV. Edgar G. Simmons II married Pearl Page and has two daughters: Pearl Page Simmons and Frances Page Simmons (recorded above).

V. Frances Simmons.

SIMMONS-HOLLEMAN DESCENDANTS

Other Dublin citizens, descendants of the Revolutionary soldier, William Simmons I, are Louise Holleman Crockett (Mrs. C. C.), George Blue Holleman and Nathaniel Green Holleman, who in 1910, after the death of their mother, Harriet Blue Holleman (Mrs. N. G.), in Buena Vista, Georgia, came to make their home in this city with their aunt, Rosa Blue Brantley (Mrs. Claude W.).

Harriet Blue (born September 5, 1868; died April 19, 1910), was married on June 19, 1888, to Nathaniel Green Holleman and had four children:

I. Lurlene Holleman, married Vilas Belk, of Beuna Vista, Georgia, three children: 1. Frances Elizabeth Belk, married Thomas R. Rogers and has two children, Beth and T. R. Rogers, Jr.; 2. Vilas Belk, married Emily Murray, and has twins, Beverly and Barbara Belk; 3. Louise Holleman Belk.

II. Louise Holleman was married, in Dublin, to Charles Campbell Crockett, a native of Virginia, and has one daughter, Rose Campbell Crockett. Mrs. Crockett is one of the leading club women of this city, a talented musician whose lovely soprano voice is an acquisition in musical and cultural circles; President of the Ladies' Auxiliary of the Henry Memorial Presbyterian Church; officer in John Laurens Chapter D. A. R. and Oconee Chapter U. D. C.

III. George Blue Holleman, married Vera Phillips, of Dublin, daughter of W. S. and Ada Owen Phillips (see Phillips genealogy), and has one daughter, Jane Holleman.

IV. Nathaniel Green Holleman, married Lucile Studdeth, of Statesboro, Georgia.

SIMMONS GENEALOGY

William Simmons I was born in Virginia in 1745; came to Georgia and was a resident of this State at the time of the American Revolution, during which he rendered active and distinguished service, being prominently mentioned in the battle of Kettle Creek, Georgia. At the close of the war he was awarded a certificate of service by Col. Elijah Clarke, and was granted large tracts of land in this state for his military services.

At the beginning of the War of 1812 William Simmons I rose to the rank of Captain, receiving his appointment on November 5, 1812, as Captain of 355th District, Company of Georgia Militia. He died in 1828.

William Simmons I was married twice: first, in 1768, to Mary King (1750-1790) and second, in 1793, to Anne King (1759-1810), sister to his first wife. By his first marriage to Mary King, William Simmons I had two sons, William Simmons (born 1769), and John King Simmons (1771-1870). By his second marriage to Anne King there was one son, Allen G. Simmons (1795-1858), and possibly others.

John King Simmons, son of William I and his first wife, Mary King Simmons, was born in Georgia in 1771; died in Houston County, Georgia, August, 1870; in 1800 was married to Sarah Bethea Middlebrooks (1776-1864) and had three children: Henry Simmons, Babe Simmons and William Pinckney Simmons. John King Simmons served in the House of Representatives from Monroe County, Georgia, 1827-1830; Justice Inferior Court, Jasper County, Georgia, November 12, 1819-October 26, 1821, and December 10, 1822-December, 1833.

William Pinckney Simmons, son of John King and Sarah Middlebrooks Simmons, was born December 25, 1809; died on January 22, 1890, in Houston County, Georgia, where he had spent the greater part of his life; married first, in 1831, Sarah Middleton (1811-1857); children by first marriage:

I. John Middleton Simmons, married Mary Elizabeth Slappey.

II. William Wright Simmons, married Alice Dennis.

III. Thomas J. Simmons, married Lee Cavendish.

IV. Eliza Simmons, married Kindred Kemp.

V. Louise Cherokee Simmons (1834-1893), married, in 1852, George Troup Holleman. (More later).

VI. Mary Frances Simmons, married first, Charles Walker, second, T. G. Holt.

VII. Parmelia Jane Simmons married Robert Holmes.

VIII. Missouri A. Simmons married R. L. Johnston.

IX. Susie Simmons married L. A. Stubbs.

William Pinckney Simmons married, second, in 1860, Mrs. Martha Woodward Stubbs and had four children:

I. Stephen Henry Simmons.

II. Martha Simmons (born June 14, 1881), married N. L. Coates.

III. Willie Georgia Simmons (born December 18, 1879), married W. A. Walker.

IV. Sarah Simmons, died young.

Dr. John Middleton Simmons I, eldest son of William Pinckney Simmons and his first wife, Sarah Middleton, was born in Crawford County, Georgia, October 15, 1839; died in Dublin, Georgia, May 29, 1904; married, first, on December 12, 1865, Mary Elizabeth Slappey (born November 28, 1843; died February 11, 1895), and had four children: David Turner Simmons, John Middleton Simmons II, Mary Slappey Simmons, Susie Elizabeth Simmons. Detailed account of the descendants of John Middleton Simmons I appears on preceding pages.

Dr. John Middleton Simmons I married, second, Mrs. Sarah Billings, no children.

William Wright Simmons, son of William Pinckney Simmons and his first wife, Sarah Middleton, was born in Crawford County, Georgia; married Alice Dennis and had four children (recorded above).

Louise Cherokee Simmons, daughter of William Pinckney Simmons and his first wife, Sarah Middleton, was born in Crawford County, Georgia, August 17, 1834; died in Marion County, Georgia, January 4, 1923; married in 1852 to George Troup Holleman and had nine children: (1) William Z. Holleman, unmarried; (2) Nathaniel Green Holleman married Harriet Blue (recorded above); (3) Robert Lee Holleman, died young; (4) Charles Alonzo Holleman, unmarried; (5) Eugenie Holleman, died young; (6) Florence Nightingale Holleman married Charles Wiley Rickerson; (7) George Troup Holleman died at the age of 17; (8) Louise Cherokee Holleman married John Wesley Adams; (9) Mary Frances Holleman married Lewis K. Potter.

DESCENDANTS OF WILLIAM SIMMONS I AND SECOND WIFE, ANNE KING

Allen G. Simmons, son of William Simmons I and second wife, Anne King, was born in 1795; died in 1858; married in 1820, Mary Cleveland, and had a son, James Marion Simmons, and possibly other children.

James Marion Simmons was born in Crawford County, Georgia,

May 29, 1828; died in Sumter County, Georgia, November 25, 1883; married on June 27, 1851, Frances E. Hollis (born May 25, 1832); and had six children: (1) Edgar G. Simmons I, (2) Robert L. Simmons, (3) Minnie B. Simmons, (4) Alice Simmons, (5) Walter C. Simmons, (6) Arthur H. Simmons.

Edgar G. Simmons I, eldest son of James Marion and Frances Hollis Simmons, (full record given above), married on October 15, 1873, Lucy Hollis, daughter of John F. Hollis, of Marion County, Georgia, and had five children: (1) Howell B. Simmons, (2) Floyd Simmons, (3) Susanne Simmons, (4) Edgar G. Simmons II, (5) Frances Simmons.

—*By Henrietta Sanders Freeman (Mrs. E. B.)*

SIMONS

James S. Simons II, was born in Columbia, South Carolina, in 1870; settled in Dublin, Georgia, in 1897; died here in 1940.

In 1900 he was President of the Young Men's Business League and President of the Dublin Cotton Exchange. A few years later he was President of the School Board; President of the Library Board and President of the Cotton Compress. He was in the cotton business.

James Simons II married Mary Pickens, of Charleston, South Carolina, in 1892. They had three children: Anne Pickens Simons; Manning Simons (born, 1925; died, 1926); James Simons Simons III.

Annie Pickens Simons married Charles Manly Smith. They have two children: Maryan Harley Smith and Dorothy Simons Smith.

James S. Simons III, married Fannie Lee Hodges, of Virginia. No children.

Parents of James S. Simons II were: James S. Simons I, born in Charleston, South Carolina, 1848, died, 1919, and Margaret Bryce Simons, born in Columbia, South Carolina, 1850, died 1902. His grandfather was Harris Simons, born in Charleston, South Carolina, 1807, died 1866. His wife was Mary I'On Wragg, born in Charleston, South Carolina, 1811, died 1878. His great grandfather was James Simons and his wife was Sarah Tucker Harris; both born in Charleston, South Carolina. He was a member of the Cincinnati Society.

Parents of Mary Pickens, wife of James S. Simons II, were: Colonel Samuel Bonneau Pickens, born in Pendleton, South Carolina, 1838, died 1891, and Anna Postell Ingraham, born 1845, died 1920. She is the great great granddaughter of General Andrew Pickens of Revolutionary fame.

—*By Mary Pickens Simons (Mrs. J. S.)*

SMITH

CHARLES U. SMITH FAMILY

Charles Uldrick Smith moved with his family to Laurens County from Augusta, Georgia, January 19, 1929; native of Hinesville, Georgia, son of Malcolm Alexander Smith, and Alice Hayman Smith; grandson of Nevin Stuart Smith and Harriett Newell McCallam Smith. Since taking up his residence in Dublin, he has been actively identified in anything which helped build the City and County of his adoption. Is Vice-Preisdent and Cashier of the Citizens and Southern Bank; member of Lions Club, of which he has served as President and Director; a member of the First Methodist Church, Chairman of its Board of Stewards; a member of the City Board of Education; has served on the Boards of the Red Cross, Chamber of Commerce and Boy Scouts.

Charles Uldrick Smith married Ruth Conley Stafford, of Hinesville, Liberty County, Georgia, June 21, 1922. She is prominently associated with the civic, social, and religious life of Dublin, member of the First Methodist Church, Parnassus Club and charter member of the Garden Club.

To this union three daughters were born: Betty Anne, a junior in the Dublin High School, born December 7, 1925; Ruth Stafford, student in Calhoun Street Junior High, born November 20, 1928; and Kathleen Stafford, student in Calhoun Street Grammar School, born February 12, 1931.

Ruth Stafford Smith is of Georgia ancestry for many generations. She is the daughter of James David Stafford, who was born April 12, 1864, in Glynn County, Georgia, and died October 28, 1930, in Liberty County, Georgia, where he is buried. He was married in Liberty County, Georgia, December 17, 1893, to Bessie Hines, the daughter of Charlton Hines and his wife, Rebecca Butler, who was the daughter of Joseph Evans Butler and Virginia Benton.

The father of James David Stafford, James Washington Stafford, born Wayne County, Georgia, January 24, 1832; died December 2, 1870, in Liberty County, Georgia, where he is buried. He was married in Liberty County, Georgia, October 13, 1853, to Rebecca Zoucks, born Liberty County, Georgia, February 14, 1830; died May 18, 1893, Liberty County, Georgia, where she is buried, the daughter of David Zoucks and his wife, Celia Harville, and the grand-daughter of Henry Zoucks and his wife, Mercy Knight, and of Samuel Harville, and his wife, Rebecca Hodge.

James Washington Stafford was the son of Robert Stafford, born March 31, 1808, Effingham County, Georgia; died September 29, 1863, Wayne County, Georgia; buried at Stafford Plantation near Tuckersville; was married in Wayne County, Georgia, December 24, 1830, to Martha Ratcliffe, born Glynn County, Georgia, September 20, 1812; died December 25, 1850; buried Waynesville, Georgia, the daughter of James Ratcliffe and his wife, Martha May.

This Robert Stafford was the son of Robert Stafford, a Revolutionary soldier of South Carolina, who moved to Georgia where he was prominent in the affairs of Screven, Effingham, and Wayne Counties. He died in Wayne County in 1829. His wife, Jane Blair, died prior to June 28, 1838, was the daughter of William Blair, who was the son of James Blair, and his wife, Sibbiah Earl, the daughter of John Earl, who came to Georgia from North Carolina in 1760. Both William Blair and Sibbiah Earl Blair served in the Revolutionary War.

—*Compiled by Margret Davis Cate (Mrs.), and Ruth Stafford Smith (Mrs. C. U.)*

SMITH

HARDY SMITH FAMILY

At the close of the Revolution a North Carolina planter, Hardy Smith (born 1757, died February, 1852), who served through that struggle and helped to achieve the independence of the Colonies, took his wife, Rebecca Thompson (to whom he was married, November 16, 1796, in Washington County, Georgia) and with his children started for the West in search of a better home. He pitched his tent on the banks of the Oconee River about ten miles below the present site of Dublin, this river then being the boundary between the "whites" and the Indians. Here he cleared a patch and established a rude home. By great industry and perseverance he succeeded in accumulating a small estate in land and negroes, and before his death was numbered among the solid men of his section. Rebecca Thompson Smith died in Laurens County in 1835.

A record of the Revolutionary services of Hardy Smith may be found in the Department of Interior, Bureau of Pensions, Washington, D. C., also in the "Roster of North Carolina Soldiers of the Revolution." He enlisted in Cumberland County, North Carolina, and served in the Militia.

Among other children were four sons: Stephen (a son by a former marriage), Hardy, Lofton and Thompson. Hardy, to whom he gave his name, as well as many of his characteristics, was born October 17, 1801, died March 27, 1864. He married, first, Honore Beacham. Their children were: Matthew, married Nettie Williams; Charlton (a well known farmer and Baptist minister of this County), married, first, Anne McLendon, second, Anne Jane Perry; Allie (born November 19, 1833, died September, 1908), married Daniel Anderson; Jane married Robert Hester.

May 22, 1836, Hardy Smith married Ann Anderson (born August

CAPTAIN HARDY SMITH

11, 1819, died November 24, 1907). She was a daughter of John Gaillard Anderson (born December 23, 1790, died, 1849), and Rachel Hester (Hollinger) born September 12, 1789. John Gaillard Anderson was the son of John G. Anderson, a pioneer settler and free holder of this County and a Revolutionary soldier. John Gaillard Anderson was married June 4, 1818, to Rachel Hester. They had three other children: Rebecca (born September 19, 1823) married Council B. Wolfe (born September 7, 1818), their only child was John Bryant Wolfe (born October 7, 1838), a well-known lawyer, merchant and farmer of this County and at one time a member of the Georgia Legislature, and also a Confederate soldier.

Daniel Anderson (born February 15, 1821, died April 27, 1896), married Allie, daughter of Hardy Smith.

Young John Anderson, the once eminent lawyer of this section, married Terence Owen, of Augusta. They had one daughter, Terence, who married Col. Estes, of Augusta.

The children of Hardy Smith and Ann Anderson were: John A., Hardy, Lofton, Rachel, Rebecca, Daniel Anderson, Henry Preston, and Ann Eliza.

John (born September 1, 1837), Rachel (born February, 1847), and Ann Eliza (born November 8, 1859), died in childhood. Rebecca (born April 9, 1849), married Frank Morris, died soon after marriage. Henry Preston (born October 30, 1856), married Emily Young.

Lofton Lamar (born December 5, 1843, died February 24, 1918), carried on the work of his father and with his mother succeeded in bringing the plantation safely through the reconstruction period. He was married January 8, 1885, to Julia Lucina Spell (born September 3, 1853, died January 11, 1927). Their children are:

Claudia Emily (Mrs. Herschel Wade Jenkins, Dublin, Georgia); Ethel Lamar (Mrs. James Simmons Devereaux), who has one daughter, Trellis Elizabeth; Nettie died in childhood; Annie Eliza (Mrs. Tom Sikes), who has six children; Edwin married Lora Cotney; Eunice (Mrs. O'Daniel Kitchens), two children, Virginia Ann and Joseph; Julia Frances (Mrs. George Comb), one son, George; Mavis (Mrs. Bocarte); Lofton; Jimmie.

Daniel Anderson Smith (born September 9, 1851; died January 7, 1919) married March 4, 1885, to Celestia Herndon (born October 15, 1869; died December 19, 1933) (See Herndon genealogy). Their children are: (1) Jane Roberta; (2) Lee Edward, graduate of Emory University Medical School, married Alma Louise Boyle, daughter of Harry Boyle, of Oakland, California. They have one daughter, Celestia Louise, the wife of Wayne Peterson, of Oakland. They have one daughter, Karen Lee. Lee Smith was a surgeon of the Naval Reserve during the World War. (3) Robert

Murphy married Lois Polhill, daughter of James B. Polhill, of Louisville, Georgia. They have one daughter, Lois Polhill. Murphy Smith served as Lieutenant in the World War.

Hardy Smith was next to bear the name which had been used through several successive generations, and also was the surname of the mother of the first Hardy. He was born October 24, 1841. Having attended the common schools of the day, he entered college at the University of Georgia, but was called away at the age of nineteen to become a soldier of the Confederacy. He was elected Lieutenant of Company H of the Fourteenth Regimental Georgia Volunteers.

During service, he was promoted to the office of Captain, in which position he led his Company at the battle of Mechanicsville. It was in this battle that he received the wound that resulted in the loss of his right arm. He then retired from active service and served as enrolling officer of the Fifth Congressional District, with headquarters in Augusta, until the surrender.

After his return from the war he was elected Clerk and Treasurer of the Superior Court (1866) and held that office until 1893, when he was elected Ordinary. He was one of the original stockholders of the Macon and Dublin Railroad and for years was Treasurer and Secretary of the Board of Directors. He was an active member of the Methodist Church.

He served for many years as Commander of "Smith Camp," a division of the United Confederate Veterans. He was much interested in this organization and became Commander of the Eastern Division with the title of Brigadier General, which office he held until his death.

On November 21, 1867, Captain Smith married Ella Few Douglas (born July 26, 1845; died June 9, 1916). Their children were:

1. Claudia Ella (born September 28, 1868), married Wm. Coney Bishop (born July 23, 1860; died July 17, 1907), a well-known farmer and merchant of this city. He was the son of Captain George W. Bishop, of Laurens County. Their children are: Mildred Anne; Adelaide (Mrs. R. E. Braddy), has two children, James Bishop and Adelaide; T. Dupree, married Lucile Hubbard, one daughter, Helen Hubbard; Olive Eugenia (Mrs. K. L. Hudson); Mary Elizabeth (Mrs. Adonis L. Gray), children, Adonis Lyle and Ariel Douglas; Claudia Helen (Mrs. Robert W. Thomas); Wm. Coney married Margaret Webster.

2. Phoebe E. (born April 8, 1870), died in childhood.

3. Arthur Peyton (born June 5, 1872; died July 16, 1906).

4. Annie (born December 18, 1874), married Geo. H. McCullough, of Brunswick, Georgia. They had eight children: Maude Peyton (Mrs. Carl Weidinger); Annie Louise (Mrs. Walter K. Sears); Cecil

Terence; Geo. Harold; Carl; Eleanor (Mrs. Sherman Wilson); Ann, Arthur; Helen.

5. Cora Adelaide (born June 29, 1877; died February 14, 19—), married Perry Fryer. They had one son, Perry, who married Clifford Johnson.

6. Nina Charlton (born October 15, 1879), married Dr. S. N. Bradshaw (born April 9, 1883). Their children are: Charlie Douglas, married Lucile Couey; James Peyton; Ella Few (Mrs. Frank Mills), one daughter, Frances C.; Helen Patia (Mrs. Pat Porter), two sons, Pat and Dickie; and George Sanford.

7. Hardy (born October 20, 1880), married Inez Sessions. Their children are: Nina Peyton (Mrs. Ross Moore); Sarah Elizabeth; Ella Louise (Mrs. Leon Brooks); Hardy, married Pauline Jackson; Rosalind Callaway; Mary Ben; Joseph Weddington; Ellen Joy; Shirley Barbara.

8. Tilman Douglas (born January 4, 1884), married Corrie LaZarus, of Atlanta.

9. Augusta Lester, married Robert Earl Camp (See Camp genealogy), who came to Dublin in early manhood and since that time has been a very successful lawyer. He has been an important figure in the life of this City and County. He is now Judge of the Superior Court. Their children are: Evelyn Douglas (Mrs. Thomas Howard Newsome), has one daughter, Ann Camp; Mary Adelaide (Mrs. John Mahoney); Sophronia Frances (Mrs. Fred Gibbs); Rosalyn (Mrs. Ben Waggner).

10. Helen Few, married Dr. S. T. Brown, now living in Savannah.

Mrs. Smith was a native of Burke County. She came to this County soon after the war with her mother and sister to make her home with a brother, Dr. Peyton W. Douglas, who was a well-known physician and surgeon of this section and was Dublin's first Mayor. Mrs. Douglas, and her daughters became very active in the life of the town at that time.

Mrs. Phoebe Douglas, Mrs. Smith and Mrs. K. H. Walker were charter members of the First Methodist Church, which was organized by Mrs. Douglas.

Mrs. Smith's father, Dr. Tilman Douglas (born in Jefferson County, Georgia, February 25, 1804), was married in 1831 to Phoebe Wambezie Charlton (born March 23, 1809; died in 1872). Their children were: 1. Octavia Jane (born January 8, 1834), married December 4, 1851, to Frederick Fell. 2. Arthur Charlton (born May 17, 1836), married, first, Mary Virginia Hankerson, June 4, 1857; second, Martha Maxwell. 3. Peyton Wade (born June 2, 1838), married Georgia Stanley, November 26, 1863. 4. Mary Frances (born May 2, 1841), married John B. Wolfe, January 24, 1861. 5. Georgia Garvin (born May 11, 1843), married Daniel B. Fisher, October 11, 1865. 6. Ella Few (Mrs. Hardy

Smith). 7. Eugenia Rebecca (born June 12, 1848), married Kinchen H. Walker. 8. Olin Capers (born January 20, 1851; died in early childhood).

Dr. Tilman Douglas was a successful physician and surgeon and a member of the Methodist Conference, having served in the Conference from 1827 to 1843. He died in Burke County, Georgia, in 1863.

He was a son of Jones Douglas who was born in Mecklenburgh, Virginia, November 25, 1779, and died in Gwinnett County, October 15, 1846. Jones Douglas served twelve months in the War of 1812 under General Andrew Jackson. His wife, to whom he was married in 1803, was Rebecca Tilman, born in Edgefield District, South Carolina, August 14, 1781, and died in Gwinnett County, March 20, 1864.

Jones Douglas was the son of David Douglas, a native of Scotland, who served for seven years in the Revolution under General Washington on the Continental line of Virginia. He married Martha Jones about 1774. Their children: James, Jones, Stephen, Jincy, Nancy, Martha, Rebecca.

Phoebe Charlton, Mrs. Smith's mother, was a descendant of Arthur Chalton (born 1722), who married Eleanor Harrison (born 1725), at All Saints Episcopal Church, Frederick City, Maryland, in 1745. Their children were: Alice; Eleanor; John Usher; Ann Phoebe, married General John Ross Key and had two children, one of whom was Frances Scott Key who wrote the "Star-Spangled Banner;" Ann Phoebe, married Roger Taney, Chief Justice of the United States in 1821; Thomas Charlton (born 1749), who married Lucy Kenan (died 1796), helped to establish the independence of the Colonies, was educatetd to be a physician, and in 1775 moved to Camden, South Carolina. He served in the war as Lieutenant and surgeon under Col. Wm. Thompson, of South Carolina. After the war, he was a member of the South Carolina Legislature. He died about 1795 as a consequence of exposure during the war. His children were: John Usher; John Kenan; Lucy; Eleanor; Phoebe Jane, married Baron Wambezie; Arthur Murdock, married Frances Mann, a daughter of Luke Mann (died about 1800). Luke Mann, who married Anne Butler in 1756, was a son of John Mann (died 1789).

Luke Mann served in the Revolution and was a member of the Provincial Congress for the Parish of St. Phillips in 1775. He is listed as a Militia Officer of St. George's Parish in 1767.

Phoebe Charlton Douglas was the daughter of Arthur Murdock Charlton and Frances Mann.

—By Mildred Bishop.

SMITH

Joseph Daniel Smith Family

Joseph Daniel Smith was born in Laurens County, Georgia, March 5, 1857, and died in Atlanta, Georgia, November 17, 1910. He is buried in Northview Cemetery in Dublin.

Two generations intervened between Joseph Daniel Smith and his ancestor, Hardy Smith, a native of North Carolina, and a Continental soldier during the Revolutionary War. This Hardy Smith had three sons, viz., Hardy, English, and Stephen, who came to Laurens County in the early 1800's, and settled on Pugh's Creek. This second Hardy Smith's son, Thomas Marcus, who was born in Laurens County on May 12, 1825, married Martha Mason, who was also born in Laurens County, November 12, 1815. The youngest son of Thomas Marcus and Martha Mason Smith was Joseph Daniel Smith.

Martha Mason Smith, mother of Joseph Daniel, was descended from two notable Virginia families, the Masons and the Turners. She was the ninth generation from the first George Mason, who in 1665 founded the family in Virginia and which was made famous by the fourth George Mason, Thomas Jefferson's instructor in statecraft. A grandfather of Martha Mason, Turner Mason, who was a North Carolinian by birth, served as a Lieutenant in the American Revolution.

By the marriage of Thomas Marcus Smith and Martha Mason there were five children: (1) William, (2) James T., (3) Henry Turner, (4) Hardy Hamilton, (5) Joseph Daniel.

Joseph Daniel Smith was thrice married, first, to Sarah Rebecca Rainey, of Laurens County, in 1875; second, to Rosalie Cook, of Columbus, Georgia, in 1885; and third, to Beulah Richardson, of Greenwood, South Carolina, in 1905.

By Joseph Daniel Smith's marriage to Sarah Rebecca Rainey there are one son and three daughters who are as follows: (1) Thomas Hardy, (2) Martha, (3) Lillian, (4) Georgia.

I. Thomas Hardy, only son of Joseph Daniel and Sarah Rebecca Rainey Smith, married Lucy Twitty.

II. Martha married Marion Abbott Kendrick and they had two sons: (1) Joseph Marion, and (2) Hyrell Smith.

III. Lillian married Hugh McCall Moore and they had one daughter and two sons, viz.: (1) Sarah, (2) James Freeman, (3) Hugh McCall, Jr.

IV. Georgia married Cornelius Alexander Weddington and they had two daughters and two sons: (1) Virginia, (2) Gladys, (3) Cornelius Alexander, Jr., (4) David Roger.

Joseph Marion Kendrick, son of Marion Abbott and Martha Smith

Kendrick, married Elizabeth Alford; and they have three children: (1) Martha Lou, (2) Joseph Marion, Jr., (3) Elizabeth Lee.

Hyrell Smith Kendrick, son of Marion Abbott and Martha Smith Kendrick, married Carolyn Summerlin and has one son, Hyrell Smith Kendrick, Jr.

Sarah Moore, daughter of Hugh McCall Moore and Lillian Smith Moore, married Benjamin Stewart Carswell and they have one daughter, Lillian, who married William Van Pelp McCane.

James Freeman Moore, son of Hugh McCall and Lillian Moore, married Nellie Micheal.

Hugh McCall Moore, Jr., married Joy Burch.

Virginia Weddington, oldest daughter of Cornelius Alexander and Georgia Smith Weddington, married Joseph Lancaster and has three children: (1) Joseph, Jr., (2) Gladys, (3) Virginia.

Gladys Weddington married Harvey Asbel.

Cornelius Alexander Weddington, Jr., married Inez Clinton.

David Roger Weddington married Minnie Ruth Knox and has one daughter, Suzanne.

By Joseph Daniel Smith's second marriage to Rosalie Cook there were born two daughters: (1) Rosalie, and (2) Gladys.

I. Rosalie married John Gordon Morrison and by this marriage there was born one son (1) John Gordon Morrison, Jr., and one daughter (2) Gladys Smith Morrison. John Gordon Morrison, Jr., married Lucile Breen. Gladys Smith Morrison married Robert Wiggins.

II. Gladys Smith, daughter of Joseph Daniel and Rosalie Cook Smith, married Ernest Talmadge Brigham (see Brigham genealogy), and they have two children: (1) Rosalie Smith, and (2) Ernest Talmadge, Jr. Rosalie Smith married Robert Musgrove Garbutt. Ernet Talmadge Brigham, Jr., unmarried.

By Joseph Daniel Smith's third marriage to Beulah Richardson there were born three daughters, viz.: (1) Beulah, (2) Josephine, (3) Rebecca. Beulah, eldest daughter of Joseph Daniel and Beulah Richardson Smith, married B. E. Brown, Jr., and they have two children: (1) Katherine, (2) Rebecca. Josephine Smith married A. L. Taylor. Rebecca Smith married John Wesley.

Sarah Rebecca Rainey, first wife of Joseph Daniel Smith, died November, 1884, and is buried in Gethsemane Church Yard.

Rosalie Cook, second wife of Joseph Daniel Smith, died June 10, 1904, and is buried in Northview Cemetery in Dublin, Georgia.

Joseph Daniel Smith established the first cotton market in Dublin, the first live stock market (Horse & Mule) in Dublin, and erected the first block of brick business houses in Dublin, yet he lived in this city only about twenty-five years. Although he never held any conspicuous public office, it is doubtful if any one man contributed more to the upbuilding of Dublin and Laurens County than did Joseph Daniel Smith.

He was not only an aggressive and enterprising business man of much public spirit, but he also cared for the better things of life. Early in life he became a member of the Methodist Church and for the remainder of his days was a constant supporter of the cause of religion.

—*By Gladys S. Brigham (Mrs. E. T.)*

SMITH

THOMAS DANIEL SMITH FAMILY

Major T. D. Smith, a native of Laurens County, was born in 1839 and in his lifetime saw Dublin grow from a struggling hamlet to a thriving city. He was the son of Thomas Peter Smith and Margaret Hill Smith. He had two brothers, Christopher Columbus and Green; two half brothers, Franklin and Guyton.

In 1868 he was married to Sarah Elmira Stokes, daughter of Cordy C. Stokes and Sarah Stanley Stokes. They had six children: Robert Lee, Thomas Cordy, Mark A., Mary M., Nancy Ellen, Sarah Frances.

Major Smith served three years in the Confederate Army as a member of the Blackshear Guards, a Company from Laurens County which formed a part of the 14th Georgia Regiment. He was in nineteen battles and saw much service in northern Virginia.

He was active in the United Confederate Veterans and organized the United Daughters of the Confederacy in Dublin. He purchased and presented to the Chapter its charter, and the Chapter was named T. D. Smith Chapter. Due to a misunderstanding which arose between him and the U. D. C. Chapter over the erection of the Confederate Monument in Dublin, the Chapter name was changed to Oconee Chapter.

He was a prominent member of the Masons, was at one time Clerk of the City Council; and at the time of his death, May, 1912, was Justice of the Peace for the Dublin District. In appreciation for the service which he had rendered to the civic life of Dublin, the bell in the courthouse tower tolled as the funeral procession passed through the city.

Children: Robert Lee, married, first, Minnie Hagen; second, Kitty Zeigler; children: Robert, Blanche, Pearl, Dora, Hugh.

Thomas C., born 1871, married Isadora Peacock; children: Sarah Martha and Frances.

Mark A., born 1882, married Belle Irwin; children: Martha, Irwin, Margaret, Mark, James.

Mary M., born 1873, married in 1909 to Freeman Walker, of Dublin; their only child, Sarah Will, married Wm. A. Legwen, of Augusta, Georgia, in 1932.

Nancy E., born 1875, married L. L. Beall; children: Sarah (Mrs. J. H. Taylor, Florida), Louise (Mrs. W. E. Cannon, Florida), James.

Sarah F., born 1879, married Stanley R. Melton, of Opelika, Alabama; their only child, Stanley, married Evelyn Ingram, Alabama.

—*By Sara Will Walker Legwin (Mrs. W. A.)*

STANLEY

James Stanley II, emigrated from Jones County, North Carolina, where the family had been prominent for a number of years, and located in Laurens County, Georgia, in 1811. He settled in the northwestern part of the County and was the progenitor of the Laurens County Stanleys. The time of his coming to Laurens can be determined by his purchase of lands at public sale on September 6, of the year above mentioned. This was four years after the County had been formed and two years following the change of the County seat from Sumpterville to Dublin. The Stanleys had therefore much to do with the early settlement of the County. For 130 years there have been Stanleys in Laurens.

The family is of unquestioned English origin, as the name was derived from a very rugged portion of Staffordshire and was first spelled Stonylea, Stonelea, Standlea, and finally Stanley. It was derived from the Saxon "Stan," a stone, and lie, lee, lege, ley, etc., a stony place, pasture, meadow, rough woodland. Some of the American Stanleys, during the Revolutionary War, as an act of patriotism, left the "n" out of the name and made it Irish. The family came to Georgia from North Carolina and there is a county there by that name spelled "Stanly," and later a town was established spelled "Stanley," like the name is now generally written.

Stanley was the family name of the Earl of Derby for whom the great racing event was named. When Georgia was chartered, June 9, 1732, the crown named James Stanley, Earl of Derby, one of the trustees. At that time there was a James Stanley in North Carolina and more were to follow, viz:. James Stanley II, who located in Laurens County, and his son, James Rowell Stanley.

James Stanley II was the ninth child and second son of James Stanley I, and his wife, Winnifred. He was born in Jones County, North Carolina, on January 23, 1771, and died April 14, 1841, in Laurens County, and is buried in the Stanley Cemetery, "The Ditch," which he established about twelve miles north of Dublin and within a half mile of his home. Members of the family were buried in the front part of the cemetery and the slaves in the rear. This cemetery was established at least in the early part of 1812 and is still maintained by the Stanley family. As it is approximately 130 years old, it is probably one of the oldest private cemeteries in Georgia still in use. The cemetery is enclosd by an iron fence. In the year 1793 Jame Stanley II was united in marriage to Leah Fordham, daughter of Benjamin Fordham, of Jones County, North Carolina. She was born September 6, 1776, and died March 9, 1853, and was buried beside her husband in the Stanley Cemetery. She was the sister of Mary Fordham, who was the second wife of John Stanley, brother of James. They had children as follows:

Hardy Brantley, born September 20, 1800, married Mary Ward, born about 1794. Ira, born September 22, 1802, married Janet Harris McCall, March 9, 1807. Needham, born November 20, 1804. James Rowell and Sarah, twins, born February 11, 1807. James Rowell was married December 17, 1829, to Mahala Coney. Mary, or Polly, born January 13, or 23, 1810. Time changed. Cathy, born June 15, 1812.

He built his first home within a hundred yards of "The Ditch." He later erected a second home near the first. This house was so well constructed that, while very old, is still standing. The timber was cut on James Stanley's plantation, was sawed at his own mill and erected largely by his own labor.

James Stanley constructed a water mill on his property which was known as the Stanley Mill, which is more than 100 years of age and is still serving the public in the northern part of Laurens County, and the southern part of Wilkinson. The stream on which it is located is almost on the line of the two counties. The mill was inherited by James Rowell Stanley and at his death was purchased by Dr. James T. Chappell and the name changed to Chappell's Mill and is still so named, although the ownership is now out of the family. The last member of the family to own the mill was the late Judge Ira Stanley Chappell, who was also the last member of the family to own and live in the home of Ira Stanley, his grandfather, which was one of the most imposing homes in Laurens County and which was destroyed by fire a number of years ago.

James Stanley entered the merchantile business under the name and style of H. B. and Ira Stanley, his two sons. He was quite a large planter, and owned some seven thousand acres. He, Governor George M. Troup, Dr. Nathan Tucker, General David Blackshear, Thomas McCall and Joel Coney were the largest land owners in Laurens.

Governor Troup, Dr. Tucker and General Blackshear lived on the east side of the Oconee River and James Stanley, Joel Coney and Thomas McCall lived on the west side.

James Stanley was a member of the Poplar Springs Baptist Church. He never sought or held public office. There are no traditions in the family as to his characteristics, but it is known that he was much interested in education and donated ten acres of ground at a cross roads, near his home, for the erection of a school building which was maintained until just a few years ago. There is no painting or photograph of him but Judge Chappell, a few years ago, described him as being "self reliant, brave, earnest, generous, a staunch friend and a good citizen."

IRA STANLEY

Ira Stanley, second son of James Stanley II, was born in Jones County, North Carolina, September 22, 1802, and came to Laurens County with his parents during the year 1811. He was educated in the county schools and by private tutors employed by his father. He was united in marriage to Janet Harris McCall, who was the twin of Margaret Sanders McCall, the youngest daughters of Thomas McCall and his wife, Elizabeth Mary Ann Smith McCall.

Ira Stanley was a man of considerable wealth and hospitality. He was one of the largest planters in the county, owning a great deal of land and quite a number of slaves. He did not believe in the slave traffic and refused to sell any of his slaves. He therefore owned many more than he needed.

After the emancipation all of the slaves who expressed a desire to remain were employed and many remained. To this day there are one or two slaves, who were young at the close of the war, and descendants of other slaves, who are still living with members of the Stanley family still owning some of the farms.

The Stanley family meet at Stanley Cemetery on the second Saturday in May of each year to decide what improvements are needed, contribute money to that end, have dinner together and discuss family affairs. At these reunions some of the old slaves are present and descendants of slaves.

Ira Stanley was an exceedingly popular man and was a very public spirited citizen. He was opposed to the liquor traffic and when a barroom was opened near his property by a preacher whose denomination was not then opposed to the use and sale of liquor, he expostulated with him and, when informed that he did not receive enough from his congregation upon which to live, Ira Stanley asked how much he made from his whiskey traffic and what investment he had in intoxicating goods. The amount was stated and he agreed to pay the preacher each month the amount of his profit, purchased the stock, had it hauled out to the side of the road and poured on the gground.

In the old days the office of sheriff was important but unremunerative. It was necessary for men of probity and wealth to take turns in filling this office. Ira Stanley was sheriff in 1825 and 1826. He was then elected a representative in the lower house of the General Assembly in 1834 and 1835. His colleague was Jeremiah H. Yopp, brother-in-law, the two having married twin daughters of James McCall.

Ira Stanley was fond of visitors and travelers were always welcome. On one occasion while on his way to Dublin, Alexander H. Stephens, of Crawfordville, spent the night with Mr. Stanley. When informed that Mr. Stanley intended to erect a new residence, Mr. Stephens called for a pen and paper and gave him a drawing of his own home. Mr. Stanley reproduced this home from Mr. Stephens' design. The home was one of the best in the county and visitors were entertained almost nightly.

Mr. Stanley was a man of great affability of manner and readily made friends of all with whom he came in contact. His integrity and honesty were above reproach; his liberality was proverbial and his generosity was unlimited. He gave his substance to the poor, and of his wisdom to all who sought it.

His children were as follows: Margaret Elizabeth, born October 15, 1828, married John Franklin Burney; Rollin Adolphus, born June 30, 1830, married Martha Rebecca Lowther; Harriett Athalia, born November 17, 1832, married Dr. James Chappell (see Chappell history); Benjamin Franklin, born September 16, 1836, married Ann Elizabeth Bass (more later); Ira Eli, born April 7, 1838, married Mary Mourman Brazeal (more later); Valeria Imogene, born August 23, 1842, died March 24, 1844; Georgia Jane Leonora, born August 20, 1845, married Dr. Peyton W. Douglas.

Ira Stanley's wife, Janet Harris McCall, was a woman of great ability and easily handled her servants, of which there were a number. She was a woman of rare charm and personality. Almost all of her widowhood was spent with the family of Dr. Peyton W. Douglas, who married Georgia Jane Leonora, her youngest daughter. Much of her widowhood was spent outside of Laurens County and she died in Atlanta, at the age of eighty-two. She was buried in the Stanley Cemetery in Laurens County.

THE McCALL ANCESTRY

The father of Mrs. Stanley was Thomas McCall, one of Laurens' largest planters and one of the most distinguished of Georgia citizens. He was a son of James McCall, who was a Lieutenant-Colonel in the Revolutionary War, and engaged in a number of battles.

At the close of the war he died from illness. Thomas McCall was married twice. Mary Ann Smith, his second wife, was the mother of Janet Harris Stanley. She was the great-great-granddaughter of the first Governor James Moore, of South Carolina, and a great-great-granddaughter of the first Thomas Smith, a landgrave, and Governor of South Carolina. She was also descended from Governor Sanders, of South Carolina. Her ancestor, Governor James Moore I, married Margaret Berringer, the stepdaughter of Sir John Yeomans, first Royal Governor of South Carolina.

Thomas McCall, before settling in Laurens, resided in Augusta,

Darien, Brunswick, and Savannah. He was named by the Governor of Georgia to the position of surveyor-general in 1786 and served until 1795.

He served in the Revolution, although quite young, and was given two land grants for services rendered. His home in Laurens was located on the west side of the river opposite the home of Governor Troup. They were great friends and frequently visited each other. Each had a skiff to convey them across the Oconee.

Thomas McCall was a celebrated grower of grapes and Governor Troup felt impelled to call attention of the General Assembly to this fact in a message which read as follows:

"The introduction of a new culture may claim the continuance of government as well from its general utility as from the difficulties attending it. Among the varieties which contribute to the comforts of man, that of the vine ranks with the first class; a culture, fellow citizens, Thomas McCall, of Laurens, distinguished alike for his science and philanthropy, has devoted many years to this culture, and his laudable zeal and patient industry gives promise of ultimate success. A temporary and limited encouragement may insure it; and good effects would be seen eventually in a diversified cultivation, in an independence of foreigners for an article of great value, and in the gradual substitution in practice of a less for a more intoxicating beverage.

"If you coincide with me in the policy of extending a fostering hand to this subject of agriculture, the kind and degree of encouragement will be regulated by a sound discretion." (Miller's Bench and Bar of Georgia, Vol. 1, page 399).

"If you coincide with me in the policy of extending a fostering hand to this subject of agriculture, the kind and degree of encouragement will be regulated by a sound discretion." (Miller's Bench and Bar of Georgia, Vol. 1, page 399).

Thomas McCall's Lauren County plantation was called "Retreat." Later it was called "Doll Neck" on account of his beautiful daughters. He also owned some property on the east side of the river.

The McCalls were of Scotch origin and were Presbyterians. They went to the north of Ireland to escape persecution and there they remained for a generation. They then came to America, first landing in Pennsylvania, finally moved to Virginia, North Carolina, South Carolina and then to Georgia. They were accompanied by the Calhoun and Harris families.

Thomas McCall's younger brother was Hugh McCall who never married. He was first an ensign, then a Lieutenant in the Paymaster's Department, then a Captain and then a Brevt Major. He wrote the first History of Georgia which was published in 1811.

In Washington, D. C., there is a Chapter of the D. A. R. named

CAPTAIN ROLLIN ADOLPHUS STANLEY

for Colonel James McCall and in Dublin the Daughters of 1812 named a Chapter for Thomas McCall. The family has a portrait of Thomas McCall in uniform and powdered wig, and in the library in Savannah there is a life-size portrait of Captain Hugh McCall.

ROLLIN ADOLPHUS STANLEY

Captain Rollin A. Stanley, the second child and first son of Ira Stanley, was born in Laurens County, June 30, 1830, and was united in marriage to Martha Rebecca Lowther, daughter of John Lowther, of Dublin. The marriage was performed at the Lowther summer home at "Van Wert," in Polk County, on the outskirts of what is now Rockmart.

He was educated in the school of Laurens County which were largely supported by his father, Ira Stanley, and was then sent to Dartmouth University. He later studied law and was admitted to the bar in Irwinton where he practiced until 1866. He then returned to Laurens County and located at Dublin where he remained for the balance of his life.

At the outbreak of the war he was residing in Irwinton and entered the Confederate Army. He was connected with the Third Georgia Regiment and remained in the army until April 14, 1862, when he was forced to retire on account of ill health. Later the relationship between President Davis and Governor Joseph E. Brown became so strained that the latter refused to grant any more requests for soldiers and organized the Georgia Militia. Captain Stanley was elected Captain of Company A, Second Regiment, Georgia State Troops, Colonel Stapleton's Regiment. He was elected Major, 16th Military District, Laurens County, but the war closed before he could be commissioned.

Captain Stanley was a member of the Dublin Baptist Church and for 25 years before his death he was superintendent of the Sunday School. He was a speaker of rare gifts and was in much demand in various parts of the State to deliver Sunday School addresses which were much enjoyed.

When the Oconee Judicial Circuit was formed he was appointed Solicitor General by Governor James M. Smith. His kind and gentle nature rebelled at having to prosecute the many who were indicted and he resigned before the term for which he was appointed had expired.

In 1891 he was elected Judge of the Court of Ordinary to succeed Judge John T. Duncan, who had died in office. He had been of great help to Judge Duncan during his long tenure of office and was well qualified to fill the position which he held until his death, March 14, 1893.

At his death the *Dublin Post* spoke of him in part as follows:

"In the discharge of his duty he performed his part well and left to the world the result of a useful life, a spotless record and an honored name. To him life's sun has set. For him life's cares are ended. While yet in the full maturity and undiminished vigor of his faculties, with not one ray of his intelligence obscured or dimmed; honored by his fellow citizens; in his home town in the midst of friends and neighbors of many years; in the bosom of those whom he loved, and who loved him, God's finger touched him and he slept."

Captain Stanley was buried in the family cemetery twelve miles north of Dublin.

Captain and Mrs. Stanley had children as follows:

Ira Lowther, born at Irwinton, February 11, 1858, married to Fannie Cassidy; Frank Rowe, born January 6, 1860, married to Ellen Ann Veronee, August 18, 1885; Mattie, born March 7, 1862, died October 23 of that year; Rollin A., born August 14, 1864, and died October 8 of that year; Harris McCall, born June 9, 1866, married Ethel Inez Stubbs, December 31, 1890; Florence Moore, born March 28, 1868, married William R. Haynes, March 18, 1891; Vivian Lee, born January 5, 1870, married Ella Mizelle Martin, April 21, 1896; Lucia Augusta, born January 2, 1874, married John S. Adams, January 20, 1895.

Martha Rebecca Lowther Stanley

Martha Rebecca Lowther, wife of Captain Rollin A. Stanley, was born in Dublin, February 23, 1835, and was married to Captain Stanley, November 13, 1856. She was the eldest daughter of John Lowther and Eliza Moore Lowther. She was a woman of endearing charms and was never known to speak in disparagement of another. Her disposition was so perfect that she either spoke kindly of everyone or said nothing at all.

She was educated in the Laurens County schools and at Milledgeville. At her funeral the minister used the declaration of Joshua, "As for me and my house we will serve the Lord." Everyone spoke of how applicable to her was this text, it illustrating her life as no other text could.

After the funeral in Dublin, which was largely attended, her remains were carried to the Stanley Cemetery and interred beside that of her husband. Besides six children, Mrs. Stanley was survived by three sisiters, viz.: Mrs. Mariah T. Doyle and Mrs. Ella Roberts, of Cedartown, and Mrs. Jesse Hardage, of Rockmart.

John Lowther

John Lowther, whose family came from Wales, was born in Bulloch County in 1801. He came to Dublin as a boy after the death of his parents in Bulloch County. He married Sarah Eliza Moore, daughter of Thomas Moore, who came to Dublin from Maryland. Salesmanship was his strong point and he entered the mercantile business when he was a young man. Although Dublin was a small town, it drew trade from adjoining counties. He sold goods to people who came from a distance as far as Tattnall County. Mr. Lowther was very successful and built a summer home at Van Wert, in Polk County, which his family enjoyed each summer. Van Wert is now almost a memory, it being adjacent to Rockmart, which, being on two railroads, grew more rapidly.

Mr. Lowther had great faith in North Georgia minerals and bought property in all of the mineral counties. At the time of his death he owned property from the eastern part of the State across to the west. Some of the land is still in the family whose members believe in the mineral value.

John Lowther, with a rare capacity for business, combining a knowledge of human nature with a friendly touch, made countless friends throughout Georgia. He was respected for his character and business sagacity and loved because of his kindly, genial nature. His passing was in early middle age, as he was only fifty-one. He left a splendid estate, for those days, including valuable land in middle Georgia.

Mr. Lowther was buried in the old cemetery in Dublin and the inscription on his monument reads:

"To have known him was to admire him. A true appreciation of his character can only be made by those who knew him best."

He was survived by his wife, Sarah Eliza, and his children, as follows:

Martha Rebecca, who married Rollin A. Stanley; Mariah, who married Dr. Edward Doyle; Mary, married to Jesse W. Hardage; Ella, who married John E. Roberts, and Florence, married to Will Otterman. The last named died young at her home in Louisiana. All of the remainder are now dead, leaving a number of children and grandchildren.

Mary Hardage had five children: Thomas, married Addie Pope; Coney; Vivian; Irma; Lucia, married J. M. Satterfield and has one child, Mary Benning Satterfield.

Ella Roberts had five children: Hughes, married Lillian Mitchell and has two children: Lillian and Hughes, Jr.; Lady, married Dr. Trumbo; Daniel, married Stella Russell; Thomas, married Sallie Williamson; Will Eph, married Mae Blair.

Maria Doyle had three children: Eva, married Mr. Whitfield and had seven children: Juanita, married W. L. McCormick; Charles, married Cora Thompson; Edwerta, married Henry Solomon and had three children: Paul, Doyle and Harry; Russell, married

Miss Seay; Luther, married Nealie Simpson; Florence, married Walter Ector; Marie; Emmett, married Cora Morgan and had two children: Exa, married Libby Steward; Robert; McDuffie, married Lorena Munford and had four children: Clarence, married Mamie Garvin; Theresa, married Burton F. Williams; Fannie Ida; Addeane.

Mrs. Lowther was descended from the quite noted Jones family, of Virginia. The first Jones of record to reach America settled in Virginia and for him the City of Petersburg was named. His first name was Peter and his son bore the same name. The family was very prominent in Colonial Virginia and several served in the House of Burgesses. There were three Jones by the name of Abraham. Martha Bugg was the daughter of the last Abraham Jones and Dr. Moore married her daughter, Martha, who was the mother of Mrs. Eliza Moore Lowther.

Several members of the Jones family made great names for themselves in Georgia. Three were named Seaborn. One of them, an uncle of Mrs. Lowther, first located in Milledgeville and was selected by Governor Troup to be master of ceremonies at a reception he gave General LaFayette. Later he moved to Columbus where he was sent to Congress and where he served two years.

Seaborn Jones erected a home in the outskirts of Columbus, known at St. Elmo, which is being preserved to this day. His daughter married General Henry Benning, a General in the Confederate Army, for whom Fort Benning was named. General Benning was also an Associate Justice of the Georgia Supreme Court.

After the death of John Lowther, Mrs. Lowther married a Dr. Coyle. She died in Rockmart and was buried in the old cemetery in Dublin.

IRA LOWTHER STANLEY

Ira Lowther, the first son of Rollin A. Stanley, was born in Irwinton, on February 11, 1858. He was eight years of age when his father returned to Laurens and made his home in Dublin. He was educated in the Dublin schools and, when Dublin *Gazette* was established, became a "printer's devil" in that office, and was the first Dublin boy to become a printer.

After being connected with the *Gazette* for some time, he and Ira Stanley Chappell established a paper at Cochran. Judge Chappell continued the paper for a time after Mr. Stanley engaged in other pursuits, in Cochran, and then moved to Cedartown. From Cedartown, Mr. Stanley went to Baird, Texas, and again was connected with a newspaper. From Baird he went to Abiline and then to Dallas.

He was one of the founders of the Dallas *Evening Herald* and then the *Times* with which the *Herald* was consolidated. He was for a considerable time secretary and treasurer of the Dallas *Times-*

Herald. He was then made foreman of the composing room and proof reader, which position he held for many years. In fact, except for being night editor of the Dallas office of the American Press Association, and later publishing a weekly paper near Dallas, he was connected with the *Times-Herald* for more than fifty years.

He wrote a special column for the paper which was widely read and was familiarly known in the office as "Boss."

Mr. Stanley, while living in Baird, was married to Mary Frances Cassidy, who was a teacher in the Baird schools. She was originally from Des Moines, Iowa, where she was born March 14, 1868. She was the daughter of Michael S. and B. Cassidy, prominent citizens of Iowa, and lived up to the traditions of her parentage and her training. She made him a loving wife and a faithful helpmate. They had three children. The first was Vivian Anastasia, born August 14, 1894; Justin Cassidy, born November 26, 1899; and David Hugh, born August 29, 1907.

Their children have been of great love and assistance to their parents and are greatly cherished. David is the only one who has married and has a son, David, Jr. Vivian is an exceptionally fine character, talented, vivacious, handsome.

Mr. Stanley's health began to fail several years ago and he was forced to take frequent vacations. He continued at work, however, and was at his post of duty just a few days before he died of pneumonia on January 5, 1941. He was buried in Dallas, where he had lived for more than half a century.

Frank Rowe Stanley

The second son of Captain Rollin A. Stanley was Frank Rowe. He was educated in the Dublin public schools. He did not care much for printing but later did follow his older brother in the office of the Dublin *Gazette*. After he became a printer he went to Gainesville and worked for the celebrated Henry Wilkes Jones Ham.

Mr. Stanley did no newspaper work after leaving the Gainesville *News* and became connected with one of the large mercantile establishments of that city. He then went to Athens where he remained for a number of years. Much of his time was spent in Millen and afterwards he went to Sandersville where he died October 1, 1918. He was buried in the Stanley Cemetery, near Dublin.

He was married while in Athens to Ellen Veronee and to them were born three children: Frank Rowe, Jr., born August 1, 1886, who married Mary Edwards; Lady Eleanor, born July 1, 1889, married to Edouard Ferdinand Henriques, August 7, 1913; William Clinton, born July 22, 1892, married to Helen Gardner Cork.

Frank Rowe Stanley, Jr., located in Americus and has a very interesting family. He became largely an automobile mechanic and stands high as such in the city of his location. He is gifted in his chosen profession, being considered one of the best in Americus. He has a good business and cares for it well. His wife comes from one of the best families in the city of his adoption. They have four children: Mae Ellen, born July 7, 1907; Edith Ardille, born March 3, 1910; Mildren Edward, born October 25, 1916; Milton Rollin, born July 27, 1924.

Lady Eleanor Henriques

The second child of Frank Rowe Stanley was Lady Eleanor. She was educated in the public schools and at Bessie Tift College, in Forsyth. She is a woman of unusual capacity and was very devoted to her father. While in New Orleans she met and married Edouard Ferdinand Henriqes, a lawyer of ability, who was special assistant to the Attorney General of the United States, with authority over admiralty, which brought him several times to Dublin, the former home of his wife's father.

He was the oldest son of Isaac Henriques and his wife, Elizabeth Calhoun Hickey, and was born in Jefferson, Texas. His father was a native of Kingston, Jamaica, and his mother, of Camden, New Jersey. He went to school at Tulane University and there graduated in law. They have children as follows: (1) Lady Helen, born October 27, 1914. She attended Louise McGee School and Sophie Newcomb College. She married Ford Thomas Hardy. They have one child, Lady Helen. (2) Elizabeth Stanley, born November 30, 1916. (3) Stanley McCall, born August 27, 1918.

William Clinton, the youngest son of Frank Rowe Stanley, went to California to live and was there married to Miss Cork. She died January 25, 1919, in Vallejo, California, leaving a daughter, Helen Clinton Stanley.

Harris McCall Stanley

Harris McCall Stanley, familiarly known to his friend as "Hal," was born June 9, 1866, and attended the Dublin public schools. He became a "printer's devil" in the office of the Dublin *Gazette*, worked his way up to the rank of editor and married the eldest daughter of the owner of the paper. Prior to becoming editor of the *Gazette* he moved to Atlanta and was connected with the Franklin Printing and Publishing Company.

On December 31, 1890, he was united in marriage to Ethel Inez Stubbs, eldest daughter of Colonel John M. Stubbs, and granddaughter of Dr. Nathan Tucker. After their marriage they lived for several years in Eastman and in 1894 moved to Savannah. While living in that city he was appointed fertilizer inspector by R. T. Nesbit, Commissioner of Agriculture. He held that position for several years.

Before leaving Dublin, Mr. Stanley was named First Lieutenant of the Dublin Light Infantry and in Eastman was elected Captain of the Eastman Volunteers. Before leaving Eastman, he was named a Lieutenant Colonel on the staff of Governor W. Y. Atkinson and held that position for four years. In Savannah, he was elected First Lieutenant of Savannah Company, Uniform Rank, Knights of Pythias, and later was made Captain and Adjutant of the First Regiment under Colonel John Juchter. Later, Mr. Stanley was appointed Colonel and Quartermaster General of the Georgia Brigade, Uniform Rank, Knights of Pythias, by General Edgar Pomeroy. He had headquarters in Atlanta and later held that same position under General Henry A. Dressen with headquarters in Savannah.

Returning to Dublin in 1897, Mr. Stanley purchased an interest in the Dublin *Courier* and became its editor. A few months later the paper was consolidated with the Dublin *Dispatch*, Mr. Stanley remaining editor-in-chief. The paper was published as a semi-weekly and a linotype machine was purchased. It is said that this was the first linotype machine sold in the South to a secular weekly, and before many small daily newspapers of the State had installed such machines. In the mean time, Mr. Stanley's younger brother, Vivian, became connected with the paper.

The *Courier-Dispatch* worked for the best interests of Dublin, Laurens County, and that section of the State. It was responsible for many improvements. The first of importance was the securing by Mr. Stanley of an appropriation from Andrew Carnegie for the erection of a public library in Dublin. A new post office building followed. Mr. Stanley then went to Washington and spent a week there working for a city delivery of mail which was secured in four or five months. In the mean time some rural free deliveries of mail were secured through Congressman W. G. Brantley, and later a full county rural mail delivery. He helped organize the Dublin Chatauqua Association and was successful in bringing to the town the best talent the country afforded.

In 1911 the Department of Commerce and Labor was created. A primary was held in December of that year to name a Democrat to run for Commissioner of Commerce and Labor, on January 12, 1912. In this primary Mr. Stanley was named, carrying every county in the State except six. He had no opposition in the general election and took office January 25, 1912. He had opposition no other time except in 1930 and in the primary election carried every county in the State.

From time to time there were improvements in the law, the major one coming in 1920 with the passage of the workmen's compensation law which took effect October 1, of that year.

Under the law, Mr. Stanley was made Ex-Officio Chairman of the Industrial Board, continuing to serve as Commissioner of Commerce and Labor. In the reorganization act of 1931 the Department of Commerce and Labor and the Industrial Board were consolidated under the title of the Department of Industrial Relations. Mr. Stanley continued as head of this department and as Commissioner of Commerce and Labor until May, 1937, when there was another reorganization. The two departments were divided, one being named Department of Labor and the other the Industrial Board. Mr. Stanley was elected Chairman of the Industrial Board and remained as such until May, 1940, when he retired, after holding public office continuously for twenty-eight years.

In 1907, Mr. Stanley was elected President of the Georgia Weekly Press Association and held that office for two years. In 1908 he was elected Corresponding Secretary of that organization and later Executive Secretary. In 1918 the name of the Association was changed to the Georgia Press Association. In 1940 Mr. Stanley retired as Executive Secretary of the Georgia Press Association and was made Secretary Emeritus for life.

Mr. Stanley united with the Knights of Pythias in 1891 and was immediately made Chancellor Commander and sent as a representative to the Grand Lodge. He attended the Grand Lodge several times and was elected to an office first in 1909 and advanced each year until he was elected Grand Chancellor in 1914.

ETHEL STUBBS STANLEY

Mrs. Stanley is a woman of deep piety, great depth of character, unbounded generosity and deep intellect. Her great interests have always been in her home, loved ones and friends.

She was educated by governesses, her father having employed one constantly for a number of years. All of her life she has been an inveterate reader and has a brilliant memory, rarely forgetting anything she has studied or read.

Mrs. Stanley inherited her father's love for flowers. She can easily give the botanical name for most flowers. At her home flowers grow everywhere and she uses all available ground for flowers and shrubbery. Her health has always been frail and she could not take an active part in outside affairs. She is a Methodist and a member of the D. A. R.

Mr. and Mrs. Stanley have three living children: Lytton McCall, born March 26, 1892, chose the newspaper profession as his career and was for a number of years connected with the Atlanta *Georgian and Sunday American*, as capitol reporter. Prior to joining the Hearst publication he was editor of the Rockmart *News*. During the first World War he was a civilian employee in the Quartermaster Corps of the United States.

Maude Stubbs, the only daughter, married John Crane Peteet, April 25, 1925, a contractor and World War veteran. For many years she has held a responsible position in the State Capitol. At present she is serving as State Treasurer to the Society of Mayflower Descendants.

Harry McCall, born August 25, 1897, was married to Jewell Shepherd on July 7, 1928. After finishing school, including two years at Donald Fraser Institute, which has now suspended, he entered the rate room of the Southern Railway and became very proficient as a rate clerk. He now holds the title of officer's assistant, with the road.

Harry Stanley is prominent in fraternal circles. He is a Past Chancellor of the Knights of Pythias; is Past Master of Pythagoras Lodge No. 41, F. & A. M.; Past High Priest of Decatur Chapter, R. A. M., and Past High Priest, Fifth Congressional District (honorary). He is also a Knights Templar. During the first World War he served in the United States Navy.

There are comparatively few couples who have had such a notable length of married life as Mr. and Mrs. Hal Stanley. On December 31, 1940, they had been living together for half a century. During that time they lost one son, John Madison, born December 18, 1898, who died suddenly August 6, 1913, while on a visit to his old home in Dublin. He was buried in West View Cemetery, in Atlanta.

FLORENCE MOORE STANLEY HAYNES

Florence Moore, the eldest daughter of Captain and Mrs. Stanley, was born March 28, 1868. She is a woman of great sweetness of character and resembled her mother in many respect. She is very popular and takes a great deal of interest in school, church, patriotic and charitable organizations. She was very studious and was among the leaders in her classes. She is an earest member of the Baptist Church and was always a devoted daughter, sister, wife and mother.

Florence Moore Stanley was united in marriage March 18, 1891, in Dublin, to William Rowell Haynes, son of Judge Mercer Haynes and Rosamond Parmeter Warren, of Allendale, South Carolina. Judge and Mrs. Haynes moved to Dublin from Griffin and he was named Judge of the County Court of Laurens County. He was at one time postmaster in Dublin.

Judge Haynes was a splendid gentleman and it was natural that his son, William Haynes, should be a man of high ideals. After finishing school, William Haynes took up railroad work and immediately after his marriage he was made agent, at Danville, for the Macon, Dublin and Savannah Railroad.

Later he was made conductor on one of the passenger trains and was employed in the office for a number of years. There was little about the railroad business that he did not know and he filled every position entrusted him with fidelity and dispatch. Leaving the railroad, he became connected with the Macon *Telegraph* and is now a traveling representative of the Macon *Telegraph and News*.

To Mr. and Mrs. Haynes were born six children: Stanley Rowell, born March 8, 1893; Helen Genevieve, born November 16, 1895; Rosamond Dismuke, born November 24, 1897, died April 11, 1906; William Russell, born August 29, 1899; Margaret Rollina and Janet Martha, twins, born July 15, 1905.

Stanley Rowell Haynes was married in Milledgeville to Martha Keith Schooler and they have three children as follows: Stanley Rowell, Jr., born December 16, 1916; Benjamin Schooler, born May 8, 1919; Florence June, born April 20, 1921. Stanley is a telegraph operator and has lived in various parts of the South and West. He is at present living in Columbus, Ohio.

Helen Genevieve was married to William Marshall Burns, in Macon, on January 26, 1918. They have two children: Helen Genevieve, born November 13, 1923, and died December 28, 1923; Rosamond Warren, born March 31, 1925. Marshall Burns is a Baptist minister and has preached and done evangelistic work throughout the South. He is now a minister at Williston, Florida.

William Russell Haynes was married to Myrtle Sessions on September 24, 1927. He is a salesman of exceptional ability and has been located in various parts of the South.

Margaret Rollina Haynes was married to Logan Edward Owen on July 23, 1925. He is connected with the Macon, Dublin & Savannah Railroad. Much of his time is spent in Dublin. They have two children: Logan Edward, Jr., and Florence Stanley Owen.

Janet Martha Haynes was married to Russell Morgan Kelly on August 28, 1926. They live in Americus and have two daughters: Sara Janet Kelly, born June 26, 1927, and Margaret Kelley. He is a field representative of the State Revenue Department.

Vivian Lee Stanley

Like his three older brothers, Vivian Lee Stanley chose the printing trade as a profession. After finishing school he entered the office of the Dublin *Post* and finally became editor of that paper. He joined his brother, Hal M. Stanley, in the purchase of the Dublin *Courier*, later becoming the *Courier-Dispatch*.

Vivian Stanley was named Dublin postmaster by President Grover Cleveland and served in that capacity during the Cleveland administration. He again served as postmaster of Dublin under the administration of Woodrow Wilson. In the interim he served on Dublin City Council, was City Clerk for three years and City Commissioner for two years.

While he was in charge of the Dublin *Courier-Dispatch* he was elected Secretary of the Georgia Prison Commission. He was made a member of the Commission upon the death of Commissioner R. E. Davidson. So far as is known Vivian and Hal Stanley were the only brothers to fill elective state offices at the same time.

Vivian Stanley took a great deal of interest in the management of convicts of the State. He was chairman of the committee which selected the site for the present State prison, in Tattnall County, and thought to be one of the most modern in the South. He was married on April 21, 1896, to Ella Mizell Martin, of Sandersville, who was a woman of charm, vivacity and agreeable manners. Her father was one of the best farmers in Washington County. She died in Atlanta on April 11, 1928, and was buried in Dublin. He was remarried in October, 1938, to Mrs. Nena Turner Ethridge, of McDonough, daughter of Judge and Mrs. Paul C. Turner. Mrs. Stanley has a charming personality and is an accomplished musician. She was educated at Lucy Cobb College, Athens, Georgia.

The children by Mr. Stanley's first wife: Martha Lowther Virginia, born September 17, 1899, and a woman of exceptional charm. She was first married to B. Frank Brown, July 12, 1915. She is now married to J. H. Whitaker, of Atlanta. She has two children by her first marriage, each of whom is very talented. B. Frank Brown, Jr., the elder, is a graduate of the University of Georgia and is now teaching in New Jersey. He is an ensign in the naval reserve. Vivian Stanley Brown is an accomplished pianist and is at present a student at the University of North Carolina.

Vivian Janet, born July 4, 1902, is married to Roy Stuart Garrett, of Montgomery, Alabama, a civil engineer of high standing. They have one daughter, Vivian Stanley, born September 5, 1927.

Eleanor Martin, born September 15, 1906, was married to Raiford Hodges, of Statesboro. He has been in the publishing business for a number of years and is now connected with an important Decatur publishing house. Their children are: Raiford, Jr., born January 2, 1932; Jane Stanley, born January 27, 1936, and Mary Eleanor, born February 16, 1941.

Rollin A. Stanley, born March 8, 1910, attended Dublin public schools and Young Harris College. His law degree was obtained from Mercer University and he practiced law in Dublin for a time. He is now connected with the Federal Bureau of Investigation. He was married to Murial Roberts, of Luthersville, and they have a son, Rollin A., Jr., born June, 1938.

William Martin Stanley, born November 27, 1912, was graduated from Young Harris College and the University of Georgia. He is at present connected with the Federal Government in Washington and is a member of the Georgia Society there. He married Mary Ada Hogaboon, of Vicksburg, Mississippi, on October 15, 1938.

LUCIA AUGUSTA STANLEY ADAMS

Lucia Augusta Stanley Adams, youngest child of Rollian A. Stanley, was born January 2, 1874. She married John Samuel Adams, of Dublin, January 20, 1895. Through her personal charm and gift for leadership many honors have been bestowed upon her. When the Thomas McCall Chapter, Daughters of 1812, was organized in Dublin she was named the first President. She had previously served as Regent of the Dublin Chapter of the D. A. R. She has been outstanding in her work in patriotic organizations and became one of the most popular and efficient State Regents of the D. A. R.

In 1937 the tombs of Hugh McCall and James Johnston were rededicated at Savannah by the Georgia Press Association, the dedicatory address being made by the late Wm. G. Sutlive, editor of the Savannah *Evening Press.* At the dedicatory, the tomb of Hugh McCall was unveiled by Mrs. Adams.

Mrs. Adams is Past State President of the Colonial Dames of the XVII Century and is now (1941) serving as President General of this organization. She is State President of the United States Daughters of 1812, also holds the National office of Curator General of the Society.

Three children were born to John Samuel and Augusta Stanley Adams, whose complete records will be found in the Adams History: Prentice, Jamie Vivian, and Frances, who married Gray Holmes and has two daughters: Nelle Gray and Augusta Stanley Holmes. Since the death of her husband Mrs. Adams spends her winters with this daughter, in New Port Richey, Florida.

—*By Maude Stanley Peteet (Mrs. J. C.)*

BENJAMIN FRANKLIN STANLEY, M.D.

Benjamin Franklin Stanley, son of Ira Stanley and his wife, Janet Harris McCall, was born September 16, 1836; attended Dartmouth College with his brother, Rollin, and was later a prominent physician and influential citizen of this section of the State; served as surgeon in the Confederate Army and was stationed for a lengthy period at Andersonville, Georgia. He died May 17, 1901, and is buried in the Stanley Burial Ground, in Laurens County, Georgia.

Dr. Benjamin F. Stanley married Ann Elizabeth Bass, daughter of John H. Bass and his wife, who was a Miss Salisbury. Children of Dr. Benjamin F. and Ann Elizabeth Stanley are:

1. Eva Bertha Stanley, married Thomas Joseph Blackshear (see Blackshear history); six children: Raphael Semmes, Thomas Joseph, Jr., Wilhelmina Elizabeth (see Kellam history), Paul David, Eva Bertha, and Renaldo Franklin.

2. Henriedda Stanley, married James Henry Duggan, M.D. (see

Duggan history); eight children: Ivey Walker, Edda Stanley, Kathleen, Nancy Elizabeth, James Henry, Sam McArthur, Charles and Lorenz.

3. Rollin Maury Stanley, married Maxie Hall, daughter of William Alford and Amelia Van Landingham Hall, of Wilkinson County, Georgia; five children: Wilkins, Elizabeth, Cora, Alfreda, and Ben Maury.

4. Lucy Mary Stanley, an accomplished musician, married Dr. Sam McArthur.

—By *Wilhelmina Blackshear Kellam (Mrs. S. M.)*

IRA ELI STANLEY

Ira Eli Stanley (born April 7, 1838, died September 6, 1895), son of Ira Stanley and his wife, Janet Harris McCall, was married on February 23, 1860, to Mary M. Brazeal (born June 8, 1838, died August 29, 1884), the daughter of Green H. Brazeal and his wife, Mary Smith. Children: 1. Rollina; 2. Henrietta Celeste, married Samuel Rice Dull (more later); 3. Henry B.; 4. Janet McCall; 5. Ira Eli; 6. Mary Josie, married Thomas Broughton Branch, one child; 7. Martha married Jack Branch, two children.

Henrietta Celeste Stanley, born December 6, 1863, at Stanley Mill, Laurens County, Georgia, married June 18, 1887, Samuel Rice Dull, born June 8, 1860, died February 10, 1919. Chosen in 1938 as one of the twelve famous women of Georgia, Mrs. S. R. Dull's life of service, unselfishness and achievements has made her one of the outstanding women of the South. She was a pioneer in the field of Home Service in the South; in 1918 she became editor of the Home Economics page of the Magazine Section of the Atlanta *Journal*. During the 20 years that she carried on this work she wrote and published her book, "Southern Cooking," which is "Dedicated to My Friends, the Women of Atlanta, of Georgia, and of the South." It became a best-seller and has been sold in every State in the Union and in seven foreign countries.

Mrs. Dull was at one time at the head of the Home Economics Department of Bessie Tift College, Forsyth, Georgia, and later aided in establishing the Domestic Science Department of the Girls' High School and Night School in Atlanta. In the mean time, she was conducting cooking schools all over the South and as far north as Delaware. The charm of her personality and the sweetness of her disposition endear her to every one with whom she comes in contact. Those who sit at her feet for advice will always appreciate the fact that a gentle Southern woman truly raised the lowliest of tasks to her level. She lives at Atlanta, Georgia.

Children of Samuel Rice Dull and his wife, Henrietta Celeste Stanley: 1. Henrietta Stanley Dull, married Dr. Abner Broach (more later); 2. Samuel Rice Dull, Jr., married Esther Hatchett; 3.

Mary Breazeal Dull, married R. E. Kottemann; 4. Louise Hawthorn Dull, married Sidney Owen; 5. Ira Cornelius Dull, died 1927, U. S. Marines.

Henrietta Stanley Dull, born October 4, 1889, married June 30, 1913, at Atlanta, Georgia, Dr. James Abner Broach, born November 10, 1883. They live at Atlanta, Georgia. Two children: 1. Dorothy McCall Broach, married William Guy Crowley (more later); 2. Mary Frances Broach.

Dorothy McCall Broach, born November 2, 1914, married April 14, 1938, William Guy Crowley, born June 19, 1905. They live at Atlanta, Georgia. One child: Henrietta Stanley Crowley, born May 28, 1940.

Mary Breazeal Dull, born August 7, 1893, married September 25, 1919, Rudolph E. Kottemann. They live at Chicago, Illinois. Five children: 1. Elizabeth Anne Kottemann; 2. Rudolph Ernest Kottemann, Jr.; 3. Walter Charles Kottemann; 4. James Broach Kottemann; 5. Jack Fraser Smith Kottemann.

—*By Dorothy Broach Crowley (Mrs. W. Guy)*

JAMES ROWELL STANLEY

James Rowell Stanley, son of James Stanley II and Leah Fordham Stanley, was born February 11, 1807, and was a life-long resident of Laurens County, where he was a farmer on an extensive scale and one of the largest land owners in the county. He married, December 17, 1829, Mahala Coney, who was born October 17, 1814. They both died in 1858 and are buried at "The Ditch," in Laurenss County. They had nine children to live to maturity, namely: Mary, Jane, Leah, Florence, Augusta, Edward Marshall, Joel Coney, and Ira Brantley. One son, James H., was killed on the battlefield in the Second Battle of Manassas.

Ira Brantley Stanley was born March 9, 1855, died August 25, 1896; married Nancy E. Fordham, daughter of Benjamin and Rosa Lord Fordham, April 18, 1883. Nancy Fordham Stanley was born September 5, 1859; died January 18, 1937, and is buried in Eastman, Georgia. Ira B. Stanley is buried at "The Ditch," in Laurens County. They had four children:

I. Rosa Augusta Stanley, who married Talley Ellington Kellam, December 16, 1903. They had five children: 1. Addie Kellam married Freeman Roy Orr, June 24, 1928, and has two sons: Freeman Roy Orr, Jr., Talley Kellam Orr. 2. Nannette Kellam married John B. Scoggins, August 18, 1933, and has one daughter: Ann Scoggins. 3. William Eustace Kellam married Julia Thomas, October 1, 1933, and has two daughters: Caroline Kellam, Rosalyn Kellam. 4. Victoria Kellam. 5 Seth Monte Kellam married Mary Emily Proctor, June, 1935, and has one son: Seth Monte Kellam, Jr.

II. Roberta Leah Stanley married Thomas L. Marchant, January 2, 1909, and has eight children: 1. Thomas L. Marchant, Jr., married Myrtle Batchelor and has two children: Billie Jack Marchant and June Marchant. 2. Martha Marchant. 3. Marie Marchant married Edward Cox; 4. Iralene Marchman; 5. George Robert Marchant. 6. Nan Marchant. 7. Joseph Isaac Marchant. 8. Eva Marchant.

III. Mala Stanley.

IV. Ira B. Stanley.

—By Rosa Stanley Kellam (Mrs. T. E.)

STUBBS

COL. JOHN MADISON STUBBS

Colonel John M. Stubbs, son of Peter and Ann Hammond Stubbs, was born in Bibb County, Georgia, August 4, 1839, and located in Laurens County in 1861. He was of English decent. Ancestors of Colonel Stubbs first settled in Virginia, later coming to Georgia. He was a grandson of Abner Hammond who was Secretary of State of Georgia in 1812. He attended Macon schools and Oglethorpe University when it was located at Milledgeville. He studied law under his cousin, Peter Stubbs, a prominent lawyer of Macon, and was admitted to the bar. On February 12, 1861, he was married to Ella Tucker, daughter of Dr. Nathan Tucker and Anna Horn Tucker. The wedding took place at "Buena Vista," in Laurens County, the home of the bride's parents.

The young couple built a home in Macon but it was destroyed by fire before they were to move in and they decided to locate in Dublin. Of this marriage there were five children: Nathan Tucker, who died in young manhood in Fort Worth, Texas; Lucien Quincy, who married Tallulah Corinne Ramsay (see Ramsay history), and became quite an important figure in Dublin, dying there on September 29, 1933; Ethel Inez, who married Harris McCall Stanley (see Stanley history); Maude Lillian, who married William Pritchett (see Pritchett history); and Ella Theodora, who died at the age of three.

Soon after his marriage the War Between the States was declared and Colonel Stubbs immediately presented himself for service. He was sent to Florida in the Quartermaster Corps, was later made a Lieutenant-Colonel and fought under Stonewall Jackson. He was always prominent among Civil War veterans and took a great deal of interest in the welfare of his brother soldiers.

After the war he began the practice of law in Dublin. His practice grew apace and he soon became one of the leading lawyers of the Oconee Judicial Circuit. Later his practice was extended to counties in the Middle and Ocmulgee Circuits. His practice included both civil and criminal law and he was successful in both branches of the profession. His law library was one of the best in Georgia.

Colonel Stubbs was an orator of distinction and his criminal practice included many prominent cases. In the civil courts he represented one side or the other of most important cases.

In addition to law he took a great interest in agriculture and civic improvements. Realizing that Dublin could not grow without newspaper aid he purchased a printing plant, named the paper the Dublin *Gazette* and turned it over without obligation or cost to one who could edit it. He was in no sense a politician, was never a candidate for public office and his advice to the editor was only that he was to work for the town, the county and the Democratic party.

Colonel Stubbs owned large holdings in Laurens County which were divided after his death. He had a great deal to do with the development of the peach industry in his section and owned a large orchard at Montrose which included 60,000 bearing trees. The orchard was destroyed by the San Jose scale, it not being known how to combat that disease at that time. Seeing the need in Dublin for a gin, grist mill and planer mill, he erected such a plant as a public service.

In Colonel Stubbs' younger days railroads were not so important as they later became. In fact, Laurens County planters opposed construction through the County of the Central of Georgia Railway. Colonel Stubbs realized that a boat line on the Oconee River was needed and he formed the Oconee River Improvement Company which purchased the "Colville" in North Carolina and brought it to Dublin. The boat, for the most part, plied between Dublin and Raoul, a station on the Oconee River between Oconee and Toomsboro.

Coming of the "Colville" revolutionized Dublin transportation and enabled the turpentine industry to develop in Laurens County. Previously steamers such as the "Silverside," "Charles Hardee" and 'Two Boys'' would come from Savannah through the inland waters to Darien and then the Altamaha and Oconee Rivers to Dublin, bringing guano and carrying back cotton. All other forms of freight were handled by wagons to Oconee, Tennille or Toomsboro.

Colonel Stubbs was very fond of outdoor life and of fishing and hunting. He organized the Forest and Stream Club and built the pleasure boat, "Gypsy." When this boat sank the "Rover" was constructed. With members these boats would ply down the Oconee to the junction with the Ocmulgee, stopping to fish or hunt as the occasion presented itself. He wa president of the company and Dublin was headquarters for the boats.

As Dublin outgrew river tranportation a railroad from Tennille was projected, but Colonel Stubbs thought that a line to Macon was

COLONEL JOHN M. STUBBS

more important and he and Colonel D. M. Hughes chartered the Macon and Dublin Railroad. As this road was being constructed, they conceived the idea of building a road from Savannah to Birmingham by way of Dublin and Macon and from Dublin to Americus, to be known as the Savannah, Dublin and Western Short Line. They spent six months in New York trying to finance the road, but conditions were against them. In the mean time the road to Macon was completed and did not owe a dollar. They financed in Illinois a line from Dublin to Vidalia, to be known as the Macon, Dublin and Savannah, the line to Macon to be included. High finance caused the loss of the entire road. They lost a great deal of their time and money, but they had the satisfaction of securing a railroad with connections to the north at Macon and to the coast via Vidalia.

Colonel Stubbs was a man of striking appearance. In fact, a typical Southern Colonel with white hair and soldierly bearing. His home was truly "Liberty Hall" and there was a constant stream of visitors coming throughout the year to enjoy his unbounded hospitality. Rarely could one be found who possessed a greater degree of open-handed generosity and whose doors were always open to friends from all parts of the State.

The spacious grounds of his home were highly cultivated and he spared no expense in obtaining rare plants and shrubs that made it a place of beauty. He brought an English gardener to Dublin who worked for a number of years landscaping the grounds and cultivating the flowers that were such a delight to visitors . The Camellia Japonicas were his greatest pride. He was associated with Prosper J. Berkmans, of Augusta, in the formation of the Georgia Horticulture Society of which he was a life member. He was also one of the founders of the Georgia Fruit Growers Association.

Colonel Stubbs was married three times. His first wife was only 37 years of age when she died. He then married Gertrude Johnson, daughter of Herschel V. Johnson, of Jefferson County, who served two terms as Governor of Georgia, was then elected to the United States Senate and was nominated for Vice-President of the United States on the ticket with Stephen A. Douglas. This ticket was defeated on account of a division among Democrats.

Following the death of his second wife, Colonel Stubbs married Victoire Lowe, a daughter of Governor Louis Lowe, of Maryland, who survived him. He died September 6, 1907, and was buried in Rose Hill Cemetery, in Macon. The Macon, Dublin and Savannah Railroad ran a special train to Macon to transport the funeral party. His death closed the earthly career of one of Georgia's great lawyers and philanthropists.

—*By Hal M. Stanley.*

Lucien Quincy Stubbs

Georgia, Laurens County, and the City of Dublin have had no more loyal and devoted son than the late Lucien Quincy Stubbs whose love and allegiance to his City, County and State superceded all thought of personal interest or ambition. Of a long line of distinguished ancestry he inherited both their high ideals and their brilliant mentality, all of which were used freely for the best interests of his community.

A born orator, he was constantly called into service to address large gatherings on all subjects of patriotic and civic interests. At the State Capitol he was a well known and influential figure, representing Laurens County in the State Legislature for several terms. As Mayor of the City of Dublin for five terms, 1887-88, 1890-92, 1896-98, 1909-11, 1919-21, he played a prominent role in directing the city government along progressive lines. It was during his administration that lights and water were installed in the City and during his last term of office that the paving of the City streets was begun.

Lucien Quincy Stubbs was the first Clerk of the City Court of Dublin, holding this important post from May, 1902, until December, 1914. During his last years he was Deputy Clerk of the United States Court, Dublin Division, also United States Commissioner of the Dublin Division. He was holding these two positions at the time of his death, September 29, 1933, and had held them from the organization of these offices here. For many years he served on the City Board of Education, and was a member of this body at the time of his death.

Lucien Quincy Stubbs was born and spent his youth on the Tucker plantation in Buckeye District of this County; the son of John Madison and Ella Tucker Stubbs; grandson of Peter and Ann Hammond Stubbs; great grandson of Peter and Mary Baradel Palmer Stubbs. He was a lineal descendant of the Revolutionary soldier, Abner Hammond; the grandson of Nathan Tucker, M.D., and his wife, Ann Horn; great grandson of Josiah and Rebecca Young Horn, pioneer settlers of this County.

Lucien Quincy Stubbs was united in marriage to a member of two of the early county families, Tallulah Corinne Ramsay, daughter of Colonel Whiteford S. and Henrietta Guyton Ramsay. (See Ramsay and Guyton genealogies). To this union were born six children, the first three of whom did not live to reach maturity: 1. Clara Guyton Stubbs; 2. Ella Ophelia Stubbs; 3. John Madison Stubbs; 4. Jeannette Ramsay Stubbs, married James Davis Glover and has four children, Corinne Ramsay Glover, James Davis Glover, Jr., Marthalu Glover, and Julia Allaphair Glover; 5. Robert Flournoy Stubbs; 6. Lucien Quincy Stubbs, Jr.

—By *Jeannette Stubbs Glover (Mrs. J. D.)*

LUCIEN QUINCY STUBBS

TUCKER

Nathan Tucker, eldest child of Gardiner Tucker and Mary Church, was born at Point Judith, R. I., January 19, 1799. He came from pioneer New England stock, one ancestor, Richard Warren, having come to America in 1620 on the Mayflower.

After some years spent in Connecticut with his Church grandparents, attending a preparatory school for Yale, the wanderlust seized him and he made several voyages to Europe. On returning from one of these trips he landed at Charleston, South Carolina, and liking the South so well he decided to remain, locating first at Fort Hawkins (now Macon), Georgia. He first took a course in law and then decided to become a physician. After preliminary work in Georgia, he graduatetd from the Philadelphia Medical College. Returning to Georgia, he located in Laurens County where he was married to Anna Horn, daughter of Josiah Horn and Rebecca Young, October 14, 1830. There were seven children by this union as follows:

Lucien Quincy Tucker, born April 12, 1832; Eugenia, born January 29, 1834; Josephine, who died in infancy; Georgia, born July 31, 1838; Ella, born March 19, 1840; Nathan, died in infancy; Ophelia, born October 6, 1844.

Lucien Quincy Tucker was sent to Princeton University and then graduated in medicine. At the outbreak of the War Between the States he entered the Confederate service and was elected Captain of one of the first companies organized in Laurens County. He gave a splendid account of himself at the front, but physicians were needed more than line officers and he was transferred to the Medical Corps. He was married to Mary Arnold Smith, of Tattnall County. His successful career as a prominent physician was cut short by his death at the age of 42.

Eugenia Tucker was married twice. Her first husband was Judge Arthur Cochran, for whom the city of Cochran was named. After his death she was married to Dr. Fitzgerald, of Macon. She was educated at Wesleyan College, as were all of her sisters, and was graduated with first honors. She organized the Adelphian Society, now the Alpha Delta Pi Sorority. There is a bench at Wesleyan dedicated to her. She was a social leader of Macon.

Georgia Tucker was married to Franklin Palmer Stubbs, of Monroe, Louisiana, who became a very prominent lawyer and planter. He was a first cousin of Colonel John M. Stubbs, who married Ella, the next daughter. Ophelia was married to Robert Flournoy, a brilliant young lawyer.

Dr. Tucker was a very prominent physician and was one of the six largest planters in the County. He owned many slaves who were extremely fond of him. He was noted for his kindness and did a great deal of charity in the County. His home was called

"Buena Vista" and was the center of hospitality. Among his patients and close friends were General David Blacksshear and Governor George M. Troup.

He was in no sense a politician, but served in the Senate in 1843-44 and was a member of the Georgia Secessional Convention. He voted against secession, as did Governor Johnson, Alexander Stephens, and others, but was very loyal to the South, although a New Englander by birth. His only son and all of his sons-in-law were officers in the Confederate Army. He died at the age of seventy at his Laurens County home. His monument was considered very handsome for the time and was the subject of much interest to the people of the surrounding country. It bears the inscription: "He was the noblest work of God, an honest man."

—By Hal M. Stanley.

WALDRON

Howard Chambless Waldron, the son of Marion Francis Waldron (born 1864; died 1940) and Minnie Goodwin Waldron (born 1868; married December 10, 1892), was born in Houston County, Georgia, December 23, 1893. When he was two years old his father and mother located in Bibb County and it was in the schools of that county and in Macon, Georgia, that he received his education.

In 1915 Mr. Waldron came to Dublin and in 1917 he became affiliated with the First National Bank of Dublin where he served as an officer until 1928 when he entered the general insurance and real estate business.

On October 12, 1921, he was married to Anna Pearl White, of Dublin. Their daughters are Maria Haynes Waldron, born June 26, 1924, and Rose Goodwin Waldron, born February 27, 1926.

Mr. Waldron has been prominently identified with religious, civic and fraternal organizations, being a member of the Board of Deacons of the First Baptist Church of Dublin, a charter member of the Exchange Club of Dublin and a member of Laurens Lodge No. 75, F. & A. M., Harmony Chapter R. A. M., Knights Templar and a member of Al Sihah Shrine Temple.

On his maternal side Mr. Waldron descends from the Hicks and Goodwin families of middle Georgia, his grandmother being Josephine Hicks before her marriage to Mr. Goodwin.

Malcom McEnnis Waldron (born, 1832; died, 1876), and Lucinda Chambless Waldron (born,, 1838; died, 1883), of Bibb County, Georgia, were his paternal grandparents. Francis C. Waldron and Mary Jane McMillen Waldron (married, November 17, 1831), were his paternal grandparents, the Waldron family coming to Georgia from Virginia. Records show that the Waldron family originally came from England as early as 1635, settling in the New England States.

Samuel Chambless (born, 1772; died, 1869), and Jane Dannelly Chambless (married, November 30, 1814), having come into Georgia in 1818 from North Carolina, were Mr. Waldron's great grandparents. Christopher Chambless, born in Rockingham County, Virginia, April 4, 1746, and died in Warren County, Georgia, in 1842, was married to Mary Taylor (a cousin of Ex-President Zachery Taylor) who was born in Orange County, Virginia, were his great, great grandparents. Christopher Chambless was a soldier from Virginia in General Nathaniel Green's command during the Revolutionary War.

—*By Anna Pearl White Waldron (Mrs. H. C.)*

WALKER

William Henry Walker was born in Stewart County, Georgia, in 1846, the son of Freeman Walker and Virginia Mitchell Walker; the grandson of Ben Persons Walker, of Taylor County, and Hannah Brantley.

At the outbreak of the Civil War he was anxious to enlist in the Confederate Army with his only brother, Benjamin, but was too young. However, shortly before the close of the war he was accepted and served at Andersonville. Benjamin was killed at the Battle of Manassas.

In 1875, William Henry Walker married Willie Delilah Finch, of Twiggs County. She was the daughter of William Finch and Sarah Zachry Finch, who was the daughter of William Zachry, of Columbia County. Mr. Walker moved his family to Laurens County in 1890 and he was a merchant in Dublin until his death in 1910. His wife survived him many years, living to the age of 81. "Grandma Walker," as she was fondly called, was a distinguished figure in church, social and patriotic club activities, being an honorary member of the United Daughters of the Confederacy. She was a member of the First Baptist Church in which she was a faithful worker. She lived with her only daughter until her death, May 22, 1938.

The children of William Henry and Willie D. Walker were as follows:

1. Freeman Walker, born in Dawson, Georgia, in 1878; married Mary M. Smith, daughter of T. D. Smith, in 1909. Their only child, Sara Will, married William A. Legwin, of Augusta, Georgia, in 1932. Freeman Walker died March 5, 1937.

2. Cicero S. Walker, married Virginia Byrd Metts, daughter of Lewis M. Metts; two children, Virginia Walker, who married Cecil E. Carroll, one daughter, Virginia Cecile Carroll, born May 31, 1938; Cicero S. Walker, Jr., married Ruth Layne, of Chattanooga, Tennessee. Cicero Walker, Sr., died November 22, 1937.

3. William Finch Walker, married Maggie Mae Matthews, of Prattsburg, Georgia; two sons: Brown and James Walker.

4. Ben P. Walker, married Mamie Dewberry, of Stillmore, Georgia, in 1908; three children: Miriam (Mrs. Wainwright), Ben, Jr., and Freeman Walker.

5. George Walker, married Nelle Kitchens, of Sandersville, Georgia, in 1911; three children: Willie Mae, George, Jr., and W. D. Walker (deceased).

6. Captain Lawrence Walker, soldier in the World War; married Ruth Beacham, in 1919; one daughter, Frances Walker. Captain Lawrence Walker died in 1923.

7. Sallie Walker, married, first, Leon Long, of Sparta, Georgia; one daughter, Maudine Long, now Mrs. Thomas S. Turner; married, second, Frank R. Zetterower, of Statesboro, Georgia; two sons: Frank Zetterower, Jr., who married Nona Thackston, of Statesboro, Georgia, and John Walker Zetterower.

—By Sara Will Walker Legwin (Mrs. W. A.)

WARREN

One of the pioneer citizens of Laurens County was Josiah Warren, locating here indeed before it was a county. Here he came in 1804, the year that we acquired from the Creek Indians the lands on which he settled, and opened up a plantation in the fork of Turkey Creek and the Oconee River. He was born in Unslow County, North Carolina, March 22, 1736, where in 1780 he married Nancy Doty, born May 15, 1763, the daughter of Benijah Doty, a member of the Provincial Congress of North Carolina. The marriage license, which is still of record, refers to him as "Josiah Warren, gent."

He served as a soldier from his native county in the American Revolution. Shortly after the peace was declared he and his wife moved to Burke County, Georgia, and settled near Brier Creek. In Burke, he was a deacon of Bark Creek Baptist Church, and in Laurens became one of the county's early magistrates. Both Mr. Warren and his wife died in the year 1809, and were buried at Poplar Springs Church. It was written long ago by one who knew them both that they were "noted for their elevated Christian character and their decided hostility to the use of alcoholic liquors."

There has always been a tradition in the family that Josiah Warren was the lone horseman who rode upon the scene at Louisville just as the "Yazoo Fraud" records were about to be burned and, producing a sun glass, handed it to James Jackson with the statement that it would require fire from Heaven to destroy the iniquity of those corrupt parchments; and that it was his glass that was used on that memorable occasion in focusing the sun's rays on the papers. Most writers of the period in telling of this most dramatic incident in our State's history, add that the horseman, immediately after the ceremony was over, rode quietly away without giving his name.

Josiah and Nancy Doty Warren were parents of fourteen children. The eldest daughter married Reverend Charles Culpepper, of Wilkinson County, a valiant soldier of the cross. It was to Mr. Culpepper and his wife to whom was committed, after the death of Mr. and Mrs. Warren, the care of the younger children. Among these were three sons, Kittrell, who became a Baptist preacher, a sketch of whom may be found in Campbell's History of the Georgia Baptists. Kittrell was the father of Rev. Dr. E. W. Warren, whose pastorates at the First Baptist Church in Macon, the First Baptist Church in Atlanta, and in Richmond, made him prominent in church circles. The second of these three sons was Lott Warren, a Senator from Laurens in the General Assembly, Solicitor-General, Judge and Congressman. He is the author of the present "one hour rule" in the National House of Representatives. His wife was Jane DeSableaux, a ward of General David Blackshear, and a daughter of a French gentleman who served with LaFayette in the Revolution. Judge Lott Warren's son was Judge L. P. D. Warren, of the Superior Courts of the Albany Circuit. The third son was Eli, for years a resident of Laurens, a Representative and State Senator from Laurens, a member of two Constitutional Conventions, in early life a Brigadier General of Militia, and who in the meridium of his life, as has been recorded by a careful historian of the time, had the largest practice of any lawyer in the State. His wife was Jane Love, daughter of another pioneer of Laurens County, Amos Love. General Warren's son, Hon. Josiah L. Warren, sat side by side with him in two Constitutional Conventions. A great grand-daughter of General Warren is Dr. Grace Warren Landrum, Dean of Women at William and Mary College in Virginia. Other descendants are the lately beloved Margaret Landrum Watkins (Mrs. F. N. Watkins), so affectionately remembered in Dublin, and her two daughters: Grace, now Mrs. Curtis William Lampson, of Richmond, Virginia, and Margaret Watkins, of Dublin. Another descendant of Josiah Warren is Mrs. Caroline O'Day, at this time Congressman at Large from the State of New York. Mrs. O'Day is a granddaughter of General Warren. Warren Grice, Associate Justice of the Supreme Court of Georgia, is also a descendant.

Of the old patriot himself, but little at this day is known, other than what is stated above. Of his personality there is little to tell. Of the battles in which he fought, the wounds, if any, he received, the campaigns in which he was engaged, his experiences on the tented field and on the march, of the hardships he endured, there are none to bear witness.

Of his descendants, eight have been lawmakers of Georgia, one, of Florida. One has been Attorney General of Georgia and now a member of Georgia's Supreme Court. Two have been Solicitors-

General of the largest circuit in Georgia. Three have been Judges of the Superior Courts. Three have sat in three different Constitutional Conventions of Georgia. Two have sat in the American Congress. Numbers of them have worn their country's uniform in the wars. Two of his sons-in-law, two of his sons, two grandsons, and two great grandsons have been preachers. Six of his descendants have served as trustees of Mercer University. There are those today in at least twenty States who trace their lineage not to some titled lord whose bones repose amid legal trappings in Westminster Abbey, but to this private soldier of the Revolution and early settler of this county, "unknown to fortune and to fame," whose venerable dust was laid beneath the sod at Poplar Springs Church, in a country graveyard "where the rude forefathers of the hamlet sleep."

—By a descendant of General Eli Warren.

WEAVER

Authentic genealogical data in the New York City Public Library states that the name of Weaver was taken from the Manor of Weever near Middlewick, Cheshire. For a long time the Weaver family was found principally in the three counties bordering on Wales, viz.: Cheshire, Shropshire and Herefordshire. The family has had a coat of arms for more than 650 years.

The Weaver families in America descended mostly from Clement Weaver, No. 42 in Welsh Pedigrees. He lived in Glastonbury, Somersetshire, England, where he married Rebecca Holbrook, on May 19, 1617. Their son, Clement, born in Glastonbury between 1617 and 1625, came to America where he married Mary Freeborn, daughter of one of the founders of Rhode Island. Many of their descendants over the United States have borne the names Clement, John, Andrew Jackson, and William.

The immediate ancestors of the Weaver families of Laurens County came from South Carolina, settling six miles from Dublin, near Poplar Springs Church, at or near what is still known as Weaver Hill. There, in the early years of the nineteenth century, lived Jethro Judson Weaver who had left South Carolina with his mother after his father was scalped by the Indians.

His first wife was an Albritton. Children: (1) Jesse, married Mary Perry (their son, John, was a prominent Alabama Baptist minister and his son, Elbert, is a prominent lawyer in Decatur, Alabama); (2) Eliza, married Eason Green. (See Green History).

Jethro Judson Weaver's second wife was Polly Ellison, married January 22, 1818. Children: 1. Jackson, died in childhood. 2. Seaborn, married Susan Ann Perry. Seaborn's son, John J., married Margaret Tillman; children: 1. James Tillman, married Olive Register; 2. Sallie, married L. A. Ryals; 3. Fannie, married Morris A.

Mertz; 4. Maggie, married first, Newman New, and second, Frank L. Butler.

On October 20, 1824, Jethro Judson Weaver married Mary Bracewell, children: 1. Mary Frances, born 1825, married, first, Drury Scarborough, four children; second, Andrew Hobbs (See Hobbs History); 2. Lucy LaFayette, born December 22, 1826, married, first, U. A. Brown, graduate of Oxford University, one son, Dan, killed in War Between the States; married, second, Enoch James St. John (1855), one son, six daughters; 3. Joseph J., married Sallie St. Clair, son, John; 4. Nathan Bracewell, born 1833, married Harriet Aycock, two sons, five daughters; 5. Amanda Malvina, married James St. Clair, two sons, five daughters; 6. Sarah Jane, married Dr. Eli Sams, two sons, four daughters; 7. Piety Comfort, married, first, William Dorsey, second, R. C. Griffith, one son; 8. William Samson, married Matilda McCarley, one son, two daughters; 9. James Madison, died in childhood; 10. Queen Elizabeth, died in childhood.

In 1846, Jethro Judson Weaver sold his plantation and slaves in Laurens County. He moved to Morgan County, Alabama, where he settled in Blue Spring Community. One daughter, Mary Frances, who married Andrew Hobbs, remained in Laurens County where her influence in home, church and community was a power for good. (See Hobbs History).

Jethro Judson Weaver died about 1870 and was buried in Blue Spring, where many of his descendants live. There his daughter, Lucy LaFayette, married her second husband, Enoch James St. John, born near Woodbury, Tennessee, October 24, 1828. They are buried near Jethro Weaver. Children: 1. Leonora Alice, born February 7, 1857, died in girlhood; 2. Mary Lydia, born March 10, 1858, married Jonathan Crow; 3. Sarah Ann, born October 1, 1859, married Louis Akin, two sons, three daughters; 4. Louisa James, born November 2, 1863, married Rev. Walter Paul McDonnald, one son, Walter Herman, one daughter, Eunice Bethsaida; 5. William Joseph, born April 29, 1865, married Emma Perry (Tennessee), four sons, four daughters; 6. Fannie Piety, born August 13, 1869, married Robert Hargrove, seven sons, two daughters; 7. Lucy Ida, born June 2, 1871 , married Campbell Self, two sons, three daughters.

The compiler of this history, Eunice Bethsaida McDonnald, is the great granddaughter of Jethro Weaver. She was born at Baileyton, Alabama, September 11, 1888, and married Dr. Thomas Burton Meadows, college professor, born February 19, 1882, at Bowdon, Georgia. Both taught several years at Georgia State College for Women, Milledgeville. Her oil painting, "Westover," a Colonial home near Milledgeville, is the property of the United States Government and hangs in the Senate Office Building, Washington, D. C., in the suite of Senator Richard B. Russell, of Georgia. Their children are: Thomas Burton, Jr., married Clara Hollinshead; Louise McDonnald Meadows; Paul McDonnald Meadows.

Information regarding the Weaver family in Alabama may be had from her through Mrs. Carl Nelson, Dublin, Georgia.
—*By Eunice McDonald Meadows (Mrs. T. B.)*

WHITE

John Thomas White, the son of Thomas Nelson White and Mary King White, was born in Houston County, Georgia, May 2, 1868. He was a grandson of Benjamin DeLane White and Mary Powell White and a great grandson of John Powell and Sarah Powell, the Powells coming from Virginia to Jones County, Georgia. His paternal great grandfather was Thomas White, who married ——— Davis and also came to Jones County, Georgia, from Virginia. His maternal grandfather and grandmother were John King, Jr., and Miriam Willims King, of Houston County. John King, Sr., and Priscilla Walker King were his great grandparents, coming to Georgia from North Carolina.

In 1887, at the age of nineteen, John Thomas White came to Laurens County, and for several years taught school in the Mount Carmel community and later was mayor and postmaster in the small town of Dexter, teaching school there also for several years.

On January 16, 1895, he was married to Anna Maria Haynes, (see Haynes genealogy), daughter of Mercer Haynes and Rosamond Warren Haynes, of Dublin, where he lived until his death on August 6, 1933.

Soon after coming to Dublin he engaged in the manufacturing of shingles and later owned and operated jointly with his son, Thomas Haynes White, a beehive factory, selling locally and extensively throughout the United States. He spent many years as a traveling representative of unusual merit.

He became a member of the Baptist Church in his early life and served as Clerk of the First Baptist Church of Dublin for a number of years.

Although Mr. White was of a quiet and unassuming nature, he was one of the best posted men of his time and, as a citizen and head of his household, he stood for the higher things of life.

Four children were born to this union, as follows:

Rosamond Nelson White, who married Kendrick Schaufele Moffett on January 5, 1918, now residing in Macon, Georgia. They have one son, Kendrick Schaufele Moffett, Jr., born October 14, 1924.

Anna Pearl White, married Howard Chambless Waldron, October 12, 1921; two daughters were born, Maria Haynes Waldron, on June 26, 1924, and Rose Goodwin Waldron, on February 27, 1926.

Thomas Haynes White, married Charlie Mae Webb on February 8, 1936, and has two children: John Thomas White II, born October 6, 1937, and Charles Haynes White, born July 31, 1940.

Martha Louise White, married Walter Dixon Pinkston, September 26, 1927, has one daughter, Mary Ann Pinkston, born August 17, 1932.

Rosamond White, graduated from Dublin High School and attended Wesleyan Conservatory at Macon, Georgia.

Anna Pearl White, graduated from Dublin High School and attended Brenau College, Gainesville, Georgia.

Thomas Haynes White, who attended school in Dublin and the Georgia Military Academy at College Park, Georgia, is a registered Civil Engineer and did government work for a number of years in the Panama Canal Zone.

Martha Louise White also completed her high school work in Dublin and graduated from Georgia State College for Women at Milledgeville, Georgia.

—*By Anna Haynes White (Mrs. J. Tom).*

WILLIAMS

George Herschel Williams was born March 5, 1870, on a farm in Bryan County, Georgia, and remained there as a farm boy until he was grown. Educated only in the common schools of his community. Moved to Swainsboro to read law in the office of his brother, R. J. Williams, and was admitted and licensed to practice in open court, October 16, 1892. Located in Wrightsville in 1893. Moved to Mt. Vernon in 1894. Moved back to Swainsboro in 1896. Married Nettie Moring in 1896. To this union were born four children: Gladstone Williams, Washington, D. C.; Berner Williams, Eastman, Georgia; G. H. Williams, Jr., died, 1918; and Antoinette, known as Beauty, now in Columbia, South Carolina.

George Herschel Williams was Representative of Emanuel County in the Legislature, 1898-99. Moved to Dublin in 1900. His first wife, Nettie Moring, died in Dublin, October 23, 1920. . In 1922 he married Jessie Rice Alsup. To this union were born two daughters, Jessie Dell, better known as Topsy, and George Williams.

Mr. Williams had but little school training, but was a student of history and his profession. He was a strong believer in the elementary branches of our public schools and was for many years President of the Board of Education, City of Dublin. He gave all of his children college educations and helped to support and educate several other boys and girls. He is a member of the Baptist Church and votes an independent ticket.

He has but little regard for secret orders and political parties. He is known as the "cornfield" lawyer, and it is said and generally understood that he feeds more people, without charge, than any man in Laurens County.

George Herschel Williams is a son of Stephen M. and Carrie

Pughsley Williams, who married in 1852. To this union were born ten children. All lived to be grown and had families, to-wit: Emma, married James Wright; Robert J., married Mollie Camp; Sidney A., married Eva Cone; William P., married Mattie Gibson; Sallie G., married Paul Purvis; Stephen G., married Jennie Roach; Carrie Bell, married J. O. Stephens; George Herschel, married, first, Nettie Moring, second, Jessie Rice Alsup; Nellie, married James Roach; Jacob Carlton, married Lizzie Williams.

Carrie Pughsley was born in Jefferson County, December 26, 1836, on the same day that her father was twenty-one years old. She died in Dublin on July 5, 1911. Her father was Robert J. Pughsley, of English ancestry, and her mother was Martha Welch, of Jeffersonville, Georgia.

Stephen M. Williams was born in Telfair County, September 12, 1826, and died in Bryan County, November 1, 1891. He was the youngest child of his father's family. He was a son of James M. Williams, who was born in Hanover County, Virginia, in 1796. He died in 1832 just across the west side of Ocmulgee River from Jacksonville, the then site of Telfair County, Georgia, where his family lived. At that time the Ocmulgee River was the line between the Whites and Indians. James M. Williams had obtained from the Indians pasture lands on their side of the river, and owned a herd of cattle, pasturing them there. He had a log house on this land and sometimes spent several days there looking after his cattle. It was thought then that all the Indians were friendly to him, but on the night of his death, he and his small son, Stephen M., spent the night in this small log house, the Indians made a raid, killed and scalped him, but the six-year-old boy, Stephen M., escaped unhurt, and was found next day. James M. Williams, the son of James Williams, was born in 1769 and died in 1820 in Hanover County, Virginia.

James Williams was the son of Colonel James Williams, who was born in Hanover County, Virginia, November 10, 1741, and married to Mary Wallace in 1762. He was an outstanding figure in the Revolutionary War; was appointed Lieutenant Colonel of State in 1776; participated in the Battle of Stono and gained a victory at Musgrove Mills. In August, 1780, was wounded and died while leading one of the attacking columns in the Battle of Kings Mountain, October 8, 1780.

Colonel James Williams was the son of Daniel Williams, born September 28, 1710, and his legal and lawful wife, Ursula Henderson. They were married October 19, 1732.

Daniel Williams was the son of John Williams, born 1679, and his legal and lawful wife, Mary Williams, born September 26, 1684.

BIBLIOGRAPHY

Columbia Encyclopedia, Volume No. 32.
Ramsay's History of South Carolina, page 344.
Moultrie's Memoirs, 220, 468, 17.
O'Neal's Annals of Newberry, South Carolina.
See National D. A. R., No. 56157.

—*By Jessie Rice Alsup Williams (Mrs. G. H.)*

INDEX

NOTE: Throughout the text appear many long lists of names. Among these are the Land Lottery list on pages 34-39; the Roster of Confederate Soldiers from Laurens County, on pages 61-63; and the early wills and marriages on pages 267-99. These lists are noted in the index. The individual names comprising them can readily be located within the lists themselves.

A. A. A., 135-36
Abolitionists, 50
Academy, Dublin, 181
Adams Family, 303-07
Adams, Benjamin, 13, 27
Adams, John Quincy, 41
Adams, John S., 80, 84, 85, 227, 306-07
Adams, Mrs. John S., 41, 99, 241, 243, 307
Adams, Lucia Augusta Stanley, 307, 508
Adams, Peter, 303
Adams, Prentice, 110, 307, 508
Agriculture in Laurens County
   Dairying, 129-30
   Livestock, 129, 132
   Lumbering and turpentining, 132
   Peach Growing, 131
   Pecan Growing, 131-32
Air mail service, 193
Albriton, John, 145
Alexander, C. T., & Sons Lumber Company, 115
Allagood, Hardy, 154
Allagood, M. L., 154
Allagood, Sarah, 154
Allgood, Edith Mae, 136
Alliance, Farmers', 94
Alsup Family, 307-08
Alsup, Angus Dillon, 307-08
Alsup, Henry Clay, 308
Alsup, Martin, 108, 110, 308
Alsup, William Byrn, 308
American Legion, Post No. 17, 255
American Legion Auxiliary, 255
Anderson, Gilliard, 25
Anthony, J. D., 163-64
Anti-federalist party, 45
Apalachicola, 29
Arnau Family, 309-10
Arnau, Albert R., 103, 309
Arnau, Miquel Marie Depalar, 309
Arnau, R. M., 92, 103, 309
Arnold, T. A., 113
Arnold, Willis Roberson, 412
Arrowheads, Indian, 5
Associations, Baptist, 160-61
Atkinson, B. C., 58

Attaway, Ezekiel, 30
Automobile dealers, 116
Autossee, 29, 30
Auxiliary, American Legion, 255
Avery, Will, 140

Bacon, B. A., 149
Bacote, Lucius T., 139
Baggett Family, 310-11
Baggett, Eva Clyde Bass, 311
Baggett, John Redding, 156, 310-11
Baggett, Morris A., 311
Baker, Jordan, 151
Baker, R. L., 152
Baker, R. T., 155
Baker, W. G., 152
Baker, W. J., 149, 151
Baker, William, 146, 153
Baldwin, Jesse, 85
Bales, William, 104
Balkcom, Thomas N., 139
Ballard Family, 311-14
Ballard, Benjamin Franklin, 313
Ballard, Elisha, 25, 312
Ballard, Frank, 51
Ballard, Laurence, 51
Ballard, Robert E., 110
Banks, Laurens County, 232-34
   Bank of Dublin, 232, 233
   Citizens' Bank, 233
   Citizens' & Southern National Bank, 234
   City National Bank, 233
   Commercial Bank of Dublin, 233
   Dublin Banking Company, 232
   Dublin-Laurens Bank, 232
   Farmers & Merchants Bank, 234
   First National Bank, 232
   Georgia State Bank, 233
   Laurens Banking Company, 232
   Southern Exchange Bank of Dublin, 233
Baptist Associations, 160-61
Baptist Churches, see Churches, Baptist
Bar, Laurens County, 80
Barbour, Thomas, 80
Barkaloo Rifles, 58, 59

Barlow, James, 240
Barnes, E. T., 113, 128, 130, 134, 464
Barnes, Mrs. E. T., 40, 243
Barnet, James, 110
Barrett, E. B., 151, 152, 178
Barron, E. D., 150
Bartlett, N. G., 105, 108, 129
Bashinski, Helen McCall, 113, 134
Bashinski, Izzie, 127
Bass, J. D., 113
Bates, John D., 58
Baxter, Andrew, 413-14
Baxter, James, 413
Baum Family, 315-17
Baum, Adolph, 95, 317
Baum, Alexander, 315
Baum, Napoleon Bonaparte, 95, 103, 315-16
Beacham, J. H., 115
Beaty, William, 18
Bedingfield Family, 317-21
Bedingfield, Edna Cornelia, 320-21
Bedingfield, H. R., 108, 320
Bedingfield, J. E., 116
Bedingfield, John Wells, 319-20
Bedingfield, Mary Caroline, 320
Bedingfield, R. A., 156, 318
Bedingfield, Sarah Jane, 321
Bedingfield, William Andrew, 318
Belcher, Mrs. G. W., 152
Bell, Ray, 139
Belleville, 39
Bennett, W. B., 83
Benton, Elijah, 151
Berryhill, Andrew, 58
Bertha Theatre, 106
Bickers, D. G., 126
Big Shoals, Battle of, 8
Bishop, G. W., 58
Bishop, Merlin, 180
Black Family, 321-22
Black, E. L., 116, 321-22
Black, Emmett, 116, 321
Black, Thomas Howard, 321
Blackshear Family, 322-27
Blackshear, A. D., 108, 324
Blackshear, Alexander, 77, 86, 122
Blackshear, Belle, 42, 324
Blackshear, D. S., 240
Blackshear, Daniel, 54
Blackshear, David, 16, 17, 23, 25, 27, 28, 29, 42, 44, 49, 79, 322-23
Blackshear, E. J., 16, 52, 83, 84
Blackshear, Everard, 57, 69, 120, 323-24
Blackshear, Fannie Hamilton, 23, 323
Blackshear, Hardeman, 85
Blackshear, James, 146, 322
Blackshear, Joseph, 25, 42
Blackshear, Julia Thweatt, 18, 69
Blackshear, M. H., 80

Blackshear, Mosley, 42
Blackshear, Robert H., 179, 324
Blackshear, T. J., 74, 75, 94, 128, 327
Blackshear, Zoe, 42
Blackshear's Ferry, 15, 16, 18, 54
 Ferrymen, 17
Blackshear Guards, 57, 58, 60
Blackshear's Mill, 54
Blackshear Road, 29
Blackshear Trail, 44, 142
Bloodworth Family, 327-28
Bloodworth, John, 327
Board of County Commissioners, 73
Board of Equalizers, 108
Board of Trade established, 104
Boat transportation company organized, 89
Boats of Oconee River, 123-25
Boll Weevil, 127
Bolton, Euri Belle, 187-88
Bond issue for schools, 95
Bond issues
 1902, 103; 1904, 103, 104; 1905, 105; 1910, 106; 1918, 106; 1919, 106; 1921, 112; 1936, 112; 1937, 112; 1939, 112
Boy Scouts, 259-60
Boykin, William, 13
Bracewell, James, 122
Braddy, R. E., 129
Branch, Jonathan, 19
Brandon, D. S., 105
Brandon & Dreyer, 103
Brantley, C. W., 104, 126
Brantley, William G., 125
Brazeal Family, 90
Brett, Annie, 148
Brewton, 198-99
Brewton & Pineora Railroad, 94
Brick building, first, erected 1876, 90
Bridge across Oconee River, 92
Brigham Family, 328-29
Brigham-Claxton Hospital, 230
Brigham-Jones Company, 103
Brigham, William Randall, 328-29
Brinson, W. W., 105
Brookins, Sara F., 139
Brown, A. T., 87
Brown, Benjamin, 13
Brown, Coke, 115
Brown, Fred L., 135
Brown, Mrs. Fred L., 249
Brown, J. L., 150
Brown, J. Ware, 152
Brown, Mattilu Burch, 138
Brown, R. E., 150
Brown & Phillips, 104
Brumby, A. V., 57, 60
Brunson, William, 110
Bryan, Thomas, 43

Bryan, William Jennings and "free coinage," 95
Bryant, Florida, 146
Buchan Family, 329-30
Buchan, John Wesley, 329
Buchanan, Reverend, 151
Buggy and harness business in 1900's, 104
Burch Family, 330-34
Burch, Alfred, 51, 153, 331
Burch, Benjamin, 332-33
Burch, Charlton O., 334
Burch, Daniel W., 331-32
Burch, F. H., 95
Burch, J. E., 96
Burch, John, 331
Burch, John Benjamin, 333-34
Burch, M. L., 84
Burch, Nathan, 179, 334
Burch, William, 333
Burch, William Gaulden, 334
Burns, W. S. & Company, 104
Bus lines, 113
Bush, D. J., 58
Bush, J. Z., 156
Bush, James, 148
Bush, Levi, 147
Bush, W. W., 98
Bush, William, 25
Buy-a-Bale Movement, 108
Byrne, John W., 127

Cadwell, 212-15
Caldwell, Charles B., 105
Calhoun, Irwin, 18
Callaway, T. W., 152
Callaway, W. S., 137
Camp Family, 335-37
Camp, Ernest, 236, 336
Camp, Joseph, 335
Camp, R. Earl, 227, 337
Campbell, A. B., 146
Cardinals, St. Louis, 113
Carnegie Library, 237-39
Carroll, Cecil, 105, 114, 135
Carroll, Dr. James C., 228
Carswell, Josephine Rowe, 71, 152
Carter, J. Warren, 108
Catholic Church, see Church, Catholic
Cawley, William, 29
Cedar Grove Community, 219-20
Cemetery, Northview, 103
Cemetery, old, 99
Citizen's Bank, 233
City Court of Dublin, 84-85
  Clerks, 84
  Judges, 84
  Sheriffs, 84
  Solicitors, 85
City National Bank, 233

City officials, 1873-1941, 117
Civic Division of Laurens County, 118
Civilian Relief Committee, 109
Chain gang established, 89
Chamber of Commerce, established, 105
  reorganized, 105
Chappell Family, 338
Chappell, Dr. James Thomas, 54, 58, 59, 338
Chappell, Ira S., 84, 338
Chappell, Mrs. I. S., 152
Chappell, Thomas II, 338
Chappell's Mill, 54
Chautauqua Week, annual, 186
Chavous, Emma C., 139
Chavous, Mrs. Vernon, 152
Cheek, Dr. Ovid, 111, 140, 420
Chehaw, 30-31
Cherry, J. R., 129, 135
Chief Kitchee, 16
Chipley, I. T., 155
Chipley, James S., 155
Chivers Family, 339-40
Chivers, O. L., Company, 115
Christian Church, see Churches, Christian
Christian Reflector, The, 50
Churches, colored
  Baptist
    Springfield Baptist Church, 175-76; Turkey Creek Church, 176
  Methodist, 176
  Other, 177
Churches, recent, 175
Churches, white
  Baptist
    Antioch, 159-60; Baker, 159; Bethesda, 152; Bethlehem, 146-48; Bethsaida, 157; Blue Springs, 156; Blue Water, 148-50; Centerville, 153; First Baptist Church of Dublin, 150-52; Jefferson Street Baptist Church, 160; Laurens Hill, 216-19; Marie, 157-58; Mount Carmel, 153; Mount Zion, 156; New Bethel, 157; New Hope, 153; Oconee, 155; Olivet, 159; Pleasant Hill, 159; Pleasant Springs, 155; Poplar Springs, 144-46; Poplar Springs (South), 157; Rock Springs, 153; Shady Grove, 154-55; Snow Hill, 156; White Springs, 156-57
  Catholic
    Dublin Catholic Church, 171
  Christian
    First Christian Church, 174
  Episcopal
    Christ Episcopal Church, 170-71

Methodist
  Boiling Springs, 165; Buckhorn, 164-65; Carter's Chapel, 169; Centenary, 170; Dexter, 202; First Methodist Church of Dublin, 165-66; Gethsemane, 165; Harmony, 170; Marvin, 168; Mount Zion, 168; New Evergreen, 169; Pine Hill, 170; Pleasant Hill, 168; Rockledge, 203-04; Thomas Chapel, 169
Pentecostal
  Dexter Pentecostal Church, 202
Presbyterian
  Henry Memorial Presbyterian Church, 171-74
Primitive Baptist
  Bay Springs, 162-63; Norris Chapel, 162; Reedy Springs, 163; Silver Leaf, 162; Union, 162
Churchwell Brothers Store, 115
Clark Family, 340-41
Clark, Arthur, 340
Clark, Calphey, 59
Clark, Fannie, 340
Clark, John, 25, 26, 39, 45, 75, 340
Clark-McQuaig Family, 341-42
Clark, Oscar, 341
Clarke, Elijah, 11, 45
Clark, J. A., 94
Claxton Family, 342-43
Claxton, Dr. E. B., 130, 140, 342
Claxton, Dr. M. Z., 116, 117, 343
Claxton-Montford Hospital, 230
Claxton Sanitorium, 230
Clerks, City Court of Dublin, listed, 84
Coats, John G., 142, 146
Coats, Robert, 27, 49, 146
Cobb, Essie Mae, 138
Cobb, Thomas R. R., 56
Cochran Family, 344-47
Cochran, Mrs. B. F., 152
Cochran, Benjamin, 344
Cochran, Frank, 179-80, 344-45
Cochran, Mrs. Guy V., 152
Cochran, M. E., 116, 132, 345
Cochran-Vason-Pearman Lineage, 346-47
Coleman Family, 347-51
Coleman, Mrs. A. A., 140
Coleman, Dr. A. T., 140, 347-48
Coleman, Mrs. A. T., 243, 251
Coleman, Elijah, 58
Coleman Hospital, 230
Coleman, Joel A., 58, 140, 349
Coleman, L. O., 58
Coleman, Mrs. R. C., 152
Coley, H. H., 127
Colville, The, 124, 125
Combs, Daniel, 51

Commerce, Chamber of, established, 105 reorganized, 105
Commercial Bank of Dublin, 233
Commissioners, County, Board of, 73
Commissioners of Laurens County, roster of, 61
Commissioners of Roads and Revenues, 74-75
  Board Members from 1896, 74-75
Coney, Joel, 49, 92, 126
Confederate Soldiers from Laurens, 61-63
Confederate States of America, 56
Confederate Veterans, Reunion 1920, 111
Confederate War, 56-69
Congressional District, changes concerning Laurens County, 118-19
Conrad, Holmes, 43
Conyers, S. V., 108
Cook, J. Eugene, 83
Cook, Needham, 50
Cook, Phil, 81
Coombs, David H., 73
Cooper, May, 87
Cordell, H. L., 138, 139
Corker, Burke, 110
Corker, F. G., 84, 98, 104
Coroners of Laurens County, 224
Cotton export firms, 127
Cotton growing, 44, 45
Cotton plantations, development of, 49
Cotton production, 124-27
Cotton production, effects of boll weevil on, 127
Cotton Warehouses, 127
Country Club, Dublin, 111
County Commissioners, Board of, 73
County Court, created 1866, 84
County Treasurers, 224
Couric, J. M., 127
Courier-Dispatch, The, 236
Courier-Herald, 236
Courier, The Dublin, 235
Court, City of Dublin
  judges, 84; sheriffs, 84; clerks, 84; solicitors, 85
Court, Clerks of, list, 82
Court, County, created 1866, 84
Court, Federal, 85
Court House and Jail, 85
Court, Inferior, 72-74
Court, Inferior, last session—1868 73
Court of Ordinary, 72-74
Court of Ordinary, created 1852, 73
Court, Superior, Laurens County, list of judges, 82
Court System, Laurens County, 75-85
Court System, Laurens County, First Indictment, 76
Cowart, Mrs. A. A., 152
Cox, W. R., 155

530

Creek, Hunger and Hardship, 3
Creek Indians, 3
Creek, Turkey, 42
Crisp, Charles F., 125
Crockett, C. C., 140
Crop Diversification, 129-132
Crop rotation program, 130-31
Cross Roads Community, 220
Crowe, Grady ., 139
Cullens, O. L., 127
Culpepper, Charles, 145
Cunningham, Lieutenant, 8
Currell Family, 351-52
Currell, George, 54, 55, 352
Currell, Henry, 59, 226, 352
Currell, Minkie, 42, 351
Currell, Palmer, 110
Currie, A. L., 150
Currie, H. M., 137
Currie, Rev. M. A., 150

Dairying, 129-30
Daley, A. F., 93
Daley, Alexa, 136
Daniel Family, 352-53
Daniel, Benjamin, 25, 352
Daniel, Cecil, 150, 179
Daniel, George, 147
Daniel, J. A., 59
Daniel, John, 353
Daniel, Robert, 13
Daniell Family, 353-55
Daniell, David G., 147, 151, 152, 178
Daniell, George W., 354
Daniell, Joseph Blackshear, 354
Daniell, Walter, 75, 140, 355
D. A. R., *see* Daughters of the American Revolution
Dasher, Martin, 55
Daughters of the American Revolution, 40, 111
Daughters of the American Revolution. John Laurens Chapter, 241-43
  Charter Members, 241
  Junior Group organized, 242
Davidson, Victor, *History of Wilkinson County*, 2, 7, 9
Davis, Alex. L., 110
Davis, George B., 108
Davis, Jefferson, 66-69
Davis, Jefferson, elected president of Confederacy, 56
Davis, John, 67, 68, 69
Davis, M. 155
Davis, W. C., 81
Dawkkins, Mrs. R. L., 149
Dealers, Automobile, 116
Deen, Elijah, 79
Deese Family, 355-56
Deese, R. F., 104, 355

Deese, R. F. & Company, 104
Democratic Party, 45
Denson, Dannie M., 139
Denson, Joseph, 13, 122
Denson, Joseph, Sr., 122
Dentists of Laurens County, 231
Department Stores, *see* Stores, Department
Department Stores in 1900's, 103-04
Derrick, Pauline, 129
De Soto, Hernando, in Laurens County and Georgia, 3
Devereaux, C. D., 140
Dexter, 199-203
Diamond's Landing, Ferry, 89-90
Diamond Landing, Indian Mound near, 2
Dispatch, The Dublin, 235
Diversification of Crops, 124-32
Divorce, first case in Laurens County, 79
Dixie Boys, 61
Dixon, Mayo, 54
Dixon, T. R., 58
Dixon, W. D., 106
Dominey, Benjamin, 58
Donaldson Family, 356-57
Donaldson, Rev. J. M., 148, 155, 178, 356
Donaldson, William H., 357
Dooley, Thomas, Capt., 8
Dorsey, Benjamin, 13
Douglas, Frederick, 60
Douglas, Jones, 488
Douglas, P. W., 58
Douglas, Dr. Peyton, 228
Dow, Lorenzo, 163
Drake, James, 78
Drew Family, 357-58
Drew, John, 357
Drug Store, first, opened 1872, 90
Dublin, named by Jonathan Sawyer, 14
Dublin, incorporated December 9, 1812, 13
Dublin, re-incorporated 1860, 54
Dublin, re-incorporated 1873, 90
Dublin Academy, 182
Dublin, Bank of, 232
Dublin, business establishments in 1900's
  blacksmith and carriage shop, 104
  buggy and harness business, 104
  department stores, 103
  drug stores, 104
  furniture factory, 104
  grocery stores, 103
  hame factory, 104
  hardware, 104
  ice factory, 104
  jewelry, 104
  livery stable, 104
  moving picture theatre, 106
  oil mill, 104

531

opera house, 106
optometrist, 104
Dublin, City of
  Charters, 117
  Chiefs of Police since 1873, 117
  City Clerks since 1873, 117
  Form of Government, 117
  Mayors since 1873, 117
  Population, 1940, 117
Dublin, City officials 1873-1941, 117
Dublin Clinic, 230
Dublin Country Club, 111
Dublin, Fire of 1885, 92
Dublin Garden Club, 252-53
Dublin, Indian Mounds near, 1-3
Dublin, Jewish Citizens in, 95
Dublin-Laurens Bank, 232
Dublin-Laurens County Council of Parent-Teacher Association see Parent-Teacher Association
Dublin, Light plant sold to Georgia Power Company, 112
Dublin Live Stock and Commission Company, 132
Dublin Mercantile Company, 95
Dublin, principal business establishments in '90's, 95
Dublin Production Credit Association, 113
Dublin, public well, 95
Dublin, Red Cross work in, 108-09
Dublin Sanitorium, 230
Dublin Sash and Door Company, 115
Dublin, in Seventies and Eighties, 90
Dublin and Southwestern Railroad, 94
Dublin Telegraph Company incorporated, 1878, 92
Dublin and Wrightsville Railroad Company, 93
Dudley, 204-06
Duett, Henry, 122
Duett, Robert, 122
Duggan Family, 358-61
Duggan, James Barnes, 359
Dull, Mrs. S. R., 509
Dunaway, Velma L., 139
Duncan Family, 361-64
Duncan, Henry, 43, 361
Duncan, John T., 84, 92, 225, 361-63
Duncan, R. H., 59, 361
Duncan, W. E., 58
Dupree, John, 155

Early, Governor, 29
Early, Peter, 75, 78
Early Marriages of Laurens County, 1809-1855, 280-99
Early Wills of Laurens County, 1809-1869, 269-79
Eastern Star, Order of, 254-55

Echols, Bernice, 129
Edge, Harry, 132
Edmondson, Dr. J. W., 111
Edwards, Christopher, 78
Elks, Benevolent and Protective Order of, 258
Ellington Family, 364-65
Ellington, Joel Franklin, 364
Ellis Health Act, 111
Ellison, James, 450
Ellison, Thomas, 450-51
Employment Service, Georgia State, 137
Episcopal Church, see Church, Episcopal
Equalizers, Board of, 108
Eubanks, Ira N., 106
Eubanks, R. W., 155
Everett, Kendall, 180
Everett, M. E., 113
Exchange Club of Dublin, 256
Expulsion of Indians, 16

Faircloth, Benjamin, 78
Faircloth, Bob, 156
Family Histories
  Adams, 303-07; Alsup, 307-08; Arnau, 309-10; Baggett, 310-11; Ballard, 311-14; Baum, 315-17; Bedingfield, 317-21; Black, 321-22; Blackshear, 322-27; Bloodworth, 327-28; Brigham, 328-29; Buchan, 329-30; Burch, 330-34; Camp, 335-37; Chappell, 338; Chivers, 339-40; Clark, 340-42; Claxton, 342-43; Cochran, 344-47; Coleman, 347-51; Currell, 351-52; Daniel, 352-53; Daniell, 353-55; Deese, 355-56; Donaldson, 356-57; Drew, 357-58; Duggan, 358-61; Duncan, 361-64; Ellington, 364-65; Felder, 365-66; Flanders, 366-68; Fordham, 368-70; Freeman, 370-75; Garrett, 375-76; Graham, 376-77; Green, 377-79; Guyton, 379-93; Haines, 394; Harrison, 395; Harvard, 396-97; Haynes, 397-98; Herndon, 398-401; Hicks, 401-03; Hightower, 404-09; Hobbs, 409-14; Horn, 414-17; Johnson, 417-19; Keen, 419-23; Kellam, 424-25; Kittrell, 425-27; Knight, 427-28; Linder, 428-32; Love, 432-34; Metts, 434; Moffett, 435; Moorman, 435-36; New, 437-38; Page, 438-40; Parker, 440-41; Peacock, 441-42; Peters, 442-43; Phillips, 443-45; Pierce, 445-46; Prescott, 447-48; Prince, 448-49; Pritchett, 449-51; Proctor, 451-52; Ramsay, 452-60; Rawls, 460-62; Rentz, 462-63; Rice, 463-67; Rowe, 467-68; Sanders, 469-74; Simmons,

474-82; Simons, 482; Smith, Charles U., 483-84; Smith, Hardy, 484-88; Smith, Joseph Daniel, 489-91; Smith, Thomas Daniel, 491-92; Stanley, 492-511; Stubbs, 511-14; Tucker, 514-15; Waldron, 516-17; Walker, 517-18; Warren, 518-20; Weaver, 520-22; White, 522-23; Williams, 523-25
Farm Agent, movement to secure, 128
Farm market in Dublin, 132
Farm Security Administration, 138-39
Farmers' Alliance, 94
Famers' Alliance Stores, 94
Farmers' Cooperative Association, 129
Farmers' Livestock Association, 129
Farmers' Supply Company, 127
Farmers' Union, 106
Farnall, Elisha, 86, 122
Faulk, U. C. B., 58
Fauna of Laurens County, 134
Federal Court, 85
Federal Court, first officers, 85
Federal Land Bank, 135
Federal Loan Agencies in Laurens County, 135
Federal Surplus Commodities, 136
Felder Family, 365-66
Felder, Thomas B., 226, 365
Felemna, 30
Ferrell, Dr. R. G., 140
Ferries on Oconee River, 123
Ferry, Blackshear's, 54
Ferry, Diamond's Landing, 89-90
Ferrymen, Blackshear's Ferry
 William Beaty, 18; J. L. Bostwick, 18; Irvin Calhoun, 18; J. C. Jones, 18; E. M. Luke, 18; D. W. Skipper, 18; D. M. Watson, 18; Joseph T. Watson, 18; R. A. Watson, 17; S. L. Weaver, 18
Fielder, James M., 60
Fincher, Martha, 136
Finn, J. M., 74, 98, 104, 105, 108, 127
Fire Company, first, organized 1878, 92
Fire Dublin, of 1885, 92
First Federal Savings & Loan Association of Dublin, 135
First National Bank, 232
Fish Trap Cut, Indian Mounds, 1
Fish, William, 396-97
Fisher, Dr. Harris, 90, 91, 228
Flanders Family, 366-68
Flanders, James Washington, 367-68
Flanders, John, 366
Flora of Laurens County, 133-34
Floral Shop, 116
Floyd, General, 30
Floyd, Mrs. W. C., 152

Fluker and Tarbutton trial, 80-81
Folsom, H. B., 40
Folsom, Robert W., 60
Fordham Family, 368-70
Fordham, Benjamin, 368
Fordham, Emma Hobbs, 146
Fordham, J. B., 44, 130
Fordham, J. I., 90
Fordham, W. J., 74
Fordham, William, 369
Fordham, Zenus, 239
Forehand, Amos, 77
Former Fraternities and Clubs, 258-59
 Benevolent and Protective Order of Elks, 258
 Fourteen Club, 259
 Improved Order of Red Men, 258
 Independent Order of Odd Fellows, 258
 Kiwanis Club, 259
 Knights of Pythias, 258
National Union, 258
 Royal Arcanum, 258
Fort, Allen, 151, 152
Fort Early, 30
Fort Hawkins, 28
Fort Mims, 28
Fort Wilkinson treaty, 10
Foster, George, 140
Fountain, Amanda, 154
Fountain of Youth, De Soto sought, 4
Four Seasons, store, 103
Fourteen Club, 259
Fowler, Simon, 13
Fox list (E. J. Blackshear), 52
Franklin County, created in 1783, 9
Fraud, Yazoo, 76
Fred Roberts Hotel, 112
Free and Accepted Masons, 253-54
Freeman Family, 370-75
Freeman, Elliott Blount, 371
Freeman, Ernest, 372
Freeman, Henrietta Sanders (Mrs. E. B.), 22, 241, 243, 245, 371-72
F. S. A., 138-39
Fulford, H. L., 113
Fulgham, Henry, 13
Fuller, Frank, 148
Fuller, J. F., 74
Fuller, J. Frank, 92
Fullford, Frank, 58
Fullwood, John, 86
Fulwood, John, 122
Fuqua, A. A., 87
Fuqua, Andrew, 50
Fuqua, Ben, 205
Fuqua, Henry, 26

Gaines, Jennie, 412
Gaines, John Richard, 413

Gaines, Richard, 413
Gaines, William Richard, 413
Garden Club, Dublin, 252-53
Garrard, Mrs. R. C., 152
Garrett Family, 375-76
Garrett, A. W., 105, 375
Gay, Frank, 153, 156
Gazetteer of Georgia, 123
Gazette, The, 235
Geeslin, J. W., 130, 137
Geiger, W. L., 151, 152
Genealogy, *see* Family Histories
Gentlewomen of the Sixties, 69-71
George M. Troup, the, 89, 124
Georgia Education Association, 184
Georgia Fruitland Company, 131
Georgia Militia Districts in Laurens County, 121
Georgia Plywood Corporation, 114
Georgia Rural Rehabilitation Corporation, 138
Georgia State Employment Service, 137
Georgia Volunteers, 234
Georgia Warehouse & Compress Company, 127
Gettys, J. M., Lumber Company, 114
Gibson, E. B., 110
Gibson, John, 13, 83
Gibson, Mrs. Thomas, 108
Gilbert, D. W., 104
Gilbert Hardware Company, 104
Gilbert, Thomas, 13
Gilder, T. R., 134
Gillman, Pearl, 128
Gin and Screw, old, 127-28
G. M. Districts in Laurens County, 121
Goldsmith, Washington L., 60
Gordy, Louis E., 110
Goulding, Dr. F. R., Jr., 111
Gove, William, 63
Grady, William vs. Sarah Grady, 79
Graham Family, 376-77
Graham, Ben, 155
Graham, G. F., 147, 148
Graham, John M., 125, 376
Graham, Latha, 148
Graham, Richard, 147
Graves, Clarence D., 152
Graves, Virginia, 136, 138, 249
Green Family, 377-79
Green, David, 156
Green, Eason, 377
Green, Dr. George F., 229
Green, Jesse J., 377
Green, John W., 94, 156, 199, 240
Green, Jule B., 96
Green, Leonard, 13
Grice, Warren, 433, 519
Griffin, Archibald, 27
Grimsley, Easter M., 154

Grimsley, R. T., 154
Grimsley, Sarah, 154
Grinstead, Dilion, 149
Grinstead, John, 122, 156
Grist Mills, 54-55
Grocery, establishments, wholesale
  Alsup Grocery Company, 115
  Cash Wholesale Grocery Company, 115
  Cochran Brothers Company, 115
  Hilburn-Bobbitt Company, 115
  W. R. Werden and Company, 115
Grocery Stores, *see* Stores, Grocery
Grocery Stores in 1900's, 103-04
Grove, Mrs. Edna B., 111
Guards, Blackshear, 58, 60
Guest, J. M., 148
Guyton Family, 379-93
Guyton, C. S., 61, 73, 90, 385
Guyton, Charles, 25, 26, 49, 87
Guyton, Dr. Charles, 228, 283
Guyton, Cincinnatus Saxon, 43, 385-86, 391-92
Guyton, Cincinnatus Saxon II, 387
Guyton, Clara, 42
Guyton, John, 25, 26, 27, 49, 382
Guyton, Joseph, 380
Guyton, Mrs. M. J., 243, 245, 246
Guyton, Moses, 25, 26, 43, 49, 382
Guyton, Moses II, 387-88
Guyton, Moses III, 389
Guyton, Moses IV, 390
Guyton, Moses Josiah, 193, 392-93
Guyton, Nathaniel, 380
Guyton, Thomas N., 50, 55, 87, 383
Gypsy, the, 124

Haines Family, 394
Haines, Alfred I., 394
Hall, S. T., 117
Hall, Dr. T. H., 229
Hall, W. J., 58
Hall, William, 122
Hampton, A. Y., 54
Hampton, Andrew, 13, 86, 122
Hampton, Benjamin, 25, 80
Hampton, James, first sheriff, 82
Hampton Mill 54
Harden, E. J., *Life of Troup,* 30
Hardware business in 1900's, 104
Hardware Stores, 117
Hardwick, Thomas W., 80
Hardwood Manufacturing Company, 114
Hargrove, A. J., 191, 265
Hargrove, Mrs. A. J., 152, 248
Harris, William A., 60
Harrison Family, 395
Harrison, Benjamin, 9
Harrison, Billy, 155
Harrison, Dr. I. H., 229
Harrison, Gainor Green, 395

Harrison, L. J., 147, 155
Harrison, Louis, 154, 155
Harrison, Macon, 395
Harrison, W. A., 155
Hart, J. F., 128, 129, 135
Hart, Mrs. J. F., 152
Hartford, 30
Hartford Road, 28
Harvard Family, 396-97
Harvard, David, 396
Harvey, J. R., 155, 156
Harvill, Iverson H., 74
Harville, Tom, 179
Harville, W. E., 148, 153, 155, 179
Harville, Mrs. W. E., 152
Haskins, W. T., 58
Hattaway, Sol, 98
Hawkins, Fort, 28
Hawkins, K. J., 80
Haygood, William M., 179
Haynes Family, 397-98
Haynes, Florence Moore Stanley, 505-06
Haynes, Mercer, 84, 92, 226, 397-98
Haynes, Mrs. Mercer, 152
Head Right Land Warrants, 9
Head-Right System, 9-10
Henderson, Annie K., 111
Henriques, Lady Eleanor, 502
Henry, R. C., 89, 104, 124, 125, 172
Hermann, Dr. J. D., 95
Herndon Family, 398-401
Herndon, Bryant A., 399
Herndon, Celestia, 399
Herndon, James, 398-99
Hesse, Joseph, 110
Hester, Maggie, 193
Hester, Thelma, 132
Hicks Family, 401-03
Hicks, Bobbie, 129, 132
Hicks, Dr. Charles, 229, 403
Hicks, Dr. Charles L., 402
Hicks, Guy M., 179
Hicks Hospital, 230
Hicks, James B., 105, 141, 402
Hicks, Nathaniel, 401
Hicks, Ralph, 78
Higdon, Charles, 13, 76
Higgins, W. F., 92, 127
High Sheriff, 82
Hightower Family, 404-09
Hightower, Bob, 106
Hightower, F. C., 151
Hightower, "Miss Genie," 106
Hightower, Gregory D., 407-08
Hightower, Mrs. J. R., 152
Hightower, James Richard, 404-05
Hightower, John Wesley, 406
Hightower, Joshua, 407-09
Hightower, Dr. R. H., 92, 105, 229, 408
Hightower, Robert Henry, 408

Hightower, Ruby Usher, 404
Hightower, T. M., & Company, 95
Hightower, William Joshua, 409
Hilbun, C. D., 108
Hilbun, Earle, 105, 117
Hilbun-Bobbitt Company, 103
Hill, Benjamin H., 56
Hill, James, 154
Hill, Joseph L., Site of Dublin purchased from, 13
Hill, Susan C., 154
Hill, Mrs. T. W., 248
Hilton, Attys P., 96
Hilton Hotel, 96
Hines, Judge J. K., 80
Histories, Family, see Family Histories
Hobbs Family, 409-14
Hobbs, Allen Lemuel, 410
Hobbs, Andy, 90, 411
Hobbs-Arnold-Gaines-Brawner Lineage, 412
Hobbs, Berry, 154
Hobbs, Bolin, 150, 151, 152, 153, 411
Hobbs, Early, 410
Hobbs, Harriet, 154
Hobbs, James Duncan, 411
Hobbs, John, 154, 409, 410
Hobbs, Jordon, 156
Hobbs, Larry, 149, 151, 152, 153, 154, 409, 410
Hobbs, Lucille Arnold, 412
Hobbs, Walter Allen, 411
Hodges, Dr. Charles A., 110, 111
Hodges, Lynwood, 117
Hog raising, 129
Hogan, Aubrin U., 137
Hogan, Edward, 13
Hogan, J. A., 126
Hogan, Marshall H., 110, 113, 132
Hogan, U. G. B., 130
Holleman, Nathan, 110
Holmes, C. L., 51
Holmes, W. L., 116
Holt, Thaddeus, 83
Home Demonstration Agent secured, 128
  Names listed, 128-29
Homes, old
  Blackshear residence, 91
  Currell residence, 91
  Dasher residence, 91
  Fuqua residence, 91
  Ramsay residence, 91
  Rowe residence, 91
  Stubbs residence, 91
  Weaver residence, 91
  Yopp residence, 91
Hooks, G. S., 96
Hooks House, 96
Hooks, T. W., 96
Hopaunee, 30, 31

Horn Family, 414-17
Horn, Anton Bender, 416
Horn, Josiah, 414
Horn, W. D., 151, 152
Horne, Michael, 77
Hospitals
   Brigham-Claxton Hospital, 230
   Claxton-Montford Hospital, 230
   Claxton Sanatorium, 230
   Coleman Hospital, 230
   Dublin Clinic, 230
   Dublin Hospital, 230
   Dublin Sanatorium, 230
   Hicks Hospital, 230
   Thompson Sanatorium, 230
Hospitals in Laurens County, 230-31
Hotel, Hilton, 96
Hotel, New Dublin, 96
Hotel, Fred Roberts, 112
Houston, Martha Lou, 19
Hudson, Laura Ann, 149
Hudson, Marbar, 149
Hudson, Mary, 149
Hudson, T. B., 85
Hughes, Dudley M., 51, 93, 207
Hughes, Hayden, 51
Hunger and Hardship Creek, 3, 27
Hurricane of 1882, 92
Hurst, W. N., 152
Hutchinson, John U., 58
Hutchinson, P. C., 117

Ice factory erected 1920, 112
Independent Order of Good Templars, 97
Indians
   Creeks, 3
   Expulsion of, 16, 45, 46
   Lower Creeks, 7
Indian arrowheads, how fashioned, 5
Indian Mounds
   Blackshear Ferry Road, 3
   Fish Trap Cut, 1
   Near Diamond Landing, 2
Indian Springs Council, 41
Indian Spring Rock, 17
Indian Troubles, 46-49
Indian Villages
   Kitchee, 3
   Ocute, 3
   Toalli, 3
Indian Wars
   Big Shoals, 8
   of 1795, 11
Inferior Court, 72-74
   Last Session 1868, 73
Inferior Court Justices, 72-73
Interracial relations in Seventies, 88-89
Irwin, Captain John, 30

Jackson, General, 30, 31

Jackson, Allen, 103, 198
Jackson, D. R., 103
Jackson, James, 45
Jackson, Maggie, 240
Jackson Stores, 103
Jails, 86
Jail, Laurens County, 77
James, Evelyn C., 139
James, Margaret, 27
Jameson Trail, 141-42
Jefferson Party, 45
Jenkins, G. V., 240
Jenkins, G. W., 58
Jenkins, L. C., 58, 59
Jenkins, Millard A., 151, 152
Jeon, John, 122
Jepeway, G. A., 132
Jewish Citizens in Dublin, 95
Johnson Family, 417-19
Johnson, Eline M., 139
Johnson, Henry, 110
Johnson, Herschel V., 56
Johnson, Israel, 54
Johnson, Israel, Mill, 54
Johnson, J. W., 155
Johnson, Pinckney McDonald, 417
Johnson, Seaborn, 418-19
Johnson, Sherman, 155
Joiner, Davis, 149, 153
Joiner, E. A., 150
Joiner, Elizabeth, 149
Joiner, H. D., 140
Joiner, Hiram, 130
Joiner, J. J., 150
Joiner, N. E., 149
Joiner, W. J., 85, 127
Jolley, O. K., 110
Jones, Adam, 83
Jones, C. C., *History of Georgia*, 2)
Jones, Horace, 148
Jones, John W., 58
Jones, Neal, 96
Jones, Samuel, 122
Jones, W. B. & M. I., Company, 95
Jones, Wilber S., 105
Jones, William B., 92
Jordan, J. W., 59
Jordan, Dr. Johnnie, 116
Jordan, M. W., 115
Jordan, Mae Allen, 140
Jordan, Opal, 138
Judges, list of, City Court of Dublin, 84
Judges, Court of Ordinary, 84
Judges, Superior Court of Laurens County, 82
Justices, Inferior Court, 72-3

Kassell, M. W., 108
Kea, Carolina Burwick, 239
Kea, Dawson, 117

Kea, W. M., 90
Kea, Wesley, 96
Keen Family, 419-23
Keen, Elizabeth, 19, 419
Keen, F. H., 103
Keen, I. T., 92
Keen, Isaac, 148
Keen, James L., 54, 421-22
Keen, James L., Jr., 75, 423
Keen, Jane 148
Keen, L. D., 105
Keen, Lawrence, 147, 421
Keen, Young, 147, 155, 420
Keen, Z. B., 155
Kellam Family, 424-25
Kellam, Russell, 424
Kellam, S. M., 105, 425
Kelley, Charles C., 60
Kelly, J. A., 125
Kelly, Rev. J. R., 148
Kellogg, Dorothy, 129
Kendrick, M. A., 104
Kilpatrick, Dr. William H., 389, 390
Kinchin, Hiram, 153
Kinchin, J. T., 153
Kinchen, James, 147
Kinchen, Tolbert, 153, 156
Kinchen, William, 239
King, Frances S., 139
Kitchee, Chief, 16
Kitchee, 3, 16
Kittrell Family, 425-27
Kittrell, Dr. C. H., 104, 105, 106, 425-426
Kittrell, Leila Brinson, 427
Kiwanis Club, 259
Knight Family, 427-28
Knight, Blewster, 180
Knight, Davis, 180
Knight, Durell W., 110
Knight, Green Bury, 240
Knight, H. A., 127
Knight, Sig, 110
Knight, W. A., 146, 427
Knight, Walter, 179
Knights of Pythias, 258
Knights Templars, State Convention 1933, 113
Ku Klux Klan, 57

Lady Washington, the, 124
LaFayette, 39-40
Lake, Enoch M., 73
Lamb, Donald, 136
Land Lottery List, 1819, 34-38
Land Lottery System, 10
Landings of Oconee River, 123
Lanier, Elizabeth Duncan, 128
Lanier, Frances, 138
Laurens, Henry, 14

Laurens, John, 12, 14-15
Laurens, John, Chapter, Daughters of the American Revolution, *see* Daughters of American Revolution
Laurens Banking Company, 232
Laurens Citizen, 236
Laurens County
  Changes in Congressional District, 118-19
  Confederate Soldiers from, 61-3
  County seat transferred to Dublin, 13
  Court System, 75-85
  Created in 1807, 12
  Geography of, 118-125
  Militia Districts, 120
  Pioneer Period, 23-38
  Population and Civic Divisions, 118
  Rainfall, 118
  Revolutionary Soldiers in, 18
  Soil and cotton production, 125-27
  Sumpterville first county seat, 12
  Temperature, 118
  Territory changed 1811, 1858, 1906, 12
  Tributary Waterways, 122
  Welfare Department, 137-38
  Whikey traffic in, 97-98
  World War dead from, 109-10
Laurens County Farmers' Club, 126-27
Laurens County Herald, 236
Laurens County Livestock Association, 106
Laurens County, Post Offices in, 194-97
Laurens County in World War, 108-11
Laurens County World War Memorial, 111
Laurens Hill, 215-16
Laurens Volunteers, 58, 59
Law, Stephen, 78
Lawyers of Laurens County, 225-27
Lee, Dr. G. R., 111, 140
Lee, James C., 59
Lee, L. B., 149, 151, 152, 153
Legion, American, 255
Lester, Mark, 114
Lester, Richard P., 60
Lewis, Roy, 110
Liberty Bonds, 108
Liberty Loan train, 109
Library, Carnegie, 237-39
"Life of Troup," E. J. Harden, 30
Light plant sold to Georgia Power Company, 112
Linder Family, 428-32
Linder-Ballard Family, 432
Linder, Berrien B., 58, 92, 428
Linder-Keen Family, 431
Linder, Mrs. L. B., 146, 148
Linder, Mrs. L. H., 148
Linder, L. L., 105

Linder, Louis Brothers, 429, 430
Linder, Nannie Bell, 148
Linder, Nannie J., 240
Linder, Tom, 5, 141, 430-31
Linder, Dr. Thomas Jacob, 51, 228, 428
Linder, "Uncle George," 262
Lingo, "Bud," 94
Lingo, William, 96
Lions Club, 255
Livestock Association, Laurens County, 106
Livestock production, 129, 132
Lock, James, 146
Lone Vidette, 63-66
Longevity in Laurens, 239-40
Lord, B. F., 93
Lord, B. H., 105
Lord, Steve, 106
Love Family, 432-34
Love, A. S., Company, 27
Love, Amos, 25, 27, 78, 86, 145, 432, 433
Love, Peter, 81, 83, 225
Lovett, 197
Lovett-Brinson, 114
Lovett, Warren P., 197
Lower Creeks, 7
Lower Uchee Trail, 141
Lowery, J. M., 74
Lowther, Ella, 42
Lowther, John, 55, 498-500
Lowther, Mary, 42
Lumber Companies, 114-15
Lumbering, 45
Lumbering and turpentining, 132

McBane, John, 122
McCall, Major Hugh, 27, 496-97
McCall, Norman, 262
McCall, Thomas, 19, 25, 27, 107, 495-97
McCall, Thomas, Chapter, United States Daughters of 1812, *see* United States Daughters of 1812
McCall, William, 13
McCall, *History of Georgia*, 8
McCormick, Colonel, 25
McCormick, Anne St. Clare, 39
McCullers, William, 80
McDaniel, Daniel, 149
McDaniel, J. R., 58
McDaniel, John D., 96
McDonald, Angus, 163
McDonald, Eunice Bethsaida, 521
McDonald, Richard, 138
McGillivray, 8, 9
McIntosh, Catherine, 39
McIntosh, Chilli, 107
McIntosh, John, 39
McIntosh, William, 41, 107
Mack, J. B., 172

Mackey, E. B., 117
Mackey, E. B., Lumber Company, 115
McLendon, Dennis, 25
McLendon, R. H. C., 58
McMahon, H. G., Dr., 140
McNeal, Daniel, 80, 225
Macon, Dublin & Savannah Railroad, 93-94
Macon Telegraph, 40
McQuaig Family, 341-42
Maddox, H. L., 153
Maddox, I. F., 140
Mahoney, J. H., 105
Mahoney, Lynette Hightower, 407
Mahoney, M. V., 93
Major, John, 144
Malone, Lucian, 116
Mann, Cader, 76
Manning, Benjamin, 147
Marriages, Early, 280-99
  Book A, 1809-1817, 280-81
  Book B, 1811-1817, 281-82
  Book C, 1813-1830, 282-87
  Book D, 1811-1836, 287-90
  Book E, 1833-1848, 291-93
  Book F, 1841-1851, 293-96
  Book G, 1840-1855, 296-99
Marshall, Daniel, 144
Marshall, E. W., 152, 155
Martin, Bob, 105
Martin, Claude, 186
Martin, George, 13
Martin, Mrs. H. H., 148
Martin, Mrs. M. E., 152
Martin, Walter E., 110
Mason, James, 110
Mason, William, 50
Masons, Dexter Lodge, 203
Masons, Free and Accepted, Laurens Lodge No. 75, 253-54
Matthews, Herbert S., 111
Matthews, James C., 111
May, Mark, 13
Mayo, Gideon, 122
Meteoric shower 1833, 45
Methodist Churches, *see* Churches, Methodist
Metts Family, 434
Metts, Blanche, 105
Metts, Frederick, 434
Metts, George, 434
Metts, George, Jr., 434
Metts, Jesse, 155
Metts, Lewis, 434
Metts, N. P., 137
Middleton, Joe, 116
Miles, Elizabeth, 149
Military Companies, 234-35
Military Rule in Georgia, 57

Militia Districts of Laurens County, 120
  1940 population of, 118
  Names of, 120-21
    Captain Hardy Griffin District, 36, 120
    Captain Leroy G. Harris District, 34, 120
    Captain Adam Jones District, 38, 120
    Captain Francis J. Ross District, 37, 120
    Captain Sion Smith District, 35, 120
Militia Muster Days, 120
Milledge, John, Gov., 79
Miller, James, 78
Miller, Stephen M., *Bench and Bar of Georgia*, I, 24-25
Miller, Warren, 92
Mills, Ante-Bellum, 54-55
  Blackshear's Mill, 54
  Chappell's Mill, 54
  Hampton Mill, 54
  Israel Johnson Mill, 54
  Shewmake Mill, 54
  Stanley Mills, 54
  Yopp Mill, 54
Mims, Fort, 28
Minter, 211
Mitchell, David B., 78, 79
Mitchell, Frances, *Georgia Land and People*, 30
Mizell, Dr. Luke, 228
Moffett Family, 435
Moffett, Alexander, 435
Moffett, Alfred N., 179, 435
Moffett, Louis, 435
Molony, Charles, 93
Monroe, James, President, 30, 41
Monroe, Lucia B., 139
Monroe, Neill, 27
Monroe, William, 78
Montford, Irwin, 113
Montrose, 51, 206-08
Moore, Bruce H., 139
Moore, Major Hugh, 69
Moore, J. F., 92
Moore, James, 122, 228
Moore, Leland, 179
Moore, Thomas, 25, 27, 227
Moore, Wesley W., 139
Moorman Family, 435-36
Moorman, David Addison, 436
Moorman, David J., 436
Moorman, Henry Ellington, 436
Moorman, Mary, 136
Moorman, Simeon Josiah, 435
Moorman, William B., 178, 435
Morgan, Audrey, 138
Morris, William, 122

Mosely, L. O., 110
Mounds and Relics, 1-3
  Blackshear Ferry Road, 3
  Near Diamond Landing, 2
  Two Indian Mounds "Fish Trap Cut" 1
Moving Picture Show, first, in Dublin, 106
Moxley, E. F., 140
Moye, Dr. C. G., 140
Mullis, M. S., 140
Murder trial, first in Laurens County, 78
Murphey, J. R., 113
"Muster Farmers" in Laurens County, 130

Nance, B., 95
National Farm Loan Association, 135
National Guard, 234-35
National Reemployment Service, 137
National Youth Association, 136
Negro, candidate for Legislature, 92
Negro, in State Legislature, 262
Negro riot, 89
Negroes, Laurens County, 261-66
Negroes, relation with former masters, 88-89
Neighbor, R. E., 152, 157-58
Nelson, Carl, 117, 140
Nelson, Mrs. Carl, 152, 248
New Family, 437-38
New Dublin Hotel, 96
New, Dr. J. E., 137, 437-38
New, Parker, 110, 438
Newspapers
  Courier-Dispatch, 236
  Courier-Herald, 236
  Dublin Courier, The, 235
  Dublin Dispatch, The, 235
  Dublin Post, The, 235
  Dublin Times, 236
  Gazette, The, 235
  Laurens Citizen, 236
  Laurens County Herald, 236
  People, The, 235
"No man's land," 81
Noles, Wright, 51
Norris, Tode, 89
Northview Cemetery, 103
Norville, Z. S., 136
N. Y. A., 136

Oatts, Dr. E. W., 116
Oconas, tribe of, 7
Oconee Chapter. United Daughters of the Confederacy, *see* United Daughters of the Confederacy
Oconee Milling Company, 129
Oconee River, the, 123-25
  Boats on the, 123-25

Ferries on the, 123
Landings on the, 123
Oconee River Steamship Company, 125
Oconee War, 8, 9-11
Oconee and Western Railroad Company, 93
Ocute, 3
Odd Fellows, Independent Order of, 258
Officers, Company H, 14th Georgia Regiment, 59-60
Officials, City of Dublin, 1873-1941, 117
Old Chicken Road, 143
Oliver, J. H., 155
O'Neal, William, 49
Opera House, 106
Order of the Eastern Star, Dexter, 202
Order of Eastern Star in Dublin, 254-55
Ordinary, Court of, 72-74, 83
 List of judges, 84
Orr, E. R., 103
Osceola, Chief, 46
Outler, Arnau, & Outler Company, 103
Overstreet, O. B., 140

Page Family, 439-40
Page, Mrs. B. B., 113
Page, J. M., 103, 439
Page, Joseph, 439
Page, Dr. Landrum, 111, 439
Page, Reba B., 138, 439
Panic, financial, 1839, 49
Parent-Teacher Association, Colored, 266
Parent-Teacher Associations, Dublin-Laurens County Council of, 249-52
 Pre-School Associations, 251-52
Parker Family, 440-41
Parker, Benjamin Franklin, 440
Parker Dairy Farm, 130
Parker, Duren, 130
Parker, George Washington, 440
Parker, Louise Scarborough, 136
Parker, William, 76
Parnassus Club, 247-49
Parrott, G. B., 140
Payne, George, 79
Peach growing industry, 131
Peacock Family, 441-42
Peacock, Anne Boisfeuillet, 442
Peacock, John Asa, 441-42
Peacock, Mrs. John Asa, 241, 243
Peacock, Mrs. Marion, 248
Peacock, R. T., 116, 441
Pecan growing, 131-32
People, The, 235
Perkins, G. W., 93
Perry Brothers Dairy, 130
Perry, Emma, 158, 186-87
Perry, Joel E., 54
Perry, L. C., & Company, 95

Perry, Louis C., 58, 59, 60
Perry, Terrell, 58
Peters Family, 442-43
Peters, Thomas, 443
Peters, William, 442
Pharis, Rev. J. L., 149
Phelps, Wiley C., 110
Phoenix Mutual Life Insurance Company, 134
Philbuck, Martha, 128
Phillips Family, 443-45
Phillips, C. W., 105, 129, 134
Phillips, William Spencer, 443-44
Physicians of Laurens County, 227-30
Pierce Family, 445-46
Pierce, Edward Clifton, 445
Pierce, Ethel Orr, 446
Pierce, Felton, 105, 110, 445
Pierce, W. W., 156
Pine Barren Speculation of 1795, 10
Pioneer Period, 23-38
Pittman, Mrs. J. C., 152
Pitts, Burton H., 50
Pitts, Lunsford C., 27
Plantations
 Horseshoe Bend, 40
 Mitchell, 40
 Rosemont, 40
Plantations, cotton, 49
Political parties
 Anti-federalist, 45
 Clarkites, 45
 Democrats, 45
 Jefferson, 45
 Populist Party, 94
 States Rights, 45
 Troupers, 45
 Whig, 45
Pollard, H. D., 93
Pollock, John, 122
Poor House, 50
Poor, Organized aid for, 50
Poor schools, 181
Pope, C. S., 103
Pope, Rev. C. W., 150
Pope, L. Cleveland, 235
Poplar Springs, Industrial School, 186-88
Population of Laurens County, 118
Populist Party, 94
Porter, Mrs. L. L., 97
Post, The Dublin, 235
Postmasters, Dublin Post Office, 192-93
Post Office, Dublin, 192-94
 Air Mail Service, 193
 New Building erected, 194
Post offices in Laurens County, 194-97
Powell Family, 446-47
Powell, Frank Wooten, 446
Powell, J. C., 74

Powell, J. B., 127
Powell, Sara Jo, 138
Presbyterian Church, see Churches, Presbyterian
Prescott Family, 447-48
Prescott, George M., 447
Price, Felix L., 60
Primitive Baptist Churches, see Churches
Prince Family, 448-49
Prince, Clifford Haynes, 448
Prince, Samuel Miles, 448
Pritchett Family, 449-51
Pritchett-Ellison Family, 450-51
Pritchett Grocery Company, 115
Pritchett, "Pet," 96
Pritchett, T. J., 104, 127, 449
Pritchett, William, 98, 104, 449
Proctor Family, 451-52
Proctor, Joseph Lindsey, 451-52
Proctor, W. H., 105
Public School System, 184-86
Public Service, Laurens County Citizens in, 221-22
  House of Representatives, 221
  State Senate, 221-22
  Beyond State, 222-23
  In County, 223-24
Pughsley, Carrie, 524
Pulaski County, created in 1808, 12
Pullen, H. T., 108
PWA, 136-37

Rabun, General, 30
Rachels & Jordon, 104
Rail fence, 77
Railroads
  Brewton and Pineora Railroad, 94
  Charter granted Wrightsville & Tennille Railroad Company 1883, 93
  Dublin-Southwestern Railroad, 94
  Dublin & Wrightsville Railroad Company, 93
  Early construction of, 49
  Macon, Dublin & Savannah Railroad, 93-94
  Oconee & Western Railroad Company, 93
  Organization discussed, 88
Ramsay Family, 452-60
Ramsay, Henrietta Guyton, 384
Ramsay, John, 457
Ramsay, Mary Guyton, 241, 243, 385, 454
Ramsay, Mattie, 152
Ramsay, Martha B., 241, 384, 454
Ramsay, W. S., 54, 57, 58, 60, 91, 101, 146, 148, 151, 152, 178, 184, 185, 244, 452-55
Ramsay, Robert Hassell, 459
Ramsay, Thomas R., 127, 385, 455-56

Rawls Family, 460-62
Rawls, B. H., 127
Rawls, Eugenia, 113
Rawls, Gussie Bell, 117
Rawls, James Julian, 400
Rawls, Napoleon Bonaparte, 461-62
Rawls, Oliver Hazard Perry, 461
Rawls, Otis Bryant, 400
Rawls, Wendell, 400
Rawls, Willis, 460
Reconstruction, 88
Recreation resorts, 106-08
  Boiling Spring, 108
  Dead River Spring, 107
  Dublin Natatorium, 108
  Pavilion, 107
  Peacock's, 107
  Rock Spring, 107
  Sessions Lake, 108
  Spivey's, 107
  Thundering Springs, 108
  Troup Spring, 107
  Wells Spring, 107
  Wilkes Spring, 107
Red Cross Work in Dublin, 108-09
Red Men, Improved Order of, 258
Reese, Stanley A., 85
Reese, W. S., 105, 113
Reforestation areas, 134
Register, A. G., 58
Register, Bob, 156
Register, John, 58
Register, T. P., 58
Reinhart, James M., 95
Reins, F. B., 111
Relics, Mounds and, 1-3
Rentz, 208
Rentz Family, 462-63
Rentz, E. P., 94, 462
Rentz, Joseph Alfred, 462-63
Representation from Laurens County, 221
Revolutionary Soldiers in Laurens County, 18
Rhiner, M. T., 113
Rice Family, 463-67
Rice, Deacon Edmund, 463
Rice, W. B., 128, 130, 463
Ricks, Charles, 148
Rifles, Barkaloo, the, 58, 59
Riggins, Samuel, 77
Riot, Negro, 89
Ritz Theatre, 106
River, the Oconee, see Oconee River
River steamer, coming of, 124
Rivers, Ed., 138
Rivers, J. J., 151
Road
  Blackshear, 29
  Hartford, 28
  Old Chicken, 143

Roads, Commissioners of, 74-75
Roberts, Drury, 78
Roberts, Fred, 105, 112
Roberts, Hansel, 78, 86
Roberts, William J., 139
Robertson, Edith, 129
Robinson, Captain, 30
Robinson, David, 89
Robinson, Hack, 127
Robinson, James F., 54
Robinson, Nelle, 129, 132
Robinson, Robert, 83, 87
Robinson, W. W., 100, 105
Robinson, Mrs. W. W., 152
Roche, W. P., 114
Rockledge, 203-04
Rocky Creek, 51
Rogers, John T., 153, 156
Rogers, M. A., 117
Rogers, W. B., 30, 127
Rose Theatre, 106
Roster Commissions in War Between the States, Laurens County, 61
Rotary Club of Dublin, 257
Rountree, Martha, 136
Rover, The, 124
Rowe Family, 467-68
Rowe, Emma Saxon Guyton, 388
Rowe, Freeman H., 54, 60, 68, 83, 89, 91, 232, 468
Rowe, Mrs. Freeman, 152
Rowe, Thomas H., 58, 60, 73, 74, 90, 92, 102, 127, 468
Rowe, Mrs. Thomas H., 152
Rowell, James, 54
Rural Rehabilitation Corporation of Georgia, 138
Russell, Reginald, 180
Rutland, Annie Perry, 240

Saffold, Adam, 83
Sammons, Bernice, 128
Sams, D. F., 117
Sanders Family, 469-74
Sanders, James B., 117, 226, 384, 454, 469, 473
Sanders, James Guyton, 384, 454, 469
Sanders, James Rabun, 471-72
Sanders, Jane, 149
Sanders, Jeremiah, 470-71
Sanders, Joshua, 470
Sanders Maternal Lineage, 473
Sanders, Otis, 117
Sanders, Rabun Clifford I, 473
Sanders, Randolph R., 110, 384, 454, 469, 470
Sanders, T. V., 105
Sanders, William Olin, 472
Sapelo Island, 29
Sarchett, Peter, 43, 90, 92

Sartin, James, 13
Satterfield, Griswold, 110
Sawyer, Jonathan
  Chose name for Dublin, 14
  Married daughter of David McCormick, 14
Scarboro, A. C., 127
Scarboro, H. S., 148, 179
Scarboro, J. F., 58
Scarborough, Daniel, 77
Scarborough, Howard C., 180
Scarborough, Nunan, 151
Scarborough, W. J., 92
Schaufele, W. F., 104
Schaufele, W. F., Company, 103
Schley, Governor William, 46
Schools, bond issues for, 95, 103
  consolidated, 188-89
  Dublin, 189-91
  Dublin Academy, 182
  Ebenezer High School, 186
  Industrial School at Poplar Springs, 186-88
  Negro, of Dublin, 265-66
  Parent-Teacher Association, 266
  Poor, 180, 181
  Public Academy, 181
  Public School System, 184-86
Sconyers, James A., 180
Scouts, Boy, 259-60
Sealey, 154
Secession, 56
Seed Loan, 135
Selective Service Boards, 139-40
Seminole and Upper Creek uprising, 46
Senators, State, from Laurens County, 221-22
Sessions, Dee, 108, 117
Seven Pines Engagement, 58
Sheep raising, 50
Sheffield, Arter, 77, 86
Shelor, Ethel, 129
Shepard, James M., 154
Shepard, Mary Ann, 154
Sheriffs, Laurens County, list, 82
Sheriffs, list of, City Court of Dublin, 84
Sherman, Selwyn Howard, 191
Sherwood, Adiel, 44, 123
Shewmake, M. A., 136
Shewmake Mill, 54
Shirley, Isaiah, 145
Shorter, Eli S., 14
Simmons Family, 474-82
Simmons, David Ramsay, 385, 455, 476, 477
Simmons, E. G., 105, 111, 478
Simmons, Edgar, II, 478-79
Simmons, H. M., 105
Simmons-Holleman Descendants, 479-80
Simmons, J. M., 104, 477-78

Simmons, Jack Whiteford, 385, 455, 476
Simmons, John M., II, 475-77
Simmons, Thomas Randolph, 385, 455, 476, 477
Simmons, William, I, 480
Simmons, William Pinckney, 385, 455, 476, 477
Simmons, William Thomas, I, 478
Simons Family, 482
Simons, James S., Jr., 105, 127, 482
Sims, Rev. S. F., 146
Slavery, 49-50
Smith, Alexander, 80
Smith, Charles U., Family, 483-84
Smith, C. U., 105, 483
Smith, Charlton, 148
Smith, G. C., 13
Smith, G. G., 19, 44
Smith, G. W., 155, 156
Smith, H. Turner, 155, 156, 178-79
Smith, Hardy, Family, 484-88
Smith, Hardy, 25, 58, 484-88
Smith, Joseph Daniel, Family, 489-91
Smith, J. D., 104, 126, 138, 148, 489-91
Smith, J. E., 103
Smith, J. M., 58, 155
Smith, James Thompson, 148, 150, 155, 178-79
Smith, Jane Roberta, 125
Smith, Lee E., 399
Smith, Lewis K., 140
Smith, M. V. B., 58
Smith, Mary C., 139
Smith, Milo, 105, 110
Smith, Mrs. Milo, 152
Smith, R. Murphy, 400
Smith, Ruth Stafford, 483
Smith, Simon, 86
Smith, T. A., 156
Smith, Thomas Daniel, Family, 491-92
Smith, T. D., 58, 244, 491-92
Smith, Mrs. T. H., 108
Smith, Theron, 110
Smith, Turner, 148
Smith, W. W., 73
Smith, Wilbur, 79
Soil of Laurens County, 125
Soldiers, Confederate, from Laurens County, 61-63
Solicitor Generals, list of, 83
Solicitors, of city court, list of, 85
Solomon, J. C., 152
Solomon, W. C., 75
Southern Cotton Oil Company, 114, 127
Southern School Journal, The, 184
Spanish-American War, 96
  Laurens County soldiers, 96
    Burch, J. E.
    Green, Jule B.
    Jones, Neal
    Kea, Wesley
    Lingo, William
    McDaniel, John D.
    Pritchett, "Pet"
    Williams, "Windy"
Spanish Period, 7
Sparks, Samuel, 13
Spivey, Jethro B., 25, 27, 86
Speight, John, 13
Springfield, 17
Stafford, James Washington, 483
Stafford, Robert, 484
Stage coach line, 142
Stallings, Judge Will, 113
Stanley Family, 492-511
  McCall Ancestry, 495-97
Stanley, Dr. Benjamin, 73, 229, 508-09
Stanley, Ethel Stubbs, 504-05
Stanley, Frank Rowe, 501-02
Stanley, H. M., 105, 127, 237-38, 502-04
Stanley, Hardy B., 145
Stanley, Ira, 25, 26, 49, 54, 146, 494-95
Stanley, Ira Eli, 509-10
Stanley, Ira Lowther, 500-01
Stanley, J. I. C., 155
Stanley, James, II, 492-94
Stanley, James Rowell, 510-11
Stanley, Martha Rebecca Lowther, 498
Stanley Mills, 54
Stanley, Rollin A., 58, 81, 91, 101, 151, 497-98, 507
Stanley, Samuel, 13
Stanley, Vivian Lee, 506-08
Stanley, Wright, 151
State vs. Green, 77-78
State vs. Tarvin, 76
States Rights Party, 45
Steamboat, coming of, 124
Steamboat transportation company, 89
Steamers built in Dublin, 125
Stephens, Alexander, elected vice-president of Confederacy, 56
Stephens, Jesse, 13
Stephens, Lucia F., 139
Stephens, R. L., 115
Stephenson, George, 86
Stevens, H. G., 104, 111, 136
Stephens, Lucia F., 139
Stevens, Needham, 122
Stinson, J. A., 130
Stock sales, 132
Stores
  Bakery, 116
  Department, 103, 115
  Grocery, 115, 116
  Hardware, 117
  Meat markets, 116
  Pharmacies, 104, 116
  Ten Cent, 116
Street, Mrs. E. S., 109

Strickland, Fisher, 135-36
Stringer, Alexander, 25
Stringer, Charles, 13
Stringer, Leonard, 86
Stringer, Noah, 25, 27
Stubbs Family, 511-14
Stubbs, John M., 89, 93, 124, 131, 226, 511-14
Stubbs, Lucien Quincy, 85, 117, 221, 514
Stubbs, Lucien Quincy, Jr., 384, 454, 514
Stubbs, Robert Flournoy, 384, 454, 514
Study Club of Dublin, Womans, 246-47
Sturgis, Thaddeus, 83
Suggs, Bruce, 117
Summerlin, A. T., 103
Sumpterville, 142
Sumpterville, first county seat of Laurens County, 12
Sunbury trail, 142
Superior Court of Laurens County, list of judges, 82
Swanton, Dr. John R., 4

Tallahassee Trail, 141
Talliaferro, W. A., 152
Tamlinson, T. M., 150
Tariff Acts, opposition to, 45
Tarpley, E. J., 95
Tarvin, George, 13
Tax collectors in Laurens County, 223
Tax Receivers of Laurens County, 223-24
Taylor, Frank M., 92
Taylor, Harry L., 140
Taylor, Travis, 136
Taylor, W. I., 148
Tecumseh, 28
Telegraph Company, incorporated 1878, 92
Telegraph, Macon, 40
Telephone exchange established 1897, 98
  Bell System 1910, 98
Ten Cent Stores, *see* Stores, Ten Cent
Tenantry in Laurens County, 129
Texas, Admission to the Union, 49
Tharpe, Charnic, 145
Theatorium, the 106
Thigpen, Marvin J., 110
Thomas, Francis, 50
Thomas, Captain Jett, 30
Thomas, Jim, 43
Thomas, John, 49, 146
Thomas, Peter, 12, 13, 75
Thomas, W. B., 93
Thompson, A. J., 74
Thompson, D. J., 153
Thompson, Margaret, 137
Thompson, Dr. William C., 140
Thompson Sanatorium, 230
Thundering Springs, 107-08
Tick eradication, 106

Tillery, J. M., 95
Tillery, W. H., 92
Times, Dublin, 236
Tindal, W. P., 117
Tingle, Christine, 138
Toalli, 3
Tompkins, W. C., 103
Toole, A. J., 93
Toole, Mrs. A. J., 243, 246
Toole, T. E., 150, 155
Toombs, Robert, 56, 69
Tornado of 1929, 112
Tracy, Dennie C., 110
Trade, Board of, established, 105
Trail, Blackshear, 44, 142
Trails
  Indian, 141-42
  Jameson, 141-42
  Lower Uchee, 141
  Sunbury, 142
Tramble and Batey Ferry, 16
Trans-Oconee Republic, 11
Transportation
  Bus lines
    Greyhound Lines, 113
    Service Coach Lines, 113
  Ferry, Diamond's Landing, 89-90
  Railroads
    Brewton & Pineora Railroad, 94
    Charter granted Wrightsville & Tennille Railroad Company 1883, 93
    Dublin & Southwestern Railroad, 94
    Dublin & Wrightsville Railroad Company, 98
    Macon, Dublin & Savannah Railroad, 93-94
    Oconee & Western Railroad Company, 93
    Railroad discussed, 88
  Steamboat, 89
Treaties, Indian
  of 1733, 7
  of 1783, 8
  Ft. Wilkinson, 10
Tributary Waterways of Laurens County, 122-23
Troup, Florida, 43
Troup, George M., 23-24, 29-30, 39-43, 45, 49, 51
Troup, Oralie, 40, 42
Troup Volunteers, 58, 59
Troupers, 39
Tucker Family, 515-16
Tucker, Lucien Quincy, 58, 515
Tucker, Dr. Nathan, 60, 146, 228
Turkey Creek, 42
Turner, James G., 125
Turpentine farms, 134
Turpentining and Lumbering, 132
Twitty, Peter, 110

544

Two Boys, the, 124
Tyner, Grover, 152
Tyre, J. B., 128
Tyre, Letcher, slaying of, 80

U. D. C., see United Daughters of the Confederacy
Underwood, Arthur S., 110
Underwood, John G., 27
Underwood, John J., 83
United Daughters of the Confederacy, Oconee Chapter, 243-45
  Charter Members, 244
  Presiding officers, 245
  State convention 1931, 113
United States Daughters of 1812, 245-46

Valde Osta, 40
Valdosta, 40
  Vallambrosa, 40, 42
Vaughn, E. W., 105
Velvet bean production, 129
Vickers, Ashley, 51
Vickers, E. A., 90
Vickers, Joseph, 13
Vickers, Stephen, 86
Vickers, Vergil, 150
Victory Loan train, 109
Vidette, The Lone, 63-66
Vigal, Dr. John A., 42
Vines, Rev. C. E., 148
Volunteers, Laurens, the, 58, 59
Volunteers, Troup, 58, 59

Wade, Peyton L., 226
Waldron Family, 516-17
Waldron, Howard Chambless, 516
Walker Family, 517-18
Walker, Ben, 205, 517
Walker, Mrs. J. W., 152
Walker, Joshua, 204-05
Walker, Lawrence, 110, 518
Walker, S. D., 156
Walker, Dr. Sidney, 111
Walker, William Henry, 517
War of 1812, 28-38
War
  Confederate, 56-69
  Revolutionary, soldiers, 18-22
  Spanish-American, 96
  World, dead, 109-10
  World, Laurens County in, 108-11
Ward, Mrs. Annie G., 254
Ward, Mrs. E. O., 129
Ward, Opal, 129
Ward, Paul, 137
Ward, W. W., 96
Ward, Mrs. W. W., 377
Ware, David, 51
Warehouses, Cotton, 127

Warren Family, 518-20
Warren, Eli, 25, 46, 225, 519
Warren, Josiah, 518
Warren, Lott, 225, 519
Warren, Polly Ann, 149
Washington County, created in 1783, 9
Water and light plant, 98
Watkins, F. N., 135
Watson, David, 13
Watson, G. R., 156
Watson, Nath, 97
Watson, P. M., Company, 132
Wayne, Robert, 43, 90
Weaver Family, 520-22
Weaver, Jethro, 25, 520-21
Weaver, Jonathan, 88
Weaver, Nathan, 13
Weaver, Seaborn, 90
Webb, Frances, 109
Webb, J. A., 155
Weddington, C. A., 105
Weddington, James, 110
Weichselbaum, Sam, Company, 103
Welch, George W., 27
Welfare Department, Laurens County, 137-38
Well, public, in Dublin, 95
Welsch, George W., 83
Wheeler's Cavalry, 88
Whig Party, 45
Whipple, A. P., Jr., 110
Whipple, Lieut. L. B., 110
Whiskey traffic in Laurens County, 97-98
White Family, 522-23
White, Mrs. Brigham, 249
White, Chris, 110
White, E. D., 75, 105
White, J. E., 108
White, Jim, 156
White, John Thomas, 522
White, Saralyn, 136
Whitehead, Gus, 43
Whittle, John, 147
Wigins, Jesse, 13
Wilkinson, Archibald Dougald, 79
Wilkes, Ellis, 138
Wilkinson, Winnelle, 137
Williams Family, 523-25
Williams, George Herschel, 523-24
Williams, Mrs. George Herschel, 152
Williams, James, 58, 524
Williams, John, 122, 524
Williams, O. O., 148
Williams, Solomon, 19, 147
Williams, Stephen M., 524
Williams, Thomas, 470
Williams, "Windy," 96
Williamson, David, 197
Williamson, James, 151, 152
Williamson, W. M., 153

Williamson, W. W., 149
Willis, Martin, 117
Wills, Early, 269-79
  Book I, 1809-1840, 269-74
  Book II, 1840-1869, 274-79
Windham, Dick, 155
Windham, Killiam, 153
Windham, Tom, 155
Witherington, J. H., 75, 103
Witherington, James R., 154
Witherington, Nancy, 154
Witherington, William A., 74, 154
Wolfe, John B., 54, 95, 225-26
Wolfe, Mrs. John B., 152
Woman's Study Club of Dublin, 246-47
Wood, Ashley, 79
Wood, Joseph M., 155
Woodard, John, 149, 150, 151
Woodard, Mary, 149
Woodard, Otis, 110
Woodmen of the World, 258
Woods, L. D., 105, 140
Woodward, E. Y., 58
Wool growing, 50
World War dead, 109-10
World War, Laurens County in, 108-11
W P A, 136-37
Wright, James W., 92
Wright, Captain Obed, 30
Wright, Wingfield, 80
Wrightsville & Tennille Railroad Company, 93
Wynn, H. H., 155

Yarborough, Joseph, 13, 50
Yarborough, William, 13, 86
Yazoo Fraud, 10, 23, 76
Y. M. C. A., 108
Yopp, Bill, 261
Yopp, J. H., 90, 94
Yopp, Jeremiah, 25, 26, 49, 150
Yopp, Jerry, 43
Yopp, John W., 54, 56, 83
Yopp Mill, 54
Yopp, Samuel, 25, 26
Yopp, Thomas McCall, 51, 57, 58, 240, 261
Young, E. Z., 155
Young Men's Business League, 104

www.ingramcontent.com/pod-product-compliance
Lightning Source LLC
Chambersburg PA
CBHW020630300426
44112CB00007B/73